W9-BYV-098

JOHN WILLIS'

THEATRE WORLD

1976–1977 SEASON

VOLUME 33

CROWN PUBLISHERS, INC.
ONE PARK AVENUE
NEW YORK, N.Y. 10016

T O
TENNESSEE WILLIAMS
the world's most respected contemporary playwright

JOHN GIELGUD and RALPH RICHARDSON
in "No Man's Land"

CONTENTS

EDITOR: JOHN WILLIS

Staff: Joseph Burroughs, Alberto Cabrera, Frances Crampon, Maltier Hagan, Ron Reagan, Stanley Reeves, William Schelble

Staff Photographers: Joseph Abeles, Bert Andrews, Ron Reagan, Van Williams

THE SEASON IN REVIEW
June 1, 1976–May 31, 1977

From a lethargic beginning, this season developed into one of the most active and satisfying in several years. In spite of inflationary costs and soaring ticket prices ($20 top), according to *Variety,* it was a record-breaker for both attendance and grosses on Broadway and the road. These were very encouraging statistics after a few discouraging years.

The emergence of several talented young American playwrights brought great hope and excitement to the New York theatre. The majority were nurtured, fortunately, in regional companies. One of them, Michael Cristofer, also a talented actor, received the Pulitzer Prize for his play "The Shadow Box." It was also voted a "Tony" for Best Play of the season. "The Texas Trilogy," by another impressive new playwright-actor, Preston Jones, deserved a more successful run. Cited by the Drama Desk as Best American Play, it consisted of three full-length plays performed in repertory with excellent performances by Diane Ladd and Fred Gwynne. The choice of Best American Play by the New York Drama Critics Circle was "American Buffalo" by another promising young playwright, David Mamet. The Circle's choice for Best Play was the English import with Tom Courtenay's Broadway debut in "Otherwise Engaged." It was voted Best Foreign Play by the Drama Desk. Other outstanding plays were "Sly Fox" with George C. Scott giving a superb comic performance, "California Suite" with two playgoers' favorites, Tammy Grimes and George Grizzard, "Gemini" transferred from Off Broadway with Danny Aiello and Anne DeSalvo in exemplary portrayals, "The Trip Back Down" that deserved more popularity and gave John Cullum a chance to display his versatility, "For Colored Girls Who Have Considered Suicide. . . ." with Trazana Beverley's Tony-Award performance for Best Supporting Actress in a play, and the British imports "Dirty Linen" in which Cecilia Hart was delightful, "No Man's Land" with memorable performances by John Gielgud and Ralph Richardson, and "Comedians" with Jonathan Pryce's Broadway debut in a Tony-Award-winning supporting performance. Julie Harris received her fifth "Tony" as Best Actress for her beautiful solo performance as Emily Dickinson in "The Belle of Amherst" that opened too late last season to be considered for awards.

An abundance of revivals was characteristic of this season, as it was of last year's. They included "The Basic Training of Pavlo Hummel" for which Best Actor "Tony" went to its star Al Pacino, Liv Ullmann as "Anna Christie," Rex Harrison and Elizabeth Ashley as "Caesar and Cleopatra," "The Innocents" with Claire Bloom, "Romeo and Juliet" with Paul Rudd and Pamela Payton-Wright, Tennessee Williams' "The Eccentricities of a Nightingale" (his rewrite of "Summer and Smoke") with Betsy Palmer, and his "Night of the Iguana" with Richard Chamberlain in a praiseworthy New York debut. Unfortunately Mr. Williams' new play "Vieux Carre" was not favorably received. Lincoln Center had New York Shakespeare Festival revivals of "The Cherry Orchard" with Irene Worth and Raul Julia, and "Agamemnon," both with unconventional direction by Andrei Serban. City Center hosted the Greek National Theatre's "Oedipus at Colonus," and Le Theatre de la Ville de Paris in "Tiger at the Gates" with Anny Duperey, Jean Mercure and Jean-Pierre Aumont.

Until the latter part of the season, except for holdovers, Broadway's musicals were primarily revivals: "Pal Joey," "The Robber Bridegroom" for which Barry Bostwick's performance won him a "Tony" for Best Actor in a Musical, "Fiddler on the Roof" with Zero Mostel re-creating his original role, "Godspell," and "Let My People Come" were both transplanted from Off Broadway, "Oh! Calcutta!" (the first naughty-nudie musical), the 1917 hit "Going Up" with Maureen Brennan again deserving applause, an all-black cast of "Guys and Dolls" with Robert Guillaume, Ernestine Jackson, James Randolph, and the show-stopping Ken Page, "A Party with Betty Comden and Adolph Green," "The King and I" with Yul Brynner and Constance Towers, "Happy End" with Meryl Streep and Christopher Lloyd that was transferred from Chelsea Theater Center, and concert productions of "She Loves Me" with Rita Moreno, Laurence Guittard, Madeline Kahn, and "Knickerbocker Holiday" with Richard Kiley and Edward Evanko.

During the third week of April, three highly praised musicals arrived to add to the mounting excitement of the season. They were the intimate and innovative "I Love My Wife" with delightful performances by Joanna Gleason, Ilene Graff, James Naughton, and Lenny Baker who received a "Tony" for Best Supporting Actor in a Musical, "Side by Side by Sondheim" with an enchanting English

cast of four, and the old-fashioned, sentimental musical spectacle "Annie," recipient of 7 "Tony" Awards, including Best Musical and Best Actress in a Musical (Dorothy Loudon), New York Drama Critics Circle citation for Best Musical, 7 Drama Desk Awards, and 5 Outer Critics Circle Awards. The "Tony" for Best Supporting Actress in a Musical went to Delores Hall of "Your Arms Too Short to Box with God." This year a controversial category was added to the list of "Tony" Awards: Most Innovative Production of a Revival. It went to "Porgy and Bess" that was performed for the first time with its entire original score by Gershwin.

An unusual number of solo performers, both on and off Broadway, appeared during the season. Among them were Hal Holbrook and his brilliant Mark Twain, Lily Tomlin, Bing Crosby, Shirley MacLaine, Red Skelton, Emlyn Williams' ever-popular "Dylan Thomas Growing Up," Fritz Weaver as Abraham Lincoln, and Len Cariou in "Sorrow beyond Dreams." Perhaps the most coveted tickets of the season were for the SRO performance by Mary Martin and Ethel Merman as a benefit gala for Friends of the Theatre and Music Collection of the Museum of the City of New York. An unforgettable experience!

Off-Broadway activity, similar to that on Broadway, had more productions and better quality than last year. Among the plays that should be mentioned are "Sexual Perversity in Chicago/Duck Variations," "The Brownsville Raid," "Monsters" with bravura performances by James Coco and Rosemary DeAngelis, Brooklyn Academy of Music Company's "The New York Idea" and "The Three Sisters" with such talent as Rosemary Harris, Denholm Elliott, Blythe Danner, Tovah Feldshuh and Ellen Burstyn, Abbey Theatre of Ireland's "The Plough and the Stars," "The Prince of Homburg," "The Crazy Locomotive," "The Farm," "My Life," "Cold Storage," "Savages," "A Night at the Black Pig," "Peg o' My Heart," "The Philanderer," "Endgame," "Dear Liar" with Jerome Kilty and DeAnn Mears, "Ashes," "Hagar's Children," "The Stronger/Creditors" with Geraldine Page and Rip Torn, "G. R. Point" with John Heard, Joe Morton and William Russ, "Scribes" with Donald Madden, Stephen Joyce, Kristoffer Tabori and Fran Brill. Notable Off-Broadway musicals were "The Club," "Lovesong," "2 by 5," "Nightclub Cantata," "Starting Here, Starting Now," "Joseph and the Amazing Technicolor Dreamcoat," "The Great MacDaddy," "Dance on a Country Grave" with Donna Theodore and Kevin Kline, "Jules Feiffer's Hold Me!," and the productions of the Light Opera of Manhattan (LOOM).

In addition to the season's outstanding performers mentioned above, the roster should include Martin Balsam, Barbara Barrie, D'Jamin Bartlett, Joanne Beretta, Anthony Call, Dixie Carter, Robert Christian, Thom Christopher, Joan Copeland, Clamma Dale, Robert Drivas, Robert Duvall, Mildred Dunnock, Joyce Ebert, Patricia Elliott, Jack Gilford, Joel Grey, Jack Gwillim, Eileen Heckart, Gloria Hodes, David Holliday, Juliette Koka, Frank Langella, Thelma Lee, Laurence Luckinbill, Sharon Madden, Joseph Maher, Roberta Maxwell, Andrea McArdle, Hector Mercado, Jan Miner, Rosemary Murphy, Estelle Parsons, Lynn Redgrave, Jess Richards, David Rounds, Maria Schell, Reid Shelton, Scott Stevenson, Chick Vennera, Jack Weston, Billy Dee Williams, and Gretchen Wyler.

Among relevant events during the year, the following should be included in the records. At the end of the season, Clive Barnes, dance and drama critic for the *New York Times,* relinquished his assignment as drama critic to devote his time entirely to dance criticism. Richard Eder succeeds him as drama critic. Manhattan Plaza Towers became the first federally subsidized apartments available for those in the performing arts. Efforts were continued to eliminate undersirable elements from the Times Square Area, and to make West 42 Street into a series of Off-Broadway theatres and showcases. New York Shakespeare Festival's Joseph Papp announced the withdrawal of his organization from Lincoln Center's Vivian Beaumont Theater complex after the open-end run of "The Cherry Orchard." Mr. Papp's departure "for financial reasons," ironically after his most successful year there, raised many questions as to the future of the Beaumont—as well as cultural institutions in general. If such organizations are to survive, it is increasingly more obvious that they must have federal support in the not-too-distant future. Again this season, those involved with the theatre became even more aware of the growing importance of regional theatres and Off Off Broadway groups as a source of life and growth for the performing arts. The prospects are optimistic.

Ralph Richardson, John Gielgud in "No Man's Land"

Left: "For Colored Girls Who Have Considered Suicide . . ."

BROADWAY CALENDAR
June 1, 1976 through May 31, 1977

Trish Van Devere, George C. Scott in "Sly Fox"

Left: Betty Comden, Adolph Green in "A Party with Comden and Green"

Andrea McArdle, Reid Shelton, Sandy in "Annie"

Tammy Grimes, George Grizzard in "California Suite"

7

BILTMORE THEATRE
Opened Wednesday, June 2, 1976*
Terry Allen Kramer and Harry Rigby by arrangement with
Circle Repertory Company present:

KNOCK KNOCK

By Jules Feiffer; Directed by Jose Quintero; Setting, John Lee
Beatty; Costumes, Jennifer Von Mayrhauser; Lighting, Dennis Pa-
richy; Sound, Charles London and George Hansen; Special Effects,
Robert E. McCarthy; Assistant Director, John H. Davis; Wardrobe
Master-Hairstylist, Franke Piazza; Production Assistant, Paul
Weiser

CAST

Cohn	Charles Durning
Abe	John Heffernan
Wiseman/Messenger/Gambler/Judge	Leonard Frey
Joan	Lynn Redgrave

Standbys: Herman O. Arbeit, Kristin Van Buren

A Comedy in three acts. The action takes place at the present time
in a small house in the woods.

Company Manager: John Corkill
Press: Henry Luhrman, Terry Lilly
Stage Managers: Robert Vandergriff, Greg Taylor

* Closed July 3, 1976 after 38 performances and 10 previews.

Charles Durning, Lynn Redgrave, Leonard Frey, John Heffernan
Top Left: Charles Durning, Lynn Redgrave, John Heffernan

Al Green

URIS THEATRE
Opened Thursday, June 3, 1976.*
Fluellen Productions, Ltd. (Reginald Fluellen, George Fluellen) presents:

AL GREEN
ASHFORD & SIMPSON

Scenery and Lighting, Michael Shere; Sound, John Venable; Choreography, George Faison; Production Assistant, Vernon Roach

A concert of songs presented in two parts.

General Managers: Reginald Fluellen, George Fluellen
Associate Manager: Jim Rouse
Press: Michael Alpert, Marilynn LeVine, Warren Knowlton, Carl Samrock, Randi Cone

* Closed June 6, 1976 after limited engagement of 7 performances.

Ashford & Simpson

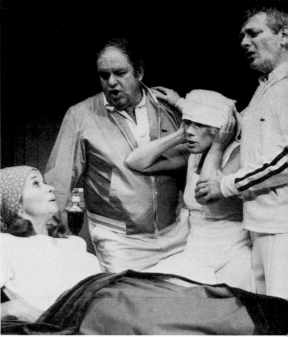

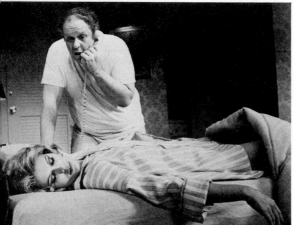

EUGENE O'NEILL THEATRE
Opened Thursday, June 10, 1976.*
Emanuel Azenberg and Robert Fryer present:

CALIFORNIA SUITE

By Neil Simon; Director, Gene Saks; Scenery, William Ritman; Costumes, Jane Greenwood; Lighting, Tharon Musser; Production Assistant, Bill Schreiner; Wardrobe Supervisor, Josephine Zampedri; Assistant to Producers, Leslie Butler; Hairstylist, Henri Chevrier

CAST

"Visitor from New York"
Hannah Warren .... Tammy Grimes†1
William Warren .... George Grizzard†2

"Visitor from Philadelphia"
Marvin Michaels........................... Jack Weston†3
Bunny............................... Leslie Easterbrook†4
Millie Michaels .... Barbara Barrie†5

"Visitors from London"
Sidney Nichols........................ George Grizzard†2
Diana Nichols .... Tammy Grimes†1

"Visitors from Chicago"
Mort Hollender .... Jack Weston†3
Beth Hollender .... Barbara Barrie†5
Stu Franklyn......................... George Grizzard†2
Gert Franklyn .... Tammy Grimes†1

STANDBYS: Tammy Grimes and Barbara Barrie, Joan Bassie; George Grizzard, John Cunningham; Leslie Easterbrook, Lani Sundsten; Jack Weston, Michael Vale

A Comedy composed of four playlets in five scenes, with one intermission. The action takes place at the present time in Suite 203 and 204 in the Beverly Hills Hotel.

Manager: Jose Vega
Press: Bill Evans
Stage Managers: Philip Cusack, Lani Sundsten

* Closed July 2, 1977 after 445 performances and 4 previews.
† Succeeded by: 1. Rue McClanahan during vacation, 2. Kenneth Haigh, David McCallum, 3. Michael Vale, Joseph Leon, Vincent Gardenia, 4. Lani Sundsten, 5. Marge Redmond

David McCallum, Tammy Grimes
Above: Leslie Easterbrook, Jack Weston

Top: Barbara Barrie, Jack Weston, Tammy Grimes,
George Grizzard Left: George Grizzard, Tammy Grimes

PALACE THEATRE
Opened Monday, June 14, 1976.*
Danny O'Donovan presents:

AN EVENING WITH DIANA ROSS

Director, Joe Layton; Musical Director, Gil Askey; Special Material, Bill Goldenberg, Bill Dyer; Additional Material, Bruce Vilanch; Lighting, John Gleason; Sound, Trevor Jordan; A Danny O'Donovan/Sagittarius Entertainment Presentation

CAST

Diana Ross
The Jones Girls
Hayward Coleman
Don McLeod
Stewart Fischer

A concert presented in two parts.

General Management: Marvin A. Krauss Associates
Management Associate: Robert I. Goldberg
Company Manager: David Wyler
Press: Solters & Roskin, Bud Westman, Josh Ellis
Stage Manager: Michael Coyte

* Closed June 26, 1976 after limited engagement of 16 performances.

Diana Ross

**Diana Ross
(also top)**

11

BROADHURST THEATRE
Opened Tuesday, June 22, 1976.*
(Moved to the Plymouth, Sept. 15, 1976; to the Ambassador, Jan. 12, 1977)
Edgar Lansbury, Stuart Duncan, Joseph Beruh and The Shubert Organization present:

GODSPELL

Conceived and Directed by John-Michael Tebelak; Based on The Gospel According to St. Matthew; Music and Lyrics, Stephen Schwartz; Lighting, Spencer Mosse; Costumes, Susan Tsu; Production Supervision, Nina Faso; Musical Director, Steve Reinhardt; Sound, Robert Minor; Associate Producer, Charles Haid; Conductor, Paul Shaffer; Executive Supervision, Al J. Isaac, Gary Gunas; Production Coordinators, Ron Bunker, Bob Skerry; Assistant to Producers, Darrell Jonas; Wardrobe Supervisor, Reet Pell; Music Coordinator, Earl Shendell; Production Assistants, Ellen Katz, Lee Minter; Original cast album by Bell Records

CAST

Lamar Alford†	Bobby Lee
Laurie Faso	Tom Rolfing
Lois Foraker	Don Scardino
Robin Lamont	Marley Sims
Elizabeth Lathram	Valerie Williams

Alternates: Kerin Blair, Bob Garrett, Michael Hoit, Kitty Rea

MUSICAL NUMBERS: "Tower of Babble," "Prepare Ye the Way of the Lord," "Save the People," "Day by Day," "Learn Your Lessons Well," "Bless the Lord," "All for the Best," "All Good Gifts," "Light of the World," "Turn Back, O Man," "Alas for You," "By My Side," "We Beseech Thee," "On the Willows," Finale

A Musical in two acts.

General Management: Marvin A. Krauss Associates
Company Manager: Gail Bell
Press: Gifford/Wallace, Glenna Freedman, Tom Trenkle
Stage Managers: Michael J. Frank, Kitty Rea

* Still playing May 31, 1977. It was transferred from Off Broadway where it had given 2118 performances after opening May 17, 1971.
† Other performers during the season were Tony Hoty, Sonia Manzano, Jeremy Sage, John-Ann Washington, Patti Mariano, Marilyn Pasekoff

Sy Friedman Photos

Top Right: Don Scardino, Robin Lamont
Below: Don Scardino (R) and company

Michael Hoit, Jeremy Sage (kneeling)

(R) Andy Rohrer (also above)

CIRCLE IN THE SQUARE THEATRE
Opened Sunday, June 27, 1976.*
Circle in the Square (Theodore Mann, Artistic Director; Paul Libin, Managing Director) presents:

PAL JOEY

Music, Richard Rodgers; Lyrics, Lorenz Hart; Book, John O'-Hara, based on Mr. O'Hara's New Yorker Magazine sketches; Director, Theodore Mann; Choreographer, Margo Sappington; Scenery, John J. Moore; Costumes, Arthur Boccia; Lighting, Ron Wallace; Musical Director, Scott Oakley; Production Associate, Atsumi Kolba; Wardrobe Supervisor, Virginia Merkel; Hairstylist, Roberto Fernandez; Production Assistants, Bill Braden, Jeff Browne, Bernard Ferstenberg, Robin Groves, Louise Knauf, Jolly Nelson, M. M. O'Flaherty; David T. Goldman, Teri Smith, Tom Smith; Music Coordinator, Earl Shendell

CAST

Mike	Harold Gary
Joey	Christopher Chadman
Kid	Terri Treas
Gladys	Janie Sell
Gail	Gail Benedict
Murphy	Murphy Cross
Rosamond	Rosamond Lynn
Marilu	Marilu Henner
Debbie	Deborah Geffner
Linda	Boni Enten
Vera	Joan Copeland
Gent	David Hodo
Ernest	Austin Colyer
Waldo the Waiter	Denny Martin Flinn
Victor	Michael Leeds
Delivery Boy	Kenn Scalice
Louis, the tenor	Adam Petroski
Melba	Dixie Carter
Ludlow Lowell	Joe Sirola
O'Brien	Ralph Farnworth

UNDERSTUDIES: Ludlow/Mike, Ralph Farnworth; Gladys, Marilu Henner; Linda, Gail Benedict; O'Brien/Louis, Austin Colyer; Melba, Rosamond Lynn; Swing Girl, Lisa Brown; Swing Boy, Richard Dodd

MUSICAL NUMBERS: "You Mustn't Kick It Around," "I Could Write a Book," "Chicago," "That Terrific Rainbow," "What Is a Man," "Happy Hunting Horn," "Bewitched, Bothered and Bewildered," "Pal Joey," "Joey Looks into the Future," "The Flower Garden of My Heart," "Zip," "Plant You Now, Dig You Later," "In Our Little Den," "Do It the Hard Way," "Take Him."

A musical in 2 acts and 12 scenes. The action takes place in Chicago during the late 1930's.

Company Manager: William Conn
Press: Merle Debuskey, Susan L. Schulman
Stage Managers: Randall Brooks, James Bernardi

* Closed Aug. 29, 1976 after 73 performances and 33 previews. Original production with Vivienne Segal and Gene Kelly opened Dec. 25, 1940 and ran for 374 performances.

Joseph Abeles, Inge Morath Photos

Top: entire cast (R) Harold Gary, Janie Sell
Below: Dixie Carter

Christopher Chadman, Boni Enten
Above: Joan Copeland

13

MOROSCO THEATRE
Opened Thursday, July 22, 1976.*
Phil Oesterman presents:

LET MY PEOPLE COME

Music and Lyrics, Earl Wilson, Jr.; Director, Phil Oesterman; Set and Lighting, Duane F. Mazey; Set and Costumes, Douglas W. Schmidt; Lighting, John Gleason; Musical Direction and Vocal Arrangements, Norman Bergen; Conductor, Glen Roven; Technical Supervisor, Mitch Miller; Wardrobe Supervisor, Clarence Sims; Original cast album by Libra Records

CAST

Brandy Alexander	Empress Kilpatrick
Joanne Baron	Dianne Legro
Dwight Baxter	Allan Lozito
Pat Cleveland	Bryan Miller
Lorraine Davidson	Rod R. Neves
Joelle Erasme	Rozaa
Yvette Freeman	Don Scotti
Paul Gillespie	Sterling Saint-Jacques
Gloria Goldman	Bryan Spencer
Tulane Howard II	Dean Tait
Bob Jockers	Lori Wagner
	Charles Whiteside

MUSICAL NUMBERS: Opening, "Mirror," "Whatever Turns You On," "Give It to Me," "Giving Life," "The Ad," "Fellatio 101," "I'm Gay," "Linda, Georgina, Marilyn and Me," "Dirty Words," "I Believe My Body," "The Show Business Nobody Knows," "Take Me Home with You," "Choir Practice," "And She Loved Me," "Poontang," "Come in My Mouth," "The Cunnilingus Champion of Company C," "Doesn't Anybody Love Anymore," "Let My People Come"

"A Sexual Musical" in two acts.

General Manager: Jay Kingwill
Press: Saul Richman, Fred Nathan
Stage Managers: Duane F. Mazey, Robert Walter, Bob Blume

* Closed Oct. 2, 1976 after 106 performances and 16 previews. It was transferred from Off Broadway where it had played 1167 performances.

Lori Wagner, Paul Gillespie

PALACE THEATRE
Opened Friday, July 9, 1976.*
HMT Associates present:

SHIRLEY MacLAINE

Directed and Staged by Tony Charmoli; Musical Director, Donn Trenner; Music either composed or arranged by Cy Coleman; Written by Fred Ebb; Additional Material, Bob Wells; Special Choreography, Alan Johnson; Lighting, Graham Large; Lighting Supervised by Richard Winkler; Special Costumes, Stanley Simmons; Sound, Mike Welsh; Wardrobe Supervisor, Patricia Hughes; Management Associates, David Wyler, Robert I. Goldberg; Wardrobe Mistress, Sydney Smith

CAST

Shirley MacLaine
and
Shirley's Gypsies:
Barbara Alston
Gary Flannery
Adam Grammis
Jo Ann Lehman
Larry Vickers

MUSICAL NUMBERS: Overture, "If My Friends Could See Me Now," "Remember Me?," "Steam Heat," "Hey, Big Spender," "I'm a Person Too," "Gypsy in My Soul," "It's Not Where You Start," "Every Little Movement Has a Meaning All Its Own," "The Hustle," "Star," "I'm a Brass Band"

Performed without an intermission.

General Management: Marvin A. Krauss Associates
Company Manager: Bernard Lang
Press: Michael Alpert, Marilyn LeVine, Warren Knowlton, Carl Samrock, Randi Cone
Stage Manager: Earl Hughes

* Closed July 24, 1976 after limited engagement of 20 performances.
Robin Platzer Photos

Shirley MacLaine (C)

Shirley MacLaine (C)
Also Top

15

BROADWAY THEATRE
Opened Wednesday, July 21, 1976.*
Moe Septee in association with Victor H. Potamkin presents:

GUYS AND DOLLS

Music and Lyrics, Frank Loesser; Book, Joe Swerling, Abe Burrows; Directed and Choreographed by Billy Wilson; Scenery, Tom H. John; Costumes, Bernard Johnson; Lighting, Thomas Skelton; Arrangements and Orchestrations, Danny Holgate, Horace Ott; Musical Director, Choral Arranger, Howard Roberts; Sound, Sander Hacker; Assistant to Director, Charles Augins; Associate Producers, Ashton Springer, Carmen F. Zollo; Entire production under the supervision of Abe Burrows; Presented in association with Frank Enterprises and Beresford Productions; Wardrobe Supervisor, Remigia Marmo; Hairstylist, Irvin Dett

CAST

Nicely-Nicely Johnson	Ken Page
Benny Southstreet	Christophe Pierre
Rusty Charlie	Sterling McQueen
Sister Sarah Brown	Ernestine Jackson
Harry the Horse	John Russell
Lt. Brannigan	Clark Morgan
Nathan Detroit	Robert Guillaume
Angie the Ox	Jymie Charles
Miss Adelaide	Norma Donaldson
Sky Masterson	James Randolph
Arvide Abernathy	Emett "Babe" Wallace
Agatha	Irene Datcher
Calvin	Bardell Conner
Martha	Marion Moore
Joey Biltmore	Derrick Bell
Master of Ceremonies	Andy Torres
Waiter	Derrick Bell
Mimi	Prudence Darby
General Cartwright	Edye Byrde
Big Jule	Walter White
Drunk	Andy Torres

THE GUYS: Derrick Bell, Toney Brealond, Jymie Charles, Bardell Conner, Nathan Jennings, Jr., Bill Mackey, Sterling McQueen, Andy Torres, Eddie Wright, Jr.

THE DOLLS: Prudence Darby, Jacquelyn DuBois, Anna Maria Fowlkes, Helen Gelzer, Julia Lema, Jacqueline Smith-Lee

UNDERSTUDIES: Nicely, Jymie Charles; Sarah, Irene Datcher; Adelaide/Gen. Cartwright, Helen Gelzer; Sky, Nathan Jennings, Jr.; Arvide, John Russell; Benny, Andy Torres; Harry, Bill Mackey; Big Jule, Toney Brealond; Agatha/Mimi, Julia Lema; Drunk, Derrick Bell; Rusty, Bill Mackey, Eddie Wright, Jr.; Swing Dancers, Alvin Davis, Freda T. Vanterpool.

MUSICAL NUMBERS: "Runyonland," "Fugue for Tinhorns," "The Oldest Established," "I'll Know," "Bushel and a Peck," "Adelaide's Lament," "Guys and Dolls," "El Cafe Felicidad," "If I Were a Bell," "My Time of Day," "I've Never Been in Love Before," "Take Back Your Mink," "More I Cannot Wish You," "Crapshooter's Dance," "Luck Be a Lady Tonight," "Sue Me," "Sit Down, You're Rockin' the Boat," "Marry the Man Today"
"A Musical Fable of Broadway" in 2 acts and 18 scenes.

General Manager: Laurel Ann Wilson
Company Manager: Donald Tirabassi
Press: Max Eisen, Barbara Glenn, Judith Jacksina
Stage Managers: R. Derek Swire, Clinton Jackson, Bonnie Sue Schloss

* Closed Feb. 13, 1977 after 239 performances and 12 previews. Original production with Sam Levene, Isabel Bigley, Vivian Blane and Robert Alda opened Nov. 24, 1950 and played 1200 performances.

Ron Reagan, Martha Swope Photos

**Top Left: Ken Page, Edye Byrde
Below: Robert Guillaume, Norma Donaldson**

**James Randolph, Ernestine Jackson
Above: Norma Donaldson**

LONGACRE THEATRE
Opened Tuesday, September 14, 1976.*
Philip Mathias and Ken Myers present:

CHECKING OUT

By Allen Swift; Director, Jerry Adler; Scenery, David Jenkins; Lighting, Ken Billington; Costumes, Carol Luiken; Production Associate, Louisa Cabot; Technical Supervisor, Sander Hacker

CAST

Florence Grayson	Joan Copeland
Bernard Applebaum	Hy Anzell
Morris Applebaum	Allen Swift
Mr. Johnson	Jonathan Moore
Dr. Theodore Applebaum	Mason Adams
Dr. Sheldon Henning	Larry Bryggman
Gilbert	Tazewell Thompson
Schmuel Axelrod	Michael Gorrin

STANDBYS AND UNDERSTUDIES: Florence, Lenore Loveman; Morris/Bernard/Axelrod, Irwin Charone; Sheldon, Kurt Garfield; Gilbert, Ron Nguvu

A comedy in 2 acts and 4 scenes. The action takes place in Morris Applebaum's apartment on West 57th Street in New York City, at the present time.

General Manager: Ken Myers
Press: Susan Bloch
Stage Managers: Murray Gitlin, Ron Nguvu

* Closed Sept. 25, 1976 after 15 performances and 4 previews.

Martha Swope Photos

Allen Swift (also top left) Above: Joan Copeland, Hy Anzell Top: Larry Bryggman, Mason Adams

BOOTH THEATRE
Opened Wednesday, September 15, 1976.*
Joseph Papp and Woodie King, Jr. present:

FOR COLORED GIRLS WHO HAVE CONSIDERED SUICIDE WHEN THE RAINBOW IS ENUF

By Ntozake Shange; Director, Oz Scott; Scenery, Ming Cho Lee; Lighting, Jennifer Tipton; Costumes, Judy Dearing; Choreography, Paula Moss; Associate Producer, Bernard Gersten; A New York Shakespeare Festival Production in association with the Henry Street Settlement's New Federal Theatre; Wardrobe Supervisor, Margaret Faison; Production Supervisor, Jason Steven Cohen

CAST

Lady in Brown	Janet League†1
Lady in Yellow	Aku Kadogo
Lady in Red	Trazana Beverley†2
Lady in Green	Paula Moss†3
Lady in Purple	Rise Collins
Lady in Blue	Laurie Carlos
Lady in Orange	Ntozake Shange†4

UNDERSTUDIES: Misses Collins, Beverley, Moss, Michele Shay; Misses League, Shange, Carlos, Kadogo, Seret Scott; Ms. Moss in "Sechita", Aku Kadogo

A program of poetry by Ntozake Shange presented without intermission.

Company Manager: Robert Frissell
Press: Merle Debuskey, Leo Stern, William Schelble
Stage Managers: John Beven, Fai Walker-Davis

* Still playing May 31, 1977
† Succeeded by: 1. Roxanne Reese, 2. Robbie McCauley, 3. Jonette O'Kelley, 4. Seret Scott, Sharita Hunt

Sy Friedman, Martha Swope Photos

Right: Trazana Beverley

Aku Kadogo, Paula Moss, Rise Collins, Janet League, Ntozake Shange, Trazana Beverley, Laurie Carlos

MINSKOFF THEATRE
Opened Thursday, September 16, 1976.*
Raymax Productions presents:

THE DEBBIE REYNOLDS SHOW

Staged and Choreographed by Ron Lewis; Musical Conductor, Tom Nygaard; Producer, Robert Fallon; Sets, Billy Morris; Lighting, Jerry Grollnek; Costumes and Gowns, Bob Mackie; Sound, Trevor Jordan; Hair Design and Supervision, Pinky Babajian; Wardrobe Supervisor, Robert O'Connell; Technical Director, Mitch Miller

CAST

Debbie Reynolds

Bruce Lea	Gene Myers
Albert Stevenson	George Eiferman
Ray Chabeau	Penny Worth
Joel Blum	Dani MiCormick
Louis McKay	Steven Lardas

ACT I: Overture, "Gee, But It's Great to Be Here," "Reach Out and Touch Somebody's Hand," "He's Got the Whole World in His Hands," "Touch a Hand," "Higher and Higher," Singers' Medley, Film Sequence and Medley, "I Ain't Down Yet," Debbie's Salute to Show Business

ACT II: Entracte, "Irene," "I'm Always Chasing Rainbows," "Alice Blue Gown," "You Made Me Love You," Premier Night Impressions, Bicentennial Salute to America

General Manager: Theatre Now, Inc.
Press: John Springer, Louis Sica, Stephanie Buzzarte
Stage Manager: Joe Lorden

* Closed Sept. 26, 1976 after 13 performances.

Debbie Reynolds (also top)

JOHN GOLDEN THEATRE

Opened Sunday, September 19, 1976.*

Ashton Springer, William Callahan, Stephens-Weitzenhoffer Productions in association with Stephen R. Friedman and Irwin Meyer present the Goodspeed Opera House Production of:

GOING UP

Book and Lyrics, Otto Harbach; Music, Louis A. Hirsch; Founded on James Montgomery's comedy "The Aviator"; Director, Bill Gile; Choreography and Production Numbers, Dan Siretta; Musical Direction and Vocal Arrangements, Lynn Crigler; Associate Producer, James L. D. Roser; Costumes, David Toser; Scenery and Lighting, Supervision, Edward Haynes; Lighting, Peter M. Ehrhardt; Special Consultant, Alfred Simon; Musical Arranger, Russell Warner; Wardrobe Master, Angelo Quilici; Production Assistant, Stephanie Austin

CAST

Miss Zonne	Pat Lysinger
Alex	Calvin McRae
Gus	Larry Hyman
John Gordon	Stephen Bray
Grace Douglas	Kimberly Farr
F. H. Douglas	Lee H. Doyle
Jules Gaillard	Michael Tartel
Hopkinson Brown	Walter Bobbie
Madeline Manners	Maureen Brennan
James Brooks	Noel Craig
Robert Street	Brad Blaisdell
Sam Robinson	Ronn Robinson
Dwayne	James Bontempo
Faye	Deborah Crowe
Howell	Michael Gallagher
Ennis	Teri Gill
Mollie	Barbara McKinley

MUSICAL NUMBERS: "Paging Mr. Street," "I Want a Determined Boy," "If You Look in Her Eyes," "Going Up," "Hello Frisco," "Down, Up, Left, Right," "Kiss Me," "The Tickle Toe," "Brand New Hero," "I'll Think of You," "Do It For Me," "My Sumurun Girl," Finale

A musical comedy in 2 acts and 4 scenes. The action takes place in 1919 in Lenox, Mass., at the Gordon Inn.

General Management: Theatre Management Associates
General Manager: Susan Chase
Company Manager: Gino Giglio
Press: Max Eisen, Irene Gandy, Barbara Glenn, Judy Jacksina
Stage Managers: Marnel Sumner, Ron Abbott, Larry McMillian

* Closed Oct. 30, 1976 after 49 performances and 4 previews. Original production with Frank Craven, Edith Day, Marion Sunshine and Frank Otto opened Dec. 25, 1917 and played 351 performances.

Ron Reagan Photos

Kimberly Farr, Brad Blaisdell (C)

20

Top: Brad Blaisdell, Kimberly Farr Left: Blaisdell Maureen Brennan, Walter Bobbie (also below)

AMBASSADOR THEATRE
Opened Monday, September 20, 1976.*
Frank Von Zerneck and Mike Wise in association with Frankie
Hewitt and The Shubert Organization present:

I HAVE A DREAM

Adapted by Josh Greenfeld from the words of Dr. Martin Luther
King, Jr.; Conceived and Directed by Robert Greenwald; Settings,
Donald Harris; Costumes, Terence Tam Soon; Lighting, Martin
Aronstein; Musical Director, Fred Gripper; Associate Producers,
Pat Lang, Theatre Now, Inc.; Assistant to Director, Amy Bloch;
Administrative Associate, Beatrice Francis; Wardrobe Supervisor,
Robin Mullen

CAST

Dr. Martin Luther King, Jr.	Billy Dee Williams†
The Woman	Judyann Elder
Singer/Actress	Sheila Ellis
Singer/Actress	Leata Galloway
Singer/Actress	Ramona Brooks
Singer/Actress	Millie Foster
Singer/Actor	Clinton Derricks-Carroll
Singer/Actress	Andrea Vereen
Accompanist	Fred Gripper

A drama in 2 acts and 3 scenes. The action takes place between
December 1955 and April 1968.

General Manager: James Walsh
Company Manager: Ronald Bruguiere
Press: Michael Alpert, Carl Samrock, Marilynn LeVine, Warren
Knowlton, Randi Cone
Stage Managers: David Clive, Janyce Ann Wagner

* Closed Dec. 5, 1976 after 80 performances and 8 previews.
† Succeeded by Moses Gunn

Martha Swope, Earl Robbin Photos

Judyann Elder, Billy Dee Williams

Moses Gunn
Top: Billy Dee Williams

Opened Tuesday, September 21, 1976.*
Robert Whitehead and Roger L. Stevens present:

A TEXAS TRILOGY

Three full-length plays by Preston Jones in repertory; Director, Alan Schneider; Scenery and Lighting, Ben Edwards; Costumes, Jane Greenwood; Assistant Director, Joan Thorne; Hairstylist, Steve Atha; Production Assistant, Katharine Allentuck; Wardrobe Supervisor, Thelma B. Davis

Lu Ann Hampton Laverty Oberlander

CAST

Claudine Hampton	Avril Gentles
Lu Ann Hampton	Diane Ladd
Billy Bob Wortman	James Staley
Skip Hampton	Graham Beckel
Dale Laverty	Everett McGill
Rufe Phelps	Walter Flanagan
Olin Potts	Thomas Toner
Red Grover	Patrick Hines
Corky Oberlander	Baxter Harris
Milo Crawford	Josh Mostel
Charmaine	Kristin Griffith

STANDBYS: for Mr. Gwynne, William Le Massena; for Lu Ann/ Martha Ann/Charmaine, Beverly Shatto; Floyd/Clarence/Maj. Ketchum, Donald Buka; Maureen/Claudine, Patricia Fay; Red/ Rufe/L. D., Joseph Warren; Skip, Everett McGill; Ramsey Eyes, Earl Sydno; Mike, Baxter Harris; Olin/Milo/Lonnie Roy, Charles Kindl; Billy Bob/Dale/Corky/Whopper, Stephen Nasuta

A drama in three acts. The action takes place in Bradleyville, Texas in the Hampton home (1953), Red Grover's bar (1963), Hampton home (1973)

General Manager: Oscar E. Olesen
Company Manager: James Walsh
Press: Seymour Krawitz, Patricia McLean Krawitz, Louise Ment, William Schelble
Stage Managers: William Dodds, Charles Kindl, Stephen Nasuta

* Closed Oct. 31, 1976 after 21 performances in repertory with "The Last Meeting of the Knights of the White Magnolia," and "The Oldest Living Graduate." "A Texas Trilogy" played 63 performances and 6 previews.

Richard Braaten Photos

Right: Baxter Harris, Diane Ladd
Top: Patrick Hines, Diane Ladd

James Staley, Diane Ladd

James Staley, Diane Ladd

BROADHURST THEATRE
  Opened Wednesday, September 22, 1976*
  Robert Whitehead and Roger L. Stevens present:

A TEXAS TRILOGY

Three full-length plays by Preston Jones in repertory; Director, Alan Schneider; Scenery and Lighting, Ben Edwards; Costumes, Jane Greenwood; Assistant Director, Joan Thorne; Hairstylist, Steve Atha; Production Assistant, Katharine Allentuck; Wardrobe Supervisor, Thelma B. Davis

The Last Meeting of the Knights of the White Magnolia

CAST

Ramsey Eyes	John Marriott
Rufe Phelps	Walter Flanagan
Olin Potts	Thomas Toner
Red Grover	Patrick Hines
L. D. Alexander	Henderson Forsythe
Skip Hampton	Graham Beckel
Colonel J. C. Kinkaid	Fred Gwynne
Lonnie Roy McNeil	Paul O'Keefe
Milo Crawford	Josh Mostel

A drama in two acts. The action takes place in Bradleyville, Texas during 1962 in the meeting room of the "Knights of the White Magnolia" on the third floor of the Cattleman's Hotel.

General Manager: Oscar E. Olesen
Company Manager: James Walsh
Press: Seymour Krawitz, Patricia McLean Krawitz, Louise Ment, William Schelble
Stage Managers: William Dodds, Charles Kindle, Stephen Nasuta

* Closed Oct. 30, 1976 after 22 performances in repertory with "Lu Ann Hampton Laverty Oberlander," and "The Oldest Living Graduate." "A Texas Trilogy" played 63 performances and 6 previews.

Richard Braaten Photos

Top: Patrick Hines, Henderson Forsythe, Paul O'Keefe, Walter Flanagan, Thomas Toner

Fred Gwynne

23

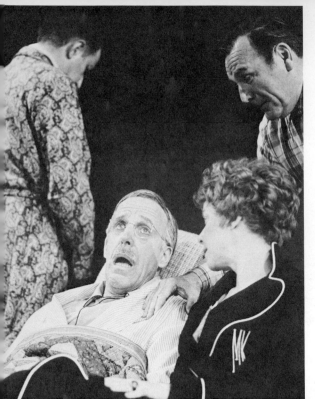

BROADHURST THEATRE

Opened Thursday, September 23, 1976.*
Robert Whitehead and Roger L. Stevens present:

A TEXAS TRILOGY

Three full-length plays by Preston Jones in repertory; Director, Alan Schneider; Scenery and Lighting, Ben Edwards; Costumes, Jane Greenwood; Assistant Director, Joan Thorne; Hairstylist, Steve Atha; Production Assistant, Katharine Allentuck; Wardrobe Supervisor, Thelma B. Davis

The Oldest Living Graduate

CAST

Colonel J. C. Kinkaid .... Fred Gwynne
Maureen Kinkaid .... Patricia Roe
Martha Ann Sickenger .... Kristin Griffith
Mike Tremaine .... Ralph Roberts
Floyd Kinkaid .... Lee Richardson
Clarence Sickenger .... Henderson Forsythe
Major Leroy W. Ketchum .... William LeMassena
Cadet Whopper Turnbull .... Paul O'Keefe
Claudine Hampton .... Avril Gentles

A drama in 2 acts and 5 scenes. The action takes place during the summer of 1962 in Bradleyville, Texas in the den of Floyd Kinkaid's ranch-style home on the outskirts of town.

General Manager: Oscar E. Olesen
Company Manager: James Walsh
Press: Seymour Krawitz, Patricia McLean Krawitz, Louise Ment, William Schelble
Stage Managers: William Dodds, Charles Kindl, Stephen Nasuta

* Closed Oct. 30, 1976 after 20 performances in repertory with "Lu Ann Hampton Laverty Oberlander," and "The Last Meeting of the Knights of the White Magnolia." "A Texas Trilogy" played 63 performances and 6 previews.

Richard Braaten Photos

Fred Gwynne, and top with Lee Richardson, Patricia Roe, Ralph Roberts

Fred Gwynne, Patricia Roe

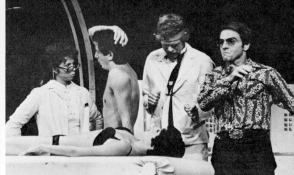

EDISON THEATRE

Opened Friday, September 24, 1976.*
Hillard Elkins, Norman Kean, Robert S. Fishko present:

OH! CALCUTTA!

Devised by Kenneth Tynan; Contributors, Jules Feiffer, Dan Greenburg, Lenore Kandel, John Lennon, Jacques Levy, Leonard Melfi, David Newman and Robert Benton, Sam Shepard, Clovis Trouille, Kenneth Tynan, Sherman Yellen; Music and Lyrics, Robert Dennis, Peter Schickele, Stanley Walden; Additional Music and Lyrics, Stanley Walden, Jacques Levy; Choreography, Margo Sappington; Musical Director, Stanley Walden; Scenery, James Tilton; Lighting, Harry Silverglat; Costumes, Kenneth M. Yount (Supervised by James Tilton); Musical Conductor, Michael Tschudin; Assistant to Director, Nancy Tribush; Projection Design, Gardner Compton; Production Manager, Sam Stickler; Entire Production Conceived and Directed by Jacques Levy; Technical Supervisor, Jim Bryne; Production Assistant, Michael Hreha

CAST

Haru Aki†1	John Hammil
Jean Andalman	William Knight
Bill Bass	Cy Moore†2
Dorothy Chansky	Coline Morse
Cress Darwin	Pamela Pilkenton†3

ACT I: "Taking Off the Robe," "Will Answer All Sincere Replies," "Rock Garden," "Delicious Indignities," "The Paintings of Clovis Trouille," "Suite for Five Letters," "One on One"

ACT II: "Jack and Jill," "Spread Your Love Around," "Was It Good for You Too?," "Coming Together Going Together"

"The World's Longest Running Erotic Stage Musical" in two acts.

General Manager: Norman Kean
Company Manager: James Fiore
Press: Les Schecter Associates, Bill Miller
Stage Managers: David Rubinstein, Maria DiDia

* Still playing May 31, 1977. Original production opened at the Eden Theatre June 17, 1969 and played 1316 performances, before moving to Broadway for 606 performances at the Belasco Theatre.
† Succeeded by: 1. Cheryl Hartley, 2. Billy Padgett, 3. Katherine Liepe

Martha Swope Photo
Ron Reagan, David Vance Photos

Top: William Knight, Pamela Pilkenton, Dorothy Chansky, Jean Andalman, John Hammil Right: Cress Darwin, William Knight

Dorothy Chansky, John Hammil

URIS THEATRE

Opened Saturday, September 25, 1976.*
(Moved Dec. 7, 1976 to Mark Hellinger)
Sherwin M. Goldman and Houston Grand Opera present:

PORGY AND BESS

Music, George Gershwin; Libretto, DuBose Heyward; Lyrics, DuBose Heyward, Ira Gershwin; Based on play "Porgy" by Dorothy and DuBose Heyward; Director, Jack O'Brien; Music Director and Chorus Master, John DeMain; Sets, Robert Randolph; Costumes, Nancy Potts; Lighting, Gilbert V. Hemsley, Jr.; Additional Scenic Elements, John Rothgeb; Choreographer and Assistant Director, Mabel Robinson; Assistant Director, Helaine Head; Musical Preparation, George Darden; Assistant Producer, Virginia Hymes; Assistant to Producers, Suzanne Greenman; Management Associate, Susan Gustafson; Production Coordinator, M. Jane Weaver; Wardrobe Mistress, Leola Edwards; Assistant Conductor, Ross Reimueller; Associate Conductor, Clay Fullum; Original cast album by RCA Victor Records.

CAST

Jasbo Brown	Ross Reimueller
Clara	Betty D. Lane
Mingo	Bernard Thacker
Jake	Curtis Dickson
Sportin' Life	Larry Marshall
Robbins	Glover Parham
Serena	Wilma Shakesnider
	or Delores Ivory-Davis
Jim	Hartwell Mace
Peter	Mervin Wallace
Lily	Myra Merritt
Maria	Carol Brice
Scipio	Alex Carrington
Porgy	Donnie Ray Albert
	or Abraham Lind-Oquendo, Robert Mosley
Crown	Andrew Smith
	or George Robert Merritt
Bess	Clamma Dale
	or Esther Hinds, Irene Oliver
Detective	Hansford Rowe
Policeman	William Gammon
Undertaker	Cornel Richie
Annie	Shirley Baines
Frazier	Raymond Bazemore
Mr. Archdale	Kenneth Barry
Strawberry Woman	Phyllis Bash
Crab Man	Steven Alex-Cole
Coroner	John B. Ross

ENSEMBLE: John D. Anthony, Shirley Baines, Earl Baker, Phyllis Bash, Kenneth Bates, Raymond Bazemore, Barbara Buck, Steven Alex-Cole, Ella Eure, Wilhelmenia Fernandez, Elizabeth Graham, Earl Grandison, Kenneth Hamilton, Betty Harris, Loretta Holkmann, Alma Johnson, Cora Johnson, Roberta Long, Hartwell Mace, Patricia McDermott, Myra Merritt, Naomi Moody, Glover Parham, William Penn, Dwight Ransom, Cornel Richie, Rodrick Ross, Alexander B. Smalls, Bernard Thacker, Mervin Wallace, Barbara Ann Webb, Wardell Woodard, Denice Woods, Barbara L. Young.

UNDERSTUDIES: Clara, Elizabeth Graham, Myra Merritt, Alma Johnson; Jake, Kenneth Hamilton, Alexander B. Smalls; Sportin' Life, Bernard Thacker; Serena, Shirley Baines; Maria, Barbara Ann Webb; Porgy, Hartwell Mace; Bess, Phyllis Bash; Detective, William Gammon; Crown, John D. Anthony; Lily/Strawberry Woman, Barbara Buck; Annie, Barbara L. Young; Peter, Kenneth Bates; Nelson/Crab Man, Dwight Ransom; Mingo, Wardell Woodard; Frazier/Undertaker, Earl Grandison; Robbins, Roderick Ross; Jim, William Penn.

MUSICAL NUMBERS: Introduction, "Brown Blues," "Summertime," "A Woman Is a Sometime Thing," "Here Come de Honey Man," "They Pass by Singin'," "Oh Little Stars," "Gone, Gone, Gone," "Overflow," "My Man's Gone Now," "Leavin' for the Promise Lan'," "It Take a Long Pull to Get There," "I Got Plenty o' Nuttin'," "Buzzard Song," "Bess, You Is My Woman Now," "Oh, I Can't Sit Down," "I Ain't Got No Shame," "It Ain't Necessarily So," "What You Want Wid Bess?," "Oh, Doctor Jesus," "I Loves You, Porgy," "Oh, Hevnly Father," "Oh De Lawd Shake de Heavens," "Oh, Dere's Somebody Knockin' at de Do'," "A Red Headed Woman," "Clara, Clara," "There's a Boat Dat's Leavin' Soon for New York," "Good Mornin', Sistuh!," "Oh, Bess, Oh Where's My Bess," "Oh Lawd, I'm on My Way"

Martha Swope Photos

An American folk opera in 2 acts and 9 scenes. The action takes place during the summer of 1935 in Charleston, S. C.

General Manager: Robert A. Buckley
Company Manager: Bill Liberman
Press: Michael Alpert, Marilynn LeVine, Warren Knowlton
Stage Managers: Helaine Head, Sally McCravey, William Gammon

* Closed Jan. 9, 1977 after 122 performances and 7 previews. Original production with Todd Duncan and Anne Wiggins Brown opened at the Alvin Theatre Oct. 10, 1935 and played 124 performances.

Top Right: Donnie Ray Albert, Clamma Dale
Below: Larry Marshall

Above: Esther Hinds, George-Robert Merritt

CIRCLE IN THE SQUARE THEATRE

Opened Sunday, September 26, 1976.*
Circle in the Square Theatre (Theodore Mann, Artistic Director; Paul Libin, Managing Director) presents:

DAYS IN THE TREES

By Marguerite Duras; Translated by Sonia Orwell; Director, Stephen Porter; Sets and Costumes, Rouben Ter-Arutunian; Lighting, Thomas Skelton; Incidental Music, Robert Dennis; Production Associates, Atsumi Kolba, Jolly Nelson; Wardrobe Supervisor, Virginia Merkel; Hairstylist, Roberto Fernandez; Production Assistants, Suzanne Koblentz, Deborah Boily, Jeffrey Browne, William Callum, Kelly Caro, Tom Causey-Smith, Arlene Grayson Simons, Helene Greece, Susan Kay, Louise Knauf, Sharon Kolberg, Ellen Meltzer, Richard Murphy, Douglas A. Nervik, M. M. O'Flaherty, James Page, Marcia Ross, Teri Smith

CAST

Mother	Mildred Dunnock
The Son	Joseph Maher
Marcelle	Suzanne Lederer
Dede	Ed Setrakian
Nightclub Guests	Helen Harrelson, Donald Linahan, Marlena Lustik

STANDBYS AND UNDERSTUDIES: Mother, Helen Harrelson; Son/Dede, Donald Linahan; Marcelle, Marlena Lustik

A play in 2 acts and 3 scenes. The action takes place in an apartment, and a nightclub in Paris during the 1960's.

Company Manager: William Conn
Press: Merle Debuskey, Susan L. Schulman
Stage Managers: James Bernardi, Donald Linahan

* Closed Nov. 21, 1976 after 69 performances and 23 previews.

Inge Morath Photos

Right: Mildred Dunnock

Mildred Dunnock, Suzanne Lederer, Joseph Maher

PALACE THEATRE
Opened Monday, September 27, 1976.*
Brannigan-Eisler Performing Arts International, Inc. presents:

SIAMSA
National Folk Theatre of Ireland

Devised and Directed by Pat Ahern; Design Consultant, Lona Moran; Choreography, Patricia Hanafin; Wardrobe Supervisor, Phyllis O'Donoghue; Technical Director, Bernard Brannigan; Production Assistants, Betsy Ross, Patricia Morinelli

CAST

The Merrymaker	Sean O'Mahony
The Gardener	Liam Heaslip
The Shoemaker	Sean Ahern
Solo Dancers	Patricia Hanafin, Jimmy Smith, Jerry Nolan, John McCarthy
Solo Singers	Mary Deady, Sean Ahern, Liam Heaslip, Sean O'Mahony
Folk Dancers	Philomena Daly, Susan Rohan, Catherine Hurley, Michael O'Shea, Aidan O'Carroll
Children	Mary Lyons, Marie O'Donoghue, Sandra O'Reilly, Catherine Spangler, Sean Heaslip, Oliver Hurley, John Fitzgerald
Musicians	Pat Kennington, Gerard Buckley, Nicholas McAuliffe, Timmy O'Shea, Pierce Heaslip, Audrey O'Carroll

"A Folk Entertainment" in two acts.

Company Manager: Martin Whelan
Press: Dan Langan
Stage Manager: Jimmy McDonnell

* Closed Oct. 2, 1976 after 8 performances.

Bord Failte Photos

Sean O'Mahoney (Center) Top Left: Liam Heaslip, Sean O'Mahoney, Sean Ahern, Mary Deady Below: Rope Dance

ALVIN THEATRE
Opened Monday, September 27, 1976.*
Dancehouse Inc. and Philip Rose present:

KINGS

Costumes, Ben Benson; Sets, John Falabella; Lighting, Thomas Skelton; Assistant Choreographer, Lynne Taylor; Technical Advisor, Mitch Miller; Production Assistant, Lester Johnson; Wardrobe Supervisor, Henry Arrango; Sound, Grayson Wideman

I. "Oedipus" by Sophocles; Adapted by John Cullum; Director, Emily Frankel; Music created by Emily Frankel. CAST: John Cullum (Oedipus), Casper Roos (Citizen), Paul Myrvold (Attendant), Graham Brown (Tiresias), E. Allan Stevens (Creon), Carol Mayo Jenkins (Jocasta), William Duell (Corinthian), Ed Preble (Herdsman), Lisa Casko (Antigone), Samantha Gold (Ismene), Chorus: Suzi Sfreddo, Cynthia Riffle, Kelly Taylor

II. "Medea"-Choreographed by Norman Walker; Music, Alban Berg. CAST: Emily Frankel (Medea), David Anderson (Jason), John David Cullum, Stephen Casko (Sons)

III. "Theseus & Hippolyta" adapted from Mary Renault's novel "Bull from the Sea"; Staged and Choreographed by Emily Frankel; Music, Miloslav Kabelac, Arvo Part. CAST: John Cullum (Theseus), Emily Frankel (Hippolyta)

An evening of dance and drama presented in three parts.

General Manager: Helen Richards, Steven Suskin
Press: Merle Debuskey, Susan L. Schulman
Stage Manager: Steve Zweigbaum

* Presented for four consecutive Monday evenings only, ending Oct. 18, 1976

Ron Reagan Photos

**Top: (Left) Emily Frankel, John Cullum
(Right) Emily Frankel**

**John Cullum, Emily Frankel,
John David Cullum**

29

HELEN HAYES THEATRE
Opened Tuesday, October 5, 1976.*
Kermit Bloomgarden and Doris Cole Abrahams in association
with Frank Milton present:

EQUUS

By Peter Shaffer; Director, John Dexter; Scenery and Costumes,
John Napier; Lighting, Andy Phillips; Sound, Marc Wilkinson;
Mime, Claude Chagrin; American Supervision by Peter Lobdell;
American Supervision of Scenery and Lighting, Howard Bay; Costumes, Patricia Adshead; Wardrobe Supervisor, Eric Harrison

CAST

Dr. Martin Dysart	Anthony Perkins†1
Alan Strang	Ralph Seymour†2
Nurse	Janet Sarno
Hester Salomon	Laurinda Barrett
Frank Strang	Page Johnson
Dora Strang	Marian Seldes†3
Horseman/Nugget	David Combs
Harry Dalton	Patrick Bedford†4
Jill Mason	Betsy Beard†5
Horses	Terence Burk, John David, Gary Faga†6, Gregory Salata†7, William Wright

UNDERSTUDIES: Dysart/Frank Strang, Patrick Bedford; Alan,
Dennis Erdman; Frank Strang, Richard Neilson; Dora/Hester, Janet Sarno; Jill/Nurse, Nancy Farngione; Horseman/Nugget, William Wright

A drama in two acts. The action takes place in Rokeby Psychiatric
Hospital in Southern England at the present time.

General Manager: Max Allentuck
Press: John Springer, Louis Sica, Michael Alpert, Marilynn
LeVine, Warren Knowlton, Carl Samrock
Stage Managers: Brent Peek, Moose Peting, David M. Everard,
Kathleen A. Sullivan

* Still playing May 31, 1977. Winner of 1975 Best Play awards from
NY Drama Critics Circle, "Tony," Drama Desk, Outer Critics
Circle, also "Tony" and Drama Desk awards for Best Director.
For original production, see THEATRE WORLD, Vol. 31.
† Succeeded by: 1. Alec McCowen, Leonard Nimoy, 2. Michael
Snyder for 4 weeks, 3. Beverly May, 4. Danny Sewell, 5. Nancy
Frangione, Ellen Parker, 6. Timothy Potter, 7. John Tyrrell

Van Williams Photos

Top: David Combs, Ralph Seymour, Anthony Perkins
Right: Marian Seldes, Ralph Seymour, Page Johnson

Leonard Nimoy, Ralph Seymour, David Combs
Above: Michael Snyder, Alec McCowen

BILTMORE THEATRE
Opened Saturday, October 9, 1976.*
John Houseman, Margot Harley, Michael B. Kapon by arrangement with The Acting Company present:

THE ROBBER BRIDEGROOM

Book and Lyrics, Alfred Uhry; Based on novella by Eudora Welty; Music Composed and Arranged by Robert Waldman; Director, Gerald Freedman; Choreography, Donald Saddler; Scenery, Douglas W. Schmidt; Costumes, Jeanne Button; Lighting, David F. Segal; Associate Producer, Porter Van Zandt; Technical Consultant, Edward Wilchinski, Jr.; Wardrobe Supervisor, Rosalie Lahm; Management Associate, Susan Gustafson; Assistant to Director, Gerald Gutierrez

CAST

Jamie Lockhart	Barry Bostwick
Clemment Musgrove	Stephen Vinovich
Rosamund	Rhonda Coullet
Salome	Barbara Lang
Little Harp	Lawrence John Moss
Big Harp	Ernie Sabella
Goat	Trip Plymale
Goat's Mother	Susan Berger
Airie	Jana Schneider
A Raven	Carolyn McCurry
Kyle Nunnery	George Deloy
Harmon Harper	Gary Epp
Norman Ogelsby	B. J. Hardin
Queenie Brenner	Mary Murray
Rose Otto	Melinda Tanner
Gerry G. Summers	Dennis Warning
K. K. Pone	Tom Westerman

UNDERSTUDIES: Jamie, George Deloy; Clemment, B. J. Hardin; Rosamund, Mary Murray; Salome, Carolyn McCurry; Little Harp, Ernie Savella; Big Harp/Kyle/Norman/Gerry/K. K., Gary Epp; Goat, Tom Westerman; Goat's Mother/Airie/Raven/Queenie, Melinda Tanner

MUSICAL NUMBERS: "Once Upon the Natchez Trace," "Two Heads," "Steal with Style," "Rosamund's Dream," "Pricklepear Bloom," "Nothin' Up," "Deeper in the Woods," "Riches," "Love Stolen," "Poor Tied Up Darlin'," "Goodbye Salome," "Sleepy Man," "Where Oh Where"

A musical performed without intermission. The action takes place in and around Rodney, Mississippi.

General Management: McCann & Nugent
Press: Merlin Group, Sandra Manley, Ron Harris, Beatrice DaSilva
Stage Managers: Mary Porter Hall, Bethe Ward

* Closed Feb. 13, 1977 after 145 performances and 12 previews

Right Center: Stephen Vinovich, Barbara Lang, Barry Bostwick Top: Rhonda Coullet, Barry Bostwick

Barry Bostwick, Rhonda Coullet, Stephen Vinovich, Barbara Lang

Ernie Sabella, Carolyn McCurry, Lawrence John Moss

BIJOU THEATRE
Opened Monday, October 11, 1976.*
Tony Conforti in association with Howard Efron and George
Tunick present:

WHEELBARROW CLOSERS

By Louis LaRusso II; Director, Paul Sorvino; Settings, Carles
Carmello, Jr.; Supervised by Ken Billington; Lighting, Leon DiLe-
one; Costumes, Jan Wallace; Supervised by Carol Luiken; Production Associates, David Silberg, Diane Matthews; Associate
Producers, Michael Bash, Howard Wesson, Irving Warhaftig

CAST

Millie Grant	Norah Foster
John Mogan	Raymond Serra
Larry Freede	Harvey Siegel
Beatrice Grant	Frances Helm
Chet Grant	James Allan Bartz
Chester Grant	Danny Aiello
Wilfred Dee	Tom Degidon

A drama in two acts. The action takes place at the present time
in the Grant household.

Company Manager: Jerry Arrow
Press: Max Eisen, Barbara Glenn, Irene Gandy, Judy Jacksina
Stage Managers: Gary Stein, Jane Barish

* Closed Oct. 16, 1976 after 8 performances and 7 previews.

Ron Reagan Photos

**Right: James Allan Bartz, Danny Aiello,
Frances Helm, Norah Foster**

**Tom Degidon, Raymond Serra, Harvey Siegel, James Allan Bartz, Norah Foster, Danny
Aiello**

LYCEUM THEATRE
Opened Tuesday, October 19, 1976.*
Marand Productions in association with Rosemary Vuocolo
and Nancy Davis presents:

BEST FRIEND

By Michael Sawyer; Director, Marty Jacobs; Setting, Andrew
Greenhut; Costumes, Miles White; Lighting, Richard Winkler; Production Consultant, Doug Taylor; Assistants to the Producers, William Michael Maher, Nancy Falls; Production Assistant, Cathy
Blaser; Wardrobe Supervisor, Ellen Anton

CAST

Carolyn Parsky .... Barbara Baxley
Mary Tagliavini .... Liz Sheridan
Anita Fitzgerald .... Mary Doyle
John McGovern .... Michael M. Ryan

UNDERSTUDIES: Carolyn, Liz Sheridan; Anita/Mary, Ingrid
Sonnichsen; John, Victor Raider-Wexler

A play in two acts. The action takes place at the present time in
an apartment on the upper West Side of New York City during late
August.

General Manager: Susan Bell
Press: Lewis Harmon, Sol Jacobson
Stage Managers: Michael Wieben, Victor Raider-Wexler, Ingrid
Sonnichsen

* Closed Oct. 23, 1976 after 8 performances and 8 previews.

Kramer-Abeles Photos

Right: Mary Doyle, Barbara Baxley

Barbara Baxley, Liz Sheridan
Above: Barbara Baxley, Michael M. Ryan

Mary Doyle, Barbara Baxley,
Michael M. Ryan

33

ETHEL BARRYMORE THEATRE
Opened Wednesday, October 20, 1976.*
Kermit Bloomgarden and John Bloomgarden and Ken Marsolais present:

POOR MURDERER

By Pavel Kohout; Director, Herbert Berghof; Scenery and Lighting, Howard Bay; Costumes, Patricia Zipprodt; Musical Director, Stanley Wietrzychowski; Hair Designs, Patrik Moreton; Produced in association with Don Mark Enterprises; Production Associate, Dona D. Vaughn; Assistant to Director, Marlene Mancini; Assistant to Producers, Noel Gilmore; Production Assistants, Mitchell Weiss, Alice Kurrus; Wardrobe Mistress, Latonia Baer

CAST

Professor Drzhembitsky	Larry Gates
Anton Ignatyevich Kerzhentsev/Hamlet	Laurence Luckinbill
First Actor/Alexey Konstantinovich Savelyov/Polonius/ Hamlet II	Kevin McCarthy
First Actress/Tatyana Nikolayevna/Queen	Maria Schell
Second Actor/Ignat Antonovich Kerzhentsev/Rector/Waiter/ Bernardo	Paul Sparer
Third Actor/Dean/Lawyer/Maj. Count Byelitsky/Kurganov/ King	Ernest Graves
Fourth Actor/Cashier/Newspaper Vendor/Conductor/Gypsy/ Francisco/Polonius II	Peter Maloney
Second Actress/Servant Girl/Katya/Flower Vendor/Gypsy Roma/Marya Vassilyevna	Julie Garfield
Third Actress/Voluptuous Mistress/Irina Pavlovna Kurganova/ Countess Byelitskaya	Ruth Ford
Fourth Actress/Slim Mistress/Duchess de Cliche-Turomel// Prologue	Felicia Montealegre
Apprentice/Gypsy Girl	Barbara Coggin
Attendants	Timothy Farmer, James Carruthers, Sean Griffin, Richard Vernon
Musicians	Stanley Wietrzychowski, Brian Koonin, Alfonso Schiapano

UNDERSTUDIES: Kerzhentsev, Sean Griffin; 1st Actress, Felicia Montealegre; Drzhembitsky/3rd Actor, Harry Young; 1st Actor, Ernest Graves; 2nd Actor, James Carruthers; 2nd Actress/Apprentice, Faith Catlin; 3rd and 4th Actress, Barbara Coggin; 4th Actor, Richard Vernon.

A drama in two acts. The action takes place during 1900 in the great hall of the St. Elizabeth Institute for Nervous Disorders, St. Petersburg, Russia.

General Manager: Max Allentuck
Company Manager: Milton Moss
Press: John Springer, Louis Sica, Stephanie Buzzarte
Stage Managers: Frederick A. DeWilde, Harry Young, Timothy Farmer

* Closed Jan. 2, 1977 after 87 performances and 8 previews.

Frederick Ohringer Photos

Top Left: Kevin McCarthy (L), Laurence Luckinbill (C) Below: Kevin McCarthy, Maria Schell, Larry Gates, Laurence Luckinbill

Maria Schell, Laurence Luckinbill

Ruth Ford, Julie Garfield, Felicia Montealegre

MOROSCO THEATRE
Opened Thursday, October 21, 1976.*
Arthur Cantor and Rose Teed present:

THE INNOCENTS

By William Archibald; Based on "Turn of the Screw" by Henry James; Director, Harold Pinter; Scenery, John Lee Beatty; Costumes, Deirdre Clancy; Supervised by Mary McKinley; Lighting, Neil Peter Jampolis; Music, Harrison Birtwistle; Associate Lighting Designer, Jane Reisman; Production Manager, Mitchell Erickson; Wardrobe Mistress, Karen Eifert; Hairstylist, Juan A. Marrero; Production Assistants, Richard Delahanty, William Goulding, Thomas Madigan, Barbara Price

CAST

Flora	Sara Jessica Parker
Mrs. Grose	Pauline Flanagan
Miss Bolton	Claire Bloom
Miles	Michael MacKay
Peter Quint	Dino Laudicina
Miss Jessel	Catherine Wolf

UNDERSTUDIES: Miss Bolton, Catherine Wolf; Miles, Toby Parker; Flora, Shelly Bruce; Mrs. Grose/Miss Jessel, Jane Groves; Peter, Paul Forste.

A drama performed without intermission. The action takes place in the drawing room of an old country house in England during the latter part of the 19th century.

Company Manager: Maurice Schaded
Press: C. George Willard, Barbara Price
Stage Manager: John Handy, Paul Forste, Dino Laudicina

* Closed Oct. 30, 1976 after 12 performances and 3 previews.

**Top: Pauline Flanagan, Michael MacKay,
Sara Jessica Parker, Claire Bloom**

Michael MacKay, Claire Bloom

35

LONGACRE THEATRE
Opened Tuesday, November 9, 1976.*
Roger L. Stevens and Robert Whitehead in association with Frank Milton presents the National Theatre of Great Britain Production:

NO MAN'S LAND

By Harold Pinter; Director, Peter Hall; Designed by John Bury; Staff Director, Sebastian Graham-Jones

CAST

Hirst	Ralph Richardson
Spooner	John Gielgud
Foster	Michael Kitchen
Briggs	Terence Rigby

STANDBYS AND UNDERSTUDIES: Spooner/Hirst, Ron Randell; Foster, Michael Miller; Briggs, Ronald Southart

A drama in two acts. The action takes place at the present time in the drawing room of Hirst's home.

Production Manager: Martin McCallum
Press: Seymour Krawitz, Louise Ment, William Schelble
Stage Manager: John Caulfield

* Closed Dec. 18, 1976 after 47 performances.

Anthony Crickmay Photos

Top: Ralph Richardson Below: John Gielgud, Terence Rigby

John Gielgud Above: Richardson, Gielgud Top: Michael Kitchen

MINSKOFF THEATRE
Opened Tuesday, November 23, 1976.*
Columbia Artists and The Republic of China present:

THE CHINESE ACROBATS OF TAIWAN

Company Director, Dr. Ching-hsien Ho; Associate Director, Yu-kuang Hsu; Head Coach, Yen-ming Chang; Coach, Lien-ch'i Chang; Wardrobe Mistress, Anne Polland; Producer, Michael Ries

PROGRAM

PART I: Chinese Carnival, The Green Ladder, Ribbon Dance, Balancing Rhapsody, Rolling Jars, Flying Chinese Dolls, Rings and Rods, Seesaw Rockets, Chinese 'Ch'i-King, Pagoda of Chairs

PART II: Dancing Plates, Jugglers' Delight, Fancy Feet, Circle of Knives, Feather Dance, Chinese Somersault, Bicycle Jamboree, Chinese Kung-Fu, Human Pyramids

Company Manager: A. Brian Liddicoat
Press: Herbert H. Breslin, Marvin R. Jenkins, Gloria L. Friedman
Stage Managers: Allison D. Liddicoat, Richmond Davis, Lisa S. Ch'en

* Closed Dec. 5, 1976 after 16 performances.

Herbert Migdoll Photos

MOROSCO THEATRE
Opened Tuesday, November 23, 1976.*
Gloria Hope Sher in association with Neal DuBrock presents:

THE ECCENTRICITIES OF A NIGHTINGALE

By Tennessee Williams; A re-write of his play "Summer and Smoke"; Director, Edwin Sherin; Scenery, William Ritman; Costumes, Theoni V. Aldredge; Lighting, Marc B. Weiss; Original Music, Charles Gross; Hairstyles and Makeup, Ted Azar; Produced in conjunction with Max W. Jacobs; Wardrobe Supervisor, Karen Eifert; Assistants to Producer, Fred Lucas, Melissa Gosnell; Production Assistant, Peter Gilbert; Sound, Grayson Wideman

CAST

Alma Winemiller	Betsy Palmer
Reverend Winemiller	Shepperd Strudwick
Mrs. Winemiller	Grace Carney
Mrs. Buchanan	Nan Martin
John Buchanan, Jr.	David Selby
Roger Doremus	Peter Blaxill
Mrs. Bassett	Jen Jones
Rosemary	Patricia Guinan
Vernon	W. P. Dremak
A Traveling Salesman	Thomas Stechschulte

A play in 2 acts and 8 scenes with epilogue. The action takes place shortly before World War I in Glorious Hill, Mississippi.

General Manager: C. Edwin Knill
Press: Seymour Krawitz, Louise Ment, Patricia M. Krawitz
Stage Managers: Henry Banister, K. Anna Moore

* Closed Dec. 12, 1976 after 24 performances and 12 previews.

Sy Friedman Photos

Left: Peter Blaxill, Betsy Palmer, Jen Jones, Grace Carney, Patricia Guinan Above: Blaxill, Jones, Guinan, W. P. Dremak, David Selby, Betsy Palmer Top: Shepperd Strudwick, Nan Mart Betsy Palmer, David Selby

David Selby, Betsy Palmer

David Selby, Nan Martin, Betsy Palmer

WINTER GARDEN
Opened Tuesday, November 23, 1976.*

NATALIE COLE

with

**The Manhattans
Herbie Hancock**

* Closed Nov. 28, 1976 after limited engagement of 6 performances.
No other details available.

MUSIC BOX THEATRE
Opened Sunday, November 28, 1976.*
Alexander H. Cohen in association with Gabriel Katzka and
Edward L. Schuman presents:

COMEDIANS

By Trevor Griffiths; Director, Mike Nichols; Designed by John
Gunter; Lighting, Ron Wallace; Scenery and Costumes, James Til-
ton; Co-Producers, Hildy Parks, Roy A. Somlyo; Associate Man-
ager, Seymour Herscher; Production Assistant, Linda Cohen; Staff
Associate, Michael Katz; Wardrobe Supervisor, Elonzo Dann;
Wardrobe Mistress, Scotty Norell; Assistant to Producers, Rita
Moriarty, Katherine Rosenfield

CAST

Caretaker	Norman Allen
Gethin Price	Jonathan Pryce†1
Phil Murray	Jeffrey DeMunn
George McBrain	Larry Lamb
Sammy Samuels	David Margulies
Mick Connor	Jarlath Conroy
Eddie Waters	Milo O'Shea
Ged Murray	John Lithgow
Mr. Patel	Jayant Blue
Bert Challenor	Rex Robbins
Club Secretary and M.C.	Robert Gerringer
Teddy	Armand Assante†2
Pianist	Woody Kessler

UNDERSTUDIES: Gethin, Jeffrey DeMunn; Sammy/Caretaker,
John Clark; Bert, Robert Gerringer; Ged/Mick, Jonathan Hogan;
George, Armand Assante; Phil/M.C., Norman Allen; Patel, Faizul
Khan

A play in two acts. The action takes place at the present time in
a secondary school, and in a workingman's club in Manchester,
England.

Company Manager: Joel Wyman
Press: Richard Hummler, Martha Mason
Stage Managers: Nina Seely, Faizul Khan

* Closed Apr. 3, 1977 after 145 performances and 39 previews.
† Succeeded by: 1. Jonathan Hogan, 2. Ted Danson

Martha Swope Photos

**Jonathan Pryce Top Right: David Margulies, Larry
Lamb, John Lithgow, Milo O'Shea, Jeffery DeMunn**

**Jonathan Pryce, John Lithgow, Jeffery DeMunn
Above: Jonathan Pryce, Milo O'Shea, David
Margulies**

PALACE THEATRE
Opened Tuesday, November 30, 1976.*
Dore Schary presents:

HERZL

By Dore Schary and Amos Elon; Based on biography of Amos Elon; Director, J Ranelli; Scenery, Douglas W. Schmidt; Costumes, Pearl Somner; Lighting, John Gleason; Assistant to Mr. Schary, Corynne Shaw; Technical Director, Mitch Miller; Wardrobe Supervisor, Angelo Quilici; Hairstylist, Joe Coscia; Assistant to Director, Carol Patella; Production Assistant, Sandy Beckwith

CAST

Theodor Herzl .... Paul Hecht
Moritz Benedikt .... Louis Zorich
Herman Bahr/Ibrahim .... Stephan Mark Weyte
Captain Henrauch/Kaiser Wilhelm .... William Kiehl
Heinrich Kana/Sultan of Turkey .... John Michalski
Arthur Schnitzler/Russian General .... Leo Bloom
Rabbi Gudeman .... Roy K. Stevens
Edouard Bacher .... Jack Axelrod
Jeanette Herzl .... Eunice Anderson
Jakob Herzl .... Roger DeKoven
Julie Herzl .... Judith Light
Nursemaid .... Rebecca Schull
Nachum Sokolov .... Ralph Byers
David Wolffsohn .... Mitchell Jason
Baron Maurice DeHirsch/Pope Pius X .... Richard Seff
Fraulein Keller .... Ellen Tovatt
Count Paul Nevlinski .... Lester Rawlins
Menachem Ussishkin .... David Tress
Martin Buber .... Saylor Creswell

UNDERSTUDIES: Theodor, Robert Murch; Julie, Ellen Tovatt; Jeanette, Rebecca Schull; Heinrich/Rabbi/Sultan, Martin Buber; Delegates, Steve Karp; Fraulein Keller/Nursemaid, Lind Selman; Sokolov, Stephan Mark Weyte; Menachem/Russian General/ DeHirsch/Butler, Jack Axelrod; Ibrahim, Saylor Creswell; Pope, Roy K. Stevens; Herman/Henrauch/Schnitzler, David Tress

A play in two acts. The action takes place between 1891 and 1897, in Vienna, Paris, Constantinople, Berlin, Vilna, Rome and Basel.

General Manager: Eugene V. Wolsk
Company Manager: Gino Giglio
Press: John Springer, Louis Sica, Suzanne Salter
Stage Managers: Frank Marino, Judith Binus, Douglas F. Goodman

* Closed Dec. 5, 1976 after 8 performances and 12 previews.

Martha Swope Photos

Top Right: Stephan Mark Weyte, Paul Hecht

Paul Hecht, Judith Light

Paul Hecht

41

URIS THEATRE
Opened Tuesday, December 7, 1976.*
Robert Paterson presents:

BING CROSBY ON BROADWAY

Staged and Directed by Robert Sidney; Lighting, Martin Aronstein; Produced by William Loeb; Management Associates, David Wyler, Robert Goldberg; Management Assistant, Lora Jeanne Martens

CAST

Bing Crosby

Rosemary Clooney	Joe Bushkin
Kathryn Crosby	Joe Bushkin Quartet
Harry Crosby III	Ted Rogers
Mary-Frances Crosby	Billy Byers Orchestra
Nathaniel Crosby	

"A Musical Entertainment" in two parts.

General Management: Marvin A. Krauss Associates
Press: Michael Alpert, Marilynn LeVine, Carl Samrock, Ted Goldsmith, Warren Knowlton, Randi Cone
Stage Manager: Robert V. Straus

* Closed Dec. 19, 1976 after limited engagement of 12 performances.

Left: Bing Crosby

Harry Crosby III, Kathryn Crosby, Bing Crosby, Mary-Frances Crosby, Nathaniel Crosby

BROADHURST THEATRE
Opened Tuesday, December 14, 1976.*
Sir Lew Grade, Martin Starger and The Shubert Organization
present:

SLY FOX

By Larry Gelbart; Based on play "Volpone" by Ben Jonson; Director, Arthur Penn; Designed and Lighted by George Jenkins; Costumes, Albert Wolsky; Technical Advisor, Mitch Miller; Wardrobe Supervisor, Josephine Zampedri; Hairstylist, Roberto Fernandez; Production Assistants, Jonathan G. Freund, Craig Wells

CAST

Simon Able	Hector Elizondo†1
Sly's Servants	Jeffrey Tambor†2, Calvin Jung, Sandra Seacat
Foxwell J. Sly	George C. Scott†3
Lawyer Craven	John Heffernan
Jethro Crouch	Jack Gilford
Abner Truckle	Bob Dishy†4
Miss Fancy	Gretchen Wyler
Mrs. Truckle	Trish Van Devere†5
Crouch's Servant	Guy King†6
Captain Crouch	John Ramsey†7
Chief of Police	James Gallery†8
First Policeman	Robb Webb†9
Second Policeman/Bailiff	Willy Switkes
Third Policeman	Joel Simon
Court Clerk	Howland Chamberlin
The Judge	George C. Scott†3

UNDERSTUDIES: Crouch, Howland Chamberlin; Sly/Judge, John Ramsey; Mrs. Truckle/Miss Fancy, Sandra Seacat; Policemen/Servants/Court Clerk/Bailiff, Joel Simon; Truckle/Chief of Police, Willy Switkes; Able/Craven, Jeffrey Tambor; Capt. Crouch, Robb Webb

A comedy in 2 acts and 7 scenes. The action takes place one day in the late 1800's in San Francisco.

General Manager: Eugene V. Wolsk
Company Manager: Manny Kladitis
Press: Merle Debuskey, Susan L. Schulman, Fred Hoot, William Schelble
Stage Managers: Henry Velez, Steven Shaw, Joel Simon

* Still playing May 31, 1977.
† Succeeded by: 1. Jeffrey Tambor, 2. Darryl Croxton, 3. Robert Preston, 4. James Gallery, 5. Beth Austin, 6. Howland Chamberlin, 7. Theodore Sorel, 8. Raleigh Bond, 9. Brooks Morton

Kramer-Abeles Photos

Top: Beth Austin, Robert Preston Right: Howland Chamberlin, George C. Scott, John Ramsey, Hector Elizondo, Jack Gilford, Bob Dishy, Trish Van Devere Below: Gilford, Gretchen Wyler

John Heffernan, Jack Gilford, Hector Elizondo Above: Elizondo, Bob Dishy, George C. Scott

CIRCLE IN THE SQUARE THEATRE
Opened Thursday, December 16, 1976.*
Circle in the Square (Theodore Mann, Artistic Director; Paul

THE NIGHT OF THE IGUANA

By Tennessee Williams; Director, Joseph Hardy; Scenery and Lighting, H. R. Poindexter; Costumes, Noel Taylor; Production Associates, Atsumi Kolba, Jolly Nelson; Wardrobe Supervisor, Virginia Merkel

CAST

Rev. T. Lawrence Shannon	Richard Chamberlain
Pedro	Gary Tacon
Maxine Faulk	Sylvia Miles
Pancho	William Paulson
Wolfgang	Ben Van Vacter
Hilda	Jennifer Savidge
Herr Fahrenkopf	John Rose
Frau Fahrenkopf	Amelia Laurenson
Hank	Matt Bennett
Miss Judith Fellowes	Barbara Caruso
Hannah Jelkes	Dorothy McGuire
Charlotte Goodall	Allison Argo
Nonno (Jonathan Coffin)	William Roerick
Jake Latta	Benjamin Stewart

UNDERSTUDIES: Shannon, John Rose; Hannah, Amelia Laurenson; Maxine, Darlene Conley; Charlotte, Jennifer Savidge; Wolfgang/Pancho/Pedro, Martin Rabbett

A drama in two acts and three scenes. The action takes place in the summer of 1940 in the Costa Verde Hotel in Puerto Barrio on the West Coast of Mexico.

Company Manager: William Conn
Press: Merle Debuskey, Susan L. Schulman, Fred Hoot
Stage Managers: Randall Brooks, James Bernardi, Martin Rabbett

* Closed Feb. 20, 1977 after 77 performances and 23 previews. Original production opened at the Royale Theatre Dec. 28, 1961 with Bette Davis, Patrick O'Neal, Margaret Leighton and played 316 performances.

Martha Swope Photos

Top: Richard Chamberlain, Dorothy McGuire, William Roerick   Right: Chamberlain, Sylvia Miles

44

**Richard Chamberlain, Dorothy McGuire
(also above)**

ST. JAMES THEATRE
Opened Monday, December 20, 1976.*
Richard Adler, Roger Berlind, Edward R. Downe, Jr. present:

MUSIC IS

Book by George Abbott; Based on Shakespeare's "Twelfth Night"; Music, Richard Adler; Lyrics, Will Holt; Director, George Abbott; Musical Numbers and Dances Staged by Patricia Birch; Musical Director, Paul Gemignani; Orchestrations, Hershy Kay; Dance and Vocal Arrangements, William Cox; Scenery, Eldon Elder; Costumes, Lewis D. Rampino; Lighting, H. R. Poindexter; Assistant Director, Judith Abbott; Production Supervisor, Mitch Miller; Management Associate, Camille Ranson; Additional Arrangements, Jim Tyler

CAST

William Shakespeare	Daniel Ben-Zali
Valentine	William McClary
Duke Orsino	David Holliday
Curio	David Brummel
Viola	Catherine Cox
Captain	Paul Michael
Clown	William Shakespeare
Maria	Laura Waterbury
Sir Toby Belch	David Sabin
Malvolio	Christopher Hewett
Olivia	Sherry Mathis
Antonio	Marc Jordan
Sebastian	Joel Higgins
Sir Andrew Aguecheek	Joe Ponazecki
First Officer	David Brummel
Second Officer	Doug Carfrae
Cupids	Helena Andreyko, Ann Crowley
Court Musicians	Donald Hettinger, Steve Uscher

MEMBERS OF THE COURT: Helena Andreyko, Doug Carfrae, Jim Corti, Ann Crowley, Dennis Daniels, Dawn Herbert, Dana Kyle, Wayne Mattson, Jason McAuliffe, Carolann Page, Susan Elizabeth Scott, Denny Shearer, Melanie Vaughan, Mimi B. Wallace

UNDERSTUDIES: Valentine/Curio, Doug Carfrae; Orsino/Captain/Antonio, David Brummel; Viola/Olivia, Carolann Page; Feste/Malvolio, William McClary; Aguecheek, Denny Shearer; Sebastian, Jason McAuliffe; Sir Toby, Paul Michael; Maria, Susan Elizabeth Scott

MUSICAL NUMBERS: "Music Is," "When First I Saw My Lady's Face," "Lady's Choice," "The Time Is Ripe for Loving," "Should I Speak of Loving You," "Dance for Six," "Hate to Say Goodbye to You," "Big Bottom Betty," "Twenty One Chateaux," "Sudden Lilac," "Sing Hi," "Blindman's Buff," "Tennis Song," "I Am It," "No Matter Where," "The Duel," "Please Be Human," "What You Will"

A musical in 2 acts and 14 scenes.

General Manager: Theatre Now, Inc.
Company Manager: Robert H. Wallner
Press: Mary Bryant, Richard Kagey
Stage Managers: Bob Bernard, Elise Warner

* Closed Dec. 26, 1976 after 8 performances and 14 previews.

Greg Gilbert, Martha Swope Photos

**Top Right: David Holliday, William McClary
Below: Joel Higgins, Sherry Mathis, Catherine Cox**

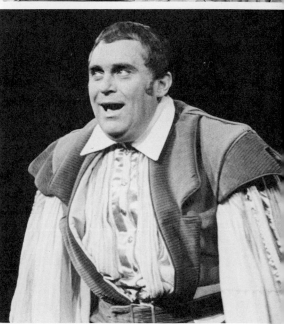

**David Sabin, Laura Waterbury, Joe Ponazecki,
Daniel Ben-Zali**

Christopher Hewett

URIS THEATRE
Opened Tuesday, December 21, 1976.*
Lee Guber, Shelly Gross and Miles Lourie present:

BARRY MANILOW ON BROADWAY

Orchestrations, Gerald Alters; Lighting Designer, Michael Newton-Brown; Supervised by Spencer Mosse; Sound Engineer, John Venable; Mr. Manilow's Clothes, Patrick Elliott; Lady Flash's Clothes, Arthur Boccia; Personal Manager, Miles Lourie; Production Coordinator, Rick Gross; Staging Consultant, Jack Hofsiss; Special Material, Bruce Sussman; Artistic Supervisor, Ken Ranaldi; Choreography, Barry Manilow and Lady Flash

CAST
Barry Manilow
Lady Flash: Debra Byrd, Reparata, Monica Burruss; The City Rhythm Band: Lee Gurst, Alan Axelrod, Keith Loving, Steven Donaghey, Harold "Ricardo" Alexander

An evening of music and songs presented in two parts.

Company Manager: David Lawlor
Press: Solters & Roskin, Joshua Ellis, Fred Nathan
Stage Managers: Chuck O'Brien, Paul Brin

* Closed Jan. 2, 1977 after limited engagement of 12 performances.

Barry Manilow

LYCEUM THEATRE

Opened Wednesday, December 22, 1976.*
Frankie Hewitt and The Shubert Organization in association with Theatre Now, Inc. present The Ford's Theatre Production of:

YOUR ARMS TOO SHORT TO BOX WITH GOD

Conceived from the Book of Matthew by Vinnette Carroll; Music and Lyrics, Alex Bradford; Additional Music and Lyrics, Micki Grant; Director, Vinnette Carroll; Choreography, Talley Beatty; Sets and Costumes, William Schroder; Set Supervisor, Michael J. Hotopp; Lighting, Gilbert V. Hemsley, Jr.; Orchestrations and Dance Music, H. B. Barnum; Choral Arrangements and Direction, Chapman Roberts; Developed by the Urban Arts Corps; Associate Manager, Steve Goldstein; Production Supervisor, Mitch Miller; Musical Supervisor, George Broderick; Assistant Conductor, Danzil A. Miller, Jr.; Wardrobe Supervisor, Jennifer Bryan

CAST

Salome Bey	Adrian Bailey
Clinton Derricks-Carroll	Deborah Lynn Bridges
Sheila Ellis	Sharon Brooks
Delores Hall	Thomas Jefferson Fouse, Jr.
William Hardy, Jr.	Michael Gray
Hector Jaime Mercado	Cardell Hall
Mabel Robinson	Bobby Hill
William Thomas, Jr.	Edna M. Krider
Derek Williams	Leone Washington
	Marilynn Winbush

MUSICAL NUMBERS: "Beatitudes," "We're Gonna Have a Good Time," "There's a Stranger in Town," "Do You Know Jeses?/ He's a Wonder," "Just a Little Bit of Jesus Goes a Long Way," "We Are the Priests and Elders," "Something Is Wrong in Jerusalem," "It Was Alone," "I Know I Have to Leave Here," "Be Careful Whom You Kiss," "Trial," "It's Too Late," "Judas Dance," "Your Arms Too Short to Box with God," "Give Us Barrabas," "See How They Done My Lord," "Come on Down," "Can't No Grave Hold My Body Down," "Didn't I Tell You," "When the Power Comes," "Everybody Has His Own Way," "I Love You So Much Jesus," "The Band"

A Biblical musical performed without intermission.

General Management: Theatre Now, Inc.
Press: Henry Luhrman, Anne Obert Weinberg, Terry M. Lilly
Stage Managers: Haig Shepherd, Robert Charles,

* Still playing May 31, 1977

Martha Swope Photos

Top: Salome Bey (above), Mabel Robinson
Right: the cast
Below: Hector Jaime Mercado (C)

Clinton Derricks-Carroll, Delores Hall

WINTER GARDEN THEATRE
Opened Tuesday, December 28, 1976.*
The Shubert Organization and Nederlander Producing Company of America, and the John F. Kennedy Center for the Performing Arts, in association with Theatre Now, Inc. (William Court Cohen, Edward H. Davis, Norman E. Rothstein) present:

FIDDLER ON THE ROOF

Book by Joseph Stein; Based on Sholom Aleichem's stories; Music, Jerry Bock; Lyrics, Sheldon Harnick; Direction and Choreography, Jerome Robbins; Settings, Boris Aronson; Costumes, Patricia Zipprodt; Lighting, Ken Billington; Orchestrations, Don Walker; Vocal Arrangements, Milton Greene; Dance Music Arranged by Betty Walberg; Music Director, Milton Rosenstock; Direction Reproduced by Ruth Mitchell; Choreography Reproduced by Tom Abbott; Production Supervisor, Mitch Miller; Technical Supervisor, Peter Mavoides; Wardrobe Supervisor, Robert Killgoar; Hairstylist, Howard Rodney; Management Associate, Camille Ranson; Assistant Conductor, Danny Rocks.

CAST

Tevye, the dairyman	Zero Mostel†1
Golde, his wife	Thelma Lee
His daughters:	
Tzeitel	Elizabeth Hale
Hodel	Christopher Callan
Chava	Nancy Tompkins
Shprintze	David Sacks
Bielke	Tiffany Bogart
Yente, the matchmaker	Ruth Jaroslow
Motel, the tailor	Irwin Pearl
Perchik, the student	Jeff Keller†2
Mordcha, the innkeeper	Leon Spelman
Lazar Wolf, the butcher	Paul Lipson
Rabbi	Charles Mayer
Mendel, his son	Paul A. Corman
Avram, the bookseller	Merrill Plaskow II
Nachum, the beggar	David Masters
Grandma Tzeitel	Duane Bodin
Fruma Sarah	Joyce Martin
Constable	Alexander Orfaly
Fyedka	Rick Friesen
Shandel, Motel's mother	Jeanne Grant
Bottle Dancers	Tog Richards, Myron Curtis, Matthew Inge, Wallace Munro
Fiddler	Sammy Bayes

VILLAGERS: Shloime the bagel man, Matthew Inge; Yitzuk the streetsweeper, Don Tull; Chaim the fishmonger, Glen McClaskey; Duvidel the seltzer man, Wallace Munro; Surcha, Lynn Archer, Label, Tog Richards, Schmeril, David Horwitz; Yakov the knifeseller, Patrick Quinn; Hershel, Myron Curtis; Fredel, Hope Katcher; Bluma, Debra Timmons; Mirala, Maureen Sadusk; Sima, Lynn Archer; Rivka, Joyce Martin; Yussel, Duane Bodin; Vladimer, Robert L. Hultman; Sasha, Wallace Munro; Bascha, Shelley Wolf.

UNDERSTUDIES: Tevye, Paul Lipson; Golde, Jeanne Grant; Motel, Paul A. Corman; Yente, Lynn Archer; Tzeitel/Fruma, Hope Katcher; Chava/Shprintze/Bielke, Debra Timmons; Lazar, Leon Spelman; Rabbi/Avram, David Masters; Perchik/Fyedka, Patrick Quinn; Hodel, Nancy Tompkins; Mendel, Matthew Inge; Constable, Glen McClaskey; Innkeeper, Merrill Plaskow II; Beggar, Tog Richards; Grandma, Wallace Munro; Fiddler, Vito Durante.

MUSICAL NUMBERS: "Tradition," "Matchmaker, Matchmaker," "If I Were a Rich Man," "Sabbath Prayer," "To Life," "Miracle of Miracles," "The Tailor, Motel Kamzoil," "Sunrise, Sunset," "Bottle Dance," "Wedding Dance," "Now I Have Everything," "Do You Love Me?," "Far from the Home I Love," "Chava," "Anatevka," "Epilogue"

A musical in two acts. The action takes place in 1905 on the eve of the revolutionary period in Anatevka, a village in Russia.

General Manager: Theatre Now, Inc.
Company Manager: Robb Lady
Press: Betty Lee Hunt, Maria Pucci, Fred Hoot
Stage Managers: Kenneth Porter, Tobias Mostel, Val Mayer

* Closed May 21, 1977 after limited engagement of 167 performances and 1 preview. Original production with Zero Mostel opened Sept. 22, 1964 at the Imperial Theatre and ran for 3242 performances. See THEATRE WORLD Vol. 21.
† Succeeded by: 1. Paul Lipson during illness, 2. Patrick Quinn.

Thelma Lee, Ruth Jaroslow
Above: Zero Mostel, Paul Lipson

Top Left: Zero Mostel, Thelma Lee, Below: Nanc
Tompkins, Elizabeth Hale, Christopher Callen

MOROSCO THEATRE

Opened Saturday, January 1, 1977.*

Adela Holzer presents:

SOMETHING OLD, SOMETHING NEW

By Henry Denker; Director, Robert H. Livingston; Scenery and Costumes, Lawrence King and Michael H. Yeargan; Lighting, Clarke Dunham; Wardrobe Supervisor, Warren Morrill; Assistant Set Designer, B. Ursula Belden; Assistant Costume Designer, Donna Tomas

CAST

Cynthia Morse	Holland Taylor
Mike Curtis	Dick Patterson
Samuel Jonas	Hans Conried
Laura Curtis	Molly Picon
Eleanor Curtis	Lois Markle
Dr. Arthur Morse	Matthew Tobin
Bruce Morse	Ahvi Spindell
Angela	Cynthia Bostick

UNDERSTUDIES: Laura, Rose Lischner; Samuel/Mike/Arthur, Frank Bara; Cynthia/Eleanor/Angela, Lynn MacLaren; Bruce, Ken Sherber

A comedy in three acts. The action takes place at the present time in the apartment of Samuel Jonas on the West Side of New York City, on a Thursday morning in spring.

General Manager: Leonard A. Mulhern
Company Manager: James Mennen
Press: Michael Alpert, Marilynn LeVine, Warren Knowlton, Carl Samrock, Randi Cone
Stage Managers: Martha Knight, Ken Sherber

* Closed Jan. 1, 1977 after one performance and 14 previews.

Sy Friedman Photos

**Hans Conried, Beryl Towbin (pre-Bdwy), Molly Picon, Matthew Tobin
Top Left: Hans Conried, Molly Picon**

LONGACRE THEATRE
Opened Tuesday, January 4, 1977.*
Philip Rose, Gloria and Louis K. Sher present:

THE TRIP BACK DOWN

By John Bishop; Director, Terry Schreiber; Scenery, Hal Tine; Costumes, Pearl Somner; Lighting, Richard Nelson; Technical Adviser, Mitch Miller; Wardrobe Supervisor, Agnes Farrell; Assistant to Director, Chris Lutz; Production Assistant, Rosemary Troyano; Hairstylist, Media Hair Design

CAST

Bobby Horvath	John Cullum
Policeman/Dave/Mechanic/Guest/ Schmidt/Man	John Randolph Jones
Factory Worker/Richie/Guest/Man	William Andrews
Factory Worker/Chuck	Charles Brant
Frank Horvath	Arlen Dean Snyder
Barbara Horvath	Doris Belack
Super Joe Weller	Anthony Call
Waitress/Guest	Gwendolyn Brown
Autograph Man/Bartender/Neighbor	Gordon Oas-Heim
JoAnn Meeghan	Jill Andre
Will Horvath	Edward Seamon
Pam	Alexa Spencer
Bar Girl/Guest	Carol Chanco
John Meeghan	Andrew Jarkowsky
Jan	Blaise Bulfair

UNDERSTUDIES: JoAnn/Barbara, Gwendolyn Brown; John, William Andrews; Jan/Pam, Carol Chanco; Super Joe, John Randolph Jones; Frank/Will, Gordon Oas-Heim; Chuck, Dean Vallas; General Understudy, Philip Oxnam

A drama in two acts. The action takes place in the spring of 1975 in Mansfield, Ohio.

General Manager: Helen Richards
Company Manager: Steven Suskin
Press: Merle Debuskey, Leo Stern
Stage Managers: Mortimer Halpern, Dean Vallas

* Closed March 6, 1977 after 70 performances and 10 previews.

Kramer-Abeles Photos

Right: Doris Belack, John Cullum
Top: Anthony Call, John Cullum

Edward Seamon, John Cullum

Edward Seamon, John Cullum, Carol Chanco, Andrew Jarkowsky

JOHN GOLDEN THEATRE
Opened Tuesday, January 11, 1977.*
Elliot Martin and Inter-Action Trust Ltd. present:

DIRTY LINEN
and
NEW-FOUND-LAND

By Tom Stoppard; Director, Ed Berman; Original London Production Designed by Gabriella Falk; Scenery and Costumes Supervised by Lawrence King and Michael H. Yeargan; Lighting, Martin Aronstein; Production Associate, Marjorie Martin; Presented by arrangement with the John F. Kennedy Center for the Performing Arts; Wardrobe Supervisor, Joseph Busheme; Hairstylist, Ted Azar; Company Coordinator, Daniel Ostroff; Production Assistants, Steven Prioletti, Charles Shain

CAST

"Dirty Linen"
Maddie .... Cecilia Hart
McTeazle, M.P. .... Francis Bethencourt
Cocklebury-Smythe, M.P. .... Remak Ramsay
Chamberlain, M.P. .... Michael Tolaydo
Withenshaw, M.P. .... Merwin Goldsmith
Mrs. Ebury, M.P. .... Leila Blake
French, M.P. .... Stephen D. Newman
Home Secretary .... Stephen Scott

"New-Found-Land"
Arthur .... Jacob Brooke
Bernard .... Humphrey Davis

UNDERSTUDIES: French/Arthur/Chamberlain, Edmond Genest; Home Secretary/Withenshaw, Michael McCarty; Cocklebury-Smythe/McTeazle, Stephen Scott; Maddie/Mrs. Ebury, Lynn Welden; Bernard, Daniel Keyes

A comedy performed without intermission. "New-Found-Land" takes place within the action of "Dirty Linen."

General Manager: Leonard A. Mulhern
Associate General Manager: David Relyea
Press: Seymour Krawitz, Patricia M. Krawitz, Louise Ment
Stage Managers: Wally Peterson, Michael McCarty

* Closed May 28, 1977 after 159 performances and 7 previews.

Right: Remak Ramsay, Francis Bethencourt, Cecilia Hart   Top: Stephen D. Newman, Michael Tolaydo, Remak Ramsay, Cecilia Hart, Merwin Goldsmith, Leila Blake, Francis Bethencourt

**Humphrey Davis, Jacob Brooke
in "New-Found-Land"**

Sy Friedman Photos

Merwin Goldsmith, Cecilia Hart

HARKNESS THEATRE
Opened Wednesday, January 12, 1977.*
A. Deshe (Pashanel) and Topol by arrangement with Ray Cooney Productions, Ltd. and Academy Theatre & Brooke Theatre, Johannesburg, present:

IPI-TOMBI

Conceived, Devised and Produced by Bertha Egnos; Original Music, Bertha Egnos; Lyrics, Gail Lakier; Choreography, Sheila Wartski; Additional Choreography, Neil McKay and members of the cast; Scenery, Elizabeth MacLeish; Lighting, Timothy Heale, John Wain; Costumes Supervised by Susan Wain; American Costume Supervision, David Toser; Sound, Sander Hacker; American Scenic Supervision, Robert Mitchell; American Lighting Supervision, Jeremy Johnson; Wardrobe Supervisor, Karen L. Eifert; Production Assistant, Adrienne Jones; Original cast album by Ashtree/Audio Fidelity Records

CAST

Count Wellington Judge, Daniel Pule, Jabu Mbalo, Matthew Bodibe, Gideon Bendile, Elliot Ngubane, Andrew Kau, Sam Hlatshwayo, Philip Gama, David Mthethwa, Shadrack Moyo, Junior Tshabalala, Simon Nkosi, Ali Lerefolo, Martha Molefe, Dorcas Faku, Lydia Monamodi, Busi Dlamini, Zelda Funani, Thembi Mtshali, Linda Tshabalsla, Betty-Boo Hlela, Dudu Nzimade, Coreen Pike, Nellie Khumalo

PROGRAM

ACT I: Village of Tsomo, The Baptism, Song of Hope, City of Gold

ACT II: Sunday on the Mines, The Township Wedding, Workaday on the Mine, The Warriors

A musical of South Africa in 2 acts and 8 scenes.

General Manager: Ralph Roseman
Press: Max Eisen, Barbara Glenn
Stage Managers: Patrick Horrigan, Barbara Dilker, Andre Love

* Closed Feb. 13, 1977 after 39 performances and 17 previews.

PLYMOUTH THEATRE
Opened Wednesday, February 2, 1977.*
James M. Nederlander, Frank Milton and Michael Codron
present:

OTHERWISE ENGAGED

By Simon Gray; Director, Harold Pinter; Settings, Eileen Diss;
Costumes, Jane Greenwood; Set Supervision and Lighting, Neil Peter Jampolis; Wardrobe Supervisor, Billie White; Management Assistant, Veronica Claypool

CAST

Simon	Tom Courtenay†
Dave	John Christopher Jones
Stephen	John Horton
Jeff	Nicolas Coster
Davia	Lynn Milgrim
Wood	Michael Lombard
Beth	Carolyn Lagerfelt

UNDERSTUDIES: Simon/Wood, Steven Sutherland; Stephen/Jeff, Michael Connolly; Dave, Jeff Rubin; Beth, Catherine Wolf; Davina, Laura Copland

A comedy in two acts. The action takes place at the present time in a house in London.

General Managers: McCann & Nugent
Company Manager: Susan Gustafson
Press: Michael Alpert, Marilynn LeVine, Warren Knowlton
Stage Managers: Ben Janney, Jeff Rubin

* Still playing May 31, 1977. Recipient of 1977 New York Drama Critics Circle Award for Best Play.
† Succeeded by Dick Cavett; Steven Sutherland on Wednesday matinees

Martha Swope Photos

Right: Lynn Milgrim, Tom Courtenay
Top: Tom Courtenay, Nicolas Coster

John Horton, Carolyn Lagerfelt, Dick Cavett
Above: Tom Courtenay, Michael Lombard

John Christopher Jones, Tom Courtenay

53

MOROSCO THEATRE
Opened Thursday, February 10, 1977.*
(Moved March 21, 1977 to Little Theatre)
Arthur Cantor and Leonard Friedman present:

A PARTY WITH BETTY COMDEN & ADOLPH GREEN

with Paul Trueblood at the piano; Miss Comden's gowns by Donald Brooks; Executed by John Fitzpatrick; Technical Director, Mitch Miller; Production Assistant, Thomas Madigan; Administrative Assistant, Barbara Price

A performance of songs and sketches written by Betty Comden and Adolph Green presented in two parts.

General Management: Jack Schlissel/Jay Kingwill
Company Manager: Mark Bramble
Press: C. George Willard
Stage Manager: Larry Bussard

* Closed Apr. 30, 1977 after 92 performances and 4 previews.

Betty Comden, Adolph Green
(also above)

54

ETHEL BARRYMORE THEATRE
Opened Wednesday, February 16, 1977.*
(Moved April 12, 1977 to Belasco Theatre)
Edgar Lansbury and Joseph Beruh present:

AMERICAN BUFFALO

By David Mamet; Director, Ulu Grosbard; Designed by Santo Loquasto; Lighting, Jules Fisher; Associate Producer, Nan Pearlman; Wardrobe Supervisor, Sydney Smith; Production Design Assistant, Fredda Slavin; Production Assistants, Lora J. Martens, M. E. Carpenter; Assistant to Producers, Darrell Jonas

CAST

Donny Dubrow .... Kenneth McMillan
Bobby .... John Savage
Walter "Teacher" Cole. .... Robert Duvall

A drama in two acts. The action takes place at the present time on a Friday in Don's Resale Junkshop.

General Management: Marvin A. Krauss Associates
Company Manager: Al J. Isaac
Press: Gifford/Wallace, Tom Trenkle, Glenna Freedman
Stage Managers: Herb Vogler, Joel Tropper

* Closed June 11, 1977 after 122 performances and 13 previews. Received New York Drama Critics Circle 1977 citation as Best American Play.

Roger Greenawalt Photos

Right: Robert Duvall

Robert Duvall, John Savage, Kenneth McMillan

Rex Harrison, Elizabeth Ashley

PALACE THEATRE
Opened Thursday, February 24, 1977.*
Elliot Martin and Gladys Rackmil, John F. Kennedy Center for the Performing Arts in association with James Nederlander present:

CAESAR AND CLEOPATRA

By George Bernard Shaw; Director, Ellis Rabb; Scenery, Ming Cho Lee; Costumes, Jane Greenwood; Lighting, Thomas Skelton; Movement Coach, Al Sambogna; Hairstylist, Paul Huntley; Directorial Assistant, William Gammon; Wardrobe Supervisor, Warren Morrill; Production Assistant, Steve Prioletti; Speech Consultant, Edith Skinner

CAST

Julius Caesar	Rex Harrison
Cleopatra	Elizabeth Ashley†
Ftatateeta	Novella Nelson
Rufio	Paul Hecht
Pothinus	Patrick Hines
Theodotus	William Robertson
Ptolemy	Roger Campo
Achillas	Mike Dantuono
Britannus	James Valentine
Lucius Septimius	John Bergstrom
Roman Sentinel	Edwin Owens
Apollodorus	Thom Christopher
Musician, a Nubian	Charles Turner
Iras	Fiddle Viracola
Charmian	Linda Martin
Court Lady	Pawnee Sills
Major Domo	Paul Rosson
Priests	Cain Richards, Ian Stuart
Slaves	Cain Richards, Joseph Scalzo, Eric Booth

UNDERSTUDIES: Caesar, James Valentine; Cleopatra, Linda Martin; Britannus, Ian Stuart; Ftatateeta/Iras/Charmian, Pawnee Sills; Pothinus/Theodotus, Paul Rosson; Achillas/Ruffio, Edwin Owens; Ptolemy, Christopher Weddle; Apollodorus/Lucius Septimus, Eric Booth; Sentinel, Charles Turner; Nubian, Cain Richards

A play in 2 acts and 6 scenes. The action takes place in 48 B.C. in Egypt.

General Managers: Leonard A. Mulhern, Maurice Schaded
Company Manager: James Mennen
Press: Betty Lee Hunt, Maria Pucci, Fred Hoot
Stage Managers: William Dodds, Michael Schaefer, Ian Stuart, Joseph Scalzo, Richard Delahanty

* Closed March 5, 1977 after 12 performances and 20 previews. Original NY production with Johnston Forbes-Robertson and Gertrude Elliott opened Oct. 30, 1906 and played 49 performances at the New Amsterdam Theatre.
† Played for two performances by Linda Martin during Miss Ashley's illness.

Richard Braaten Photos

**Rex Harrison, Elizabeth Ashley,
Novella Nelson**

**Paul Hecht, Thom Christopher, Elizabeth Ashley,
Rex Harrison**

Right: Bill Lazarus, Jerry Stiller, Loney Lewis
Top: Zohra Lampert, Michael Vale, Constance
Forslund, Frank Piazza, Jerry Stiller,
Bill Lazarus

THE LITTLE THEATRE
Opened Wednesday, March 2, 1977.*
Charles Grodin presents:

UNEXPECTED GUESTS

By Jordan Crittenden; Director, Charles Grodin; Scenery, Stuart Wurtzel; Costumes, Joseph G. Aulisi; Lighting, Cheryl Thacker; Production Supervisor, Richard Scanga; Assistant to Director, Kris Koczur

CAST

Vince Provenzano	Frank Piazza
Harry Mullin	Jerry Stiller
Gordon	Bill Lazarus
M. J. Nyberg	Michael Vale
Mrs. Mullin	Anne Ives
Mr. Mullin	Loney Lewis
Susan Beckerman	Constance Forslund
Melissa Mullin	Zohra Lampert
Delivery Man	Robert Costanzo
Man	Robert Earl Jones

UNDERSTUDIES: Harry, Bill Lazarus; Melissa/Susan/Mrs. Mullin, Sandy Gabriel; Vince/Nyberg/Gordon/Mr. Mullin, Robert Costanzo

A comedy in two acts. The action takes place at the present time on an October evening in a home in Southern California.

Company Manager: John Corkill
Press: Michael Alpert, Marilynn LeVine, Warren Knowlton, Randi Cone
Stage Managers: John Brigleb, Ellsworth Wright

* Closed March 13, 1977 after 14 performances and 22 previews.

Zohra Lampert, Frank Piazza,
Jerry Stiller

IMPERIAL THEATRE
Opened Tuesday, March 15, 1977.*
Emanuel Azenberg and Dasha Epstein present:

HAL HOLBROOK
in
"MARK TWAIN TONIGHT!"

Production Supervisor, Bennett Thompson; Production Associate, Cathy Blaser; Assistant to the Producers, Leslie Butler; Production Assistants, Mary Jo Slater, Karen Wood

Mr. Holbrook as Mark Twain presents, in two parts, selections from Mr. Twain's writings.

Manager: Jose Vega
Company Manager: Earl Shendell
Press: Bill Evans, Susan Bell, Kevin Ottem

* Closed March 26, 1977 after limited engagement of 12 performances and 1 preview.

**Hal Holbrook
as Mark Twain**

CIRCLE IN THE SQUARE THEATRE
Opened Thursday, March 17, 1977.*
Circle in the Square (Theodore Mann, Artistic Director; Paul Libin, Managing Director) presents:

ROMEO AND JULIET

By William Shakespeare; Director, Theodore Mann; Scenery, Ming Cho Lee; Costumes, John Conklin; Lighting, Thomas Skelton; Music, Thomas Pasatieri; Fights and Fencing, Patrick Crean, Erik Fredricksen; Wigs and Hair Styles, Paul Huntley; Textual Adviser, Diana Maddox; Production Associates, Atsumi Kolba, Jolly Nelson; Wardrobe Supervisor, Virginia Merkel; Hairdresser, Michael Wasula; Production Assistants, William Callum, Louise Knauf, Sharyn Kolberg, Leslie McCullough, M. M. O'Flaherty, Christine Pittel, Paul Schneeberger, Teri Smith.

CAST

Chorus/Musician/Guard	Jim Broaddus
Sampson/Watchman	Christopher Loomis
Gregory/Chief Watch	Dennis Lipscomb
Peter	Dennis Patella
Abram/Friar John/Watchman	Peter Van Norden
Balthasar	Michael Forella
Benvolio	Ray Wise
Tybalt	Armand Assante
Capulet	Lester Rawlins
Lady Capulet	Delphi Harrington
Montague	Tom Klunis
Lady Montague	Helen Harrelson
Prince Escalus	Richard Greene
Romeo	Paul Rudd
Paris	John V. Shea
Juliet	Pamela Payton-Wright
Nurse to Juliet	Jan Miner
Mercutio	David Rounds
Rosaline	Lisa Pelikan
Cousin Capulet/Watchman	Erik Fredricksen
Friar Laurence	Jack Gwillim
Musician/Guard	K. C. Kelly
Apothecary	Daniel Ben-Zali
Paris' Page	Mark Cohen
Ladies of Verona	Ruth Livingston, Jennifer Savidge

UNDERSTUDIES: Romeo, John V. Shea; Juliet, Lisa Pelikan; Nurse, Helen Harrelson; Mercutio/Paris, Dennis Lipscomb; Capulet/Montague, Daniel Ben-Zali; Lady Capulet/Lady Montague, Ruth Livingston; Escalus/Friar John/Abram, Jim Broaddus; Sampson/Servant/Watchman/Gregory/Peter/Balthasar, K. C. Kelly; Friar Laurence, Peter Van Norden; Tybalt/Benvolio/Chorus, John Rose

A tragedy performed in two acts. The action takes place in Verona and Mantua.

Company Manager: William Conn
Press: Merle Debuskey, David Roggensack
Stage Managers: Randall Brooks, James Bernardi, K. C. Kelly

* Closed May 22, 1977 after 77 performances and 23 previews.

Martha Swope Photos

Top Right: Paul Rudd, Pamela Payton-Wright, Jack Gwillim

Ray Wise, Paul Rudd, David Rounds

Jan Miner

BILTMORE THEATRE
Opened Thursday, March 24, 1977.*
Ron Delsener presents:

LILY TOMLIN
in
"Appearing Nitely"

Written and Directed by Jane Wagner and Lily Tomlin; Staged by George Boyd; Music, Jerry Frankel; Lighting, Daniel Adams; Costume, J. Allen Highfill; Sound, Jack Mann; Associate Producer, George Boyd; Additional Material, Cynthia Buchanan, Lorne Michaels, Patricia Resnick; Executive Producer, Michael Tannen.

A solo performance presented in two parts with Miss Tomlin and the characters she creates.

General Management: Marvin A. Krauss Associates
Company Manager: Robert I. Goldberg
Press: The Merlin Group Ltd., Sandra Manley
Stage Manager: Brian Meister

* Closed June 12, 1977 after a limited engagement of 96 performances.

Lily Tomlin

TOWN HALL

Opened Tuesday, March 29, 1977.*

Richard Grayson and John Bowab present "Broadway in Concert at Town Hall":

SHE LOVES ME

Book, Joe Masteroff; Based on play by Miklos Laszlo "Parfumerie," and film made from it "The Shop around the Corner"; Music, Jerry Bock; Lyrics, Sheldon Harnick; Director, John Bowab; Musical Director, Wally Harper; Gowns, Donald Brooks; Lighting, Ken Billington; Director's Assistant, Joey Patton; Production Assistant, Patricia Morinelli

CAST

Ladislav Sipos	Tom Batten
Arpad	George David Connolly
Ilona Ritter	Rita Moreno
Steven Kodaly	Laurence Guittard
Georg Nowack	Barry Bostwick
Mr. Maraczek	George Rose
Customers	Bette Glenn, Marti Bucklew, Janet McCall
Amalia Balash	Madeline Kahn
Keller	Michael Hayward Jones
Waiter	John LaMotta
Choraler	William James

UNDERSTUDIES: Ilona/Amalia, Bette Glenn; Georg/Steven/Arpad/Keller, William James; Mr. Maraczek, Tom Batten; Ladislav/Waiter, Michael Hayward Jones

MUSICAL NUMBERS: "Good Morning, Good Day," "Sounds While Selling," "Days Gone By," "No More Candy," "Three Letters," "Tonight at 8," "I Don't Know His Name," "Perspective," "Goodbye Georg," "Will He Like Me," "Ilona," "I Resolve," "A Romantic Atmosphere," "Tango Tragique," "Mr. Nowack, Will You Please," "Dear Friend," "Try Me," "Where's My Shoe," "Vanilla Ice Cream," "She Loves Me," "A Trip to the Library," "Grand Knowing You," "12 Days to Christmas," Finale.

A musical in 2 acts and 10 scenes.

Company Manager: Gino Giglio
Press: Betty Lee Hunt, Maria Pucci, Fred Hoot
Stage Managers: Ben Sprecher, T. L. Boston, Michael Hayward-Jones

* Closed April 17, 1977 after limited engagement of 24 performances. Original production with Jack Cassidy, Barbara Cook, Barbara Baxley and Daniel Massey opened April 23, 1963 and played 301 performances.

Ken Howard Photos

Rita Moreno, George Rose Top Right: George Rose, Barry Bostwick, Rita Moreno, Madeline Kahn

Madeline Kahn, Barry Bostwick

BIJOU THEATRE
Opened Wednesday, March 30, 1977.*
Arthur Shafman International, Ltd. presents:

MUMMENSCHANZ

Production Supervisor, Christopher Dunlop; Production Adviser, Richard G. Miller; Production Associates, Evelyn Gross, Susan Balsam

CAST

Andres Bossard
Floriana Frassetto
Bernie Schurch

A program of mime in two parts with the use of masks, flexible body wrappings, props and costumes.

Company Manager: John Scott
Press: Jeffrey Richards, Michael Ellis, Barbara Carroll
Stage Manager: Patrick Lecoq

* Still playing May 31, 1977.

Top Right: Andres Bossard, Floriana Frassetto, Bernie Schurch

MOROSCO THEATRE
Opened Thursday, March 31, 1977.*
Lester Osterman, Ken Marsolais, Allan Francis and Leonard Soloway present the Mark Taper Forum/Long Wharf Theatre Production of:

THE SHADOW BOX

By Michael Cristofer; Director, Gordon Davidson; Setting, Ming Cho Lee; Costumes, Bill Walker; Lighting, Ronald Wallace; Associate Producers, Philip Getter, Bernard Stuchin; Wardrobe Supervisor, Joseph Busheme; Assistant to Producers, Louise Edmonson; Hairstylist, Patrick D. Morton

CAST

The Interviewer	Josef Sommer†1
Cottage 1:	
Joe	Simon Oakland†2
Steve	Vincent Stewart
Maggie	Joyce Ebert†3
Cottage 2:	
Brian	Laurence Luckinbill†4
Mark	Mandy Patinkin†5
Beverly	Patricia Elliott†6
Cottage 3:	
Agnes	Rose Gregorio
Felicity	Geraldine Fitzgerald†7

A drama in two acts. The action takes place at the present time in three cottages on the grounds of a large hospital.

Company Manager: Robert H. Wallner
Press: Betty Lee Hunt, Maria Pucci, Fred Hoot
Stage Manager: Franklin Keysar

* Still playing May 31, 1977. Winner of 1977 Pulitzer Prize and "Tony" Award for Best Play.
† Succeeded by: 1. Stephen Keep, 2. Clifton James, 3. Sloane Shelton, 4. Josef Sommer, 5. David Rasche, 6. Gwyda DonHowe, 7. Mary Carver

Top: Vincent Stewart, Joyce Ebert, Simon Oakland
Right: Laurence Luckinbill, Patricia Elliott, Mandy Patinkin

Geraldine Fitzgerald, Rose Gregorio

MARTIN BECK THEATRE
Opened Thursday, April 7, 1977.*
Edgar Bronfman, Jr. for Sagittarius Entertainment presents:

LADIES AT THE ALAMO

By Paul Zindel; Director, Frank Perry; Scenery, Peter Larkin; Costumes, Ruth Morley; Lighting, Marc Weiss; Assistant to Director, Lynn Forman; Assistant to Producer, Liza Lerner; Production Assistant, Patti Hassler; Hairstylist, Steve Atha; Wardrobe Supervisor, Agnes Farrell

CAST

Dede Cooper	Estelle Parsons
Bella Gardner	Eileen Heckart
Suits	Susan Peretz
Joanne Remington	Rosemary Murphy
Shirley Fuller	Jan Farrand

UNDERSTUDIES: Dede/Bella, Marie Cheatham; Joanne/Shirley, Jan Bowes; Suits, Maureen Sadusk

A drama in two acts. The action takes place at the present time in The Remington Room of a multi-million dollar theater complex in Texas City, Texas.

General Manager: James Walsh
Press: Michael Alpert, Warren Knowlton, Randi Cone, Sandy Mandel
Stage Managers: Marnel Sumner, Maureen Sadusk

* Closed April 23, 1977 after 20 performances and 3 previews.

Martha Swope Photos

Susan Peretz, Estelle Parsons

Top: Rosemary Murphy, Estelle Parsons, Eileen Heckart

IMPERIAL THEATRE
Opened Thursday, April 14, 1977.*
By arrangement with Gabriel Katzka and Edward L. Schuman,
Alexander H. Cohen presents:

ANNA CHRISTIE

By Eugene O'Neill; Director, Jose Quintero; Scenery and Light-
ing, Ben Edwards; Costumes, Jane Greenwood; Hair Styles and
Makeup, J. Roy Helland; Co-Producers, Hildy Parks, Roy A. Som-
lyo; Production Associate, Seymour Herscher; Assistant to Director,
Ben Levit; Production Assistant, Kathleen Mazzocco; Staff Asso-
ciate, Patrick Maloney; Staff Assistants, Lawrence Fecho, Debra
Wise; Technical Supervisors, Arthur Siccardi, Joseph Monaco;
Wardrobe Supervisor, Kathleen Foster

CAST

Johnny-the-Priest	Richard Hamilton
Longshoremen	Edwin McDonough, Vic Polizos
Larry	Ken Harrison
Postman	Jack Davidson
Chris Christopherson	Robert Donley
Marthy Owen	Mary McCarty
Anna Christie	Liv Ullmann
Sailors	Vic Polizos, Ken Harrison
Johnson	Jack Davidson
Mat Burke	John Lithgow

UNDERSTUDIES: Marthy, Elsa Raven; Mat/Larry, Edwin
McDonough; Chris, Richard Hamilton; Johnny-the-Priest, Jack Davidson; Postman/Longshoreman/Sailor, Alan Coleridge

A drama in four acts, performed with two intermissions. The
action takes place in the fall of 1912 in Johnny-the-Priest's saloon
near South Street in New York City, and on the barge "Simeon
Winthrop."

Company Manager: Charles Willard
Press: Richard Hummler, Martha Mason
Stage Managers: George Martin, Alan Coleridge

* Closed July 30, 1977 after limited engagement of 124 performances and 3 previews. The original production with Pauline
Lord, George Marion and Frank Shannon opened Nov. 2, 1921
at the Vanderbilt Theatre and played 177 performances. It received the 1922 Pulitzer Prize for Best Play.

Martha Swope Photos

Right: Liv Ullmann

Liv Ullmann, John Lithgow, Robert Donley

Mary McCarty, Liv Ullmann

ETHEL BARRYMORE THEATRE
Opened Sunday, April 17, 1977.*
By arrangement with Joseph Kipness, Terry Allen Kramer and
Harry Rigby present:

I LOVE MY WIFE

Book and Lyrics, Michael Stewart; Music Composed and Arranged by Cy Coleman; From a play by Luis Rego; Director, Gene Saks; Scenery, David Mitchell; Lighting, Gilbert V. Hemsley, Jr.; Costumes, Ron Talsky; Musical Direction, John Miller; Sound, Lou Gonzalez; Associate Producer, Frank Montalvo; Musical Numbers Staged by Onna White; Technical Supervisor, Mitch Miller; Production Assistant, Jon Puleo; Wardrobe Supervisor, Clarence Sims

CAST

Cleo	Ilene Graff
Monica	Joanna Gleason
Wally	James Naughton
Stanley	Michael Mark
Quentin	Joe Saulter
Harvey	John Miller
Norman	Ken Bichel
Alvin	Lenny Baker

UNDERSTUDIES: Quentin, Warren Benbow; Harvey, Michael Mark; Norman, Joel Mofsenson; Stanley, Michael Sergio

MUSICAL NUMBERS: "We're Still Friends," "Monica," "By Threes," "A Mover's Life," "Love Revolution," "Someone Wonderful I Missed," "Sexually Free," "Hey There, Good Times," "Lovers on Christmas Eve," "Scream," "Everybody Today Is Turning On," "Married Couple Seeks Married Couple," "I Love My Wife"

A musical in two acts. The action takes place at the present time in Trenton, N. J.

General Management: Jack Schlissel, Jay Kingwill
Press: Henry Luhrman, Anne Obert Weinberg, Terry M. Lilly
Stage Managers: Bob Vandergriff, Tony Manzi

* Still playing May 31, 1977.

Martha Swope Photos

Left: Lenny Baker, Joanna Gleason , Ilene Graff, James Naughton also top with Ken Bichel, Michael Mark, Joseph Saulter, John Miller

Ilene Graff, Lenny Baker, James
Naughton, Joanna Gleason

James Naughton, Lenny Baker

THE MUSIC BOX
Opened Monday, April 18, 1977.*
Harold Prince in association with Ruth Mitchell, by arrangement with The Incomes Company, Ltd. presents:

SIDE BY SIDE BY SONDHEIM

Music and Lyrics by Stephen Sondheim, and Music by Leonard Bernstein, Mary Rodgers, Richard Rodgers, Jule Styne; Director, Ned Sherrin; Musical Director, Ray Cook; Musical Staging, Bob Howe; Continuity, Ned Sherrin; Pianists, Danie Troob, Albin Konopka; Scenery, Peter Docherty; Costumes, Florence Klotz; Lighting, Ken Billington; Scenery Supervision, Jay Moore; Musical Supervision, Paul Gemignani; Sound, Jack Mann; Original cast album and tapes by RCA Records

CAST

Millicent Martin
Julie N. McKenzie
David Kernan†
Ned Sherrin

STANDBYS: Mr. Sherrin, Fernanda Maschwitz; Ms. Martin, Carol Swarbrick; Ms. McKenzie, Bonnie Schon; Mr. Kernan, Jack Blackton

MUSICAL NUMBERS: "Comedy Tonight," "Love Is in the Air," "If Momma Was Married," "You Must Meet My Wife," "The Little Things You Do Together," "Getting Married Today," "I Remember," "Can That Boy Foxtrot," "Company," "Another Hundred People," "Barcelona," "Marry Me a Little," "I Never Do Anything Twice," "Bring on the Girls," "Ah, Paree!," "Buddy's Blues," "Broadway Baby," "You Could Drive a Person Crazy," "Everybody Says Don't," "Anyone Can Whistle," "Send in the Clowns," "We're Gonna Be All Right," "A Boy Like That," "I Have a Love," "The Boy from . . .," "Pretty Lady," "You Gotta Have a Gimmick," "Losing My Mind," "Could I Leave You?," "I'm Still Here," "Conversation Piece," "Side by Side by Side"

"A Musical Entertainment" in two parts.

General Manager: Howard Haines
Press: Mary Bryant, Bruce Cohen
Stage Managers: John Grigas, Artie Masella

* Still playing May 31, 1977.
† Succeeded by Larry Kert

Martha Swope Photos

**Top: Ned Sherrin, Julie N. McKenzie,
David Kernan, Millicent Martin**

Millicent Martin, Julie N. McKenzie

TOWN HALL
Opened Tuesday, April 19, 1977.*
Richard Grayson and John Bowab present "Broadway in Concert at Town Hall" with:

KNICKERBOCKER HOLIDAY

Book and Lyrics by Maxwell Anderson; Music, Kurt Weill; Director, John Bowab; Musical Direction, Bill Brohn; Gowns, Donald Brooks; Lighting, Ken Billington; Produced in association with Joseph Harris, Wardrobe Mistress, Gail McLaughlin; Production Assistant, Patricia Morinelli; Director's Assistant, Joey Patton

CAST

Washington Irving	Kurt Peterson
Marshall Schermerhorn	Gerard Russak
Mistress Schermerhorn	Genette Lane
Van Rensselaer	John Dorrin
Roosevelt	Gene Varrone
Vanderbilt	Elliot Savage
Tienhoven	Eric Brotherson
Van Cortlandt	Walter Charles
Brom Broeck	Edward Evanko
First Girl	Maida Meyers
Second Girl	Alyson Bristol
Third Girl	Susan Rush
Tenpin	Clay Causey
Tina Tienhoven	Maureen Brennan
Pieter Stuyvesant	Richard Kiley
General Poffenburg	John Leslie Wolfe
Soldiers	Ed Dixon, Orrin Reiley

UNDERSTUDIES: Stuyvesant, John Dorrin; Broeck/Irving, Ed Dixon; Tina, Maida Meyers; Poffenburgh/Van Rensselaer/ Roosevelt/Tienhoven/Vanderbilt, Walter Charles; Tenpin/Van Cortlandt, Orrin Reiley; Mistress Schermerhorn, Susan Rush

MUSICAL NUMBERS: "Introduction and Washington Irving Song," "Clickety-Clack," "Entrance of the Council," "Hush Hush," "There's Nowhere to Go but Up," "It Never Was You," "How Can You Tell an American?," "Will You Remember Me?," "Stuyvesant's Entrance," "One Touch of Alchemy," "The One Indispensable Man," "Young People Think about Love," "September Song," "All Hail, the Political Honeymoon," "Ballad of the Robbers," "Sitting in Jail," "We Are Cut in Twain," "The Army of New Amsterdam," "To War!," "Our Ancient Liberties," "May and January," "The Scars," "Dirge for a Soldier," "No, Ve Vouldn't Gonto Do It," Finale.

A musical in two acts and three scenes with a prologue. The action takes place in Washington Irving's study in 1809, and at The Battery in 1647.

Company Manager: Gino Giglio
Press: Betty Lee Hunt, Maria Pucci, Fred Hoot
Stage Managers: Ben Sprecher, Frank Birt, Orrin Reiley

* Closed April 30, 1977 after 16 performances. Original production with Walter Huston and Ray Middleton opened Oct. 19, 1938 at the Ethel Barrymore Theatre and ran for 168 performances.

Ken Howard Photos

Richard Kiley, Maureen Brennan, also top with Edward Evanko

Robyn Finn, Donna Graham, Diana Barrows, Danielle Brisebois, Andrea McArdle, Janine Ruane, Shelley Bruce in "Annie"

Sandy with Andrea McArdle

ALVIN THEATRE
Opened Thursday, April 21, 1977.*
Mike Nichols presents:

ANNIE

Book, Thomas Meehan; Based on "Little Orphan Annie" comic strip; Music, Charles Strouse; Lyrics, Martin Charnin; Musical Numbers Choreographed by Peter Gennaro; Director, Martin Charnin; Producers, Irwin Meyer, Stephen R. Friedman, Lewis Allen; Settings, David Mitchell; Costumes, Theoni V. Aldredge; Lighting, Judy Rasmuson; Musical Direction, Peter Howard; Orchestrations, Philip J. Lang; Produced by Alvin Nederlander Associates, Inc.-Icarus Productions; Produced in association with Peter Crane; Assistant to Mr. Charnin, Sylvia Pancotti; Assistant Conductor, Robert Billig; Technical Coordinator, Arthur Siccardi; Wardrobe Supervisor, Adelaide Laurino; Production Assistants, Janice Steele, Stephen Graham; Hairstylists, Ted Azar, Charles LaFrance; Original cast recording by Columbia Records

CAST

Molly	Danielle Brisebois
Pepper	Robyn Finn
Duffy	Donna Graham
July	Janine Ruane†
Tessie	Diana Barrows
Kate	Shelley Bruce
Annie	Andrea McArdle
Miss Hannigan	Dorothy Loudon
Bundles McCloskey/Sound Effects Man/Ickes	James Hosbein
Dog Catcher/Jimmy Johnson/Honor Guard	Steven Boockvor
Dog Catcher/Bert Healy/Kaltenborn's Voice/ Hull	Donald Craig
Sandy	Himself
Lt. Ward/Morganthau	Richard Ensslen
Harry/FDR	Raymond Thorne
Sophie the Kettle/Cecille/A Star to Be/ Bonnie Boylan/Perkins	Laurie Beechman
Grace Farrell	Sandy Faison
Drake	Edwin Bordo
Mrs. Pugh/Connie Boylan	Edie Cowan
Annette/Ronnie Boylan	Penny Worth
Oliver Warbucks	Reid Shelton
Rooster Hannigan	Robert Fitch
Lily	Barbara Erwin
Fred McCracken/Howe	Bob Freschi
NBC Page	Mari McMinn

HOOVERVILLE-ITES, POLICEMEN, SERVANTS, NEW YORKERS: Laurie Beechman, Steven Boockvor, Edwin Bordo, Edie Cowan, Donald Craig, Richard Ensslen, Barbara Erwin, Bob Freschi, James Hosbein, Mari McMinn, Penny Worth

STANDBYS AND UNDERSTUDIES: Annie, Kristen Vigard; Warbucks, Raymond Thorne; Miss Hannigan, Penny Worth; Grace, Mari McMinn; Rooster, Steven Boockvor; Duffy/Pepper/Kate/Tessie, Janine Ruane; Molly, Shelley Bruce; July, Donna Graham; FDR/Harry, Donald Craig; Lily, Edie Cowan; Drake/Bert, Bob Freschi; Sandy, Arf; Ensemble Alternate, Don Bonnell

MUSICAL NUMBERS: "Maybe," "It's the Hard-Knock Life," "Tomorrow," "We'd Like to Thank You," "Little Girls," "I Think I'm Gonna Like It Here," "N.Y.C.," "Easy Street," "You Won't Be an Orphan for Long," "You're Never Fully Dressed without a Smile," "Something Was Missing," "I Don't Need Anything but You," "Annie," "A New Deal for Christmas"

A musical in 2 acts and 13 scenes. The action takes place December 11–25, 1933 in New York City.

General Management: Gatchell & Neufeld Ltd.
Company Manager: Drew Murphy
Press: David Powers
Stage Managers: Janet Beroza, Jack Timmers, Patrick O'Leary, Roy Meachum

* Still playing May 31, 1977. Received 1977 New York Drama Critics Circle and "Tony" Awards for Best Musical. Among the other six "Tonys" it received was Best Actress in a Musical for Dorothy Loudon.
† Succeeded by Kathy-Jo Kelly

Martha Swope Photos

Top Right: Andrea McArdle, Reid Shelton Below: Robert Fitch, Dorothy Loudon, Barbara Erwin

Andrea McArdle, Sandy Faison, Reid Shelton

LONGACRE THEATRE
Opened Sunday, April 24, 1977.*
Moe Septee and Carmen F. Zollo present the Theatre Company of Boston Production of:

THE BASIC TRAINING OF PAVLO HUMMEL

By David Rabe; Director, David Wheeler; Scenery, Robert Mitchell; Costumes, Domingo Rodriguez; Lighting, David F. Segal; Technical Coordinator, Arthur Siccardi; Wardrobe Supervisor, Grisha Mynova; Production Assistants, Karen Van Zandt, Lee Kappelman, Pamela Singer; Hairstylist, Nino Raffaello; Special Consultant for Music and Sound, Peter Judd

CAST

Pavlo Hummel	Al Pacino
Yen	Tisa Chang
Ardell	Gustave Johnson
First Sergeant Tower	Joe Fields
Corporal Jackson	Jack Kehoe
Squad:	
Parker	Max Wright
Kress	Larry Bryggman
Pierce	Lance Henriksen
Hinkle	Paul Guilfoyle
Hendrix	John Aquino
Parham	Damien Leake
Burns	Gary Bolling
Ryan	Michael Dinelli
Gomez	Kevin Maung
Captain Saunders	Brad Sullivan
Mickey	Ron Hunter
Sorrentino	Andrea Masters
Mrs. Hummel	Rebecca Darke
Jones	Don Blakely
Vietnamese Boy	Kevin Maung
Mamasan	Anne Miyamoto
Sergeant Brisbey	Richard Lynch
Sergeant Wall	Sully Boyar
Private Grennel	Gary Bolling
Captain Miller	Brad Sullivan
First Viet Cong	Kevin Maung
Second Viet Cong	Tisa Chang
Vietnamese Farmer	Anne Miyamoto
Lieutenant Smith	Brad Sullivan

UNDERSTUDIES: Ardell/Burns, Damien Leake; Corporal/Hendrix, Ron Hunter; Hendrix/Hinkle, Kevin Maung; Mrs. Hummel, Andrea Masters; Jones, Gary Bolling; Kress, John Aquino; Pierce, Michael Dinelli; Ryan, Paul Guilfoyle; Mrs. Sorrentino/1st VC, Tisa Chang; Tower, Don Blakely; 2nd VC/Yen, Anne Miyamoto

A drama in two acts. The action takes place in The United States Army, 1965–67.

General Manager: Laurel Ann Wilson
Press: Max Eisen, Judy Jacksina, Barbara Glenn
Stage Managers: Patrick Horrigan, Barbara Dilker

* Still playing May 31, 1977. Original NY production with William Atherton opened May 19, 1971 at the Public/Newman Theater and played 365 performances.

Al Pacino, Tisa Chang, Anne Miyamoto
Above: Joe Fields, Al Pacino

Al Pacino, Richard Lynch
Top Left: Andrea Masters, Al Pacino

BROADWAY THEATRE
Opened Tuesday, April 26, 1977.*
Harold Leventhal and Samuel Gesser present:

NANA MOUSKOURI ON BROADWAY
with
The Olympians

Musical Director, Georges Kokkinos; General Management, Theatre Now, Inc. (William Court Cohen, Edward H. Davis, Norman E. Rothstein); Assistant to Producers, Irene Allong; Sound, Doug Beveridge, Denis Gray; Lighting, Doug Franklin; The Olympians: Georges Kokkinos, Yussuf Allie, Vangelis Paraskevas, Stilianos Calathopoulos, Bernard Papillon

A program of songs in two parts. The songs were announced at each performance.

General Management: Theatre Now, Inc.
Press: Seymour Krawitz, Patricia M. Krawitz
Stage Manager: Gerald Larteau

* Closed May 1, 1977 after a limited engagement of 7 performances.

Nana Mouskouri

71

Opened Monday, May 2, 1977.*
Lee Guber and Shelly Gross present:

THE KING AND I

Music, Richard Rodgers; Book and Lyrics, Oscar Hammerstein 2nd; Based on novel "Anna and the King of Siam" by Margaret Landon; Entire Production Directed by Yuriko; Original Choreography by Jerome Robbins; Settings, Peter Wolf; Costumes, Stanley Simmons; Based on original costumes by Irene Sharaff; Lighting, Thomas Skelton; Musical Supervisor, Milton Rosenstock; Musical Director, John Lesko; Sound, Richard Fitzgerald; Associate Producer, Fred Walker; Hairstylist, Werner Sherer; Technical Supervisor, Mitch Miller; Wardrobe Master, Elonzo Dann; Assistant to Director, Susan Kikuchi; Hairdressers, Bobby Abbott, Alan D'Angerio; Assistant Conductor, Fred Manzella; Assistant to Producers, Marilyn Wise

CAST

Captain Orton	Larry Swansen
Louis Leonowens	Alan Amick
Anna Leonowens	Constance Towers
The Interpreter	Jae Woo Lee
The Kralahome	Michael Kermoyan
The King	Yul Brynner
Tuptim	June Angela
Lady Thiang	Hye-Young Choi
Prince Chulalongkorn	Gene Profanato
Princess Ying Yaowalak	Julie Woo
Lun Tha	Martin Vidnovic
Sir Edward Ramsay	John Michael King

ROYAL DANCERS AND WIVES: Su Applegate, Jessica Chao, Lei-Lynn Doo, Dale Harimoto, Pamela Kait, Susan Kikuchi, Faye Fujisaki Mar, Sumiko Murashima, Libby Rhodes, Cecile Santos, Hope Sogawa, Mary Ann Teng, Patricia K. Thomas

PRINCESSES AND PRINCES: Ivan Ho, Clark Huang, Annie Lam, Connie Lam, Jennifer Lam, Paul Siu, Tim Waldrip, Kevan Weber, Kym Weber, Julie Woo, Mary Woo

NURSES AND AMAZONS: Sidney Smith, Marienne Tatum, Patricia K. Thomas, Rebecca West

PRIESTS AND SLAVES: Kaipo Daniels, Barrett Hong, Jae Woo Lee, Ric Ornellas, Simeon Den, Chandra Tanna, Robert Vega

STANDBYS AND UNDERSTUDIES: King, Michael Kermoyan; Anna, Margot Moser, Marianne Tatum; Kralahome, Jae Woo Lee; Lady Thiang, Sumiko Murashima; Lun Tha, Robert Vega; Tuptim, Pamela Kalt; Prince, Ivan Ho; Louis, Tim Waldrip; Simon, Patricia K. Thomas; Angel, Faye Fujisaki Mar; Uncle Thomas, Hope Sogawa; Topsy, Libby Rhodes

MUSICAL NUMBERS: "I Whistle a Happy Tune," "My Lord and Master," "Hello, Young Lovers," "March of the Siamese Children," "A Puzzlement," "Royal Bangkok Academy," "Getting to Know You," "We Kiss in a Shadow," "Shall I Tell You What I Think of You?," "Something Wonderful," "Western People Funny," "I Have Dreamed," "The Small House of Uncle Thomas," "Shall We Dance?," Finale

A musical in two acts. The action takes place in and around the King's Palace in Bangkok, Siam, during the 1860's.

General Manager: Theatre Now, Inc.
Company Manager: Robb Lady
Press: Solters & Roskin, Joshua Ellis, Milly Schoenbaum, Fred H. Nathan
Stage Managers: Ed Preston, Conwell Worthington, Thomas J. Rees

* Still playing May 31, 1977. Original production with Gertrude Lawrence and Yul Brynner opened March 29, 1951 at the St. James Theatre and played 1246 performances.

Michael Baumann/Fuji Photos

Top Right: Yul Brynner, Constance Towers
Below: Susan Kikuchi, Yul Brynner

Yul Brynner, Constance Towers

MARTIN BECK THEATRE
Opened Saturday, May 7, 1977.*
Michael Harvey and The Chelsea Theater Center (Robert Kalfin, Artistic Director; Michael David, Executive Director) present:

HAPPY END

Music, Kurt Weill; Lyrics, Bertolt Brecht; Book and Lyrics Adapted by Michael Feingold; Original German play by Elisabeth Hauptmann; Directed and Staged by Robert Kalfin, Patricia Birch; Scenic Design, Robert U. Taylor; Costumes, Carrie F. Robbins; Lighting, Jennifer Tipton; Musical Direction, Roland Gagnon; Associate Producer, Wilder Luke Burnap; Hairstylist and Makeup, Patrik D. Moreton; Technical Supervisor, Mitch Miller; Assistant Director, Peter Byrne; Assistant Musical Director, David Krane; Wardrobe Mistress, Latonia O. Baer

CAST

The Gang:
Bill Cracker .... Christopher Lloyd
Sam "Mammy" Wurlitzer .... Benjamin Rayson
Dr. Nakamura ("The Governor") .... Tony Azito[1]
Jimmy Dexter ("The Reverend") .... John A. Coe
Bob Marker ("The Professor") .... Robert Weil
Johnny Flint ("Baby Face") .... Raymond J. Barry
Lady in Gray ("The Fly") .... Grayson Hall
Miriam, the barmaid .... Donna Emmanuel
The Army:
Lt. Lillian Holiday ("Hallelujah Lil") .... Meryl Streep[2]
Major Stone .... Liz Sheridan
Capt. Hannibal Jackson .... Joe Grifasi
Sister Mary .... Prudence Wright Holmes
Sister Jane .... Alexandra Borrie
Brother Ben Owens .... Christopher Cara
A Cop .... David Pursley
The Fold .... Kristin Jolliff, Frank Kopyc,
Tom Mardirosian, Martha Miller, Victor Pappas

UNDERSTUDIES: Bill, Bob Gunton; Lillian, Alexandra Borrie; Sister Jane, Donna Emmanuel; Miriam/Sister Mary, Kristin Jolliff; Capt. Jackson, Frank Kopyc; Baby Face/Cop, Tom Mardirosian; Maj, Stone/The Fly, Martha Miller; Nakamura/Marker, Victor Pappas; Wurlitzer/Dexter, David Pursley; Brother Owens, Christopher Cara

MUSICAL NUMBERS: Prologue, "The Bilbao Song," "Lieutenants of the Lord," "March Ahead," "The Sailors' Tango," "Brother, Give Yourself a Shove," "Song of the Big Shot," "Don't Be Afraid," "In Our Childhood's Bright Endeavor," "The Liquor Dealer's Dream," "The Mandalay Song," "Surabaya Johnny," "Ballad of the Lily of Hell," "The Happy End."

A musical in 3 acts and 4 scenes with a prologue. The action takes place in Chicago in December of 1915.

General Management: Jack Schlissel, Jay Kingwill
Company Manager: Albert Poland
Press: Susan Bloch, Sally G. Christiansen, Francis X. Tobin
Stage Managers: Mark Wright, Charles Kindl, Christopher Cara

* Closed July 10, 1977 after 75 performances. Transferred from the Chelsea Theater Center where it opened March 8, 1977 and played 56 performances.
†Succeeded by: 1. Victor Pappas, 2. Janie Sell

Martha Swope Photos

Benjamin Rayson, Tony Azito, Christopher Lloyd, Grayson Hall, Donna Emmanuel, Robert Weil, Raymond J. Barry, John A. Coe

Janie Sell
Above: Christopher Lloyd, Meryl Streep

ST. JAMES THEATRE
Opened Wednesday, May 11, 1977.*
Golden Eagle Productions, Inc. and George R. Nice, in association with Ruth Hercolani, present:

VIEUX CARRE

By Tennessee Williams; Director, Arthur Allan Seidelman; Set and Lighting, James Tilton; Costumes, Jane Greenwood; Incidental Music, Galt MacDermot; Associate Producers, Milton Justice, Eleanor Fortus, May Grindrod, Christopher Rote, Myles Spector; Sound, Gary Harris; Wardrobe Supervisor, Warren Morrill; Hairstylist, Joseph Blitz

CAST

Writer	Richard Alfieri
Mrs. Wire	Sylvia Sidney
Nursie	Gertrude Jeanette
Jane	Diane Kagan
Painter	Tom Aldredge
Blake	Reb Brownell
Angel	Grace Carney
Miss Carrie	Iris Whitney
Mrs. Wayne	Olive Deering
Tye	John William Reilly
Photographer	Jed Cooper
First Patrolman	Bill Perley
Second Patrolman	Reb Brownell
Judge (Voice)/Guide	Robert Colson
Ida	Toni Darnay
Bess	Lois Holmes
Ella	Sharon Morrison

UNDERSTUDIES: Mrs. Wire/Mrs. Wayne, Toni Darnay; Writer, Jed Cooper; Jane, Sharon Morrison; Painter, William Perley; Miss Carrie/Angel, Lois Holmes; Nursie, Lil Henderson; Ferguson, Robert Colson; Policemen/Guide, William Pomeroy; Photographer/Tye, Reb Brownell

A drama in two acts. The action takes place in the late 1930's in the French Quarter of New Orleans, LA.

General Manager: C. Edwin Knill
Company Manager: Morry Efron
Press: David Lipsky
Stage Managers: Lee Murray, William Pomeroy, Robert Colson

* Closed May 15, 1977 after 6 performances and 11 previews.

Joseph Abeles Photos

Left: Richard Alfieri, Tom Aldredge Top: Alfieri, Sylvia Sidney, Iris Whitney, Olive Deering

Richard Alfieri, Sylvia Sidney

John William Reilly, Diane Kagan

BROADWAY THEATRE
Sunday, May 15, 1977.*
Friends of the Theatre and Music Collection of the Museum of the City of New York present:

MARY MARTIN   ETHEL MERMAN
TOGETHER ON BROADWAY
Cyril Ritchard, Narrator

Producer, Anna Sosenko; Staged by Donald Saddler; Musical Direction, Jay Blackton; Conductor for Miss Martin, John Lesko; Conductor for Miss Merman, Eric Knight; Lighting, Ken Billington; Sound, Joe Donohue; Projections, Sheppard Kerman; Miss Merman's Clothes and Miss Martin's Evening Pants, Morty Sussman; Miss Martin's Dresses, Jean-Louis; Production Assistants, Jamie Haskins, Merle Hubbard, Marvin Jenkins

A program of songs from productions in which they appeared, sung by Miss Merman and Miss Martin.

Manager: Victor Samrock
Press: Bob Ullman, Louise Weiner Ment, Richard Kornberg
Stage Managers: Robert Borod, Robert Schear, Paul Diaz, Mark Gerolmo

* Performed for one night only as a benefit for the Theatre and Music Collection of the Museum of the City of New York

Martha Swope Photos
Top: Ethel Merman Right: Mary Martin
Right Center: Martin, Merman

Ethel Merman, Cyril Ritchard

75

Toller Cranston

PALACE THEATRE
Opened Thursday, May 19, 1977.*
Dennis Bass and Robin Cranston Present:

TOLLER CRANSTON'S
THE ICE SHOW

Produced and Directed by Myrl A. Schreibman; Set Design, Anthony Sabatino, William H. Harris; Costumes, Miles White; Lighting, D. Scott Linder; Sound, Jack Shirk; Choreography and Staging, Brian Foley; Additional Choreography, Ellen Burka; Music Supervision, Bill Courtney; Skating Consultant, Bill Turner; Original Music, Al Kasha, Joel Hirshhorn; Production Supervisor, Mitch Miller; Hairstylists, Werner & Sherer; Executive Producers, Dennis Bass, Robin Cranston

CAST

Toller Cranston

Jim Millns & Colleen O'Connor	Gordon McKellen, Jr
Ken Shelley	Candy Jones & Don Fraser
Wendy Burge	Barbara Berezowski & David Porter
Kathy Malmberg	Jack Courtney & Emily Benenson
Elizabeth Freeman	Janet & Mark Hominuke

Presented in 2 acts and 5 scenes.

General Management: Theatre Now, Inc.
Press: Seymour Krawitz, Patricia M. Krawitz
Stage Managers: Joe Lorden, Judith Binus, Jack Gianino

* Closed July 10, 1977 after 60 performances and 2 previews.

Martha Swope Photos

THE LITTLE THEATRE

Opened Saturday, May 21, 1977.*
Jerry Arrow and Jay Broad representing Circle Repertory
Company and PAF Playhouse present:

GEMINI

By Albert Innaurato; Director, Peter Mark Schifter; Supervised
by Marshall W. Mason; Setting, Christopher Nowak; Costumes,
Ernest Allen Smith; Lighting, Larry Crimmins; Sound, Leslie A.
DeWeerdt, Jr.; Production Assistants, James Arnemann, Terry Gus-
morino; Wardrobe Supervisor, Kathy Powers; Hairstylist, Jose An-
selmi

CAST

Francis Geminiani	Robert Picardo
Bunny Weinberger	Jessica James
Randy Hastings	Reed Birney
Judith Hastings	Carol Potter
Herschel Weinberger	Jonathan Hadary
Fran Geminiani	Danny Aiello
Lucille Pompi	Anne DeSalvo

A comedy in 2 acts and 4 scenes. The action takes place June 1
& 2, 1973 in the Geminiani-Weinberger backyard in South Philadelphia, PA.

General Manager: Jerry Arrow
Company Manager: Robert Lussier
Press: Rima Corben
Stage Managers: Fred Reinglas, Dennis Purcell

* Still playing May 31, 1977.

Ken Howard Photos

**Right: Reed Birney, Jessica James, Danny Aiello,
Robert Picardo, Anne DeSalvo, Carol Potter**

**Aiello, DeSalvo, Potter, Birney, Picardo
Above: Carol Potter, Robert Picardo**

Carol Potter, Jonathan Hadary

BROADWAY PRODUCTIONS FROM OTHER SEASONS
THAT PLAYED THROUGH THIS SEASON

ANTA THEATRE
Opened Tuesday, March 2, 1976.*
J. Lloyd Grant, Richard Bell, Robert M. Cooper, Ashton Springer in association with Moe Septee present the Media House Production of:

BUBBLING BROWN SUGAR

Book, Loften Mitchell; Based on a concept by Rosetta LeNoire; Director, Robert M. Cooper; Musical Direction, Danny Holgate; Choreography and Musical Staging, Billy Wilson; Sets, Clarke Dunham; Lighting, Barry Arnold; Costumes, Bernard Johnson; Projections, Lucie D. Grosvenor, Clarke Dunham; Sound, Joel S. Fichman; Additional Music, Danny Holgate, Emme Kemp, Lillian Lopez; Choral Arrangements, Chapman Roberts; Hairstylists, Gene Sheppard, Stanley James; Originally presented by the AMAS Repertory Theatre; Production Supervisor, I. Mitchell Miller; Props, Bob Anderson; Production Coordinator, Sharon Brown; Production Associate, Trudy Brown; Wardrobe Mistress, Linda Lee

CAST

Skip/Young Checkers .... Lonnie McNeil†1
Bill/Time Man/Bumpy/M.C. ...... Vernon Washington†2
Ray/Young Sage .... Newton Winters†3
Carolyn/Gospel Lady/Nightclub Singer .... Carolyn Byrd
Norma .... Karen Grannum†4
Gene/Gospel Lady's Son .... Alton Lathrop
Helen .... Dyann Robinson
Laura .... Charlise Harris†5
Marsha/Young Irene .... Vivian Reed†6
Tony/Waiter/Dutch .... Anthony Whitehouse
Irene Paige .... Josephine Premice
John Sage/Rusty .... Avon Long
Checkers/Dusty .... Joseph Attles
Jim/Nightclub Singer .... Chip Garnett†7
Ella .... Ethel Beatty
Judy/Dutch's Girl .... Barbara Rubenstein
Charlie/Count .... Barry Preston†8
The Solitunes .... Alton Lathrop, Lonnie McNeil†1,
Ursuline Kairson, Newton Winters†3
Chorus .... Susan Edwards, Murphy Cross,
Nedra Dixon, Emme Kemp, Stanley Ramsey, Amii Stewart,
Marilyn Johnson, Ira Hawkins

STANDBYS AND UNDERSTUDIES: Marilyn Johnson (Irene/Gospel Lady/Nightclub Singer), Cecelia Norfleet (Marsha/Young Irene), Clebert Ford (Sage/Checkers), Clyde-Jacques Barrett (Bill/Time Man/Bumpy/M.C.), Ira Hawkins (Jim/Nightclub Singer), Susan Edwards (Judy), E. Lynn Nickerson (Tony/Charles/Waiter/Count), Amii Stewart (Ella), Dance Alternates: Leona Johnson, David Cameron

MUSICAL NUMBERS: "Harlem '70," "Bubbling Brown Sugar," "That's What Harlem Is to Me," "Bill Robinson Specialty," "Harlem Sweet Harlem," "Nobody," "Goin' Back in Time," "Some of These Days," "Moving Uptown," "Strolling," "I'm Gonna Tell God All My Troubles," "His Eye Is on the Sparrow," "Swing Low, Sweet Chariot," "Sweet Georgia Brown," "Honeysuckle Rose," "Stormy Monday Blues," "Rosetta," "Sophisticated Lady," "In Honeysuckle Time," "Solitude," "C'mon Up to Jive Time," "Stompin' at the Savoy," "Take the A Train," "Harlem Time," "Love Will Find a Way," "Dutch's Song," "Brown Gal," "Pray for the Lights to Go Out," "I Got It Bad," "Harlem Makes Me Feel!," "Jim Jam Jumpin' Jive," "There'll Be Some Changes Made," "God Bless the Child," "It Don't Mean a Thing"

A musical revue in 2 acts and 9 scenes. The action takes place in Harlem at the present time, and between 1920 and 1940.

General Managers: Ashton Springer, Susan Chase
Company Managers: Carolyne A. Jones, Stephanie Austin
Press: Max Eisen, Barbara Glenn, Judy Jacksina
Stage Managers: Ron Abbott, Kenneth Hanson, E. Lynn Nickerson

* Still playing May 31, 1977. For original production, see THEATRE WORLD vol. 32.
† Succeeded by: 1. Clinton Keen, 2. David Bryant, Stanley Ramsey, 3. Clyde-Jacques Barrett, 4. Renee Brailsford, 5. Yolanda Raven, 6. Ursuline Kairson, 7. Milt Grayson, 8. Denny Shearer.

Bert Andrews Photos

Denny Shearer, Barbara Rubenstein
Top: Joseph Attles, Ursuline Kairson,
Josephine Premice, Avon Long

FORTY-SIXTH STREET THEATRE
Opened Tuesday, June 1, 1975.*
Robert Fryer and James Cresson present:

CHICAGO

Book, Fred Ebb, Bob Fosse; Music, John Kander; Lyrics, Fred Ebb; Based on play "Chicago" by Maurine Dallas Watkins; Directed and Choreographed by Bob Fosse; Settings, Tony Walton; Costumes, Patricia Zipprodt; Lighting, Jules Fisher; Musical Director, Stanley Lebowsky; Orchestrations, Ralph Burns; Dance Music Arrangements, Peter Howard; Sound, Abe Jacob; Hairstylist, Romaine Green; Produced in association with Martin Richards, Joseph Harris and Ira Bernstein; Managerial Associate, Frank Scardino; Wardrobe Supervisor, Louise Van Dine; Assistant Conductor, Art Wagner; Production Assistant, Vicki Stein; Assistant Choreographer, Tony Stevens; Assistant to Director, Kathryn Doby; Original cast album by Arista Records

CAST

Velma Kelly	Chita Rivera†1
Roxie Hart	Gwen Verdon†2
Fred Casely	Christopher Chadman†3
Sergeant Fogarty	Richard Korthaze
Amos Hart	Barney Martin†4
Liz	Cheryl Clark†5
Annie	Michon Peacock†6
June	Candy Brown†7
Hunyak	Graciela Daniele†8
Mona	Pamela Sousa†9
Martin Harrison	Michael Vita†10
Matron	Mary McCarty†11
Billy Flynn	Jerry Orbach†12
Mary Sunshine	M. O'Haughey
Go-to-Hell Kitty	Charlene Ryan†13
Harry	Paul Solen†14
Aaron	Gene Foote†15
The Judge	Ron Schwinn†16
Court Clerk	Gary Gendell†17

STANDBYS AND UNDERSTUDIES: Candace Tovar (Roxie), Elaine Cancilla (Velma), Mace Barrett (Billy), Georgia Creighton (Matron/Mary Sunshine), Richard Korthaze (Amos), Dance Alternates: Hank Brunjes, Monica Tiller

MUSICAL NUMBERS: "All That Jazz," "Funny Honey," "Cell Block Tango," "When You're Good to Mama," "Tap Dance," "All I Care About," "A Little Bit of Good," "We Both Reached for the Gun," "Roxie," "I Can't Do It Alone," "Chicago after Midnight," "My Own Best Friend," "I Know a Girl," "Me and My Baby," "Mister Cellophane," "When Velma Takes the Stand," "Razzle Dazzle," "Class," "Nowadays," "Keep It Hot," "R.S.V.P."

A "musical vaudeville" in two acts. The action takes place in the late 1920's in Chicago, Illinois.

General Managers: Joseph Harris, Ira Bernstein
Press: The Merlin Group, Cheryl Sue Dolby, Harriett Trachtenberg, Ron Harris
Stage Managers: Ed Aldridge, Craig Jacobs, Paul Phillips, Jay S. Hoffman

* Still playing May 31, 1977. For original production, see THEATRE WORLD Vol. 32.
† Succeeded by: 1. Lenora Nemetz, 2. Lenora Nemetz, Liza Minnelli, Ann Reinking, 3. Gary Gendell, 4. Rex Everhart, 5. Carla Farnsworth, 6. Joan Bell, 7. Karen G. Burke, Sally Neal, 8. Sandra Brewer, Candace Tovar, 9. Debra Lyman, 10. Jerry Yoder, 11. Alaina Reed, 12. Steve Elmore during vacation, 13. Fern Fitzgerald, Gina Ramsel, 14. Ron Schwinn, 15. Laurent Giroux, Jeremy Blanton, 16. David Kottke, 17. Ross Miles.

Martha Swope Photos

Top Right: Jerry Orbach, Ann Reinking

Ann Reinking, Lenora Nemetz

David Thome, Donna Drake, Jim Litten, Janet Wong, Justin Ross, Vicki Frederick, Kathrynann Wright, Christopher Chadman, Gillian Scalici, Sandahl Bergman, Edward Love, Don Percassi, Deborah Geffner, Mitzi Hamilton, Paul Charles, George Pesaturo, Loida Iglesias Top: Vicki Frederick, Kurt Johnson

Donna Drake, Kathrynann Wright, Gilliam Scalici

80

SHUBERT THEATRE
Opened Sunday, October 19, 1975.*
Joseph Papp presents a New York Shakespeare Festival Production in association with Plum Productions:

A CHORUS LINE

Conceived, Choreographed and Directed by Michael Bennett; Book, James Kirkwood, Nicholas Dante; Music, Marvin Hamlisch; Lyrics, Edward Kleban; Co-Choreographer, Bob Avian; Musical Direction and Vocal Arrangements, Don Pippin; Associate Producer, Bernard Gersten; Setting, Robin Wagner; Costumes, Theoni V. Aldredge; Lighting, Tharon Musser; Sound, Abe Jacob; Music Coordinator, Robert Thomas; Orchestrations, Bill Byers, Hershy Kay, Jonathan Tunick; Assistant to Choreographers and Dance Captain, Baayork Lee; Wardrobe Mistress, Alyce Gilbert; Production Manager, Andrew Mihok; Original cast album by Columbia Records

CAST

Roy	Scott Allen†1
Kristine	Renee Baughman†2
Sheila	Kelley Bishop†3
Val	Pamela Blair†4
Mike	Wayne Cilento†5
Butch	Chuck Cissel†6
Larry	Clive Clerk†7
Maggie	Kay Cole†8
Richie	Ronald Dennis†9
Tricia	Donna Drake†10
Tom	Brandt Edwards†11
Judy	Patricia Garland†12
Lois	Carolyn Kirsch†13
Don	Ron Kuhlman†14
Bebe	Nancy Lane†15
Connie	Baayork Lee†16
Diana	Priscilla Lopez†17
Zach	Robert LuPone†18
Mark	Cameron Mason†19
Cassie	Donna McKechnie†20
Al	Don Percassi†21
Frank	Michael Serrecchia†22
Greg	Michael Stuart†23
Bobby	Thomas J. Walsh†24
Paul	Sammy Williams†25
Vicki	Crissy Wilzak
Audre	Fern Fitzgerald
Rick	Cameron Mason†26
Jarad	John Mineo

UNDERSTUDIES: Tim Cassidy (Don/Greg/Bobby), Crissy Wilzak (Val/Judy/Kristine), Clive Clerk (Zach), Patti D'Beck (Diana/Bebe/Tricia/Vicki), Cynthia Carrillo Onrubia (Maggie/Connie), Fern Fitzgerald (Sheila), Larry G. Bailey (Richie), Sandahl Bergman (Cassie), David Fredericks (Mark/Larry), Deborah Geffner (Sheila), Danny Ruvolo (Greg/Bobby/Larry/Mike/Al), Rene Clemente (Paul)

MUSICAL NUMBERS: "I Hope I Get It," "I Can Do That," "And . . . ," "At the Ballet," "Sing!," "Hello Twelve, Hello Thirteen, Hello Love," "Nothing," "Dance: Ten; Looks: Three," "The Music and the Mirror," "One," "The Tap Combination" "What I Did for Love," Finale

A musical performed without intermission. The action takes place at an audition at the present time in this theatre.
Company Manager: Harris Goldman
Press: Merle Debuskey, Bob Ullman, Richard Kornberg
Stage Managers: Jeff Hamlin, Peter Von Mayrhauser, Zane Weiner, Danny Ruvolo
* Still playing May 31, 1977. Cited as Best Musical by NY Drama Critics Circle, winner of Pulitzer Prize, and "Tony" Awards for Best Musical, Best Book, Best Score, Best Director, Best Lighting, Best Choreography, and a Special Theatre World Award was presented to every member of the creative staff and original cast.
† Succeeded by: 1. Danny Ruvolo, 2. Cookie Vasquez, Deborah Geffner, 3. Kathrynann Wright, 4. Barbara Monte-Britton, Karen Jablons, Mitzi Hamilton, 5. Don Correia, Jim Litten, 6. Edward Love, Larry G. Bailey, 7. Adam Grammis, 8. Lauree Berger, Donna Drake, 9. Winston DeWitt Hemsley, Edward Love, 10. Jo Speros, Cynthia Carrillo Onrubia, 11. Rene Clemente, Cameron Mason, 12. Sandahl Bergman, 13. Vicki Frederick, Cheryl Clark, Patti D'Beck, 14. David Thome, 15. Gillian Scalici, 16. Lauren Kayahara, Janet Wong, 17. Carole Schweid, Rebecca York, Loida Iglesias, 18. Joe Bennett, Eivind Harum, Kurt Johnson, 19. Paul Charles, 20. Ann Reinking, Vicki Frederick, 21. Bill Nabel, John Mineo, Ben Lokey, 22. Tim Cassidy, 23. Justin Ross, 24. Christopher Chadman, 25. Danny Ruvolo, George Pesaturo, 26. David Fredericks

Martha Swope Photos

Ellen March, Frank Piegaro

EDEN THEATRE
Opened Monday, February 14, 1972.*
(Moved June 7, 1972 to Broadhurst Theatre, November 21, 1972 to Royale Theatre)
Kenneth Waissman and Maxine Fox in association with Anthony D'Amato present:

GREASE

Book, Music and Lyrics, Jim Jacobs, Warren Casey; Director, Tom Moore; Musical Numbers and Dances Staged by Patricia Birch; Orchestrations, Michael Leonard; Musical Supervision, Vocal and Dance Arrangements, Louis St. Louis; Scenery, Douglas W. Schmidt; Costumes, Carrie F. Robbins; Lighting, Karl Eigsti; Musical Direction, Jeremy Stone; Sound, Jack Shearing; Hairstylist, John Delaat; Production Supervisor, T. Schuyler Smith; Assistant to Producers, Linda Schultz; Assistant to Director, Nancy Robbins; General Management, Theatre Now, Inc.; Original cast album by MGM Records.

CAST

Miss Lynch	Dorothy Leon†1
Patty Simcox	Ilene Kristen†2
Eugene Florczyk	Tom Harris†3
Jan	Garn Stephens†4
Marty	Katie Hanley†5
Betty Rizzo	Adrienne Barbeau†6
Doody	James Canning†7
Roger	Walter Bobbie†8
Kenickie	Timothy Meyers†9
Sonny LaTierri	Jim Borelli†10
Frenchy	Marya Small†11
Sandy Dumbrowski	Carole Demas†12
Danny Zuko	Barry Bostwick†13
Vince Fontaine	Don Billett†14
Johnny Casino	Alan Paul†15
Cha-Cha DiGregorio	Kathi Moss
Teen Angel	Alan Paul†15

UNDERSTUDIES: Danny Zuko, Frank Piegaro; Female roles, Forbesy Russell, Ann Travolta; Male roles, John Fennessy, Jim Langrall, Greg Zadikov

MUSICAL NUMBERS: "Alma Mater," "Summer Nights," "Those Magic Changes," "Freddy, My Love," "Greased Lightnin'," "Mooning," "Look at Me, I'm Sandra Dee," "We Go Together," "Shakin' at the High School Hop," "Born to Hand-Jive," "Beauty School Drop-Out," "Alone at a Drive-in Movie," "Rock 'n' Roll Party Queen," "There Are Worse Things I Could Do," "All Choked Up," Finale.

A rock musical in 2 acts and 12 scenes. The action takes place in the late 1950's.

General Manager: Edward H. Davis
Company Manager: Camille Ranson
Press: Betty Lee Hunt, Maria Cristina Pucci, Fred Hoot
Stage Managers: Lynne Guerra, Steve Beckler, John Fennessy

* Still playing May 31, 1977. For original production, see THEATRE WORLD Vol. 28.
†Succeeded by: 1. Sudie Bond, Ruth Russell, 2. Joy Rinaldi, Carol Culver, Katherine Meloche, 3. Barrey Smith, Stephen Van Benschoten, Lloyd Alann, 4. Jamie Donnelly, Randee Heller, Rebecca Gilchrist, Mimi Kennedy, Cynthia Darlow, 5. Meg Bennett, Denise Nettleton, Marily Henner, Char Fontane, Diane Stilwell, 6. Elaine Petricoff, Randee Heller, Livia Genise, Judy Kaye, 7. Barry J. Tarallo, 8. Richard Quarry, John Driver, Michael Tucci, Ray DeMattis, 9. John Fennessy, Jerry Zaks, Michael Tucci, Danny Jacobson, 10. Matt Landers, Albert Insinnia, David Paymer, 11. Ellen March, Joy Rinaldi, Jill P. Rose, Forbesy Russell, 12. Ilene Graff, Candice Earley, Robin Lamont, 13. Jeff Conaway, John Lansing, Lloyd Alann, Treat Williams, 14. Jim Weston, John Holly, Walter Charles, 15. Bob Garrett, Philip Casnoff, Joe Rifici, Philip Casnoff, Frank Piegaro

Joseph Abeles Photos

**Top Left: Treat Williams, Robin Lamont
Below: Cynthia Darlow, Ray DeMattis**

CORT THEATRE
Opened Tuesday, May 28, 1974.*
Edgar Lansbury, Joseph Beruh, Ivan Reitman present:

THE MAGIC SHOW

Book, Bob Randall; Songs, Stephen Schwartz; Magic, Doug Henning; Direction and Dances, Grover Dale; Setting, David Chapman; Costumes, Randy Barcelo; Lighting, Richard Nelson; Musical Director, Stephen Reinhardt; Dance Arrangements, David Spangler; Assistant to Director, Jay Fox; Associate Producer, Nan Pearlman; Audio, Phil Ramone; Management Associates, Al Isaac, Gary Gunas; Wardrobe Supervisor, Teena Maria Charlotta; Music Coordinator, Earl Shendell; Production Assistants, Sam Cristensen, Darrell Jonas, Walter Wood, Lee Minter; Assistant to Producers, Darrell Jonas

CAST

Manny	Robert LuPone†1
Feldman	David Ogden Stiers†2
Donna	Annie McGreevey†3
Dina	Cheryl Barnes†4
Cal	Dale Soules†5
Doug	Doug Henning†6
Mike	Ronald Stafford†7
Steve	Loyd Sannes†8
Charmin	Anita Morris†9
Goldfarb	Sam Schact

STANDBYS AND UNDERSTUDIES: Steven Peterman (Doug), Baillie Gerstein (Cal/Donna), Sharron Miller (Charmin/Dina), Nicholas Wyman (Feldman/Goldfarb), Richard Balestrino (Mike/Steve), Jay Fox (Manny), Christopher Lucas (Manny).

MUSICAL NUMBERS: "Up to His Old Tricks," "Solid Silver Platform Shoes," "Lion Tamer," "Style," "Charmin's Lament," "Two's Company," "Goldfarb Variations," "Doug's Act," "A Bit of Villainy," "West End Avenue," "Sweet, Sweet, Sweet," "Before Your Very Eyes."

A magic show with music performed without intermission.

General Management: Marvin A. Krauss Associates
Company Managers: Gary Gunas, Bob Skerry
Press: Gifford/Wallace, Glenna Freedman, Tom Trenkle
Stage Managers: Herb Vogler, Jay Fox, John Actman, Brennan Roberts

* Still playing May 31, 1977. For original production, see THEATRE WORLD Vol. 30.
† Succeeded by: 1. Clifford Lipson, 2. Timothy Jerome, Kenneth Kimmins, 3. Lisa Raggio, 4. Lynne Thigpen, 5. Gwendolyn Coleman, 6. Jeffrey Mylett, Joseph Abaldo, 7. Robert Brubach, 8. T. Michael Reed, Christopher Lucas, 9. Loni Ackerman, Louisa Flaningam

**Lynne Thigpen, Joseph Abaldo, Lisa Raggio
Top: Louisa Flaningam, Robert Brubach,
Joseph Abaldo, Christopher Lucas**

Top: Joseph Abaldo, Dale Soules

IMPERIAL THEATRE
Opened Monday, October 23, 1972.*
(Moved March 15, 1977 to Minskoff Theatre)
Stuart Ostrow presents:

PIPPIN

Book, Roger O. Hirson; Music and Lyrics, Stephen Schwartz; Direction and Choreography, Bob Fosse; Scenery, Tony Walton; Costumes, Patricia Zipprodt; Lighting, Jules Fisher; Musical Direction, Rene Wiegert, Milton Setzer; Orchestrations, Ralph Burns; Dance Arrangements, John Berkman; Sound, Abe Jacob; Hairstylist, Ernest Adler; Associate Conductor, Joseph Klein; Wardrobe Supervisor, A. T. Karniewich; Assistants to Director, Louis Quick, Kathryn Doby; Original cast album by Motown Records

CAST

Leading Player	Ben Vereen[1]
Pippin	John Rubinstein[2]
Charles	Eric Berry
Lewis	Christopher Chadman[3]
Fastrada	Leland Palmer[4]
Sword Bearer	John Mineo[5]
The Head/Field Marshall	Roger Hamilton
Berthe	Irene Ryan[6]
Beggar	Richard Korthaze[7]
Peasant	Paul Solen[8]
Noble	Gene Foote[9]
Catherine	Jill Clayburgh[10]
Theo	Shane Nickerson[11]

STANDBYS AND UNDERSTUDIES: Dean Pitchford (Pippin), Quitman Fludd III (Leading Player), Dortha Duckworth (Berthe), Verna Pierce (Catherine), Sparky Shapiro (Theo), Roger Hamilton (Charles), Virginia MacColl (Fastrada), John Windsor (Pippin)

MUSICAL NUMBERS: "Magic to Do," "Corner of the Sky," "Welcome Home," "War Is a Science," "Glory," "Simple Joys," "No Time at All," "With You," "Spread a Little Sunshine," "Morning Glow," "On the Right Track," "Kind of Woman," "Extraordinary," "Love Song," Finale

A musical in 8 scenes performed without intermission. The action takes place in 780 A.D. and thereabouts, in the Holy Roman Empire and thereabouts.

General Managers: Joseph Harris, Ira Bernstein
Company Manager: Nancy Simmons
Press: Solters/Roskin, Milly Schoenbaum, Nini Finkelstein, Fred Nathan
Stage Managers: Lola Shumlin, John H. Lowe III, Herman Magidson, Andy Keyser, Paul Bowen, Roger Bigelow

* Closed June 12, 1977 after 1944 performances. For original production see THEATRE WORLD Vol. 29.
† Succeeded by: 1. Samuel E. Wright, Irving Lee, Ben Harney, Northern J. Calloway, 2. Dean Pitchford, Michael Rupert, 3. Justin Ross, Jerry Colker, 4. Priscilla Lopez, Patti Karr, Antonia Ellis, 5. Ken Urmston, 6. Lucie Lancaster, Dorothy Stickney, Fay Sappington, 7. Larry Merritt, Roger Bigelow, Ken Miller, 8. Chet Walker, John Windsor, 9. Larry Giroux, Bryan Nicholas, 10. Betty Buckley, Joy Franz, 11. Douglas Grober, Shamus Barnes

Martha Swope Photos

Top Right: Northern J. Calloway, Michael Rupert
Below: Antonia Ellis

Company in "War"

Michael Rupert Joy Franz

ALVIN THEATRE

Opened Tuesday, January 7, 1975.*
(Moved March 29, 1977 to Mark Hellinger Theatre)
Philip Rose, Gloria and Louis K. Sher present:

SHENANDOAH

Book, James Lee Barrett, Peter Udell, Philip Rose; Based on screenplay of same title by James Lee Barrett; Music, Gary Geld; Director, Philip Rose; Choreography, Robert Tucker; Scenery, C. Murawski; Lighting, Thomas Skelton; Costumes, Pearl Somner, Winn Morton; Orchestrations, Don Walker; Musical Direction, Richard Parrinello; Dance Arrangements, Russell Warner; Originally presented at the Goodspeed Opera House; Hairstylist, Werner Sherer; Technical Adviser, Mitch Miller; Wardrobe Supervisor, Lee Decker; Production Assistant, Rosemary Troyano; Original cast album by RCA Records.

CAST

Charlie Anderson	John Cullum†1
Jacob	Ted Agress†2
James	Joel Higgins†3
Nathan	Jordan Suffin†4
John	David Russell
Jenny	Penelope Milford†5
Henry	Robert Rosen
Robert (The Boy)	Joseph Shapiro†6
Anne	Donna Theodore†7
Gabriel	Chip Ford†8
Reverend Byrd	Charles Welch†9
Sam	Gordon Halliday
Sergeant Johnson	Edward Penn
Lieutenant	Marshall Thomas
Tinkham	Charles Welch†10
Carol	Casper Roos
Corporal	Gary Harger
Marauder	Gene Masoner†11
Engineer	Ed Preble†12
Confederate Sniper	Craig Lucas†13

ENSEMBLE: Tedd Carrere, Dennis Cooley, Stephen Dubov, Richard Flanders, Kathleen Gordon, Gary Harger, David Cale Johnson, Robert Johanson, Sherry Lambert, Gene Masoner, Paul Myrvold, Dan Ormond, Casper Roos, J. Kevin Scannell, Emily Bindiger, E. Allan Stevens, Marshall Thomas, Matt Gavin, James Ferrier, Joe Howard, Timothy Wallace, Martin Walsh, Kevin Wilson, Suzy Brabeau

UNDERSTUDIES: Gene Masoner (Jacob), James Ferrier (James), Kevin Wilson (Nathan), Matt Gavin (John), Robert Johanson (Henry), Gibby Gibson (Robert), Christopher Blount (Gabriel), Suzy Brabeau (Jenny), Kathleen Gordon (Anne), Richard Flanders (Sam), Casper Roos (Charlie/Byrd/Johnson), J. Kevin Scannell (Carol), E. Allan Stevens (Tinkham/Marauder), Dan Ormond (Cpl/Engineer)

MUSICAL NUMBERS: "Raise the Flag of Dixie," "I've Heard It All Before," "Pass the Cross to Me," "Why Am I Me," "Next to Lovin' I Like Fightin'," "Over the Hill," "Pickers Are Comin'," "Meditation," "We Make A Beautiful Pair," "Violets and Silverbells," "It's a Boy," "Freedom," "Papa's Gonna Make It All Right," "The Only Home I Know"

A musical in two acts with a prologue. The action takes place during the Civil War in the Shenandoah Valley of Virginia.

General Manager: Helen Richards
Press: Merle Debuskey, Leo Stern, William Schelble
Stage Managers: Steve Zweigbaum, Arthuro E. Porazzi, Sherry Lambert

* Closed Aug. 7, 1977 after 1050 performances. For original production, see THEATRE WORLD Vol. 31.
† Succeeded by: 1. William Chapman until Mr. Cullum's return June 6, 1977, 2. Roger Berdahl, 3. Wayne Hudgins, Paul Myrvold, 4. Craig Lucas, Kevin Wilson, 5. Maureen Silliman, Emily Bindiger, 6. Mark Perman, Steve Grober, 7. Leslie Denniston, 8. Bent Carter, David Vann, Donny Cooper, Tony Holmes, 9. P. L. Carling, 10. Richard Flanders, 11. Joe Howard, 12. E. Allan Stevens, 13. Dennis Cooley, Robert Johanson

Sy Friedman Photos

**Top: John Cullum, Gordon Halliday
Below: (L) William Chapman**

William Chapman, David Russell, Leslie Denniston, Wayne Hudgins, Roger Berdahl, Gordon Halliday, Maureen Silliman

MAJESTIC THEATRE
Opened Sunday, January 5, 1975.*
(Moved May 25, 1977 to Broadway Theatre)
Ken Harper presents:

THE WIZ

Book, William F. Brown; Based on L. Frank Baum's "The Wonderful Wizard of Oz"; Music and Lyrics, Charlie Smalls; Director, Geoffrey Holder; Choreography and Musical Numbers staged by George Faison; Musical Direction, Tom Pierson; Settings, Tom H. John; Costumes, Geoffrey Holder; Lights, Tharon Musser; Orchestrations, Harold Wheeler; Vocal Arrangements, Charles H. Coleman; Dance Arrangements, Timothy Graphenreed; Manager, Jose Vega; Sound, Richard J. C. Miller; Wardrobe Supervisors, Joseph Potter, Frank Green; Associate Conductor, Jack Jeffers; Special Effects, Ronald Vitelli; Wigs and Makeup, Stanley James; Original cast album by Atlantic Records

CAST

Aunt Em	Tasha Thomas†1
Toto	Nancy†2
Dorothy	Stephanie Mills
Uncle Henry	Ralph Wilcox†3
Tornado	Evelyn Thomas†4
Munchkins	Phylicia Ayers-Allen, Leslie Butler, Joni Palmer, Andy Torres, Carl Weaver, Lois Hayes, Howard Porter
Addaperle	Clarice Taylor†5
Yellow Brick Road	Ronald Dunham, Eugene Little, John Parks, Kenneth Scott, Paul Hoskins, Kevin Jeff, Rodney Green, Chuck Thorpes
Scarecrow	Hinton Battle†6
Crows	Wendy Edmead, Frances Morgan, Thea Nerissa Barnes, Renee Rose
Tinman	Tiger Haynes
Lion	Ted Ross†7
Kalidahs	Philip Bond, Pi Douglass, Rodney Green, Evelyn Thomas, Andy Torres, John Parks, Alma Robinson, Wendy Edmead, Kwame Johnson, Bruce Taylor, Gayle Turner
Poppies	Lettie Battle, Leslie Butler, Eleanor McCoy, Frances Morgan, Joni Palmer, Renee Rose, Pat Estwick, Lois Hayes
Field Mice	Phylicia Ayers-Allen, Pi Douglass, Carl Weaver, Ralph Wilcox, Sam Harkness, Howard Porter
Gatekeeper	Danny Beard†8
The Wiz	Andre DeShields†9
Evillene	Mabel King†10
Lord High Underling	Ralph Wilcox†3
Soldier Messenger	Carl Weaver
Winged Monkey	Andy Torres†11
Glinda	Dee Dee Bridgewater†12

UNDERSTUDIES: Dorothy, Gayle Turner, Pat Estwick; Tin Man, Howard Porter, Victor Willis; Lion, Toney Watkins, Victor Willis; Scarecrow, Carl Weaver, Alvin McDuffie; Addaperle, Ruth Brisbane; Evillene, Ruth Brisbane; Wiz, Kwame Johnson, Toney Watkins, Victor Willis; Glinda, Phylicia Ayers-Allen, Janyse M. Singleton; Aunt Em, Deborah Burrell, Wendy Edmead; Swing Dancers-Singers, Al Perryman, Carl Hardy, Demarest Grey, Dyane Harvey, Christina Kimball

EMERALD CITY CITIZENS: Thea Nerissa Barnes, Pat Estwick, Leslie Butler, Wendy Edmead, Lois Hayes, Keith Harris, Alvin McDuffie, Frances Morgan, Claudia Lewis, Ronald Dunham, Rodney Green, Eugene Little, Kenneth Scott, Alwin Taylor, John Parks, Pat Estwick, Renee Rose, Alma Robinson, Paul Hoskins, Kevin Jeff, Bruce Taylor, Kwame Johnson, Phylicia Ayers-Allen

MUSICAL NUMBERS: "The Feeling We Once Had," "Tornado Ballet," "He's the Wizard," "Soon as I Get Home," "I Was Born on the Day Before Yesterday," "Ease on Down the Road," "Slide Some Oil to Me," "Mean Ole Lion," "Kalidah Battle," "Be a Lion," "Lion's Dream," "Emerald City Ballet," "So You Want to Meet the Wizard," "What Would I Do if I Could Feel," "No Bad News," "Funky Monkeys," "Everybody Rejoice," "Who Do You Think You Are," "If You Believe," "Y'All Got It!," "A Rested Body Is a Rested Mind," "Home"

A musical in 2 acts and 16 scenes with a prologue.

General Managers: Emanuel Azenberg, Eugene V. Wolsk
Company Manager: Susan Bell
Press: Merlin Group, Sandra Manley, Elizabeth Rodman, Ron Harris
Stage Managers: Christopher Kelly, Robert Burland, Steven Shaw, Donald Christy, Clint Jakeman

Martha Swope Photos

* Still playing May 31, 1977. For original production see THEATRE WORLD Vol. 32.
† Succeeded by: 1. Esther Marrow, 2. Westy, 3. Al Fann, Toney Watkins, 4. Wendy Edmead, 5. Jozella Reed, 6. Gregg Burge, 7. James Wigfall, Ken Page, 8. Toney Watkins, 9. Alan Weeks, Mr. DeShields returned Jan. 24, 1977, 10. Edye Byrde, Theresa Merritt, Ella Mitchell, 11. Keith Harris, Kevin Jeff, 12. Deborah Burrell

**Top Right: Tiger Haynes, Stephanie Mills
Below: Andre DeShields**

BROOKS ATKINSON THEATRE
Opened Thursday, March 13, 1975.*
Morton Gottlieb, Dasha Epstein, Edward L. Schuman, and
Palladium Productions present:

SAME TIME, NEXT YEAR

By Bernard Slade; Director, Gene Saks; Scenery, William Ritman;
Costumes, Jane Greenwood; Lighting, Tharon Musser; Associate
Producers, Ben Rosenberg, Warren Crane; Wardrobe Supervisor,
Penny Davis; Hairstylist, Angela Gari

CAST

Doris . . . . Ellen Burstyn†1
George . . . . Charles Grodin†2
Standbys: Rochelle Oliver, Peter DeMaio

A comedy in two acts and six scenes. The action takes place in a
guest cottage of a country inn in Northern California from 1951 to
1975.

General Manager: Ben Rosenberg
Company Manager: Martin Cohen
Press: Solters/Roskin, Milly Schoenbaum, Fred Nathan
Stage Managers: Warren Crane, Kate Pollock, J. S. McKie, Jr.

* Still playing May 31, 1977. For original production, see THE-
ATRE WORLD Vol. 31.
† Succeeded by: 1. Joyce Van Patten, Loretta Swit, Sandy Dennis,
Hope Lange, 2. Conrad Janis, Ted Bessell, Don Murray

Top Left: Sandy Dennis, Ted Bessell

Hope Lange, Don Murray

Don Murray, Hope Lange

BROADWAY PRODUCTIONS FROM PAST SEASONS THAT CLOSED THIS SEASON

Title	Opened	Closed	Performances
Equus	10/24/74	9/11/76	781
Me and Bessie	10/22/75	12/5/76	453
My Fair Lady	3/25/76	2/20/77	384
Very Good Eddie	12/21/75	9/5/76	307
The Royal Family	12/30/75	7/18/76	233
Pacific Overtures	1/11/76	6/27/76	206
The Runner Stumbles	5/18/76	10/31/76	198
Who's Afraid of Virginia Woolf?	4/1/76	7/11/76	120
The Belle of Amherst	4/28/76	8/8/76	117
Something's Afoot	5/27/76	7/18/76	74

OFF-BROADWAY PRODUCTIONS

PROVINCETOWN PLAYHOUSE
Opened Wednesday, June 9, 1976.*
Xander Productions, Inc. presents:

PAVILION

By Marshall Yaeger; Director, Eve Brandstein; Scenic Design, John Pitt; Lighting, Patricia Moeser; Producers, Lois Bailey, David Bailey; Associate Producer, Michael Martorella; Assistant to Producers, Diane Guide; Costumes, Lois Bailey, Diane Guide; Production Assistant, Diane George

CAST

Mom .... Joan See
Dad .... David Bailey
Sam .... Richard Hayes
Julie .... Maura Kramer
Davis Blair .... Peter Reznikoff

A play in 3 acts and 4 scenes. The action takes place during Memorial Day weekend 1963 in a pavilion on an estate in Minnesota.

Press: Sol Jacobson, Lewis Harmon
Stage Managers: Nancy Robbins, Elicia Rinaldi

* Closed June 20, 1976 after 11 performances and 1 preview.

**David Bailey, Maura Kramer, Joan See,
Peter Reznikoff**

NEW FOLLIES THEATRE
Opened Thursday, June 10, 1976.*
(Moved Sept. 8, 1976 to Gate Theatre; Nov. 17, 1976 to Cricket Theatre)
Joseph Tiraco and Donald Elliott present:

GREENWICH VILLAGE FOLLIES

Music, Lyrics and Vignettes by Ronnie Britton; Conceived and Directed by Mr. Britton; Costumes, by Kapton; Lighting, Steve Loew; Musical Director, Max Lifchitz; Assistant Musical Director, Carl Troop; Production Assistant, Jeff Gibson; Makeup Consultant, Wendy Kaplan; Stage Manager, Joe Pino

CAST

Linda David†	Jacqueline Carol
Lance Marcone	Ronaeld Smith
Danny Freedman	Philippe de Brugada
Gregory Cook	Marisa Lyon

ACT I: Overture, Introduction, "Greenwich Village Follies," "Let Me Sing!" "Hello, New York," "Le Grand Rape," "You Show Me Yours," "Quartet for Losers," "Nude with Violin," "We Wanna Star," "Rock 'n' Roll Star," "Long Ago, or Yesterday?," "I've Been in Love," "Most Unusual Pair"

ACT II: "Melody of Manhattan," "Merry-Go-Round," "Bicentennial March," "Look at Me," "That Girl with the Curls," "Ole Soft Core," "Ballet Erotique," "The Expose," "Garbage-Ella," "Pandora," Finale

A revue in two acts.

* Still playing May 31, 1977.
† During the season the following succeeded various members of the cast: Coco Colos, Donna Noack, Lola Holman, Ronald St. Pierre, James St. Pierre, Lee Parker, Anthony Piazza, Samantha, Mikel Cusson, Linda Ipanema, Jeff Maron, Wendy Kaplan

Ray Blakey Photo

**(kneeling) James St. Pierre, Mikel Cusson, Lance Marcone,
Susan Bluckman, Samantha, Brenda Dattel**

THEATRE FOUR
Opened Monday, June 14, 1976.*
Pegasus III presents:

BEWARE THE JUBJUB BIRD

By Sandra Jennings; Director, Harold Guskin; Set and Lighting, Lee Goldman; Music, Sandra Jennings, Richard Cameron; Management Associates, Thelma Cooper, Amy Gitlin; Pianist, Richard Cameron

CAST

Lisa .... Jenny Sanford
Daniel .... Kevin Kline
Jason .... Peter G. Skinner
Jean .... Cheryl Scammon
Owen .... Jared Sakren
Understudies: Jason, Jared Sakren; Owen, Scott Wilcox

A play in 2 acts and 5 scenes. The action takes place at the present time in New York City in the apartments of Daniel and Lisa, and Jason, and in the theatre.

General Management: Dorothy Olim Associates
Company Manager: Donald Joslyn
Press: David Powers
Stage Manager: Janet Sonenberg

* Closed June 15, 1976 after 2 performances.

Scott Wilcox Photo

Kevin Kline, Jenny Sanford, Peter G. Skinner

CIRCLE IN THE SQUARE
Opened Tuesday, June 15, 1976.*
Heartsong Productions in association with Drew Murphy presents:

BECOMING

By Gail Edwards and Sam Harris; Settings, Dan Leigh; Lighting, Martin Tudor; Costumes, Dee Dee Fote; Musical, Lawrence J. Blank; Production Supervisor, James Zitlow; Sound, David Congdon; Additional Costumes, Nolan Drummond; Directed and Choreographed by John Mineo; Associate Producer, Dennis I. Gould

CAST

Norman .... Norman Meister
Anne .... Anne Sward
Gail .... Gail Edwards

MUSICAL NUMBERS: "It Feels So Good to Be Alive Today," "Believe in You," "It's Not Easy to Change Your Life," "Goin' Back to That Feelin'," "Mama," "Valentine Song," "Lonely Times," "Lordy," "Choices," "Birthday Song," "From Now On," "Let It Be Today," "Love Me Lightly," "Freer Love," "Look Inside," "Let's Get Started"

A musical in two acts.

General Manager: Drew Murphy
Press: Max Eisen, Judy Jacksina

* Closed June 16, 1976 after 2 performances and 6 previews.

**Anne Sward, Gail Edwards, Norman Meister
in "Becoming"**

CHERRY LANE THEATRE
Opened Wednesday, June 16, 1976.*
Lawrence Goossen and Jeffrey Wachtel present:

SEXUAL PERVERSITY IN CHICAGO
and
DUCK VARIATIONS

By David Mamet; Director, Albert Takazauckas; Set and Costumes, Michael Massee; Lighting, Gary Porto; Music Composed by George Quincy; Associate Producer, Jean Halbert; Production Coordinator, Linda Jackson; Assistant Producer, Peter Lopez

CAST

"Sexual Perversity in Chicago"
Bernard Litko .... F. Murray Abraham
Deborah Soloman .... Jane Anderson
Danny Shapiro .... Peter Riegert
Joan Webber .... Gina Rogers
The action takes place around the North Side of Chicago during a period of nine weeks one summer.

"Duck Variations"
George S. Aronovitz .... Michael Egan
Emil Varec .... Mike Kellin

The action takes place in a park at the present time.

Press: Jean Halbert
Stage Managers: William LaRosa, Peter Reed Glazer

* Closed Apr. 17, 1977 after 273 performances and 8 previews.

Shaun Considine, Burke Photos

GOOD SHEPHERD-FAITH CHURCH
Wednesday, June 30, 1976.*
Musical Theatre Lab presents:

SAINTS

Book and Lyrics, Merle Kessler; Music, William Penn; Director, Edward Berkeley; Choreography, Nora Peterson; Musical Direction, Bob Goldstone; Project Producer, Steve Kimball; Technical Director, William Stiegel

CAST

Martha Harris .... Jane Altman
Zeke .... Dennis Bailey
Elias Hancock .... Ralph Bruneau
Dr. MacIntire/Judge .... Yusef Bulos
Cindie .... Joanna Churgin
Ann .... Kathryn Cordes
Amy .... Jill Eikenberry
Will/Stone .... Dann Florek
Ruthie/Mrs. Stone .... Robin Groves
Loretta/Boo .... Deborah Johnson
Sarah .... Heather Lupton
Ollie .... Bob Picardo
Badger Cleese .... Dean Pitchford
Aaron .... Nick Plakias
Pa/Governor .... Steve Pudenz
Joseph Tucker .... Terry Quinn
Jemima .... Marti Rolph
Eben/Mr. Seymour .... Tom Tofel

MUSICAL NUMBERS: "I Am the Sign," "In the Sweet By and By," "Mama Lazarus," "I Can't Walk on Water," "The Old Rabbit Hole," "What Will Daddy Say?," "Stand by Me," "It's Hard I Know," "O My Soul," "Remember Love," "Death Comes Like a Thief," "Bastard for the Lord," "Night Is a Weapon," "The Ladies Come from Baltimore," "The Years Are Burning," "I Believe in Survival," "See the River Flow," "Let It Fall," "This Darkness," "Sweet Jesus, Blessed Savior"

A musical in two acts.

Production Manager: Robert Schear
Stage Manager: Paul Diaz

* Closed July 11, 1976 after limited engagement of 10 performances. No photos available.

Top Right: Gina Rogers (top), Jane Anderson, and Below: with F. Murray Abraham, Peter Riegert

Michael Egan, Mike Kellin in "Duck Variations"

89

Bob Slater, Connie Day

Opened Thursday, July 1, 1976.*
Guy Lombardo presents:

SHOWBOAT

Music, Jerome Kern; Book and Lyrics, Oscar Hammerstein 2nd; Based on novel by Edna Ferber; Director, John Fearnley; Choreographer, Robert Pagent; Scenery, John W. Keck; Costumes, Winn Morton; Lighting, Richard Nelson; Musical Director, Jay Blackton; Entire production under supervision of Arnold Spector; Assistant to Director, Ruth Bedford; Wardrobe Mistress, Agnes Farrell; Hair Designer, Werner Sherer; Assistant Conductor, Robert Stanley; Choral Director, Robert Monteil

CAST

Windy	Robert Pagent
Steve	Bob Slater
Pete	Ralph Vucci
Queenie	Alyce Webb
Parthy Ann Hawks	Lizabeth Pritchett
Capt. Andy Hawks	Max Showalter
Ellie	Connie Day
Frank	Lee Roy Reams
Rubberface	Jimmy Powers
Julie	Beth Fowler
Gaylord Ravenal	Robert Peterson
Vallon	John Dorrin
Magnolia	Barbara Meister
Joe	Edward Pierson
Backwoodsman	Lee Cass
Jeb	Dale Muchmore
Landlady	Irma Rogers
Jim	Lee Cass
Jake	Kevin Wilson
Man with guitar	Don Bonnell
Doorman at Trocadero	Eugene Edwards
Mother Superior	Elaine Bunse
Kim	Karen DiBianco
Old Lady on the levee	Irma Rogers

TOWNSPEOPLE: Helena Andreyko, Ellie Bowman, Elaine Bunse, Jean Busada, Patricia Cort, Karen DiBianco, Roslyn Dixon, Doris Galiber, Mickey Gunnersen, Sherry Lambert, Janette Moody, Kathleen Robey, Irma Rogers, Renee Spector, Lorice Stevens, Dixie Stewart, Maggie Stewart, Russell Anderson, Don Bonnell, Larry Cahn, Peter Clark, Donald H. Coleman, Jeff Delson, Eugene Edwards, Paul Flores, Ted Goodridge, Franz Jones, James Kennon-Wilson, Dale Muchmore, Don Oliver, Sean Power, Jimmy Rivers, David Weatherspoon, Kevin Wilson, Swing: Laurie Scandurra, Robert Montiel

UNDERSTUDIES: Ravenal, Bob Slater; Magnolia, Dixie Stewart; Capt. Andy, John Dorrin; Julie/Ellie, Sherry Lambert; Joe, Don Oliver; Parthy Ann, Elaine Bunse; Frank, Don Bonnell; Queenie, Roslyn Dixon; Windy, Lee Cass; Steve, Dale Muchmore; Vallon, Peter Clark

MUSICAL NUMBERS: "Grand Opening," "Cotton Blossom," "Show Boat Parade," "Ballyhoo," "Only Make Believe," "Old Man River," "Can't Help Lovin' That Man," "I Might Fall Back on You," "Dance Specialty," "Life upon the Wicked Stage," "You Are Love," "Levee Dance," "At the Fair," "Why Do I Love You?," "Bill," "Goodbye, My Lady Love," "After the Ball," Finale

A musical in two acts. The action takes place during the 1880's and into the 1920's, aboard the showboat "Cotton Blossom," in Mississippi River towns, and in Chicago during the 1893 World's Fair.

Company Manager: Sam Pagliaro
Press: Saul Richman
Stage Managers: Mortimer Halpern, Bernard Pollock, Ralph Vucci

* Closed Sept. 5, 1976 after 67 performances.

Liz Lombardo Photos

Top: Barbara Meister, Lizabeth Pritchett, Max Showalter, Robert Peterson Below: Edward Pierson, Alyce Webb, Barbara Meister, Beth Fowler

TOP OF THE VILLAGE GATE
Opened Tuesday, October 5, 1976.*
Wayne Starr in association with Thomas Hannan and Charles Kalan presents:

LOVESONG

By Michael Valenti; Original Idea Conceived by Henry Comor; Orchestrations and Vocal Arrangements, Michael Valenti; Musical Numbers Staged by John Montgomery; Musical Director, David Krane; Set, Jack Logan; Lighting, Martin Friedman; Media Design, Bruce Shenton; Costumes, Joan Mayo; Choreographic Assistant, Michael Perrier

CAST

Melanie Chartoff
Sigrid Heath
Ty McConnell
Jess Richards

MUSICAL NUMBERS: "What Is Love," "Did Not," "When I Was One-and-Twenty," "Bid Me Love," "A Birthday," "Sophia," "Many a Fairer Face," "Maryann," "When We're Married," "To My Dear and Loving Husband," "I Remember," "April Child," "Song," "What Is a Woman Like?," "Let the Toast Pass," "Echo," "Open All Night," "A Rondelay," "Just Suppose," "Unhappy Bella," "Young I Was," "Jenny Kiss'd Me," "Indian Summer," "The Fair Dissenter Lass," "Blood Red Roses," "So, We'll Go No More A-Roving," "An Epitaph"

A musical entertainment in two acts.

General Manager: Jay Kingwill
Company Manager: Mark Bramble
Press: Alan Eichler
Stage Managers: Martin Friedman, Bobby Kneeland

* Closed Oct. 24, 1976 after 23 performances.

Jarry Lang Photos

Right: Melanie Chartoff, Ty McConnell, and top with Sigrid Heath, Jess Richards

CARNEGIE HALL
Wednesday, October 6, 1976.*
The Carnegie Hall Corp. by arrangement with the Asia Society Performing Arts Program presents:

MARTIAL ARTS OF KABUKI

From the National Theatre Institute of Japan; Directors, Nakamura Matagoro, Onoe Kuroemon, Bando Yaenosuke

CAST

Nakamura Matajiro	Miyawaki Shinji
Nakamura Mataichi	Tanaka Shinji
Kishi Nobutaka	Nakamura Namio
Kihara Hirokazu	Matsuoka Yutaka
Koike Mitsuyosh	Motohashi Norio

Traditional classical Japanese theatre presented in two parts.

* One performance only.

THEATRE FOUR
Opened Tuesday, October 12, 1976.*
The Chelsea Theater Center by arrangement with Arthur Cantor presents:

EMLYN WILLIAMS
as
DYLAN THOMAS GROWING UP

A solo performance in two parts devised by Emlyn Williams from the stories of Dylan Thomas; Lighting and Production Supervisor, Robert Crawley; Personal Assistant to Mr. Williams, Brian Stashick

PRESS: Susan Bloch, Lester Gruner

* Closed Oct. 24, 1976 after limited engagement of 16 performances. Returned Friday, Nov. 26, 1976 for 20 additional performances, closing Dec. 12, 1976.

Emlyn Williams

VILLAGE GATE DOWNSTAIRS
Opened Monday, October 18, 1976.*
Judy Gordon and Jack Temchin present:

2 BY 5

Music, John Kander; Lyrics, Fred Ebb; Conceived and Directed by Seth Glassman; Setting and Costumes, Dan Leigh; Lighting, Martin Tudor; Musical Director, Joseph Clonick

CAST

D'Jamin Bartlett
Kay Cummings
Danny Fortus
Shirley Lemmon
Scott Stevensen

MUSICAL NUMBERS: Overture, "Cabaret," "Willkommen," "Yes," "Sing Happy," "Mein Herr," "Seeing Things," "The World Goes Round," "Love Song," "The Money Song," "Sign Here," "My Own Best Friend," "Losers," "Military Man," "Only Love," "Why Can't I Speak?," "Me and My Baby," "Isn't This Better," "Home," "Maybe This Time," "Ring Them Bells," "Mr. Cellophane," "Among My Yesterdays," "I Don't Remember You," "Class," "Broadway, My Street," "New York, New York," "On Stage," "Ten Percent," "Razzle Dazzle," "A Quiet Thing," "Cabaret"

A "musical cabaret" in two parts.

General Management: Drew Murphy
Press: Jeffrey Richards, Elaine Bestmann, Larry Ersland
Stage Manager: Mark Rubinsky

* Closed Dec. 5, 1976 after 57 performances.

92 **D'Jamin Bartlett, Scott Stevensen, Danny Fortus, Shirley Lemmon, Kay Cummings**

CIRCLE IN THE SQUARE DOWNTOWN
Opened Thursday, October 14, 1976.*
Circle in the Square (Theodore Mann, Artistic Director; Paul Libin, Managing Director) presents:

THE CLUB

By Eve Merriam; Director, Tommy Tune; Musical Direction and Arrangements, Alexandra Ivanoff; Costumes and Set, Kate Carmel; Lighting, Cheryl Thacker.

CAST

Johnny	Marlene Dell
Bertie	Gloria Hodes
Algy	Joanne Beretta
Freddie	Carole Monferdini
Bobby	Julia J. Hafner
Maestro	Memrie Innerarity
Henry	Terri White

Understudies: Frolic Taylor, Gerta Grunen

A "musical diversion" performed without intermission. All the songs are from the period 1894–1905.

Press: Merle Debuskey, David Roggensack
Stage Managers: Gene Taylor, Frolic Taylor, Gerta Grunen

* Still playing May 31, 1977.

Martha Swope Photos

**Right: Julie J. Hafner, Gloria Hodes,
Carole Monferdini, Joanne Beretta
Top: Joanne Beretta, Carole Monferdini,
Gloria Hodes, Julie J. Hafner**

Terri White, Marlene Dell

Gloria Hodes, Julie J. Hafner

Opened Monday, November 1, 1976.*
The Yael Company and Norman Kean present:

DON'T STEP ON MY OLIVE BRANCH

Book, Harvey Jacobs; Composer-Lyricist, Ron Eliran; Conceived, Choreographed and Directed by Jonathan Karmon; Musical Director, David Krivoshei; Sound, Sander Hacker; Setting and Projections, James Tilton; Lighting, William H. Batchelder; Costumes, Pierre D'Alby; Assistant to Mr. Karmon, Alan Fox; Musical Coordinator, Michael Tschudin; Production Supervisor, Sam Stickler; Technical Directors, Tom Healy, Frank Treubig, Jim Piotti; Production Assistant, Michael Hreha; Hairstylist, Robert Sachs-Takada

CAST

Rivka Raz	Donald Ronci
Ron Eliran	Karen DiBianco
Ruthi Navon	Carla Farnsworth
Riki Gal	David Kottke
Hanan Goldblatt	Joel Robertson
Gail Benedict	Lisa Gould Rubin
Darleen Boudreaux	Daniel Stewart
	John Windsor

MUSICAL NUMBERS: "Moonlight," "The World's Greatest Magical Act," "I Believe," "Only Love," "My Land," "We Love a Conference," "Come with Me," "Tired Heroes," "Have a Little Fun," "I Hear a Song," "I Live My Life in Color," "Young Days," "Somebody's Stepping on My Olive Branch," "It Was Worth It," "Jerusalem"

A musical performed without intermission. The action takes place at the present time at a border settlement in Israel.

Manager: Charles Artesona
Press: Max Eisen, Irene Gandy, Barbara Glenn, Judy Jacksina
Stage Managers: Daniel E. Early, Karen Winer

* Closed Nov. 14, 1976 after 16 performances and 16 previews.

Top Left: Rivka Raz, Ron Eliron

Riki Gal, Rivka Raz, Ruthi Navon

Opened Friday, November 12, 1976*
Dume Spanish Theatre (Herberto Dume, Producer-Artistic Director) presents:

LA VOZ HUMANA
and
EL BELLO INDIFFERENTE

By Jean Cocteau; Direction and Sets, Herberto Dume; Costumes, Serge Pinckney; Assistant Director, Claudio Mauricio; Press, William Perez

CAST

"La Voz Humana"
Norberto Kerner

"El Bello Indiferente"
Pablo de la Torre
Jorge Cretari

* Closed December 5, 1977 after limited engagement of 12 performances.

Rafael Llerena Photo

Pablo de la Torre, Jorge Cretari

94

CITY CENTER 55th STREET THEATRE
Opened Wednesday, November 10, 1976.*
Brannigan-Eisler Performing Arts International presents the
National Theatre of Greece (Alexis Minotis, Director General)
in:

OEDIPUS AT COLONUS

By Sophocles; Director, Alexis Minotis; Translated from Ancient
Greek By Ioannis Gryparis; Set, Kl. Klonis; Costumes, Dionyssis
Fotopoulos; Music, Theodoros Antoniou; Choreography, Maria M.
Horss; Musical Direction, Elli Nikolaidi

CAST

Antigone	Olga Tournaki
Oedipus	Alexis Minotis
Stranger	Grigorios Vafias
Ismene	Maria Skountzou
Theseus	Vassilis Kanakis
Creon	Ghikas Biniaris
Polynices	Christos Parlas
Messenger	Stelios Vokovits

Performed without intermission.

and

KNIGHTS

By Aristophanes; Director, Alexis Solomos; Translated by Nikos
Styroeras; Sets and Costumes, Giorgos Vakalo; Music, Stavros Xar-
chakos; Choreography, Dora Tsatsou-Symeonidi; Musical Direction, Elli Nikolaidi

CAST

Demosthenes	Theodoros Sarris
Nicias	Kostas Kokkakis
Sausage-seller	Stelios Vokovits
Paphlagon	Ghikas Biniaris
Demos	Pandelis Zervos

Performed without intermission

Press: Daniel Langan, Marshall Ballou

* Closed Nov. 14, 1976 after a limited engagement of 7 performances (3 of "Oedipus" and 4 of "Knights")

WHITMAN HALL
Saturday, November 20, 1976.*
Paul Elliott presents The Young Vic Company in:

THE TAMING OF THE SHREW

By William Shakespeare; Director, Denise Coffey; Designed by
Carl Toms; Music, Michael Lankester; Wardrobe Supervisor, Harriet Wallerstein

CAST

Lucentio	Richard Warwick
Tranio	Peter O'Farrell
Biondello	Arthur Blake
Baptista Minola	Hugh Hastings
Gremio	Job Stewart
Hortensio	Gavin Reed
Bianca Minola	Denise Coffey
Katherina Minola	Joanna McCallum
Petruchio	David Henry
Grumio	Ian Trigger
Curtis	Job Stewart
A Pedant of Mantua	Barrie Rutter
A Tailor	Norman Abrams
Vincentio	Alan Coates
A Widow	Judy Wilson
Servants	Sally Anne Newton, Norman Abrams
Musicians	Alan Coates, Sally Anne Newton

A comedy performed in two acts.
General Manager: John H. deLannoy
Company Manager: L. Liberatore
Press: Danny Banks
Stage Managers: Ian Drake, Rita Guenigault, Norman Abrams,
Martin John Logan

* Presented for one performance only.

**Alexis Menotis
as
Oedipus**

David Henry, Ian Trigger

THE TOP OF THE GATE

Opened Sunday, January 9, 1977.*
Charles Hollerith, Jr. and Rosita Sarnoff present the Music-Theatre Performing Group/Lenox Arts Center Production (Lyn Austin/Mary D. Silverman, Executive Directors) of:

NIGHTCLUB CANTATA

Conceived, Composed and Directed by Elizabeth Swados; Sets, Patricia Woodbridge; Lighting, Cheryl Thacker; Costumes, Kate Carmel; Associate Producer, Martha Sturtevant; Piano, Judith Fleisher; Percussion, William Milhizer; Management Associate, Thelma Cooper; Wardrobe Mistress, Marjorie Horne; Production Assistant, Neatherly Batsell

CAST

Karen Evans   Shelley Plimpton
Rocky Greenberg   David Schechter
Paul Kandel   Elizabeth Swados
JoAnna Peled   Mark Zagaeski

MUSICAL NUMBERS: "Things I Didn't Know I Loved," "Bestiario," "Bird Chorus," "Bird Lament," "Ventriloquist and Dummy," "The Applicant," "To the Harbormaster," "Adolescents," "Indecision," "Dibarti," "In Dreams Begin Reesponsibilities," "Are You with Me?," "Raga," "Waking This Morning," "Pastrami Brothers," "The Ballad of the Sad Cafe," "Isabella," "Waiting," "The Dance," "On Living"

A musical entertainment performed without intermission.

General Management: Dorothy Olim Associates
Company Manager: Gail Bell
Press: Mary Bryant, Richard Kagey, Bruce Cohen
Stage Managers: Susan D. Greenbaum, Karen Evans

* Closed May 15, 1977 after 145 performances.

Martha Swope Photo

JoAnna Peled, Shelley Plimpton, Paul Kandel, Rocky Greenberg, Karen Evans, Mark Zagaeski, David Schechter

ASTOR PLACE THEATRE

Opened Thursday, January 13, 1977.*
James J. Wisner presents:

THE COCKEYED TIGER

Written and Directed by Eric Blau; Choreography, Gemze de Lappe, Buzz Miller; Musical Score, Bert Kalmar, Harry Ruby; Original Music and Lyrics, Nicholas Meyers, Eric Blau; Sets and Costumes, Donald Jensen; Lighting, Crimmins & Smith; Arrangements, Nicholas Meyers, Nicholas Archer, Jimmy Wisner; Production Assistants, Ellen Zalk, Richard W. Graham; Special Consultant to Producer, John A. Vaccaro

CAST

Kishka Control . . . . James Nisbet Clark
Larry Seasoner . . . . Robert Matthews
Walda Barbras . . . . Chris Campbell
Rhoda Boston . . . . Wendy Wolfe
Rosetta Bensonhurst . . . . Janet McCall
Richard Bucharest . . . . Leon Morenzie
Rani Bengali . . . . Joseph Neal
The Tiger (a.k.a. Tigris, Tigris) . . . . Jack Scalici
Lilly Marlena Littleflea . . . . Elly Stone

MUSICAL NUMBERS: "The Littleflea Hop," "God Is Good to Me," "Tyger, Tyger," "Whoopie," "Hold Me Thusly," "My Dream of the South of France," "It's a Long, Long March to Kansas City," "We're Together at Kishka," "Good Times," "You've Got to Be a Tiger, Tiger," "We're Four of the Three Musketeers," "Tulip Told Tale," "Show Me a Rose," "America I Like You," "Daddy Oh!," "You Were a Hell of a Crowd Tonight"

A musical in two acts. The action takes place at the present time in the newly refurbished facsimile of the old and celebrated Klub Kishka at Broome and Houston Street in New York City.

General Manager: Lily Turner
Company Manager: Donald Joslyn
Press: Jeffrey Richards, Lewis Harmon
Stage Manager: George Allison Elmer

* Closed Jan. 14, 1977 after two performances.

Elly Stone, Jack Scalici

96

92nd STREET YM-YWHA/KAUFMANN AUDITORIUM
Opened Sunday, January 23, 1977.*
The Paper Bag Players (Judith Martin, Director) presents:

GRANDPA

Written and Designed by Judith Martin; Music, Donald Ashwander; Lighting, Robby Monk; Technical Director, John W. Lloyd; Coordinators, Edith Harnik, Susan G. Baerwald; Administrators, Judith Liss, Nancy Lloyd; Stage Manager, Peter Jablonski

CAST

Irving Burton
Judith Martin
Jeanne Michels
Virgil Roberson
Donald Ashwander

MUSICAL NUMBERS: "Getting Older," "Worrying," "Stolen Sneakers," "A Long Story," "Fast Dance," "It's Just Not Fair," "Can You Tell Me What's Happened to Kurtz?," "Bubble Gum," "A Great Big Kiss," "Born Leader," "Dancing Partners," "When You're Older," "Growing Up," "Changing"

A revue about growing older performed without intermission.

* Closed March 27, 1977 after limited engagement of 20 performances.

Right: Jeanne Michels, Irving Burton

PROMENADE THEATRE
Opened Monday, February 7, 1977.*
Jeff Britton presents:

CASTAWAYS

Book, Anthony Stimac, Dennis Andersen, Ron Whyte; Music, Don Pippin; Lyrics, Steve Brown; Director, Tony Tanner; Scenery, Scott Johnson; Lighting, Richard Winkler; Costumes, Patricia McGourty; Orchestrations, Bill Brohn; Musical Director, Dorothy Opalach; Associate Producers, Jimmy Merrill, Michael Shepley; Assistant to Producer, Karen S. Garber; Production Assistant, Michael Ellis; Technical Director, Gary Shevett; Wardrobe Mistress, Latonia Baer

CAST

Mate	Gibby Brand
Mr. Cooke	Joel Kramer
Adele	Maureen Maloney
Mr. Lewis	Stephen James
Mrs. Cooke	June Squibb
Mr. Noah	Wayne Sherwood
Mrs. Kendall	Kathleen Widdoes
Second Mate	Danie Ziskie
Captain	Rick Ladson

MUSICAL NUMBERS: "Exits and Entrances," "Isn't She," "She Can't Resist Me," "I Won't Love a Soldier Boy," "The Chase," "Kind Sir," "Could Such a Face Be False," "Old Glory," "She Would Be a Soldier," "My Love," "Whipperwill," "Dumplings," "Call Back the Times," "This Dawn," Finale

A musical performed without intermission.

General Manager: Paul B. Berkowsky
Press: Shirley Herz
Stage Managers: Robert Schear, Paul Diaz

* Closed Feb. 7, 1977 after 1 performance and 13 previews.

June Squibb, Joel Kramer, Maureen Maloney, Wayne Sherwood, Rick Ladson, Daniel Ziskie, Gibby Brand
Above: Kathleen Widdoes

THE PLAYHOUSE
Opened Monday, February 14, 1977.*
Michael Ross and Eddie Vallone present:

PIAF ... A REMEMBRANCE

By David Cohen; Conceived by Milli Janz; Director, Lee Rachman; Settings and Lighting, Ralph Alswang; Costumes, Robert Troie; Music Arranged and Conducted by John Marino

CAST

Theo Sarapo	Gregory Salata
Louis Leplee	Edmund Lyndeck
Marcel Cerdan	Lou Bedford
Edith Piaf	Juliette Koka
Loulou Barrier	Douglas Andros
Henri/Young Doctor	Donald Hampton

UNDERSTUDIES: Piaf, Monique Leboeuf; Leplee/Barrier, Owen Rachleff; Sarapo/Cerdan, Donald Hampton

MUSICAL NUMBERS: "Padam," "Bal Dans Ma Rue," "L' Etranger," "Bravo pour le Clown," "Mon Dieu," "L'Accordioniste," "Mon Menage a Moi," "Milord," "La Vie en Rose," "Les Trois Cloches," "Under Paris Skies," "La Goulante du Pauvre Jean," "Hymne a l'Amour," "La Foule," "Les Blouses Blanches," "Non, Je Ne Regrette Rien"

A play with music in two acts.

General Manager: David Lawlor
Press: David Powers
Stage Managers: Robert J. Bruyr, Amelia Haywood

* Closed March 6, 1977 after 24 performances and 16 previews.

Martha Swope Photos

Left: Juliette Koka, and below with Gregory Salata, Lou Bedford, Edmund Lyndeck

BARBARANN THEATRE RESTAURANT
Opened Monday, March 7, 1977.*
Steve Abrams, Mary Jo Slater and Scott Mansfield in association with Morton Schwartz present:

STARTING HERE, STARTING NOW

Lyrics, Richard Maltby, Jr.; Music, David Shire; Director, Richard Maltby, Jr.; Choreography, Ethel Martin; Musical Director, Robert W. Preston; Costumes, Stanley Simmons; Lighting, Joan Liepman; Assistant to Producers, Susan Julian; Originally produced at Manhattan Theatre Club

CAST

Loni Ackerman
Margery Cohen
George Lee Andrews

A musical revue

General Management: Gatchell & Neufeld
Press: Betty Lee Hunt, Maria Pucci, Fred Hoot
Stage Manager: Joan Liepman

* Closed June 19, 1977 after 120 performances.

George Lee Andrews, Margery Cohen, Loni Ackerman

ASTOR PLACE THEATRE
Opened Thursday, March 10, 1977.*
Adela Holzer presents:

MONSTERS

"Side Show" by William Dews and "The Transfiguration of Benno Blimpie" by Albert Innaurato; Director, Robert Drivas; Sets and Costumes, Ruben De Saavedra; Lighting, Ian Calderon; Assistant to Director, Tony de Santis, Martin Jackman; Production Assistant, Beth-Ellen Keyes; Wardrobe Mistress, Debbie Lundie

CAST

"SIDE SHOW":
Jeffrey .... Richard DeFabees
Arnold .... Robert Drivas
"THE TRANSFIGURATION OF BENNO BLIMPIE"
Benno .... James Coco
Old Man .... Peter Carew
Mother .... Rosemary DeAngelis
Girl .... K. McKenna
Father .... Roger Serbagi

UNDERSTUDY for Mr. Coco and Mr. Carew, Henry Ferrentino

Two one-act plays performed with one intermission.

General Manager: Leonard A. Mulhern
Company Manager: Donald Joslyn
Press: Michael Alpert, Marilynn LeVine, Warren Knowlton, Randi Cone
Stage Managers: Larry Forde, Tony de Santis

* Closed May 1, 1977 after 61 performances and 8 previews.

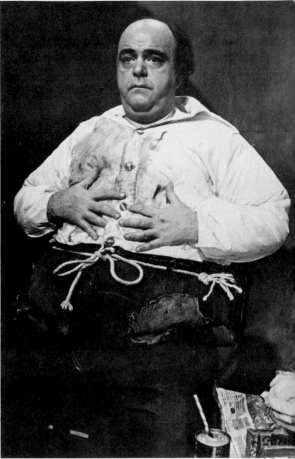

James Coco

Red Skelton

CARNEGIE HALL
Saturday, March 12, 1977.*
Arthur Shafman International, Ltd. presents:

RED SKELTON IN CONCERT

Musical Director, Norm Krone; All Music composed by Red Skelton

Mr. Skelton performed a program of pantomimes and verbamimes without intermission.

Press: David Powers

* Presented for two consecutive performances.

ACTORS PLAYHOUSE
Opened Monday, March 14, 1977.*
Free Space Ltd. presents:

MOVIE BUFF

Book and Lyrics, Hiram Taylor; Music and Lyrics, John Raniello; Director, Jim Payne; Musical Direction and Arrangements, Donald G. Jones; Choreography, Jack Dyville; Sets, Jimmy Cuomo; Costumes, Carol Wenz; Lighting, Jo Mayer; Technical Directors, Brad Richart, Coleman Rupp; Production Assistants, Ruth DiPasquali, Steven Shapine; Piano, Donald G. Jones; Percussionist, Matt Patuto

CAST

Spirit of the 1930's	Charlie Scatamacchia
Mike Williams	Jim Richards
Joanne Simpson	Deborah Carlson
Velma	Nora Cole
Sally Smith	Nancy Rich
Tom	Mark Waldrop
Mildred (Gloria DeWilde)	Mary Travizo
Robert Robbins (Butch)	Keith Curran

MUSICAL NUMBERS: "Silver Screen," "Something to Believe In," "Movietown, U.S.A.," "You Are Something Very Special," "Where Is the Man," "Movie Stars," "May I Dance with You?," "Tell a Little Lie or Two," "Song of Yesterday," "The Movie Cowboy," "Reflections in a Mirror," "All-Talking, All-Singing, All-Dancing," "Coming Attractions," "Tomorrow"

A musical in two acts. The action takes place at the present time in New York City.

General Manager: Jim Payne
Press: Herb Striesfield
Stage Managers: Jessie Frank, Thom Mitchell

* Closed Apr. 3, 1977 after 22 performances and 18 previews.

Emma Landau Photo

Entire cast of "Movie Buff"

18th STREET PLAYHOUSE
Opened Friday, March 18, 1977.*
Robin Swados presents:

HELLO AND GOODBYE

By Athol Fugard; Director, Franklyn Lenthall

CAST

Johnny	Robin Swados
Hester	Joyce O'Connor

A tragi-comedy in two acts. The action takes place during the summer of 1965 in Port Elizabeth, South Africa.

Stage Manager: Mark Hoist

* Closed April 3, 1977 after limited engagement of 12 performances.

Robin Swados, Joyce O'Connor

WASHINGTON SQUARE CHURCH
Opened Tuesday, March 29, 1977.*
American Writers Theatre Foundation presents the Writers
Theatre Workshop production of:

AN AWFULLY BIG ADVENTURE

By Thomas M. Fontana; Music, Mark Hardwick; Lyrics, Martha
Shaver; Director, Walter Bobbie; Sets and Lighting, Mary E. Brach-
mann; Costumes, Judy Fauvell; Technical Director, David Laundra;
Props, Debbie Osterwald; Producer, Linda Laundra

CAST

Charles Fontana
Jerry Lee
Melinda Peterson
Margot Rose
Patricia Webb
Brian T. Whitehill

Performed without intermission.

Stage Managers: Victoria Bradshaw, David R. Domedian

*Closed April 2, 1977 after limited engagement of 5 performances.

**Top Right: Charles Fontana (Standing), Jeffry Lee,
Margot Rose, Melinda Peterson**

NYU LOEB CENTER
Tuesday, March 29, 1977.*
New York University Loeb Center presents:

SIMON KUDROV'S CHARACTERS
AND IMAGES

Director and Producer, Simon Kudrov; Musical Direction, Eve-
ning Chime: Lev Zennona, Piano/Organ/Vocalist, and Valery
Tokarev, Bass Guitar/Balalaika/Vocalist; Art Direction, Natalia
Kudrov

PROGRAM

PART I: Introduction, Stubborn Mule, Wall, Sculptor, Operation,
Nothing But Trouble
PART II: Bullfight, New Face for a Samurai, Made in U.S.A.

* Presented for one performance only.

Right Center: Simon Kudrov

TOWN HALL
Wednesday, March 30, 1977.*
Interludes presents:

ANNA RUSSELL IN CONCERT
with
Frank Bartholomew

A solo performance of Miss Russell's characters and sketches.

* Presented for one performance only.

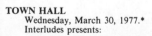

Anna Russell

PROMENADE THEATRE
Opened Monday, April 11, 1977.*
Jule Styne and Joseph Kipness present:

JOCKEYS

By Frank Spiering and Milton Katselas; Script Supervision, Michael Shurtleff; Director, Milton Katselas; Choreographer and Associate Director, Gerald Arpino; Designed by Peter Wexler; Music Composed by Bernardo Segall; Sound, Gary Harris; Associate Producers, Dorothy Dicker, Charlotte Dicker; Martial Arts Choreography, Dan DiVito; Production Supervisor, Fritz Holt; Management Associate, David Wyler; Associate Choreographer, James Howell; Wardrobe Supervisor, Pat Britton; Associate Designer, Tom Schwinn; Production Assistants, Eric Angelson, Warren Stockwell, Travis Stockley; Sound, Ellen Zalk

CAST

Angel Quiton	Chick Vennera
Queenie	David Nichols
Fausto	Alfred Mancini
Jockeys .. Nicholas B. Daddazio, Danie Faraldo, John Widlock	
Mr. T	Thaao Penghlis
Lisa	Simone Griffeth
Danny Levitt	Richard Forbes
Louis	Daryl Roach
Anise	Pamela Poitier
Angel's Father	Harry Davis

STANDBYS AND UNDERSTUDIES: Lisa, Kathy Knowles; Angel, Daniel Faraldo; Fausto, Nicholas B. Daddazio; Queenie, John Widlock

A play with music performed without intermission. The action takes place at the present time in many places in New York City.

General Management: Marvin A. Krauss Associates
Press: The Merlin Group, Harriett Trachtenberg, Ron Harris, Beatrice DaSilva
Stage Manager: Daryl Roach

* Closed April 17, 1977 after 8 performances.

**Simone Griffeth, Chick Vennera,
Thaao Penghlis**

AMDA THEATRE
Opened Monday, April 18, 1977.*
Sally E. Parry and Peter M. Paulino present:

LET'S FACE IT!

Music and Lyrics, Cole Porter; Book, Herbert and Dorothy Fields; Adapted, Directed and Choreographed by Jeffery K. Neill; Musical Direction and Special Arrangements, Wendell Kindberg; Additional Arrangements, Frederick S. Roffman; Production Design, Chas W. Roeder; Lighting, Peggy Moran; Technical Crew, Ed Moran, Peter Roehr, Tim Buller, Frank Dunn, Michael Broccio

CAST

Winnie Potter	Tacey Phillips
Muriel McGillicuddy	Barbara Niles
Jean Blanchard	Shelley Werk
Polly Lee	Martha Daly
Madge Hall	Sandra Wheeler
Helen Marcy	Suzanne Kaszynski
Dorothy Crowthers	Charla Mann
Mollie Wincor	Lila Goodman
Rose Gunther	Rosemary D'Alessandro
Cornelia Abigail Pidgeon	Gerladine Hanning
Judge Henry Clay Pidgeon	Bill Collins
Nancy Collister	Marilyn Hudgins
George Collister	Allan N. Smith
Maggie Watson	Renee Orin
Julian Watson	Norman Beim
Eddie Hilliard	Howard Pinhasik
Frankie Burns	Robert Zanfini
Phillip	Edwin Dekker
Jules	Brett Moore
John	Bob Laconi
Andy	Ron Carnavil
Lt. Wiggins	Ralph Bowers
Jerry Walker	Ira Denmark
Parker & Daniels	Suzanne Kaszynski, Edwin Dekker
Eddie Fatootsie	Edwin Dekker

MUSICAL NUMBERS: "Milk, Milk, Milk," "A Lady Needs a Rest," "Jerry, My Soldier Boy," "Let's Face It!," "Farming," "Everything I Love," "Ace in the Hole," "You Irritate Me So," "Get Yourself a Boy," "Hey, Good Lookin'," "Rub Your Lamp," "Cuttin' a Persian Rug," "Revenge," "I've Got Some Unfinished Business with You," "Let's Not Talk about Love," "I Hate You Darling," "A Little Rumba Numba," "Shootin' the Works for Uncle Sam"

A musical in 2 acts and 7 scenes. The action takes place in 1941 on Decoration Day weekend.

Press: David Lipsky
Stage Managers: Sally Parry, John Vought

* Closed May 1, 1977 after limited engagement of 12 performances.

(Mark Fracasso Photo)

Entire cast of "Let's Face It!"

CITY CENTER 55th STREET THEATRE
Opened Wednesday, April 20, 1977.*
Le Treteau de Paris/Jean DeRigault in association with 55th
Street Dance Theatre Foundation presents Le Theatre de la
Ville (Jean Mercure, Animateur-Directeur) in:

THE TROJAN WAR WILL NOT TAKE PLACE

By Jean Giraudoux; Director, Jean Mercure; Sets and Costumes,
Yannis Kokkos; Incidental Music, Marc Wilkinson; Wardrobe Su-
pervisor, Jesse Hope; Management Associate, Veronica Claypool;
Lighting, Serge Peyrat; Set and Costumes Supervised by William
Ritman; Lighting Supervision, Martin Aronstein

CAST

Andromaque	Dominique Jayr
Cassandre	Isa Mercure
Servantes Virginie Duvernoy, Bernadette Lange, Helene Zanicoli	
Hector	Jose-Maria Flotats
Paris	Bernard Giraudeau
Vieillards	Eugene Berthier, Jean-Marie Bon
Priam	Regis Outin
Demokos	Maurice Chevit
Hecube	Jandeline
Le geometre	Bernard Veron
Anchise	Michel Salina
Polyxene	Anne-Laure Meury
Helene	Anny Duperey
Messagers	Michel Feder, Jean-Luc Russier
La Paix	Djanet Lachmet
Troilus	Pascal Sellier
Abneos	Angelo Bardi
Busiris	Jean Mercure
Suivant de Busiris	Serge Peyrat
Oiax	Lionel Baylac
Ulysse	Jean-Pierre Aumont
Le gabler	Lafleur
Olpides	Coussonneau
Un marin	Serge Peyrat
Garde	Georges Joannon
Iris	Jenny Arasse

A play in two acts. The action takes place in and around the
Palace of Troy.

General Manager: McCann & Nugent
Company Manager: James Mennen
Press: Arthur Rubine, Ted Goldsmith
Stage Manager: Alain Tartas

* Closed April 30, 1977 after limited engagement of 13 performances.

Dominique Jayr, Jose-Maria Flotats

TRUCK & WAREHOUSE THEATRE
Opened Wednesday, April 27, 1977.*
The Ridiculous Theatrical Company presents:

DER RING GOTT FARBLONJET

Written, Directed, Sets and Costumes by Charles Ludlam; Music,
Jim McElwaine; Lighting, Richard Currie; Sound, Robert Carey;
Film, Andrew Horn

CAST

Twoton (Nobodaddy of the Gods)	Adam Macadam
Donner (God of Thunder)/Rosseweisse	Robert Reddy
Froh (God of Rain, Sun, Fruits)/Schwertleita	Stephen Holt
Loge (God of Fire and Lies)/Siegmund/Bear	Georg Osterman
Fricka (Goddess of Lawful Wedlock)/Gunther	Ethyl Eichelberger
Freia (Goddess of Youth and Beauty)/Grimgerde	Suzanne Peters
Eartha (The Earth Mother)/Sieglinda/Gutruna	Black-Eyed Susan
Flosshilde/Ninny	Everett Quinton
Woglinde/Helmvige/Bird	Beverly Brown
Welgunde/Valtrauta	Ericka Brown
Fasdolt/Siegfried	John D. Brockmeyer
Fafner/Hagen	Richard Currie
Alverruck	Bill Vehr
Brunnhilda	Lola Pashalinski
Gerhilda	Janine Day
Ortlinda	Denise Day
Siegruna	Debra Crane
Norns	Everett Quinton, Beverly Brown, Ericka Brown
Hunding (A Gesundheit)	Richard Currie
Vassals and Heathen Onlookers	Robert Grindstaff, Randy Buck, Suzanne Peters, Stephen Holt, Robert Reddy, Debra Crane

Performed in four acts.

General Management: New Arts Management
Press: Alan Eichler
Stage Manager: Richard Gibbs

* Still playing May 31, 1977

Martha Morgan Photo

**Lola Pashalinski, John D. Brockmeyer,
Beverly Brown in "Der Ring . . ."**

ACTORS PLAYHOUSE

Opened Thursday, April 28, 1977.*

Peter Copani and Victor Papa present The People's Performing Company's production of:

NEW YORK CITY STREET SHOW

Book, Music and Lyrics, Peter Copani; Additional Music, Christian Staudt, David McHugh, Ed Vogel; Musical Arrangements, Eric W. Diamond, John Kroner; Choreography, Charles Goeddertz; Set, Jim Chestnut; Lighting, Richard Harper; Musical Director, Steven Oirich; Production Assistant, John Copani; Entire production Conceived and Directed by Peter Copani

CAST

Sergio	Bob Arcaro
Meri	Eva Charney
Jesus	Rob DeRosa
Anita	Florie Freshman
Vernon	Hubert Kelly
Xena	Deborah Malone
Gina	Theresa Saldana
Bob	Richard Woods

MUSICAL NUMBERS: "American Dream," "Who Can Say?," "God Is in the People," "A Special Man," "Strawberries, Pickles and Ice Cream," "Hail, Hail," "Kung Fu," "One of Us," "When You Are Together," "If Jesus Walked," "Bad but Good," "Make Them Hate," "Corruption," "Wait and See," "Hanging Out," "Love Is Beautiful"

A musical in 6 scenes with a prologue performed without intermission.

Press: Herb Striesfield
Stage Manager: Ron Lawrence

* Closed May 15, 1977 after 21 performances.

THEATRE FOUR

Opened Wednesday, May 4, 1977.*

Saul Novick, Marion Brasch, Leonard Finger present the Lion Theatre Company production of:

PEG O' MY HEART

By J. Hartley Manners; Director, Gene Nye; Set, Miguel Romero; Costumes, David James; Lighting, Joseph Spencer; Assistant to Director, John Guerrasio; Dialect Coach, Liz Smith; Production Assistants, Paul Baretsky, Jay Embree; Props, Pam Belyea

CAST

Jarvis	Gibson Glass
Bennett	Mary E. Baird
Mrs. Chichester	Kathleen Tremaine
Ethel, her daughter	Sandra Halperin
Alaric, her son	Jim Ricketts
Brent	Donovan Sylvest
"Peg"	Sofia Landon
Montgomery Hawkes	Ken Costigan
"Jerry"	Allan Carlsen

A comedy in three acts. The action takes place in the living room of Regal Villa, Mrs. Chichester's house in Scarborough, England, in early summer.

Company Manager: David Lawlor
Press: Shirley Herz, Frank Prince
Stage Manager: Andrea Naier

* Closed May 15, 1977 after 15 performances and 1 preview.

VANDAM THEATRE

Opened Friday, May 20, 1977.*

Shelter West Company presents:

LANDSLIDE AT NORTH STATION

By Ugo Betti; Translation, G. H. McWilliam; Director, Dan Mason; Assistant Director, Robert Rigley; Set, Charls Baum; Lighting, Marsha Imhof; Technical Directors, James Conway, Bud Rich; Costumes, Annick Leymarie

CAST

Parsc	Stuart Rudin
Holand	Sam Rittenberg
Goetz	Joel M. Freedman
Jud	William Preston
Manrico Giuseppetti	Roberto Monticello
Anselmo Bret	Rick Richardson
Riccardo Gaucker	James Maxson
Short-Sighted Witness/Kurz Junior	Peter Reznikoff
Woman with baby/Giovanna Burke	Eleanore Auer
Girl from the cafe	Laurie Latham
Elderly Woman/Beatrice Mosca	Edith Amsterdam
Lucrezio	David F. Louden
Menjura	Michael Detmold
Man wearing a shiny suit	Jay W. Merek
Anna Gaucker	Trudi Mathes
Kurz Senior	Maurice Blanc
Carmelo Aiello	Ron Harris
Felici Imparato	Brent Collins
Orsola Nasca	Dorothy Kobs

A play in three acts. The action takes place at the present time in a foreign city.

Press: Ron Harris
Stage Managers: Cindy DePaula, Stephen B. Real

* Closed June 5, 1977 after limited engagement of 12 performances. (No photos available)

**Sofia Landon, Jim Ricketts, Kathleen Tremaine
in "Peg o' My Heart"**

CHERRY LANE THEATRE

Opened Sunday, May 22, 1977.*
Richard Barr presents:

I WAS SITTING ON MY PATIO THIS GUY APPEARED I THOUGHT I WAS HALLUCINATING

By Robert Wilson; Co-Directors, Robert Wilson, Lucinda Childs; Music, Alan Lloyd; Lighting, Beverly Emmons; Set, Robert Wilson, Christina Giannini; Clothes, Scaasi; Film, Greta Wing Miller, Byron Lovelace; Production Coordinator, Robert Lo Bianco; Technical Director, Jim Grant; Sound, Jim Neu; Assistant to Producer, Jerry Sirchia

CAST

Lucinda Childs
Robert Wilson

A play in two acts.

General Manager: Bolen High
Press: The Merlin Group Ltd., Sandra Manley

* Closed May 29, 1977 after 8 performances.

Lucinda Child
Above: Robert Wilson

OFF CENTER THEATRE

Opened Tuesday, May 24, 1977.*
Polaris Repertory Company (Bob Horen, Artistic Director; Erle Bjornstad, Executive Director) presents:

THE SUNDAY PROMENADE

By Lars Forssell; Translated from Swedish by Harry G. Carlson; Director, Bob Horen; Executive Producer, Will Mott; Setting, Elfi Von Kantzow; Costumes and Lighting, Jay B. Keene; Promenade Song, Ardis Cavin; Sound, Regis Caddic; Production Assistant, Dan Lutzky; Wardrobe Supervisor, Jo Tanner

CAST

Justus Corlander, a grocer	Edward Stevlingson
Elsa, his wife	Mary Carter
Suleima, his mother	Kathleen Claypool
Angelica, his deaf mute daughter	K. T. Baumann
Carl Michael, his elder son	Greg Johnson
Willy, his younger son	John Guerrasio
Ragnar Ruriksson, a rector	Thomas Barbour
Abraham, a clerk	Bruce Bouchard
Miss Attie	Suzanne Granfield
Mr. Ambergriss, Game Preserve Supervisor	Edwin Young
Mr. Ploughman, the sheriff	Don Lochner

A comedy-drama in three acts with an epilogue. The action takes place early in July at the turn of the century in the dining-room of Mr. Corlander's home in a small city in Sweden.

Press: Max Eisen, Judy Jacksina
Stage Manager: Malcolm Ewen

* Closed June 5, 1977 after 12 performances and 6 previews.

EASTSIDE PLAYHOUSE

Opened Tuesday, May 31, 1977.*

LLORDS' INTERNATIONAL

A program of "music and Marionettes for adults" performed by Daniel Llords in repertory, including "Don Quixote," "Firebird," "Les Petit Riens," "Petrouchka," "Fantasy on Faust," "Holiday," "Paris 1890," "Commedia," "Die Musikmeister," "Capriccio," "Shakespeare"

* Closed June 26, 1977 after 32 performances.

Daniel Llords

ACTORS' ALLIANCE, INC.

First Season

PROVINCETOWN PLAYHOUSE
June 24-July 10, 1976 (18 performances)

THE TAVERN by George M. Cohan; Director, Michael Posnick; Costumes, Peg Schierholz; Setting, Vicki Paul; Lighting, Burt J. Patalano; Stage Manager, Kimerley Francis Kearsley; Press, Alan Eichler, CAST: Tom Jarus, Robin G. Eisenman, Robert Costanzo, William Arrigon, William Newman, Margaret Donohue, Jack Poggi, Martha Miller, Sara Louise, Terrence O'Hara, Robert Coluntino, Peter DeLaurier, Martin Brandfon, Thomas MacGreevy

July 14-25, 1976 (13 performances)

LULLABY By Don Appell; Director, William Arrigon. CAST: Peter DeLaurier, Kathryn Arrigon, Paul Lieber, Eda Reiss Merin

July 30-August 15, 1976 (14 performances)

HAY FEVER By Noel Coward; Setting, Vicki Paul; Costumes, Peg Schierholz; Lighting, Burt J. Patalano. CAST: Michael Varna, Sara Louise, Pat Maniccia, Nina Polan, William Newman, Thomas MacGreevy, Isabel Grandin, Terrence O'Hara, Margaret Donohue

TOWNHOUSE OF THE ADAMS SCHOOL
April 1-3, 1977 (4 performances)

BREAK OF NOON by Paul Claudel; Director, William Arrigon; Special Music, Bill Mesnick. CAST: Nina Polan, Evan Thompson, James Higgins, William Arrigon, Michael Varna

April 15-May 1, 1977 (11 performances)

UNCLE VANYA by Anton Chekhov; Director, Bruce Jordan; New Translation, Jack Poggi; Costumes, Kathe Berl; Stage Manager, Rachel Lindhart; Press, Alan Eichler, CAST: Eda Reiss Merin, William Newman, Jack Poggi, Donald Pace, Margaret Donohue, Marsha Korb, William Arrigon, Cynthia Mason, Michael Scanlan

May 21-29, 1977 (8 performances)

THE LAST WAR by David Scanlan; Based on "Draussen vor der Thur" by Wolfgang Borchert; Director, William Newman; Environment, Kathryn Arrigon; Company Manager, Donald Pace; Stage Manager, Isabel Grandin. CAST: Paul Lieber, Frederick Good, Peter DeLaurier, Andrea Cullen, Nina Polan, Ceal Phelan, Homer Foil, Charlotte Louise, Thomas Sminkey, Jeanne Schlegel, Victor Argo

Press: Alan Eichler

Ron Reagan, Martin Brandfon Photos

**Top Right: Terrence O'Hara, Martha Miller
in "The Tavern" Below: Paul Lieber, Kathryn
Arrigon in "Lullaby"**

**Sara Louise, Martha Miller, Jack
Poggi in "The Tavern"**

"Hay Fever"

ACTORS STUDIO

Lee Strasberg, Artistic Director

ACTORS STUDIO
Opened Thursday, December 2, 1976.*

FROM THE MEMOIRS OF PONTIUS PILATE

By Eric Bentley; Director, Ed Setrakian; Scenic Designer, Sally Locke; Costumes, Margradel Hicks; Lighting, Jay Cohen; Executive Producer, Carl Schaeffer; Producer, Anna Antaramian; Musical Composer, Harold Seletski; Production Assistants, Kay Cortez, Linda Mulvihill, Christine Von Dohln, Rosalie Adamo; Studio Coordinator, Ellen Chenoweth; Stage Manager, Howard Meadow

CAST

Pilate	Jack Holland†1
Yeshu	Geoffrey Holder
Guards	Sheldon Elman, Scott Kasdin, Richard Livert, David Scholar
Barabbas	Mel Bernstein
Stephen	Jack Leustig
Judas	John Costopoulos
Caiaphas	Murray Moston
Herod Antipas	Ed Kovens
Annas	Rudy Bond†2

A drama in two acts.

* Closed Dec. 19, 1976 after a limited engagement of 12 performances.

†Succeeded by: 1. Joe Ragno, 2. Salem Ludwig

Jack Hollander, Geoffrey Horne

Michael Moriarty

Joanna Miles

ACTORS STUDIO
Opened Friday, January 14, 1977.*

ALFRED DIES

By Israel Horovitz; Production Supervisor, Ben Levit; Set, Paul Eads; Lighting, Spencer Mosse; Costumes, Susan Tsu; Executive Producer, Carl Schaeffer; Producer, Anna Antaramian; Technical Director, Ken Fillo; Studio Coordinator, Ellen Chenoweth; Wardrobe Supervisor, Lynne Cherry; Stage Managers, Joe Carbone, Pat De Rousie, Stephen Jobes

CAST

Alfred	Michael Moriarty
Lynch	Dominic Chianese
Emily	Joanna Miles
Roxy	Madeleine Thornton-Sherwood

A drama in three acts. The action takes place at the end of June and beginning of July in a storage room under the bandstand at the Commons in Wakefield, Massachusetts

* Closed Jan. 30, 1977 after limited engagement of 11 performances.

AMERICAN PLACE THEATRE

Wynn Handman, Director
Julia Miles, Associate Director
Thirteenth Season

AMERICAN PLACE THEATRE
Opened Thursday, October 17, 1976.*
The American Place Theatre presents:

JACK GELBER'S NEW PLAY: REHEARSAL

Written and Directed by Jack Gelber; Set Supervision, Henry Millman; Lighting, Edward M. Greenberg; Technical Director, Edward Gianfrancesco; Wardrobe Mistress, Tommy Rowland; Adminstrative Assistant, David Logan Morrow

CAST

Tommy	John McCurry
Guard	Jack Hollander
Ernst	Sam Schacht
Karl	Martin Shakar
Danny	Robert Burgos
Rufus	Darryl Croxton
Scott	Lane Smith
Fat	Fred Kareman
Arlene	Grayson Hall

A play in two acts. The action takes place at the present time on stage during a rehearsal.

Press: Jeffrey Richards, Joe Wolhandler,
Stage Managers: Errol Selsby, Rene Mainguy

* Closed Oct. 24, 1976 after 31 performances.

AMERICAN PLACE THEATRE
Opened Sunday, January 23, 1977.*
The American Place Theatre (Wynn Handman, Director; Julia Miles, Associate Director) presents:

HOLD ME!

Adapted from Jules Feiffer's cartoons; Director, Caymichael Patten; Sets, Kert Lundell; Costumes, Ruth Morley; Lighting, Edward M. Greenberg; Choreography, Dalienne Majors; Technical Director, Edward Gianfrancesco; Wardrobe Mistress, Tommy Rowland

CAST

Geraldine Brooks†
Kathleen Chalfant
Paul Dooley
Dalienne Majors
Michael Tucci
Understudies: Dan Strickler, Maria Cellario
An entertainment in two parts.

Company Manager: Alan C. Wasser
Press: Jeffrey Richards Associates, Barbara Carroll
Stage Managers: Nancy Harrington, Rene Mainguy

* Closed Jan. 31, 1977 and re-opened Saturday, February 19, 1977 at Chelsea Westside Cabaret Theater as "Jules Feiffer's Hold Me!." Closed May 15, 1977 after 100 performances.
† Succeeded by Cynthia Harris

**Left Center, Jane Galloway, Regina Baff,
Guy Boyd, Conard Fowkes in "Domino Courts"**

**Martin Shakar, Sam Schacht
in "Jack Gelber's New Play"**

AMERICAN PLACE THEATRE
Opened Thursday, December 2, 1976.*
The American Place Theatre presents:

DOMINO COURTS COMANCHE CAFE

By William Hauptman; Director, Barnet Kellman; Sets, Henry Millman; Costumes, Carol Oditz; Lighting, Edward M. Greenberg; Technical Director, Edward Gianfrancesco; Wardrobe Mistress, Tommy Rowland; Technicians, David Sheppard, Bob Lampel; Production Assistant, Victoria Butler

CAST

"COMANCHE CAFE" (A Prologue)

Ronnie	Jane Galloway
Mattie	Sasha Von Scherler

The action takes place on a Sunday morning in the 1930's outside the Comanche Cafe, a roadside diner in southern Oklahoma.

"DOMINO COURTS"

Floyd	Guy Boyd
Ronnie	Jane Galloway
Roy	Conard Fowkes
Flo	Regina Baff

The action takes place four years later at the Domino Courts, a tourist cabin in southern Oklahoma.

Press: Jeffrey Richards, Joe Wolhandler, Barbara Carroll
Stage Managers: Richard S. Viola, Andrea Naier

* Closed Dec. 12, 1976 after 29 performances.

Martha Holmes Photos

**Michael Tucci, Paul Dooley, Dalienne Majors,
Geraldine Brookes, Kathleen Chalfant, Jules Feiffer**

AMERICAN PLACE THEATRE
Opened Sunday, January 30, 1977.*
The American Place Theatre presents:

ISADORA DUNCAN SLEEPS WITH THE RUSSIAN NAVY

By Jeff Wanshel; Director, Tom Haas; Costumes, Bobbi Owen;
Assistant to Director, Joy Javits; Musical Director, Russell Walden;
Dance Consultant, Linda Tarnay; Technical Director, Edward
Gianfrancesco; Wardrobe Mistress, Tommy Rowland; Technician,
Frank Hoffman; Production Assistant, Frank Quist

CAST

Author	David Ackroyd
Producer	Robert Lesser
Isadora Duncan	Marian Seldes
Narrator	Howard Ross
Deidre Duncan	Daphne Youree
Patrick Duncan	Luke Youree
Raymond Duncan/Oscar Beregi/Paris Singer	Richard Council
Andre Beaunier/Heinrich Thode/ Stanislavsky	Christopher Curry
Mother Duncan/Loie Fuller/Walt Whitman	Anita Dangler
Auguste Rodin/Gordon Craig/Honorable Lew Shanks	Dennis Jay Higgins
Gypsy/Anna Pavlova/Angel	Annette Kurek
Alexander Gross/Sergei Essenin/Walter Rommel	Peter Lownds
Ivan Miroski/German Entrepreneur/Lenin	David Rasche

Understudy: Tanny McDonald

A play performed without intermission.

Press: Jeffrey Richards Associates, Barbara Carroll
Stage Managers: Errol Selsby, Peter Gelblum

* Closed Feb. 20, 1977 after 36 performances.

Marian Seldes (C) in "Isadora Duncan Sleeps with the Russian Navy"

AMERICAN PLACE THEATRE
Opened Wednesday, April 6, 1977.*
The American Place Theatre presents:

COLD STORAGE

By Ronald Ribman; Director, Joel Zwick; Sets, Kert Lundell;
Costumes, Ruth Morley; Lighting, Edward M. Greenberg; Techni-
cal Director, Edward Gianfrancesco; Wardrobe Mistress, Tommy
Rowland

CAST

Friedrich Reisen	Paul Sparer
Joseph Parmigian	Martin Balsam
Richard Landau	Michael Lipton
Miss Madurga	Julie Carmen

Understudy: Sanford Morris

A play in two acts and three scenes. The action takes place in 1941
in a police station in Portugal, and in June 1976 on a hospital roof
garden in New York City.

Press: Jeffrey Richards Associates, Barbara Carroll, Michael Ellis
Stage Managers: Richard S. Viola, Jeffrey Rowland

* Closed May 8, 1977 after 47 performances.

Martin Balsam in "Cold Storage"

BROOKLYN ACADEMY OF MUSIC

Harvey Lichtenstein, President
Judith E. Daykin, General Manager

BROOKLYN ACADEMY OF MUSIC
Opened Tuesday, November 9, 1976.*
Brannigan-Eisler Performing Arts International in association
with Zagreb Concert Management presents the U. S. debut of
the Gavella Theatre of Zagreb, Groatia, Yugoslavia, in:

THE KERMESS

By Miroslav Krleza; Director, Dino Radojevic; Designed by
Zlatko Bourek; Costumes, Diana Bourek; Language Adviser, Dr.
Bratoljub Klaic; Technical Director, Miho Verveger, Dee Doucette,
Sr.; Production Coordinator Patricia Morinelli; Production Assistant, Betsy Ross

CAST

Toll Collector	Ivo Fici
Villager from Sestine	Ante Dulcic
Drunken Tanner	Zvonimir Ferencic
Tanner's Wife	Zdenka Anusic
Townsman	Bozidar Boban
Lady Citizens	Vjera Zagar-Nardelli, Ljubica Jovic, Helena Buljan
Fat Citizen	Mato Ergovic
Old Turk	Djuro Utjesanovic
Master Japica	Drago Krca
Mamica	Marija Kohn
Guests	Ljubomir Kapor, Boris Miholjevic, Zlatko Vitez
Peddler	Fahro Konjhodzic
Butcher	Mladen Serment
Margit	Ljiljana Gener
Stella	Zdenka Hersak
Blind Man	Mirko Vojkovic
Man Servant	Ivo Rogulja
Madame	Nada Subotic
Lola	Inga Apelt
Hajnal	Ljubica Mikulicic
Janez	Pero Kvrgic
Ruffian	Drago Mestrovic
Stijef	Josip Marotti
Fortune Teller	Vesna Smiljanic
First Gentleman	Emil Glad
Magician	Mladen Budiscak
Magician's Assistant	Biserka Ipsa
Anka	Semka Sokolovic
Hercules	Kresimir Zidaric
Cripple	Vlatko Dulic
Soldier	Zorko Rajcic
Coachmen	Stevo Krnjajic, Mladen Budiscak, Slavko Brankov
Peasants	Drago Mitrovic, Dusko Valentic, Mladen Budiscak

The action takes place in Zagreb at the beginning of this century
during an annual fair.

Press: Tomislav Slavica, Daniel Langan
Stage Managers: Drazen Grunwald, Clarke Thornton

* Closed Nov. 10, 1976 after limited engagement of two performances.

The Kermess

Angela Newman, Siobhan McKenna, John Kavanagh, Cyril Cusack

BROOKLYN ACADEMY OF MUSIC PLAYHOUSE
Opened Wednesday, November 17, 1976.*
The Brooklyn Academy of Music presents the Abbey Theatre
of Ireland in:

THE PLOUGH AND THE STARS

By Sean O'Casey; Director, Tomas MacAnna; Setting and Costumes, Bronwen Casson; Lighting, Leslie Scott; Lighting Supervisor,
William Mintzer; Production Manager, Brian Collins; State Directors, Bill Hay, Finola Eustace; Sound, Nuala Golden; Assistant to
Director, Bryan Murray

CAST

Commandant Jack Clitheroe	Clive Geraghty
Nora Clitheroe	Sorcha Cusack
Peter Flynn	Bill Foley
Young Covey	John Kavanagh
Fluther Good	Cyril Cusack
Bessie Burgess	Siobhan McKenna
Mrs. Gogan	Angela Newman
Mollser	Bernadette Shortt
Captain Brennan	Desmond Cave
Lieutenant Langon	Bryan Murray
Rosie Redmond	Maire O'Neill
Barman	Geoffrey Golden
Woman from Rathmines	Aine Ni Mhuiri
The Figure	Peadar Lamb
Sergeant Tinley	Philip O'Flynn
Corporal Stoddard	Niall O'Brien
Messenger from Arnotts	Robert Carlile

A play in four acts performed with one intermission. The action
takes place during November of 1915 and Easter week of 1916.

Company Manager: Chuck Eisler
Press: Charles E. Ziff, Kate MacIntyre, Kay Green
Stage Managers: Tommy Woods, Billie Morton

* Closed Nov. 28, 1976 after limited engagement of 16 performances.

BROOKLYN ACADEMY OF MUSIC LEPERCQ SPACE
Opened Tuesday, November 30, 1976.*
The Brooklyn Academy of Music presents:

IN MY FATHER'S TIME

Devised, Written and Performed by:

EAMON KELLY

A solo performance of Irish wit, nostalgia, and humor told by a cast of characters created by Mr. Kelly.

* Closed Dec. 5, 1976 after limited engagement of 8 performances.

Ken Howard Photos

Eamon Kelly

BROOKLYN ACADEMY OF MUSIC OPERA HOUSE
Opened Thursday, December 30, 1976.*
The Brooklyn Academy of Music presents:

JOSEPH AND THE AMAZING TECHNICOLOR DREAMCOAT

By Tim Rice and Andrew Lloyd Webber; Staged and Directed by Frank Dunlop; Choreography, Graciela Daniele; Designed by Nadine Baylis; Costume Supervisor, Dona Granata; Setting Supervisor, John Pitts; Lighting, F. Mitchell Dana; Sound, Abe Jacob; Musical Director, Steve Margoshes

CAST

Narrator	Cleavon Little
Jacob	Tony Hoty
Ladies	Mary Jane Houdina, Marybeth Kurdock, Jill Streisant
Joseph	David-James Carroll
Reuben	Stuart Pankin
Simeon	Adam Grammis
Levi	Paul Kreppel
Napthali	Don Swanson
Isaachar	Ron Taylor
Asher	William Parry
Dan/Baker	Kurt Yahjian
Zebulun	Craig Schaefer
Gad/Butler	David Patrick Kelly
Benjamin	Leonard John Crofoot
Judah	Robert Rhys
Potiphar	Terry Eno
Mrs. Potiphar	Virginia Martin
Pharaoh	Jess Pearson
Egyptian/Ishmaelite	Richard Seer and the Brooklyn Boys Chorus

A musical in 2 acts and 18 scenes.

General Manager: Berenice Weiler
Press: Charles E. Ziff, Kate MacIntyre, Kay Green
Stage Managers: Frank Bayer, Barbara-Mae Phillips

* Closed Jan. 9, 1977 after a limited engagement of 22 performances.

Cleavon Little (C)
Above: David-James
Carroll

111

BROOKLYN ACADEMY OF MUSIC LEPERCQ SPACE

Opened Tuesday, March 29, 1977.*
Berlin Now Festival of Goethe House New York presents the
Schiller Theater Berlin in:

WAITING FOR GODOT

By Samuel Beckett; Staged by Mr. Beckett; Set and Costumes,
Matias; Lighting, Heinz Hohenwald; Technical Director, Julian
Herrey; Makeup, Wener Siebert; Translation by Elmar Tophoven

CAST

Estragon	Horst Bollmann
Vladimir	Stefan Wigger
Lucky	Klaus Herm
Pozzo	Carl Raddatz
A Boy	Torsten Sense

A play in two acts, performed in German.

Press: Charles E. Ziff, Kate MacIntyre, Kay Green

* Closed April 3, 1977 after limited engagement of 7 performances.

**Carl Raddatz, Samuel Beckett, Stefan Wigger
rehearsing "Waiting for Godot"**

BROOKLYN ACADEMY OF MUSIC PLAYHOUSE

Opened Friday, March 18, 1977.*
The Brooklyn Academy of Music presents the Brooklyn
Academy of Music Theatre Company in:

THE NEW YORK IDEA

By Langdon Mitchell; Director, Frank Dunlop; Setting, William
Ritman; Costumes, Nancy Potts; Lighting, F. Mitchell Dana; Administrative Director, Berenice Weiler

CAST

Grace Phillimore	Diana Kirkwood
Miss Heneage	Margaret Hamilton
Thomas	Jerome Collamore
Mrs. Phillimore	Justine Johnston
William Sudley	Ralph Clanton
Cynthia Karslake	Blythe Danner
Phillip Phillimore	Stephen Collins
Tim Fiddler	Leon Russom
Rev. Matthew Phillimore	Edward Zang
Vida Phillimore	Rosemary Harris
John Karslake	Rene Auberjonois
Sir Wilfred Cates-Darby	Denholm Elliott
Benson	Holly Villaire
Brooks	Alek Primrose
Nogam	George David Connolly

UNDERSTUDIES: Phillip/Sir Wilfrid, Alek Primrose; Mathew/-
John, Leon Russom; Grace/Vida, Holly Villaire; Sudley/Nogam,
Jerome Collamore; Benson/Cynthia, Diana Kirkwood

A comedy in four acts performed with one intermission. The
action takes place in May 1906 in New York in Phillip Phillimore's
living room, Mrs. Vida Phillimore's boudoir, and John Karslake's
study.

General Manager: Berenice Weiler
Press: Charles E. Ziff, Kate MacIntyre, Kay Green
Stage Managers: Frank Bayer, Barbara-Mae Phillips, George
Connolly, Sandra McKnight

* Closed April 10, 1977 after limited engagement of 28 performances.

**Blythe Danner, Stephen Collins
Above: Diana Kirkwood, Margaret Hamilton,
Justine Johnston**

BROOKLYN ACADEMY OF MUSIC PLAYHOUSE

Opened Tuesday, May 3, 1977.*
The Brooklyn Academy of Music presents the BAM Theatre Company in:

THE THREE SISTERS

By Anton Chekhov; Translated by Stark Young; Director, Frank Dunlop; Setting, William Ritman; Costumes, Nancy Potts; Lighting, F. Mitchell Dana; Administrative Director, Berenice Weiler; Hairstylist, Karol Coeyman; Speech Consultant, Edith Skinner

CAST

Olga Prozoroff	Rosemary Harris
Masha	Ellen Burstyn
Irina Prozoroff	Tovah Feldshuh
Audrey Prozoroff	Stephen Collins
Natalia Ivanovna	Holly Villaire
Fyodor Illyitch Kulygin	Rex Robbins
Anfisa	Margaret Hamilton
Ferapont	Ralph Clanton
Maid	Diana Kirkwood
Lt. Col. Vershinin	Denholm Elliott
Staff Capt. Solyony	Rene Auberjonois
Lt. Baron Tusenbach	Austin Pendleton
Tchebutykin	Barnard Hughes
2nd Lt. Fedotik	Stuart Pankin
2nd Lt. Roday	David Patrick Kelly
Orderly	Robert Windslow

A drama in four acts performed with one intermission. The action takes place in the house of the Prozoroff family in a garrison town of provincial Russia.

General Manager: Bernice Weiler
Press: Charles E. Ziff, Kate MacIntyre, Kay Green
Stage Managers: Frank Bayer, Barbara-Mae Phillips, Robert Windslow, William Tynes

* Closed May 15, 1977 after limited engagement of 24 performances.

Martha Swope Photos

Austin Pendleton, Tovah Feldshuh
Above: Rosemary Harris, Tovah Feldshuh,
Ellen Burstyn

BIL BAIRD THEATER

Opened Friday, October 15, 1976.*
The American Puppet Arts Council (Arthur Cantor, Executive Producer) presents:

BIL BAIRD'S MARIONETTES
in
DAVY JONES' LOCKER

Book, Arthur Birnkrant, Waldo Salt; Music and Lyrics, Mary Rodgers; Director, Bill Dreyer; Designed and Produced by Bil and Susanna Baird; Lighting, Peggy Clark; Musical Director and Arranger, Alvy West

CAST

Nick	Olga Felgemacher
Billy/Miranda	Rebecca Bondor
Mr. Merriwether/Davy Jones	Peter B. Baird
First Goon	Neil Bleifeld
Capt. Scorn/Sea Monster	William Toast Burkett
Paddlefoot	Ronnie

A musical in two acts. The action takes place on a deserted island in the Bahamas, aboard the ship of Capt. Fletcher Scorn, and in Davy Jones' Locker.

General Manager: William Glass
Press: C. George Willard, Barbara Price
Stage Manager: Steve Login

* Closed Jan. 16, 1977 after 97 performances.

"Davy Jones' Locker"

CHELSEA THEATER CENTER

Robert Kalfin, Artistic Director
Michael David, Executive Director
Burl Hash, Productions Director

BROOKLYN ACADEMY OF MUSIC
Opened Wednesday, October 27, 1976.*
(Moved November 3, 1977 to Theatre Four)
The Chelsea Theater Center presents:

THE PRINCE OF HOMBURG

By Heinrich Von Kleist; English Version, James Kirkup; Adapted and Directed by Robert Kalfin; Scenery, Christopher Thomas; Costumes, Ruth Morley; Lighting, Marc B. Weiss; Music, Mel Marvin; Hairstylist, Patrik D. Moreton; Special Consultant, Erlo Van Waveren; Period Movement Adviser, Cindia Huppeler; Technical Directors, James Burke, Howard Rood; Assistant to Director, Bruce Connor; Production Assistants, Eric Bashford, Nelson Christianson, Tom Donahue, Richard Hageman, Paul Mobray

CAST

Prince Friedrich Arthur of Homburg	Frank Langella
Count Hohenzollern	George Morfogen
Friedrich Wilhelm	K. Lype O'Dell
His Wife	Jane Staab
Princess Natalia of Orange	Patricia Elliott
Baron Goltz	Peter Burnell
Count Reuss	Frank Anderson
Colonel Hennings	Jon Peter Benson
Colonel Truchss	William Myers
Field-Marshall Dorfling	Larry Swansen
Colonel Kottwitz	Roger DeKoven

UNDERSTUDIES: Peter Burnell (Prince of Homburg), Charles Conwell (Goltz), Randy Danson (Wilhelm's Wife/Natalia), Robert Einenkel (Hohenzollern/Hennings/Reuss/Truchss), William Yers (Wilhelm/Kottwitz/Dorfling)

A play in three acts.

General Manager: William Craver
Press: Susan Bloch, Lester Gruner
Stage Managers: Sherman Warner, Chuck Conwell

* Closed Nov. 21, 1977 after 40 performances.

Martha Swope Photos

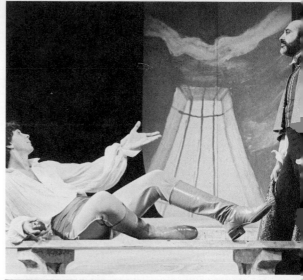

**George Morfogen, Roger DeKoven, Frank Langella, K. Lype O'Dell, William Myers, Larry Swansen
Top: Frank Langella, George Morfogen**

Frank Langella, K. Lype O'Dell

Roger DeKoven, Jon Peter Benson, George Morfogen, Larry Swansen, Frank Langella, K. Lype O'Dell, Frank Anderson William Myers

114

BROOKLYN ACADEMY OF MUSIC
Opened Tuesday, November 30, 1976.*
(Moved December 12, 1976 to Theatre Four)
Chelsea Theater Center presents:

LINCOLN

By Saul Levitt; Director, Carl Weber; Scenery, Lawrence King; Costume Coordinator, Carol Spier; Lighting, William Mintzer; Music, Mel Marvin; Film, Bedrich Batka, Francis Lee, Fred von Bernewitz; Sound, Edwin Pryor; Hairstylist, Patrik D. Moreton; Assistant to Director, Anna Randall; Production Assistant, Cathleen Stinson; Technical Directors, James Burke, Howard Rood

CAST

Fritz Weaver
as
Abraham Lincoln

A solo performance in three parts.

General Manager: William Craver
Press: Susan Bloch, Lester Gruner
Stage Managers: Phillip Price, Jill Marshall

* Closed Dec. 26, 1977 after 32 performances.

Martha Swope Photo

Fritz Weaver

BROOKLYN ACADEMY OF MUSIC
Opened Tuesday, January 18, 1977.*
(Moved to Theatre Four February 4, 1977)
The Chelsea Theater Center presents:

THE CRAZY LOCOMOTIVE

By Stanislaw Witkiewicz; Translated by Danie C. Gerould and C. S. Durer; Director, Des McAnuff; Scenery, Douglas Schmidt; Costumes, Carol Oditz; Lighting, Burl Hash; Electronic Music and Orchestration, Pril Smiley; Makeup, Claudia Kaneb; Assistant Director, Karen Gerst; Sound, Peter Byrne; Film Sequences, Scott Morris

CAST

Nicholas Slobok (Travaillac)	Dwight Schultz
Julia Tomasik	Lin Shaye
Siegfried Tenser (Prince Carl)	Garnett Smith
Sophia Tenser/Erna Abracadabra/ Jeanne Cackleson	Glenn Close
First Gendarme	John Scoullar
Valery Bean	Peter Bartlett
Minna, Countess de Barnhelm	Prudence Wright Holmes
Miss Mira Bean	Linda Scoullar
Turbulence Guster	Joe Palmieri
Conductor	Bob DeFrank
Third Thug	Lee Cotterell
John Cackleson/First Thug	John Jellison
Dr. Marcellus Riftmaker/Second Thug	Dennis Lipscomb
Second Gendarme/Doctor's Assistant	Mark C. Peters

UNDERSTUDIES: Lee Cotterell (Valery), Robert Einenkel (Siegfried/Riftmaker/Turbulence/Thugs/Gendarme), Rosalind Harris (Julia/Sophia/Mira/Minna/Jeanne), John Jellison (Nicholas), Dennis Lipscomb (Cackleson), John Scoullar (Conductor)

A play in two acts.

General Manager: William Craver
Press: Susan Bloch, Lester Gruner, Frank Tobin
Stage Managers: Ginny Freedman, James Harker

* Closed Feb. 13, 1977 after 29 performances.

Martha Swope Photo

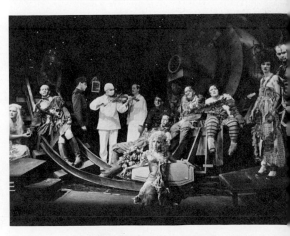

"The Crazy Locomotive"

"Mrs. Murray's Farm"

BROOKLYN ACADEMY OF MUSIC
Opened Tuesday, March 8, 1977.*
The Chelsea Theater Center and Michael Harvey present:

HAPPY END

Music, Kurt Weill; Lyrics, Bertolt Brecht; Original German play by Dorothy Lane; Book and Lyrics Adapted by Michael Feingold; Musical Staging, Patricia Birch; Director, Michael Posnick; Scenery, Robert U. Taylor; Costumes, Carrie F. Robbins; Lighting, Jennifer Tipton; Musical Director, Roland Gagnon; Film, Scott Morris; Hairstylist, Patrik D. Moreton; Assistant Director, Peter Byrne; Assistant Musical Director, David Krane; Wardrobe Mistress, Latonia O. Baer; Production Assistants, Daniel Quinn, Karen Gerst

CAST

Bill Cracker	Christopher Lloyd†1
Sam "Mammy" Wurlitzer	Benjamin Rayson
Dr. Nakamura ("Governor")	Tony Azito
Jimmy "Reverend" Dexter	John A. Coe
Bob "Professor" Marker	Robert Weil
Johnny "Baby Face" Flint	Raymond J. Barry
Lady in Gray ("The Fly")	Grayson Hall
Miriam, the barmaid	Donna Emmanuel
Lt. Lillian Holiday ("Hallelujah Lil")	Shirley Knight†2
Major Stone	Liz Sheridan
Capt. Hannibal Jackson	Joe Grifasi
Sister Mary	Prudence Wright Holmes
Sister Jane	Alexandra Borrie
Brother Ben Owens	Bob Gunton†3
A Cop	David Pursley
The Fold	Kristin Jolliff, Frank Kopyc,
	Tom Mardirosian, Martha Miller, Victor Pappas

UNDERSTUDIES: Alexandra Borrie (Lillian), Donna Emmanuel (Jane), Bob Gunton (Bill), Kristin Jolliff (Miriam/Mary), Frank Kopyc (Jackson), Tom Mardirosian (Baby Face/Cop), Martha Miller (Major/Fly), Victor Pappas (Nakamura/Marker), David Pursley (Wurlitzer/Decter)

MUSICAL NUMBERS: Prologue, "Bilbao Song," "Lieutenants of the Lord," "March Ahead," "Sailors' Tango," "Brother, Give Yourself a Shove," "Song of the Big Shot," "Don't Be Afraid," "In Our Childhood's Bright Endeavor," "The Liquor Dealer's Dream," "Mandalay Song," "Surabaya Johnny," "Ballad of the Lily of Hell," "Happy End"

A musical in 3 acts and 4 scenes. The action takes place in Chicago during December 1915 in Bill's Beer Hall, and the Salvation Army Mission.

General Manager: William Craver
Press: Susan Bloch, Lester Gruner, Sally Christiansen, Francis X. Tobin
Stage Managers: Mark Wright, Christopher Cara

* Closed Apr. 3, 1977 after 32 performances. Resumed performances Tuesday, Apr. 12 after being re-directed by Robert Kalfin, and with Meryl Streep as Lt. Lillian Holiday. Closed Apr. 30, 1977 after 24 performances to move to Broadway where it opened May 7, 1977.
† Succeeded by: 1. Bob Gunton, 2. Meryl Streep, 3. Christopher Cara

(Martha Swope Photo)

CIRCLE REPERTORY COMPANY

Marshall W. Mason, Artistic Director
Jerry Arrow, Executive Director
Eighth Season

CIRCLE REPERTORY COMPANY THEATRE
Opened Wednesday, June 30, 1976.*
The Circle Repertory Company presents:

MRS. MURRAY'S FARM

By Roy London; Directors, Neil Flanagan, Marshall W. Mason; Music, Michael Valenti; Setting, John Lee Beatty; Costumes, Jennifer von Mayrhauser; Lighting, John P. Dodd; Sound, Charles London, George Hansen; Technical Director, Robert Yanez; Assistant to Directors, Amy Schecter; Wardrobe Mistress, Margot Avery

CAST

Barbara Warren	Nancy Snyder
Willa Hooper	Sharon Madden
Arnold Westerly Apthorpe	Burke Pearson
Israel James	Danton Stone
Mrs. Robert Murray	Tanya Berezin
Peter Roome, Jr	Michael Ayr
British Soldiers	Terence Foley, Peter Sherin
Lt. Dawson	Bruce Gray
Mrs. Joshua Loring	Nancy Killmer
General William Howe	James Perkinson

A play in two acts. The action takes place on September 16, 1776 at Murray Hill on Manhattan Island.

Company Manager: Dennis Purcell
Press: Rima Corben
Stage Managers: David Clow, Amelia R. Haywood

* Closed Aug. 1, 1976 after 41 performances and 7 previews.

Arlene Avril Photo

**Christopher Lloyd, Shirley Knight
in "Happy End"**

**Debra Mooney, Jack Gwillim
in "The Farm"**

CIRCLE REPERTORY COMPANY THEATRE
Opened Sunday, November 28, 1976.*
The Circle Repertory Company presents:

A TRIBUTE TO LILI LAMONT

By Arthur Whitney; Director, Marshall W. Mason; Setting, John Lee Beatty; Costumes, Jennifer von Mayrhauser; Lighting, Dennis Parichy; Original Music, Norman L. Berman; Sound, Charles London; Assistant to Director, Lawrence Smith; Wardrobe Supervisor, Jenny Feder; Technical Director, Robert Yanez

CAST

Oliver Fuller	William Hindman
Tommy Alvarez	Francis Walsh
Bebe Bernstein	Helen Stenborg
Pauline Johnson	Claris Erickson
Harry Shannon	Burke Pearson
Joe Bernstein	Jack Davidson
Miss Lili Lamont	Leueen MacGrath

A play in two acts. The action takes place at the present time on a rainy July evening in a basement on a side street off lower Fourth Avenue in New York City.

Company Manager: Dennis Purcell
Press: Rima Corben
Stage Managers: Fred Reinglas, Burke Pearson

* Closed Jan. 2, 1977 after 36 performances and 6 previews.

Ken Howard Photo

**Jo Henderson, William Hurt, Claire Malis,
Douglass Watson, Nancy Snyder in "My Life"**

CIRCLE REPERTORY COMPANY THEATRE
Opened Sunday, October 10, 1976.*
The Circle Repertory Company presents:

THE FARM

By David Story; Director, Marshall W. Mason; Setting, John Lee Beatty; Costumes, Laura Crow; Lighting, Dennis Parichy; Wardrobe Mistress, Jenny Feder; Technical Director, Robert Yanez; Assistant to Director, Steven Gomer

CAST

Wendy	Debra Mooney
Jennifer	Trish Hawkins
Brenda	Nancy Snyder
Slattery	Jack Gwillim
Mrs. Slattery	Ruby Holbrook
Albert	Michael Ayr
Arthur	Jeff Daniels

A play in 3 acts and 5 scenes. The action takes place in November of the present year in an ancient farmhouse in Northern England.

Company Manager: Dennis Purcell
Press: Rima Corben
Stage Managers: Dave Clow, LauraSue Epstein

* Closed Nov. 14, 1976 after 36 performances and 6 previews.

(Ken Howard Photo)

Leueen MacGrath

CIRCLE REPERTORY COMPANY THEATRE
Opened Sunday, January 23, 1977.*
The Circle Repertory Company presents:

MY LIFE

By Corinne Jacker; Director, Marshall W. Mason; Setting, David Potts; Lighting, Dennis Parichy; Costumes, Kenneth M. Yount; Original Music, Norman L. Berman; Sound, Charles London; Technical Directors, Robert Yanez, Joe Musco; Assistant to Director, Mark Milliken; Wardrobe Mistress, Gail Peretsman

CAST

Perdita Mason	Claire Malis
Edward Howe	William Hurt
Grandfather	Christopher Reeve
Father	Roger Chapman
Mother	Tanya Berezin
Wallace Howe	Douglass Watson
Laura Howe Winchester	Jo Henderson
Young Eddie	Jeff Daniels
Sally	Nancy Snyder

A play in three acts. The action takes place on a September evening in San Francisco, and the summers before.

Company Manager: Dennis Purcell
Press: Rima Corben
Stage Managers: Amy Schecter, David Oisher

* Closed Feb. 27, 1977 after 36 performances and 6 previews.

(Ken Howard Photo)

CIRCLE REPERTORY COMPANY THEATRE
Opened Tuesday, February 8, 1977.*
Circle Repertory Company Afterpiece Theater presents:

THE PASSING OF CORKY BREWSTER

By Jerry L. Crawford; Director, Daniel Irvine; Technical Director, Robert Yanez; Sound, David Oisher

CAST

Sharon Madden
as
Grace Turley

A one-act comedy. The action takes place last October in a small town in central Iowa.

Press: Rima Corben
Stage Managers: Fred Reinglas, LauraSue Epstein

* Closed Feb. 13, 1977 after limited engagement of 5 performances. Returned Tuesday, March 22–27, 1977 for 5 additional performances.

(Ken Howard Photos)

Ken Kimmons, Kate Kelly, Sharon Madden, Jason McAuliffe in "For Love or Money" Above: Sharon Madden in "Passing of Corky Brewster"

CIRCLE REPERTORY COMPANY THEATRE
Opened Tuesday, March 8, 1977.*
The Circle Repertory Company in association with PAF Playhouse presents:

GEMINI

By Albert Innaurato; Directory, Peter Mark Schifter; Setting, Christopher Nowak; Costumes, Ernest Allen Smith; Lighting, Larry Crimmins; Wardrobe Supervisor, Kathy Powers

CAST

Francis Geminiani..........................Robert Picardo
Bunny Lowenstein ....Jessica James
Randy Hastings.............................Reed Birney
Judith Hastings............................Carol Potter
Marshall Lowenstein.....................Jonathan Hadary
Fran Geminiani............................Danny Aiello
Lucille Grande ....Anne DeSalvo

A comedy in two acts and four scenes. The action takes place in the Geminiani-Lowenstein backyard in South Philadelphia on June 1 & 2, 1973.

Company Manager: Dennis Purcell
Press: Rima Corben
Stage Managers: Fred Reinglas, James Arneman

* Closed May 1, 1977 after 56 performances and 7 previews to move to Broadway

CIRCLE REPERTORY COMPANY THEATRE
Opened Tuesday, March 29, 1977.*
Circle Repertory Company Afterpiece Theater presents:

FOR LOVE OR MONEY

Music, Jason McAuliffe; Lyrics, Jay Jeffries; Director, Susan Lehman; Musical Director, Daniel Glosser; Designer, Michael Massee; Choreographer, Kathie Kallaghan; Technical Director, Robert Yanez; Assistant Musical Director, Steve Rosenthal

CAST

Kate Kelly
Ken Kimmins
Sharon Madden
Jason McAuliffe

A musical entertainment performed without intermission.

MUSICAL NUMBERS: "Other Alternatives," "Geography," "That Happy Melody," "Brief Encounter," "Confessional," "Where Have I Been All My Life?," "Snap Decision," "Taboo or Not Taboo," "Counterpoint," "Mamma's Cooking," "Living Love"

Press: Rima Corben
Stage Manager: Peter Jablonski

* Closed April 10, 1977 after 9 performances.

CIRCLE REPERTORY COMPANY THEATRE
Opened Sunday, May 15, 1977.*
The Circle Repertory Company Afterpiece Theater presents:

CABARET THEATRE
(New York Times)

Written by Gloria Allen, Brooks Porter, James Tobin; Music, Jeffrey Nissim; Director, Ann Raychel; Costumes, Karen Miller; Lights, Curt Ostermann; Sets, Terry Burns

CAST

Octavio Ciano
Daniel Dassin
Marion Levine
John A. Murray
Maria Normal
Brooks Porter
Kevin Wade

Press: Rima Corben
Stage Managers: Ric Barrett, Carol Patella

* Closed June 27, 1977 after limited engagement of 4 performances.

CIRCLE REPERTORY COMPANY THEATRE
Opened Tuesday, May 17, 1977.*
Circle Repertory Company Afterpiece Theater presents:

WHAT THE BABE SAID

By Martin Halpern; Director, Amy Schecter; Costumes, Nina Friedman; Lights, April Webster; Project Director, Daniel Irvine

CAST

Sal Salerno............................... Mitchell Jason
Buck Benson .... Dan Hamilton

The action takes place at the present time in the visiting manager's office of a Major League baseball team. Performed without intermission.

Press: Rima Corben
Stage Managers: Rita Calabro, Gretchen Pasanen

* Closed June 3, 1977 after limited engagement of 9 performances.

CIRCLE REPERTORY COMPANY THEATRE
Opened Thursday, May 19, 1977.*
The Circle Repertory Company presents:

EXILES

By James Joyce; Director, Rob Thirkield; Settings, David Potts; Costumes, Jennifer von Mayrhauser; Lighting, Dennis Parichy; Music, Norman L. Berman; Sound, Charles London; Wardrobe Supervisor, Gary Stangl: Technical Directors, Robert Yanez, Joe Musco; Staff Assistant, Suzanne Koblentz; Staff Assistant, Brian Ross

CAST

Richard Rowan............................. Alan Jordan
Bertha.................................. Stephanie Gordon
Archie .... Anthony Austin
Robert Hand............................. Neil Flanagan
Beatrice Justice .... Nancy Killmer
Brigid...................................... Ele Logan

A play in three acts. The action takes place in the early 1900's during the summer in the suburbs of Dublin, Ireland.

Company Manager: Dennis Purcell
Press: Rima Corben
Stage Managers: Bob Lampel, Larry Smith

* Closed June 12, 1977 after 26 performances and 9 previews.

Ken Howard Photos

Stephanie Gordon, Alan Jordan Above: Neil Flanagan, Nancy Killmer, Anthony Austin, Alan Jordan, Stephanie Gordon, Eleanor Logan

CLASSIC STAGE COMPANY

Christopher Martin, Artistic Director
Leonard Edelstein, Managing Director
John Shannon, Production Manager

ABBEY THEATRE
October 1, 1976–April 24, 1977

COMPANY

Christopher Martin, Karen Sunde, Tom Donaldson, Peter Van Norden, Frank Dwyer, Noble Shopshire, Carol Flemming, Ara Watson, Darrie Lawrence, Martin Treat, Marcia Hyde, Sam Blackwell, Wayne Wofford, Harlan Schneider, Jerri Iaia, Jennifer Reed, Michael Kolba, Kevin McClarnon, Peter Galman

GUEST DESIGNERS: David Chapman, Harry Lines, Evelyn Thompson

PRODUCTIONS

In Rotating Repertory: "Heartbreak House" by Bernard Shaw, "Tartuffe" by Moliere (*World Premiere* of Christopher Martin's verse translation), *New York Premiere* of Edward Bond's "Bingo," "The Homecoming" by Harold Pinter, and *American Premiere* of new version of Jean Genet's "The Balcony" by Terry Hands and Barbara Wright

Gerry Goodstein Photos

**Christopher Martin
in "The Homecoming"**

THE CLASSIC THEATRE

Nicholas John Stathis, Producer
Maurice Edwards, Artistic Director

CENTRAL ARTS THEATRE
June 18–July 2, 1976 (12 performances)
TROPICAL MADNESS by Stanislaw Witkiewicz; Translated by
Danie C. Gerould; Director, Maurice Edwards; Design, Ikuyo
Garber; Costumes, Sarah Nash Gates; Lights, Anthony Borovicka;
Sound, Jason Rosenfield; Stage Manager, Marilyn Daljord; Techni-
cal Consultant, Terry Hunter. A drama in three acts. CAST: Frank
Biancamano (Richard Golders), Elizabeth Reavy (Elinor Golders),
Tom Bahring (Mr. Price), Elizabeth Ballard (Georgiana Fray),
Woodrow Garrian (Albert Britchello), Lydia Edwards (Bertha
Britchello), Christina Lenz (Lily Radcliffe), Craig Wyckoff (Tom
Radcliffe), Carl Palusci (Jack Britchello), Osiris Delosrios (Jim/
Dan)

CARAS NUEVAS
January 13–30, 1977 (12 performances)
THE CONSPIRACY OF FEELINGS by Yurii Olyesha; Translated
by Daniel C. and Eleanor S. Gerould; Director, Maurice Edwards;
Set, Sal Rasa; Costumes, Ruth Thomason; Lighting, Osiris Delosrios, Annie Rech; Music, Robert Bonfiglio, Richard Einhorn;
Stage Managers, Mary Malloy Adams, Susan Jonas; Technical Di-
rector, Michael A. Fink; Set Collaborator, Robert Maloney; A
drama in 7 scenes. CAST: Jerry Richkin (Andrei), Ron Johnston
(Ivan), Nels Hennum (Nikolai), Linda Lodge (Valya), Albert Ama-
teau (Solomon), Barbara Winkler (Annichka), Marilyn Ballard Dal-
jord (Lizaveta), Jeff Gold (Her Husband), Thomas Charles (1st
Tenant/Mikhail), Lucille Paisley (Woman Celebrating Name Day),
Teri Owen (Zinochka), Annie Rech (Lady in Green), John Rothman
(Young Man/Vic), John Copeland (Old Man), Anthony Ristoff (2nd
Tenant/Old Man), Jeff Gold (Guest/Safraonov), Arnold Victor (4th
Tenant/Drunk Guest/Fessenkov), Ted Gargiulo (3rd Tenant/Doc-
tor/Harman)

CARAS NUEVAS
February 3–20, 1977 (12 performances)
SHADOW OF A GUNMAN by Sean O'Casey; Director, Lawrence
Zucker; Sets, Steve Duffy; Lights, Mary Moran, Osiris Delosrios;
Costumes, David Samuel Menkes; Sound, Edward R. Fitzgerald;
Assistant Director, Thomas Bahring; Stage Managers, Marilyn Bal-
lard Daljord, Nancy Johnson; Technical Director, Michael Fink;
Dialecticians, Robin Reiter, Steve Gavis. CAST: Thomas Bahring
(Donal), John McPeak (Seamus), Jack Biser (Maguire), Franz Robi-
now (Landlord/Auxiliary Officer), Linda Cook (Minnie), Richard
Stack (Tommy), Anne-Frances Thom (Mrs. Henderson), Frederick
Rein (Gallogher), John Copley-Quinn (Adolphus), Bettyann Leese-
berg (Mrs. Grigson)

Michael Zettler Photos

**Tom Bahring, Linda Cook
in "Shadow of a Gunman"**

120

**"Tropical Madness" Below: Marilyn Rockafellow,
George Riddle "Autumn Serenade"**

CARAS NUEVAS
March 11–27, 1977 (12 performances)
EACH IN HIS OWN WAY by Luigi Pirandello; English version,
Arthur Livingston; Director, Maurice Edwards; Set, Sal Rasa, Rob-
ert Maloney; Costumes, David Samuel Menkes; Lighting, Annie
Rech, Osiris Delosrios; Stage Manager, Mary Malloy Adams; Tech-
nical Director, Michael A. Fink; Fencing Staged by Edward Easton.
CAST: Julia Curry (Delia), Thomas MacGreevy (Michele), Elaine
Eldrige (Livia), Walter Wright (1st Gentleman), Donald Pace (2nd
Gentleman), John Archibald (1st Young Man), Frank Askin (2nd
Young Man), Brigid Moynahan (1st Young Lady), Aimee Philpott
(2nd Young Lady), Thomas Sminkey (Doro), Roger Boxill (Diego),
Osiris Delosrios (Filippo), Roger Kozol (Francesco) Frank Laurino
(Prestino), Edward Easton (Fencing Master), Madeline Rockower
(Amelia), Robert Foresta (Baron), Mary Malloy Adams (Stage
Manager), Gerald Richkin (Business Manager), Walter Wright (1st
Drama Critic), Annie Rech (2nd Drama Critic), Arnold Victor (3rd
Drama Critic), Donald Pac (Old Author), Stephen Zufa (Spectator),
Ann McCormack (Supporter of Pirandello), Brigid Moynahan (An-
tagonist of Pirandello)

CARAS NUEVAS
April 8–18, 1977 (12 performances)
AUTUMN SERENADE by Wesley St. John; Directors, Anthony
Ristoff, George Riddle; Technical Director, James Sorkin; Stage
Manager, Donna Williams; Press, Marilyn Ballard Daljord. Three
inter-related one-act plays. CAST: George Riddle (Max), Marilyn
Rockafellow (Cindy), Gerda Shepard (Margaret), Anthony Ristoff
(Harry)

CARAS NUEVAS
May 6–23, 1977 (12 performances)
ROSMERSHOLM by Henrik Ibsen; New translation by Rolf
Fjelde; Director, Cyril Simon; Set, Tony Giovannetti; Costumes,
David Samuel Menkes; Lighting, Annie Rech; Music, David Hol-
lister; Stage Manager, Mary Malloy Adams; Production Assistants,
Karen Craig, Marlene Scheuermann. A play in 4 acts. CAST: Paul
Vincent (John Rosmer), Kathryn Harrold (Rebecca West), Jack
Axelrod (Dr. Kroll), William Myers (Ulrik Brendel), Jeffrey Spolan
(Peter Mortensgaard), Norma Frances (Mrs. Helseth)

THE CONSPIRACY

Lester Shane, Executive Director

EAST FIFTH STREET

July 31–August 1, 1976 (2 performances)
STREET SCENE by Elmer Rice; Director, Ricka Kanter; Stage Manager, Jill Pester; Props, Tina Reddy; Lights, Danny Loewenthal; Sound, Tom Edlun. CAST: Burt Sorkey (Abraham), Susan King (Greta), Kae Colman (Emma), Carol Levitt (Olga), Danny Levine (Willie), Kathy O'Callaghan (Anna), Dennis Southers (Daniel), Peter Jolly (Frank), Brian Russo (George/1st Policeman), Gordon Blackman (Steve), Lola Conrad (Agnes), Roy Finamore (Carl), Martha Jacobs (Shirley), Paul Georges (Filippo), Bonnie Murphy (Alice), Sarah Chodoff (Laura), Vanessa West (Mary), Ricky Snyder (Charlie), Lester Shane (Samuel), Nancy Hendrickson (Rose), Kenny Marino (Harry), Suzanne Peters (Mae), Rick Ericson (Dick/Intern), Paul J. Ott (Vincent), Herve Wiener (Dr. Wilson/Mailman/Officer Murphy), George Cocorelis (Marshal/Iceman/New Tenant), Scott W. Glenn (Fred/Man), Marjorie Gross (1st College Girl/2nd Nursemaid), Yolanda Kempley (2nd College Girl/Woman/Grocery Boy), Gail Michelson (Music Student/New Tenant), Laura Hawkins (1st Nursemaid)

STAGE 73

September 9–19, 1976 (8 performances)
SUMMER AND SMOKE by Tennessee Williams; Director, Lester Shane; Producers, Lynn Lowry, Lester Shane; Lighting, Joe Mangine; Stage Managers, Susi Mara, Clay Hapaz, Diana Doussant. A play in 2 acts and 15 scenes. CAST: Peter Brouwer (John, Jr.), Nancy Hendrickson (Nellie), Ricka Kanter (Grace), Norman Rene (Vernon), Susan King (Rosemary), Dennis Southers (Roger), Warrington Winters (Rev. Weinmiller), Kathy O'Callaghan (Mrs. Winemiller), Lynn Lowry (Alma), Andrea Masters (Rosa), Joe Daly (Dr. Buchanan, Sr.), Lester Shane (Archie)

STAGE 73

December 4–19, 1976 (6 performances)
BIRDBATH by Leonard Melfi; Director, Norman Rene; Setting, Paul Berizzi; Lighting, Rick Belzer; Stage Manager, Susie Mara. CAST: Nancy Hendrickson (Velma Sparrow), John Seeman (Frankie Basta)

STAGE 73

April 21–May 1, 1977 (12 performances)
HEDDA GABLER by Henrik Ibsen; Translation, Christopher Hampton; Director, Lester Shane; Producer, Lynn Lowry; Lighting, Rick Belzer; Stage Manager, Susi Mara. CAST: Charles Antalosky (Tesman), Susan King (Bertha), Margaret Thomson (Aunt Julia), Lynn Lowry (Hedda), Nona Pipes (Mrs. Elvsted), Roger Brown (Judge Brack), Patrick Watkins (Eilert Lovborg)

THE NIGHTHOUSE

May 11–20, 1977 (8 performances)
THE WAGER by Mark Medoff; Director, Norman Rene; Designer, Bob Wolff; Stage Manager, Susi Mara; Technical Director, Roger Middleton; Lighting, Rick Belzer; Properties, Laine Courtney; Slides, Paul Berizzi. CAST: Sheldon Epps (Leeds), John Seeman (Ward), Anne Twomey (Honor), Michael Hagerty (Ron)

(Kim Snyder Photo)

Lynn Lowry, Patrick Watkins in "Hedda Gabler"

COUNTERPOINT THEATRE COMPANY

Howard Green, Artistic Director
Paulene Reynolds, Managing Director
Fred Berry, Company Manager

COUNTERPOINT THEATRE

October 8–25, 1976 (12 performances)
OLD TIMES by Harold Pinter; Director, Howard Green; Scenery and Lights, Barbara Schwartz; Costumes, Ernesto Leston; Stage Manager, Cindy Russell. CAST: Paulene Reynolds (Kate), Len Auclair (Deeley), Jacqueline Barnett (Anna)

November 26–December 13, 1976 (12 performances)
THE PLAY'S THE THING by Ferenc Molnar; Director, Howard Green; Set, T. Byrne; Costumes, Ernesto Leston, Petrea Macdonald; Lights, Cindy Russell; Props, Bob Butler; Stage Manager, Ilene Dube. CAST: Arthur Anderson (Mansky), Sam Gray (Sandor), John Seidman (Albert), Elek Hartman (Dwortnitschek), Linda Geiser (Ilona), Ed Crowley (Almady), Roy Sorrels (Mell), Footmen: Fred Berry, Bob Butler

January 28–February 14, 1977 (12 performances)
PLAYING WITH FIRE by August Strindberg; Director, Charles Maryan; Set, Atkin Pace; Costumes, Lana Fritz; Lights, Patrick Mann; Stage Manager, Cindy Russell. CAST: Kevin Kline (Son), Francesca de Sapio (Daughter-in-Law), Barbara Stanton (Mother), George Hall (Father), Elizabeth Kemp (Cousin), Alan Coates (Friend)

LUNCH HOUR by John Mortimer. (same credits as above) CAST: Elizabeth Kemp (Girl), George Hall (Man), Barbara Stanton (Manageress)

March 18–April 4, 1977 (12 performances)
AWAKE AND SING! by Clifford Odets; Director, Terry Walker; Set, Patrick Mann; Costumes, Petrea Macdonald; Lights, Gerald J. Dellasala, Gary Marks; Stage Managers, Bryan Bradley, Emily Agin. CAST: Elek Hartman (Myron), Hope Cameron (Bessie), Clement Fowler (Jacob), Tanny McDonald (Hennie), Michael Mantel (Ralph), Morris Alpern (Schlosser), Howard Green (Moe), Daniel Pollack (Uncle Morty), Robert Tennenhouse (Sam)

May 6–23, 1977
HOW HE LIED TO HER HUSBAND and OVERRULED
Two one-acts by George Bernard Shaw; Director, Howard Green; Set, Patrick Mann; Costumes, Petrea Macdonald; Lights, Jac Yager, Gary Marks; Assistant to Director, Emily Agin; Stage Manager, Bryan Bradley. CAST: "How He Lied to Her Husband": John Seidman (Apjohn), Tanny McDonald (Aurora), Doug Stender (Bompas) "Overruled": Fran Brill (Mrs. Juno), Doug Stender (Lunn), Saylor Creswell (Mr. Juno), Tanny McDonald (Mrs. Lunn)

Jacqueline Barnett, Len Auclair,
Paulene Reynolds in "Old Times"

THE CUBICULO

Philip Meister, Artistic Director
Elaine Sulka, Managing Director
Dinah Carlson, Publicity Director

THE CUBICULO

October 7–16, 1976 (7 performances)
A DRINK AT THE WELL by Galt MacDermot and Norman Matlock; Lighting, Blu Lambert; Technical Director, Ben Donenberg. A musical revue. CAST: Marilyn LaGrone-Amaral, Norman Matlock, Sheila Scott-Wilkinson

October 21–November 13, 1976 (12 performances)
MISTER McMANNIS, WHAT TIME IS IT? by William Schlottmann; Directed by the Author; Sets and Lighting, Marilyn Reed; Sound, Joe Restuccia; Lighting, Juno Sobel; Stage Manager, Mabel Alexander; Production Assistant, Alan Rathe; Technical Director, Bob Lampel; Associate Producer, Katherine Kish; Press, Laura Melim. A play in two acts. CAST: Olive Deering (Emily), Joseph Julian (Arnold McMannis), Joan Kaye (Customer), Wayne Duncan (Arlo)

November 18–28, 1977 (8 performances)
ONCE AND FOR ALL by Robert Gordon; Director, Edward M. Cohen; Sets, Bil Mikulewicz; Costumes, Louise M. Herman; Lights, Paul Leavin; Stage Manager, Andy Lopata. A play in 3 scenes. CAST: Michael Brody (Mister Winston), Robert Haufrecht (Al), Gloria Barret (Ruth), Ron Johnston (Charlie)

January 4–6, 1977 (3 performances)
A MARK TWAIN MEDLEY based on the works of Mark Twain; Director, Sue Lawless; Set, Joan Ferncheck; Costumes, Sharon Hollinger; Pianist, Robert McDowell; Lighting, Ron Daley; Stage Manager, Rob Granfors. CAST: Andy Chase, Natalie Dame, Rob Granfors, Debbie McLeod, Paul Richards, Stephen M. Stylinski

January 7–9, 1977 (3 performances)
SPOON RIVER ANTHOLOGY based on book by Edgar Lee Masters; Music, Folk and Traditional; Director, Sue Lawless; Set, Joan Ferncheck; Costumes, Sharon Hollinger; Pianist, Robert McDowell; Lighting, Ron Daley; Stage Manager, Rob Granfors. CAST: same as "Mark Twain Medley"

February 7–8, 1977 (2 performances)
TALES TOLD TO THE SPHINX - a program of mime theatre by Peter Lobdell; Lighting, Ron Daley; Sound, Charles Horowitz; Masks and Costumes, Jane Stein, Pamela Scofield, Peter Lobdell; Voice of the Sphinx, Ching Valdes; Pyramid, Roxy Wright, Al Cook

February 24–March 19, 1977 (12 performances)
THE RECRUITING OFFICER by George Farquhar; Director, Philip Meister; Movement Director, Marlene Pennison; Production Coordinator, Jenny Cornuelle; Music Composed and Directed by Judy Kurzer; Stage Managers, Michael McConkey, Dennis O'-Reilly; Costumes, Sharon Hollinger; General Manager, Deborah Teller; Program Coordinator, Dinah Carlson; Technical Director, Ron Daley. A vaudeville treatment of a Restoration farce. CAST: Anthony Ristoff (Balance), Ralph Nilson (Worthy), Paul Welsh (Capt. Plume), Peter Gallman (Capt. Brazen), James Doerr (Kite), George Ayer (Bullock), Lou Quinones (Coster/Smith/Constable), Lloyd Kay (Scale/Appletree/Butcher), Sally Mercer (Melinda), Khalisa Dawn Gray (Silvia), Eve Packer (Lucy), Kimberly Cole (Rose)

March 23–24, 1977 (2 performances)
CHOPIN LIVES! by Robert Guralnik and Harold Guskin; Director, Harold Guskin; Costume, Marion Smiley; Technical Director, Ron Daley. A recital-monologue in two parts performed by Robert Guralnik

April 7–24, 1977 (12 performances)
TOO MANY THUMBS by Robert Hivnor; Director, John Olon-Scrymgeour; Set, Jane Thurn; Lights, Nicole LeBrun; Costumes, Kimberly Cole; Production Coordinator, Dinah Carlson; Technical Director, Ron Daley. A comedy in 2 acts and 5 scenes. CAST: Renee Lippin (Psyche), Charles Lutz (Arthur), Michael McConkey (Johnson), Terry Markovich (Dr. Macklebee), Kate Weiman (Jenny), Ron Carrier (Thumbs), Paul Andor (Dr. Block)

April 24–May 14, 1977 (10 performances)
NOBODY HEARD THE LIONS ROAR by Leslie Holzer; Director, Lawrence Hoff; Sets, William Holzer; Lighting, Joan Klaus, Donna Brady; Press, Herb Striesfield; Wardrobe, Ellen Beck-Meyer; Stage Managers, David A. Ticotin, Francine Gindi. A comedy in 2 acts and 4 scenes. CAST: Tony Kraber (Steele Worthington), Lou Quinones (Heyjo Klitzino), Missie Zollo (Nina Martin)

Robert Guralnik in "Chopin Lives"
Above: Peter Lobdell
Top: "The Recruiting Officer"

Pictures of People Photos

EQUITY LIBRARY THEATRE

George Wojtasik, Managing Director
Lynn Montgomery, Production Director

EQUITY LIBRARY THEATRE
Opened Thursday, October 14, 1976.*
Equity Library Theatre presents:

FIORELLO!

Book, Jerome Weidman, George Abbott; Music, Jerry Bock; Lyrics, Sheldon Harnick; Direction and Choreography, William Koch; Musical Director, Thomas Helm; Scenery, Richard B. Williams; Costumes, Deborah Shaw; Lighting, Isaac Waksul; Hairstylist, J. Alexander Scafa; Assistant Choreographer, Ellen Zalk; Tap Choreographer, Diane Maggio; Wardrobe Mistress, Cindy Dangle

CAST

Fiorello LaGuardia	Frank Kopyc
Neil	Bill Biskup
Morris	Michael McCarty
Mrs. Pomerantz	Anne Korzen
Lopez/Senator/Red Baron/Bodyguard	Ryon C. Garee
Zapatella/Heckler/German/Butler	Ernie Semento
Dora	Alexandra Korey
Marie	Ann Hodapp
Ben Marino	Christopher Wynkoop
Dealer Louis/Commissioner	Mark Zimmerman
Ed Peterson/Judge	Donald L. Norris
Tony/Soldier/Bodyguard/Reporter	Bruce Kent
Cardplayer/Soldier/Announcer Chadwick	Hardy Phippen
Tenor Cardplayer/German/Frantic	Karl Heist
Cardplayer/Heckler/Politician	Glen Agrin
Seedy Man/Oilcan Harry/King Victor Emmanuel/Frankie Scarpini	Sheldon Silver
Nina/Maid	Sophie Schwab
Sophie/Cutie	Kathryn Boule
Floyd	Frank Luz
Thea	Verna Pierce
Washington Secretary/Florence	Mary Rocco
Bella/Cutie	Diane Maggio
Lena/Cutie	Chris Jamison
Newsreel Rooster/Cutie	Rochelle Seldin
Mitzi	Debbi Morell

MUSICAL NUMBERS: "On the Side of the Angels," "Politics and Poker," "Unfair," "Marie's Law," "The Name Is LaGuardia," "The Bum Won," "I Love a Cop," "Cop Dance," "Till Tomorrow," "Home Again," "When Did I Fall in Love," "Gentleman Jimmy," "Jimmy Dance," "Little Tin Box," "The Very Next Man," Finale

A musical in 2 acts and 20 scenes. The action takes place in NYC and Washington, DC.

Press: Sol Jacobson, Lewis Harmon
Stage Managers: Sally Hassenfelt, Kit Harding, Jim Fauvell

* Closed Oct. 31, 1976 after limited engagement of 22 performances.

(Gary Wheeler Photo)

Sophie Schwab, Mary Rollo, Chris Samison, Frank Kopye, Kathryn Boule, Rochelle Seldin, Alexandra Korey

EQUITY LIBRARY THEATRE
Opened Tuesday, November 11, 1976.*
Equity Library Theatre presents:

HEARTBREAK HOUSE

By George Bernard Shaw; Director, Alfred Gingold; Scenery, Michael Molly; Lighting, William D. Anderson; Costumes, David Murin; Sound, Bill Odell; Hairstylist, Maggie Raywood; Flutists, Didi Charney, Ulrich Childs

CAST

Ellie Dunn	Sofia Landon
Nurse Guinness	Naomi Riseman
Captain Shotover	Ben Slack
Ariadne Utterword	Martha Miller
Hesione Hushabye	Sharon Laughlin
Mazzini Dunn	Peter Murphy
Hector Hushabye	Tom Crawley
Boss Mangan	Bernie Passeltiner
Randall Utterword	Kermit Brown
Billy Dunn	Marshall Rosenblum

A play in three acts. The action takes place in Capt. Shotover's house in Sussex, England.

Press: Lewis Harmon, Sol Jacobson
Stage Managers: Zoya Wyeth, Robert Reich, Rena Rockoff

* Closed Nov. 21, 1976 after limited engagement of 14 performances.

(Gary Wheeler Photo)

Sharon Laughlin, Martha Miller, Ben Slack

123

EQUITY LIBRARY THEATRE

Opened Thursday, December 2, 1976.*
Equity Library Theatre presents:

THE BOYS FROM SYRACUSE

Music, Richard Rodgers; Lyrics, Lorenz Hart; Book, George Abbott; Based on "Comedy of Errors" by William Shakespeare; Director, Marc Jordan Gass; Musical Direction Mark T. Long; Choreography, Nina Janik; Musical Numbers and Tap Sequences, Mark Jordan Gass; Additional Musical Arrangements, Hugh McElyea; Sets, Jim Chestnutt; Costumes, Tom Hansen; Lighting, Marcia Madeira; Assistant Director, Lisa Lindstrom; Fights, R. Mack Miller

CAST

Sergeant	Ken Waller
Duke	Bruce Sherman
Aegeon	Joshua Michaels
Antipholus of Ephesus	Dana Coen
Dromio of Ephesus	Michael Makman
Tailor	Randy Skinner
Antipholus of Syracuse	Jerry Yoder
Dromio of Syracuse	T. Galen Girvin
Merchant of Syracuse	Robert Ari
Apprentice	David Monzione
Angelo	Jack Hoffman
Corporal	Andy Ferrell
Luce	Judith Moore
Andriana	Lisby Larson
Luciana	Karyn Cole
Maids	Lynda Kay Hamil, Lynn Marlowe, Kay Walbye
Sorcerer	Anthony Lawrence
Courtesan	Susan Edwards
Fatima	Paige Massman
Courtesan	Sharon Bruce
Courtesan/Seeress/Emelia	Rebecca Malka

MUSICAL NUMBERS: "I Had Twins," "Dear Old Syracuse," "What Can You Do with a Man?," "Falling in Love with Love," "The Shortest Day of the Year," "This Can't Be Love," "Ladies of the Evening," "He and She," "You Have Cast Your Shadow on the Sea," "Come with Me," "Big Brother," "Sing for Your Supper," "Oh, Diogenes," Finale

A musical in 2 acts and 11 scenes. The action takes place in Ancient Greece.

Press: Sol Jacobson, Lewis Harmon
Stage Managers. Michael Swafford, Valerie L. Imbarrato, Carolyn Brooks

* Closed Dec. 19, 1976 after limited engagement of 22 performances.

(Gary Wheeler Photo)

**Michael Makman, Anthony Lawrence
in "The Boys from Syracuse"**

EQUITY LIBRARY THEATRE

Opened Thursday, January 13, 1977.*
Equity Library Theatre presents:

TWELFTH NIGHT

By William Shakespeare; Director, Richard Mogavero; Set, Michael Sharp; Lighting, Robby Monk; Costumes, Donna Meyer; Weaponry, Eric Uhler; Hairstylist, J. Alexander Scafa; Music Coordinators, Randee Berman, Didi Charney; Wardrobe Mistress, Robin Schram

CAST

Orsino	Michael Maurice
Curio/Priest	Robert Zukerman
Valentino/Officer #1	Dana Hart
Musician/Lady in waiting	Didi Charney
Musician/Lady in waiting	Randee Berman
Viola	Pam Rogers
Sea Captain/Officer #2	Stan Buturla
Sir Toby Belch	Jared Matesky
Maria	Marie Tommon
Sir Andrew Aguecheek	Richard Peterson
Feste	Bill Roberts
Lady Olivia	Judy Levitt
Malvolio	Ronald Willoughby
Sebastian	Michael LaGue
Antonio	Jim Broaddus
Fabian	Cameron Smith

A comedy in 2 acts and 18 scenes. The action takes place in Illyria and the nearby seacoast.

Press: Sol Jacobson, Lewis Harmon
Stage Managers: Victoria Merrill, William F. Condee, Gina Willens

* Closed Jan. 23, 1977 after limited engagement of 14 performances

Gary Wheeler Photo

**Pam Rogers, Richard Peterson
in "Twelfth Night"**

COME BACK, LITTLE SHEBA

By William Inge; Director, Ron Troutman; Scenery, Linda Skipper; Lighting, Jeremy Craig Johnson; Costumes, Sharon Buchs; Original Music, David Friedman; Assistant Director, Robin Thomsen; Sound, Bill O'Dell; Props, Robin Schram

CAST

Doc	Stan Lachow
Marie	Shelli Place
Lola	Joan Lowell
Turk	Edward O'Ross
Postman	Del Willard
Mrs. Coffman	Elaine Grollman
Milkman	Allen Fitzpatrick
Messenger	Stephen Stewart-James
Bruce	David Okarski
Ed Anderson	Mark Weston
Elmo Huston	Nick Harrison

A play in 2 acts and 6 scenes. The action takes place in an old house in a run-down neighborhood of a Midwestern city.

Press: Lewis Harmon, Sol Jacobson
Stage Managers: K. Anna Moore, Stephen Stewart-James, Ana Pacheco

* Closed Feb. 20, 1977 after limited engagement of 14 performances.

Gary Wheeler Photo

Top Right: Joan Lowell, Elaine Grollman

**Donna Liggitt Forbes (L), Ed Dixon,
Cathy Brewer-Moore (R)**

WONDERFUL TOWN

Book, Joseph Fields, Jerome Chodorov; Based on their play, "My Sister Eileen," and the stories of Ruth McKenney; Music, Leonard Bernstein; Lyrics, Betty Comden, Adolph Green; Director, Bolen High; Choreographer, Dennis Grimaldi; Music Director, James Stenborg; Set, Darrell K. Keister; Costumes, William Campbell; Lighting, Craig Miller; Pianos, James Stenborg, Tony Grealis; Drums, Bruce Pachtman; Millinery, Fran Rosethal; Hairstylist, Gary Stavens; Assistant to Director, Sue Breeze; Props, Judith Klug

CAST

Guide/Editor/Shore Patrol/Policeman	Stephen Howard
Appopolous	Loukas Skipitaris
Helen	Elizabeth Austin
Wreck	Paul Ukena, Jr.
Violet	Melanie Winter
Valenti	Bruce Robinson
Eileen	Donna Liggitt Forbes
Ruth	Cathy Brewer-Moore
Strange Man/Cadet/Policeman	Michael Gallagher
Drunk/Cadet/Policeman	Patrick Hardy
Drunk/Cadet/Policeman	Rick DeFilipps
Robert Baker	Ed Dixon
Associate Editor/Cadet/Ruth's Escort	Bill Nolte
Mrs. Wade	Patty O'Brien
Frank Lippencott	Jamie Widdoes
Delivery Boy/Cadet/Policeman	Jerry Ziaja
Chick Clark	Richard Stack

GREENWICH VILLAGERS: Riselle Bain, Laura DuDell, Terry Gene, Susan Streater, Rick DeFilipps, Michael Gallagher, Patrick Hardy, Stephen Howard, Bill Nolte, Brad Witsger, Jerry Ziaja

MUSICAL NUMBERS: "On Christopher Street," "Ohio," "One Hundred Easy Ways," "What a Waste," "Story Vignettes," "A Little Bit of Love," "Pass the Football," "Conversation Piece," "A Quiet Girl," "Conga," "My Darlin' Eileen," "Swing," "It's Love," "Dance at the Vortex," "Wrong Note Rag"

A musical in 2 acts and 13 scenes. The action takes place in New York City in 1935.

Press: Sol Jacobson, Lewis Harmon
Stage Managers: Don Judge, Pat Trott, Daniel Morris, Kathleen Robey

* Closed March 27, 1977 after limited run of 22 performances.

Gary Wheeler Photo

ARSENIC AND OLD LACE

By Joseph Kesselring; Director, Susan Schulman; Scenery, Patrick Mann; Lighting, Joel Levine; Costumes, Wendy Pierson; Music Composed by Andy Bloor; Wardrobe Mistress, Bebe Sacks Landis; Props, Rose Podrasky, Vicki Sussman; Hair Stylists, Rick Zuccarelli, Jackie Nicole

CAST

Abby Brewster	Frances Pole
Rev. Dr. Harper	Robert Davis
Teddy Brewster	Herbert DuVal
Officer Brophy	Michael A. Hartman
Officer Klein	Rick Petrucelli
Martha Brewster	Georgia Southcotte
Elaine Harper	Sarah Brooke
Mortimer Brewster	Chet Carlin
Mr. Gibbs	Jim Fitzpatrick
Jonathan Brewster	William Metzo
Dr. Einstein	James Cook
Mr. Hoskins	J. Mauer
Mr. Spenalzo	M. Judith
Officer O'Hara	Anthony Scipio
Lt. Rooney	Russell Costen
Mr. Witherspoon	Mike J. Murray

A comedy in 3 acts and 4 scenes. The action takes place in the Brewster home in Brooklyn in 1941.

Press: Lewis Harmon, Sol Jacobson
Stage Managers: Victor A. Gelb, Judy Mauer

* Closed April 24, 1977 after limited engagement of 14 performances.

Gary Wheeler Photo

Top Right: Georgia Southcotte, Frances Pole, William Metzo in "Arsenic and Old Lace"

SILK STOCKINGS

Music and Lyrics, Cole Porter; Book, George S. Kaufman, Leueen MacGrath, Abe Burrows; Set, William Rowe; Lighting, Paul Mathiesen; Costume Coordination, Joyce Aysta; Musical Direction and Arrangements, Robert Plowman; Musical Staging and Choreography, Karin Baker; Director, Richard Michaels

CAST

Brankov	Armin Shimerman
Ivanov	Neil Elliot
Bibinski	David St. James
Desk Clerk/Reporter	Van Craig
Mlle. Fabour/Anna	Jan Maris
Peter Boroff	James LeVaggi
Steve Canfield	Mark Zimmerman
Choreographer/Photographer	Terry Brown
Guards	Van Craig, Karl Heist
Russian Ballerinas	Elaine Horton, Lynne Fursa, Debra Pigliavento, Wendy Stuart
V. Markovitch	David Emge
Vera/Shopgirl	Jan Neuberger
Nina Yoschenko	Carolyn Kirsch
Janice Dayton	Carole Schweid

ENSEMBLE: Terry Brown, Van Craig, Lynne Fursa, Karl Heist, Elaine Horton, Debra Pigliavento, Wendy Stuart, and Pit Singers: Marsha Best, Marilyn Hiratzka, Charles Whiteside

MUSICAL NUMBERS: "Too Bad," "Ode to a Tractor," "Stereophonic Sound," "Paris Loves Lovers," "Chemical Reaction," "All of You," "Satin and Silk," "Silk Stockings Ballet," "Without Love," "Fated to be Mated," "Josephine," "Silk Stockings," "The Red Blues."

A musical in two acts. The action takes place in Paris and Moscow in the late 1930's.

Press: Sol Jacobson, Lewis Harmon
Stage Managers: Barry J. W. Steinman, Debbie Ann Thompson, Dolly Colby

* Closed May 22, 1977 after limited engagement of 22 performances.

Gary Wheeler Photo

Mark Zimmerman, Carolyn Kirsch in "Silk Stockings"

EQUITY LIBRARY THEATRE INFORMALS

George Wojtasik, Managing Director
Lynn Montgomery, Production Director
Ann B. Grassilli, Producer ELT Informals

LINCOLN CENTER LIBRARY & MUSEUM
Equity Library Theatre Informals Series presents:
September 23–25, 1976 (3 performances)

RICHARD ERICSON ANDERS: Production Concept and Staging, Patrick Arena; Musical Director/Piano, Elliot Finkel; Lighting, Merrie Handfinger; Percussion, Jim Erwin; Bass, Perry Sheldon

October 18–20, 1976 (3 performances)
WORDS AND FOUR PLAY with Music by Martin Silvestri; Book and Lyrics, Tony Tanner; Director, Jeffrey Dunn; Musical Direction and Arrangements, John Kroner; Scenery, Harry Lines; Lighting, Merri Handfinger, Tommy Kennedy; Costumes, E. Susan Erenburg; Stage Managers, Roger Shea, Ed Chemaly; Assistant Musical Director, Daniel Glosser; Choreographic Assistant, William Michael Maher. CAST: Susan Marchand (Julie), Greg Macosko (Bill), Charles Ryan (Ted), Marilyn Pasekoff (Buzz)

December 6–8, 1976 (3 performances)
PLAY ME, ZOLTAN by Lucas Myers; Director, Charles Maggiore; Set, Randi Frank; Lighting, Daniel Ionazzi; Costumes, Cynthia Goatley; Assistant Director, Susan Loughran; Stage Manager, Esther Kamalay; Production Assistant, Jim Fainberg. CAST: Al Nazario (Rafael), Jerry Matz (Zoltan), Carolyn Chrisman (Lilli), Sonny Adams (Effie), Herb Aronson (Costas), Margo Duke (Liana) Lynne Charnay (Liesl), Leslie Barrett (Warfield), Nancy LeBrun (Evelyn), Ron Lawrence (John), Ruth Livingston (Catherine), Joan Mollison (Zuszsi)

January 24–26, 1977 (3 performances)
THE STRUGGLE BETWEEN MEN AND WOMEN AS SEEN THROUGH OPERA and ANTIGONE: Narration written by Stuart Michaels; Director, Stuart Michaels; Musical Director, Norman Carey; Sets and Costumes, Gina Taulane; Lights, Paul Mathiesen; Stage Manager, Joanne Maiello; Assistant Musical Director, Lois Poppe; Narrator, Tad Motyka. Part I: Duets and Arias from five operas sung by Donna Casella, Sally Mitchell, Jay Pierce, Tad Motyka, George Maguire, Betsy Beard, Linda Mulrean, Neil Semer, Part II: "Antigone" with music and libretto by Lou Rodgers, and sung by Trude Wallace or Donna Emmanuel (Antigone), Betsy Beard (Ismene), Jay Pierce (Warrior), Linda Mulrean (Messenger), Donna Casella or Sally Mitchell (Eurydice), Lois Poppe (Calliope), Tad Motyka (Haemon), George Maguire (Creon), Neil Semer (Tiresias)

February 7–9, 1977 (3 performances)
DIVERTISEMENT directed by Jack Dyville; Musical Director, Donald Gordon Jones; Original Music, Thomas Helm; Lighting/ Stage Manager, Larry Brumer; Assistant Choreographer, David Westphal. CAST: Jacki Garland, Lois Hathaway, Kurt Johnson, Mary Ann Strossner

March 21–23, 1977 (3 performances)
SVENGALI WAS A LADY! by Allen S. Houston; Director, Sam As-Said; Production Manager, Woody Eney; Costumes, Richard MacKay; Set, D. John Armstrong; Technical Director, Richard Blankenship; Stage Manager, Ellen Katz. CAST: William Pitts (Roger), Carolyn Mignini (Lulu), Sam As-Said (Sammy), Sherry Eney (Sally), Doreen Dunn (Marj), Hal Studer (Gentleman Caller)

April 18–20, 1977 (3 performances)
MILLIONS OF MILES by Elliot Taubenslag, and MOLLY BLOOM freely adapted by Donna Wilshire from the last chapter of James Joyce's novel "Ulysses"; Director, Donna Wilshire; Designer/Technical Director, Roger Paradiso; Assistant to Director, Felicia Balicer; Stage Managers, Gregory Roach, Neal Brilliant. CAST: "Millions of Miles": Rod Houts (Walter Knoblock), Elaine Grollman (Edna Brennan), Patricia Guinan (Katherine Knoblock), "Molly Bloom": Helga Kopperl (Molly)

May 16–18, 1977 (3 performances)
NOT BACK WITH THE ELEPHANTS conceived and directed by David Pursley; a collage of scenes, sketches and commentaries about the theatre and its inhabitants from the pages of "Vanity Fair" magazine; David Krane at the piano. CAST: Reathel Bean, Richard Blair, Linda Daugherty, Jack Godby, Julie Kurnitz

(No photos available)

HUDSON GUILD THEATRE

Craig Anderson, Producing Director
Dennis Luzak, Production Manager

HUDSON GUILD THEATRE
October 13–31, 1976 (12 performances)
THE DIARY OF ANNE FRANK by Frances Goodrich and Albert Hackett; Director, Craig Anderson; Set, Tom Warren; Lighting, Rick Belzer; Costumes, Michele Suzanne Reisch; Technical Director, Art Soyk; Stage Managers, Edward Fitzgerald, Fran Albin. CAST: Stan Lachow (Mr. Frank), Susan Willerman (Miep), Fran Anthony (Mrs. Van Daan), Louis Terenne (Mr. Van Daan), Mark Winkworth (Peter), Dorothy Lancaster (Mrs. Frank), Catherine Schreiber (Margot), Susan Sharkey (Anne Frank), Bob Horen (Mr. Kraler), John Wylis (Mr. Dussel), Princess (Mooshi)

November 5-21, 1976 (11 performances)
THE WOBBLIES by Stewart Bird and Peter Robilotta; Director, C. R. Portz; Set, Bruce Monroe; Projections, Peter Smallman; Lighting, Gregg Marriner; Costumes, Louise Martinez; Musical Direction, Martin Burman; Assistant Director, Stewart Bird; Props, Larry May; Production Manager, Terry Uppenberg; Stage Manager, Michael DeMarzo. CAST: C. R. Portz (Vandeveer), Peter McRobbie (Nebbeker), Alfred Cherry (Judge Landis), William G. Schilling (Narrator), Larry Fleischman (J. T. Doran), Walter Blocher (William D. Haywood), Alan Bluestone (Hooten/Samuel Gompers/Organizer/William Wood/Congressman Berger), David Kabat (Tussy/J. Edgar Hoover/Shorty/John Golden), Phil Levy (Spy/-Clarence Darrow/Otto Stolp/Len), Bette Craig (Elizabeth Gurley Flynn/Stenographer/Dr. Shapley), Jennifer Thompson (Camella Teoli/Haywood's Daughter)

December 2-19, 1976 (12 performances)
THE ADMIRABLE CRICHTON by J. M. Barrie; Director, Craig Anderson; Sets, Mary Beth Mann; Lighting, Rick Belzer; Costumes, Michele Suzanne Reisch; Props, Dott Dolson; Music, Andy Bloor; Technical Director, Art Soyk; Stage Manager, Edward R. Fitzgerald. CAST: Jarion Monroe (Mr. Crichton), Richmond Hoxie (Hon. Ernest Woolley), Claudia Zahn (Lady Agatha Lasenby), Robyn Reeves (Lady Catherine Lasenby), Leah Chandler (Lady Mary Lasenby), Lucky Noll (Rev. John Treherne), Thomas Barbour (Earl of Loam), Lowry Miller (Lord Brocklehurst), Elizabeth Swain (Tweeny), J. Douglas James (Naval Officer), Dorothy Lancaster (Lady Brocklehurst), Servants: Mark Barnhart, Anne Brisk, Barbara Hladsky, J. Douglas James, Robert Lagersen, Robin Reiter, Naomi Rossabi, Art Soyk, Mary Lois Vann, Lawrence Zucker

(Simon Robert Newey Photo)

**Claudia Zahn, Leah Chandler, Robyn Reeves
in "The Admirable Crichton"**

HUDSON GUILD THEATRE

January 11–30, 1977 (24 performances)
CREDITORS and THE STRONGER and MISS JULIE by August
Strindberg; New translation by Palaemona Morner, R. Spacek; Sets,
John Wright Stevens, Rick Belzer; Costumes, Madeline O'Connor;
Choreography, John Montgomery; Music, Andy Bloor; Stage Managers, James W. Pentecost, Dan Zittel; Production Assistants,
Jeremy Peterson, John Kerr. Performed in repertory. CAST: "The
Stronger" (Rip Torn, Director) with Geraldine Page (Mrs. X), Amy
Wright (Mrs. Y), Judith L'Heureux (Waitress), "Creditors" (James
Kendell, Director) with John Heard (Adolf), Rip Torn (Gustav),
Geraldine Page (Tekla), Tom Hurt (Waiter), Amy Wright, Jeremy
Peterson, "Miss Julie" (James Kendell, Director) with Geraldine
Page (Kristin), Rip Torn (Jean), Amy Wright (Miss Julie), Peter
Jolly (Count), Musicians: Elise Bernhardt, Lucinda Zeising, Farm
Folk: Kim Ameen, Pat Graf, Tom Hurt, Russel Martin Hubert,
Peter Jolly, Judith L'Heureux, William Perley, Jeremy Peterson

February 24– March 13, 1977 (13 performances)
SAVAGES by Christopher Hampton; Director, Gordon Davidson;
Indian Scenes, Kenneth Brechner; Settings and Costumes, Sally
Jacobs; Lighting, John Gleason; Stage Managers, Wendy Caster,
Larry Harbison; Makeup, Robert Ryan; Motion Picture Sequence,
Gregory S. Dinallo. CAST: Joseph Maher (Alan West), Stephen
Joyce (Mark Crawford), Alice Drummond (Mrs. West), Mandy
Patinkin (Carlos) Leslie Barrett (Maj. Brigg), Ernie Fierron (Chief/-
Bert), Louis Beachner (Rev. Penn), Valcour Lavizzo (Kumai), Saylor Creswell (Investigator), Shelly Desai (Ataide Pereira),
Integrados: Glenn Cabrera, Donald F. Berman, Jose Montalbo,
Tribe: Josette Bailey, Raul Aranas, Hortensia Colorado, Orlando
Dole, Martin Marinaro, Katherine Jeannette Riley, Ted Sod

April 22–May 15, 1977
DANCE ON A COUNTRY GRAVE Book, Music, and Lyrics,
Kelly Hamilton; Based on Thomas Hardy's "The Return of the
Native"; Director, Robert Brewer; Musical Sequences Staged and
Choreographed by Dennis Grimaldi; Musical Direction and Arrangements, Bill Grossman; Setting, Tom Warren; Costumes,
Donna Meyer; Lighting, Curt Osterman; Assistant Musical Director, Eric Diamond; Stage Managers, Barbara Goldstein, Mary Jane
DeFroscia. CAST: Ghost Children: Bella Sirugo, Carol Sirugo,
Gena Feist, Sam Freed (Diggory Ven), Donna Theodore (Eustacia
Vye), Mike Dantuono (Damon Wildeve), Fiddle Viracola (Susan
Nunsuch), Gail Kellstrom (Tess), Susan Berger (Olly Dowden),
Paul Rosson (Grandfer Cantle), Timothy Wallace (Timothy Fairway), John B. Giletto (Humphrey), Kate Kelly (Thomasin Yeobright), Elizabeth Owens (Mrs. Yeobright), Trip Plymale (Christian
Cantle), Deborah McHale (Jane Orchard), Carmen Peterson (Bathsheba), Jim Frank (Sam), Kevin Kline (Clym Yeobright)

Press: Howard Atlee, Clarence Allsopp, Becky Flora

Marinaro, Simon Robert Newey Photos

**Top Right: Alfred Cherry, Walter Blocher,
C. R. Portz in "The Wobblies" Below:
Joseph Maher, Stephen Joyce
in "Savages"**

**Catherine Schreiber, Stan Iachow, Dorothy
Lancaster in "Diary of Anne Frank"**

**Donna Theodore, Kevin Kline
in "Dance on a Country Grave"**

JOSEPH JEFFERSON THEATRE COMPANY

Cathy Roskam, Executive Director
Connie Alexis, General Manager

THE LITTLE CHURCH AROUND THE CORNER
October 27–November 13, 1976
U. S. A. by Paul Shyre and John Dos Passos; Director, John Henry Davis; Musical Director, Norma Curley; Choreographer, Merry Lynn Katis; Set, Raymond C. Recht; Costumes, A. Christina Giannini; Lighting, Francis Roefaro; Technical Director, Gerald Weinstein; Costume Mistress/Technical Assistant, Judyth Goldschmidt; Stage Managers, Evan Canary, Dominic A. Cammarota; Press, Anne Einhorn, Joyce Reed. CAST: John Getz (Moorehouse), Reathel Bean (Debs/Joe Williams/Edgecombe/Bingham), Allan Carlsen (Dick Savage/Ollie Taylor), Nita Novy (Janey Williams), Linda Barnhurst (Gertrude), Anne C. Twomey (Eleanor Stoddard/Isadora)

December 1–18, 1976 (12 performances)
THE WELL adapted from Noh Plays by Seymour Reiter; Music, Mitsuo Kitamura; Director, Julianne Boyd; Choreography, Kazuko Hirabayashi; Set and Costumes, Bill Groom; Lighting, Boyd Masten; Technical Director, Gerald Weinstein; Costume Mistress, Andy Hoppe; Stage Manager, Abigail Harper. CAST: Ralph Braun (Priest), Sonya Baehr (Girl), Cris Groenendaal (Husband), Richard T. Alpers (Boatman), Bill Randolph (1st Officer), Sheldon Silver (2nd Officer), Ensemble: Martha Ihde, Marcy Jellison, Nancy Cook, Leslie Middlebrook, Gary Barker, Alston Campbell, Richard T. Alpers, Bob White, Instrumentalists: Ron Leighty, Bob Ford, Deborah Knaack

February 2–19, 1977 (12 performances)
JOHNNY BELINDA by Elmer Harris; Director, William Koch; Set, Gerald Weinstein; Costumes, Cindy Polk; Lighting, Richard B. Williams; Sound, William Stallings; Props, Cherie M. Secter; Stage Managers, Evan Canary, Judyth Goldschmidt; Assistant to Director, Jim Fauvell; Costume Mistress, Judith Fauvell; Props, Debbie Carter. CAST: June Stein (Belinda), Reathel Bean (Dr. Jack), David Mack (Jimmy Dingwell), Robert Lanchester (Black McDonald), Frank Luz (Locky McCormick), Jan Granger (Stella), Linda Lashbrook (Mrs. McKee), Beverly Knapp (Lizzie/Mrs. McKee), Ruth Wallman (Gracie/Mrs. Lutz), Mark Hattan (Andy McPhearson/Rev. Tidmarsh)

PRINCE GEORGE HOTEL
April 27–May 14, 1977 (12 performances)
SKATERS by Ted Pezzulo; Director, Bill Herndon; Set, Bill Groom; Costumes, A. Christina Giannini; Lighting, Ronald B. Lindholm; Technical Director, Gerald Weinstein; Production Coordinator, William Stallings; Props, Richard George; Stage Managers, Marion Finkler, Dominic A. Cammarota. CAST: Jennifer Dawson (Nurse Dedrick), Rosemary McNamara (Carrie Monte), Richard Zavaglia (Nick Monte), Roger DeKoven (Wilhelm Kurtz), Anita Bayless (Freda Belden), Demo DiMartile (Andy Monte)

Michael Uffer Photos

Top Right: Reathel Bean in "U.S.A."
Below: June Stein, Frank Luz
in "Johnny Belinda"

Anita Bayless, Rosemary McNamara,
Richard Zavaglia, Roger DeKoven in "Skaters"

Sonya Behr
in "The Well"

LION THEATRE COMPANY

Directors, Gene Nye, Garland Wright
Managing Director, Ellie Meglio

LION THEATRE COMPANY

July 4–25, 1976 (18 performances)
LOVE'S LABOUR'S LOST by William Shakespeare; Director, Gene Nye; Set, John Arnone; Lighting, Frances Aronson; Costumes, Rita Barbera; Choreography, Kathy Kramer; Music Written and Performed by Carol Hall; Music Produced by Bob Sakayawa; Sound, Maureeen Forrester; Production Assistants, Jerry Franklin, David Silberger; Stage Managers, Ian McCall, Eric Segal. CAST: David Gallagher (King of Navarre), Chip Brenner (Berowne), Michael J. Cutt (Longaville), Bram Lewis (Dumaine), Gibson Glass (Dull), John Guerrasio (Costard), Ray Fry (Don Adriano de Armado), Joshua Daniel (Mote), Janice Fuller (Jaquenetta), Leland Moss (Boyet), Linda Carlson (Princess of France), Wanda Bimson (Maria), Mary Wright (Katharine), Eda Zahl (Rosaline), Greg Michaels (Sir Nathaniel), Ron Van Lieu (Holofernes), Jeremiah Trebor (Marcade), Lords: Jim McClure, Greg Grove

August 3–22, 1976 (18 performances)
A NIGHT AT THE BLACK PIG by Charles Nolte; Director, Larry Carpenter; Costumes, David Murin; Lighting, Frances Aronson; Set, Miguel Romero; Music, Gregg Almquist; Production Assistant, Jerry Franklin; Stage Managers, Ian McColl, Eric Segal; Props, Maureen Forrester; Company Director, Garland Wright. CAST: Dawn Didawick (Geraldine), Wanda Bimson (White Roach), Ron Van Lieu (Ola Hannson), John Arnone (Gunnar Heiberg), Helga Kopperel (Laura), Warrington Winters (Dr. Asch), Monica Merryman (Aspasia), David Chandler (Popoffsky), Janice Fuller (Mama Turke), James McLure (Kitchen Rat), Sarah Brooke (Mitzi), Murray Moss (Newspaperman), Julie MacKenzie (Frida Uhl), John Genke (Richard Dehmel), Lorraine James (Mme. Geyer), Mary E. Baird (Emancipated Woman), Ted Forlow (Strindberg), Kim Ameen (Blind Margaret), Gregg Almquist (Wirsen/Police Lt.), Dean Tulipane (Policeman/Bartender)

September 2–26, 1976 (20 performances)
MARATHON '33 by June Havoc; Direction and Design, Garland Wright; Musical; Direction, John McKinney; Costumes, David James; Lighting, Frances Aronson; Props, Michael Badalucco; Stage Managers, Ian McColl, Dorothy Maffei, Don Wright. CAST: Chip Brenner (Mr. James), Jack Deisler (Beezer), Mary E. Baird (Matron/ Angel), Dean Tulipane (Pete), William Metzo (Rudd/M.C.), Barbara LeBrunn (Evie), Cynthia Frost (Sugar Hips Johnson), Jeff Eagle (Lusty), Lynn Martin (Rita Marimba/Melba Marvel), Steven Burney (Scotty Schwartz), Evalyn Baron (Pearl Schwartz), Susan Nell Schneider (Robin), Cliff Cannon (Robin's Partner), Haskell Gordon (Bozo), Reuben Schafer (Abe O'Brien), Peter Johl (Beefy/Forbes), Donna Gabel (Mick), Maryin Brasch (Helen Bazoo), Sally Sockwell (Ida/Pinky), David Dean (Red/Hinky), Herman O. Arbeit (Dankle), Richard Stack (Patsy), Julie MacKenzie (June), Mary Ellen Ashley (Flo Marconi), Steven Burch (Al Marconi), Bella Jarrett (Rae Wilson), David MacEnulty (Schnozz), Janice Fuller (Mrs. Beckett-Jones/Nightclub Star), Jonathan Slaff (Minister/Spectator), Quincy Long (Legionaire/Spectator), Young Spectators: Barbara Arbeit, Vincent Metzo

LION THEATRE COMPANY

October 19–November 7, 1976 (18 performances)
A BIRD IN THE HAND by George Feydeau; Translated and Adapted by Edward Stern, Anne Ward Stern; Director, Leland Moss; Costumes, Susan Denison; Set and Lights, Jim Stewart; Musical Adviser, John McKinney; Technicians, Steve Burney, Clif Gannon; Stage Managers, Don Wright, Linda Robin Morris. CAST: Haskell Gordon (Pacarel), Maria Cellario (Martha), Brian Hartigan (Landernau), Laurie Heineman (Julie), Janice Fuller (Amandine), David Gallagher (Tiburce), Gene Nye (Dufausett), Ron Van Lieu (Lanoix de Vaux)

November 26–December 23, 1976 (24 performances)
VISIONS OF KEROUAC by Martin Duberman; Director, Kenneth Frankel; Set, John Arnone; Lighting, Frances Aronson; Costumes, Ruth A. Wells; Sound, Bernie Wajchman, Stephen Nasuta, Arthur Karp; Stage Managers, Alma Negro, Jim McLure, Linda Morris. CAST: James Handy (Cameron), Lane Smith (Jack Kerouac), Brian Hartigan (Wiman), Gregg Almquist (Carber), Tom Foley (Moore), Robert Picardo (Irwin), Joe Pantoliano (Raphael), Michael Wager (Hubbard), Katharine Manning (Ruthie), William Russ (Cody), Kristen Griffith (Mary Lou), Chip Brenner (Officer), Julia Barr (Evelyn), Daniel Keyes (Emil Kerouac), Blance Dee (Gabrielle Kerouac), Morgan Kester (Tristessa), Gabriel Yorke (Simon), Jack Deisler (Cacoethes), Darlene Wasko (Princess), John Spencer (Japhy), Brett Clarin (Timmy), Jim McLure (Joey), Barbara Tarbuck (Stella Kerouac)

January 28–March 27, 1977 (52 performances)
PEG O' MY HEART by J. Hartley Manners; Director, Gene Nye; Set, Miguel Romero; Lighting, Joseph Spencer; Costumes, David James; Assistant to Director, John Guerrasio; Dialect Coach, Liz Smith; Technical Director, Thom Shovestull; Props, Pam Belyea, Stage Managers, Andrea Naier, Mary E. Baird; CAST: Gibson Glass (Jarvis), Mary E. Baird (Bennett), Kathleen Tremaine (Mrs. Chichester), Sandra Halperin (Ethel), Jim Ricketts (Alaric), Donovan Sylvest (Brent), Sofia Landon (Peg), Ken Costigan (Montgomery Hawkes), Allan Carlsen (Jerry)

April 15–May 15, 1977 (18 performances)
FOR THE USE OF THE HALL by Oliver Hailey; Director, Ron Van Lieu; Lights, James Chaleff; Set, Miguel Romero; Costumes, David Murin; Assistant Director, Mitch Kaplan; Production Manager, Dorothy Maffei; Stage Manager, Laurie F. Stone; Props, Jay Embree; Production Assistants, Shelli Shier, Charles Kopelman. CAST: Eileen Burns (Bess), David Gallagher (Allen), Sharon Laughlin (Charlotte), Evalyn Baron (Terry), Barbara LeBrunn (Alice), Ted Tinling (Martin)

Sharon Laughlin, David Gallagher in "For the Use of the Hall"

(Ron Reagan Photo)

Top: Laurie Heineman, Ron Van Lieu in "Bird in the Hand" Below: Lane Smith, William Russ in "Visions of Kerouac"

(Nathaniel Tileston Photo)

THE LIGHT OPERA OF MANHATTAN

William Mount-Burke, Producer-Director
Raymond Allen, Associate Director

EASTSIDE PLAYHOUSE

June 2, 1976–May 29, 1977

Producer-Director, William Mount-Burke; Associate Director, Raymond Allen; Business Manager-Press, Mark J. L. Somers; Stage Manager-Choreographer, Gerald Gotham; Assistant Musical Director, Brian Molloy; Musical Assistant, J. Michael Bart; Sets, Elouise Meyer, Bill Schroder; Lighting, Peggy Clark; Costumes, George Stinson, Bill Schroder

COMPANY

PRINCIPALS: Raymond Allen, Diane Armistead, Paula Bailey, Jeanne Beauvais, Christopher Biehn, Tom Boyd, Dennis Britten, Maureen Burns, Dennis Curran, Elizabeth Devine, Rebecca Dorman, Dennis English, Susan Greenleaf, Lloyd Harris, Michael Harrison, G. Michael Harvey, Nancy Hoffman, Paul Huck, Edward Hustwit, Michael Irwin, Joanne Jamieson, Clevedon Kingston, Joan Lader, Peter Ludwig, David Mallard, Ethel Mae Mason, Rob Main, Georgia McEver, Terry McNulty, Mary Moore, Joanne Morris, James Nadeaux, Rhea Nierenstein, Elaine Olbrycht, John Palmore, Kristin Paulus, Vashek Pazdera, Gary Pitts, Steven Polcek, Gary Ridley, Julio Rosario, Kenneth Sieger, Richard Smithies, Elizabeth Tanner, James Weber, Eleanor Wold, Mark Wolff, Rosemarie Wright, Kathryn Zetto

CHORUS: Stephen Anderson, Colette Antosca, Gail August, Eric Brothers, Ellen Brown, Stephen Brown, Elizabeth Campbell, Philip Carrubba, Jan Downing, Louis Esposito, Jim Farnsworth, Carol Felner, Christine Fontanelli, Queenie Goldman, Barbara Guerard, Corrina Hall, Ed Harrison, Stuart Jahre, Douglas James, Nelson Jewell, Lee Kelley, Louis Klaff, Lisa Landis, Christy Larimer, Amy Lavietes, Constance Little, Anne Marie Lowell, David Marjules, Mary Miller, Maureen McNamara, Vicki Piper, Frank Prieto, Jo Shelnutt, Elizabeth Spellman, Jack Sweeney, Andrea Wright

PRODUCTIONS

"The Student Prince," "The Merry Widow," "Naughty Marietta," "The Vagabond King," "H.M.S. Pinafore," "The Mikado," "The Pirates of Penzance," "Ruddigore," "Princess Ida," "The Yeoman of the Guard," "Utopia, Limited"

Arlene Avril Photos

Right Center: Georgia McEver, Raymond Allen in "The Student Prince" Above: Michael Harrison in "The Merry Widow" Top: Georgia McEver, Raymond Allen in "Yeoman of the Guard"

Raymond Allen, Eleanor Wold in "The Mikado"

Kenneth Sieger, Jeanne Beauvais, Gary Ridley in "The Merry Widow"

131

MANHATTAN THEATRE CLUB

Artistic Director, Lynne Meadow; Managing Director, Barry Grove; Associate Artistic Director, Stephen Pascal; Associate Director, Thomas Bullard; Press, Robert Pontarelli, Caryn Katkin; Technical Director, Robert Buckler; Business Manager, Stanley Bernstein; Administrative Assistant, Diane de Mailly; Technical Assistant, Betsy Tanner; Playwright-in-Residence, Jonathan Levy; Sound Designers, George Hansen, Charles London

June 3–12, 1976
THE WISE WOMAN AND THE KING by Carl Orff; Director, David Shookhoff; Set and Costumes, Steve Rubin; Lighting, Dennis Parichy; Musical Director, Robert Rogers; Additional Musical Staging, Sam Bayes; Stage Manager, Rachael Lindhart. CAST: David Anchel, Sean Barker, Thomas Brooks, Gary Crow-Willard, Harry Danner, Ray Hickman, Gloria Johnson, Keith Lockhart, John Shackelford

October 20–November 14, 1976 (24 performances)
CHILDREN by A. R. Gurney, Jr.; Based on story by John Cheever; Director, Melvin Bernhardt; Set, Marjorie Kellogg; Costumes, Patricia McGourty; Lighting, Arden Fingerhut; Stage Manager, Mark Paquette. CAST: Holland Taylor (Barbara), Dennis Howard (Randy), Nancy Marchand (Mother), Swoosie Kurtz (Jane), Gary Smith (Pokey)

October 27–November 21, 1976
CRACKED TOKENS with Robert Frania, Joann A. Lipari, Pam Moller, John Slavin, Mary Steenburgen

A TOAST TO COMDEN AND GREEN directed by Norman L. Berman; Musical Director, Jim DeHaven; New Vocal Arrangements, Donald Oliver; Stage Manager, James Harker. CAST: Barbara Hartman, Scott Robertson, Carole Schweid, Michael Wickenheiser

November 4–21, 1976 (18 performances)
CLAW by Howard Barker; Director, Stephen Pascal; Set, John Gisondi; Costumes, Rachel Kurland; Lighting, Carol Waaser; Stage Manager, Amy Shecter. CAST: Peter Boyden (Lusby), Michael Burg (Lily), Clarence Felder (Biledew), Alan Hawkridge (Noel), Dale Hodges (Christine), Marion Lines (Angie), Geraldine Sherman (Mrs. Biledew), John Tillinger (Clapcott), Y York (Nora)

November 24–December 19, 1976
THEATRE SONGS BY MALTBY AND SHIRE directed by Richard Maltby, Jr.; Music, David Shire; Lyrics, Richard Maltby, Jr.; Stage Manager, Joan Liepman; Musical Director, Tom Babbitt. CAST: Loni Ackerman, Margery Cohen, Michael Tucci

December 2–19, 1976 (12 performances)
BALLYMURPHY by Michael Neville; Director, Ronald Roston; Set, Ernest Allen Smith; Costumes, Joyce Aysta; Lighting, Cheryl Thacker; Stage Manager, Maureen Lynett; Sound, Ellen Zalk. CAST: Neal Arluck (Pvt.), Larry Bryggman (Mickey O'Hanlon), Christopher Curry (Seamus O'Neil), Jay Devlin (Rusty), Bernard Frawley (Fr. Conde Lynch), John Gallogly (Liam), Danny Holland (Cpl.), Roy London (Paddy), Sam McMurray (Otis), Meg Myles (Maggie), Kevin Ottem (Alfie), James Rebhorn (Fr. Gerry Powers), John C. Vennema (Jimmy), Daniel Ziskie (Lt.)

December 8, 1976–January 2, 1977 (24 performances)
ASHES by David Rudkin; Director, Lynne Meadows; Set, John Lee Beatty; Costumes, Jennifer von Mayrhauser; Lighting, Dennis Parichy; Stage Manager, Zane Weiner; Sound, George Hansen, Charles London; Dialogue Coach, Gordon Jacoby. CAST: Penelope Allen (Woman), Roberta Maxwell (Anne), Brian Murray (Colin), John Tillinger (Man)

January 12–23, 1977
SONGS BY GOGGIN AND LORICK; Music, Dan Goggin; Lyrics, Robert Lorick; Stage Manager, Frank Root. CAST: Dan Goggin, Ann Hodapp, Elaine Petricoff, Marvin Solley

January 19–February 13, 1977 (24 performances)
BOESMAN AND LENA by Athol Fugard; Director, Thomas Bullard; Set, Atkin Pace; Costumes, Rachel Kurland; Lighting, Spencer Mosse; Dialect Coach, Gordon Jacoby; Stage Manager, Maureen Lynett. CAST: Robert Christian (Boesman), Frances Foster (Lena), Paul Makgoba (Old African)

Ken Howard Photos

**Clarence Felder, Alan Hawkridge in "Claw"
Top: Holland Taylor, Nancy Marchand,
Swoosie Kurtz, Dennis Howard in "Children"**

**Robert Christian, Frances Foster in "Boesman
and Lena" Above: Neal Arluck, Kevin Ottem
in "Ballymurphy"**

MANHATTAN THEATRE CLUB

January 26–February 20, 1977
SONGS FROM "NELL" directed by David Shookhoff; Music, Peter Schickele; Lyrics, Diane Lampert; From a new musical with book by Dennis Turner and William Green; Design Consultant, Rachel Kurland; Stage Manager, Malcolm Ewen; Musical Director, Jim DeHaven; Additional Musical Staging, Lisa Reswick. CAST: Johanna Albrecht, Sean Barker, Catherine Cox, Thomas Alan Rowe

January 27–February 13, 1977
BILLY IRISH by Thomas Babe; Director, Barry Marshall; Set, Eugene Warner; Costumes, Ken Yount; Lighting, Cheryl Thacker; Stage Manager, Dorothy Maffei; Sound, George Simonson. CAST: Michael Austin, Malcolm Groome, Toni Kalem, Bruce McGill, Lane Smith

February 24–March 13, 1977 (18 performances)
QUAIL SOUTHWEST by Larry Ketron; Director, Andy Wolk; Set, James Joy; Costumes, Susan Tsu; Lighting, Toni Goldin; Stage Manager, Will Maitland Weiss. CAST: Stephanie Gordon (Evy), Munson Hicks (Werth), Zina Jasper (Virginia), Toni Kalem (Barbara), Dick Latessa (Brigan), Amy Nathan (Kerra), Drew Snyder (Caldren), Margot Stevenson (Mrs. Garrett)

March 9–April 3, 1977
SONGS BY SIEGAL & JOSEPH directed by Denny Martin Flinn; Music, Donald Siegal; Lyrics, Robert Joseph; Musical Director, Donald Siegal; Stage Manager, Stephen B. Real. CAST: Kathleen Dezina, Annie McGreevey, Hal Watters

March 2–27, 1977 (18 performances)
THE GATHERING by Edna O'Brien; Director, Austin Pendleton; Set, Patricia Woodbridge; Costumes, Kenneth M. Yount; Lighting, Cheryl Thacker; Stage Manager, Maureen Lynett. CAST: Jane Cronin (Lil O'Shea), Louis Zorich (Jamie O'Shea), Nancy Donohue (Helen), Barbara eda-Young (Carmel), John Gallogly (Gurnet), Molly Scoville (Mrs. Gurnet), Sloane Shelton (Peg), Maria Tucci (Emer), Alan Mixon (Teddy)

Maria Tucci, Alan Mixon in "The Gathering" Top: Amy Nathan, Drew Snyder in "Quail Southwest"

April 6–May 1, 1977
SONGS FROM "THE CONFIDENCE MAN" based on the novel by Herman Melville; Libretto, Ray Errol Fox; Music, Jim Steinman; Lyrics, Ray Errol Fox; Director, Gui Andrisano; Musical Director, Bobby Blume; Stage Manager, John Michael Stringer. CAST: David Eric, Walter Niehenke, Joyce Nolen, Norman Snow

April 7–24, 1977
STATUES/EXHIBITION/THE BRIDGE AT BELHARBOUR by Janet Neipris; Director, Stan Wojewodski, Jr.; Sets, David Potts; Costumes, Bob Wojewodski; Lighting, Ian Calderon; Stage Manager, Paul Schneeberger; Three one-act plays. CAST: Laura Esterman, Michael Higgins, Mark Lonow, Ed Seaman

May 4–29, 1977 (24 performances)
IN THE SUMMER HOUSE by Jane Bowles; Director, Stephen Hollis; Set, John Kasarda; Costumes, Rachel Kurland; Lighting, Dennis Parichy; Original Music, Michael Valenti; Stage Manager, Susana Meyer. CAST: William Carden, Carolyn Coates, Leora Dana, Maria Duval, Christine Estabrook, Janice Fuller, Kristin Griffith, Juliette Modica, Francisco Prado, Antonia Rey, Lupe Garnica, Michael Greif, James Modica, Yvonne Rosetti, Jeff Shandler

May 4–22, 1977
FOUR YEARS AFTER THE REVOLUTION: Theatre Songs by Richard Peaslee; Director, Allan Albert; Costumes, Ann Wallace; Lighting, Dick Williams; Choreography, Dennis Dennehy; Stage Manager, Charles Kopelman. CAST: Shelley Barre, Ralph Bruneau, Jill Eikenberry, James Seymour

May 19–29, 1977 (8 performances)
THE LAST STREET PLAY by Richard Wesley; Director, Thomas Bullard; Set, David Potts; Costumes, Judy Dearing; Lighting, Dennis Parichy; Stage Manager, Amelia R. Haywood. CAST: Morgan Freeman (Zeke), Richard E. Gant (Eldridge), Yvette Hawkins (Rita), Brent Jennings (Tiny), J. Herbert Kerr (Lucky), Roscoe Orman (Frankie), Maurice Woods (Braxton)

May 25–June 12, 1977
NEW COMPOSER'S CABARET directed by Jack Allison; Musical Director, Michael Karp; Stage Manager, Paul Fitzmaurice. CAST: Linda Daugherty, Richard Dunne, Grenoldo Frazier, Sarilee Kahn

Ken Howard Photos

Yvette Hawkins, Roscoe Orman in "The Last Street Play" Above: Carolyn Coates, William Carden in "In the Summer House"

NEGRO ENSEMBLE COMPANY

THEATRE DE LYS
Opened Sunday, December 5, 1976.*
The Negro Ensemble Company (Douglas Turner Ward, Artistic Director; Robert Hooks, Executive Director; Frederick Garrett, Administrative Director; Gerald S. Krone, Director of Special Projects) presents:

THE BROWNSVILLE RAID

By Charles Fuller; Director, Israel Hicks; Set, Neil Peter Jampolis; Costumes, Mary Mease Warren; Lighting, Sandra L. Ross; Production Assistant, Ron Lewis; Technical Director, Dik Krider; Sound, Gwen Gilliam; Wardrobe Supervisor, Marzetta Jones

CAST

Pvt. John Holliman	Adolph Caesar
Pvt. James Newton	Charles Weldon
Sgt. Major Mingo Saunders	Douglas Turner Ward
Pvt. Dorsey Willis	Reyno
Cpl. Clifford Adair	Samm-Art Williams
Pvt. Reuben Collins	Bill Cobbs
Cpl. Boyd Conjers	Arthur French
The Captain	Lawrence Keith
Pvt. Richard Johnson	Wayne Elbert
Dolly Saunders	Ethel Ayler
Orderly	Charles Brown
Mayor Combs	Robert Fitzsimmons
Theodore Roosevelt	Owen Hughes
Emmett Scott	Graham Brown
Major Blocker	William Mooney
General Garlin	Frank Hamilton
Sentry	Sam Finch

A drama in three acts. The action takes place during 1906 in Brownsville, Texas.

General Manager: Coral Hawthorne
Press: Howard Atlee, Clarence Allsopp, Becky Flora
Stage Manager: Horacena J. Taylor

* Closed Feb. 27, 1977 after 112 performances.

Charles Weldon, Samm-Art Williams, Charles Brown, Bill Cobbs, Reyno, Wayne Elbert in "The Brownsville Raid"

THEATRE DeLYS
Opened Wednesday, April 13, 1977.*
The Negro Ensemble Company (Douglas Turner Ward, Artistic Director; Robert Hooks, Executive Director; Frederick Garrett, Administrative Director; Gerald S. Krone, Director of Special Projects) presents:

THE GREAT MacDADDY

By Paul Carter Harrison; Music, Coleridge-Taylor Perkinson; Director, Douglas Turner Ward; Choreography, Dianne McIntyre; Scenery, William Ritman; Lighting, Sandra L. Ross; Technical Director, Dik Krider; Technical Coordinator, Joe Gandy; Wardrobe Supervisors, Herman Cortez, Kaydette Grant; Production Assistant, Marvin Brown

CAST

MacDaddy	Charles Weldon
Scag/Photographer/Skull/Sheriff/Scarecrow/ Humdrum	Bill Mackey
Old Woman/Momma/Mother Faith	Barbara Montgomery
Deacon Jones/Dude/Cowboy	Norman Jacob
Young Woman/Niggertoe/Song	Carol Maillard
Young Man/Dude/Signifyin' Baby	Charles Brown
Wine/Old Grandad/Soldier/Poppa/ Blood Leader	Graham Brown
Shine/Dude/Blood Son	Reyno
Dancer	Joella Breedlove
Leionah	Lynn Whitfield
Bartender/Skulleton/Middlesex	Carl Gordon
Mrs. Middlesex	Charliese Drakeford
Eagle	Newton Winters
Stagolee/Scagolee/Skulleton	Frankie R. Faison
Red Woman/Tree/Dance	Freda T. Vanterpool
Community Members	Kenneth Frett, Jennifer Jarrett, Maggie Stewart, Dennis Williams

A musical in two acts. A ritualized African/American event beginning in the 1930's, and progressing forward and backward in time.

General Manager: Coral Hawthorne
Press: Howard Atlee, Clarence Allsopp, Becky Flora
Stage Managers: Horacena J. Taylor, Clinton Turner Davis

* Closed May 22, 1977 after 48 performances and 8 previews.

Lynn Whitfield, Charles Weldon in "The Great MacDaddy"

THE NEW DRAMATISTS, INC.

Chairman of the Board, L. Arnold Weissberger; President, Mary K. Frank; Administrative Director, Stephen Harty; Workshop Coordinator, Peter Kozik; Administrative Assistant, Deborah Openden; Technical Director, Kenneth Fillo.

June 7–10, 1976 (6 performances)
KEROUAC by Martin Duberman; Director, Kenneth Frankel; Assistant to Director, Arthur Karp; Lights, Michael White; Stage Managers, Michael White, Bob Acito, Paul Lambert, Alma Negro. CAST: James Handy (Cameron), David Chandler (Wiman), Lane Smith (Kerouac), Gregg Almquist (Carver/Cacoethes), Tom Foley (Moore), Daniel Keyes (Emil Kerouac), Blanche Dee (Gabrielle Kerouac), Joe Pantoliano (Raphael), Robert Picardo (Irwin), Katharine Manning (Ruthie/Tristessa), Reno Roop (Wm. Hubbard), William Russ (Cody), Rolanda Mendels (Marylou), Julia Barr (Evelyn), Lynn Lowry (Princess), Tom Bair (Japhy), Jeffrey Lane (Simon), Brett Clarin (Timmy), Bertina Johnson (Billie), Paul Lambert (Joey), Patricia Stewart (Stella Kerouac)

Thursday, September 16, 1976
THE PROMOTION OF ARTAUD WISTAAR by Steven Somkin; Director, Warren Kliewer; Lighting, Ken Fillo. CAST: Ruth Baker (Felicia), Roby Brown (Apple), Bill Cosgriff (Henderson), Ed Crowley (Pfeffer), Ned Farster (Sorites), Mary Gallagher (Imogene), Lance Hewett (Caddis), David Kabat (Lawrence), Terry Layman (Artaud), John Lloyd (Messenger), George Salerno (Berry), Caroline Yaeger (Lily)

Monday, September 20, 1976
THE BESERKERS by Warren Kliewer; Director, Cliff Goodwin. CAST: David Aaron (Johan), Jonathan Bolt (Oscar), Cathy Cieciuch (Young Elizabeth), Joanne Cieciuch (Alice), Gloria Maddox (Elizabeth)

Thursday, October 21, 1976
BRIXTON RECOVERY by Jack Gilhooley; Director, Cliff Goodwin; Lighting, Greg Buch; Stage Manager, Dan Morris. CAST: Shirley Brown (Shirley), Richard Stack (Mickey)

Thursday, November 11, 1977
THE TWO MARYS by Warren Kliewer; Director, Cliff Goodwin; Stage Directions, Deborah Openden. CAST: Nancy Franklin (Mary Williams), Bryan Hull (John Williams), Peter Kozik (Jimmy Selby), Michelle Larue (Mary Petersen)

November 16–20, 1976 (5 performances)
EVEN THE WINDOW IS GONE by Gene Radano; Director, Shan Covey; Lighting, Jo Mayer; Music, Tom Piazza; Costumes, Linda Roots; Stage Manager, Sal Miraldi; Production Assistant, Francine Gindi. CAST: Shelly Batt (Bonnie), Jack Deisler (Domenick), Laura Dowling (Shirley), Susan Marshall (Landlady), Mary Moon (Carmella), William Ostroff (Mel), Garnett Smith (Paul), Diane Tyler (Florence), Dorothy Wilens (Mother), Dan Ziskie (Sal)

December 2–7, 1976 (6 performances)
THE WAKEFIELD PLAYS by Israel Horovitz; Director, John Dillon; Lighting, Arden Fingerhut; Set, Bil Mikulewicz; Costumes, Susan Tsu; Stage Manager, Pat DeRousie. CAST: John Cazale (Will), Nancy Chesney (Margaret), Dominic Chianese (Sam), Joanna Miles (Emily), Michael Moriarty (Alfred), Peg Murray (Roxy)

December 14–18, 1976 (5 performances)
BULL FIGHT COW by Allen Davis III; Director, Warren Kliewer; Set and Lighting, Kenneth Fillo; Stage Manager, Kathleen Phelan. CAST: William Newman (Calvin), Michael McCleery (Ted), Albert M. Ottenheimer (Hiram), Martha Galphin (Drucinda), Shirley Bodtke (Jinkie), Hank Smith (Gumbah)

Friday, January 7, 1977
LUST by Steven Somkin; Director, Andrew Harris; Stage Directions, Jamie Farbman. CAST: Ronnie Harris (Adele), Ruth Baker (Madeleine), Richard Ehrhart (Richard), George Salerno (Bernard), Cyndy Aimes (Dora), Ed Crowley (Charles), Bruce Bouchard (Bobby), Nicholas Levitin (Auctioneer)

Friday, January 14, 1977
THE COUNTERPART CURE by Jeff Kindley; Director, Bill Gile; Stage Directions, Laura Solodkin. CAST: David Berman (Mr. Thimble), Brad Blaisdell (Wallace Fitler), Barbara Coggin (Miss Flagg), Georgia Creighton (Mrs. Bunt), Dick Pohlers (Dr. Paradine), Tom O'Rourke (Figaro Pontoon), John Remme (Elmo Roper), Ellen Sandler (Nurse Caribou)

Warren Kliewer, Nicholas Levitin Photos

Michael McCleery, Martha Galphin, Bill Newman, Albert Ottenheimer, Shirley Bodtke, Hank Smith in "Bull Fight"

Ed Crowley, Ruth Baker in "Lust"

Phil Rubenstein, Tony Turco, Paul Michael, Joe Sorbello, Asher Stern, Bob Costanzo in "The Mute Who Sang"

NEW DRAMATISTS INC.

January 23–26, 1977 (5 performances)
THE BESERKERS by Warren Kliewer; Director, Cliff Goodwin; Set, Douglas Lebrecht; Lighting, Priscilla Cooper; Costumes, Linda Roots; Music Composed by Tom Piazza; Played by Robin Alvarado; Sound, Regina Mullen; Production Assistants, Ed Lapine, Wendy Tulipan, Laurie Robbins. CAST: Janine Geary (Alice Franz), Bonnie Deroski (Elizabeth Franz), Paul McCrane (Johann Franz), Barbara Tarbuck (Mrs. Franz), Robert Chamberlain (Oskar Pakula)

Wednesday, February 2, 1977
THE GIRL OF THE GOLDEN WEST by Maurice Noel; Director, Michael Bavar. CAST: Bonnie Leu Banyard (Calamity Jane), Meredith Rile (Nan), Michael Oakes (Toby), Tony Savage (Wild Bill)

THE BRIDE OF HITLER by Maurice Noel; Director, Michael Bavar. CAST: Darryl Croxton (Spider Man), Jane Altman (Aimee McPherson), Jane Norvell (Eva Peron)

Friday, February 4, 1977
LUNATICS AND LOVERS by Stephen Foreman. CAST: Rusty Russ (Josh), Joe Pantaliano (Frog), Maureen Garrett (Jamba), Tom Bair (Homer), Graham Beckel (Cal), Jayne Haynes (Smoke), Bertina Johnson (Solange), Kerry Welch (Bardo), Morgan Kester (Merlinda), Steve Ommerle (Quincy), David Laden (Fat Poppa), Pamela Hartford (Woman), Michael McCleery (Man), Jim Handy (Narrator)

Monday, February 7, 1977
GANDHIJI by Rose L. Goldemberg; Director, Elinor Renfield. CAST: Bob Balaban (Gandhi), Richard Fancy (1st Actor), Dana Gladstone (2nd Actor), Katina Commings (1st Actress), Patricia Cray (2nd Actress), Glenn Cabrera (3rd Actor), Dan DaSilva (Little Boy), Lisa Hope Schiller (Little Girl), Ingrid Sonnichsen (Narrator)

Thursday, February 10, 1977
NEST OF VIPERS by Stuart Vaughan. CAST: Paul Sparer (James), Gregory Abels (Overbury), Kevin Kline (Carr), Sharon Laughlin (Frances), Pat Falkenhain (Ann), Tom Waites (Henry), Howard Renensland (Essex/Weston), Roy Sorrels (Reeves), Shiela Grenham (Turner), Peter Kozik (Villiard)

February 16–20, 1977 (5 performances)
LUST by Steven Somkin; Director, Andrew Harris; Set, Letch Hudgins; Lighting, Kenneth Fillo; Assistant Director, Pamela Hartford; Props, Janet Heath; Stage Manager, Paul Lambert; Production Assistant, Arthur Moore; Dances Staged by Naomi Brunswick; Costumes, June Lowe. CAST: Ronnie Harris (Adele), Ruth Baker (Madeleine), Richard Ehrhart (Richard), Nicholas Levitin (Bernard), Ruth Gregory (Dora), Ed Crowley (Charles), Bruce Bouchard (Bobby), Howard Renensland (Auctioneer), Bidders: Joe Tripician, Janet Heath, Pamela Hartford, Arthur Moore

Friday & Saturday, February 25–26, 1977 (2 performances)
WHAT DO I DO ABOUT HEMINGWAY? by Enid Rudd; Director, Barbara Rosoff; Stage Manager, Kathleen Phelan. CAST: Trip Plymale (Martin), Lin Shaye (Lucy), George Riddle (Dr. Redding), Rebecca Schull (Elsie), Paul Marin (Arthur), Freddy Valle (Josef), Joan Kelleher (Roberta), Richard Husson (Mervin), Shirley Bodtke (Cynthia), Myra Stennett (Carol), Richard Moore (Yogi)

Sunday & Monday, February 27–28, 1977 (2 performances)
YOU ARE WHAT YOU ARE by David Trainer; Director, Alfred Gingold; Stage Manager, Bill McComb. CAST: Rick Lieberman (Rob), Susan Vare (Ellie), Jack Axelrod (Pete), Katherine Manning (Paula), James Allan Bartz (Mike), Joni Fritz (Toni)

Friday & Saturday, March 4–5, 1977 (2 performances)
WORKING LATE by Donald Wollner; Director, Dana Roberts. CAST: Edmund Williams (Francis), Joan Grant (Miss Josephson), Lawrence Johnson (Bill), Anita Keal (Dorothy), Alfred Cherry (Joe), Carl Moebus (Ernie)

Friday & Saturday, March 18–19, 1977 (2 performances)
MOCKING BIRD by William Parchman; Director, Julie Boyd. CAST: China Chen (Daughter), Anne Miyamota (Mother), Freddy Mao (Father), Harsh Nayyar (Mr. Ito), Harry Wong (Steward), Ernest Abuba (Samurai)

MARY HAMILTON by William Parchman; Director, Julie Boyd. CAST: Tom Bair (Will), Susan Sharkey (Mary Hamilton), Dolores Kenan (Queen), Edmund Williams (King), Jan Granger (Mary C), Diane Blumberg (Mary S), Elly Weiss (Mary B), Peter Boyden (Guard/Sheriff), William Robertson (Old Man)

Friday & Saturday, April 1–2, 1977
LOSERS by Donald Wollner; Director, Ellen Sandler; Stage Directions, John Lloyd. CAST: David Little (Dave Ehrlich), Stephen Deroski (Sandy Ehrlich), Bob Powell (Willie), Joseph Jamrog (Arnie), Howard Renensland (Gary), Joan Grant (Jeanne), John Lloyd (Waiter)

Wednesday, April 6, 1977
MOTHER RYAN by Maurice Noel; Director, Paul Schneider. CAST: Barbara eda-Young (Lorraine), Mark Metcalf (Richard), Sloane Shelton (Mrs. Newman), Parker McCormick (Judy), Olympia Dukakis (Mother Ryan), Robin Leary (Radio Woman), John Lloyd (Rev. Marcus)

Friday & Saturday, April 15–16, 1977 (2 performances)
ARTISTS FOR THE REVOLUTION by Eric Thompson; Director, Thomas Gruenewald; Stage Manager, Tracy Cohen. CAST: David Rosenbaum (Street Vendor), Elizabeth Franz (Francoise), Edward Binns (Philippe), Maurice Copeland (Edouard), Nicholas Kepros (Maximilien), Chris Weatherhead (Anne), Richard Council (Paul), Joan Shepard (Marie), Peter Coffeen (Narrator/Rene), Evan Thompson (Jean-Nicholas)

Wednesday, April 20, 1977
THE TWO MARYS by Warren Kliewer; Stage Directions, Chris Hanckel. CAST: Jonathan Bolt (Prof. Williams), Nancy Franklin (Mrs. Mary Williams), Michele LaRue (Mary Petersen), Peter Kozik (Jimmy)

May 9–12, 1977 (4 performances)
A NEW WORLD! with Book and Lyrics by Marian Winters; Music, Albert Hague; Staged by Marian Winters; Lighting, Ned Hallick; Stage Managers, Allan Benjamin, Thomas P. Carr, Rianna Bryceland, Wendy Dillon. CAST: Elsa Raven (Narrator), Stanley Grover (Wm. Brewster), Barbara Andres (Mary Brewster), Court Miller (Winslow Bradford), Penelope Bodry (Dora Bradford), Adam Leitner (Trevor Brewster), William J. Coppola (John Carver), J. Kevin Scannell (John Crackston), Steve Nisbet (John Goodman), Steve Jennings (William White), Richard Mathews (Tom Tinker), Michael Medeiros (Miles Standish), Mary Ellen Ashley (Rose Standish), Lynn Ann Leveridge (Susanna White), Gary Cookson (1st Sailor), Robert Resnikoff (Official/Billington), Thomas P. Carr (Isaac Allerton/2nd Sailor/Wm. Button), Alan North (Master Jones), Jay Lowman (John Alden), Jonathan Slaff (Edward Macken), Sam Stoneburner (Mate Clark), Dan Duckworth (Stephen Hopkins), Valerie Beaman (Priscilla Mullins), Barbara Kolsun (Liz Hopkins), Roger Alan Brown (Squanto), Richard Maggiong (Samoset), Ensemble: Rianna Bryceland, David Cahn, Thomas P. Carr, Gary Cookson, Pamela Knowles, Susan Kay Logan, Jonathan Slaff

May 24–28, 1977 (6 performances)
THE MUTE WHO SANG by Gene Radano; Director, Frank Scaringi; Set and Lighting, Robert Lewis Smith; Stage Managers, Carol Baer, Eileen Sullivan; Props, Debbie Wantuch. CAST: Paul Michael (Tano), Anna Berger (Filomena), Ralph Monaco (Johnny), Joe Sorbello (Dave), David Potts (Vic), Tony Turco (Rosario), Bob Costanzo (Nick), Phil Rubenstein (Fat the Barber), Asher Stern (Don Pasquale)

(No photos available)

NEW YORK SHAKESPEARE FESTIVAL AT LINCOLN CENTER

Joseph Papp, Producer
Bernard Gersten, Associate Producer

VIVIAN BEAUMONT THEATER
Opened Thursday, February 17, 1977.*
Joseph Papp presents:

THE CHERRY ORCHARD

By Anton Chekhov; New English version by Jean-Claude van Itallie; Director, Andrei Serban; Scenery and Costumes, Santo Loquasto; Lighting, Jennifer Tipton; Incidental Music, Elizabeth Swados; Dance arranged by Kathryn Posin; Assistant Director, Richard Jakiel; Assistant to Director, Wes Jensby; Production Assistant, Pamela Singer; Hairstylist, J. Roy Helland; Supervision of Wigs, Hair and Makeup, Marlies Termine, Kathy Jones; Wardrobe Supervisor, James Roberts; Sound, Joseph Dungan

CAST

Lopakhin, Yermolay Alexeyevich .... Raul Julia
Dunyasha, the maid .... Meryl Streep
Yepikhodov, Semyon Panteleyevich .... Max Wright
Anya, Mme. Ranevskaya's daughter .... Marybeth Hurt
Ranevskaya, Lyobiv Andreyevna .... Irene Worth
Varya, her adopted daughter .... Priscilla Smith
Gayev, Leonid Andreyevich .... George Voskovec
Charlotta Ivanovna, governess .... Cathryn Damon
Simeonov-Pishchik, a landowner .... C. K. Alexander
Yasha, a valet .... Ben Masters
Firs, an old valet .... Dwight Marfield
Trofimov, Pyotr Sergeyevich .... Michael Cristofer
A Vagrant .... Jon DeVries
Stationmaster .... William Duff-Griffin
Guests, Peasants .... John Ahlburg, Suzanne Collins,
    Christine Estabrook, C. S. Hayward, Diane Lane, Jim Siering

UNDERSTUDIES: Gerry Gamman (Lopakhin/Yepikhodov), Jacqueline Brookes (Ranevskaya), Suzanne Collins (Varya), Maury Cooper (Firs/Gayev), Jon DeVries (Trofimov), William Duff-Griffin (Pishchik), Christine Estabrook (Anya/Dunyasha), Elizabeth Franz (Charlotte), C. S. Hayward (Vagrant), Jim Siering (Yasha)

A comedy in 4 acts performed with 2 intermissions. The action takes place on Madame Ranevskaya's estate in Russia from May to October.

General Manager: Robert Kamlot
Press: Merle Debuskey, Faith Geer
Stage Managers: Julia Gillett, Stephen McCorkle

* Closed April 10, 1977 after limited engagement of 62 performances. Re-opened with some cast changes on Tuesday, June 28, 1977.

Sy Friedman Photos

Top Right: Dwight Marfield, C. K. Alexander, Priscilla Smith, Irene Worth, George Voskovec, Ben Masters, Michael Christofer Below: Raul Julia, Max Wright, Meryl Streep

George Voskovec, Irene Worth, C. K. Alexander, Ben Masters

Irene Worth, Raul Julia

VIVIAN BEAUMONT THEATER
Opened Wednesday, May 18, 1977.*
Joseph Papp presents:

AGAMEMNON

Conceived by Andrei Serban and Elizabeth Swados using fragments of the original Greek play by Aeschylus and Edith Hamilton's translation; Director, Andrei Serban; Music Composed by Elizabeth Swados; Scenery, Douglas W. Schmidt; Costumes, Santo Loquasto; Lighting, Jennifer Tipton; Associate Producer, Bernard Gersten; Production Supervisor, Jason Steven Cohen; Assistants to Director, Maude Dinand, Wes Jensby; Production Assistant, Julie Hymen; Wardrobe Supervisor, James Roberts; Sound, Joseph Dungan; Production Manager, Andrew Mihok; Technical Director, Mervyn Haines, Jr

CAST

Clytemnestra/Cassandra	Priscilla Smith
Agamemnon/Aegisthus	Jamil Zakkai
Chorus Leader	George Voskovec
Iphigenia	Diane Lane

CHORUS: Stuart Baker-Bergen, Patrick Ennis Burke, Suzanne Collins, Gretel Cummings, Jerry Cunlifee, Jon DeVries, Helena D. Garcia, Natalie Gray, Kathleen Harris, C. S. Hayward, Rodney Hudson, Onni Johnson, Paul Kreppel, Paula Larke, Roger Lawson, Esther Levy, Mimi Locadio, Tom Matsusaka, Valois Mickens, Joseph Neal, William Parry, Justin Rashid, Peter Schlosser, Jai Oscar St. John, Eron Tabor, John Watson, Beverly Wideman

UNDERSTUDIES: Natalie Gray (Clytemnestra), Valois Mickens (Cassandra), George Touliatos (Chorus Leader)

Performed without intermission

General Manager: Robert Kamlot
Press: Merle Debuskey, Faith Geer
Stage Managers: Julia Gillett, Richard Jakiel

*Closed June 19, 1977 after limited run of 38 performances and 23 previews. Opened at Delacorte Theater in Central Park on Tuesday, Aug. 2, 1977 with cast changes and played through Aug. 28, 1977.

Joseph Abeles Photos

Priscilla Smith, Jamil Zakkai

Priscilla Smith (C)
Top: Priscilla Smith, George Voskovec

NEW YORK SHAKESPEARE FESTIVAL PUBLIC THEATER

Joseph Papp, Producer
Bernard Gersten, Associate Producer

PUBLIC/ANSPACHER THEATER
Opened Tuesday, June 1, 1976.*
Joseph Papp presents:

FOR COLORED GIRLS WHO HAVE CONSIDERED SUICIDE WHEN THE RAINBOW IS ENUF

By Ntozake Shange; Director, Oz Scott; Choreography, Paula Moss; Costumes, Judy Dearing; Lighting, Victor En Yu Tan; Mural, Ifa Iyaun; Music for "I Found God in Myself" by Diana Wharton; Originally produced by Henry Street Settlement New Federal Theater (Woodie King, Jr., Producer); Wardrobe Mistress, Kathy Roberson; Production Supervisor, Jason Steven Cohen; Production Manager, Andrew Mihok; Technical Director, Mervyn Haines, Jr.

CAST

Lady in brown	Janet League
Lady in yellow	Aku Kadogo
Lady in red	Trazana Beverley
Lady in green	Paula Moss
Lady in purple	Rise Collins
Lady in blue	Laurie Carlos
Lady in orange	Ntozake Shange

Performed without intermission.

General Manager: Robert Kamlot
Press: Merle Debuskey, Bob Ullman, Bruce Cohen, Richard Kornberg
Stage Managers: John Beven, Aku Kadogo

* Closed Aug. 29, 1976 after 103 performances and 17 previews. Moved to Broadway Friday, Sept. 10, 1977.

Martha Swope Photo

PUBLIC/NEWMAN THEATER
Opened Thursday, June 3, 1976.*
The New York Shakespeare Festival (Joseph Papp, Producer) presents:

REBEL WOMEN

By Thomas Babe; Director, Jack Hofsiss; Music, Catherine MacDonald; Lyrics, Barbara Bonfigli; Setting, John Lee Beatty; Costumes, Carrie F. Robbins; Lighting, Neil Peter Jampolis; Assistant to Director, Jason LaPadura; Sound, Roger Jay; Props, Bill Brosnahan; Wardrobe Mistress, Melissa Adzima

CAST

Tussie	Deloris Gaskins
Katharine King	Deborah Offner
Mrs. Mary E. Law	Leora Dana
Mrs. Mary Law Robarts	Kathryn Walker
First Soldier	Eric Anthony Roberts
Second Soldier	Mark Kologi
Third Soldier/Civilian	David Dean
Maj. Robert Steele Strong	Mandy Patinkin
Dr. Samuel Sutler	John Glover
Gen. William Tecumseh Sherman	David Dukes
Lt. Henry Hitchcock	Peter Weller
Soldiers	Ralph Byers, Tracey Walter

A play in three acts. The action takes place in the summer home of the Law Family in Vidalia, GA., Dec. 5–6, 1864.

General Manager: Robert Kamlot
Press: Merle Debuskey, Bob Ullman, Bruce Cohen, Richard Kornberg
Stage Managers: Peter von Mayrhauser, Penny Gebhard

* Closed June 13, 1976 after 14 performances and 32 previews.

Frederic Ohringer Photo

Janet League, Ntozake Shange

Kathryn Walker, Deborah Offner, Leora Dana, David Dukes 139

PUBLIC/NEWMAN THEATER

Opened Saturday, February 5, 1977.*
Joseph Papp presents:

MARCO POLO SINGS A SOLO

By John Guare; Director, Mel Shapiro; Setting, John Wulp; Costumes, Theoni V. Aldredge; Lighting, Jennifer Tipton; Production Assistant, Jory Johnson; Props, Varel McComb, Deborah Sohmer; Wardrobe Supervisor, Melissa Adzima; Technical Director, Mervyn Haines, Jr.; Production Supervisor, Jason Steven Cohen

CAST

Diane McBride	Madeline Kahn
Tom Wintermouth	Chris Sarandon
Freydis	Sigourney Weaver
Stony McBride	Joel Grey
Lusty McBride	Chev Rodgers
Mrs. McBride	Anne Jackson
Larry Rockwell	James Jansen
Frank Schaeffer	Larry Bryggman

A comedy in 2 acts and 3 scenes. The action takes place on the island of Trollenthor, forty miles off the coast of Norway in the early spring of 1999.

General Manager: Robert Kamlot
Press: Merle Debuskey, Bob Ullman, Richard Kornberg
Stage Managers: D. W. Koehler, Sally Campbell

* Closed March 6, 1977 after 35 performances and 29 previews.

(John Wulp Photos)

Joel Grey Right: Sigourney Weaver, Anne Jackson Top: Madeline Kahn, Chris Sarandon, James Jansen

PUBLIC/ANSPACHER THEATER

Opened Wednesday, February 9, 1977.*
Joseph Papp presents:

ASHES

By David Rudkin; Director, Lynne Meadows; Setting, John Lee Beatty; Costumes, Jennifer von Mayrhauser; Lighting, Dennis Parichy; Sound, George Hansen, Charles London; A New York Shakespeare Festival production in association with the Manhattan Theatre Club; Production supervisor, Jason Steven Cohen; Assistant Director, Andy Wolk; Props, William G. Bell; Wardrobe Supervision, Rosalie Wells; Technical Director, Mervyn Haines, Jr.

CAST

Colin	Brian Murray†1
Anne	Roberta Maxwell†2
Man	John Tillinger
Woman	Penelope Allen

UNDERSTUDIES: Anne/Woman, Marian Clarke; Colin/Man, Steven Gilborn

A drama performed without intermission.

General Manager: Robert Kamlot
Press: Merle Debuskey, Bob Ullman, Richard Kornberg
Stage Managers: Zane Weiner, Darrell Ziegler

* Closed July 3, 1977 after 167 performances.
†Succeeded by: 1. Joe Fabiani, 2. Dianne Wiest

(Barry Kramer Photo)

Roberta Maxwell, Brian Murray

140

PUBLIC/LuESTHER HALL

Opened Wednesday, March 16, 1977.*
Joseph Papp presents the New York Shakespeare Festival Workshop Production of:

MUSEUM

By Tina Howe; Director, Richard Jordan; Movement, Loren Hightower; Scenery and Lighting, Robert Yodice; Costumes, Patricia McGourty; Production Supervisor, Jason Steven Cohen; Wardrobe, Lucy Robinson, Rita Barbera; Technical Director, Mervyn Haines, Jr.

CAST

Mrs. Salt/Ada Bilditsky/Lillian	Barbara Coggin
Hans Durheim	Tom Crawley
Elizabeth Sorrow/Kate Siv/Woman	Brenda Currin
Bob Lamb/Steve Williams	Clifford David
Will Willard	Bill Elverman
Jean-Claude/Mr. Gregory/Elderly Man	Pierre Epstein
Guard	Henderson Forsythe
Blakey/Zoe Calverrio	Kathryn Grody
Peter Ziff/Second Guard	Dan Hedaya
Liz/Julie Jenkins	Swoosie Kurtz
Harriet Pogol/Tink Solheim	Margaret Ladd
Mr. Salt/Bill Plaid/1st Guard	Michael Miller
Annette Froebel/Barbara Castle/Harriet	Joan Pape
Michael Wall	Les Roberts
Maggie Snow/Barbara Zimmer/Woman	Barbara Spiegel
Chloe Trap/Elderly Woman	Helen Stenborg
Francoise/May	Sasha von Scherler
Hollinsford/Giorgio Calverrio	Stephan Weyte
Carol/Gilda Norris	Penney White

Performed without intermission.

General Manager: Robert Kamlot
Press: Merle Debuskey, Bob Ullman, Richard Kornberg
Stage Managers: Louis Rackoff, Frank DiFilia

* Closed March 27, 1977 after 24 performances.

(No photos available)

PUBLIC/MARTINSON HALL

Opened Wednesday, March 23, 1977.*
Joseph Papp presents a New York Shakespeare Festival/New Playwrights Theatre of Washington production of:

HAGAR'S CHILDREN

By Ernest Joselovitz; Director, Robert Graham Small; Music, Randy Lee Ross; Scenery and Lighting, Clarke Dunham; Associate Producer, Bernard Gersten; Production Supervisor, Jason Steven Cohen; Props, Varel McComb; Wardrobe Mistress, Ellen Roberts; Technical Director, Mervyn Haines, Jr.

CAST

Esther Roxburg	Carmen Vickers
Oliver Davidson	Lloyd Davis, Jr.
Diana	Dorothy Hayden
Rob	Brian Wiese
Sharon	Jan Dorn
Mervin	Tri Garraty
David	Thomas Simpson
Tom Hervala	Gardner Hathaway
The Sheriff	Mark Simon

UNDERSTUDIES: Anne Barclay (Esther), Jacklyn Maddux (Diana/Sharon), Nathaniel Robinson (Oliver), Gardner Hathaway (Mervin/Rob/David)

A drama in two acts. The action takes place at Bridgehaven Farm on the day and night before Christmas of 1971.

General Manager: Robert Kamlot
Press: Merle Debuskey, Bob Ullman, Richard Kornberg
Stage Managers: Lenny Pass, Barbara Alpert

* Closed May 15, 1977 After 63 performances.

Fred Ohringer Photos

Top Right: Jan Dorn, Thomas Simpson

Jan Dorn, Carmen Vickers, Ti Garraty

PUBLIC/LuESTHER HALL
Opened Wednesday, April 27, 1977.*
The New York Shakespeare Festival (Joseph Papp, Producer) presents:

ON-THE LOCK-IN

Book, Music and Lyrics, David Langston Smyrl; Conceived and Directed by Robert Macbeth; Scenery, Karl Eigsti; Lighting, Victor En Yu Tan; Costumes, Grace Williams; Musical Direction, George Stubbs; Musical Arrangements, Paul Griffin; Associate Producer, Bernard Gersten; Production Supervisor, Jason Steven Cohen; Wardrobe Supervisor, Karen Perry Kain

CAST

Houndog	David Langston Smyrl
Frankie	Manuel Santiago
Mess Hall	Harold Cromer
Home Boy	Billy Barnes
Jerry	Henry Baker
Dude	Thomas M. Brimm II
Rock	Ezra Jack Maret
The Guard	Leon Thomas
Jazz	Alan Weeks
Small Times	Henry Bradley
Abdu	Don Jay
Musicians	George Stubbs (piano), Chris White (bass), Al Harewood (drums)

MUSICAL NUMBERS: "Whatever It Happens to Be," "Dry Mouth with No Water," "Born to Lose," "Sister Paradise," "Peace Will Come," "Circumstances," "42nd Street Blues," "Talkin' Blues," "Marlene," "Alone"

A musical performed without intermission. The action takes place at the present time in a house of detention.

General Manager: Robert Kamlot
Press: Merle Debuskey, Bob Ullman, Richard Kornberg
Stage Managers: Toby Scott Macbeth, George Lee Miles

* Closed June 5, 1977 after 47 performances and 15 previews.

(Martha Swope Photo)
Sy Friedman Photos

Leon Thomas in "On-the Lock-In"

PUBLIC/NEWMAN THEATER
Opened Tuesday, May 17, 1977.*
The New York Shakespeare Festival (Joseph Papp, Producer) in association with Sanctuary Theatre Workshop presents:

THE STRONGER
and
CREDITORS

By August Strindberg; Translated by Palaemona Morner and R. Spacek; Director, Rip Torn; Settings, John Wright Stevens; Costumes, Carrie F. Robbins; Lighting, Ian Calderon; Associate Producer, Bernard Gersten; Originally produced by Hudson Guild Theatre (Craig Anderson, Producing Director); Technical Director, Mervyn Haines, Jr.; Production Supervisor, Jason Steven Cohen; Wardrobe Supervisor, Melissa Adzima; Props, Deborah Sohmer; Hairstylist, Kathy Jones

CAST

"THE STRONGER"

Mlle. Y	Geraldine Page
Mrs. X	Amy Wright
Waitress	Judith L'Heureux

The action takes place in a coffee house for ladies

"CREDITORS"

Adolf	John Heard
Gustav	Rip Torn
Tekla	Geraldine Page
Women	Amy Wright, Judith L'Heureux
Waiter	Tom Hurt

The action takes place in a drawing room at a beach resort.

UNDERSTUDIES: Gustav, David Brooks; Adolf, Tom Hurt; X/Y/Tekla, Judith L'Heureux

General Manager: Robert Kamlot
Press: Merle Debuskey, Bob Ullman, Richard Kornberg
Stage Managers: James Pentecost, Sally Campbell

* Closed June 5, 1977 after 24 performances and 32 previews.

Top: Amy Wright, Geraldine Page in "The Stronger"
Below: John Heard, Page, Rip Torn in "Creditors"

THE PHOENIX THEATRE

T. Edward Hambleton, Managing Director
Marilyn S. Miller, Executive Director
Daniel Freudenberger, Producing Director

MARYMOUNT MANHATTAN THEATRE
October 28–November 7, 1976 (12 performances)
LADYHOUSE BLUES by Kevin O'Morrison; Director, Tony Giordano; Scenery and Lighting, James Tilton; Costumes, Fred Voelpel; Production Manager, Barbara Carrellas; Administrative Assistant, Bruce Levy; Technical Director, Paul Everett; Production Assistants, Judy Mauer, David Rosenberg; Press, Gifford/Wallace, Tom Trenkle; Stage Manager, Tom Aberger. CAST: Christine Estabrook (Eylie), Cara Duff-MacCormick (Helen), Mary-Joan Negro (Dot), Jo Henderson (Liz), Gale Garnett (Terry)

November 25–December 5, 1976 (12 performances)
CANADIAN GOTHIC/AMERICAN MODERN by Joanna M.Glass; Director, Daniel Freudenberger; Scenery and Lighting, James Tilton; Music Composed and Performed by Arthur Miller; General Manager, Marilyn S. Miller; Assistant General Manager, Louise M.Bayer; Technical Director, Paul Everett; Costume Coordinator, Patricia Smith; Production Assistant, Leslie Yudell; Stage Managers, Tom Aberger, David Rosenberg. CAST: "Canadian Gothic": Tom Aldredge (Father), Joanna Merlin (Mother), Mary-Joan Negro (Jean), John Kauffman (Ben), "American Modern": Tom Aldredge (Mike), Joanna Merlin (Pat)

December 16, 1976–January 2, 1977 (16 performances)
MARCO POLO by Jonathan Levy; Director, Lynne Meadow; Scenery and Lighting, James Tilton; Costumes, Carrie F. Robbins; Assistant Director, Andrew Wolk; Technical Director, Paul Everett; Production Assistant, Leslie Yudell; Stage Managers, Tom Aberger, Stephen Stewart-James, Edward Courtien. CAST: Luis Avalos (Maffeo Polo), Mark Campo (Musician), Bernard Frawley (Kublai Khan), Dick Latessa (Nicolo Polo), Robert Rogers (Musician), Barry Snider (Achmed), David Berman (Counselor 1), Christien Estabrook (Princess Kogatin), Nicholas Hormann (Yellow Lama), Joel Polis (Prop Man), Jeremy Sage (Marco Polo), Brent Spiner (Counselor 2), Jerry Zaks (Harlequin).

January 13–23, 1977 (14 performances)
February 8–20, 1977 (16 performances)
A SORROW BEYOND DREAMS by Peter Handke; Translation, Ralph Manheim; Adapted and Directed by Daniel Freudenberger; Scenery, Lighting, Projections, James Tilton; Technical Director, Paul H. Everett; Costume Coordinator, Beba Shamash; Production Assistant, Shannah Green; Press, Gifford/Wallace, Tom Trenkle; Stage Managers, Tom Aberger, David Rosenberg. CAST: Len Cariou (The Writer)

April 7–17, 1977 (12 performances)
G. R. POINT by David Berry; Director, Tony Giordano; Scenery, James Tilton; Lighting, Arden Fingerhut; Costumes, Frances Ellen Rosenthal; Technical Director, Paul H. Everett; Stage Managers, Tom Aberger, David Rosenberg; Production Assistants, Scott Baldinger, Martha McDonnell, Charlotte Volage. CAST: Frank Adu (Deacon), Lori Tan Chinn (Mama-San), Woody Eney (Lt. Johnston), John Heard (Micah), Brent Jennings (K.P.), Joe Morton (Shoulders), Francisco Prado (Tito), William Russ (Zan), Donald Warfield (Straw)

May 26–June 5, 1977 (12 performances)
SCRIBES by Barrie Keeffe; Director, Keith Hack; Scenery and Lighting, James Tilton; Costumes, Frances Ellen Rosenthal; Technical Director, Ric Barrett; Sound, Oriole O'Neill; Production Assistants, Margaret Giusto, Martha McDonnell, Barbara Rosenthal; Stage Managers, Tom Aberger, David Rosenberg; Wardrobe Supervisor, Linda Lucero. CAST: Fran Brill (Lorraine), Leonardo Cimino (Dan), Russell Horton (Arnold), Jeffrey Jones (Roy), Stephen Joyce (Hunt), Donald Madden (Charlie), Ann McDonough (Janet), Alan North (Reg), Don Scardino (David), Kristoffer Tabori (Spud), George Taylor (Dick)

Roger Greenawalt Photos

Top Right: Mary-Joan Negro, Cara Duff-MacCormick, Gale Garnett, Christine Estabrook in "Ladyhouse Blues"

Below: John Heard, Lori Chinn, Joe Morton in "G. R. Point"

"Scribes" Above: Len Cariou in "A Sorrow beyond Dreams" 143

PLAYWRIGHTS HORIZONS, INC.

Robert Moss, Executive Director
Philip Himberg, Producing Director
Productions Manager, Zoya Wyeth; Business Manager, Jim Swaine;
Literary Manager, Andre Bishop; Press, Joan Egan; Business Administrator/Queens, Ira Schlosser; Technical Directors, Charles Tyndall, Mary Calhoun, Christie Heiss

PLAYWRIGHTS HORIZONS
and
QUEENS THEATER-IN-THE-PARK

June 3–13, 1976 (8 performances)
DEAR RUTH by Norman Krasna; Director, Robert Moss; Set and Costumes, Greg Etchison; Lights, Tony Santoro; Stage Managers, Ian McColl, Deborah Butt. CAST: Peter Bartlett, Carolyn Borger, Jim Broaddus, Mary Louise Burke, James Carruthers, Frank Cento, John Gilpin; Margaret Gwenver, Carolyn Hurlburt, Jo Anne Sedwick

June 3–13, 1976 (8 performances)
PARADISE by Steven Shea; Director, Paul Cooper; Set, Christopher A. Nowak; Lights, Harry Itzkowitz. CAST: Elliot Burtoff, Kathleen Chalfant, Jillian Lindig, John Guerrasio, Greg Johnson, Ron Johnston.

June 15–19, 1976 (5 performances)
THE INVESTIGATION OF J.T. by Richard Ploetz; Director, Lewis Pshena; Sets, Nancy Winters; Lights, William D. Anderson; Costumes, Robert Lord-Taylor; Stage Manager, Melissa Hager. CAST: Madeline Berger, Rod Houts, Dorothy Levine, Marvin Peisner, Bill Steele, Fred Stuthman.

June 15–19, 1976 (5 performances)
REUNION, Book by Dennis Andersen, Lyrics by Jim Billings, Music by Dennis Arlan; Director, Jim Billings; Sets, Nancy Winters; Lights, William D. Anderson. CAST: Alan Baker, Mary Boylan, Carolyn Friday, Eleanor Cody Gould, Thomas Jamerson, Kristin Jolliff, Rose Lischner, Joyce McDonald, William Robertson, Eugene Rohrer, Monona Rossol, Michael Sander, Wayne Sherwood.

June 22–26, 1976 (5 performances)
GILBERT and THE KNIGHT OF THE TWELFTH SAUCER by David S. Meranze and Marc Alan Zagoren; Director, Stuart H. Ross; Set, Nancy Winters; Lights, William D. Anderson; Stage Manager, Nancy Harrington. CAST: Peter Alzado, Frank Anderson, Craig Carlson, Mark Fleischman, Suzanne Gilbert, Robert Ground, Elaine Grollman, Eda Reiss Merin, Judith Morley, Linda Scoullar.

June 22–26, 1976 (5 performances)
OCTOBER WEDDING by Dorothy Louise; Director, William Schorr; Set, Nancy Winters; Lights, William D. Anderson; Costumes, Thomas McKinley; Stage Manager, Roxy Wright. CAST: Faith Catlin, Helen Harrelson, Larry Lott, Randall Merrifield, Valerie Morrell, Amy Nathan, Christopher Pitney, Bee Swanson.

June 22–26, 1976 (5 Performances)
STORMBOUND by Larry Ketron; Director, Jessica Levy; Sets, Nancy Winters; Lights, William D. Anderson; Stage Manager, David Rosenberg. CAST: Elizabeth Franz, Marlena Lustik, Art Pingree, Bill Tatum.

"Dear Ruth" Below: Harry Goz, Lynn Lipton in "Born Yesterday"

PLAYWRIGHTS HORIZONS

June 24–July 4, 1976 (8 performances)
THE TAVERN by George M. Cohan; Director, Ronald Miller; Set and Costume, Amanda Klein; Lights, Tony Santoro; Stage Manager, Julia Ervin. CAST: Jim Broaddus, Elliott Burtoff, Larry Carr, Denis Cleary, Jeffrey DeMunn, Robert Horen, Greg Johnson, David Kabat, Jillian Lindig, Jim Loren, Joan Lowell, Chip Lucia, Andrea Masters, Adrien Royce.

June 29–July 3, 1976 (5 performances)
MONTPELIER PA-ZAZZ, Book and Lyrics by Wendy Wasserstein, Music by David Hollister; Director, Donald Warfield; Sets, Nancy Winters and Donald Warfield; Lights, William D. Anderson; Costumes, V. Jane Suttell; Stage Manager, Alvin Ho. CAST: Bess Armstrong, Jonathan Charnas, Peggy Harner, Bonnie Hellman, Gayle Kelly Landers, Jill Medow, Nancy New, Debbe Renee, Charles Ryan, Harris Shore, Sally Sockwell, Jeffrey Spolan, Elizabeth Stockhammer, Frederic Stone.

June 29–July 3, 1976 (5 performances)
THE COUNTRY CLUB by James P. Staley; Director, Georgia Fleenor; Sets, Nancy Winters; Lights, William D. Anderson; Costumes, Mary Alice Orito; Stage Manager, Camille Monte. CAST: Tom Berenger, Kathleen Coyne, Herbert Duval, Richard Harmel, Charles T. Harper, Susan Kellerman, Robert Sevra.

June 29–July 3, 1976 (5 performances)
THE BODY PARTS OF MARGARET FULLER by E. M. Broner; Director, Robert Moss; Sets, Nancy Winters; Lights, William D. Anderson. CAST: Kathleen Chalfant, Margaret Gwenver, Jayne Haynes, Carolyn Hurlburt, Robyn Goodman, Ellen Parks, Jane Sanford, Jo Anne Sedwick, Lin Shaye, Jane Staab, Elizabeth Swain.

July 15–25, 1976 (8 performances)
BORN YESTERDAY by Garson Kanin; Director, Caymichael Patton; Sets, Amanda Klein; Lights, Paul Kaine; Costumes, Amanda Klein; Stage Management, Marjie Klein and David Gawlikowski. CAST: Tom Bade, Andre Bishop, Kathleen Chalfant, Stan Edelman, Harry Goz, Lynn Lipton, Richmond Hoxie.

September 25–October 10, 1976 (12 performances)
BABES IN ARMS, Music by Richard Rodgers, Lyrics by Lorenz Hart, Book by George Oppenheimer, based on the original book by Rodgers and Hart; Director, Peter Mark Schifter, Choreography, Bob Bowyer; Musical Direction, Jim Fradrich; Sets, Christopher Hacker; Lights, William D. Anderson; Costumes, Greg Etchison; Stage Manager, Lewis Pshena. CAST: Peggy Atkinson, Jo Ann Bruggeman, Larry Carr, Rick De Filips, Richard Ferrugio, Robin Field, Jonathan E. Freeman, Arthur Howard, Maj-lis Jalkio, Deborah Lake, Bill Lamb, Joan Lowell, Karen Magid, Cathy McCann, Tacey Phillips, Barbara Saturn, Alan Skolnick, Dan Taylor, Kathy Winston.

Nathaniel Tileston Photos

"The Body Parts of Margaret Fuller"

PLAYWRIGHTS HORIZONS

October 2–24, 1976 (12 performances)
BOO HOO by Philip Magdalany; Director, Michael Flanagan; Sets, Mark Winkworth; Lights, Jeffrey Schissler; Costumes, David James; Stage Manager, Beverly Randolph. CAST: Elaine Kerr, Patricia O'Connell, Anna Shaler.

October 10–23, 1976 (9 performances)
MAD DOGS by George Shea; Director, Stuart H. Ross; Sets, Bill Ruggieri; Lights, Barbara Kopit; Costumes, Beth Juda; Sound, Nancy Harrington; Stage Manager, Karen Nothman. CAST: George Bamford, Lauren Barnes, Michael Bierne, Gary Cookson, William Da Prato, Gil Frazier, Gariel Gribetz, Bebe Landis, Nick La Padula, Scott Redman, Gabrielle Sinclair, David Tabor, Eric Uhler, Jim Swaine.

October 30–November 21, 1976 (15 performances)
THE DYBBUK by S. Ansky; Director, Philip Himberg; Choreography, Carol Kastendieck; Sets, Nancy Winters; Lights, Mary Calhoun; Costumes, Mimi Maxmen; Musical Supervisor, Philip Campanella; Stage Manager, Amy Chase. CAST: Robin Bartlett, Betty Bernstein, Teresa Castonguay, Kenneth L. Chomont, Tobias Haller, Michael Hardstark, Rod Houts, Elaine Grollman, Peter Johl, Susan McVeigh, Robert Nersesian, Catherine Olim, Michael Nobel, Sanford Seeger, Martin Siegel, Madeline Shaw, Laurel Weber, Arn Weiner, Lee Wilkof, Randall Merrifield.

November 11–28, 1976 (15 performances)
RIO GRANDE by Martin Sherman; Director, Leland Moss; Sets and Lights, Jeffrey Schissler; Costumes, Michael J. Cesario; Stage Manager, Judy Mauer. CAST: Bill Conway, Irene Dailey, Lynn Lobban, Joan Lowell, Michael Morin, David Rasche, Kathrin King Segal.

December 4–19, 1976 (14 performances)
THE RIVALS by Richard Brinsley Sheridan; Director, Robert Moss; Associate Director, Stuart H. Ross; Sets, John Gisondi; Lights, Patrika Brown; Costumes, Michael J. Cesario; Stage Manager, Paula Ellen Cohen. CAST: John Abajian, Joel Brooks, Maria Cellario, Tom Crawley, Ronald Frazier, Margaret Gwenver, David Keith, Carolyn Olga Kruse, Lynda Myles, Stuart H. Ross, Sy Travers, Kermit Brown.

December 11–19, 1976 (8 performances)
GEMINI by Albert Innaurato; Director, Peter Mark Schifter; Sets, Christopher Nowak; Lights, Larry Cummings; Costumes, Ernie Smith; Stage Manager, Belle Baxter. CAST: Reed Birney, Jonathan Hadary, Jessica James, Tom Mardirosian, Jon Polito, Anne De Salvo, Sigourney Weaver.

December 19, 1976–January 8, 1977 (12 performances)
REBECCAH (The cycle play: part one) in association with The Rebeccah Company; by Karen Malpede; Director, Tina Shepard; Designed by Marcie Begleiter; Music, Sybille Hayn and Ellen Maddow; Lights, Beth Helen Glick. CAST: Jan Cohen, Sybille Hayn, Ellen Maddow, Ann Cain McGinnis, Gloria Mojica, Tina Shepard, Pam Verge, Lois Weaver.

Nathaniel Tileston Photos

Ann Shaler, Elaine Kerr in "Boo Hoo"
Below: Irene Dailey in "Rio Grande"

PLAYWRIGHTS HORIZONS

January 19–23, 1977 (5 performances)
JUST LIKE THE NIGHT by David Rimmer; Director, Barry Keating; Lights, Pat Stearn; Stage Manager, Paula Cohen. CAST: Loren Brown, Griffin Dunne, Joel Polis, Fanny Spiess.

January 22–February 6, 1977 (12 Performances)
HAY FEVER by Noel Coward; Director, Marshall Oglesby; Lights, William Anderson; Sets, Donato Moreno; Costumes, Polly Smith; Stage Manager, Belle Baxter. CAST: Valerie Beaman, Robert Baines, Elaine Bromka, Bill Elverman, Margaret Hall, Judith McGilligan, Jon Stevens, Frederick Wessler.

February 3–20, 1977 (13 performances)
STOP THE PARADE by Marsha Sheiness; Director, Harold Scott; Lights, Patrika Brown; Sets, Paul Eads; Costumes, Mary Alice Orito; Music, Kathrin King Segal; Stage Manager, Judy Mauer. CAST: Maria Cellario, Dallas Greer, Jayne Haynes, J. R. Horne, Ernest Lehrer, Quincey Long, Joseph Mays, Jackie Nicole, Scott Robinson, Steve Simpson, Robert Sevra.

February 7 & 14, 1977 (2 performances)
MADEMOISELLE COLOMBE by Jean Anouilh; Book by Albert Harris; Music, Michael Valenti; Lyrics, Edwin Dulchin; (based on English adaptation by Louis J. Kronenberger); Director, Albert Harris. CAST: Nancy Andrews, Candice Earley, Bill Hedge, Kristin Jolliff, I. W. Klein, Robert Manzari, Richard Marr, Ty McConnell, Tad Motyka, Keith Perry, Naomi Riseman, Richard Rossomme, Steve Rotblatt, Norman Weiler.

February 8 & 9, 1977 (2 performances)
TRADE-OFFS by Lonnie Carter; Director, Richard Vos; Sets, Karen Wise. CAST: Sarah Fairfax, Franz Jones, Bob Lawrence, Kennley Noble, Tony Rutledge, Grant J. Stewart.

February 10–20, 1977 (8 performances)
RAMBLINGS by Gus Kaikkonen; Director, Michael Montel; Lights, David F. Segal; Sets, Stuart Wurtzel; Costumes, Michael P. Dennison; Sound, Ken Fillo; Stage Manager, Pat De Rousie CAST: Sarah Chodoff, Maurice D. Copeland, Joshua Rogoff Heitler, Trish Johnson, Elizabeth Lawrence, David Leary, Kaiulani Lee, Gene Lindsey, Morrie Piersol, William Sadler, Sloane Shelton.

February 26–March 13, 1977 (12 performances)
THE MOUSETRAP by Agatha Christie; Director, Larry Carpenter; Lights, Frances Aronson, Sets, Miguel Romero; Costumes, Michael J. Cesario; Sound, Philip Campanella; Stage Manager, Camille Monte. CAST: Mary Carter, Renato Cibelli, Dana Hart, Douglas Jones, Julia MacKenzie, Robert Molnar, Jon Stevens.

Lynda Myles, Ronald Frazier, Margaret Gwenver in "The Rivals"

PLAYWRIGHTS HORIZONS

March 10–27, 1977 (13 performances)
FAIR WEATHER FRIENDS by Philip Magdalany and Kenneth Pressman; Director, Richard Place; Lights, William D. Anderson; Sets, Christina Weppner; Costumes, Marcie Begleiter; Stage Manager, Belle Baxter. CAST: Pat Lysinger, Elaine Rinehart, Deborah Savadge, Bill Tatum, Douglas Travis, Frederick Wessler.

March 4–6, 1977 (4 performances)
WHITE PIANO adapted and directed by Christopher Adler from the Al Rose adaptation of Portions of Storyville; Musical Direction and Arrangements, Yolanda Segovia; Choreography, Lonnie McNeil; Lights, Michael Krones; Stage Manager, Chip Mitchell. CAST: Loretta Abbott, Georgia Cobb, Debra Greenfield, Maggie Gorril Hasafa, Dolly Jonah, Gary Q. Lewis, Frank Mastracola, Sherry Mathis, Thomas Lord Sullivan, Maggie Tucker, Bea Winde.

March 19 & 20, 1977 (2 performances)
UNCOMMON WOMEN and OTHERS by Wendy Wasserstein; Director, Chris Cox; Stage Manager, David Rosenberg. CAST: Alice Elliot, Marlene Fisher, Eleanor Cody Gould, Laurie Heineman, Steven Liska, Naomi Mitty, Nita Novy, Mary Portiser, Ann Sachs, Paula Wagner.

March 26 & 27, 1977 (2 performances)
INNOCENT THOUGHTS AND HARMLESS INTENTIONS by John Heuer; Director, James Nicola; Lights, Carlos Castanon; Stage Manager, Carlos Castanon. CAST: Dennis Bailey, Brian Brownlee, Cara Duff-MacCormick, Thomas Everett, Emmett Foster, Thomas Hulce, David Patrick Kelly, Lani Miyazaki, Jess Osuna, Michael Rieder, Tony Simotes.

April 8–May 1, 1977 (13 performances)
JACQUES BREL IS ALIVE AND WELL AND LIVING IN PARIS, production conception, English lyrics, additional material by Eric Blau and Mort Shuman based on Brel's lyrics and commentary, Music by Jacques Brel; Director, Stuart H. Ross; Musical Director, Norman L. Berman; Lights, Pat Stearn; Sets, Stephen P. Edelstein; Costumes, Patricia Adshead, Stage Manager, Andy Lopata. CAST: Jonathan Ball, Peter Bartlett, Jan Buttram, Susan Cella; Musicians, Vicki Carter, Bruce Pachtman, Brian Connie.

April 13–May 1, 1977 (17 performances)
FOR THE USE OF THE HALL by Oliver Hailey (Co-produced with the Lion Theatre Company); Director Ron Van Lieu; Lights James Chaleff, Sets, Miguel Romero; Costumes, David Murin; Stage Manager, Laurie F. Stone. CAST: Evalyn Baron, Eileen Burns, David Gallagher, Sharon Laughlin, Barbara Le Brunn, Ted Tinling.

Deborah Savadge, Frederick Wessler, Elaine Rinehart, Bill Tatum in "Fairweather Friends" Below: Susan Cella, Jan Buttram in "Jacques Brel Is Alive . . ."

PLAYWRIGHTS HORIZONS.

April 28–May 7, 1977 (8 performances)
S.W.A.K. (SEALED WITH A KISS) by Sally Ordway; Director, Geraldine Court; Lights, Joan Racho; Assistant to the Director, Vicki Sussman; Stage Manager, Jonathan Gans. CAST: Annie Abbott, Quincy Long, John Lordan, Raleigh Miller, Virginia Stevens, Kathren Troll, Margaret Warncke.

May 7–22, 1977 (12 performances)
STAGE DOOR by Edna Ferber and George S. Kaufman; Director, Robert Moss; Lights, William D. Anderson; Sets, Richard B. Williams; Costumes, Michael J. Cesario; Stage Manager, Belle Baxter. CAST: Doug Baldwin, Nancy Boykin, Jani Brenn, Mary Louise Burke, Kathleen Coyne, Dorie Don Vito, Carole Doscher, Sarah Fairfax, Jack Gilpin, Joan Jaffe, Sherri Kotimsky, Rita Litton, Julia MacKenzie, Lynn Martin, Parker McCormick, Judith McIntyre, Jerry C. Nelson, JoAnne Sedwick, Jane Staab, Dan Tedlie, Penny White.

May 12 & 13, 1977 (2 performances)
A TALE FOR CHRISTMAS EVE by Susan Jack; Director, Alfred Gingold; Stage Manager, Yari. CAST: Andy Backer, Ellen Barber, Kathleen Gray, Gene Gross, Jane Hoffman, Murray Horwitz, Fredric Stone, Allen Swift, Bob Temliak.

May 17–28, 1977 (8 performances)
EARTH WORMS by Albert Innaurato; Director, David Schweizer; Lights, Ian Calderon; Sets, Christopher Nowak; Costumes, William Ivey-Long; Stage Manager, Bonnie Panson; Music, Richard Weinstock. CAST: Richard Cox, Gene Davis, Michael Egan, Cara Duff-MacCormick, Jonathan Frakes, Elaine Grollman, Richard Hayes, Peter Jolly, David Keith, Jeffrey Knox, Matthew Kristov, Ellie Schadt.

Nathaniel Tileston Photos

Ron Hale, Julia MacKenzie in "Stage Door"

PUBLIC PLAYERS

J. Perry McDonald, Producer-Director

CENTRAL ARTS THEATRE
June 2–13, 1976 (12 performances)
BOHEMIAN SUMMER conceived and directed by J. Perry McDonald; Assistant to Director, Iris Grossman; Costumes, Max Navarre; Lighting, Ricki Klein; Setting, Charles McDonough; Stage Manager, Andrea Larson. CAST: John Sheehan, Nancy Frangione, Jim Hackett, Dorothy Fielding, Thomas Merritt, David Leopold, Mark Hoyt, Carl Brown

THEATRE OF THE OPEN EYE
September 3–12, 1976 (13 performances in repertory)
A WOMAN OF NO IMPORTANCE by Oscar Wilde; Director, J. Perry McDonald; Associate Producer, Iris Grossman; Stage Managers, Pat Pell, John Sheehan; Lighting, Pat Stern; Set, Charles McDonough; Costumes, Clifford Capone; Music, Gilbert & Sullivan's "Utopia Limited." CAST: Leslie O'Hara (Alice), Alexandra Johnson (Hester), David McCarver (Gerald), Mimi Weddell (Lady Caroline), Don Hampton (Francis), William Simington (Sir John), Joan Turetzky (Lady Hunstanton), Roger Tiberii (Lord Illingworth), Peggy Cooper (Mrs. Allonby), Kathleen Eaton (Lady Stutfield), Sasha Nanus (Mrs. Arbuthnot)

THE IMPORTANCE OF BEING EARNEST by Oscar Wilde; Same credits as above. CAST: Sasha Nanus (Merriman), Roger Tiberii (Lane), David McCarver (Algernon), Don Hampton (Worthing), Peggy Cooper (Lady Bracknell), Leslie O'Hara (Gwendolen), Kathleen Eaton (Miss Prism), Alexandra Johnson (Cecily), William Simington (Rev. Chasuble), Charles McDonough (Gardener)

VAN DAM THEATRE
February 17–March 1, 1977 (12 performances)
MR. DORIAN GRAY, SIR: OR PROF. CHEN-TUNG'S MAGIC LANTERN HORROR SHOW by Charles McDonough and Christopher Pumpkin; Loosely based on Oscar Wilde's "The Picture of Dorian Gray"; Media Design, Bruce Shenton; Producer, Iris Grossman; Sets, Andre St. Jean; Lighting, Ricki Klein; Costumes, Stephanie; Choreographer, Giancarlo Calabrese; Assistant to Director, Ingrid Geiffert. CAST: Alan Coates (Valet/Dorian Gray), Greg Michaels (Groom/Lord Henry/ Herod/Adrian), Sasha Nanus (Housekeeper/Lady Wotton), Pat Pell (Maid/Sybil/Salome/Hag), John Sheehan (Gardener/Vane/ Flynn), Malcolm Stewart (Butler/-Basil/Alan), Joan Turetzky (Cook/Lady Bradden/Mrs. Vane/Mrs. Campbell), Mimi Weddell (Laundress/Lord Fermor/Mrs. Leaf/-Lady Diana), Emilie Roberts (Music Hall Singer)

TOSOS
April 14–May 8, 1977 (16 performances)
AS YOU LIKE IT by William Shakespeare; Director, J. Perry McDonald; Producer, Iris Grossman; Sets, Charles McDonough; Lighting, Ricki Klein; Stage Manager, Kristine Holtvedt; Costumes, Mes Habits; Music, Stephen de Pietri. CAST: Sam Baker (Adam), Brian Benben (Oliver), James Bergen (Touchstone), Stuart Bernstein (Charles/Messenger), Carl Brown (Silvius), Nancy Cooney (Phebe), Stephen de Pietri (Amiens), Elbert L. Dinkins, Jr. (Sir Oliver Martext), Hunter Keble-Johnston (LeBeau), Greg Michaels (Orlando), Sasha Nanus (Rosalind/Ganymede), Lee Owens (Duke, Sr./Duke Frederick), Richard Pierce (Corin), Mary Ann Renz (Celia/Aliena), Emilie Roberts (Audrey), Gene Thomas (Jaques)

"The Importance of Being Earnest"
(Joseph Griffith Photo)

George Dal Lago, Victoria Vergara, Juan M. Aguero, Tony Diaz in "Everything Not Compulsory . . ."
(Ron Schwinn Photo)

PUERTO RICAN TRAVELING THEATRE

Miriam Colon, Executive Director
Administrator, Allen Davis III; Directors, Pablo Cabrera, Miriam Colon, Alba Oms; Sets, Robert Strohmeier, Carlos Carrasco; Costumes, Maria Ferreira, Benito Gutierrez-Soto; Lighting, Dan Bartlett, Larry Johnson, Robert Strohmeier, David Segal; Stage Managers, Ron Cappa, Toni Fernandez, Norberto Kerner, Steven Stewart-James, Manuel Yeskas; Press, Alan Eichler, Margarita Morales, Dylcia Pagan

LABORATORY THEATRE
June 25–July 18, 1976 (29 performances)
THE DINNER GUEST by Manuel Martinez Mediero; Translated by Ignacio Perez; Director, Alba Oms; Music, Arthur Jenkins; Choreography, Ernesto Gonzalez; Producer, Miriam Colon; Production Assistant, Jeanette Collazo; Sound, Toni Fernandez; Stage Manager, Norberto Kerner. CAST: Norberto Kerner (Father), Tony Diaz (Son), Ernesto Gonzalez (Guest), George Dal Lago (Butler) and EVERYTHING NOT COMPULSORY IS STRICTLY FORBIDDEN by Jorge Diaz; Other credits same as above. CAST: Luis Avalos (Gentleman), Eva De La O (Lady), Tony Diaz (Placido), Ernesto Gonzalez (Epifanio)

NEW YORK CITY PARKS
August 17–September 12, 1976 (22 performances)
ELEUTERIO, THE COQUI adapted by Pablo Cabrera, Miriam Colon and Rosa Luisa Marquez from a short story by Tomas Blanco; Songs, Rafael Hernandez; Director, Pablo Cabrera; Costumes, Benito Gutierrez-Soto; Set, Robert Strohmeier; Lights, Dan Bartlett; Stage Manager, Ron Cappa; Sound, Gary Harris; Producer, Miriam Colon; Associate Producer, Allen Davis III. CAST: Carlos Cestero (Narrator), Emmanuel Logrono (Eleuterio), Iraida Polanco (Mole Cricket), Ramon Pena (Cricket), Jose Machado (Bull Frog), Tony Diaz (Crow), Norberto Kerner (Sandpiper), Lauren Barnes (Tringa), Elia Enid (Pusilla), with EVERYTHING NOT COMPULSORY IS STRICTLY FORBIDDEN by Jorge Diaz; Other credits same as above. CAST: Tony Diaz (Gentleman), Victoria Vergara (Lady), Juan M. Aguero (Placido), George Dal Lago (Epifanio)

MANHATTAN CENTER
Saturday, April 30, 1977
LA CARRETA by Rene Marques; Director, Norberto Kerner; Producer, Miriam Colon. CAST: Marquitos Armendariz, Emil Belasco, Octavio Ciano, Peter John Deliz, Gloria Irizarry, Carmen Maya, Maria Norman, Iraida Polanco, Jaime Tirelli, Freddy Valle, Lucy Vega

FIREHOUSE THEATRE
May 19–June 12, 1977 (16 performances)
I TOOK PANAMA by Luis A. Garcia and Teatro Popular de Bogota; Translation, Tony Diaz; Costumes, Maria Ferreira; Lighting, David Segal; Music, Galt MacDermot; Movement, Julie Arenal; Director, Alba Oms; Producer, Miriam Colon. CAST: Juan M. Aguero, Luis Avalos, Carlos Carrasco, Peter John Deliz, Edouard DeSoto, Tony Diaz, Daniel Faraldo, Norberto Kerner, Juan Vaquer, Teresa Yenque, and CHORUS: Eddie Blanco, Eloida Hulbert, Pedro Morales, Carmen Rosario, Isabel Saez, Donaldo Spano, Manuel Torres

RICHARD MORSE MIME THEATRE

Richard Morse, Director
Ian Wilder, Production Director

RICHARD MORSE MIME THEATRE
December 22–26, 1976; February 18–April 16, 1977

COMPANY

Richard Morse

Rasa Allen	Charles Penn
Lee Copenhaver	Tina Sakai
Gjertine Johansen	Byam Stevens

REPERTOIRE: "Flirtations," "Leash to Leash," "Concert," "Fish Story," "Baseball," "Gargoyles of Notre Dame," "Death of a Poet," "Confuzione under the Balcone," "Pierrot's Lunar Fantasy," "At Court," "Five in the Afternoon," "Circus Rags," "Arrivals, Crush Hour," "Elevator," "Restaurant," "On Mad. Ave.," "Faucet," "Basketball," "Football," "Not Quite the Last Tango," "Civic Improvement," "Commedia," "Departures"

(Eric Jacobsen Photo)

Dick Shawn, Carol Teitel in "The World of Sholem Aleichem" Above: Richard Morse Mime Theatre

ROUNDABOUT THEATRE

Gene Feist, Producing Director
Michael Fried, Executive Producer
Mary Beth Carroll, General Manager
Eleventh Year

ROUNDABOUT THEATRE/STAGE TWO
Opened Wednesday, June 9, 1976.*
Roundabout Theatre presents:

A MONTH IN THE COUNTRY

By Ivan Turgenev; In a new adaptation by David Morgan; Director, Ronald Roston; Set, James R. Grant; Lighting, Dan Koetting; Costumes, Nancy L. Johnson; Sound, David Achelis; Technical Adviser, Lewis Mead

CAST

Schaaf	Fred Miller
Anna	Dolores Samperi
Lizaveta	Diane Tarleton
Natalya	Ella Luxembourg
Rakitin	John K. Carroll
Kolya	Ross Conrad
Beliayev	Jeff Rubin
Mattvei	Gerald Walker
Shpigelsky	Bernie Passeltiner
Vera	Vivian Kaye
Katya	Anastasia Nicole
Bolshintsov	Henry Ferrentino
Arkady	Richard Leighton

A play in three acts. The action takes place on the estate of Arkady Segeitch Yslaev on four days in the summer of 1831.

Press: Mark Arnold
Stage Manager: Cameron A. Thompson

* Closed June 26, 1976 after a limited engagement of 12 performances.

ROUNDABOUT THEATRE/STAGE ONE
Opened Tuesday, July 12, 1976.*
Roundabout Theatre presents:

THE WORLD OF SHOLEM ALEICHEM

By Arnold Perl; Director, Larry Arrick; Set, Akita Yoshimura; Costumes, Dianne Chapman; Lighting, Cheryl Thacker; Music, Robert DeCormier; Musical Supervision, Barbara Damasher; Sculpture, Jordan Steckel; Costume Supervision, David Chapman; Hairstylist, Robert Baker; Technical Director, Lewis Mead; Sound, Douglas Nolan; Wardrobe, Dorian Lo Pinto

CAST

Mendele/Aaron Katz	Dick Shawn
The Melamed/Prosecuting Angel/Principal	Michael Tucker
Rifkele/2nd Angel/2nd Woman	Suzanne Shepherd
Rabbi David/Bontche Schweig/Man	Jack Aaron
Angel Rochele/Defending Angel/Woman	Michele Shay
Stranger/Presiding Angel/Tutor/Dodi	Ed Hall
Rifkele's Friend/6th Angel/Hannah	Carol Teitel
Goatseller/3rd Angel/Aunt Reba	Rita Karin
Villager/1st Angel/Man	Mark Blum
Villager/4th Angel/Kholyava	Derek Meader
Villager/5th Angel/Moishe	Paul Regina

Presented in two parts.

Company Manager: Barbara Price
Press: Mark Arnold
Stage Managers: Douglas F. Goodman, J. R. Grant

* Closed Aug. 8, 1976 after 67 performances.

Gerry Goodstein Photo

Opened Wednesday, September 29, 1976.*
Roundabout Theatre presents:

THE PHILANDERER

By George Bernard Shaw; Director, Stephen Hollis; Set, Eldon
[...]der; Costumes, Christina Giannini; Lighting, Dan Koetting;
[...]riginal Score, Philip Campanella; Hairstylist, Robert Baker; Tech-
[...]cal Director, Frederick W. Fisher; Technical Coordinator, R. J.
[...]rick; Costume Supervisor, Nancy L. Johnson; Assistant Pro-
[...]cer, Gary Levine; Executive Assistant, Josephine Feagley; Ad-
[...]nistrative Assistants, Arthur Pearson, Martin Gewirtz

CAST

[...]onard Charteris	Donald Madden
[...]ace Tranfield	Marion Lines
[...]ia Craven	Cara Duff-MacCormick
[...]seph Cuthbertson	Ralph Clanton
[...]olonel Daniel Craven	George Ede
[...]lvia Craven	Pamela Brook
[...]. Percy Paramore	Jack Bittner
[...]e Page	William Perkiss

A comedy in three acts. The action takes place in London during
[...]93 in the drawing room of a flat in the Victoria district, the library
[...] the Ibsen Club, and in Dr. Paramore's reception room in Saville
[...]w.

General Manager: Mary Beth Carroll
Press: Mark Arnold
Stage Manager: Robert Neu

Closed Oct. 24, 1976 after 50 performances.

Frederic Ohringer PHotos

[...]ight: Cara Duff-MacCormick, Donald Madden
[...] Ralph Clanton, Cara Duff-MacCormick, Pamela
[...]ok, Donald Madden, Marion Lines, George Ede

Opened Thursday, October 14, 1976.*
Roundabout Theatre presents:

THE REHEARSAL

By Jean Anouilh; Director, Anthony Stimac; Set, Miguel Romero;
Costumes, David Murin; Original Score, Philip Campanella; Lighting, William Otterson; Technical Director, R. J. Turick; Assistant
to Director, Richard Earhardt; Wardrobe Supervisor, Teri Rosario-
Vasquez

CAST

The Countess	Elizabeth Owens
Damiens	Don Perkins
The Count	Barry Boys
Hortensia	Jean DeBaer
Hero	Philip Kerr
Villebosse	Edward Cicciarelli
Lucile	Alexandra Isles

A comedy in two acts. The action takes place during April 1952
in a chateau near LeMans.

General Manager: Mary Beth Carroll
Press: Mark Arnold
Stage Manager; Andrew Bales

* Closed Jan. 16, 1977 after 98 performances.

Amnon Nomis Photos

[...]arry Boys, Alexandra Isles, Elizabeth Owens
[...]bove: Alexandra Isles, Barry Boys, Philip Kerr

ROUNDABOUT THEATRE/STAGE ONE
Opened Wednesday, January 19, 1977.*
Roundabout Theatre presents:

JOHN GABRIEL BORKMAN

By Henrik Ibsen; Director, Gene Feist; Adapted by Mr. Feist; Original Score, Philip Campanella; Technical Director, R. J. Turick; Assistant to Director, Bonnie Panson; Props, Susan Stasiuk; Sound, Glennis Milliken

CAST

John Gabriel Borkman .... Robert Pastene
Gunhild Borkman .... Gale Sondergaard
Erhart Borkman .... Jeffrey David Pomerantz
Ella Rentheim .... Jan Farrand
Fanny Wilton .... Valerie French
Vilhelm Foldal .... Truman Gaige
Frida Foldal .... Madelon Thomas
Hulda .... Carolyn Sullivan

Understudy: Carolyn Sullivan

A drama in four acts performed with one intermission. The action takes place during a winter evening at Rentheim Manor some distance from Christiania, the Norwegian captial.

Company Manager: David Krimm
Press: Mark Arnold
Stage Manager: Robert Neu

* Closed Feb. 13, 1977 after 43 performances.
Amnon Nomis Photo

Jan Farrand, Robert Pastene, Gale Sondergaard

ROUNDABOUT THEATRE/STAGE TWO
Opened Thursday, February 24, 1977.*
Roundabout Theatre presents:

ENDGAME

By Samuel Beckett; Director, Gene Feist; Set, James Grant; Costumes, Nancy Johnson, Lighting, Frances Aronson

CAST

Hamm .... Gordon Heath
Clove .... Jake Dengel
Nagg .... Charles Randall
Nell .... Suzanne Shepherd

General Manager: Mary Beth Carroll
Press: Mark Arnold
Stage Manager: Franklin Davis

* Closed May 22, 1977 after 80 performances.

Peter Krupenye Photo

Charles Randall, Gordon Heath, Suzanne Shepherd

ROUNDABOUT THEATRE/STAGE ONE
Opened Thursday, April 28, 1977.*
Roundabout Theatre presents:

DEAR LIAR

By Jerome Kilty from the letters of Mrs. Patrick Campbell and George Bernard Shaw; Director, Mr . Kilty; Set, Robin Sherman; Costumes, Nancy L. Johnson; Lighting, R. J. Turick; Musical Supervision, Philip Campanella

CAST

George Bernard Shaw .... Jerome Kilty
Mrs. Patrick Campbell .... DeAnn Mears

Presented in two parts: Act One from 1899 to 1914, and Act Two from 1914 to 1939.

Company Manager, David Krimm
Press: Mark Arnold
Stage Managers: Errol Selsby, Frank Davis, Paul Moser

* Closed June 12, 1977 after 53 performances.

Peter Krupenye Photo

Jerome Kilty, DeAnn Mears

SPANISH THEATRE REPERTORY

Gilberto Zaldivar, Producer

GRAMERCY ARTS THEATRE

Opened Thursday, June 3, 1976 (still in repertory)
LA FIACA by Ricardo Talesnik; Director, Rene Buch; Designed by Robert Federico; Production Manager, Vivian de Angelo. CAST: Raul Davila (Nestor), Graciela Mas (Marta), Rene Sanchez (Peralta), Jusan Villarreal or Roberto Antonio (Jauregui, Ofelia Gonzalez (La Madre), Alfonso Manosalvas (Balbiani)

Opened Sunday, October 24, 1976 (still in repertory)
LA PIPA AZUL by Maggie Crespo; Director, Norberto Kerner; Lights, Robert Federico; Costumes, Maria Ferreira; Production Manager, Alberto Tore. CAST: Ofelia Gonzalez (Wife), Rene Sanchez or Norberto Kerner (Salesman), Vivian de Angelo (Salesgirl), Frank Robles (Husband)

November 13, 1976–February 19, 1977 (18 performances)
DONA ROSITA, LA SOLTERA by Federico Garcia Lorca; Director, Rene Buch; Design, Robert Federico; Costumes, Maria Ferreira; Assistant to Director, Alberto Tore; Visual Effects, Skip Ronglin; Musical Director, Juan Viccini. CAST: Ofelia Gonzalez, Lolina Gutierrez, Alfonso Manosalvas, Virginia Rambal, Raoul Alphonse, Tony Diaz, Roberto Antonio, Mirtha Cartaya, Vivian de Angelo, Juan Carlos Jimenez, Luisa Leschin, Graciela Mas, Nereida Mercado, Maria Norman, Rene Sanchez, Braulio Villar, Haydee Zambrana

November 26–28, 1976 (4 performances)
OKEY by Isaac Chocron; Director, Rene Buch; Set, Mario Arellano; Lights, Robert Federico; Costumes, Rene Sanchez; Production Manager, Alberto Tore; Assistant to Director, Tony Wagner; Stage Manager, Virginia Rambal. CAST: Velia Martinez (Mina), Griselda Noguera (Angela), Mario Ernesto Sanchez (Franco)

November 29, 1976–March 13, 1977 (4 performances)
RETABLO DE VIDA Y MUERTE by Mercedes Rein and Mario Morgan; Music, Federico Garcia Virgil; Singer, Jose Eduardo Brenila; Guitar, Daniel Queiros; Costumes, Guma Zorrilla; Director, Mario Morgan. CAST: Estela Medina

December 9, 1976–January 30, 1977 (15 performances)
LA MAXIMA FELICIDAD by Isaac Chocron; Director, Pablo Cabrera; Design, Robert Federico; Production Manager, Alberto Tore; Stage Manager, Virginia Rambal. CAST: Francisco Prado (Pablo), Maria Norman (Perla), Octavio Ciano (Leo)

Opened Saturday, February 5, 1977 (still in repertory)
LA DECENTE by Miguel Mihura; Director, Rene Buch; Design, Robert Federico; Costumes, Rene Sanchez; Assistant to Director, Vivian de Angelo; Production Manager, Alberto Tore. CAST: Alfonso Manosalvas (Roberto), Mirtha Cartaya (Nuria), Rene Sanchez (Miranda), Frank Robles or Juan Villarreal (Pepe), Maria Norman or Graciela Mas (Genara), Ofelia Gonzalez (El Ama)

Opened Sunday, February 13, 1977 (still in repertory)
EL CENSO by Emilio Carballido; Director, Delfor Peralta; Lights, Robert Federico; Production Manager, Alberto Tore. CAST: Virginia Rambal (Herlinda), Frank Robles (Census Taker), Vivian de Angelo (Dora), Alfonso Manosalvas (Paco), Maria Norman (Concha), Ofelia Gonzalez

Opened Tuesday, March 1, 1976 (still in repertory)
LA CELESTINA by Fernando de Rojas; Director, Rene Buch; Design, Robert Federico; Production Manager, Alberto Tore. CAST: Ofelia Gonzalez (Celestina), Virginia Rambal or Maria Norman (Areusa), Roberto Antonio (Calisto), Teresa Yenque (Elicia), Mirtha Cartaya (Melibea), Braulio Villar (Parmeno), Alfonso Manosalvas (Pleberio), Julio Hara (Sempronio)

Opened Wednesday, March 16, 1977 (still in repertory)
LA DAMA DUENDE by Pedro Calderon de la Barca; Director, Rene Buch; Design, Robert Federico; Production Manager, Alberto Tore; Costumes, Ofelia Gonzalez; Musical Director, Juan Viccini. CAST: Virginia Rambal (Angela), Mirtha Cartaya (Beatriz), Braulio Villar (Cosme), Teresa Yenque or Nereida Mercado (Isabel), Nino Roger or William Perez (Juan), Julio Hara (Luis), Roberto Antonio (Manuel), Mateo Gomez or Juan Carlos Jimenez (Rodrigo), Nereida Mercado or Patricia Jimenez Rojo (Clara)

Sunday & Monday, April 10–11, 1977 (2 performances)
GRUPO TEATRAL UNIVERSITARIO DE VALLADOLID DE ESPANA in two plays by Cervantes: "El Retablo de Las Maravillas" and "El Viejo Celoso." CAST: Juan A. Quintana, Yolanda Bolado, Jose Urbistondo, Jose Gonzalez, Juan Miralles, Orencio Frutos, Idoia Kamiruaga, Mery Maroto, Ramon Serrada, Julio de Benito

(Gerry Goodstein Photos)

Opened Sunday, April 24, 1977 (still in repertory)
AMOR DE DON PERLIMPLIN CON BELISA EN SU JARDIN by Federico Garcia Lorca; Director, Christopher Martin; Lights, Robert Federico; Costumes, Ofelia Gonzalez; Production Manager, Alberto Tore. CAST: Alfonso Manosalvas (Don Perlimplin), Vivian de Angelo (Belisa), Ofelia Gonzalez (Marcolfa), Virginia Rambal (Mother)

April 25 and May 2, 1977 (2 performances)
HOLA . . . HOLA . . . 1, 2, 3 three monologues: "La Voz Humana" by Jean Cocteau, "Perdon, Numero Equivocado" by L. Fletcher, and "Pobre Sra. de Smith" by Noel Coward; Translated by China Zorrilla; Costumes, Guma Zorrilla; Lights, Robert Federico; Production Manager, Braulio Villar; Production Assistant, Alberto Tore; Stage Manager, Virginia Rambal. CAST: China Zorrilla

May 18–22, 1977 (6 performances)
LOS FANTASTIKOS with Book and Lyrics by Tom Jones; Music, Harvey Schmidt; Director, Rene Buch; Design, Mario R. Arellano; Lights, Robert Federico; Choreography, Josefina R. Arellano; Costumes, Rene Sanchez; Musical Director, Julio Gutierrez; Special Collaboration, Margot Ros. CAST: Chamaco Garcia (Narrator), Ana Margarita Martinez Casado (Girl), Mario Martin (Boy's Father), Hector Fernandez (Boy), Rene Alejandro (Girl's Father), Carlos Poce (Actor), Francisco Fernandez-Suarez (Mute), Rene Sanchez (Man Who Dies)

Press: Marian Graham

Top Right: Ofelia Gonzalez, Rene Sanchez in "La Pipa Azul" Below: Braulio Villar in "La Dama Duende"

Above: Velia Martinez, Griselda Noguera, Mario Ernesto Sanchez in "Okey"

THE STAGE COMPANY

Artistic Director, Robert D. Simons; Managing Director, Lindsay Gambini; Business Manager, Gary Hotvedt; Press, Bruce Cohen, Marilynn LeVine, Gerry Santangelo; Administrative Assistants, Polly Glasser, Helene Greece.

FLUSHING TOWN HALL

November 17–December 8, 1976 (21 performances)
TWELFTH NIGHT by William Shakespeare; Director, Robert D. Simons; Scenery, Elliot Gerber; Costumes, Patricia Adshead; Lights, Gary Weathersbee; Special Music, Logan Pope; Technical Director, Gary Hotvedt; Stage Managers, Gary Weathersbee, Arlene Grayson. CAST: Arlene Grayson (Viola), James Fleetwood (Sir Toby), Bill Nunnery (Aguecheek), Nancy Nutter (Maria), Ian O'Connell (Feste), Jerry Rodgers (Malvolio), Linda Sherwood (Olivia), Robert Barnes (Fabian), Edward Conery (Orsino), Michael Hill (Sebastian), Gerry Santangel (Valentine), Michael Seidenberg (Curio), John Wyeth (Antonio).

January 5–19, 1977 (16 performances)
CHILD'S PLAY by Robert Marasco; Director, Lucia Victor; Scenery, Robert E. Franklin; Costumes, Patricia Adshead; Lighting, Gary Weathersbee; Stage Managers, Gary Weathersbee, Jerry Rodgers. CAST: Peter Bosche (Jerome Malley), George Cavey (Fr. Griffin), Michael Hennessey (Paul Reese) Jerry Rodgers (Fr. Mozian), Evan Thompson (Joseph Dobbs), Roy Lavitt (Carre), John Feiden (Medley), Jerry Peluso (Banks), Owen Flaherty (Jennings), Billy Van Dyke (O'Donnell), Dan Da Silva (Shea), Bernard Ferstenberg (Wilson), Tucker Howard (McArdle), Evan Turk (Travis)

February 16–March 9, 1977 (24 performances)
WHAT THE BUTLER SAW by Joe Orton; Director, Lucia Victor; Scenery, Robert E. Franklin; Lights, Jo Mayer; Stage Managers, Arlene Grayson; Costume Coordinator, Susanna Howard; Production Coordinator, Valerie Simmons; Technical Director, Charles LeFehr. CAST: Kim Ameen (Geraldine Barclay), Edward Conery (Sgt. Match), Kensyn Crouch (Dr. Prentice), Stephen Currens (Nicholas Beckett), Joyce Krempel (Mrs. Prentice), Sy Travers (Dr. Rance)

March 30–April 13, 1977 (16 performances)
EYE FOR AN I by Lucia Victor; Director, Miss Victor; Costumes, Michael J. Cesario; Scenery, Robert E. Franklin; Lights, Jo Mayer; Props, Billy Van Dyke, Laura Kornstein; Production Coordinator, Theodore Pappas; Stage Manager, Arlene Grayson. CAST: Don Draper (Theodore Jurgann), Robert Aberdeen (Gabe Grotofski), Constance Dix (Louisa Jurgann), Michale Hennessey (Frank Thompson), Kathleen Swan (Eleanora Jurgann), Robert Barnes (Norris), Warren Ball (Dr. White), Joseph Grzetic (Jackson), Joseph Martin (Joe), Billy Van Dyke (Santini)

May 12–June 2, 1977 (22 performances)
I DO! I DO! by Tom Jones (Book and Lyrics) and Harvey Schmidt (Music); Director, Joseph G. Rodgers; Scenery, Eddie Feldman; Lights, Jo Mayer; Costumes, Kate Bergh; Musical Director, Randy Barnett; Choreography, Theodore Pappas; Stage Manager, Dan Early; Wardrobe, Sylvia Gruen. CAST: Meg Bussert (Agnes), John Stratton (Michael)

Cast of "Six Characters in Search of an Author"
(Theatre Off Park)

152

THEATRE OFF PARK

Executive Directors, Martin deMaat, James Howe
Associate Director, Patricia Flynn Peate

THEATRE OFF PARK

August 5–15, 1976 (8 performances)
SIX CHARACTERS IN SEARCH OF A PLOT consists of scene developed by the cast and Director Martin deMaat; Words an Music, Thom McCleister, Dan Gruver; Stage Managers, Stace Griffin, Thomas Farrington; Lighting, Bob McAndrew; Pianis Tom Garro. CAST: Marsha Clark, Sharon Good, Thom Mc Cleister, Patricia Meaney, Raymond Riberdy, Martin Shapiro

November 4–14, 1976 (8 performances)
KRAPP'S LAST TAPE by Samuel Beckett; Directed by Jame Howe; Set and Costumes, James Howe; Lights, Martin deMaa Film, Graphcild and Skywalls. CAST: John Capodice (Krapp with COME AND GO by Samuel Beckett; Other credits same a above. CAST: Jane Crawley (Vi), Erica Brown (Ru) Suzanne Co lins (Flo), and NIGHT by Harold Pinter; Other credits same a above. CAST: Richard Broad (Man), Jane Crawley (Woman)

December 2–19, 1976 (12 performances)
THE LAST DAYS OF THE WITCHITA KID by Carla Conwa Director, Donald Warfield; Set, Paty; Stage Managers, Lind Lucero, Kurt Feuer; Lights, Bernita Robinson, James Shewalte CAST: Nicholas Guest (Tony), Tina Austin (Margie), Robert Hi (Sonny), Gayle Kelly Landers (Sue Ellen), Shannon McG (Freddy), Regina David (Teresa), Chester Clarke (Frank), L Archer Tardell (Torey), Michael Houlihan (Sean), Gary Cox (M chael), Kurt Feuer (Timothy)

February 18–20, 1977 (3 performances)
JOURNEY by Ronn Tombaugh; Adapted and Directed by Lest Malizia; Lighting, Larry Johnson; Stage Managers, Arlene Rit Melissa Taylor; Technician, Jim Harwell. CAST: Ned Osterho (Boy), Joseph Mauck (Father), Ray Robertson (Friend), Mauree McDonald (Mother), Leslie Blake (Lady), Nora Baetz (Friend)

April 7–24, 1977 (12 performances)
EMIGRES by Slawomir Mrozek; Translation, Maciej and Teres Wrona with Robert Holman; Director, Tim Curnen; Set, John W Jacobsen; Lighting, Stan Salfas; Sound, Steve Rich; Stage Manage Christine S. Banas; Production Manager, Aileen M. Smith; Techn cal Director, Jonathan McCormick; Props, Judy Hamil. CAST Marcus Smythe, Kelly Monaghan

Top: Ian O'Connell, Maggie Da Silva, Linda
Sherwood (seated) in "Twelfth Night" Below:
Kathleen Swan, Constance Dix, Don Draper,
Michael Hennessey in "Eye for an I" (Stage Co.)

OFF-BROADWAY PRODUCTIONS FROM OTHER SEASONS THAT PLAYED THROUGH THIS SEASON

SULLIVAN STREET PLAYHOUSE
Opened Tuesday, May 3, 1960.*
Lore Noto presents:

THE FANTASTICKS

Book and Lyrics, Tom Jones; Suggested by Edmond Rostand's "Les Romanesques"; Music, Harvey Schmidt; Director, Word Baker; Original Musical Direction and Arrangements, Julian Stein; Designed by Ed Wittstein; Associate Producers, Sheldon Baron, Dorothy Olim, Robert Alan Gold; Assistant to the Producer, Thad Noto; Production Assistant, John Krug

CAST

The Narrator	David Brummel†1
The Girl	Sarah Rice†2
The Boy	Ralph Bruneau†3
The Boy's Father	Lore Noto
The Girl's Father	Arthur Andersen†4
The Actor	Seamus O'Brien†5
The Man Who Dies	James Cook†6
The Mute	Tom Flagg†7
At the piano	William F. McDaniel
At the harp	Pattee Cohen

MUSICAL NUMBERS: Overture, "Try to Remember," "Much More," "Metaphor," "Never Say No," "It Depends on What you Pay," "Soon It's Gonna Rain," "Rape Ballet," "Happy Ending," "This Plum Is Too Ripe," "I Can See It," "Plant a Radish," "Round and Round," "They Were You," Finale

A musical in two acts.

Press: Bob Pribble, Anthony Noto
Stage Managers: Ned Levy, Anthony Rasemus

* Still playing May 31, 1977. For original production, see THEATRE WORLD Vol. 16.
† Succeeded by: 1. Keith Charles, Joe Gagliano, 2. Betsy Joslyn, 3. Bruce Cryer, 4. David Vogel, 5. Donald Babcock, 6. Bill Preston, Liam O'Begley, 7. John Thomas Waite

Cast of "The Fantasticks"

Jane Galloway, Sally Sockwell, Susan Merson in "Vanities"

WESTSIDE THEATER
Opened Monday, March 22, 1976.*
The Chelsea Theater Center, the Lion Theatre Company, and Playwrights Horizons present:

VANITIES

By Jack Heifner; Director, Garland Wright; Scenery, John Arnone; Lighting, Patrika Brown; Costumes, David James; Wardrobe Mistress, Gertrude Sloan

CAST

Kathy	Jane Galloway
Mary	Susan Merson
Joanne	Kathy Bates†

MITZI E. NEWHOUSE THEATER
Opened Wednesday, April 21, 1976.*
The New York Shakespeare Festival (Joseph Papp, Producer)
presents:

STREAMERS

By David Rabe; Director, Mike Nichols; Setting, Tony Walton; Costumes, Bill Walker; Lighting, Ronald Wallace; Production Assistant, Kathy Talbert; Wardrobe Master, Al Calamoneri; Production Supervisor, Jason Steven Cohen; Production Manager, Andrew Mihok

CAST

Martin	Michael Kell
Richie	Peter Evans
Carlyle	Dorian Harewood†1
Billy	Paul Rudd†2
Roger	Terry Alexander
Sgt. Rooney	Kenneth McMillan†3
Sgt. Cokes	Dolph Sweet†4
M. P. Officer	Arlen Dean Snyder†5
Hinson, M. P.	Les Roberts†6
Clark, M. P.	Mark Metcalf†7
M. P.	Miklos Horvath†8

UNDERSTUDIES: Thomas A. Stewart (Richie/Clark/Hinson/Martin/M.P. Officer), Howard E. Rollins, Jr. (Carlyle/Roger), Bernie McInerney (Cokes/Rooney), Ted LePlat (Billy/Martin/M.P.)

A drama in two acts. The action takes place in 1965 in an army barracks in Virginia.

General Manager: Robert Kamlot
Press: Merle Debuskey, Faith Geer
Stage Managers: Nina Seely, Miklos Korvath, Tom Gardner

* Closed June 5, 1977 after 478 performances and 17 previews. For original production, see THEATRE WORLD Vol. 32.
† Succeeded by: 1. Kene Holliday, 2. Mark Metcalf, Peter Weller, 3. Joseph Bova, 4. Philip Bosco, 5. Bernie McInerney, 6. Howard E. Rollins, Jr., 7. Ted LePlat, 8. Thomas A. Stewart

Martha Swope Photos

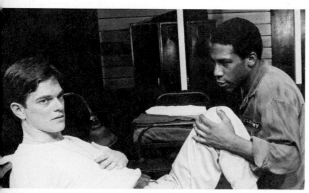

Thomas A. Stewart, Kene Holliday Top Right: Peter Evans, Mark Metcalf, Terry Alexander, Dolph Sweet, Kenneth McMillan

Bernie McInerney, Thomas A. Stewart, Ted LePlat, Terry Alexander, Kene Holliday, Howard Rollins, Jr., Peter Weller (prone)

OFF-BROADWAY PRODUCTIONS FROM OTHER SEASONS THAT CLOSED THIS SEASON

Title	Opened	Closed	Performance
Let My People Come	1/8/74	7/4/76	1167
Women Behind Bars	4/20/76	1/26/77	324
The Threepenny Opera	5/1/76	1/23/77	306

PRODUCTIONS THAT OPENED AND CLOSED BEFORE SCHEDULED BROADWAY PREMIER

THE BAKER'S WIFE

Book, Joseph Stein; Based on "La Femme du Boulanger" by Marcel Pagnol and Jean Giono; Music and Lyrics, Stephen Schwartz; Director, Joseph Hardy†1; Choreography, Dan Siretta†2; Settings, Joe Mielziner; Costumes, Theoni V. Aldredge; Lighting, Jennifer Tipton; Musical Direction, Don Jennings†3; Dance Arrangements, Daniel Troob; Orchestrations, Thomas Pierson; Production Supervisor, Lucia Victor; Sound, Robert Maybaum; Wardrobe Master, Gene Wilson; Associate Conductor, Larry Hochman; Presented by David Merrick; Opened Tuesday, May 11, 1976 in the Dorothy Chandler Pavilion in Los Angeles, and closed Nov. 13, 1976 at Kennedy Center Opera House.

CAST

Teacher	Timothy Jerome
Antoine	Gordon Connell
Barnaby	Pierre Epstein
Therese	Portia Nelson
Henriette	Darlene Conley
Claude	Benjamin Rayson†4
Le Marquis	Keene Curtis
Colette	Tara Leigh
Melissa	Cynthia Parva
Simone	Jean McLaughlin
Denise	Teri Ralston
Priest	David Rounds
Aimable	Chaim Topol†5
Genevieve	Carole Demas†6
Dominique	Kurt Peterson
Raoul	Tony Schultz
Jean-Paul	Bill Mullikin

UNDERSTUDIES: Michael Quinn (Aimable/Antoine/Claude), Bill Mullikin (Le Marquis/Priest/Teacher/Barnaby), Denise Lor (Denise/Therese/Henriette), Teri Ralston (Genevieve), Francisco Lagueruela (Dominique/Raoul)

MUSICAL NUMBERS: "Welcome to Concorde," "A Little Taste of Heaven," "Gifts of Love," "Bread," "Proud Lady," "Serenade," "Meadowlark," "Any-Day-Now Day," "Something's Got to Be Done," "Romance," "Endless Delights," "The Luckiest Man in the World," "If I Have to Live Alone," "Where is the Warmth?," Finale

A musical in two acts. The action takes place in a small village in Provence, France, in the recent past.

General Manager: Helen L. Nickerson
Company Manager: G. Warren McClane
Press: Solters/Roskin, Joshua Ellis, Milly Schoenbaum, Fred H. Nathan
Stage Managers: Robert Borod, Pat Trott, Kathleen Robey

† Succeeded by: 1. John Berry, 2. Robert Tucker, 3. Robert Billig, 4. Charles Rule, 5. Paul Sorvino, 6. Patti LuPone

Martha Swope Photos

Right: Tara Leigh, Jean McLaughlin, Keene Curtis, Cynthia Parva Above: Kurt Peterson, Patti LuPone, Topol (R)

Keene Curtis (L), David Rounds (C), Paul Sorvino (R)

Patti LuPone, Paul Sorvino

THE BED BEFORE YESTERDAY

By Ben Travers; Director, Lindsay Anderson; Scenery, John Lee Beatty; Costumes, Mary McKinley; Lighting, Neil Peter Jampolis; Assistant to Director, Louis Pulvino; Wardrobe, Sam Elterman; Production Assistants, William Goulding, Thomas Madigan, Barbara Price; Production Manager, Mitchell Erickson; Associate Producer, Eric Friedheim; Presented by Arthur Cantor by arrangement with H. M. Tennent; Opened Friday, October 22, 1976 at the Playhouse in Wilmington, DE., and closed January 15, 1977 at the Poinciana Theatre in Palm Beach, FL.

CAST

Victor Keene	Elliott Reid
Alma	Carol Channing
Mrs. Holly	Barbara Lester
Aubrey	Henry Dibling
Ella	Caroline McWilliams
Lolly Tucker	Ludi Claire
Felix	Barry Vigon
Fred Castle	Paxton Whitehead
Taxi Driver	John Neville-Andrews

A comedy in two acts and six scenes. The action takes place in the spring and summer of 1930 in Alma's house in Brompton Mews, London.

Company Manager: Ken Krezel
Press: Solters & Roskin, Milly Schoenbaum, Fred Nathan
Stage Managers: T. L. Boston, Richard Delahanty

Martha Swope Photos

Elliott Reid, Carol Channing

Carol Channing, and Left with Ludi Claire

THE DREAM

By Richard Lortz; From the book by Lucy Freeman; Director, Edwin Sherin; Scenery, William Ritman; Costumes, Theoni V. Aldredge; Lighting, Marc B. Weiss; Special Effects, Charles Gross; Wardrobe Mistress, Agnes Farrell; Assistant to Director, Emilie Fanchon Condon; Production Associate, Ada Green; Presented by Joel W. Schenker; Opened Monday, Feb. 7, 1977 at the Forrest Theatre in Philadelphia, PA, and closed there Feb. 12, 1977.

CAST

Dr. William Ames	Lee Richardson
Lt. Lonegan	Michael Higgins
Elaine Thomas	Barbara Baxley
Susan Michaels	Louise Sorel
James Browne	Michael Wager
Norma Dodd	Ann Wedgeworth
Jonathan Thomas	Keith Charles

UNDERSTUDIES: Lynda Myles (Elaine/Norma/Susan), Frank Latimore (Ames/Lonegan), Wayne Carson (Jonathan/James)

A play in two acts. The action takes place in the middle of the summer at the present time.

General Manager: Victor Samrock
Company Manager: G. Warren MacLane
Press: Max Eisen, Barbara Glenn, Judy Jacksina
Stage Managers: John Actman, Wayne Carson

(No photos taken)

HELLZAPOPPIN

Written by Abe Burrows, Bill Heyer, Hank Beebe; Based on format by Olson and Johnson; Music, Jule Styne, Hank Beebe, Cy Coleman; Lyrics, Carolyn Leigh, Bill Heyer; Director, Jerry Adler; Choreography, Donald Saddler; Scenery and Lighting, Robert Randolph; Costumes, Alvin Colt; Hairstylist, Joe Tubens; Sound, Jack Shearing; Musical Supervision, Elliot Lawrence; Orchestrations, Ralph Burns; Dance Music, Gordon Lowry Harrell; Musical Conductor, John Lesko; Co-Producers, Hildy Parks, Roy A. Somlyo; Associate Conductor, Louis Brown; Production Assistants, Susan Guernsey, Juliet Wise; Wardrobe Supervisor, Elonzo Dann; Wardrobe Mistress, Betty Lee Matelli; Presented by Alexander H. Cohen in association with Maggie and Jerome Minskoff; Opened Monday, Nov. 22, 1976 at the Mechanic Theatre in Baltimore, MD., and closed Jan. 22, 1977 at the Colonial Theatre in Boston, MA.

CAST
Jerry Lewis
Lynn Redgrave

Mace Barrett	Brandon Maggart
Tom Batten	Michael Mann
Marie Berry	P. J. Mann
Terry Calloway	Dana Jo Moore
Jill Choder	Rick Pessagno
Susan Danielle	Rodney Reiner
Herb Edelman	Terry Rieser
Mercedes Ellington	Catherine Rice
Joey Faye	Jeff Richards
Robert Fitch	Tudi Roach
Trudie Green	Jane Robertson
Lisa Guignard	Karen St. George
Lisa Haapaniemi	Fred Siretta
Bob Harvey	Robin Stone
Peter Heuchling	The Villams
Gwen Hillier	The Volantes
Justine Johnston	Bob Williams & Louie
Holly Jones	Melanie Winter
Leonardo	

MUSICAL NUMBERS: "Hellzapoppin," "A Husband, A Lover, A Wife," "Bouncing Back for More," "Eighth Avenue," "Once I've Got My Cane," "Hello, Mom," "Back to Him," "A Hymn to Her," "A Miracle Happened," "One to a Customer," Finale

"A musical circus" in two acts.

Company Manager: Seymour Herscher
Press: David Powers
Stage Managers: Marnel Sumner, Michael Turque, Phil DiMaggio

Martha Swope Photos

Top Right: Lynn Redgrave, Mace Barrett, Brandon Maggart Below: Lynn Redgrave, Jerry Lewis

Jerry Lewis, Herb Edelman, Lynn Redgrave

Joey Faye, Jerry Lewis

(Failure to submit material necessitated several omissions)

THE BELLE OF AMHERST

By William Luce; Compiled by Timothy Helgeson; Director, Charles Nelson Reilly; Scenery and Lighting, H. R. Poindexter; Costumes, Theoni V. Aldredge; Hair Design, Ray Iagnocco; Production Supervisor, George Eckert; A Dome/Creative Image Production; Presented by Mike Merrick and Don Gregory. Opened Monday, Sept. 13, 1976 at Kennedy Center, Washington, DC, and closed May 27, 1977 in Berkeley, CA.

CAST

JULIE HARRIS

A play in two acts based on the life and works of Emily Dickinson. The action takes place in the Dickinson home in Amherst, Massachusetts, between 1845 and 1886.

General Manager: James Awe
Company Manager: Charles Willard
Press: Seymour Krawitz, Gertrude Bromberg
Stage Managers: George Eckert, Berny Baker

For original NY production, see THEATRE WORLD Vol. 32. Miss Harris received a 1977 "Tony" Award (her fifth) for Best Actress.

Sy Friedman Photo

Julie Harris

BUBBLING BROWN SUGAR

Book, Loften Mitchell; Based on concept by Rosetta LeNoire; Director, Robert M. Cooper; Choreography and Musical Staging by Billy Wilson; Musical Direction and Arrangements, Danny Holgate; Sets, Clarke Dunham; Lighting, Barry Arnold; Costumes, Bernard Johnson; Projections, Lucie D. Grosvenor and Clarke Dunham; Hairstylist, Gene Sheppard; Choral Arrangements; Musical Conductor, William Foster McDaniel; Production Supervisor, I. Mitchell Miller; Production Coordinator, Sharon Brown; Wardrobe Supervisor, Olga Anderson; Presented by J. Lloyd Grant, Richard Bell, Robert M. Cooper, Ashton Springer in association with M.G.B. Associates Ltd.; Opened June 22, 1976 at the Shubert Theatre in Chicago, and still touring May 31, 1977.

CAST

Skip	Ronald "Smokey" Stevens
Bill/Time Man/M.C.	Charles "Honi" Coles
Ray/Young Sage	Robert Melvin
Carolyn/Nightclub Singer	Marilyn Johnson
Norma	Yolanda Graves
Gene/Young Checkers	Marcus B. F. Brown
Helen	Vikki Baltimore
Laura	Nancy-Suzanne
Marsha/Young Irene	Ursuline Kairson
Newsboy/Gospel Lady's Son/Nightclub Singer	Keith Davis
Tony/Waiter/Dutch	Alan Zampese
Irene Paige	Mable Lee
John Sage/Dusty	Vernon Washington
Checkers/Rusty	Jay Flash Riley
Jim	J. Edward Adams
Ella	Terri Burrell
Judy/Dutch's Girl	Stephanie Kurz
Charlie/Count	Richard Casper
Gospel Lady	Lucille Futrell Harley
The Solitunes	Marcus B. F. Brown, Ronald "Smokey" Stevens, Keith Davis, Ursuline Kairson
Bumpy	Hugh Hurd
Singers	Marilyn Johnson, Hugh Hurd, Dolly Lauria, William Bremer

MUSICAL NUMBERS: See Broadway production, page 78

A musical revue in 2 acts and 9 scenes. The action takes place in Harlem at the present time, and between 1920 and 1940.

General Manager: Ashton Springer
Company Manager: Douglas Helgeson
Press: Max Eisen, Maurice Turet
Stage Managers: Jack Welles, Femi Sarah Heggie, Nancy-Suzanne

Mable Lee

BULLY

By Jerome Alden; Director, Peter H. Hunt; Setting and Costumes, John Conklin; Lighting, Peter H. Hunt; General Management, Theatre Now, Inc. (William Court Cohen, Edward H. Davis); Production Supervisor, Mitch Miller; Production Assistants, Sam Anderson, Joel Rosenzweig, Raul Moncada; A George Spota and Four Star International presentation; Opened Thursday, Feb. 10, 1977 in Wilmington, DE., and closed June 12, 1977 at the Ahmanson Theatre, Los Angeles, CA.

CAST

JAMES WHITMORE

"An adventure with Teddy Roosevelt" in two acts.

Company Manager: John Caruso
Press: Mary Bryant, Sol Jacobson, Bruce Cohen
Stage Managers: Martha Knight, Leanna Lenhart

Ken Howard Photo

James Whitmore

A CHORUS LINE

Conceived, Directed and Choreographed by Michael Bennett; Book, James Kirkwood, Nicholas Dante; Music, Marvin Hamlisch; Lyrics, Edward Kleban; Setting, Robin Wagner; Costumes, Theoni V. Aldredge; Lighting, Tharon Musser; Sound Abe Jacob; Co-choreographer, Bob Avian; Orchestrations, Bill Byers, Hershy Kay, Jonathan Tunick; Music Direction and Vocal Arrangements, Don Pippin; Musical Direction, Larry Blank; Associate Producer, Bernard Gersten; Presented by the New York Shakespeare Festival (Joseph Papp, Producer) in association with Plum Productions; Opened Monday, May 3, 1976 at the Royal Alexandra Theatre, Toronto, Can., and still playing May 31, 1977. For original NY production, see THEATRE WORLD Vol. 31.

CAST

Paul	Tommy Aguilar
Jarad	Michael Austin
Kristine	Christine Barker
Al	Steve Baumann
Vicki	Nancy Dafgek†1
Tom	Mark Dovey†2
Maggie	Jean Fraser†3
Frank	Troy Garza
Val	Mitzi Hamilton†4
Zach	Eivind Harum
Mike	Jeff Hyslop
Diana	Loida Iglesias†5
Louis	Anthony Inneo
Greg	Andy Keyser†6
Bobby	Ron Kurowski
Connie	Jennifer Ann Lee
Lois	Wendy Mansfield
Judy	Yvette Mathews†7
Richie	A. William Perkins
Barbara	Martie Hatem Ramm
Larry	T. Michael Reed
Butch	Ken Rogers
Cassie	Sandy Roveta†8
Mark	Timothy Scott
Roy	Don Simione
Sheila	Jane Summerhays
Bebe	Miriam Welch
Tricia	Nancy Wood
Don	Ronald Young†9

For musical numbers, see Broadway Calendar, page 80

General Manager: Emanuel Azenberg
Company Manager: Maurice Schaded
Press: Merle Debuskey, Horace Greeley McNab
Stage Managers: Jeff Hamlin, Martin Herzer, David Taylor, Michael Austin

† Succeeded by: 1. Judy Burns, 2. Ron Stafford, 3. Betty Lynd, 4. Karen Jablons, 5. Gina Paglia, 6. Mark Dovey, 7. Murphy Cross, 8. Pamela Sousa, 9. Brandt Edwards

Martha Swope Photos

Jane Summerhays, Eivind Harum, Sanda Roveta

A CHORUS LINE

Conceived, Choreographed and Directed by Michael Bennett; Book, James Kirkwood, Nicholas Dante; Music, Marvin Hamlisch; Lyrics, Edward Kleban; Setting, Robin Wagner; Costumes, Theoni V. Aldredge; Lighting, Tharon Musser; Sound, Abe Jacob; Co-choreographer, Bob Avian; Orchestrations, Bill Byers, Hershy Kay, Jonathan Tunick; Music Coordinator, Robert Thomas; Music Direction and Vocal Arrangements, Don Pippin; Musical Direction, Arthur Rubinstein; Associate Conductor, Tom Hancock; Associate Producer, Bernard Gersten; Presented by the New York Shakespeare Festival (Joseph Papp, Producer) in association with Plum Productions; Opened Tuesday, May 11, 1975 at the Curran Theatre in San Francisco, and still playing May 31, 1977; For original NY production, see THEATRE WORLD Vol. 31.

CAST

Kristine	Renee Baughman†1
Val	Pamela Blair
Roy	Tim Cassidy
Mark	Paul Charles†2
Maggie	Kay Cole†3
Mike	Don Correia
Richie	Ronald Dennis
Judy	Patricia Garland
Greg	Andy Keyser
Don	Ron Kuhlman†4
Bebe	Nancy Lane
Connie	Baayork Lee†5
Diana	Priscilla Lopez†6
Zach	Robert LuPone†7
Cassie	Donna McKechnie†8
Vicki	Mary Ann O'Reilly
Bobby	Scott Pearson†9
Al	Don Percassi
Sheila	Charlene Ryan†10
Larry	Roy Smith
Butch	Sam Tampoya
Tom	Danny Taylor
Frank	Claude R. Tessier
Paul	Sammy Williams
Lois	Lee Wilson
Tricia	Rebecca York†11

For musical numbers, see Broadway Calender, page 80

General Manager: Emanuel Azenberg
Company Managers: Peter Neufeld, Douglas C. Baker
Press: Merle Debuskey, Judi Davidson
Stage Managers: Jeff Hamlin, Patricia Drylie, Frank Hartenstein, Andy G. Bew, Peter von Mayrhauser

† Succeeded by: 1.Cookie Vasquez, 2. Jimmy Roddy, 3. Donna Drake, Lisa Donaldson, 4. Dennis Edenfield, 5. Lauren Kayahara, 6. Chris Bocchino, 7. Joe Bennett, 8. Ann Reinking, Vicki Frederick, Pamela Peadon, 9. Michael Austin, 10. Kelly Bishop during illness, 11. Linda Dangcil

Baayork Lee, Sammy Williams, Donna Drake, Jimmy Roddy, Pamela Blair, Don Correia, Cookie Vazquez, Dennis Edenfield, Patricia Garland, Andy Keyser, Ann Reinking, Scott Pearson, Charlene Ryan, Don Percassi, Nancy Lane, Ronald Dennis, Chris Bocchino Top: Roy Smith, Pamela Peadon, Joe Bennett

EMLYN WILLIAMS AS CHARLES DICKENS
and
DYLAN THOMAS GROWING UP

Two programs devised by Emlyn Williams from the works of Charles Dickens and Dylan Thomas; Lighting and Production Supervision, Robert Crawley; Personal Assistant to Mr. Williams, Brian Stashick; Presented by Arthur Cantor; Press, C. George Willard, Barbara Price; Opened Sept. 14, 1976 in New Haven, and closed March 26, 1977 in Buffalo, NY.

CAST
EMLYN WILLIAMS

A solo performance presented in two parts.

**Emlyn Williams
as Charles Dickens**

DON'T BOTHER ME, I CAN'T COPE

By Micki Grant; Conceived and Directed by Vinnette Carroll; Choreography, Edmond Kresley; Assistant Director, Clinton Derricks; Lighting, Ken Billington; Musical Arrangements, Danny Holgate; Costumes, William Schroder; Musical Director, George Broderick; Production Supervisor, Roger Franklin; Presented by Tom Mallow in association with James Janek; Management, American Theatre Productions; Production Assistants, Richard Martini, Jerry R. Moore; Opened Tuesday, June 1, 1976 at the Charles Playhouse in Boston, and closed there Jan. 2, 1977.

For original NY production, see THEATRE WORLD Vol. 28.

CAST

Cheryl Bailey	Dwayne Phelps
Alberta Bradford	Jai Oscar St. John
Allyne De Chalus	Linda Sallee
Bobby Hill	Steiv Semien
Carleton Jones	Beauris Allen Whitehead
Pat Lundy	Gregory Wright
Jali'a Murry	

MUSICAL NUMBERS: "I Gotta Keep Movin'," "Harlem Intro," "Lock Up the Dog," "Harlem Street," "Lookin' over from Your Side," "Don't Bother Me, I Can't Cope," "Children's Rhymes," "Ghetto Life," "So Long, Sammy," "You Think I Got Rhythm?," "Time Brings About a Change," "So Little Time," "Thank Heaven for You," "Show Me That Special Gene," "My Love's So Good," "Men's Dance," "They Keep Comin'," "My Name Is Man," "All I Need," "Questions," "Love Mississippi," "It Takes a Whole Lot of Human Feeling," "Good Vibrations," "Prayer," "Sermon," "Fighting for Pharaoh," "We Gotta Keep Movin'"

A "musical entertainment" in two acts.

General Manager: Don Joslyn
Press: Charles J. Cohen
Stage Manager: Robert I. Cohen

Bert Andrews Photos

Boston Company

DON'T BOTHER ME, I CAN'T COPE

Production credits same as above; Opened Friday, June 11, 1976 at the Marines Theatre, San Francisco, CA., and closed there July 25, 1976.

CAST

Renee Brailsford	Clinton Keen
Nell Carter	Nat Morris
Leslie Dockery	Linda Sallee
Billy Dorsey	Steiv Semien
Sheila Ellis	Charlaine Woodard
Every Hayes	

Press: Cheryle Elliott, Jim Kerber

Every Hayes (Kneeling)

DON'T BOTHER ME, I CAN'T COPE

Production Credits same as above; Musical Director, Howard L. Grate; Direction and Choreography, Edmond Kresley after original; Opened Thursday, September 16, 1976 at Keppel Auditorium, Salisbury, NC, and closed December 12, 1976 in Fort Lauderdale, FL.

CAST

Adrian Bailey	Linda Griffin
Helen Castillo	Alphanzo Harrison
Bill Dorsey	Elaine Holloman
Yvette Freeman	Nat Morris
Sandy Gilfillan	Karen Waldron-Ramsey
Elijah Gill	John-Ann Washington
Ernest Griffin	

General Manager: James Janek
Company Manager: Irving Sudrow
Press: Howard Atlee, Clarence Allsopp
Stage Managers: Donald Moss, Luis Montero

Michael Snyder, Ken McDonnell, Ken Howard

EQUUS

By Peter Shaffer; Director, John Dexter; Scenery and Costumes, John Napier; Lighting, Andy Phillips; Supervised by Howard Bay; Costumes, Patricia Adshead; Production Supervisor, Brent Peek; Presented by Kermit Bloomgarden and Doris Cole Abrahams in association with Frank Milton; After playing one week in New York, opened at Kennedy Center, Washington, D.C., Sept. 13, 1976 and closed in Toronto, Canada, Apr. 23, 1977; For original NY production, see THEATRE WORLD Vol. 31.

CAST

Martin Dysart	Douglas Campbell
Alan Strang	Keith McDermott
Nurse	Kathleen Betsko
Hesther Salomon	Jillian Lindig
Frank Strang	Dalton Dearborn
Dora Strang	Catherine Byers
Horseman/Nugget	Kai Wulff
Harry Dalton	Richard Neilson
Jill Mason	Roxanne Hart
Horses	Milledge Mosely, Albert Ownes, Michael Rathay, Gerard Surerus, L. B. Williams

UNDERSTUDIES: Dalton Dearborn (Dysart), Michael Snyder (Alan), Richard Neilson (Frank), Kathleen Betsko (Dora/Hesther), Carolyn Hurlburt (Jill/Nurse), Michael Rathay (Horseman/Nugget), Gerard Surerus (Horses)

A drama in two acts. The action takes place at the present time in Rokeby Psychiatric Hospital in Southern England.

General Manager: Max Allentuck
Company Manager: Jo Rosner
Press: John Springer Associates, Harry Davies, Michael Alpert Associates, Warren Knowlton
Stage Managers: William Schill, Gerard Surerus, Carolyn Hurlburt

Van Williams Photos

EQUUS

By Peter Shaffer; Director, John Dexter; Scenery and Costumes, John Napier; Lighting, Andy Phillips; Sound, Marc Wilkinson; Mime, Claude Chagrin, Peter Lobdell; Production Supervisors, Robert Borod, Brent Peek; American Supervision of Scenery and Lighting, Howard Bay; and Costumes, Patricia Adshead; Wardrobe Supervisor, Eric Harrison; Presented by Kermit Bloomgarden, Doris Cole Abrahams in association with Frank Milton; Opened Tuesday, Nov. 18, 1975 at the Wilbur Theatre, Boston, MA., and closed April 24, 1977 at the Studebaker Theatre in Chicago; For original NY production, see THEATRE WORLD Vol. 31.

CAST

Martin Dysart	Brian Bedford[†1]
Alan Strang	Dai Bradley[†2]
Nurse	Mary Hara[†3]
Hesther Salomon	Sheila Smith[†4]
Frank Strang	Humbert Allen Astredo
Dora Strang	Delphi Lawrence[†5]
Horseman/Nugget	Richard Marshall[†6]
Harry Dalton	Danny Sewell[†7]
Jill Mason	Penelope Willis[†8]
Horses	Joseph Capelli, Mark Hanks, Tom Rolfing, Patrick Watkins, Mark Shannon, Gary Faga, Michael Paliotti, Steve Buck, Edward Trotta, Steve Ward, David Wende

UNDERSTUDIES: Humbert Allen Astredo (Dysart), Marc Vahanian (Alan), Danny Sewell (Frank), Mary Hara (Hesther/Dora), Dorothy French (Jill/Nurse), Joseph Capelli (Dalton), Mark Hanks (Horseman/Nugget), Michael Paliotti (Horses)

A drama in two acts. The action takes place in Rokeby Psychiatric Hospital in Southern England at the present time.

General Manager: Max Allentuck
Company Managers: John Bloomgarden, Harold Kusell
Press: Richard Spittel, Dan Kephart, Michael Alpert Associates
Stage Managers: Nicholas Russian, Robert Borod, Mark Shannon, Dorothy French, Anne B. Sullivan, Michael Paliotti

† Succeeded by: 1. Ken Howard, 2. Michael Snyder, 3. Joan Ulmer, 4. Cathryn Damon, Angela Wood, 5. Betty Miller, 6. David Ramsey, Ken McDonell, 7. John Wardwell, 8. Johanna Leister

Van Williams Photos

(C) Douglas Campbell, Keith McDermott

Ellen Parker, Bill Barrett

GREASE

Book, Music and Lyrics, Jim Jacobs, Warren Casey; Director, Tom Moore; Scenery, Douglas W. Schmidt; Costumes, Carrie F. Robbins; Musical Numbers and Dances Staged by Patricia Birch; Orchestrations, Michael Leonard; Vocal and Dance Arrangements, Louis St. Louis; Musical Direction, Thom Janusz; Assistant to Producers, Linda Schulz; Production Associate, Camille Ranson; Associate Conductor, Ben Sloane; Hairstylist, Barbara Zmed; General Management, Theatre Now, Inc.; Presented by Kenneth Waissman and Maxine Fox in association with Anthony D'Amato; Opened Sunday, October 10, 1976 at the Shubert Theatre in Boston, MA., and still touring May 31, 1977; For original NY production, see THEATRE WORLD Vol. 28.

CAST

Sonny LaTierri	David Paymer
Miss Lynch	Shirl Bernheim
Patty Simcox	Amanda Castle
Eugene Florczyk	Jimmie F. Skaggs
Jan	Pippa Pearthree
Marty	Sandra Zeeman
Betty Rizzo	Lorelle Brina
Doody	Bill Vitelli
Roger	Vincent Otero
Kenickie	Paul Regina, Jr.
Frenchy	Peggy Lee Brennan
Sandy Dumbrowski	Andrea Walters
Danny Zuko	Adrian Zmed
Johnny Casino	Bill Beyers
Vince Fontaine	Steve Fifield
Cha-Cha DiGregorio	Joene Lewis
Teen Angel	Bill Beyers

UNDERSTUDIES. Lori A. Jaroslow, Caryn Richman, Michael Brindisi, Peter Heuchling

MUSICAL NUMBERS: see Broadway Calendar, page 81

A musical in two acts and twelve scenes. The action takes place in the 1950's.

General Manager: Edward H. Davis
Company Manager: Peter H. Russell
Press: Betty Lee Hunt, Kevin C. O'Connor
Stage Managers: Michael Martorella, Gege Martorella, Michael Brindisi

EQUUS

By Peter Shaffer; Director, John Dexter; Associate Director, Brent Peek; Lighting Consultant, Ken Billington; Costume Coordinator, Eric Harrison; Wardrobe Supervisor, Darrell Reed; Supervision of Mime, Peter Lobdell; Production Assistants, Richard Martini, Jerry R. Moore; Associate Producer, James Janek; Presented by Tom Mallow by arrangement with Kermit Bloomgarden and Doris Cole Abrahams; Tour Management, American Theatre Productions; Opened Sept. 24, 1976 in the Municipal Auditorium, Burlington, VT., and closed Dec. 19, 1976 at the Theatre Maisenneuve, Montreal, Canada; For original NY production, see THEATRE WORLD Vol. 31.

CAST

Martin Dysart	David Leary
Alan Strang	Bill Barrett
Nurse	Lacy J. Thomas
Hesther Salomon	Stanja Lowe
Frank Strang	John Carpenter
Dora Strang	Ruth Klinger
Horseman/Nugget	Peter Phillips
Harry Dalton	Herbert DuVal
Jill Mason	Ellen Parker
Horses	Peter DeLaurier, Rory Kelly, David MacEnulty, Timothy Potter, Alan Spitz

A drama in two acts. The action takes place at the present time in Rokeby Psychiatric Hospital in Southern England.

General Manager: James Janek
Company Manager: Robert Ossenfort
Press: Max Gendel
Stage Managers: Barry Andrew Kearsley, Peter DeLaurier

Adrian Zmed, Andrea Walters

JESUS CHRIST SUPERSTAR

Music, Andrew Lloyd Webber; Lyrics, Tim Rice; Director, William Daniel Grey; Musical Direction, Robert Brandzell; Setting, Frank Desmond; Costumes, Barbara Sabella; Choreography, Kelly Carrol; Wardrobe Supervisor, Pixie Esmond; Entire production under the supervision of Mammoth Productions; Presented by Hal Zeiger; Opened Tuesday, January 11, 1977 in Kalamazoo, MI., and closed April 24, 1977 in Stratford, CT; For original NY production, see THEATRE WORLD Vol. 28.

CAST

Jesus of Nazareth	William Daniel Grey
Judas Iscariot	Patrick Jude
Mary Magdalene	Joy Garrett
Pontius Pilate	Randy Wilson
Caiaphas	Christopher Cable
Annas	Steve Schochet
Priests	Doug Lucas, Garon Douglass
Simon	Shelly Safir
Peter	Ken Hilliard
Soldiers	Alan Blair, George Bernhard
Apostles	Kelly St. John, David Cahn, Norman Meister
Maid by fire	Joy Kohner
Soul Girls	Freida Williams, Mara Joyce, Pauletta Pearson
King Herod	Paul Ainsley

Understudies: Kelly Carrol, Bradley Jones

A musical in two acts.

Stage Managers: Chuck Linker, Donald Moss, Alan Blair

No photos available.

Katharine Hepburn, Paul Harding
Top: Charlotte Jones, Katharine Hepburn

A MATTER OF GRAVITY

By Enid Bagnold; Director, Noel Willman; Scenery, Ben Edwards; Costumes, Jane Greenwood; Lighting, Thomas Skelton; Production Assistant, Katharine Allentuck; Wardrobe Supervisor, Colin Ferguson; Hairstylist, Ron Lewis; Presented by Robert Whitehead and Roger L. Stevens; Opened Wednesday, Sept. 29, 1976 in the Auditorium Theatre, Denver, CO., and closed at the Mechanic Theatre in Baltimore, MD, May 14, 1977; For original NY production, see THEATRE WORLD Vol. 32.

CAST

Dubois	Charlotte Jones
Estate Agent	Miller Lide
Mrs. Basil	Katharine Hepburn
Nicky	Richard Kelton
Shatov	Paddy Croft
Herbert	Paul Harding
Elizabeth	Wanda Bimson
Tom	Gary Tomlin

UNDERSTUDIES: Barbara Colton (Dubois/Shatov), Miller Lide (Herbert), Karen Bernhard (Elizabeth), Bill Becker (Agent), Charles McCaugh (Tom)

A comedy in three acts. The action takes place at the present time in a room of an old English country house.

General Manager: Oscar E. Olesen
Company Manager: David Hedges
Press: Seymour Krawitz, Gertrude Bromberg, William Schelble
Stage Managers: Ben Strobach, Bill Becker

Sy Friedman Photos

Katharine Hepburn

ME AND BESSIE

Conceived and Written by Will Holt and Linda Hopkins; Director, Robert Greenwald; Musical Direction, Howlett Smith; Special Dance Sequences, Lester Wilson; Setting, Donald Harris; Costumes, Pete Menefee; Lighting, William H. Batchelder; Presented by Norman Kean; Opened Feb. 1, 1977 in Miami's Coconut Grove Playhouse, and still playing May 31, 1977; For original NY production, see THEATRE WORLD Vol. 32.

CAST

Bessie Smith	Linda Hopkins
Man	Thomas M. Pollard
Woman	Gerri Dean

MUSICAL NUMBERS: "I Feel Good," "God Shall Wipe All Tears Away," "Moan You Mourners," "New Orleans Hop Scop Blues," "Romance in the Dark," "Preach Them Blues," "A Good Man Is Hard to Find," "T'Ain't Nobody's Bizness if I Do," "Gimme a Pigfoot," "Put It Right Here," "You've Been a Good Ole Wagon," "Trombone Cholly," "Jazzbo Brown," "After You've Gone," "Empty Bed Blues," "Kitchen Man," "Mama Don't 'Low," "Do Your Duty," "Fare Thee Well," "Nobody Knows You When You're Down and Out," "Trouble."

General Managers: Maria DiDia, Jim Fiore
Company Manager: Doris Buberl
Press: Les Schecter, Bill Miller
Stage Manager: Sam Stickler

Thomas M. Pollard, Linda Hopkins, Gerri Dean

NATIONAL SHAKESPEARE COMPANY

Artistic Director, Philip Meister; Managing Director, Elaine Sulka; Scenic Design, Associated Theatrical Designers; Costumes, Sharon Hollinger; Lighing, Bob Lampel; Opened Monday, Oct. 4, 1976 in Machias, ME., and closed Apr. 24, 1977 in New Britain, CT.

CAST

"ROMEO AND JULIET"
Directed by Philip Meister

Escalus/Apothecary	Julian Bailey
Paris	K. C. Kizziah
Montague/Mercutio	Kirk Wolfinger
Capulet	Marc Weishaus
Romeo	Kim Traeger
Benvolio	Stephen Root
Tybalt	Bert Kruse
Friar Laurence	Harvey S. Wilson
Peter/Friar John	Samuel Green
Lady Capulet	Alison Edwards
Juliet	Nancy Hammill
Nurse	Catey Reiman

"COMEDY OF ERRORS"
Directed by Sue Lawless

Solinus/Balthazar/Officer	Julian Bailey
Jailer/Emilia	Harvey S. Wilson
Egeon/Merchant	Bert Kruse
1st Merchant/Angelo/Pinch	Kirk Wolfinger
Antipholus of Ephesus	Kim Traeger
Antipholus of Syracuse	K. C. Kizziah
Dromio of Ephesus	Stephen Root
Dromio of Syracuse	Marc Weishaus
Adriana	Alison Edwards
Luciana	Nancy Hammill
Courtesan/Luce	Catey Reiman

"TWELFTH NIGHT"
Directed by Mario Siletti

Orsino	Bert Kruse
Sebastian	Kim Traeger
Sea Captain/Antonio	Samuel Green
Valentine/Curio	Stephen Root
Sir Toby Belch	Julian Bailey
Sir Andrew Aguecheek	K. C. Kizziah
Malvolio	Kirk Wolfinger
Feste	Marc Weishaus
Olivia	Alison Edwards
Viola	Nancy Hammill
Maria	Catey Reiman

Company Manager: Kirk Wolfinger
Press: Dinah Carlson
Stage Managers: Harvey S. Wilson, K. C. Kizziah

"Twelfth Night"
Above: "Romeo and Juliet"

PACIFIC OVERTURES

Book, John Weidman; Additional Material, Hugh Wheeler; Music and Lyrics, Stephen Sondheim; Director, Harold Prince; Choreographer, Patricia Birch; Scenery, Boris Aronson; Costumes, Florence Klotz; Lighting, Tharon Musser; Orchestrations, Jonathan Tunick; Musical Direction, Paul Gemignani; Dance Music, Daniel Troob; Kabuki Consultant, Karuki Fujimoto; Wardrobe Supervisor, Adelaide Laurino; Associate Conductor, Bill Grossman; Technical Supervisor, John J. Moore; Presented by Harold Prince in association with Ruth Mitchell, and the Los Angeles Civic Light Opera Co.; Opened Tuesday, Aug. 31, 1976 in the Dorothy Chandler Pavilion, and closed in San Francisco's Curran Theatre on Dec. 18, 1976.

CAST

Reciter/Shogun/Jonathan Goble	Mako
Abe/First Councillor	Yuki Shimoda
Manjiro	Sab Shimono
2nd Councillor/Old Man/French Admiral	James Dybas
Shogu's Mother/Merchant/American Admiral	Alvin Ing
3rd Councillor/Samurai's Daughter	Freddy Mao
Kayama	Isao Sato
Tamate/Samurai/Storyteller/Swordsman	Soon-Teck Oh
Servant/Commodore Perry	Haruki Fujimoto
Observers	Alvin Ing, Ricardo Tobia
Fisherman/Wrestler/Lord of the South	Jae Woo Lee
Son/Priest/Noble	Timm Fujii
Grandmother/Wrestler/Japanese Merchant	Conrad Yama
Thief/Samurai/Soothsayer/Warrior/Russian Admiral	Mark Hsu Syers
Adams/Samurai/Noble	Ernest Abuba
Williams/Lord of the South	Larry Hama
Shogun's Wife	Freda Foh Shen
Physician/Madam/British Admiral	Ernest Harada
Priest/Boy	Gedde Watanabe
Shogun's Companion/Dutch Admiral	Patrick Kinser-Lau
Girls	Timm Fujii, Patrick Kinser-Lau, Gedde Watanabe, Leslie Watanabe
Imperial Priest	Tom Matsusaka
British Sailors	Timm Fujii, Patick Kinser-Lau, Mark Hsu Syers

MUSICAL NUMBERS: "The Advantages of Floating in the Middle of the Sea," "There Is No Other Way," "Four Black Dragons," "Chrysanthemum Tea," "Poems," "Welcome to Kanagawa," "Someone in a Tree," "Lion Dance," "Please Hello," "A Bowler Hat," "Pretty Lady," "Next"

A musical in two acts. The action takes place in Japan in July of 1853 and from then on.

General Manager: Howard Haines
Press: Mary Bryant, Martin Shwartz
Stage Managers: George Martin, John Grigas, Carlos Gorbea

Van Williams Photo

RAISIN

Book, Robert Nemiroff, Charlotte Zaltzberg; Based on Lorraine Hansberry's play "A Raisin in the Sun"; Music, Judd Woldin; Lyrics, Robert Brittan; Scenery, Robert U. Taylor; Costumes, Bernard Johnson; Lighting, William Mintzer; Directed and Choreographed by Donald McKayle; Musical Director and Conductor, Jack Holmes; Production Supervisor, Nate Barnett; Associate Producers, Sydney Lewis, Jack Friel, Irving Welzer; Executive Associates, Charles Briggs, Will Mott; Wardrobe Supervisor, Betty D'Aloia; Opened Tuesday, Dec. 9, 1975 at the Playhouse, Wilmington, DE, and still touring May 31, 1977; for original NY production, see THEATRE WORLD Vol. 30.

CAST

Pusher	Le'Von Campbell
Victim	Loretta Abbott†1
Ruth Younger	Mary Seymour†2
Travis Younger	Darren Green†3
Mrs. Johnson	Sandra Phillips
Walter Lee Younger	Autris Paige†4
Beneatha Younger	Arnetia Walker
Lena "Mama" Younger	Virginia Capers
Bar Girl	Zelda Pulliam
Bobo Jones	Irving Barnes
Willie Harris	Walter P. Brown†5
Joseph Asagai	Milton Grayson
Pastor	Roderick Sibert†6
Pastor's Wife	Kay Barnes
Karl Lindner	Stacy McAdams

PEOPLE OF THE SOUTHSIDE: Eddie Jordan, Cleveland Pennington, Renee Warren, Zelda Pulliam, Irving Barnes, Roderick Sibert, Corliss Taylor, Kay Barnes, Ned Wright, Charles E. Grant, Jacqueline Derouen, Maxine Brown

MUSICAL NUMBERS: Prologue, "Man Say," "Whose Little Angry Man," "Runnin' to Meet the Man," "A Whole Lotta Sunlight," "Booze," "Alaiyo," "African Dance," "Sweet Time," "You Done Right," "He Come Down This Morning," "It's a Deal," "Sidewalk Tree," "Not Anymore," "Measure the Valleys"

A musical in two acts. The action takes place in the 1950's in Chicago, Illinois.

General Manager: John Corkill
Company Manager: Kimo Gerald
Press: Max Eisen, Fred Weterick
Stage Managers: Anthony Neely, Bert Wood, Sheila R. Phillips, Stacy McAdams

† Succeeded by: 1. Bonita Jackson, 2. Vanessa Shaw, 3. Lacy Darryl Phillips, 4. Gregg Baker, 5. Roderick Sibert, 6. Isaac Clay

Mako (C)

Top: Vanessa Shaw, Gregg Baker, Lacy Darryl Phillips

THE ROYAL FAMILY

By George S. Kaufman and Edna Ferber; Director, Ellis Rabb; Scenery, Oliver Smith; Costumes, Ann Roth; Lighting, John Gleason; Original Music, Claibe Richardson; Wardrobe Supervisor, Bryan Brice; Assistant to Director, Richard Humphrey; Hairstylist, Charles Lo Presto; Presented by Burry Fredrik and Sally Sears; Opened Tuesday, Oct. 12, 1976 at the Wilbur Theatre in Boston, and closed at the Curran Theatre in San Francisco, CA., Feb. 19, 1977.

CAST

Della	Fran Salisbury
Jo	Nicholas Martin
Hallboy	Terry Layman
McDermott	Sherman Lloyd
Herbert Dean	Richard Woods
Kitty Dean	Laura Stuart
Gwen Cavendish	Ellen Fiske
Perry Stewart	Forrest Buckman
Fanny Cavendish	Eva LaGallienne
Oscar Wolfe	Sam Levene
Julie Cavendish	Carole Shelley
Tony Cavendish	Leonard Frey
Chauffeur	George Gitto
Gilbert Marshall	Donald Barton
Hallboys	George Gitto, Shawn Smith
Gunga	Edward Earle
Miss Peake	Betty Low

UNDERSTUDIES: Laura Stuart (Julie), Betty Low (Fanny/Kitty/Ella), George Gitto (Tony/Gilbert), Edward Earle (Oscar/Herbert/Gilbert), Terry Layman (Perry), Kathy Connell (Gwen/Miss Peake), Shawn Smith (Jo/McDermott)

A comedy in three acts. The action takes place in the duplex apartment of the Cavendishes in the East Fifties in New York City during 1927–28.

General Manager: David Lawlor
Company Manager: Fred Cuneo
Press: Shirley Herz, Bev Kelley
Stage Managers: Susie Cordon, Elliott Woodruff, Shawn Smith

Martha Swope Photo

**Top Right: Sam Levene, Carole Shelley,
Eva LeGallienne, Leonard Frey
Below: cast of "The Royal Family"**

SAME TIME, NEXT YEAR

By Bernard Slade; Director, Gene Saks; Scenery, William Ritman; Costumes, Jane Greenwood; Lighting, Tharon Musser; Wardrobe Supervisor, Donald Grubler; Hairstylist, Vincent Tucker; Associate Producers, Ben Rosenberg, Warren Crane; Presented by Morton Gottlieb, Dasha Epstein, Edward Schuman, and Palladium Productions; Opened Tuesday, July 20, 1976 at the Parker Playhouse, Ft. Lauderdale, FL., and still touring May 31, 1977; For original NY production, see THEATRE WORLD Vol. 31.

CAST

Doris	Barbara Rush
George	Tom Troupe

Standbys: Elizabeth Lowry, J. P. Bumstead

A comedy in 2 acts and 6 scenes. The action takes place in a guest cottage of a country inn in Northern California from 1951 to 1975.

General Manger: Ben Rosenberg
Company Manager: Martin Cohen
Press: Solters/Roskin, Milly Schoenbaum, David Polland
Stage Managers: Warren Crane, Peter B. Mumford, J. P. Bumstead

Tom Troupe, Barbara Rush

VERY GOOD EDDIE

Book, Guy Bolton; Music, Jerome Kern; Based on a farce by Phillip Bartholomae; Lyrics, Schuyler Greene; Director, Bill Gile; Dances and Musical Numbers Staged by Dan Siretta; Scenery and Lighting, Fred Voelpel; Costumes, David Toser; Musical Direction, Edward Strauss; Musical Arrangement, Russell Warner; Assistant Conductor, Manford Abrahamson, Jr.; Wardrobe Supervisor, Cindy Chock; Presented by David Merrick, Max Brown and Byron Goldman; Opened Monday, Oct. 4, 1976 at the Hanna Theatre, Cleveland, OH., and closed Jan. 8, 1977 at the Shubert Theatre in Boston, MA.

CAST

Steward	Benny Baker
Dick Rivers	Russ Beasley
Mme. Matroppo	Travis Hudson
Elsie Lilly	Sharon Werner
M. de Rougemont	Ed Dixon
Georgina Kettle	Spring Fairbank
Eddie Kettle	J. J. Jepson
Percy Darling	John Sloman
Elsie Darling	Virginia Seidel
Al Cleveland	Benny Baker
Lily Pond	Candy Darling
Crystal Poole	Kim Carter
Carrie Closewell	Beverly Hartz
Alwys Innit	Lisa Paden
Tayleurs Dumme	J. Keith Ryan
Dayr Thurst	Les Johnson
Dustin Stacks	Don Detrick
Rollo Munn	James J. Mellon

UNDERSTUDIES: Jon Engstrom (Eddie), Candy Darling (Elsie Darling), Nancy Evers (Mme. Matroppo), J. Keith Ryan (Dick), Les Johnson (de Rougemont), Don Detrick (Percy), Barbara Pearl (Georgina), Spring Fairbank (Elsie Lilly), Barbara Pearl (Swing Girl)

MUSICAL NUMBERS: "We're on Our Way," "Some Sort of Somebody," "13 Collar," "Bungalow in Quogue," "Isn't It Great to Be Married," "Good Night Boat," "Left All Alone Again Blues," "Hot Dog!," "If You're a Friend of Mine," "Wedding Bells Are Calling Me," "Honeymoon Inn," "I've Got to Dance," "Moon of Love," "Old Boy Neutral," "Babes in the Wood," "Katy-Did," "Nodding Roses," Finale

A musical in 2 acts and 3 scenes. The action takes place in June of 1913 on a Hudson River Dayline, and in the lobby of Honeymoon Inn in the Catskill Mountains.

General Manager: Helen L. Nickerson
Company Manager: Morry Efron
Press: Max Eisen, Robert W. Jennings
Stage Managers: Ben Kranz, John J. Bonanni, Jon Engstrom

CORRECTION: In THEATRE WORLD Vol. 32 (1975–76), page 32, Bill Gile was erroneously credited with staging the dances and musical numbers. Bill Gile was the director, and Dan Siretta staged the dances and musical numbers for the Broadway production as they did for this production.

Martha Swope Photo

(C) J. J. Jepson, Virginia Seidel

Kamal (C)

THE WIZ

Book, William F. Brown; Based on L. Frank Baum's "The Wonderful Wizard of Oz"; Music and Lyrics, Charlie Smalls; Direction and Costumes, Geoffrey Holder; Setting, Tom H. John; Lighting, Tharon Musser; Musical Direction and Vocal Arrangements, Charles H. Coleman; Choreography and Musical Numbers staged by George Faison; Manager, Jose Vega. Opened Wednesday, June 16, 1976 at the Ahmanson Theatre in Los Angeles, and still touring May 31, 1977; For original NY production, see THEATRE WORLD Vol. 31.

CAST

Aunt Em/Glinda	Roz Clark
Toto	Patches
Dorothy	Renee Harris
Uncle Henry/Gatekeeper/Lord High Underling	George Bell
Tornado	Regina Bell
Munchkins	Sharon Brown, Charlotte Neveu, Keith Simmons, Patience Valentine, Tony Walker
Addaperle	Vivian Bonnell
Yellow Brick Road	Leon Jackson, Eran Smith, Dan Strayhorn, Lewis Whitlock
Scarecrow	Charles V. Harris
Crows	Ruth Ashton, Jamilah Hunter, Cindy McGee
Tinman	Ben Harney
Lion	Ken Prymus
Kalidahs	Sharon Brown, Le'Von Campbell, Tenaj Davis, Keith Simmons, Siri Sat Nam Singh, Patience Valentine, Rony Walker
Poppies	Ruth Ashton, Regina Bell, Jamilah Hunter, Cindy McGee, Charlotte Neveu
Field Mice	Perry Peyton, Patience Valentine, Tony Walker, Vince Willis
The Wiz	Kamal
Evillene	Carolyn Miller
Soldier Messenger	Tony Walker

UNDERSTUDIES: Dorothy, Sharon Brown, Sylvia Striplin; Lion, George Bell; Scarecrow, Tony Walker; Tinman, Siri Sat Nam Singh, Dan Strayhorn; Addaperle, Charlotte Neveu; Evillene, Sulanya Conway; Wiz, Leon Jackson; Glinda/Aunt Em, Peggie Blue; Swing Dancers, Stanley Dalton, Karen McDonald, Graciele Simpson

MUSICAL NUMBERS: see Broadway Calendar, page 85

A musical in 2 acts and 16 scenes with a prologue.

General Mangers: Emanuel Azenberg, Eugene V. Wolsk
Company Manager: David W. Payne
Press: Merlin Group, Sandra Manley
Stage Managers: Kathleen A. Sullivan, Fred Seagraves, Jeanne Fornadel

Martha Swope Photo

AMERICAN SHAKESPEARE THEATRE

Stratford, Connecticut
June 8, - September 12, 1976
Twenty-second Season

Michael Kahn, Artistic Director; President, Konrad Matthaei; Managing Director, William Stewart; Press, Gerald S. Lennick, Richard Pheneger, Gurtman & Murtha, Gladys Shaw, Joan Mirsky; Production Manager, Lo Hardin; Stage Managers, Suzanne Egan, Peter DeNicola; Wardrobe Mistress, Helen McMahon; Hairstylist, Barbara Duly; Production Assistant, Larry Mengden; Assistant Director, Ben Levit; Music Director and Conductor, Herbert Kaplan; Assistant Conductor, Walter Wich; Business Manager, Donald Bundock

COMPANY

Eileen Atkins, Jeanne Bartlett, Powers Boothe, Frank Borgman, Richard Dix, Tovah Feldshuh, Victor Garber, Jack Gwillim, Sarah-Jane Gwillim, George Hearn, Bette Henritze, Will Hussung, Anne Ives, Philip Kerr, William Larsen, Barbara Lester, Anna Levine, Tom McDermott, Don Murray, Wyman Pendleton, Sarallen, Marshall Shnider, Josef Sommer, Theodore Sorel, John Tillinger, Maria Tucci

PRODUCTIONS

"The Winter's Tale" and "As You Like It" by William Shakespeare, and "The Crucible" by Arthur Miller; all directed by Michael Kahn.

Martha Swope Photos

Right: Eileen Atkins, Tom McDermott, April Shawhan, Victor Garber in "As You Like It"

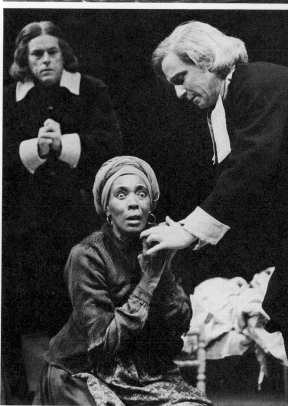

Maria Tucci, Philip Kerr, Bette Henritze in "Winter's Tale" Above: Don Murray, Tovah Feldshuh in "The Crucible"

Richard Dix, Sarallen, George Hearn in "The Crucible"

ALABAMA SHAKESPEARE FESTIVAL

Anniston, Alabama
July 16 - August 21, 1976

Martin L. Platt, Artistic Director, Bruce Hoard, Associate Director; Stage Managers, Dickson Lane, Alvin Balin; Assistant to Director, Patti McCrory; Sets and Lighting, Robert Moeller; Costumes, Lynne Emmert; Wardrobe Supervisor, Darrel Smith; Props, Steve Frye, Mary Ann O'Neal; Production Assistants, Darrel Smith, Mary Ann O'Neal, Sharon Pierce

COMPANY

Charles Antalosky, Alvin Balin, Leslie Blake, Kathy Chandler, Andrew Cole, Stefan Cotner, Kim Crow, Andre Degas, Robert Egan, Kathleen Forbes, Richard Gruppenhoff, Bruce Hoard, Charles Hutchins, Lester Malizia, Judith Marx, Michael O'Brien, Robert Rieben, Elizabeth Schuette, Ronald Stanley Sopyla, J. Allen Suddeth, Mark Varian, Sean Lancaster, Hank Snider, Darrel Smith, Dara Caldwell, Michael Caldwell

PRODUCTIONS

"King Lear," "The Winter's Tale," "The Miser," all directed by Martin L. Platt, and "The Merry Wives of Windsor" directed by Bruce Hoard

Martin L. Platt Photos

**Judith Marx, Charles Antalosky
in "Merry Wives of Windsor" (Alabama)**

CHAMPLAIN SHAKESPEARE FESTIVAL

Burlington, Vermont
July 8 - August 28, 1976
Eighteenth Season

Producer-Director, Edward J. Feidner; Gerard E. Moses, Director; Stage Managers, Andrew Mack, Joan Kennedy; Costumes, Polly Smith, W. K. Fauser; Scenery and Lighting, W. M. Schenk; Production Designer, Lisa Devlin; Technical Director, Dan Boeple; Business Manager, Barbara Phillips; Press, Heidi Racht; Choreographer, Evelyne Germaine; Production Staff, Mary Bashaw-Horton, Melanie Donovan, Betsy Ellis, Liz Herold, Cynthia Hodder, Wendy Pearce, Merrill Reynolds, Mark Shepardson, Holly Young

COMPANY

Dennis Lipscomb, Alan Altshuld, Lorraine Barrett, Dan Baumgarten, Michele Benedict, Jonathan Bourne, Kent Cassella, Daniel Cournoyer, Susan Dunlop, Hamilton Gillett, David Godkin, Charles Kerr, James Kowal, Peter Kurth, Jock MacDonald, Kevin Meconi, Sara O'Neil, Greg Patnaude, John Bruce Patton, Steven Pinsler, Jose Angel Santana, Paul F. Ugalde

PRODUCTIONS

"The Tragedy of King Richard II" and "The Comedy of Errors" directed by Edward J. Feidner, "The Tragedy of King Lear" directed by Gerard E. Moses

Charles Trottier Photos

**Dennis Lipscomb as Richard II
(Champlain)**

COLORADO SHAKESPEARE FESTIVAL

Boulder, Colorado
July 23 - August 15, 1976

Directors, Robert Benedetti, Lee Potts, Ricky Weiser; Stage Managers, Cynthia Noel Macy, Greg Sullivan; Set Designer, Steven J. Griffith; Costumes, David A. Busse, Deborah M. Dryden; Press, Trish McAdams

COMPANY

Tony Amendola, Gigi Benson, Priscilla Davis, Mark M. Dumas, Jeff Eiche, Craig Ferwerda, Brian Fitzsimmons, Craig R. Gardner, Lynda B. Styles, John W. Toth, Peter D. Giffin, Shirley Grubb, Roger Holzberg, Barbara L. MacCameron, Cynthia Noel Macy, Joan Keogh McAfee, David K. Miller, Kevin Patrick O'Brien, Denis R. Williams, David Arthur Walker, Charles Wilcox, Laurie O'Brien, Mary Olseon, Carl A. Rahal, Catherine L. Romey, Richard Rorke, Ed Sampson, Ivan Schechtman, Steve Smith, Thomas D. Williams, Stephen Yarian, Mark Zetterberg

PRODUCTIONS

"The Comedy of Errors" directed by Robert Benedetti, "The Tempest" directed by Lee Potts, "King John" directed by Ricky Weiser

Tom Byers Photos

**Charles Wilcox, David Miller
in "The Tempest" (Colorado)**

GLOBE OF THE GREAT SOUTHWEST

Odessa, Texas
June 18 - August 22, 1976
Eighth Season

Producing Director, Charles David McCally; Founder, Marjorie Morris; Press, Wanda Snodgrass; Costumes, James Maynard; Stage Managers, Joe McNeely, Joe Dunckel, Michael Rowan; Technical Director, Sets and Lighting, Gregory Edwin Wurz; Choreographers, Patricia Angelin Skemp, Billy Nelson; Hairstylist and Makeup, James Maynard; Choral Directors, Bob Welborn, Harold Lewallen

COMPANY

Charles Benton, Don Carr, Marta Rovelstad Caulfield, Michael Rowan, Patricia Angelin Skemp, William Hutson, Douglas Koth, Marilynn Meyrick, David W. Crawford, Peter B. Nichols, James Bottom, Harvey S. Wilson, Michael Roe, Deborah Bigness, Joe Dunckel, James Maynard, Gregory Edwin Wurz, Virgil L. Wilson, Jr., Brett Elise McCally Joseph D. McLendon, Rhonda Clark, Bill Gibbs, James Whitmire, Billy Nelson, Joe McNeely, Bob Coward, Craig Cooper

PRODUCTIONS

"A Midsummer Night's Dream" and "The Merry Wives of Windsor" by William Shakespeare, "The Life of Christ" by Regina Walker McCally, all staged and directed by Charles David McCally

Marta Rovelstad Caulfield, James Bottom in "A Midsummer Night's Dream" (Globe)

GREAT LAKES SHAKESPEARE FESTIVAL

Lakewood, Ohio
June 24, - October 10, 1976

Vincent Dowling, Artistic Director; Business Manager, Mary Bill; Press, Bill Rudman; Set Designer, John Ezell; Costumes, Susan Tsu, Susan Rita Murar; Lighting, Mark Kruger, William Plachy; Stage Managers, Robert Stevenson, Olwen O'Herlihy; Technical Directors, Richard Archer, Ray Barnhart; Guest Directors, John Dillon, William Glover

COMPANY

Robert Black, Tom Blair, John Q. Bruce, V. G. Dowling, Robert Elliott, Jonathan Farwell, Leslie Geraci, Bernard Kates, Sally Mertz, Edith Owen, Robert Scogin, Debbie Stover, Henry Strozier

PRODUCTIONS

"The Tempest" by William Shakespeare, "Dear Liar" by Jerome Kilty, "The Devil's Disciple" by George Bernard Shaw, directed by Vincent Dowling, "Ah, Wilderness!" by Eugene O'Neill directed by John Dillon, "Romeo and Juliet" by William Shakespeare, directed by William Glover

Center: Edith Owen, Bonnie Sacks in "Romeo and Juliet" Right: Vincent Dowling, Sally Mertz in "Dear Liar"

Sally Mertz, Bernard Kates in "Ah, Wilderness!"

GLOBE PLAYHOUSE

Los Angeles, California
June 1, 1976 - May 31, 1977

Producing Organization, The Shakespeare Society of America; Founder-Executive Producer, R. Thad Taylor; Business Manager, Susan Marrone; Artistic Director, DeVeren Bookwalter; Managing Directors, Shannon Eubanks, Karen McLaughlin; Stage Managers, Tony McGuffin, Greg Elliott, Jon Palo, B. J. Grogan, Steve Munsie, William Carlin, Bob Reddy, Lou Clayton; Sets, Laurelyn Palo, Kathleen Bishop; Costumes, Judy Barnett, Ellen Sedor, Jerri Grammer, Louise Hayter, Michael Shere, Kathleen Bishop, Karen Jean Sanders, Margo Upham; Lighting, Keith Gonzales, Fred Plotnick, Rob Esselstein, George Gizienski, Phil Matel; Music, Steve Meigs, Shannon Eubanks, Chris Kuhni, Myron Dyal, Craig Zehms; Directors, Robert Ravan, Harry Mastrogeorge, John Flynn, Karen McLaughlin, Ben Martin, Martin L. Platt, Stephen Roberts, Keith Langsdale

PRODUCTIONS AND CASTS

THE COMEDY OF ERRORS with James Ralston, Ed Garrabrandt, William Forward, Keith Langsdale, Gregory Elliot, Steven D. Schwartz, David Meyers, Stephen Leon, James O'Kleshen, William Kux, Richard Baker, Tina Deane, Kathleen Bishop, Margaret Hepburn, Cristina Bramlet, Dinah Anne Rogers, John Sherwood

A CRY OF PLAYERS by William Gibson, with Richard S. Fullerton, Cal Thomas, Joan Montgomery, David Meyers, Jennifer Youngs, Hersha Parady, Robert Chapel, Richard Baker, James O'Kleshen, William Kux, Mark Fairchild, Richard T. Guilfoyle, Leslie Thompson, Philip Carey Jones, James Ralston, Jennifer Warner, Thomas Mahard, Robert Gray, Steve Meigs

THE MERCHANT OF VENICE with William Forward, Craig Fisch, John Megna, David Meyers, Mark Pint, Steven D. Schwartz, Kathleen Bishop, Sarah Boulton, Cristiana Bramlet, Allan Rich, Antar Mubarak, William Kux, Peter Brocco, Michael Ross-Oddo, Anne Potts, David Cramer, Richard T. Guilfoyle, Mark Fairchild, Rob Curtin, Bronia Dearle, Lynn Farrell, Joan Montgomery, John Nestler

MUCH ADO ABOUT NOTHING with Shannon Eubanks, Ann Greer, Margaret Hepburn, Judy Barnett, Oren Curtis, Michael Ross-Oddo, Julia Benjamin, Gaetano BonGiovanni, Rob Curtin, Bradley Thrush, Lane Davies, Greg Elliott, Robert Shea, Jon Palo, Keith Langsdale, Robert Almanza, Pat Haggerty, William Gunther, Barry Gremillion, James Ralston, Larry Eisenberg

JULIUS CAESAR with Ed Knight, Karen McLaughling, Tom McGowan, John-Frederick Jones, DeAnn Mears, Peter Ellenstein, Frank Savino, Rob Curtin, Ludwig Boneberg, Larry Eisenberg, Pat Torelle, Ed Harris, Allan Stone, Harlan Greene, Ira Zucker, William Gunther, Barry Gremillion, Michael Ross-Oddo, Richard Winnie, Virgil Stratton, Angelynne Bruno, Gil Peters, Bob Reddy, Karen Shaffer, Carola Warfield, Richard Moss, Art Hannes

AS YOU LIKE IT with Lane Davies, Robert Rieben, Beaumont Bruestle, James Ralston, Cristiana Bramlet, Shannon Eubanks, Robert Almanza, Tom McGowan, Larry Eisenberg, Robert Wexler, Charles Hutchins, Allan Almeida, Phylis Ward Fox, Rhonda Jackson, Stacy Stein, Jean-Francois Wood

KING LEAR with George Coulouris (Guest Star), B. J. Grogan, John Wood, John Flynn, Ed Knight, Lee Corrigan, Oren Curtis, Larry Eisenberg, Rob Curtin, Joe Madalis, Steve Hartley, Sarah Boulton, Phylis Ward Fox, Victoria Carver, Larry Vigus, Robert Reddy, Michael Ross-Oddo, Tom McGowan, Phil Kellamus

HENRY IV PART I with Ed Knight, Christopher J. Brown, Michael Augenstein, Ed Garrabrandt, Derek Woolley, Frank Geraci, Oren Curtis, Steve Hartley, Greg Elliot, Dale Swann, Charles Moll, Dan Mahar, Charlie Dell, Jack Phillips, Evan Cole, Jennifer Williams, Andrea Comsky, Bette Jinette, Steve Stuart, Robert S. Gibson, Nigel Bullard, Leo McCormick, Rocco Williams, Bob Reddy, Shannon Eubanks, Anita Barry, Desiree Butler, Margaret Hepburn, Sue Marrone

HENRY IV PART II with Steve Munsie, Derek Woolley, William Rothlein, John Evans, Vince Brocato, Tom Fuccello, Ralph Steadman, Ann Bronston, Tony Haig, Craig Zehms, Paul Brennan, Dale Swann, V. Phipps Wilson, Randy Russell Ferrier, Michael Ross-Oddo, Evan Cole, Robert Gray, John Megna, Andrea Comsky, Rhonda Jackson, Douglas J. Stevenson, Ron Harper, Paul Kawecki, Beaumont Bruestle, Philip Carey Jones, R. H. Forward, Michael Augenstein, Terence Hallmark, Kevin Ackerman, Jason Michas

Mitchell Rose Photos

"Julius Caesar" Above: "As You Like It"
Top: George Coulouris as King Lear
Below: "Merchant of Venice"

NATIONAL SHAKESPEARE FESTIVAL

Old Globe Theatre/San Diego, California
June 1, - September 12, 1976
Twenty-seventh Season

Producing Director, Craig Noel; General Manager, Robert McGlade; Art Director, Peggy Kellner; Press William B. Eaton; Technical Director, Terry Kempf; Stage Directors, Jack O'Brien, Dan Sullivan, Edward Payson Call; Costumes, Peggy Kellner, Steven Rubin, Tom Rasmussen; Lighting, Donald Harris; Composers, Conrad Susa, Carol Lees; Dramaturge, Diana Maddox; Sound, Dan Dugan; Props, Steve Carmack, Roger Mask; Combats Staged by Anthony DeLongis; Stage Managers, Tom Corcoran, Diana Clarke

COMPANY

G. W. Bailey, Robert Burke, Patricia Conolly, Tom DeMastri, John Devlin, Byron Jennings, Michael Keenan, Barry Kraft, William Marshall, Sandy McCallum, Pamela Payton-Wright, Carolyn Reed, Adrian Sparks, Benjamin Stewart, Ray Stewart, G. Wood, Peter Aylward, Leonardo DeFilippis, Matthew Faison, Kelsey Grammer, V. Craig Heidenreich, Gregg Henry, Zachary Lewis, Ann Matthews, Walter Pienkowski, Michael T. Rega, Maureine Saari, Arnaldo Santana, Douglas Sheehan, Jamey Sheridan, Caroline Smith, Deborah Taylor, Dan Speaker, James Avery, William Mallory, Robin Taylor, Lindy Nisbet, Sandy Tinker, Michael Wayne, Kelly Ward, Damon Younger, Sunny Langton, Charan Levitan

PRODUCTIONS

"As You Like It" directed by Jack O'Brien, "Othello" directed by Dan Sullivan, "Troilus and Cressida" directed by Edward Payson Call, "Rodgers and Hart: A Musical Celebration" directed by Wayne Bryan

Bill Reid Photos

Top Left: Robert Burke, Patricia Connolly in "As You Like It" Below: (front) Robin Taylor Kelly Ward, Charan Levitan, William Mallory, (Top) Sandy Tinker, Damon Younger, Lindy Nisbet, Michael Phillips in "Rodgers and Hart: A Musical Celebration"

**Barry Kraft in "Troilus and Cressida"
Above: Pamela Payton-Wright, G. Wood
in "Troilus and Cressida"**

**Pamela Payton-Wright, William Marshall
in "Othello"**

NEW JERSEY SHAKESPEARE FESTIVAL

Drew University/Madison, N. J.
June 29 - December 5, 1976
Twelfth Season

Paul Barry, Artistic Director; Press, Ellen Barry; Stage Managers, Jon Froscher, Dale Allan Vivirito; Lighting, Gary C. Porto; Sets, David M. Glenn; Costumes, Dean H. Reiter, Jean Steinlein; Assistant Producer, Barnett Lippmann; Administrative Assistants, Leon Berger, Lillia Burwasser; Musical Director, Linda C. Calvert; Stage Directors, Paul Barry, Davey Marlin-Jones; Original Music, Stewart Turner, Dean Powell

COMPANY

Clayton Berry, Eric Booth, Michael Capanna, Mary Case, Lynn Cohen, David Connell, Dottie Dee, Kenneth Gray, Earl Hindman, J. C. Hoyt, Patricia Kilgarriff, Robert Machray, Susanne Marley, Michael McCarty, Ann McCurry, Edwin J. McDonough, Katherine McGrath, Jocelyn Meng, Timothy Meyers, Judy Noble, William Preston, Naomi Riseman, Molly Scoville, Eileen Shannon, Ronald Steelman, Earl Theroux, Michael Zeke Zacarro, Barbara Adinaro, Dean Barclay, Sandra Biano, Marilyn Rae Block, Debbie Bloom, Patrick Boynton, Roger M. Brady, Melinda Bruno, Kathleen Burns, Joan Certa, Marilyn Cervino, Susanne K. Chopp, Mark L. Churchill, Victoria Constan, Patrick Crea, John Devaney, C. J. Dishian, Richard Dorfman, Patsy Ann Durbin, Rob Ernest, Gail Fitzgibbons, Sandra Fong, Marianne Fraulo, Brenda Friend, Barbara Gato, Barbara Goldberg, Chris Grandy, Carol Dawn Greene, William Haggerty, Suzanne Hall, Grace Harvey, Hariet Haygood, Sharon Johnston, Akim Kaiser, Claudia Kavenagh, John Kegley, Laurie Keough, Susie Kuche, Mary Lou Lauricella, Russell Lawyer, Jason Lee, Karen Makowski, Peter Manzione, Uriel Menson, Jana Miller, Richard Moore, Peter Motson, Scott Nangle, Cynthia Nicholson, Helen Oravetz, Marcela Ourednik, Camille Palmer, Louise Quinn, John Rathburn, Tom Regnier, Gloria Rice, Marcy Rubin, Allen Salzberg, Michael Sears, Howard Shalwitz, Maura Silverman, Laura Simonds, Ron Skorton, Diana Swack, Stewart Turner, Donald J. Watson, Caryn Wexler, William Weir, Susan Yates, Leslie Yudell

PRODUCTIONS

"The Tempest" and "Henry V" by William Shakespeare, "The Best Man" by Gore Vidal, "The Devil's Disciple" by George Bernard Shaw, "Private Lives" by Noel Coward, "Stop the World—I Want to Get Off" by Anthony Newley and Leslie Bricusse, "The Playboy of the Western World" by John Millington Synge, "Of Mice and Men" by John Steinbeck
Phil Degginger, Blair Holley Photos

Right: Clayton Berry, Katherine McGrath in "Private Lives" Above: Eric Booth (C) as Henry V

"Playboy of the Western World"
Top Right: Ann McCurry, Paul Barry in "Stop the World. . . ."

Clayton Berry, J. C. Hoyt, Susanne Marley in "The Tempest"

174

NEW YORK SHAKESPEARE FESTIVAL

Delacorte Theater/Central Park
New York, N. Y.
June 24, - August 29, 1977
Twentieth Season

Producer, Joseph Papp; Associate Producer, Bernard Gersten; General Manager, Robert Kamlot; Press, Merle Debuskey, Bob Ullman, Bruce Cohen; Production Manager, Andrew Mihok; Administrative Manager, Duane Wolfe; Assistant to the Producer, Marilyn Lebowitz; Technical Director, Mervyn Haines, Jr.; Prop Master, Leslie E. Rollins; Produced in cooperation with the City of New York

June 24, - July 25, 1976

HENRY V

By William Shakespeare; Director, Joseph Papp; Setting, David Mitchell; Costumes, Timothy Miller; Lighting, Martin Aronstein; Music, William Elliott; Battles, Lee Breuer, Erik Fredricksen; Production Supervisor, Jason Steven Cohen; Stage Managers, Louis Rackoff, Richard S. Viola, Robert Kellogg; Assistant Directors, Sam Waterston, Wilford Leach; Technical Director, Darrell Ziegler; Wardrobe Master, Elonzo Dann; Production Assistants, Andy Lopata, Cary Mazer

CAST

Michael Moriarty (Chorus), Paul Rudd (Henry V), Clarence Felder (Duke of Exeter), Jay O. Sanders (Earl of Westmoreland), Gilbert Cole (Duke of Gloucester), Stephen Lang (Duke of Bedford), Jeremiah Supple (Earl of Warwick), Maurice Copeland (Archbishop/Governor), Bruce McGill (Ambassador of France/ Duke of Orleans), John C. Capodice (Bardolph), Ben Slack (Nym), Philip Bosco (Pistol), Sasha von Scherler (Mistress Quickly/Isabel), Jaime Nontilla (Boy), Stephen Daley (Earl of Cambridge/Duke of Bourbon), William M. Hurt (Lord Scroop/Interpreter/John Bates), Erik Fredricksen (Sir Thomas Grey/Salisbury/Duke of Alencon), Gerry Bamman (Gower), Joseph Bova (Fluellen), William Youmans (Alexander Court), Suzanne Collins (His Wife), Jerome Dempsey (Charles VI), Lenny Baker (Dauphin), Barton Heyman (Constable), Tom Klunis (Montjoy), Meryl Streep (Katherine), Don Plumley (MacMorris), Valerie French (Alice), Walter McGinn (Michael Williams), Ensemble: Nancy Boykin, Stephen Brennan, Joseph Carberry, Charles Clemetson, Charles Conwell, John Ferraro, F. Kenneth Freedman, Bradford Gottlin, Gabriel Gribetz, Ron Jacobson, Dennis Krausnick, John Lordan, Christopher McHale, Robert Vincent Park, Paul John Perri, Peter Phillips, Michael Rieder, Daniel Riviera, William Sadler, Mel Shrawder, Mark Simon, Tony Simotes, Theodore Sod, Peter Van Norden, Ricardo Velez, Bernard Velinsky, Tom Villard

August 11 - 29, 1976

MEASURE FOR MEASURE

By William Shakespeare; Director, John Pasquin; Setting and Costumes, Santo Loquasto; Lighting, Martin Aronstein; Music, William Penn; Stage Managers, Frank Bayer, Jason LaPadura; Technical Director, Darrell Ziegler; Props, Stephen Zorthian; Wardrobe Master, Elonzo Dann; Production Assistant, K. C. Schulberg

CAST

Sam Waterston (Vicentio), John Cazale (Angelo), Ron Randell (Escalus), David Haskell (Claudio), Lenny Baker (Lucio), Joseph Regalbuto (Gentleman 1), Jake Dengel (Gentleman 2), John Seitz (Provost), Mark Simon (Justice), Steven Gilborn (Friar Thomas), Jeffrey Tambor (Elbow), Michael Tucker (Froth), Howard E. Rollins, Jr. (Pompey), Walt Gorney (Abhorson), Jay O. Sanders (Barnardine), Meryl Streep (Isabella), Caroline McWilliams (Mariana), Robin Mary Paris (Juliet), Judith Light (Francisca), Ruby Holbrook (Mistress Overdone), Harlan Schneider (Servant), Ensemble: Beverleigh Banfield, Katherine Braun, Ann Bronston, Frances Hardman Conroy, Gabriel Gribetz, Cheryl Tafathale Jones, Jolly King, Michael Kolba, Christopher McHale, Marilyn McIntyre, Nathaniel Robinson, William T. Sadler, Tony Simotes

Frederic Ohringer Photos

Top Right: Paul Rudd, Meryl Street in "Henry V"

Lenny Baker, Meryl Streep, John Cazale in "Measure for Measure"

Denis Arndt as King Lear Left: "Henry VI Part 2"
Top: Jean Smart, Allen Nause in "Much Ado about
Nothing"

OREGON SHAKESPEARE FESTIVAL

Ashland, Oregon
June 12, - September 19, 1976
Forty-first Season

Angus L. Bowmer, Founder-Consultant; Producing Director, Jerry Turner; General Manager, William Patton; Scenic Designers, Richard L. Hay, Byron Olson; Costumes, Jeannie Davidson, Phyllis Corcoran; Lighting, Dirk Epperson, Jerry L. Glenn, Thomas White; Production Coordinator, Pat Patton; Technical Director, R. Duncan MacKenzie; Stage Directors, Pat Patton, Jerry Turner, James Edmondson, Will Huddleston, Michael Leibert, James Moll; Choreographer, Judith Kennedy; Music Director, Todd Barton; Fight Director, David L. Boushey; Props, Michael Becker; Wardrobe Mistress, Susan Rosamund Smith; Sound, Daniel Rose; Stage Managers, Dennis Bigelow, Wendy Chapin, Jeffrey Hirsch; Hairstylists, Candy Neal, Ranny Beyer

COMPANY

Bruce Abbott, Denis Arndt, Larry R. Ballard, Virginia Bingham, John A. Caldwell, Ruth Cox, Michael Day, Joseph DeSalvio, James Edmondson, William Ferriter, Keith Grant, Mark Grover, Sands Hall, Warren Hansen, Mark Harelik, Christine Healy, Will Huddleston, Jerry Jones, Marilyn Jones, Philip L. Jones, Bob Kallus, Dan Kremer, Roberta Levitow, Brian Lynner, Martin Mackey, Delores Y. Mitchell, Dan Moore, William Moreing, Barry Mulholland, Brian Mulholland, Allen Nause, Judd Parkin, JoAnn Johnson Patton, Kristin Anne Patton, Shirley Patton, Rex Rabold, Jon Rome, Jean Smart, Brad Smith, Jane Stevens-Jones, Charles Taber, Brian Thompson, Gordon Townsend, Mary Turner, John Warren Tyson, Bruce Williams, David Williams, Cal Winn, Ron Woods, Kathleen Worley, and Dancers: Bruce Abbott, Bruce Geller, Jim Giancarlo, Jo Goff, Mark Grover, Mary Molodovsky, Dan Moore, Kristin Anne Patton, Suzanne Seiber, Charles Taber, Leslie Velton

PRODUCTIONS

"King Lear" directed by Pat Patton, "Much Ado about Nothing" directed by James Edmondson, "Henry VI Part 2" directed by Jerry Turner, "Comedy of Errors" directed by Will Huddleston, "The Devil's Disciple" directed by Michael Leibert," "The Little Foxes" directed by James Moll

Hank Kranzler Photos

Barry Mulholland, Joe DeSalvio in "Comedy of
Errors" Above: Denis Arndt, Brian Thompson
in "The Devil's Disciple"

STRATFORD FESTIVAL OF CANADA

Stratford, Ontario
June 7 - September 26, 1976
Twenty-fourth Season

Artistic Director, Robin Phillips; General Manager, Bruce Swerdfager; Directors, Robin Phillips, William Hutt, Urjo Kareda; Executive Producer, John Hayes; Production Manager, Jack Hutt; Technical Director, Robert Scales; Assistant to Artistic Director, Margaret Ryerson; Designers, Daphne Dare, Polly Bohdanetzky, Janice Lindsay, John Pennoyer; Press, Anne Selby, Douglas Allan, Richard Wolfe, Betty Ross, Elaine Jones; Music, Berthold Carriere, Raffi Armenian; Stage Managers, Nora Polley, Vincent Berns, Colleen Stephenson, Michael Benoit, Raymond Burton Early, Heather Kitchen, Tom Patterson

PRODUCTIONS AND CASTS

THE WAY OF THE WORLD by William Congreve, with Alan Scarfe, Jeremy Brett, Frances Fagan, Stuart Hutchison, Gregory Wanless, Keith Batten, Keith Baxter, Bernard Hopkins, Mia Anderson, Domini Blythe, Maggie Smith, Jackie Burroughs, Jan Kudelka, Larry Lamb, Jessica Tandy, Barbara Stephen, Peter Hutt, Cathy Wallace, Tony van Bridge

HAMLET by William Shakespeare, with Richard Monette, Paul Butt, Don Hunkin, Victor A. Young, Stephen Russell, Graeme Campbell, Michael Liscinsky, Patricia Bentley-Fisher, Marti Maraden, Richard Partington, Robin Nunn, Richard Curnock, Bill Ballantyne, John Goodlin, Barbara Budd, Melody Ryane, William Merton Malmo, Richard Whelan, Jack Wetherall, Paul Batten, Robert G. More, Pat Galloway, and at Avon Stage with Nicholas Pennell as Hamlet

THE MERCHANT OF VENICE by William Shakespeare, with Hume Cronyn, Lewis Gordon, Nick Mancuso, Rod Beattie, Robert Benson, James Hurdle, Gregory Wanless, Jackie Burroughs, Denise Fergusson, Martin Donlevy, Bernard Hopkins, Mervyn Blake, Stuart Hutchison, Dorian (Joe) Clark, Frank Maraden, Domini Blythe, David Fox-Brenton, Max Helomann, Wally Bondarenko, Jan Kudelka, Peter Hutt, Bob Baker, William Needles, Larry Lamb, Gerald Isaac, Bruce French

THE TEMPEST by William Shakespeare, with William Hutt, Don Hunkin, Stephen Russell, Eric Donkin, Jack Wetherall, Graeme Campbell, Richard Curnock, Victor A. Young, Richard Whelan, Barry MacGregor, Richard Partington, Bill Ballantyne, Paul Batten, Paul Butt, John Goodlin, Michael Liscinsky, William Merton Malmo, Robert More, Robin Nunn, Marti Maraden, Nicholas Pennell, Richard Monette, Patricia Bentley-Fisher, Barbara Budd, Melody Ryane, Pat Galloway, Gerald Isaac

ANTONY AND CLEOPATRA by William Shakespeare, with Keith Baxter, Maggie Smith, Alan Scarfe, Max Helpmann, Robert Benson, Jan Kudelka, Patricia Idlette, Gregory Wanless, Jack Roberts, Nick Mancuso, Dorian (Joe) Clark, Domini Blythe, Lewis Gordon, David Fox-Brenton, Bob Baker, James Hurdle, Keith Batten, Mervyn Blake, Joel Kenyon, Larry Lamb, Daniel Buccos, Rod Beattie, Wally Bondarenko, William Needles, Frank Maraden, Bernard Hopkins, Paul Batten

Right Center: Jeremy Brett, Jessica Tandy in "Midsummer Night's Dream" Above: Nicholas Pennell, Michael Liscinsky, Pat Galloway in "Hamlet"

THE IMPORTANCE OF BEING EARNEST by Oscar Wilde, with Richard Curnock, Barry MacGregor, Nicholas Pennell, William Hutt, Pat Galloway, Marti Maraden, Amelia Hall, Eric Donkin, Graeme Campbell

MEASURE FOR MEASURE by William Shakespeare, with William Hutt, Douglas Rain, Tony van Bridge, Daniel Buccos, Richard Monette, Rod Beattie, Keith Batten, William Needles, Peter Hutt, Jack Roberts, Joel Kenyon, Frank Maraden, Lewis Gordon, Larry Lamb, Robert Benson, Gregory Wanless, Martha Henry, Jackie Burroughs, Mia Anderson, Barbara Stephen, Domini Blythe, Maggie Smith

EVE by Larry Fineberg, with Jessica Tandy, James Edmond, Les Carlson, Richard Partington, Louis Zorich, Melody Ryane

A MIDSUMMER NIGHT'S DREAM by William Shakespeare, with Jessica Tandy, Jeremy Brett, Mia Anderson, William Needles, Richard Partington, Nick Mancuso, Denise Fergusson, Jack Roberts, Hume Cronyn, Bernard Hopkins, Rod Beattie, Richard Whelan, Larry Lamb, Dorian (Joe) Clark, Tom Kneebone, Jan Judelka, Gregory Wanless, Bob Baker, Stephen Russell, Daniel Buccos

THREE SISTERS by Anton Chekhov, with Martha Henry, Marti Maraden, Maggie Smith, Amelia Hall, Patricia Bentley-Fisher, Michael Liscinsky, Frank Maraden, William Hutt, Eric Donkin, Bill Ballantyne, Keith Baxter, Alan Scarfe, Richard Curnock, Pat Galloway, Victor A. Young, Robert G. More, Melody Ryane, Eugene Laszkiewicz, Larry Greenberg, David Martin

Zoe Dominic, Robert C. Ragsdale Photos

Maggie Smith, Marti Maraden, Amelia Hall, Martha Henry in "Three Sisters" Top Right: Pat Galloway, William Hutt, Nicholas Pennell in "The Importance of Being Earnest"

SHAKESPEAREAN THEATER OF MAINE

Monmouth, Maine
July - September 5, 1976
Seventh Season

Artistic Director, Earl McCarroll; General Manager, Glen Cooper; Business Manager, Helen Rhodes Hochman; Stage Manager, James J. Thesing; Sets, Karen Schulz; Lighting, Paul Gallo; Costumes, Joyce Aysta; Technical Director, Drew Field; Press, Karen A. Longwell.

COMPANY

Earl McCarroll, Bob Burrus, Patricia Daniels, John H. Fields, June Helmers, Robert Johanson, Lee McClelland, Dana Mills, Charyl Moore, Ronald Parady, James J. Thesing, Herman Tuider, Peter Michael Webster, Vebe Borge, Jeffry G. Cismoski, Matthew Cohen, Priscilla Entersz, Richard Haverinen, Verne Hendrick, Nicholas G. Kaledin, James D. Lannon, Lorna C. Littleway, Aaron Lustig, Michael O'Brien, Katharine Pantzer

PRODUCTIONS

"A Midsummer Night's Dream" and "Antony and Cleopatra" directed by Earl McCarroll, Moliere's "The Imaginary Invald" directed, translated and Music by Robert Johanson, "King Henry IV Part I" directed by James J. Thesing, and *World Premiere* of "The King Who Stole the Shadows" by Peter Michael Webster

D. A. Fuller, Harold Gabriel Marshall Photos

Dana Mills, Lorna Littleway in "Midsummer Night's Dream" Left: Bob Burrus, Lee McCleland in "Antony and Cleopatra" Top: Robert Johanson, John H. Fields in "Henry IV"

THEATRE VENTURE '77

Beverly, Massachusetts
May 2 - 23, 1977

Managing Director, Stephan Slane; Manager, Theda Taylor; Press, Peter Downs; Assistants to Manager, Tom David, Randall Rosenbaum; Stage Manager, Jerry Litwin; Sound, Dan Richard Preston; Props, Venixe St. Pierre

PRODUCTION AND CAST

JULIUS CAESAR by William Shakespeare; Director, Ada Brown Mather; Set, Eve Lyon; Lighting, Theda Taylor; Costumes, Halliday Wallace. CAST: William Kiehl (Caesar), Gordon Gould (Brutus), George F. Maguire (Cassius), David Bulasky (Marcus Antonius), Terry Layman (Casca), Peter Marklin (Decius Brutus), Dick St. George (Cimber), Jack Cornwall (Cinna the Conspirator), Michael Arabian (Trebonius), Kathleen Forbes (Portia), Michelle Henthorn (Calpurnia), John Tallman (Marullus/Soothsayer), Andrew P. Glant (Cinna the Poet)

Peter Downs Photos

Peter Marklin, William Kiehl, Dick St. George, George Maguire in "Julius Caesar" (Venture '77)

PROFESSIONAL RESIDENT COMPANIES

(Failure to meet deadline necessitated several omissions)

ACT: A CONTEMPORARY THEATRE

Seattle, Washington
June 17–December 30, 1976
Twelfth Season

Artistic Director, Gregory A. Falls; General Manager, Andrew Witt; Press, Louise Mortenson; Technical Director, Phil Schermer; Musical Director, Stan Keen; Directors, Gregory A. Falls, Robert Loper, Paul Lee; Stage Managers, Eileen MacRae Murphy, Michael Weholt; Sets, William Forrester, Jerry Williams, Shelley Henze Schermer; Costumes, Sally Richardson; Props, Peter Hardie; Lighting, Phil Schermer, Richard Devin

PRODUCTIONS AND CASTS

SIZWE BANZI IS DEAD by Athol Fugard, John Kani, Winston Ntshona, with Joe Fields, Mel Johnson, Jr.

THE TIME OF YOUR LIFE by William Saroyan, with Lori Abrahamson, Richard E. Arnold, John Aylward, Erik Barnes, Kurt Beattie, Karen Kee Campbell, Maury Cooper, Christopher "Spider" Duncan, Karen Eastman, Patricia Estrin, Dean Gardner, Tom Hill, Will Hughes, Karen Joshi, Robert MacDougall, James W. Monitor, Robert E. Oram, Sally Pritchard, Kathryn Stalter, Robert Taeschner, James Taylor, A. C. Weary, Stanley Yale

SCAPINO adapted by Frank Dunlop and Jim Dale from Moliere, with Kurt Beattie, Maury Cooper, Christopher "Spider" Duncan, Patricia Estrin, Jay Fernandez, Dean Gardner, Jim Jansen, Karen Joshi, Jo Leffingwell, Robert MacDougall, James W. Monitor, Robert E. Oram, A. C. Weary

DESIRE UNDER THE ELMS by Eugene O'Neill, with Richard Arnold, John Aylward, Robert Cornthwaite, Karen Eastman, Frank H. Ferrel, Martin LaPlatney, Robert MacDougall, Richard Marion, Tanny McDonald, K. Nelsen, Jeffrey L. Prather, Leah Sluis, Stanley Yale

RELATIVELY SPEAKING by Alan Ayckbourn, with Donald Ewer, Katherine Ferrand, Mark Geiger, Margaret Hilton

BOCCACCIO adapted by Kenneth Cavander from Boccaccio's "Decameron" with Megan Dean, Robert MacDougall, Beth McDonald, Marnie Mosiman, Frederick Sperberg, Kelly Walters, A. C. Weary

Right: Karen Eastman, Maury Cooper, John Aylward in "The Time of Your Life" Top: Jim Jansen, James Monitor, Christopher Duncan in "Scapino!"

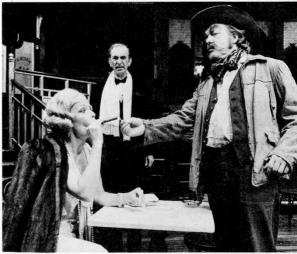

Joe Fields, Mel Johnson, Jr. in "Sizwe Bansi Is Dead"

Margaret Hilton, Donald Ewer in "Relatively Speaking"

179

ACTORS THEATRE OF LOUISVILLE

Louisville, Kentucky
October 4, 1976–May 22, 1977

Jon Jory, Producing-Director; Administrative Director, Alexander Speer; Associate Director, Trish Pugh; Press, Ronnie McNulty; Directors, Jon Jory, Steve Robman, Israel Hicks, Elizabeth Ives, Ken Frankl, Charles Kerr, Patrick Henry, Ray Fry, Robert Brewer; Sets, Paul Owen, Richard Gould, Richard Kent Wilcox; Costumes, Kurt Wilhelm, Paul Owen; Lighting, Vincent Faust, Paul Owen, Ron Wallace, James E. Stephens; Props, Stephen McDowell, Peter Show; Technical Director, Joseph Ragey; Costumiere, Mary Lou Owen; Stage Managers, Elizabeth Ives, Don Johnson, Marvin Sprague, Nan Wray, William McNulty, David Rosenak, James Lannon, Kimberly Francis Kearsley.

COMPANY

Jim Baker, Bob Burrus, William Cain, Barry Corbin, Joseph Costa, Peggy Cowles, Andrew Davis, Dawn Didawick, Marji Dodrill, Kathleen Doyle, Earle Edgerton, Lee Anne Fahey, Matthew Faison, John H. Fields, Ray Fry, Harry Groener, Georgia Heaslip, Vinnie Holman, Daniel Hugh-Kelly, Will Hussung, Ken Jenkins, Victor Jory, Michael Kevin, Susan Kingsley, James Lannon, Michael Laskin, Damien Leake, Ruth Maynard, Vaughn McBride, William McNulty, William Metzo, John Napierala, John Newton, Adale O'Brien, C. C. H. Pounder, Dennis Predovic, Marcell Rosenblatt, Bill Schoppert, James Secrest, Howard Lee Sherman, Patrick Tovatt, Deborah Trissell, Nan Wray, Daniel Zippi.

PRODUCTIONS

"The Best Man," "Tea with Dick and Jerry," "Vanities," "Sexual Perversity in Chicago," "Medal of Honor Rag," "Much Ado about Nothing," "A Christmas Carol," "The Resistible Rise of Arturo Ui," "Who's Afraid of Virginia Woolf?," "The Matchmaker," "Diary of Anne Frank," "The Rainmaker," "Table Manners," "Round and Round the Garden," and *Premieres* of "Reunion," "The Gin Game," "Indulgences in the Louisville Harem"

David S. Talbott Photos

Right: Adale O'Brien, William McNulty, Peggy Cowles, Ray Fry in "Table Manners" Above: Andrew Davis, Joseph Costa, Patrick Tovatt, Barry Corbin, Michael Kevin, Bob Burrus in "The Resistible Rise of Arturo Ui"

Victor Jory, William Cain (above) Top Right: Will Hussung, Georgia Heaslip in "The Gin Game"

Lee Anne Fahey, Daniel Zippi, Dawn Didawick, Joseph Costa in "The Matchmaker"

ALLEY THEATRE

Houston, Texas
October 16, 1976–May 29, 1977

Producing Director, Nina Vance; Sets, Matthew Grant; Costumes, Michael Olich; Lighting, Jonathan Duff; Technical Director, William C. Lindstrom; Press, Bob Feingold; Business Manager, Bill Halbert; Producing Associate, H. Wilkenfeld; Assistant to Miss Vance, George Anderson; Directors, Beth Sanford, Ted Follows, Leslie Yeo; Production/Company Manager, Bettye Fitzpatrick; Stage Managers, George Anderson, Rutherford Cravens, Trent Jenkins

PRODUCTIONS AND CASTS

THE STY OF THE BLIND BIG by Phillip Hayes Dean, with Louise Jenkins, Carl Gordon, Frances Foster, Gilbert Lewis

THE DOCK BRIEF by John Mortimer, with Kenneth Wickes, Kenneth Dight, David Wurst

THE COLLECTION by Harold Pinter, with Kenneth Dight, Brian Tree, Michael Ball, Margo McElroy

YOU NEVER CAN TELL by George Bernard Shaw, with Michael Ball, Cristine Rose, Rutherford Cravens, Bob Thompson, Jane MacIver, Pamela Brook, Margo McElroy, Leslie Yeo, Kenneth Dight, David Wurst, Philip Davidson, David E. Chadderdon, Doug Gens, Nelson Heggen, James Kelly, Chip Pankey, Peggy Ann Byers, Carol Lee Lang, Alice J. Rhoades, Linda Woodruff

THE CORN IS GREEN by Emlyn Williams, with Philip Davidson, Concetta Tomei, A. J. Rhoades, Lillian Evans, Bob Thompson, Maggie Askey, Cristine Rose, Kate Reid, James Kelly, Christopher Gaze, Doug Gens, Nelson Heggen, Chip Pankey, Carl Davis, Peggy Ann Byers, Randy Cheramie, Carol Lee Lang, Vernon Grote, Nikjon Kovalevsky, Chris Lewis

LOOT by Joe Orton, with Bernard Frawley, Sarah Hardy, Trent Jenkins, David K. Johnson, Kenneth Dight, David Wurst

THE RUNNER STUMBLES by Milan Stitt, with Randy Cheramie, Anthony Manionis, Lillian Evans, Philip Davidson, Cristine Rose, Bettye Fitzpatrick, David Wurst, Bob Thompson, Concetta Tomei

ENDGAME by Samuel Beckett, with Robert Symonds, Sheldon Epps, Victoria Zussin, Bernard Frawley

HOW THE OTHER HALF LOVES by Alan Ayckbourn, with Lillian Evans, Cristine Rose, Robert Symonds, David Wurst, Trent Jenkins, Judy Mueller

Alan B. Currie Photos

Right: Frances Foster, Gilbert Lewis in "Sty of the Blind Pig" Above: Cristine Rose, Anthony Manionis in "The Runner Stumbles"

Christopher Gaze, Kate Reid in "The Corn Is Green" Top Right: Robert Symonds, Sheldon Epps in "Endgame"

Pamela Brook, Michael Ball in "You Never Can Tell"

181

ALLIANCE THEATRE COMPANY

Atlanta, Georgia
January 13–June 4, 1977

Producing Director, David Bishop; Artistic Director, Fred Chappell; Administrative Director, Victoria Mooney; Press, Sandra Johnson; Production Designer, Michael Stauffer; Production Manager, Baxter Joy; Stage Managers, Allen Wright, Dickson Lane, Trey Altemose; Costumes, Martha Kelly; Sets, Michael Stauffer, Phillip Jung; Lights, Cassandra Henning, Michael Stauffer; Technical Director, Erik Magnuson; Guest Artists, Kent Paul, Harold Scott, Charles Kerr, Fannie Flagg

PRODUCTIONS AND CASTS

SCAPINO directed by Fred Chappell, with Christopher Allport, Tom Arcuragi, Harriet Bass, David Braucher, Howard Brunner, Marianne Hammock, Clayton Landey, Susan Larkin, Gib Manegold, John McCorckle, John Milligan, Albert Sanders, Morgan Williams, Jim Word

HEDDA GABLER directed by Kent Paul, with Christopher Allport, Dana Ivey, Susan Larkin, Erica Cast Rhodes, Reno Roop, Mary Nell Santacroce

COME BACK TO THE 5 AND DIME JIMMY DEAN, JIMMY DEAN by Ed Graczyk, directed by Fred Chappell (professional premiere), with Fannie Flagg, Pamela Burrell, Diane Deckard, Kristin Griffith, Dana Ivey, Linda Kampley, Richard Loder, Erika Petersen, Georgia Southcotte

MISALLIANCE directed by Harold Scott, with David Braucher, Peter Burnell, Patricia Falkenhain, Marianne Hammock, Dana Ivey, Richard Loder, K. Lype O'Dell, Reno Roop, William Trotman

ALL THE WAY HOME directed by Fred Chappell, with Meg Brush, Peter Burnell, Patricia Falkenhain, Travis L. Fine, Anne Haney, Christopher Hogenson, Mimi Honce, Dana Ivey, Rory Kelly, Philip Kraus, Dickson Lane, K. Lype O'Dell, Alexander Reed, Mary Nell Santacroce, Wendy Walker

HENRY IV PART I directed by Fred Chappell, with Trey Altemose, David Braucher, Morris Brown, Peter Burnell, Stuart Culpepper, Scott E. DePoy, James M. Gough, Marianne Hammock, Jeroy Hannah, Ted Henning, Dana Ivey, Sonny Knox, Philip Kraus, Clayton Landey, Dickson Lane, Ian MacMillan, Gib Manegold, Donald C. Moore, K. Lype O'Dell, Jim Peck, Anthony Scaben, Wendy Walker

WHO'S AFRAID OF VIRGINIA WOOLF? directed by Charles Kerr, with Carol Morley, Lou Bedford, Jill O'Hara, Dennis Howard

VANITIES directed by Fred Chappell, with Jane Dentinger, Bette Glenn, Patricia Miller

Charles Rafshoon Photos

Right: Carol Morley, Lou Bedford in "Who's Afraid of Virginia Woolf?" Top: Pamela Burrell, Fannie Flagg, Dana Ivey in "Come Back to the 5 and Dime, Jimmy Dean"

"The Lovers"
(American Mime Theatre)

AMERICAN MIME THEATRE

New York, N.Y.
Twenty-fifth Season

Director, Paul J. Curtis; Administrator, Jean Barbour; Counsel, Joel S. Charleston

COMPANY

Jean Barbour
Charles Barney
Paul J. Curtis
Dale Fuller
Jean Gennis
Lynda Hodges

Deda Kavanagh
Andrew Levitt
Michael O'Brien
Toni Stanley
Arthur Yorinks
Mr. Bones

REPERTORY: "The Lovers," "The Scarecrow," "Dreams," "Hurly-Burly," "Evolution," "Sludge," "Six," "Work in Progress," "Abstraction"

AMERICAN CONSERVATORY THEATRE

San Francisco, California
October 1976–May 1977

William Ball, General Director; Executive Producer, James B. McKenzie; Executive Director, Edward Hastings; Production Manager, Benjamin Moore; Stage Managers, James Haire, James L. Burke, Suzanne Fry, Anne Salazar, Marian Li; Technical Director, Stan Ouse; Wardrobe, Barbara Hayes-Ouse; Scenery, Robert Blackman, Robert Dahlstrom, Ralph Funicello, John Jensen, Richard Seger; Costumes, Robert Blackman, Cathy Edwards, Robert Fletcher, Robert Morgan, Walter Watson; General Manager, Charles Dillingham; Press, Cheryle Elliott, Jim Kerber; Stage Directors, William Ball, Allen Fletcher, Edward Hastings, Nagle Jackson, Tom Moore, Jack O'Brien, Laird Williamson, Eugene Barcone, Paul Blake, Sabin Epstein, Dolores Ferraro, James Haire, David Hammond

COMPANY

Wayne Alexander, Candace Barrett, Joseph Bird, Raye Birk, Earl Boen, Joy Carlin, Daniel Davis, Barbara Dirickson, Peter Donat, Franchelle Stewart Dorn, Sabin Epstein, Janice Garcia, Michael Keys-Hall, Charles Hallahan, Harry Hamlin, John Hancock, Lawrence Hecht, Elizabeth Huddle, Amy Ingersoll, Gregory Itzin, Daniel Kern, Anne Lawder, Deborah May, Delores Y. Mitchell, William Paterson, Susan E. Pellegrino, Ray Reinhardt, Stephen St. Paul, Francine Tacker, Tony Teague, Sydney Walker, Marrian Walters, Al White, J. Steven White, James R. Winker, Peter Arnoff, Libby Boone, Catherine Brickley, Julie Brown, Marilyn Kay Caskey, George Ceres, Richard Christopher, Peter Davies, Heidi Davis, Raymond E. Dooley, Nancy Erskine, Ann Foorman, Mike Gainey, Benjamin Louis Jurand, Margaret Kienck, Noel Koran, Anita Maynard, Carol Miller, Thomas R. Oglesby, Michael T. Rega, Priscilla Shanks, Freda Foh Shen, Ronald Stanley Sopyla, Bruce Williams, Christopher Wong, Alan Blumenfeld, Charles Coffey, Bill Ferriter, Michael Hill, Barta Heiner, Katherine James, Alice Travis

PRODUCTIONS

"Othello" by William Shakespeare, "Man and Superman" by George Bernard Shaw, "Equus" by Peter Shaffer, "A Christmas Carol" by Charles Dickens, "Knock Knock" by Jules Feiffer, "The Bourgeois Gentleman" by Moliere, "Valentin and Valentina" by Mihail Roshchin (American Premiere), "Travesties" by Tom Stoppard, "Peer Gynt" by Henrick Ibsen

William Ganslen Photos

Right: Barbara Dirickson, Peter Donat in "Man and Superman" Above: Ray Birke, Barbara Dirickson in "Travesties"

Elizabeth Huddle, J. Steven White in "Valentin and Valentina" Top Right: Deborah May, John Hancock in "Othello"

Janice Garcia, Harry Hamlin in "Equus"

ARENA STAGE

Washington, D. C.
October 8, 1976–June 26, 1977

Producing Director, Zelda Fichandler; Executive Director, Thomas C. Fichandler; Production Coordinator, George Spalding; Press, Thomas O'Connor; Directors, Edward Payson Call, David Chambers, Liviu Ciulei, Martin Fried, Norman Gevanthor, Thomas Gruenewald, Alan Schneider, Douglas C. Wager; Sets, Zack Brown, Sally Cunningham Karl Eigsti, Grady Larkins, Santo Loquasto, Tony Straiges; Costumes, Zack Brown, Linda Fisher, Jennifer von Mayrhauser, Marjorie Slaiman; Lighting, Robert Crawley, Hugh Lester, William Mintzer; Composers Robert Dennis, Mel Marvin; Stage Managers, Gully Stanford, John Charlesworth, John J. Mulligan, Jane Neufeld, Florine (Sissy) Pulley, Ellen Raphael; Technical Director, Henry R. Gorfein.

COMPANY

Eunice Anderson, Stanley Anderson, Richard Armstrong, Dulcie Arnold, Andy Backer, Richard Bauer, Gary Bayer, Liese Behringer, Janis Benson, Joseph Bieber, Bill Blanchard, Roy Brocksmith, Helen Burns, Russell Carr, Leslie Cass, Rodney Chiles, Breena Clarke, Joel Colodner, Joan Croydon, Terrence Currier, Leora Dana, Donald Davis, J. Robert Dietz, Lance Davis, Lydia deGreeve, Laura Esterman, Brendan Fawcett, Robert Fisher, David Garrison, Julie Garfield, William Godsey, Max Gulack, Mark Hammer, Trish Hawkins, Jackie Hays, I. M. Hobson, John Hollis, Dick Hoseman, Mary Irey, John B. Jellison, Brent Jennings, Grace Keagy, Laurie Kennedy, Swoosie Kurtz, Damien Leake, Stuart Lerch, Christopher McHale, Marilyn McIntyre, Howard Marsden, Michael Mertz, John J. Mulligan, Meg Myles, Tania Myren, Terry O'Quinn, Joan Pape, Nadia Parsons, Anthony Pasqualini, Robert Pastene, Linda Patchell, Chuck Patterson, Ted Polites, Robert Prosky, Mark Robinson, Theodore Rose, John P. Ryan, Jay O. Sanders, John Seitz, April Shawhan, Sloane Shelton, Lisa Sloan, Shepard Sobel, Phyllis Somerville, Katherine Squire, Frank Stoegerer, Steven Sullivan, Dolores Sutton, Kristoffer Tabori, David Teeple, James Tolkan, Paula Trueman, Kate Van Burek, Eric Weitz, Bart Whitman, Dianne Wiest, Nathan Wilansky, MacArthur Wilder, Ann Williams, Jobeth Williams

PRODUCTIONS

"Saint Joan" by George Bernard Shaw, "Saturday, Sunday and Monday" by Eduardo de Filippo, "Play" by Samuel Beckett, "Streamers" by David Rabe, "Singers" by Steven Stosny, "Porch" by Jeffrey Sweet, "Scooping" by Richard Nelson, "Exhibition" by Janet Neipris, "Living at Home" by Anthony Giordano, "The Autumn Garden" by Lillian Helman, "The Lower Depths" by Maxim Gorky, "A History of the American Film" by Christopher Durang, and *American Premieres* of "Forever Yours, Marie-Lou" by Michel Tremblay, "That Time" and "Footfalls" by Samuel Beckett, and "Catsplay" by Istvan Orkeny

George de Vincent, Alton Miller Photos

Left: Roy Brocksmith, Joe B. Mann, Terrence Currier, John Seitz, Richard Bauer, Jay O. Sanders, Mark Hammer in "The Lower Depths" Above: Brent Jennings, Terry O'Quinn, Joel Colodner in "Streamers"

184   **"A History of the American Film" Top: I. M. Hobson, Helen Burns, Eunice Anderson in "Catsplay"**

Howard Witt, Marilyn McIntyre, Laura Esterman, Leslie Cass in "Forever Yours, Marie-Lou"

ARLINGTON PARK THEATRE

Arlington Heights, Illinois
June 1, 1976–May 31, 1977

Producing Director, Harvey Medlinsky; Managing Director, Walter Perner, Jr.; Business Manager, Suzanne Ruetenick; Press, Zonka and Zonka, Jill Goldberg; Stage Managers, Richard Jellum, James T. McDermott; Technical Director, William B. Fosser; Props, Sandy Lewis; Sets and Lighting, William B. Fosser

PRODUCTIONS AND CASTS

SUITE IN TWO KEYS by Noel Coward, with Richard Kiley, Theresa Wright, Jan Farrand, Spain Logue, Richard Barr (Director)

SABRINA FAIR by Samuel Taylor, with Martin Milner, Maureen O'Sullivan, Sylvia Sidney, Heather MacRae, Robert Urich, Richard Bowler, Marie Brady, Barrie Moss, Harold J. Kennedy (Director)

THE SUNSHINE BOYS by Neil Simon, with Milton Berle, Jack Gilford, Jerry Houser, Louise Jenkins, Andrea Laki, George Tountas, H. George Bruckman, Harvey Medlinsky (Director)

THAT CHAMPIONSHIP SEASON by Jason Miller, with William Conrad, Danny Aiello, Michael Fairman, Eddie Jones, Peter Masterson, Jerry Adler (Director)

THE MOUSETRAP by Agatha Christie, with David McCallum, Katharine Houghton, Kurt Kasznar, Bruse Gray, Dennis McGovern, Nancy Cushman, Leon Shaw, Daryn Kent, Tony Tanner (Director)

RODGERS AND HART with John Gavin, Constance Towers, Tony Tanner, Beth Fowler, Lee Roy Reams, Toni Kaye, John Fearnley (Director)

World Premiere of AN ALMOST PERFECT PERSON by Judith Ross, with Colleen Dewhurst, Richard Schaal, George Hearn, Zoe Caldwell (Director)

TWO FOR THE SEESAW by William Gibson, with Dyan Cannon and Don Murray, Harvey Medlinsky (Director)

BAREFOOT IN THE PARK by Neil Simon, with James MacArthur, Hans Conried, Barbara Britton, Lucy Saroyan, Damon Reicheg, Harvey Medlinsky (Director)

ROOM SERVICE by John Murray and Allen Boretz, with Shelley Berman, Alan Sues, Ron Palillo, Douglas Mellor, Ray Lonergan, Mark Fletcher, Mary T. Wonderlick, Vicki Kaywood, Louis Plante, Robert E. Ingham, Joe Rodgers, Jerry Toulos, George Buse, Richard Hutt, Harvey Medlinsky (Director)

THE BIG KNIFE by Clifford Odets, with James Farentino, Michele Lee, Nehemiah Persoff, Mike Nussbaum, Robert E. Ingham, Kim Zimmer, Marji Bank, Jack Callahan, Nathan Davis, Cynthia Baker Johnson, Don Blackwell, Gordon Oas-Heim, Harvey Medlinsky (Director)

Tony Romano Photos

**Milton Berle, Jack Gilford in "The Sunshine Boys"
Above: Michele Lee, James Farentino, Nehemiah
Persoff in "The Big Knife"**

**Top: Colleen Dewhurst in "An Almost Perfect
Person" Left: Don Murray, Dyan Cannon
in "Two for the Seesaw"** 185

ASOLO STATE THEATER

Sarasota, Florida
June 1, 1976–May 31, 1977

Executive Director, Richard G. Fallon; Artistic Director, Robert Strane; Managing Director, Howard J. Millman; Sets, John Scheffler, Jim Chestnutt, Peter Harvey, David Chapman, Robert C. Barnes; Lighting, Martin Petlock; Costumes, Catherine King, Flozanne John; Technical Director, Victor Meyrich; Stage Managers, Marian Wallace, Stephanie Moss

COMPANY

Martha J. Brown, Ken Costigan, Kelly Fitzpatrick, James Hillgartner, David S. Howard, Pamela Lewis, Dennis Michaels, Bette Oliver, Barbara Reid, Steven Ryan, Isa Thomas, Bradford Wallace, Stephen Van Benschoten, Susan Borneman, Deanna Dunagan, Trent Jones, William Leach, Mary Ed Porter, Walter Rhodes, Frederick Sperberg, Milt Tarver, Cathy S. Chappell, Nora Chester, Janice Clark, Jim Crisp, Jr., John Gray, Stephen Joseph, David Kwiat, Clark Niederjohn, Patricia Oetkin, Frederic-Winslow Oram, Donna Pelc, Robert Stallworth, Romulus E. Zamora, Linda Burnham, Fred Davis, Molly DePree, Bill Herman, Peter Ivanov, Beth Lincks, Paul Murray, Steven J. Rankin, Deborah Unger, John C. Wall, Kathleen Archer, Maryann Barulich, Howard A. Branch, Jr., Ritch Brinkley, Tom Case, Lou Ann Csaszar, John Green, Arthur Hanket, Angela L. Lloyd, Jean McDaniel, Kim Ivan Motter, Joseph Reed, Robert Walker

GUEST ARTISTS: Eberle Thomas, John Franceschina, Lee Kalcheim, Jack Gilhooley, Peter Maloney, Amnon Kabatchnik, Brian McFadden, James Donlon, Normand Beauregard, Neal Kenyon

PRODUCTIONS

"Boy Meets Girl," "Streetcar Named Desire," "The Music Man," "Look Homeward, Angel," "The Ruling Class," "Cat on a Hot Tin Roof," "Waltz of the Toreadors," "Desire under the Elms," "Knock Knock," "The Sea Horse," "Oh, Coward!," "Two for the Seesaw," "Serenading Louie," and *World Premieres* of "The Quibbletown Recruits," "Win with Wheeler," "1776 . . . and All That Jazz," "Mummer's End," "My Love to Your Wife"

Gary Sweetman Photos

Right: Martha J. Brown, Steven Ryan in "The Quibbletown Recruits" Above: Isa Thomas, Bette Oliver, William Leach in "Mummer's End" Top Right: "Win with Wheeler"

Susan Borneman in "My Love to Your Wife"

Stephen Van Benschoten, Bette Oliver, Pamela Lewis in "Look Homeward, Angel"

**Rita Gardner, Ilsebet Tebesli in "Sweet Mistress"
Top: Sharon Morrison, John Christopher Jones
in "The Glass Menagerie" Right: "You Can't
Take It with You"**

BARTER THEATRE

Abingdon, Virginia
April 5–October 17, 1976

Artistic Director-Manager, Rex Partington; Business Manager, Owen Phillips; Business Manager, Pearl Hayter; Staff, James Franklin, Carr Garnett, Don Coleman, Bennet Averyt, Ken Swiger, Lucy Bushore, Walter Wood, Clayton Austin, Tony Partington, Lisa Crego, Steve Woolf, Sigrid Insull, John Olon, John Going, Bryon Grant, Elizabeth Covey, Michael Mantel, Parmelee Welles, Ira Wallach, David Spangler, Susan Dias, Charles Maryan, John Lesko, William Van Keyser, Grant Clifford Logan

COMPANY

Virginia Mattis, Dan Dietch, Sharon Morrison, John Christopher Jones, Cleo Holladay, Peggity Price, Yolande Bryant, Paul Meacham, Robert Rutland, Eric Conger, William Thompson, Holly Cameron, Pete Edens, Gale McNeeley, George Clark Hosmer, Dorothy Marie, Joseph Costa, Carol Haynes Rogers, Stanley Flood, Wayne Knight, Tyson Stephenson, Margaret Lunsford, Mark Dempsey, Michelle Reilley, Mary Shelley, Ellen Painter, Gloria Zaglool, Josephine Nichols, Robert Blackburn, James Tolkan, Gwendolyn Brown, Sarah Hofman, Gwyllum Evans, Bruce McPherson, Allison Pickrell, Alicia Quintano

PRODUCTIONS

"The Glass Menagerie," "You Can't Take It with You," "The Threepenny Opera," "Democracy," "The Matchmaker," "Relatively Speaking," "Beyond the Fringe"

**Right Center: Joseph Costa, Mary Shelley
in "Democracy"**

**Michelle Reilley, Mark Dempsey, Mary Shelley,
Gloria Zaglool (kneeling) in "Threepenny Opera"**

BODY POLITIC THEATRE LABORATORY

Chicago, Illinois
September 1976–June 1977

Executive Director, James A. Shiflett; Artistic Director, Ned Schmidtke; Producing Director, Sharon Phillips; Press, Carmencita DiPuma; Stage Managers, Anthony Petito, Patrick Waddell, Sean O'Connor; Sets, Dean Taucher, Nels Anderson; Costumes, Susan T. Gayford, Kaye Nottbusch, Julie A. Nagel

PRODUCTIONS AND CASTS

WHO'S HAPPY NOW? by Oliver Hailey, with Ann Eggert, Bette Forsyth, John C. Kavan, Daniel M. Therriault, Jack Wallace, Joseph Slowik (Director)

KNOCK KNOCK by Jules Feiffer, with Steve Marmer, Suzanne Quinlan, Harry Stopek, Robert B. Swan

World Premiere of JOHNNIE WILL by Victor Power, with Barry Cullison, Jim Dexter, Sharon Ferguson, Maureen Gallagher, George Heller, Jane MacIver, Lynn Mansbuach, David S. Moore, Ned Schmidtke (Director)

Mark Doyel Photo

**Right: Jack Wallace
in "Who's Happy Now?"**

CALIFORNIA ACTORS THEATRE

Los Gatos, California
October 1, 1976–May 15, 1977

Executive Director, Sheldon Kleinman; Artistic Director, James Dunn; Corporation Directors, Francine Gordon, Sheldon Kleinman, James Dunn; Dramaturge, Dakin Matthews; Sets, Ronald Krempetz; Technical Director, Hal Henderson; Lighting, Robert Klemm, Ray Garrett; Costumes, Barbara Affonso, Sarah Godbois; Stage Managers, Frank Silvey, Robert Steiger; General Manager, Harvey Landa; Press, Barbara Kieve, Carol Torchia, Celia Welterlien

COMPANY

Susan Leigh Brashear, Martin Ferrero, Gina Franz, Bonnie Gallup, David Daniel Haney, Karen Hensel, Tary Ismond, Byron Jennings, Karen Kreider, Matthew J. Locricchio, Dakin Matthews, Scott Paulin, Tom Ramirez, Carolyn Reed, Carl Reggiardo, Kurtwood Smith, John Vickery, Terry Wills, Anita Birchenall, Richard Bradshaw

PRODUCTIONS

"Hamlet" by William Shakespeare and adapted by James Dunn; "Blithe Spirit" by Noel Coward, directed by Terry Wills; "The Good Woman of Setzuan" by Bertolt Brecht, directed by James Dunn; "The Odd Couple" by Neil Simon, directed by G. W. Bailey; "The Rainmaker" by N. Richard Nash, directed by James Dunn; "The Innocents" by William Archibald, directed by Anne McNaughton; "Rashomon" by Fay and Michael Kanin, directed by Kurtwood Smith, and *World Premiere* of "Bierce Takes on the Railroad" by Philip A. Bosakowski

H. J. Susser Photos

**"Blithe Spirit" Above: "The Rainmaker"
Right Center: Byron Jennings as Hamlet**

CENTER THEATRE GROUP
AHMANSON THEATRE

Los Angeles, California
October 13, 1976–June 4, 1977

Robert Fryer, Managing Director; Manager, Charles Mooney; Production Coordinator, Michael Grossman; Press, Rupert Allan, Gail Crooks, James H. Hansen; Assistant Manager, Barbara Stocks; Technical Supervisor, H. R. Poindexter; Administrative Coordinator, Joyce Zaccaro

PRODUCTIONS AND CASTS

A MATTER OF GRAVITY by Enid Bagnold; Director, Noel Willman; Scenery, Ben Edwards; Costumes, Jane Greenwood; Lighting, Thomas Skelton. CAST: Katharine Hepburn, Charlotte Jones, Miller Lide, Richard Kelton, Paddy Croft, Paul Harding, Wanda Bimson, Gary Tomlin

THE GUARDSMAN by Ferenc Molnar; English Version, Grace I. Colbrun; Hans Bartsch; Acting Version, Philip Moeller; Director, Robin Phillips; Designed by Daphne Dare; Lighting, F. Mitchell Dana; Production Associate, Robert Linden; Stage Managers, William O'Brien, Timothy Askew. CAST: Maggie Smith, Brian Bedford, Victor Buono, Mary Savidge, Cathy Wallace, Richard Whelan, Harriet Medin, Timothy Askew

LONG DAY'S JOURNEY INTO NIGHT by Eugene O'Neill; Director, Peter Wood; Designed by Carl Toms; Lighting, H. R. Poindexter; Stage Managers, Milt Commons, Lawrence Maynard, Duchess Dale. CAST: Charlton Heston, Deborah Kerr, Andrew Prine, Robert Burke, Nora Heflin

MERTON OF THE MOVIES by George S. Kaufman and Marc Connelly; Director, Burt Shevelove; Set, John Conklin; Costumes, Noel Taylor; Lighting, Tharon Musser. CAST: Richard Thomas, Annette O'Toole, Brian Avery, Patrick J. Cronin, Barry Cutler, Mickey Deems, Zale Kessler, Barry Michlin, Marilyn Lea Nix, Anne O'Donnell, Peggy Rea, Joe Ross, Fran Ryan, Benjamin Stewart, Herb Vigran, John Volstad, Byron Webster, Erik Howell, Amy Allen, Tobias Andersen, Stefan Fischer, Michael Keenan, Helen Noyes, Bill Story, Robert Wexler

Right: Brian Bedford, Victor Buono, Maggie Smith in "The Guardsman" Top: Annette O'Toole, Richard Thomas, Amy Allen in "Merton of the Movies"

Robert Burke, Deborah Kerr, Charlton Heston, Andrew Prine in "Long Day's Journey into Night"

Katharine Hepburn in "A Matter of Gravity"

189

CENTER THEATRE GROUP
MARK TAPER FORUM

Los Angeles, California
July 15, 1976–July 3, 1977

Gordon Davidson, Artistic Director; General Manager, William P. Wingate; Associate Director, Edward Parone; Press, Stanley F. Kaminsky, Nancy Hereford, Anthony Sherwood, Leigh Charlton; Lighting, Tharon Musser; Production Manager, John De Santis, Technical Director, Robert Calhoun; Stage Managers, Don Winton, Madeline Puzo, Richard Serpe

PRODUCTIONS AND CASTS

THE ROBBER BRIDEGROOM by Alfred Uhry (Book/Lyrics), Robert Waldman (Music); Director Gerald Freedman; Choreography, Donald Saddler; Sets, Douglas W. Schmidt; Costumes, Jeanne Button; Lights, David F. Segal. CAST: Barry Bostwick, Stephen Vinovich, Rhonda Coullet, Barbara Lang, Lawrence John Moss, Ernie Sabella, Trip Plymale, Susan Berger, Jana Schneider, Carolyn McCurry, George DeLoy, Gary Epp, B. J. Hardin, Mary Murray, Melinda Tanner, Dennis Warning, Tom Westerman, Kyle Nunnery, Harmon Harper, Norman Ogelsby, Queenie Brenner, Rose Otto, Gerry G. Summers, K. K. Pone

ICE by Michael Cristofer; Director, Jeff Bleckner; Designed by John DeSantis. CAST: Cliff DeYoung, Ron Rifkin, Britt Swanson. *World Premiere.*

VANITIES by Jack Heifner; Director, Garland Wright; Scenery, John Arnone; Costumes, David James; Lighting, F. Mitchell Dana. CAST: Lucie Arnaz, Stockard Channing, Sandy Duncan

TRAVESTIES by Tom Stoppard in repertory with THE IMPORTANCE OF BEING EARNEST by Oscar Wilde; Director, Edward Parone; Setting, Ralph Funicello; Costumes, Peter J. Hall; Lighting, Tharon Musser; Music, Carol Lees. CAST: David Dukes, Corale Browne, Herbert Foster, Nicholas Hammond, Jean Marsh, Richard Sanders, Anita Gillette, Neil Flanagan, Jane Connell

A HISTORY OF THE AMERICAN FILM by Christopher Durang; Director, Peter Mark Schifter; Sets, John Conklin; Costumes, Joe I. Tompkins; Lighting, J. Mitchell Dana. CAST: Udana Power, Robert Walden, June Gable, Alice Playten, Richard Lenz, Jane Connell, Teri Ralston, Roger Robinson, Barry Dennen, Frank O'Brien, Lu Leonard, Gordon Connell; in repertory with ANGEL CITY by Sam Shepard; Director, Robert Calhoun. CAST: Ron Silver, Paul Sand, Loren Pickford, Edward Winter, Larry Hankin, Aileen Fitzpatrick

World Premiere of LEANDER STILLWELL by David Rush; Director, John Dennis; Designers, Charles Berliner, F. Mitchell Dana. CAST: Dorothy Chace, Nathan Cook, Brenda J. Davis, Doug Franklin, Noreen Hennessy, E. Lamont Johnson, Hal Landon, Jr., Allan Lurie, Michael McNeilly, Tony Papenfuss, Randy Pelish, Rick Vartorella, Alfre Woodard; in repertory with BUGS/GUNS by Doris Baizley; Music, Harry Aguado; Lyrics, Doris Baizley, Harry Aguado. CAST: Nathan Cook, Brenda J. Davis, Noreen Hennessy, Hal Landon, Jr., Michael McNeilly, Tony Papenfuss, Rick Vartorella, Alfre Woodard

Steven Keull Photos

Left: Anita Gillette, David Dukes in "Travesties"
Above: Aileen Fitzpatrick, Paul Sand
in "Angel City"

Coral Browne, Nicholas Hammond, Jean Marsh i
"The Importance of Being Earnest" Top Left: Ro
Rifkin, Britt Swanson, Cliff DeYoung in "Ice"
Below: Lu Leonard, Barry Dennen, Alice Playte
in "A History of the American Film"

Sandy Duncan, Lucie Arnaz, Stockard Channing
in "Vanities"

CENTER THEATRE GROUP
MARK TAPER FORUM

IMPROVISATIONAL THEATRE PROJECT

Director, John Dennis; Manager, Michael Lonergan; Stage Manager, Richard Serpe; Writer, Doris Baizley; Designer, Charles Berliner; Music Composed by Harry Aguado; Lyrics, Doris Baizley, Harry Aguado; CAST: Nathan Cook, Brenda J. Davis, Noreen Hennessy, Hal Landon, Jr., Michael McNeilly, Tony Papenfuss, Rick Vartorella, Alfre Woodard.

FORUM LABORATORY

Director, Robert Greenwald; Associate Director, John Sullivan; Manager, Michael Lonergan; Production Managers, Erik Brenmark, Diane Keil; Stage Managers, Mark Armarino, Tish Iversen, Robert Kahn, Diane Keil, James T. McDermott, Richard W. McKibben, Kim Miyori, Gary Raileanu, Sarah Rodman, Ron Schultz, Richard Serpe, Jason Shubb

PRODUCTIONS AND CASTS

CONVICTIONS by the members of the Terminal Island Correctional Institution Drama Workshop; Directors, Vickie Rue, Jeremy Blahnik; Designers, Thomas Walsh, Barbara Ling. CAST: Kathie Andrews, Doris Brown, Rico Chetty, Maxine Ford, Bill Gabriels, Rodni Hardison, Charlie Hines, Deborah Long, Marque S. Lynche, Jimmy Matthews, Rhennae Moore, Sally Moore, Kenny Nills, Mel Taylor, Herman Thomas, Daniel White-Odudua, Betty Winn.

NO PLACE TO BE SOMEBODY by Charles Gordone and JUMP STREET performed by the Terminal Island Prison Drama Workshop

CONJURING AN EVENT by Richard Nelson; Director, John Dennis; Designers, Charles Berliner, Julie Weiss, Brian Gale; Music, Steven Wells, and the Urban Boubon Band. CAST: Brenda J. Davis, Philip Baker Hall, Milt Kogan, Michael McNeilly, Barry Moore, Tony Papenfuss

HEY, RUBE! by Janet McReynolds; Director, Robert Calhoun. CAST: Frances Bay, Vincent Cobb, Al Dunlap, Elizabeth Farley, Aileen Fitzpatrick, Elizabeth Franz, Lorry Goldman, Nora Heflin, Betty Jinnette, Karyn Kronenbourg, Lauren Levian, James Luisi, V. Phipps-Wilson, Mallory Sandler, Diana Scarwid

DADDY'S DUET by Clifford Turknett; Director, Gordon Hunt. CAST: Neil Flanagan, Barbara Iley, Robert LuPone, Paul Zegler.

A HOUSE FOR ROSIE by Leonora Thuna; Director, Jeremy Blahnik. CAST: Phillip R. Allen, Dimitra Arliss, Bert Conway, Frank Geraci, Robert Machray, Richard Marion, Ruth Manning.

SAFE HOUSE by Nicholas Kazan; Director, Vickie Rue. CAST: Catlin Adams, Jonathan Banks, Terri Carson, Michael Cavanaugh, Jane Elliot, Art LaFleur, L. Gray, Alex Henteloff

THE MIDDLE AGES by A. R. Gurney, Jr.; Director, Gordon Hunt. CAST: Cliff DeYoung, Keene Curtis, Toni Lamond, Kitty Winn

THE FISHER KING by Daniel Algie; Directors, Mako, Shizuko Hoshi. CAST: Shizuko Hoshi, Alberto Isaac, Clyde Kusatsu, Dana Lee, Soon Tech Oh, Yuki Shimoda, Keone Young

GETHSEMANE SPRINGS by Harvey Perr; Director, John Sullivan. CAST: Eileen Brennan, Tyne Daly, David Barlow, Devin Goldenberg, Arlene Golonka, Melanie Mayron, Ron Rifkin, Carol Rossen, Robert Rovin, Harvey Solin, Joyce Van Patten.

NEVADA by David Kranes; Director, Jack Bender. CAST: Kay Cole, Hugh Gillin, Susan Heldfond, Ed Lowe, Adrienne Marden, Frank McCarthy, John Medici, Dennis Redfield, John Ritter, Tom Sauber

FORCE OF HABIT by Thomas Bernhard; Translation, Michael Feingold; Director, Don Winton. CAST: Sara Ballantine, Jack Collins, Jeff Katz, George McDaniel

Gordon Hunt, Robert Kahn Photos

Right Center: Toni Lamond, Cliff DeYoung, Keene Curtis, Kitty Winn in "The Middle Ages" Above: Robert LuPone, Paul Zegler, Neil Flanagan in "Daddy's Duet" Top: "Bugs"

Devon Goldenberg, Carol Rossen, Arlene Golonka in "Gethsemane Springs"

CENTER STAGE

Baltimore, Maryland
October 22, 1976–May 15, 1977

Artistic Director, Stan Wojewodski, Jr.; Managing Director, Peter W. Culman; Administrative Director, Peter B. England; Business Manager, Jane S. Moss; Press, Paula Marmon, Linda Kinsey; Designer, Charles Cosler; Costumier, Elizabeth P. Palmer; Stage Managers, William Yaggy, Amy Leveen; Sound Technician, Kevin Carney; Technical Director, Robert Murphy; Lighting, Ian Calderon

PRODUCTIONS AND CASTS

SHE STOOPS TO CONQUER by Oliver Goldsmith, with Paul C. Thoman, Carol Gustafson, Donna Welby, Michael Haney, Tana Hicken, Christine Baranski, Roland Bull, Jim Broaddus, Dan Diggles, Dan Szelag, Roland Bull, Caleb Childs, Tim McCusker, Ken Tipper, Thomas G. Waites

WHEN YOU COMIN' BACK, RED RYDER? by Mark Medoff, with Dan Diggles, Tana Hicken, Pat Karpen, Michael Medeiros, John Straub, Paul C. Thomas, Thomas G. Waites, Donna Welby

MISALLIANCE by George Bernard Shaw, with Dan Diggles, Davis Hall, Linda Alper, Nanette Rickert, Joseph Warren, Paul C. Thomas, Ron Seibert, Christine Baranski, Donald Warfield, Arne Zaslove (Director)

TOYS IN THE ATTIC by Lillian Hellman, with Anne Lynn, Louis Markle, Tommy Hicks, Ruby Holbrook, Walter Jones, Beeson Carroll, Deborah Offner, Robert Wirtz, Kevin Mangan

THE FIRST BREEZE OF SUMMER by Leslie Lee, with Ronny Clanton, Peter Wise, Dorothi Fox, Claudia McNeil, Bill Cobbs, Juanita Bethea, Elizabeth Van Dyke, Tommy Hicks, Walter Jones, Davis Hall, Norman Mizell Wilkerson III, Terry Scott, Barney Cohen, Verna Day, William Jay, Woodie King, Jr. (Director)

KNOCK KNOCK by Jules Feiffer, with Robert Pastene, Herman O. Arbeit, Bess Armstrong, Edmond Genest

A SORROW BEYOND DREAMS by Peter Handke, with Len Cariou; Daniel Freudenberger, Director.

Richard Anderson Photos

Top Right: Claudia McNeil in "The First Breeze of Summer" Below: "Misalliance"

CENTER STAGE THEATRE

Austin, Texas
June 1976–May 1977

Artistic Director-Manager, Ken Johnson; Guest Directors, Mavourneen Dwyer, Alva Hascall; Technical Directors, John Rathman, Mike Sullivan; Costumes, Francis Mauldin, Lynn Capri, Wanda McMurray, Ann Lind, Stephen McMillan; Business Manager, Silver Battle; Press, Bob Kobarg; Assistant to Director, Debi Kline

COMPANY

Ann Armstong, Cindy Banks, George Barilla, James Belcher, John Bernadoni, Greg Bayless, Annie Bordon, Carolee Brown, Carter Bryant, Bill Buchannan, Tony Bove, Susan Brady, Thomas Byrne, Kathleen Boulton, Bill Breaux, John Brown, Jerry Conn, Barbara Corbin, Mary Courtney, Gordon Cole, Troy Dale, Dave Davis, Scott Dawes, John Dodson, Joe Dockery, Mavourneen Dwyer, Oscar Duran, Mitch Etter, Wayde Frey, Roger Gorton, Marilyn Gunter, Jeff Gillam, Olin Fite, Don Fenner, Betsey Fath, Barbara Flores, Ken Evert, Oliver Handley, Cookie Hascall, Patricia Hadley, Tom Heard, Richard James, Kim Jones, Nancy Jones, Donald Janda, Cliff King, Carol Gabriel, Jane Herrick, Ethel Little, John Lowrey, Linda McClelland, Jim McKenna, Stephen McMillan, Charles Harveson, Standish Meacham, Michael Meyerson, Janis Moffit, Timothy Miller, Taylor Maddux, Cadeline Olds, Constance O'Hearne, Ivy Lipscomb, Claire Price, Debi Klein, Ray Peevey, Cindy Pflughft, Wanda Pierce, Karen Pippin, Sharon Porter, Vickie Purgason, Mary Reynold, Lee Ripley, Patti Romines, Walter Sleeth, Sam Sanchez, Judy Scott, Joanne Schmidt, Mike Sullivan, Kathleen Scafe, Susan Shofner, Ron Swift, Maurice Thompson, Lester Simmons, Maggie Strub, Doug Scherer, Steve Uzzell, Anne Threlkeld, Scottie Wilkinson, Larry Williams, Christine Wallis

PRODUCTIONS

"Little Mary Sunshine," "Born Yesterday," "What the Butler Saw," "The Cherry Orchard," "Kiss Me, Kate," "Two for the Seasaw," "The Royal Family"

Ken Johnson Photos

John Lowery, Carter Bryant, Carolee Brown in "Born Yesterday"

CINCINNATI PLAYHOUSE IN THE PARK

Cincinnati, Ohio
October 26, 1976–June 5, 1977

Producing Director, Michael Murray; General Manager, Robert W. Tolan; Assistant to Mr. Murray, Jerri Roberts; Assistant to Mr. Tolan, Barbara Steiger Platt; Business Manager, Yodie Mitchell; Administrative Assistants, David Carter, Ron Sayers; Press, Lanni Johnston Brengel; Production Managers, Richard Lukaszewicz, Kent Koefler; Costumes, Annie Peacock Warner, Prue Warren, Jill Hamilton, Maureen Flanagan Bird: Props, Roger Abell, Nancy Gilmore, Kathy Duvall; Stage Managers, J. P. Valente, Ken Stauffer; Sound, Kim Zimmerman; Lighting, Neil Peter Jampolis, Jane Resiman, Dennis Parichy; Sets, Paul Shortt, Neil Peter Jampolis, John Lee Beatty, Karl Eigsti; Stage Directors, Michael Murray, John Going, Robert Brewer, Geoff Garland.

PRODUCTIONS AND CASTS

CAT ON A HOT TIN ROOF by Tennessee Williams, with Ellen Barber, Ronnie B. Baker, Carole Lockwood, Melissa Wolfe, Karen Husman, Kurt Froehlich, Kent Rizley, Elizabeth Moore, Richard Dix, Edwin Dundon, Luke Sickle

OLIVER! by Lionel Bart, with Tim Waldrip, Tim Rail, I. M. Hobson, Helena Humann, Viola Feldman, Judith Claire, Keith Perry, Susan Willis, Beth Scholten, Ron Bommer, John Wylie, David Parkes, Howard Krakovsky, Patrick Downey, Joy Garrett, Ginger Timberlake, George Massey, George Brengel, Luke Sickle, Virginia Payne, David Vesper, and Etha Arren, John Beran, Sheelagh Bevan, David Centers, Peter Franz, Robert Greenlea, Cory Johnson, Cliff Logan, Sean McCarthy, Previn Moore, Brad Powell, Chris Vaughan, Elaine Eckstein, Gary McGurk, Richard Pruitt, Dan Seymour, Diane Smith, Robert Stocker, David Upson

A MONTH IN THE COUNTRY by Ivan Turgenev, with David Upson, Marian Baer, Brenda Curtis, Paul Collins, Susan Willis, Chris Sullivan, Bradley Boyer, Pamela Rohs, John Wylie, Robin Groves, Mitchell Edmonds, Luke Sickle

WHEN YOU COMIN' BACK, RED RYDER? by Mark Medoff, with Raynor Scheine, Mia Dillon, Patrick McCullough, Luke Sickle, Karen Shallo, Duncan Hoxworth, Kent Broadhurst, Sharon Goldman

HEARTBREAK HOUSE by George Bernard Shaw, with Claudia Zahn, Nancy Cushman, John Wylie, Kathleen O'Meara Noone, Jo Henderson, Douglas Fisher, Stephen Arlen, Richard Dix, Keith Perry, Ron Steelman

THE HOSTAGE by Brendan Behan, with Joyce Krempel, Moultrie Patten, Viola Feldman, David Ursin, Ennis Smith, II, Georgia Neu, Ralph Redpath, Lloyd Harris, Ron Steelman, Jane Lowry, Linda Dunlevy, Terrence O'Hara, Michael Shooner, Richard Niles

Sandy Underwood Photos

Right: Kent Broadhurst, Karen Shallo in "When You Comin' Back, Red Ryder?" Above: Moultrie Patten, Linda Dunlevy, Joyce Krempel in "The Hostage"

Brenda Curtis, John Wylie in "A Month in the Country" Top Right: "Heartbreak House"

"Oliver"

193

COMPANY THEATRE

Los Angeles, California
June 1, 1976–May 31, 1977

COMPANY: Alan Abelew, Polita Barnes, Dierdre Berthrong, Gar Campbell, Laurence Cohen, Milton Earl Forrest, Myrna Gawryn, Susan Gelb, Barbara Grover, Daniel Grace, Nancy Hickey, Jerry Hoffman, Karen Jeter, Lori Landrin, Paul Linke, Marcina Motter, Andrew Parks, Louie Piday, Jerry Pojawa, Michael Prichard, Roxann Pyle, Russel Pyle, Dennis Redfield, Jack Rowe, Billy Schaffner, Trish Soodik

GUEST ARTISTS: Joedy Barnes, John Brumfield, Cris Capen, George Carter, Michael Dare, Tony DeFonte, Stephen Downs, Madison Mason, Andrew Masset, Bruce McGuire, Constance Mellors, Liz Palmer, Michael Sheehan

PRODUCTIONS: "Aucassin and Nicolette" (*World Premiere* of an original musical by Stephen Downs), "Lear" by Edward Bond

Right: Alan Abelew (standing), Louis Piday, Daniel Grace, Barbara Brover in "Lear"
(Sindy Hawke Photo)

Below: Madison Mason in "Aucassin and Nicolette"
(Lisa Powers Photo)

CLARENCE BROWN COMPANY

Knoxville, Tennessee
November 1976–April 1977

Director, Ralph G. Allen; Honorary Chairman, Clarence Brown; Associate Directors, Thomas Cooke, Fred Fields, Albert Harris, Wandalie Henshaw, Anthony Quayle; General Manager, Julian Forrester; Director of Design, Robert Cothran; Technical Director, Robert Field; Design Staff, Marianne Custer, Barry Daniels, Steven Kennedy, Robert Mashburn; Company Manager, Margaret Wheeler; Press, Gary Haun; Stage Managers, Pat Bailey, David Keith, D. Bradley Thomas, Barrett Nolan

PRODUCTIONS AND CASTS

GHOSTS by Henrik Ibsen, with Mary Jane McGee, Gregg Almquist, Jay Doyle, Wandalie Henshaw, Kenneth Gray

THE NEW MAJESTIC FOLLIES & LYCEUM GARDENS REVUE by Ralph G. Allen, with Joe E. Ross, Gene Bell, Bernerd Engel, Richard Galuppi, Rick Spivey, Donna King, Ann Connors, Becky Gelke, Jo Ann Havrilla, Diane Nicole, Donna Pelc, Libby Rhodes, Laurie Winn, Lisa Brinegar, Cindy Leake, Chris Grabenstein, Debbie Freeberg, Bill Smith, Robin Whitehead, Lee Wittenberg, and Jimmy Mathews

THE TAX COLLECTOR freely adapted from Lesage's "Turcaret" by Ralph Allen, with June Havoc, Gregg Almquist, Judith Calder, Jay Doyle, Patricia Fay, Kenneth Gray, John Krich, Timothy Meyers, Harriet Nichols, Larry Bounds, Anthony White

Donna King in "The New Majestic Follies"
Above: Gregg Almquist, June Havoc, Ken Gray in "The Tax Collector"

CLEVELAND PLAY HOUSE

Cleveland, Ohio
September 28, 1976–May 1,1977

Director, Richard Oberlin; Associate Director, Larry Tarrant; Assistant Director, Robert Snook; Scenic Director, Richard Gould; Administrative Coordinator, Nelson Iseikeit; Press, William Lempke, Paula Bond, Sherry Tarrant, Walter Heid; Resident Directors, Jonathan Farwell, Richard Halverson, Paul Lee, Evie McElroy, Richard Oberlin, William Rhys; Guest Directors, John Dillon, Eddie Gasper, Jack Lee, Dorothy Silver; Resident Designers, Harriet Cone, Eugene Hare, Barbara Leatherman, Estelle Painter, David Smith, Joseph P. Tilford; Guest Designers, Arden Fingerhut, Maura Smolover, James Tilton, Stuart Wurtzel; Company Manager, Stanley R. Suchecki; Stage Managers, Eugene Hare, Richard Oberlin, Stanley R. Suchecki, Bennett E. Taber, Larry Tarrant, Ray Barnhart, Pamela Sprosty; Technical Director, Joseph P. Tilford

ACTING ENSEMBLE

Norman Berman, Sharon Bicknell, Cynthia Brown, John Buck, Jr., Dan Desmond, Jo Farwell, Jonathan Farwell, June Gibbons, Wesley Grant, Richard Halverson, Allen Leatherman, Paul Lee, Andrew Lichtenberg, Lizabeth Mackay, Evie McElroy, Richard Oberlin, William Rhys, James Richards, Tedd Rawlins, George C. Simms, Robert Snook, Wayne S. Turney, Daryl Champine, John Danielich, Carol Schultz

GUEST ARTISTS: Kenneth Albers, Yolande Bavan, Clayton Corzatte, Charlotte Fairchild, David O. Frazier, Mary Gallagher, George Gould, Dee Hoty, Myrna Kaye, Charles Keating, J. J. Lewis, Susan Ludlow, Spencer McIntyre, Christina Moore, Ralph Neeley, Selena Nystrom, Dorothy Paxton, Dale Place, Rhonda Plymate, Sheila Smith, John Leslie Wolfe, Emlyn Williams

PRODUCTIONS

"Emlyn Williams as Charles Dickens," "The Sunshine Boys" by Neil Simon, "The Cat and the Fiddle" by Jerome Kern and Otto Harbach, "Are You Now or Have You Ever Been" by Eric Bentley, "A Moon for the Misbegotten" by Eugene O'Neill, "The Yellow Jacket" by George C. Hazelton and Benrimo, "The Twain Shall Meet" compiled by Clayton Corzatte and Susan Ludlow, "Man and Superman" by George Bernard Shaw, "Ladyhouse Blues" by Kevin O'Morrison, "Macbeth" by William Shakespeare," "Table Manners" (Part I of "The Norman Conquests") by Alan Acykbourn

Herbert Ascherman, Jr. Photos

Right Center: "Man and Superman"

Above: Evie McElroy, Ken Albers, Paul Lee in "Moon for the Misbegotten"

"Ladyhouse Blues" Top Right: Sheila Smith in "The Cat and the Fiddle"

James Richards, Daryl Champine in "The Yellow Jacket"

DALLAS THEATER CENTER

Dallas, Texas
October 5, 1976–Aug. 1

Managing Director, Paul Baker; Assistant Director, Mary Sue Jones; Press, Lynn Trammell; Stage Directors, Ken Latimer, Bryant J. Reynolds, Ryland Merkey, Robyn Flatt, John Henson, John Logan; Sets, John Henson, Steve Wallace, Yoichi Aoki, Kathleen Latimer, Peter Wolf; Costumes, Cheryl Denson, Pamela Jensen, Denise Drennen, Paul Buboltz, Michael Krueger; Lighting, Linda Blase, Randy Moore, Robin Crews, Sally Netzel, Wayne Lambert; Stage Managers, M. Randall Russell, Robert Bovard, Suzanne Chiles, Don White, Paul R. Bassett, John Nichols, Carolyn Pines.

COMPANY

Yoichi Aoki, Linda Blase, Judith Davis, Cheryl Denson, Keith Dixon, John Figlmiller, Robyn Flatt, Martha Robinson Goodman, John Henson, Allen Hibbard, Mary Sue Jones, Preston Jones, Kathleen Latimer, Sallie Laurie, John Logan, Rebecca Logan, Steven Mackenroth, Ryland Merkey, Norma Moore, Randy Moore, Louise Mosley, Sally Netzel, Patti O'Donnell, Mona Pursley, Bryant J. Reynolds, Synthia Rogers, Mary Rohde, Glenn Allen Smith, John R. Stevens, Randolph Tallman, Jacque Thomas, Matt Tracy, Lynn Trammell

PRODUCTIONS

"Sherlock Holmes and the Curse of the Sign of Four" by Dennis Rosa, "Once in a Lifetime" by Kaufman and Hart, "Scapino" adapted by Dunlop and Dale, "Three Sisters" by Chekhov, "Something's Afoot" by McDonald, Vos and Gerlach, and *World Premieres* of "Sam" by Sally Netzel, and "Santa Fe Sunshine" by Preston Jones

Linda Blase Photos

Left: Rebecca Logan, Cheryl Denson, Alex Winslow Celeste Varricchio in "Something's Afoot" Above: John Figlmiller, Randy Moore in "Sherlock Holmes" Top: Ruth Cantrell, Paul Buboltz, Judith Davis, Randy Moore, Sally Netzel in "Santa Fe Sunshine"

Jacque Thomas, Ryland Merkey in "Sam"

Mona Pursley, Norma Moore, Mary Rohde in "Three Sisters"

DETROIT REPERTORY THEATRE

Detroit, Michigan
November 4, 1976–June 26, 1977

Artistic Director, Bruce E. Millan; Administrative Assistant, Marylynn Kacir; Audience Development, Robert Williams; Sets, Bruce E. Millan, John Knox; Costumes, Marianna Hoad; Lighting, Dick Smith, Mary Payne, Jack Slater; Stage Manager, Jesse Newton; Stage Directors, Bruce E. Millan, Robert Williams, Dee Andrus, Barbara Busby

PRODUCTIONS AND CASTS

WEDDING BAND by Alice Childress, with Joilette Payne, Ria Armstron, Frenchy Hodges, Myrenna Hawthorne, Yolanda Williams, Reginald Crawford, Jack Slater, William Boswell, Cheryl Lemans, Dee Andrus

THE PETRIFIED FOREST by Robert Sherwood, with William Boswell, Mark Bennett, Willie Hodges, Donald Douglas, Mark Murri, LuJuana Taylor, Sharon Castleberry, David Jeffrey, Bill McGowan, Jessie Newton, Renate Walker, Robert Williams, John McCollum

THE MATCHMAKER by Thornton Wilder, with William Boswell, Scott McCue, Willie Hodges, Ruth Palmer, Kleph Chase, John W. Hardy, Robert Williams, Barbara Busby, Michael Joseph, Marge Miller, Alisa Foster, Van Little, Chris DuPree

THE LITTLE DOG LAUGHED by Joe Schneiders (*World Premiere*), with Dee Andrus, Council Cargle, Alisa Foster, John W. Hardy, Willie Hodges, Scott M. McCue, Marge Miller, Mark Murri, Jesse Newton, Beverly Whatley

Buzz Sawyer Photos

Top Right: Dee Andrus, Scott M. McCue, Jesse Newton, Council Cargle in "The Little Dog Laughed" Below: "The Petrified Forest"

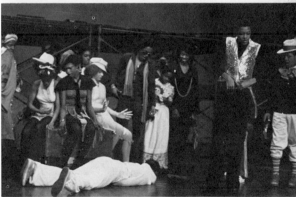

THE FAMILY

New York, N.Y.
Fifth Season

Artistic Director, Marvin Felix Camillo; Administrator, Joseph L. Green; Workshop Supervisor, Bette Howard; Administrative Assistant, Al Black; Counselor, Jose Maldonado; Press, Faith Geer, Carol Winfield, Malika Whitney; Lighting, Spencer Moss; Scenery, David Mitchell; Technical Adviser, Don Koehler

COMPANY

Ellen Cleghorne, Malika Whitney, Carlos Juan Febry, Audrey Taylor, Ife Shipp, Raymond Ruiz, Luis Torres, Rodney Cleghorne, Everett Ensley, Diedre Marcelle, Darryl Yates, Pamela Goodrich, Sam Harrington, Laramarie Davis, A. D. Cannon, Gwynne Tomlan, Harriet Brown, Bette Howard, Rodney Rincon, Winston Lovett, Jimmy Hayeson, Amy Bibb, Jacqueline Wilson, Linda Harrison, Jose Maldonado, Lloyd James Evans, Marilyn Worrell, Monica Williams, Feliz Pitre, Felipe Torres, Ayana Phillips, Emily Rodriguez, Hector Colon, Maria Ramos, J. J. Johnson, Lauren Marshall, Jose Felix Guzman II, Marie Rodriquez, Marvin Feliz Camillo, Jr., Mark Low, Morace T. Landy, Sam King, Carol Winfield, Jenny Kellan, Willie Peartree, Pinkie McCullough, Maxine Sharrock, Al Black, Carlos Cummings, Thom Santiago, Mark Surles, Garrison Ferrer, Norman Marcelle, Fran Ficklen, Chris Currie, Lawrence Griffin, Alphonso Douglas

PRODUCTIONS

"Straight from the Ghetto," "Clara's Ole Man," "The Proposal," "The Blacks," "Looking for Tomorrow," "Noah's Ark"

Mark 6 Photos

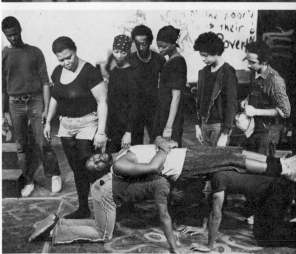

**"Straight from the Ghetto"
Above: "Noah's Ark"**

197

FOLGER THEATRE GROUP

Washington, D. C.
October 15, 1976–June 26, 1977

Producer, Louis W. Scheeder; General Managers, Larry Verbit, Michael Sheehan; Press, Linda Lehman; Company Manager, Mary Ann deBarbieri; Technical Director, G. Kerry Comerford; Stage Managers, Pamela Horner, Laura Burroughs; Lighting, Arden Fingerhut, Hugh Lester, Elizabeth Toth; Costumiere, Karen M. Hummel; Sets, Raymond C. Recht, David Chapman, John Kasarda, Franco Colavecchia; Costumes, Bob Wojewodski, Jennifer von Mayrhauser, Karen M. Hummel; Choreography, Virginia Freeman

PRODUCTIONS AND CASTS

THE FOOL: SCENES OF BREAD AND LOVE by Edward Bond (*American Premiere*), with Linda Atkinson, Paul Collins, Albert Corbin, David Cromwell, James Dean, Earle Edgerton, David Garrison, Pat Gebhard, John Gilliss, Robert Hagen, June Hansen, Terry Hinz, Joanne Hrkach, Kenneth Kelleher, Richard Madden, Barry MacMillan, Steven Nowicki, Donald Parker, Joseph Pinckney, Louis Schaefer, Anne Stone, Frederic Warriner

MUCH ADO ABOUT NOTHING by William Shakespeare, with Andy Backer, Mary Carney, Albert Corbin, David Cromwell, James Dean, Clement Fowler, Kurt Garfield, Steven Gilborn, John Gilliss, Carlos Juan Gonzalez, Robert Hagen, Joanne Hrkach, Joseph Michael Hume, Richard Madden, Steven Nowicki, Etain O'Malley, Louis Schaefer, Jo Spiller, Steven Sullivan, John Tillotson, Frederic Warriner

MUMMER'S END by Jack Gilhooley (*World Premiere*), with Jean Barker, Mary Carney, John Gilliss, John LaGioia, David Little, Anne Stone, Joseph Sullivan, Marie Wallace, Frederic Warriner

BLACK ELK SPEAKS by Christopher Sergel (*World Premiere*), with Kenry "Kaimu" Bal, Carl Battaglia, Carlos Carrasco, Didi Charney, Clayton Corbin, Donald Davidson, Richard de Angelis, David Forman, Susan Galbraith, John Gilliss, Carlos Juan Gonzalez, Carlo (Inali) Grasso, Jane Lind, Michael Medeiros, Betsy Revard, Maria Antoinette Rogers, Michael Sutton, Jerry ver Dorn, Quentin Vidor, Toni Wein

A MIDSUMMER NIGHT'S DREAM by William Shakespeare, with Anthony Call, Albert Corgin, David Cromwell, Andrew Davis, John Elko, John Hertzler, Terry Hinz, Joanne Hrkach, Barry MacMillan, Deborah Mayo, Steven Nowicki, Scott Miller, Elizabeth Perry, Marcia Elaine Phillips, Marcell Rosenblatt, John Shuman, Count Stovall, Richard Wright

Top Right: Clayton Corbin, Carlos Carrasco in "Black Elk Speaks" Below: John LaGioia in "Mummer's End"

Jonelle Allen, Michael Davis, Barbara Heuman, Irving Lee (front) in "The All Night Strut"

FORD'S THEATRE SOCIETY

Washington, D. C.
September 7, 1976–July 31, 1977

Executive Producer, Frankie Hewitt; General Manager, Maury Sutter; Assistant to Producer, Margaret Jones; Press, Alma Viator, Michael Howe; Technical Director, Tom Berra; Wardrobe Mistress, Hillary Gibbs Paul; Chairman of the Board, Williard F. Rockwell, Jr.; Stage Directors, Vinnette Carroll, Garland Wright, Fran Charnas; Sets, William Schroeder, John Arnone, Richard Ferrer; Costumes, William Schroeder, David James, Carol Oditz; Lighting, Gilbert Hemsley, Jr., Patrika Brown, Barry Arnold; Stage Managers, Lani Ball, Sam Ellis; Choreographers, Talley Beatty, Arthur Faria

PRODUCTIONS AND CASTS

YOUR ARMS TOO SHORT TO BOX WITH GOD by Vinnette Carroll and Alex Bradford, with Salome Bey, Alex Bradford, Sharon Brooks, Thomas Jefferson Fouse, Jr., Cardell Hall, Delores Hall, William Hardy, Jr., Jan Hazell, Bobby Hill, Artartus Jenkins, Aisha Khabeera, Hector Jaime Mercado, Zola Shaw, William Thomas, Jr.

VANITIES by Jack Heifner, with Valorie Armstrong, Sarah Harris, Patricia Richardson

THE ALL NIGHT STRUT! by Fran Charnas, with Jonelle Allen, Michael Davis, Barbara Heuman, Irving Lee, Melanie Adam, Nedra Dixon, Leslie Dockery, Brenda Holmes, Bobby Longbottom, Jack Magradey, Liz Morris, Charles Neal, Eric Riley, Christina Saffran, Jeff Spielman, Michelle Stubbs, Gary Sullivan

GEORGE STREET PLAYHOUSE

New Brunswick, N. J.
October 8, 1976–May 21, 1977

Producing Director, Eric Krebs; Managing Director, John Herochik; Artistic Director, Bob Hall; Administrative Assistant, Mary Matro ; Press, Shelley Glotzer; Stage Manager, Lois J. Kier; Stage Directors, Bob Hall, Dino Narizzano, David Rubinstein, Eric Krebs, Peter Bennett

PRODUCTIONS AND CASTS

THAT CHAMPIONSHIP SEASON by Jason Miller, with P. J. Barry, James Handy, Alfred Hinckley, Russ Hubert, Stewart Steinberg

BROTHERS by Eric Krebs (*World Premiere*), with Mark Blum, John Corey, Robert McIllwaine, Aleen Malcolm, Bronwyn Rucker

OH! COWARD! (words and music by Noel Coward) with William Graves, Ruth Haye, Jay Kirsch

A MIDSUMMER NIGHT'S DREAM by William Shakespeare, with Robert Engel, Laure Mattos, Paul Panfiglio, Nona Pipes, Dwight Collins, David Richmond, Debra Jo Rupp, Anita Sorel, John Del Regno, Richard Spore, Jason Tyler, Lee Wilkof

THE MOUSETRAP by Agatha Christie, with John Benson, Victoria Boothby, Dana Coen, Jeanne Cullen, Suzanne Heitman, Eric Loeb, Samuel Maupin, Paul Panfiglio

THE MEMOIRS OF CHARLIE POPS by Joseph Hart, with Andy Backer, Rita Bascari, Robert Costanzo, Harris Laskawy, Susan Kay Logan, Gloria Matthews, Peter Webster

WAITING FOR GODOT by Samuel Beckett, with Samuel Maupin, John Vennema, Eric Loeb, Michael Burg, Stevie Eichenbaum

**Alfred Hinckley
in "That Championship Season"**

**Left Center: Victoria Boothby, Dana Coen
in "The Mousetrap"**

GEVA THEATRE

Rochester, N. Y.
October 6, 1976–April 12, 1977

Artistic Directors, Donald MacKechnie, Gideon Y. Schein; Managing Director, Jessica L. Andrews; Technical Director, David Herwitz; Stage Managers, Timothy Toothman, Joel Elins; Production Assistants, Terri Belli, Edward Colcord, Geoffrey Hobin; Sets, David Herwitz, Donald MacKechnie; Costumes, Danica Eskind, Madeline Cohen; Stage Directors, Donald MacKechnie, Gideon Y. Schein, Gary Reineke; Press, John C. Marks

COMPANY

Roger Forbes, Lisa Evans, Cyril Mallett, Thora Nelson, Patricia Doyle, Josh Burton, Timothy Landfield, Merle Louise, Garrison Botts, Martha Jacobs, Bruce Jordon, Christopher McCann, Greg Thornton, Frederick Nuernberg, Larry Carr, Barbara McCameron, Jay Alan Ginsberg, Ed M. Colcord, Bill Stienfeldt, John Quinn, Dorothy Lancaster, Virginia Anton, Tim Leary, Toby Gold, Roger Kenyon, Mike Thomas

PRODUCTIONS

"Private Lives" by Noel Coward, "Relatively Speaking" by Alan Ayckbourn, "The Birthday Party" by Harold Pinter, "Much Ado about Nothing" by William Shakespeare, "Sleuth" by Anthony Shaffer, "Tartuffe" by Moliere, "I Do! I Do!" by Tom Jones and Harvey Schmidt, "The Loves of Betsy Ross" by Arlene Brent Fanale, "Limerickle and Other Tripe" by Larry Carr and Bruce Cornwell, "Husbands and Lovers" by Franz Molnar, "Happy Moments in Mime" by Bob Berky, "How He Lied to Her Husband" by George Bernard Shaw, "The Life of Mary Jemison"

(Pat Thornton Photo)

Roger Forbes, Cyril Mallet in "Sleuth"

GOODMAN THEATRE

Chicago, Illinois
October 1, 1976–June 12, 1977

Artistic Director, William Woodman; Managing Director, John Economos; Business Manager, Janet Wade; Associate Artistic Director, Gregory Mosher; Associate Managing Director, Roche Schulfer; Press, Ron Christopher, Lewis Lazare; Production Manager, Joseph E. Bates; Sound, David Rice; Sets, Richard Oates, Joseph Nieminski, Marjorie Kellogg, John Jensen, Beverly Sobieski, Dean Taucher, Michael Merritt, Maher Ahmad; Costumes, Marsha Kowal, Michelle Demichelis, Virgil C. Johnson, James Edmund Brady; Lighting, Pat Collins, F. Mitchell Dana, Gilbert V. Hemsley, Jr., Robert Christen; Stage Managers, Peter Dowling, Christine Lawton, Ruth Rinklin, Joseph Drummond, Martin Lazarus; Stage Directors, William Woodman, George Keathley, Gene Lesser, Gregory Mosher, Dennis Zacek, Gary Houston, Sidney Eden

PRODUCTIONS AND CASTS

DESIGN FOR LIVING by Noel Coward, with Carrie Nye, Richard Clarke, Brian Murray, David Dukes, Jane MacIver, Louis Plante, Marty Levy, Aviva Crane, Owen Sullivan, Judith Ivey, Frank Barrett

LONG DAY'S JOURNEY INTO NIGHT by Eugene O'Neill, with Edward Binns, Frances Hyland, Drew Snyder, John V. Shea, Sonja Lanzener

THE SHOW-OFF by George Kelly, with Eugene J. Anthony, Woody Eney, Jane Hoffman, Robert Ingham, Carolyn Kirsch, W. H. Macy, Edgar Meyer, Michael Tezla, Carol Williard, O. J. Eney

RICHARD III by William Shakespeare, with Richard K. Allison, Michael Arceal, Barry Boys, Pauline Brailsford, Donald Brearley, George Brengel, Bruce Burgun, William Carey, Patricia Fraser, Allison Giglio, Ann Goldman, Dirk Hacker, Michael Hawkins, Benjamin Hendrickson, Matthew Kimbrough, Marty Levy, Jonathan Lyon, William Mowry, Fern Persons, Jack Roberts, Norman Snow, Matt Stephens, Owen Sullivan, Nicolas Surovy, Michael Tezla, Norman Tobin, Jerome Bobis, Robert L. Garcia, Ira Goldstein, Dennis Ryan, Daniel Shapiro, John C. Silverman

STREAMERS by David Rabe, with Richard K. Allison, Robert Christian, Donald Corren, Richard Cox, J. J. Johnston, W. H. Macy, Michael O'Dwyer, Ted Raymond, Ron Relic, Meshach Taylor

DON JUAN by Moliere in a new translation by Christopher Hampton, with Robert Guillaume, Glenn Kovacevich, Nicolas Surovy, Brenda Curtis, Judith Ivey, Andrew Rohrer, Fay Hauser, Bruce Rodgers-Wright, Joseph Bell, Gus Kaikkonen, Steven Williams, Michael Tezla, Steve Merle, William Mowry

SIZWE BANZI IS DEAD by Athol Fugard, John Kani, Winston Ntshona, with Meshach Taylor, Lionel Smith

THE SPORT OF MY MAD MOTHER by Ann Jellicoe, with John Kenny, Chris Raynolds, Judith Ivey, Keith Szarabajka, Donald Corren, Claudia Bohard, Arlene Schulfer

A LIFE IN THE THEATRE by David Mamet (*World Premiere*), with Mike Nussbaum, Joe Mantegna

KASPAR by Peter Handke, with J. Pat Miller, Harold Yee, Robert Strom, Mark Hutter, Christopher Raynolds, Randall Smith

GEORGE JEAN NATHAN IN REVUE by Sidney Eden, based on writings of George Jean Nathan, with Tony Mockus, Ray Rayner, Tony Lincoln, Geraldine Kay

Left Center: Mike Nussbaum (seated), Joe Mantegna in "A Life in the Theatre" Tony Mockus in "George Jean Nathan in Revue" Above: Frances Hyland, Edward Binns, Drew Snyder, John V. Shea in "Long Day's Journey into Night" Top: Brian Murray, Carrie Nye, David Dukes in "Design for Living" Norman Snow, Jonathan Lyon in "Richard III"

Fay Hauser, Nicolas Surovy, Judith Ivey in "Don Juan"

GUTHRIE THEATER

Minneapolis, Minnesota
June 14, 1976–February 26, 1977

Artistic Director, Michael Langham; Managing Director, Donald Schoenbaum; Associate Directors, Stephen Kanee, Ken Ruta; Production Manager, Jon Cranney; Musical Director and Conductor, Dick Whitbeck; Lighting Designer, Duane Schuler; Voice and Movement, Fran Bennett; Technical Production, Terry Sateren, Bruce Margolis, Sioux Saloka; Production Assistant, Wendy Sasse; Stage Managers, Michael S. Vacius, Charlotte Green, Emily Mann, Paddy McEntee; Props, Veda Hyde; Sound, Scott Herner; Costumes, Jack Edwards, Robert Morgan, Andrew F. Mihelcic IV; Wardrobe, Evelyn Bongard, Mary Jean Gauthier; Administrative Director, Donald Michaelis; Press, Dennis Babcock, Melissa R. Cohen; Sets, Desmond Heeley, John Conklin, Jack Barkla, Ralph Funicello, Sam Kirkpatrick; Stage Directors, Michael Langham, Peter Nichols, Stephen Kanee, Ken Ruta

COMPANY

Fran Bennett, Barbra Berlovitz, Leta Bonynge, Barbara Bryne, Cynthia Carle, Jeff Chandler, Oliver Cliff, Robert Colston, Susan Dafoe, Lance Davis, Peter Michael Goetz, Russell Gold, Michael Gross, Wiley Harker, Tom Hegg, Cheryl Tafathale Jones, Dennis Kennedy, Mark Lamos, Karen Landry, Meredith Lane, Tony Mockus, Jane Murray, Guy Paul, John Pielmeier, Christopher Pennock, Kathleen Marie Perkins, Richard Russell Ramos, Ken Ruta, Dominique Serrand, Victoria Thompson, Harley Venton

PRODUCTIONS

"The Matchmaker," "The Winter's Tale," "Rosencrantz and Guildenstern Are Dead," "Cat on a Hot Tin Roof," "A Christmas Carol," "Doctor Faustus," "An Enemy of the People," "The National Health," Julie Harris in "The Belle of Amherst," Len Cariou in "A Sorrow Beyond Dreams," James Whitmore in "Bully"

Steve Rouch, Mike Paul, Robert Wilson Photos

Top: "Cat on a Hot Tin Roof" Below: "An Enemy of the People" Right: Michael Gross, Mark Lamos in "Doctor Faustus"

Mark Lamos, Jeff Chandler, Christopher Pennock in "Rosencrantz and Guildenstern Are Dead" Above: "The National Health"

HARTFORD STAGE COMPANY

Hartford, Connecticut
September 17, 1976–June 12, 1977

Producing Director, Paul Weidner; Managing Director, William Stewart; Press, Dave Skal, Marilyn Sponzo; Business Manager, Alan Toman; Technical Director, Randy Engels; Directors, Edward Albee, Jack Going, Irene Lewis, Paul Weidner; Sets, John Conklin, David Jenkins, Hugh Landwehr, Santo Loquasto; Costumes, Claire Ferraris, Santo Loquasto, Robert Mackintosh, Caley Summers; Lighting, Ian Calderon, David Chapman, Peter Hunt, John McLain, Steve Woodring; Stage Managers, Fred Hoskins, Gary Lamagna, Dru Strange

COMPANY

Maureen Anderman, Joan Astley, Samuel Barton, Jeff Brooks, Barbara Caruso, Veronica Castang, Cynthia Crumlish, Dan Diggles, Beth Dixon, Walter Flanagan, Suzanne Ford, Ted Graeber, Cynthia Herman, Lois Holmes, Jeffrey Horowitz, Thomas Hulce, Maggie Jackson, William Jay, Carol Mayo Jenkins, Mel Johnson, Jr., Angela Lansbury, Chip Lucia, Richard Mathews, Ruth Maynard, Mary McTigue, Neil Napolitan, John Newton, Terry O'Quinn, David O. Petersen, Margaret Phillips, William Prince, Jack Ryland, Anne Shropshire, Nick Smith, Stephen Stout, Jane Ellen Unger, Alice White, Jerry Zaks

PRODUCTIONS

"The Glass Menagerie" by Tennessee Williams, "The Blood Knot" by Athol Fugard, "The Waltz of the Toreadors" by Jean Anouilh, "Candida" by George Bernard Shaw, "Workman! Whoever You Are . . .", and *Premieres* of "Counting the Ways" and "Listening" by Edward Albee, and "A History of the American Film" by Christopher Durang

David Robbins, Gerry Goodstein, Lanny Nagler Photos

**Right: "The Glass Menagerie" Below:
Margaret Phillips in "Waltz of the Toreadors"**

**"A History of the American Film"
Top Right: William Prince, Angela Lansbury,
Maureen Anderman in "Listening"**

**Thomas Hulce, Barbara Caruso
in "Candida"**

Theodore Sorel, Mike Kellin, Ralph Byers
in "Death of a Salesman" Right: Carol Teitel,
Lenka Peterson in "Arsenic and Old Lace" Below:
Paul Collins, Earle Hyman in "As to the Meaning
of Words"

HARTMAN THEATRE COMPANY

Stamford, Connecticut
November 3, 1976–May 15, 1977
Second Season

Producing Directors, Del and Margot Tenney; Managing Director, Daniel B. Miller; General Manager, Stanley D. Silver; Press, Steve Rothman, Debbie Weiner; Production Manager, Roger Meeker; Music Director, Barbara Damashek; Sound, Charles Pistone; Assistant to Producers, Stephen S. Hicks; Sets, Zack Brown, J. D. Ferrara, Robert VerBerkmoes, Akira Yoshimura; Costumes, Zack Brown, David Murin, Gerda Proctor; Stage Managers, Joseph Kavanagh, Peggy Peterson; Costumes, Gerda Proctor, June Stearns, Janice Fitzpatrick; Wardrobe, Renee Lutz; Production Assistants, John Jefferson, Karen Wiltshire; Technical Directors, David McWilliams, Bruce Bixler; Props, J. D. Ferrara; Stage Directors, Del Tenney, Mel Shapiro, Jerry Blunt, John Dillon, Larry Arrick

PRODUCTIONS AND CASTS

THE REASON WE EAT by Israel Horovitz (World Premiere), with Estelle Parsons, Ron Faber, Robert Balaban, Diana Davila

ARSENIC AND OLD LACE by Joseph Kesselring, with Carol Teitel, Ted Lewis, Gary F. Martin, Ed Rice, Charles Piston, Lenka Peterson, Tiina Cartmell, Austin Pendleton, John Vichiola, Theodore Sorel, Ron Faber, Henson Keys, James Brick, Ted Lewis

TARTUFFE by Moliere, with Lenka Peterson, George Morforgen, Margot Tenney, Eric R. Christiansen, Tiina Cartmell, Ed Rice, Theodore Sorel, Caroline Kava, James Brick, Austin Pendleton, Henson Keys, Rosalyn R. Farinella, Leo Holder, Gary F. Martin

DEATH OF A SALESMAN by Arthur Miller, with Mike Kellin, Carol Teitel, Ralph Byers, Theodore Sorel, Stephen Berenson, Margot Tenney, Alfred Hinckley, Earle Hyman, Gary F. Martin, Susan Smyth, Henson Keys, Tiina Cartmell, Robin Reif

AS TO THE MEANING OF WORDS by Mark Eichman (World Premiere), with Earle Hyman, Tina Rose Rosselli, Paul Collins, George Dzundza, Alfred Hinckley, Deloris Gaskins, Theodore Sorel, Dominic Chianese, Ralph Byers, Margot Tenney

HE WHO GETS SLAPPED by Leonid Andreyev, freely adapted by Larry Arrick with music by Barbara Damashek, with Richard Kavanaugh, Ed Waterstreet, Jr., Linda Bove, Theodore Sorel, Dominic Chianese, Carmen de Lavallade, Deborah Offner, Gregory Salata, Joel Kramer, James Brick, Earle Hyman, Barbara Damashek, Bill Patton, Rebecca Rabinowitz, Laurel Schmidt, David Pilot, Joan Friedman, Phil Soltanoff, Susan Smyth, Lyle Carney

David Robbins, Gerry Goodstein Photos

**Estelle Parsons
in "The Reason We Eat"**

203

INDIANA REPERTORY THEATRE

Indianapolis, Indiana
October 15, 1976–April 9, 1977

Producing Director, Benjamin Mordecai; Artistic Director, Edward Stern; Business Manager, Stewart Slater; Press, Gayle Gordon; Stage Directors, Gerardine Clark, John Going, William Guild, Charles Kerr, Leland Moss, John S. Patterson, Edward Stern, Arne Zaslove; Sets, Ursula Belden, John Doepp, Christopher Hacker, Eric Head, Van Phillips, Raymond C. Recht, Thomas Taylor Targownik; Costumes, Carol H. Beule, Susan Denison, Florence L. Rutherford, Susan Tsu; Lighting, Bridget Beier, Susan Dandridge, Charles Gotwald, Joel Grynheim, Timothy K. Joyce, Ralph John Merkle, Michael Orris Watson; Production Manager, Chris Armen; Stage Managers, Jody Boese, Mayo Anne Brainerd, Joel Grynheim, Ralph John Merkle

PRODUCTIONS AND CASTS

THE LAST MEETING OF THE KNIGHTS OF THE WHITE MAGNOLIA by Preston Jones, with Robert Blackburn, Leo Murmester, Henry Butler, Hank Frazier, Dale Helward, Michael Hendricks, Conrad McLaren, Robert Scogin, William Trotman

WHEN YOU COMIN' BACK, RED RYDER? by Mark Medoff, with Leo Murmester, Lisa Goodman, Dale Helward, Michael Hendricks, Bernard Kates, Sharon Madden, Robert Scogin, Sara Woods

THE THREEPENNY OPERA by Bertolt Brecht and Kurt Weill, with John Aylward, Kurt Beattie, Clayton Berry, Gerald Burgess, Leo Murmester, Katherine Carlson, Jack L. Davis, Igors Gavon, Lisa Goodman, Robert Harbin, Michael Hendricks, Bella Jarrett, Montgomery Kuklenski, Priscilla Lindsay, Sharon Madden, Demetra Pittman, Anna Maria Rail, Robert Scogin, Diane Tarleton, Jeffery V. Thompson, Janet Wilson, Sara Woods

WHO'S AFRAID OF VIRGINIA WOOLF by Edward Albee, with Tanya Berezin, Robert Elliott, Bernard Kates, Gun-Marie Nilsson

THE TEMPEST by William Shakespeare, with John Abajian, Linda Atkinson, Patrick Beatey, Gerald Burgess, Katherine Carlson, David Chandler, Deborah Chernin, Jack L. Davis, Randall Duk Kim, Laura Elmore, Igors Gavon, Michael Hendricks, Bernard Kates, Montgomery Kuklenski, Priscilla Lindsay, Karen Mahoney Littman, Demetra Pittman, Robert Scogin, Jeffery V. Thompson, Margaret Whitton, Mark Wilson, Robin Wilson

THE BRIXTON RECOVERY by Jack Gilhooley (*World Premiere,*) with Leo Murmester, Elizabeth Van Dyke

PRIVATE LIVES by Noel Coward, with John Abajian, Katherine Carlson, Nicholas Hormann, Priscilla Lindsay, Sara Woods

SLEUTH by Anthony Shaffer, with Bernard Kates, Thomas Stechschulte

MISS JULIE by August Strindberg, with Leo Murmester, Janice Fuller, Linda Selman

LIFT EV'RY VOICE and MUSICAL MIRAGE EXPRESS '77 with Gerald Burgess, Michael Hendricks, Elizabeth Machlan, Demetra Pittman, Alvin Lee Sanders

McGuire Studio Photos

Top: "Who's Afraid of Virginia Woolf?" Right: "Last Meeting of the Knights . . ." Below: "Private Lives"

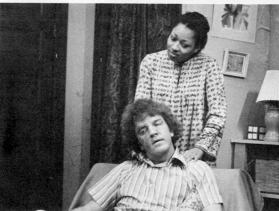

Mike Hendricks in "When You Comin' Back, Red Ryder?" Above: "The Brixton Recovery"

JOHN F. KENNEDY CENTER FOR THE PERFORMING ARTS

Washington, D. C.
June 12, 1976–May 28, 1977

Chairman, Roger L. Stevens; Executive Director, Martin Feinstein; Press, Frank Cassidy

PRODUCTIONS AND CASTS

FIDDLER ON THE ROOF by Joseph Stein, Jerry Bock and Sheldon Harnick, with Zero Mostel. See Broadway Calendar

D'OYLY CARTE IN GILBERT AND SULLIVAN with John Reed, John Ayldon, Meston Reid, Julia Goss, Patricia Leonard, Janet Metcalfe, Kenneth Sandford, Michael Rayner, Geoffrey Shovelton, Lyndshie Holland, Barbara Lilley, James Conroy-Ward, Michael Buchan, Barry Clark, Jon Ellison, Gareth Jones, Paul Waite, Michael Westbury, Caroline Baker, Patricia Ann Bennett, Gillian Burrows, Anne Egglestone, Beti Lloyd-Jones, Glynis Prendergast in "The Mikado," "H.M.S. Pinafore," and "The Pirates of Penzance"

THE MAGNIFICENT YANKEE by Emmet Lavery, with James Whitmore, Audra Lindley, Emery Battis, Jack Murdock, Louis Beachner, Aileen Fitzpatric, Ross Bickell, Tom Blank, Edmund Gaynes, Robert Gibbons Arthur Hammer, Jerry Hoffman, Randy Pelish, Peter Ratray, Fred Slyter, Colin Vogel

EL CAPITAN by John Philip Sousa, with Linda Kowalski, Maryanne Telese, Scott Pedersen, Scott Reeve, Lanny Green, Edgar Moore, Stephen Dickson, Jack Eddleman, Joseph Warner, Martha Williford

THE BELLE OF AMHERST by William Luce, with Julie Harris. See National Touring Companies

THE BAKER'S WIFE by Joseph Stein and Stephen Schwartz, with Topol, Patti LuPone, Kurt Peterson, Keene Curtis. See Productions That Opened and Closed before Broadway Premiere.

NO MAN'S LAND by Harold Pinter, with John Gielgud and Ralph Richardson. See Broadway Calendar

MUSIC IS by George Abbott, Richard Adler and Will Holt. See Broadway Calendar

DIRTY LINEN & NEW-FOUND-LAND by Tom Stoppard. See Broadway Calendar

TRAVESTIES by Tom Stoppard, with John Wood, Jack Bittner, James Booth, Elzbieta Chezevska, Ronald Drake, Charles Kimbrough, Lynne Lipton, Katherine McGrath

CAESAR AND CLEOPATRA by George Bernard Shaw, with Rex Harrison and Elizabeth Ashley. See Broadway Calendar

ANNIE by Thomas Meehan, Charles Strouse, Martin Charnin, with Andrea McArdle, Dorothy Loudon, Reid Shelton. See Broadway Calendar

SHENANDOAH by James Lee Barrett, Peter Udell, Philip Rose, Gary Geld, with Howard Keel, Barbara Marineau, Deborah Combs, Dennis Romer, James D'Apollonia, Robert Henderson, Jeff Yonis, David Vann, Martin Meredith, James Howard Laurence, Stuart Silver, Jack Straw, Michael Feeley

JIM THORPE, ALL-AMERICAN by Saul Levitt, with T. J. Boyle, Sam Blackwell, Tom McLaughlin, Robert DeFrank, Curt Hostetter, Malcolm McKinnon, Leslie Feagan

THE ARCHBISHOP'S CEILING by Arthur Miller *World Premiere,* directed by Arvin Brown, with John Cullum, Bibi Andersson, Tony Musante, Douglass Watson, Josef Sommer, Bara-Cristen Hansen

SHIRLEY MacLAINE and Shirley's Gypsies. See Broadway Calendar

Right Center: "Jim Thorpe, All-American"
Above: Ronald Drake, John Wood, James Booth,
Charles Kimbrough, Katherine McGrath in "Travesties"
Top: John Cullum, Bara-Cristen Hansen, Bibi
Andersson in "The Archbishop's Ceiling"

Audra Lindley, James Whitmore
in "The Magnificent Yankee" 205

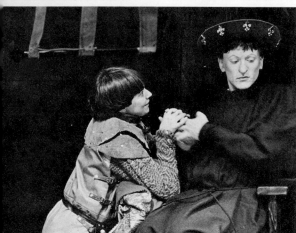

LONG WHARF THEATRE

New Haven, Connecticut
October 8, 1976–July 3, 1977

Artistic Director, Arvin Brown; Executive Director, M. Edgar Rosenblum; Press, Rosalind Heinz; Stage Directors, Arvin Brown, Gordon Davidson, Martin Fried, Michael Lindsay-Hogg, Mike Nichols, Steven Robman, Eric Thompson; Sets, Edward Burbridge, John Conklin, David Jenkins, Marjorie Kellogg, Ming Cho Lee, David Mitchell, Steven Rubin; Costumes, Michele S. Reisch, Carrie F. Robbins, Mary Strieff, Bill Walker; Lighting, Jamie Gallagher, Judy Rasmuson, Ronald Wallace; Stage Managers, Anne Keefe, Franklin Keysar, Nina Seely

PRODUCTIONS AND CASTS

ALPHABETICAL ORDER by Michael Frayn (*American Premiere*), with Roderick Cook, Mary Fogarty, Valerie French, John Horton, Richard Mathews, Jeanne Ruskin, Josef Sommer

THE AUTUMN GARDEN by Lillian Hellman, with Carolyn Coates, Alice Drummond, Joyce Ebert, Mary Fogarty, Victor Garber, Carmen Mathews, John McMartin, Charlotte Moore, James Noble, Susan Sharkey, Josef Sommer, Richard Bernard Turner

HOME by David Storey, with Emery Battis, Mary Fogarty, Bette Henritze, J. Frank Lucas, Everett McGill

THE SHADOW BOX by Michael Cristofer, with Joyce Ebert, Patricia Elliott, Geraldine Fitzgerald, Rose Gregorio, Clifton James, Laurence Luckinbill, Mandy Patinkin, Josef Sommer, Vincent Stewart

ST. JOAN by George Bernard Shaw, with Emery Battis, Rudy Bond, James Cahill, Roy Cooper, Neil Hunt, Timothy Jerome, Ben Kapen, Richard Mathews, Everett McGill, Robert Murch, John Neville-Andrews, Michaelan Sisti, Josef Sommer, William Swetland, Kristoffer Tabori, Kitty Winn

ABSENT FRIENDS by Alan Ayckbourn (*American Premiere*), with Jacob Brooke, Dale Hodges, Anne Jackson, Joseph Maher, Christina Pickles, Eli Wallach

THE ROSE TATOO by Tennessee Williams, with Emery Battis, Tom Berenger, Shirley Bryan, Glenn Close, Mary Fogarty, Avril Gentles, Linda Hunt, Toni Kalem, Steven Keats, Jack Marks, Gloria Matthews, Rita Moreno, Estelle Omens, William Swetland, Mary Testa, Grace Woodard

THE GIN GAME by D. L. Coburn, with Hume Cronyn, Jessica Tandy

William L. Smith Photos

Steven Keats, Rita Moreno in "The Rose Tattoo"
Above: Kitty Winn, Kristoffer Tabori in "St. Joan"

Top: Eli Wallach, Joseph Maher in "Absent Friends"
Left: Charlotte Moore, Joyce Ebert, John McMartin in "The Autumn Garden"

LORETTO-HILTON REPERTORY THEATRE

Webster Groves, Missouri
October 13, 1976–April 9, 1977

Managing Director, David Frank; Consulting Director, Davey Marlin-Jones; General Manager, Charles Seymour, Jr.; Assistant General Manager, Michael Pitek, III; Press, Noeli Lytton Wotawa; Sets, John Kavelin, Karen R. Connolly, Atkin Pace; Costumes, John Carver Sullivan, Katherine Reich, Bill Walker; Lighting, Peter E. Sargent, Glenn Dunn; Technical Director, Jack Conant; Guest Stage Directors, Carl Schurr, Hal Scott

COMPANY

Robert Bays, Brendan Burke, Alan Clarey, Ellen Crawford, Robert Darnell, Joneal Joplin, Wil Love, Robert Spencer, Henry Strozier, Margaret Winn, James Anthony, John Cothran, Jr., Patrick Desmond, Cara Duff-MacCormick, Augustine Dunn, Louis Edmonds, Mike Genovese, Al Grab, Stephen McKinley Henderson, Benjamin Hendrickson, Louise Jenkins, Duane Jones, Stephen Keep, Patricia Kilgarriff, Susanne Marley, Joan Matthiessen, Ann McDonough, Mark Robbins, Carl Schurr, Charles Siegel, Sherry Skinker, Nicolas Surovy, Elliott Vileen, Carlene Watkins, Steven Worth

PRODUCTIONS

"Billy Budd" by Chapman and Coxe, "The Eccentricities of a Nightingale" by Tennessee Williams, "The Beaux Stratagem" by George Farquhar, "The House of Blue Leaves" by John Guare, "The Front Page" by Charles MacArthur and Ben Hecht

Michael Estman Photos

"The Beaux Stratagem"

MANITOBA THEATRE CENTRE

Winnipeg, Manitoba, Canada
September 30, 1976–May 14, 1977

Artistic Director, Arif Hasnain; General Manager, Gregory Poggi; Press, Max Tapper; Production Manager, Dwight Griffin; Technical Director, Neil McLeod; Stage Directors, Alex Dmitriev, Edward Gilbert, Arif Hasnain, Eric Steiner, Richard Digby-Day, David Calderisi, Voigt Kempson, Richard Cottrell; Sets and Costumes, Grant Guy, Mark Negin, Peter Wingate, Robert Doyle, Doug McLean; Lighting, Bill Williams, Peter Wingate, Bryn Finer, Robert Reinholdt, Nicholas Cernovitch

PRODUCTIONS AND CASTS

BERLIN TO BROADWAY WITH KURT WEILL by Gene Lerner, with Ross Douglas, Joan Karasevich, Dorothy Poste, Don Samuels

TWELFTH NIGHT by William Shakespeare, with Rodger Barton, Richard Blackburn, James Blendick, Richard Burleson, Susan Cox, John Greer, Peter Haworth, David Jemblen, Irene Hogan, Deborah Kipp, John-Peter Linton, Mina Erian Mina, Marrie Mumford, Graeme C. Norman, Ron O'Krancy, Anton Rodgers, Cedric Smith, Howard Story

ALL OVER by Edward Albee, with Myra Carter, Dan Cawthon, Alan Gifford, Howard Hicks, Budd Knapp, Walter Massey, Anne Murray, Harry Nelken, Sandra Scott, Anne Shropshire

CANADIAN GOTHIC/AMERICAN MODERN by Joanna M. Glass, with Janet Barkhouse, Irena Mayeska, Tim Sikyea, Neil Vipond

BEAUTY AND THE BEAST by William Glennon, with Frank Adamson, Gloria Bien, Tom Butler, Margot Charlton, Alexe Duncan, Michael Davis, David Gillies, Janet Laine Green, Robert More, Michael Petty, Brenda Roy

RELATIVELY SPEAKING by Alan Ayckbourn, with Robin Bailey, Peter Dvorsky, Irene Hogan, Marti Maraden

FABLES HERE AND THEN by David Feldshuh, with David Bentley, Jay Brazeau, David Gillies, Gina Laight, Lynda Langford, Sharon Noble, Robin Nunn

DAMES AT SEA by George Haimsohn and Robin Miller, with Trudy Bayne, Don Bradford, Edda Gburek, Cynthia Parva, Michael Ricardo, Patrick Young

WAITING FOR GODOT by Samuel Beckett, with George Buza, Michael Davis, Clive Endersby, Dennis Robinson, Peter Rogan

THE CRUCIBLE by Arthur Miller, with Robin Bailey, Eleanor Beecroft, James Blendick, Doreen Brownstone, James B. Douglas, Alexe Duncan, Richard Farrell, Cliff Gardner, Edda Gburek, Alan Gifford, Jill Harris, Peter Haworth, Philip Kerr, Deborah Kipp, Cynthia Parva, Jacquie Presly, Sandi Ross, Howard Storey, Sean Sullivan, Tim Whelan

ALPHA BETA by E. A. Whitehead, with Elisabeth LeRoy, Peter Rogan

SHE STOOPS TO CONQUER by Oliver Goldsmith, with Zoe Alexander, Robin Bailey, Margaret Barton, James Blendick, Jay Brazeau, Ian Deakin, Alex Dmitriev, Edward Greenhalgh, Robin Marshall, Kate McDonald, Fiona Ried, Howard Storey, Hutchison Sandro, R. H. Thomson

Gerry Kopelow Photos

"Fables Here and Then" Above: Neil Vipond, Irene Mayeska in "American Modern"

MARRIOTT'S LINCOLNSHIRE THEATRE

Lincolnshire, Illinois
June 22, 1976–June 19, 1977

Producer, Richard S. Kordos; Press, Bill Wilson, John Rade-wagon, Aaron D. Cushman; Sets, Jeffrey Harris; Stage Manager, Paul A. Ferris; Technical Director-Lighting Designer, Pat Nesladek; Costume Coordinator, Susan Clare, Props, Jeffrey Harris, Barbara Harris; Stage Directors, Jack Cassiday, Richard S. Kordos, Al Cairo, Dominic Missimi, Tony Mockus, George Keathley

PRODUCTIONS AND CASTS

WAIT UNTIL DARK by Frederick Knott, with Jack Cassidy, Barry Cullison, Frank Loverde, Connie McGrail, Wesley Pfenning, Thomas Stechschulte, Owen Sullivan

BUS STOP by William Inge, with Edie Adams, Pete Candoli, Beverly Feldt, Anne Haney, Barry Hope, Robert Ingham, Tony Lincoln, Chelcie Ross

THE SECRET AFFAIRS OF MILDRED WILD by Paul Zindel, with Nanette Fabray, Robb Alton, Eugene J. Anthony, Ron Beattie, Anne L. Edwards, Lillian Evans, Mary Seibel, Allison Giglio Tezla

I DO! I DO! by Tom Jones and Harvey Schmidt, with Ed Ames, Jeannine Ann Cole

ACCENT ON YOUTH by Samson Raphaelson, with Ricardo Montalban, Tim Halligan, Art Kassul, Ted Liss, Carole Lockwood, Mary Seibel, Kim Zimmer

SEND ME NO FLOWERS by Norman Barasch, Carroll Moore, with Bill Bixby, Mike Arcesi, Brenda Benet, George Brengel, Dee Dee Dolan, Bret Hadley, Dennis Kennedy, Roger Mueller

THE GLASS MENAGERIE by Tennessee Williams, with Maureen Stapleton, Ralph Byers, Penelope Reed, Owen Sullivan

David H. Fishman, Joseph Jedd Photos

Left: Barry Hope, Chelcie Ross, Edie Adams in "Bus Stop" Top: Ron Beattie, Eugene Anthony, Nanette Fabray in "Secret Affairs of Mildred Wild"

208   **Wesley Pfenning, Jack Cassidy in "Wait until Dark"**

Penelope Reed, Maureen Stapleton, Ralph Byers in "The Glass Menagerie"

MASSACHUSETTS CENTER REPERTORY COMPANY

Boston, Massachusetts
April 19–May 29, 1977

Producing Director, Janice Cashell; Producers, Stephen M. Mindich, John Zurick, Jonathan R. Yates; General Managers, Laurel Ann Wilson, Donald Tirabassi; Press, Patt Dale; Business Managers, Alan Clark, Richard E. Miller; Sets and Lighting, Howard Bay; Costumes, Pearl Somner; Technical Director, Vincent DiGabrielle; Production Supervisor, Dick LaViolette; Stage Managers, Peter Lawrence, Joan Tolentino, Lo Hardin, Mark R. Paquette, R. Derek Swire, Michael Haney, Connie Roderick

PRODUCTIONS AND CASTS

THE DANCE OF DEATH by August Strindberg, directed by Stephen Porter, with Ben Gazzara, Colleen Dewhurst, George Hearn, Joan Tolentino, Annette Miller

LONG DAY'S JOURNEY INTO NIGHT by Eugene O'Neill, directed by Michael Kahn, with Jose Ferrer, Kate Reid, Len Cariou, Ben Masters, Laurie Kennedy

CANDIDA by George Bernard Shaw, directed by Jeffrey Hayden, with Eva Marie Saint, Paul Benedict, Mary Jay, Peter Maloney, Frank Hamilton, John Rubinstein

William L. Smith Photos

Top: George Hearn, Ben Gazzara, Colleen Dewhurst in "Dance of Death"

Kate Reid, Jose Ferrer, Len Cariou, Ben Masters in "Long Day's Journey into Night"

McCARTER THEATRE COMPANY

Princeton, N. J.
October 5, 1976–April 19, 1977

Producing Director, Michael Kahn; General Manager, Edward A. Martenson; Production Manager, Mark S. Krause; Press, David Wynne; Business Manager, Marsha Senack; Technical Director, Mitchell Kurtz; Guest Directors, Kenneth Frankel, Gene Lesser, Stephen Porter; Scenic Designers, Michael H. Yeargen, Lawrence King, Marjorie Kellogg, Tony Straiges, David Jenkins, Zack Brown; Costumes, Jane Greenwood, Carrie F. Robbins, Jeanne Button, Laura Crow, Zack Brown; Lighting, John McLain, Pat Collins; Stage Managers, Suzanne Egan, R. L. Barr, Audrey A. Frankowski

COMPANY

Michael Allinson, Irwin Atkins, Christine Baranski, Beverly Barbieri, Daniel Barton, Louis Beachner, Alice Beardsley, Powers Booth, Shirley Bryan, Marian Clarke, Richard Clarke, Glenn Close, Jane Cronin, Richard Dix, Oliver Dixon, George Dzundza, David Edelman, Mitchell Edmonds, Thomas Eley, Patricia Elliott, Patricia Falkenhain, Christopher Gaze, Ted Graeber, Jane Groves, Sarah-Jane Gwillim, Mary Hayden, Anthony Holland, Lawrence Holofcener, Patrick Horgan, George Clark Hosmer, Gloria Irizarri, Ann Johnson, Jeffery Jones, Nicholas Kepros, Shirley Knight, Stephen Lang, Christopher Leggette, Barbara Lester, Tom MacDermott, David MacEnulty, Paul McCrane, Beth McDonald, Katherine McGrath, Anthony McKay, Donald Madden, John Milligan, Vivian Nathan, James Noble, Meg Wynn Owen, Jim Oyster, Eric Roberts, Randy Rydell, Sarallen, Stephen Sheld, Lewis J. Stadlen, Robert Stattel, William Swetland, Barbara Tarbuck, Eric Tavaris, James Tolin, George Touliatos, Maria Tucci, Fiddle Viracola, Peter Vogt, Kathryn Walker, Kenneth Welsh

PRODUCTIONS

"A Streetcar Named Desire" by Tennessee Williams, "Major Barbara" by George Bernard Shaw, "The Physicists" by Friedrich Durrenmatt, "Design for Living" by Noel Coward, "The Night of the Tribades" by Per Olov Enquist (*American Premiere*), "Angel City" by Sam Shepard (*World Premiere*)

Cliff Moore Photos

**Top: Shirley Knight in "A Streetcar Named Desire"
Right: Meg Wynn Owen, Michael Allinson in "Design for Living" Below: Maria Tucci, Robert Stattel in "Major Barbara"**

Kathryn Walker, Donald Madden, Patricia Elliott in "Night of the Tribades" Above: Eric Tavaris, Anthony McKay, Lewis J. Stadlen in "Angel City"

MEADOW BROOK THEATRE

Rochester, Michigan
October 7, 1976–May 22, 1977

Artistic Director, Terence Kilburn; Managing Director, David Robert Kanter; Directors, Terence Kilburn, Charles Nolte, Vincent Dowling, John Ulmer, Don Price; Stage Managers, R. Joseph Mooney, James Riggs, James Corrigan; Technical Director, Peter Hicks; Costumes, Mary Lynn Bonnell; Sound, Thomas Spence; Wardrobe, Janice Scott; Sets, Don Beckman; Props, Carolyn Hull; Business Manager, Vincent L. Ammann

COMPANY

Dennis Bailey, Terence Baker, Dan C. Bar, Arthur Barsamian, Laurie Allen Becker, Mary Benson, R. J. Bonds, Lynn Bradford, Thom Bray, Brenda Broome, Norman Colborne, James Corrigan, J. L. Dahlmann, Stephen Daley, Elizabeth Dallas, Kevin Daly, Frank Dent, Annette DiFilippo, Joyce Feurring, Cheryl Giannini, Christa Gievers, Frederika Gray, William Halliday, Patricia Harless, Roger Hilborn, Richard Hilger, Elizabeth Horowitz, Corrin Kason, Kimberly Kirkpatrick, Terence Marinan, Margaret Morrissey, Elisabeth Orion, John Petlock, Phillip Piro, Patricia Reilly, Melanie Resnick, George Romaine, Carl Schurr, Thomas C. Spackman, Ernie Stewart, Fred Thompson, Marcia Lynn Watkins, James Winfield GUEST ARTISTS: Fran Brill, David Canary, Booth Colman, Harry Ellerbe, Donald Ewer, William Hurt, Richard Jamieson, William LeMassena, Donald C. Moore, Clive Rosengren, Polly Rowles, Peter Walker, Marie Wallace

PRODUCTIONS

"Man and Superman," "The Night of the Iguana," "The School for Wives," "When You Comin' Back, Red Ryder?," "Sleuth," "The Merchant of Venice," "The Show-Off," "Dames at Sea"

Dick Hunt Photos

Polly Rowles, Harry Ellerbe in "The Show-Off"
Below: "Man and Superman"

"The Merchant of Venice"
Above "Dames at Sea"

"When You Comin' Back, Red Ryder?"

MILWAUKEE REPERTORY THEATER

Milwaukee, Wisconsin
September 17, 1976–May 29, 1977

Artistic Director, Nagle Jackson; Managing Director, Sara O'Connor; Business Manager, Peggy Rose; Press, Richard Bryant; Directors, William Glover, Nagle Jackson, Robert Lanchester, Daniel Mooney, Kent Paul, Sanford Robbins, Walter Schoen; Sets and Lighting, Christopher M. Idoine, R. H. Graham, Pete Davis, Sam Garst, Valerie Kuehn, Seth Price; Costumes, Ellen M. Kozak, Elizabeth Covey, Linda Fisher, Rosemary Ingham, Joanne Karaska; Stage Manager, Fredric H. Orner

COMPANY

Jim Baker, Tom Blair, Emma Angeline Butler, Shellie Chancellor, Peggy Cowles, Kelvin Davis, Montgomery Davis, Bill Henry Douglas, Gina Franz, Bob Gossett, Elaine Hausman, Dana Hibbard, John Mansfield, Durward McDonald, William McKereghan, Mary Lowry, Daniel Mooney, James Pickering, Rose Pickering, Michael Pierce, Penelope Reed, Steven Ryan, Bennett Sargent, Ruth Schudson, Franklyn Seales, James Secrest, Bruce Somerville, Sirin Devrim Trainer, G. Wood, Eda Zahl, Michael Plunkett, Patricia Schmidt, Kevin Schwartz, T. A. Taylor

PRODUCTIONS

"Death of a Salesman," "Private Lives," "Volpone," "Vanties," "The Birthday Party," "The Dog Ran Away," "Domino Courts," "A Christmas Carol" adapted by Nagle Jackson (*Premiere*), *World Premieres* of "The Trial of the Moke" by Daniel Stein, "In Memory of" by Kevin Schwartz

Jack Hamilton Photos

Franklyn Seales, Emma Angeline Butler in "The Trial of the Moke" Top: Steven Ryan, Mary Lowry, Daniel Mooney in "Private Lives"

MISSOURI REPERTORY THEATRE

Kansas City, Missouri
June 24, 1976–February 26, 1977

Producing Director, Patricia McIlrath; Staff Directors, James Assad, Francis J. Cullinan; Production Manager, David Dannenbaum; Stage Manager, Joseph DePauw; Technical Director, Alan Kibbe; Costumes, Vincent Scassellati, Baker Smith; Lighting, Joseph Appelt, Curt Osterman; Sound, Bruce Richardson; Press, David Stuart Hudson, Donna Woodward; Sets, John Ezell, G. Philippe de Rosier, Frederic James, James Joy, Judy Juracek, Barbara Medlicott, Kathryn Ann Scheutze; Guest Directors, Thomas Gruenewald, John O'Shaughnessy, John Reich, Alan Schneider

COMPANY

Walter W. Atamaniuk, Susan Borneman, Richard C. Brown, Dalton Cathey, Liza Cole, John Cothran, Ellen Crawford, Lynn Cohen, Ron Durbian, Marty Greene, Paul Hough, Earnest Hudson, Jeannine Hutchings, Michael LaGue, John Maddison, Lou Milandra, Alice White

PRODUCTIONS

"The Drunkard" adapted by Francis J. Cullinan, "Don Juan of Flatbush" by Stanley Taikeff (*World Premiere*), "The Great White Hope" by Howard Sackler, "The Heiress" by Ruth and Augustus Goetz, "Who's Afraid of Virginia Woolf?" by Edward Albee, "Once in a Lifetime" by George S. Kaufman and Moss Hart, "The Glass Menagerie" by Tennessee Williams, "The Orphans" by James Prideaux (*World Premiere*)

William Turner, Robin Humphrey in "The Orphans"
Above: "Don Juan of Flatbush"

NEW REPERTORY PROJECT

Kingston, R. I.

Director, J. Ranelli; Designer, Robert Steinberg; Administrator, Bonnie Bosworth; Stage Managers, Douglas Goodman, Otis Snell, Peter Frechette

COMPANY

David Berman, Joel Brooks, Tom Griffin, Jane Macdonald, Nancy Mette, Nancy Foy, Jeanne Rusking, Alan Woolf, Chel Chenier, Joseph White, Mary Dyer, Robert Gutcheon, Maury Klein, Jan Grant, Mary Testa, Tracey Patterson

PRODUCTIONS

Premieres of "The Resurrection of Jackie Cramer" by Frank Gagliano with music by Raymond Benson, "The Conversion of Aaron Weiss" by Mark Medoff

Robert Steinberg Photos

"One Flew over the Cuckoo's Nest"
Above: "Once upon a Mattress"

OKLAHOMA THEATER CENTER

Oklahoma City, Oklahoma
October 6, 1976–April 24, 1977

Artistic Director, Lyle Dye, Jr.; Business Director, Russ Walton; Press, Patricia Cacy; Technical Director, Rober B. Drummond; Directors, Alan Langdon, Lyle Dye, Jr., Bob Sykes, Robert Raider Sloan, Cheri Ingram, Garry Charter, Nancy Nell Hanks, Paul A. Nutt, Richard B. Darby; Sets, Sheldon Wilhelm, Dale Hall, Del Unruh, Ray Larson, Van Grubbs, Paula Large, Sandy Kimerer, Tim Lynch, Cynthia Adler, Roger B. Drummon; Lighting, Roger B. Drummond, David Pape, Del Unruh, Tim Lynch, Dan Summerford; Costumes, Vicki Holden, Robert E. Zahn, Chuck Larsen, David M. Scott; Musical Directors, Jim Followell, Ralph Duncan; Choreographer, Cheri Ingram

PRODUCTIONS AND CASTS

DON'T DRINK THE WATER with Brian Kagan, Bert Slocombe, Don Spence, Richard B. Darby, A. Bea Hester, David Earl Hodges, Judith Miller, Norman Fogel, David Taylor, Dale Basler, John Thompson, Carolyn Capron, Susan Rush, Michael McCoy, Dick Alexander, Chris Correy, Judy Hansen, Drew Self, Vickie Wiginton, Linda Rowland, Larry Bailey, Mike Jones

THE CORN IS GREEN with Vernon Wall, Cecilia Bristow, Richard B. Darby, Mary Patterson, Clyde Martin, Charlotte Franklin, Laura Walker Chandler, Sue Long, Steve Martin, Bud Flanagan, Sam Burris, Mark Schommer, Alan Runge, Woody Walker, Dante Walkup, Jennie Allen, Elizabeth Harris, Caroline Specht

ONCE UPON A MATTRESS with Garry Charter, Judith Miller, Megan Mullaly, Loren Vandagriff, Diane Perkins, Dale Basler, Lara Teeter, Charles Unger, Elaine Pfleiderer, Linda Parrish-Hunt, Michael James, Anthony Hume, Jan Sparlin-Zenner, Cheryl Kinion, Mariann Myers, Laurie Plath, Robin Stephens, John Chandler, Rodney Guinn, Keith Taggart, Jeff VanNoy, Ben Wear

SLEUTH with Charlie Dickerson and Rick Shields

6 RMS RIV VU with Danny Shadid, Vera Trunk, Mike Druce, Carol C. Collier, Warren L. Dickson, Mary S. Patterson, Anita Ciaccia, Jeff VanNoy

ANNE OF THE THOUSAND DAYS with Kathy Milligan, Bill Brewer, George Kuebler, Ray Henderson, Dan Summerford, Nick Backes, Vernon Wall, Ben Wear, Thelma Joslyn Coburn, Elizabeth Anne Harris, Jeff VanNoy, Retha Oliver, Kelly J. McDonald, Kenneth Hamilton, Don Spence, Daniel J. Christianens, James Burton, Jon B. Womastek, Roy Burney

GODSPELL with Clarence Briggs, Dana Jo Cornett, Richard B. Darby, Cherie Belinda Grubbs, Mary H. Hart, Paul A. Nutt, Kay Rentzel, Kerry Robertson, R. James Rodda, Kent Rone, Lara Teeter, Billie Thrash, Russ Walton

THE KILLING OF SISTER GEORGE with Toni Ingram, Karen Thomas, Suzanne Charney, Leah Hunnicutt

THE HOUSE OF BLUE LEAVES with David Earl Hodges, Larry J. Hise, Marilyn Morris, Merrilyn B. Gibson, Sue Rush, Charles Unger, Jean Smith, Shana Ledet, Stephanie Sheehan, Steve Sawyer, Buck Compton

ONE FLEW OVER THE CUCKOO'S NEST with Winford Imotichey, Michael Erickson, Robert D. Worthen, Joan Pickard, Katherine Womack, Raymond Dean Slaten, Robert White, John Webb, John Farris, John Bigelow, Tim Lynch, Roy Burney, Gerald Hartzell, Anthony DeGiusti, Glenda Thompson, Stephen R. Smith, James L. Tyra, Richard L. Wawro, Ben Hunt, Chris Porter, John Patterson, Rebecca Lee, Regina Johnson

THE LAND OF THE DRAGON with Zon Kordic, Drew Self, Dana Taylor, Steve Huntress, Shana Ledet, Jean Smith, Iris Slocombe, Ken Shade, Alan Amick, Steve Sawyer, Skip Cain, Jim Robinson

TOAD OF TOAD HALL with Ruth A. Allison, Louise Cole, Linda Rogers, Julie Roberts, Mike McLaughlin, Dale Basler, Jay Davis, Terrel W. Neugebauer, Dante Walkup, Jenny Allen, Cheryl E. Rixman, Darrell William Graham, Sam Walker, Sam Burris, Marti Sparks, Cathryn Spaulding

Dave Stanton Photos

Top Center Left: Joel Brooks in "The Conversion of Aaron Weiss"

PAF PLAYHOUSE

Huntington Station, N. Y.
October 1, 1976–May 28, 1977

Producer, Jay Broad; Associate Producer, Joel Warren; Business Manager, Michael Maso; Stage Managers, Agnes Albright, David Schieve, William Gensel; Press, Susan Bloch, Sallie Baton; Directors, John Stix, Ernestine Perrie, Jay Broad, Peter Mark Schifter, Ronald Roston, Jonathan Bolt, Edward Stern; Sets, Eldon Elder, David Chapman, Douglas F. LeBrecht, Christopher Nowak, Ernest Allen Smith; Costumes, Catherine Hiller, Diane Finn Chapman, Jania Szatanski, Ernest Allen Smith, William Shroder; Lighting, Leslie A. DeWeerdt, Jr., Richard Winkler, Edward Effron, Larry Crimmins, Marc B. Weiss; Technical Director, Eric Marantz

PRODUCTIONS AND CASTS

THE SIGNALMAN'S APPRENTICE by Brian Phelan (*American Premiere*), with John Wardwell, Bernard Frawley, Douglas Ball

HOW TO ROB A BANK by David S. Lifson (*American Premiere*), with Alfred Drake, Chevi Colton, Sal Carolo, Larry Spinelli, Francesca DeSapio, Jean Barker, Joe DeSantis, George Salerno

IN MEMORY OF LONG JOHN SILVER by Jamie Oliviero, William Pisarra, Zizi Roberts (*Premiere*), with Kathleen Dezina, Krys Murphy, Jamie Oliviero, William Pisarra, Zizi Roberts

GEMINI by Albert Innaurato (*Premiere*), with Robert Picardo, Reed Birney, Carol Potter, Jonathan Hadary, Danny Aiello, Anne DeSalvo

PATRICK HENRY LAKE LIQUORS by Larry Ketron (*Premiere*), with Don Plumley, James Hilbrandt, Earl Hammond, Diane Stilwell, Lynn Lowry, John C. Vennema, Sharon Madden, Tom Mason, Tara Loewen, William Tripoli, Ron Kagel

THE BRIGHT AND GOLDEN LAND by Harry Granick (*World Premiere*), with Paul Lieber, Pierre Epstein, Estelle Omens, Jack Hollander, Bea Tendler, Florence Anglin, John Madden Towey, Peggy Atkinson

THE BRIXTON RECOVERY by Jack Gilhooley, with Leo Murmester, Yah ee

Joan James Photos

Left: Leo Burmester, Yah ee in "The Brixton Recovery" Top: Estelle Omens, Pierre Epstein in "The Bright and Golden Land"

Alfred Drake in "How to Rob a Bank"

Krys Murphy, Kathleen Dezina, Zizi Roberts in "In Memory of Long John Silver"

PHILADELPHIA DRAMA GUILD

Philadelphia, Pennsylvania
November 3, 1976–March 27, 1977

Artistic Director, Douglas Seale; Managing Director, James B. Freydberg; Chairman of the Board, Elkins Wetherill; Stage Directors, Douglas Seale, Douglas Campbell; Artistic-Administrative Coordinator, Lillian Steinberg; Sets, John Kasarda; Costumes, Dona Granata; Lighting, Spencer Mosse; Stage Managers, Gerald Nobles, Rusty Swope; Press, Kirby F. Smith; Props, Blair Kersten; Technical Director, Alan Trumpler

PRODUCTIONS AND CASTS

HEARTBREAK HOUSE by George Bernard Shaw, with Valerie Von Volz, Betty Leighton, Tony van Bridge, Louise Troy, Moya Fenwick, Gillie Fenwick, James Valentine, Ronald Bishop, Jeffrey Jones, Edward Atienza

ENTER A FREE MAN by Tom Stoppard, with Betty Leighton, Domini Blythe, Sam Kressen, Rudolph Willrich, Eric Uhler, James Valentine, Edward Atienza, Louise Troy

FIVE FINGER EXERCISE by Peter Shaffer, with Carolyn Coates, Lee Toombs, Jack Gwillim, Linda Hunt, John Glover

BLITHE SPIRIT by Noel Coward, with Ann Crumb, Carolyn Coates, Peter Pagan, Donald Ewer, Lois de Banzie, Betty Leighton, Louise Troy

HAMLET by William Shakespeare, with John Glover, David Leary, William LeMassena, Donald Symington, Powers Boothe, Robert Beseda, Peter Phillips, Eric Uhler, James E. Maxwell, William Buell, Michael Morin, Rusty Swope, Thomas Markus, Louise Troy, Sherry Steiner, Betty Leighton, Lois de Banzie, Michael Boyle, Gene Colebank, Tony Conaway, Larry Coxe, Robert DiCerbo, David Dotterer, Patrick Kerr, Andrew Massey, John Melancon, Gary D. Murphy, Joseph Torrisi, Peter Watts, Ann Crumb, Jeanne Drake, Terry Gahagan, Barbara Massey, Jona Huber, Deborah Marszalec, Eve Oswald, Natalie Strauss

Peter Lester Photos

Top Left: Louise Troy, Edward Atienza in "Enter a Free Man" Right: Carolyn Coates, John Glover in "Five Finger Exercise" Below: Carolyn Coates, Donald Ewer, Betty Leighton, Lois de Banzie, Peter Pagan in "Blithe Spirit"

Tony van Bridge, Valerie von Volz in "Heartbreak House"

PITTSBURGH PUBLIC THEATER

Pittsburgh, Pennsylvania
September 29, 1976–January 23, 1977

General Director, Ben Shaktman; Managing Director, Karl Gevecker; Business Manager, Cynthia J. Tutera; Press, Christine Hurst; Stage Directors, Ben Shaktman, Woodie King, Jr.; Sets, Peter Wexler, John Jensen, Karl Eigsti; Costumes, David Toser, Witney Blausen, Karl Eigsti; Lighting, Bennet Averyt; Stage Managers, David Rosenak, Patricia Hannigan; Technical Director, Dan Krehbiel; Costume Mistress, Anne Watson; Props, Cornelia Twitchell

PRODUCTIONS AND CASTS

UNCLE VANYA by Anton Chekhov (*World Premiere* translation by Michael Henry Heim), with Christopher Bernau, Veronica Castang, Joan Croydon, Jenifer Henn, Antoinette Kray, Raymond Leghart, William Roerick, Jack Ryland, Michael Thompson

SIZWE BANZI IS DEAD by Athol Fugard, John Kani, Winston Ntshona, with Joe Morton, Joe Seneca

KING HENRY V by William Shakespeare, with Robertson Carricart, Thomas Arson, Veronica Castang, Douglas Gordon, John Grassilli, Robert Grossman, Greg Johnson, Stefan Klum, John Long, Paul Milikin, Peter Murphy, James Newell, Charles Noel, Lawrence Pressman, Jack Ryland, John Scanlan, Gisele Stephanopoli, George Taylor, Michael Thompson

Jack Weinhold, Nancy Adam Photos

Jack Ryland, Christopher Bernau in "Uncle Vanya"
Top: Joe Morton, Joe Seneca in "Sizwe Banzi
Is Dead" Right Center: Lawrence Pressman
as "King Henry V"

SEATTLE REPERTORY THEATRE

Seattle, Washington
October 13, 1976–June 5, 1977

Artistic Director, Duncan Ross; Producing Director, Peter Donnelly; Costumes, Lewis D. Rampino, Nanrose Buchman; Technical Director, Floyd Hart; Production Manager, Marc Rush; Stage Managers, Jay Moran, Rod Pilloud; Press, Shirley Dennis, Marnie Andrews; Assistant to Director, Jeff Bentley; Company Manager, Charles Younger; Guest Directors, George Abbott, Reginald Denham, Garland Wright, John Going, Robert Loper, Gwen Arner, Glenda Dickerson, Larry Carpenter; Guest Designers, Eldon Elder, Robert Blackman, Jerry Williams, Robert Dahlstrom, Michael Mayer, John Shaffner, H. R. Poindexter, Richard Devin, Cynthia J. Hawkins, Scott Hawthorn

PRODUCTIONS AND CASTS

MUSIC IS by George Abbott (*World Premiere*) See Broadway Calendar

ANNA CHRISTIE by Eugene O'Neill, with Gardner Hayes, Loren Foss, Ralph Steadman, Richard Riehle, Jeffrey L. Prather, Wallace Rooney, Molly Dodd, Kaiulani Lee, Jonathan Frakes

THE MOUSETRAP by Agatha Christie, with Eda Zahl, Jeffrey Jones, Richard Bresthoff, Joan Norton, Gardner Hayes, Katherine Ferrand, John Capodice, Dennis Robertson

CAT ON A HOT TIN ROOF by Tennessee Williams, with Katherine Ferrand, David Darlow, Elizabeth Topping, Anne Gee Byrd, John Capodice, Marjorie Nelson, Beda Elliott, Walter Flanagan, Gardner Hayes, Richard Riehle, Tee Dennard, Kevand Topping, Abigail Deleers, Jason Wells, Andrew Petersen

THE SHOW-OFF by George Kelly with Anne Gee Byrd, Josephine Nichols, Darcy Pulliam, Vern Taylor, Sydney G. Smith, Warren Buck, Robert Moberly, Richard Riehle, Loren Goss

EQUUS by Peter Shaffer, with James Ray, Mark Buchan, Paul C. Thomas, Margaret Hilton, Katherine Ferrand, Kimberly Ross, Adrian Sparks, Jeffrey L. Prather, Jean Smart, Dana Cox, Leo Howes, Clayton Richardson, Martin Rotondi, Craig Turner

BINGO by Edward Bond, with Archie Smith, Kurt Beattie, Robert MacDougall, Gardner Hayes, John Aylward, Ralph Steadman, Mark Murphey, Marjorie Nelson, Cynthia Crumlish, Kathy Lichter, Jean Marie Kinney

ONCE UPON A TIME by Alexey Arbuzov, translated by Ariadne Nicolaeff (*American Premiere*), with Philip Minor, Robin Haynes, John Gilbert, Lisa Goodman, Charles Michael Wright, Ralph Steadman

SUZANNA ANDLER by Marguerite Duras, translated by Barbara Bray, with Eve Roberts, Joe Horvath, Judith Ann Roberts, Gardner Hayes

BOESMAN AND LENA by Athol Fugard, with Zaida Coles, William Jay, Paul Mokgaba

VANITIES by Jack Heifner, with Jane Bray, Dawn Didawick, Nancy New

Greg Gilbert Photos

Right: Mark Buchan (C), James Ray (R) in "Equus"
Above: Kaiulani Lee, Wallace Rooney in "Anna Christie"

Robert Moberly in "The Show-Off" Top Right:
Eve Roberts in "Suzanna Andler"

Zaida Coles, Paul Makgoba
in "Boesman and Lena"

SAN FRANCISCO MIME TROUPE

San Francisco, California
June 1, 1976–May 31, 1977

Technical Director, Trina Johnson; Writer, Joan Holden; Press, Angus Mackenzie

COMPANY: Marie Acosta, Bruce Barthol, Daniel Chumley, Lonnie Ford, Deb'bora Gilyard, Arthur Holden, Melody James, Ed Levey, Barry Levitan, Sharon Lockwood, Esteban Oropeza, Patricia Silver, David Topham

PRODUCTIONS: *World Premieres* of "False Promises" and "Nos Enganaron"

**San Francisco Mime Troupe
in "False Promises"**

SPANISH THEATRE REPERTORY

Miami, Florida
June 1, 1976–March 27, 1977

Producers, Gilberto Zaldivar, Mario R. Arellano; Associate Producer, Robert Federico; Artistic Director, Rene Buch; General Administrator, Nancy Zaldivar; Press, Lidia Hernandez, Marian Graham; Sets, Mario R. Arellano; Lighting, Robert Federico; Costumes, Rene Sanchez

PRODUCTIONS AND CASTS

OKEY by Isaac Chocron, with Velia Martinez, Griselda Noguera, Mario Ernesto Sanchez

LA FIACA by Ricardo Talesnik, with Raul Davila, Graciela Mas, Rene Sanchez, Juan Villarreal, Carlos Gerardo, Ofelia Gonzalez

VIDAS PRIVADAS by Noel Coward, with Blanquita Amaro, Osvaldo Calvo, Ana Margarita Martinez Casado, Chamaco Garcia

LA VALIJA by Julio Mauricio, with Amelia Bence, Roberto Antonio, Raul Davila

EL AMOR DE DON JUAN by Rene Buch based on work by Jose Zorilla, with Jose Rodriguez, Ana Margarita Martinez Casado, Chamaco Garcia, Mario Martin, Lolina Gutierrez, Lourdes Alvarez-Pedroso, Chabela Amaya, Jorge Dore, Rey Fernandez, Patricia Jimenez-Rojo, Jorge Perez, Pedro de Pool, Johnny Rojas, Sergio Dore, Martha Casanas

UNA MUJER MY. . .DECENTE by Miguel Mihura, with Osvaldo Calvo, Rosa Felipe, Virginia Alonso, Manolo Villamil

LOS FANTASTIKOS by Tom Jones and Harvey Schmidt, with Chamaco Garcia, Ana Margarita Martinez Casado, Mario Martin, Hector Fernandez, Rene Alejandro, Carlos Poce, Francisco Fernandez-Suarez, Rene Sanchez

LOS TITERES DE BERTHA CAMEJO with Bertha Camejo, Manolo Reyes, Johnny Rojas, Patricia Jimenez Rojo, Camejo-Blanco Children

RETABLO DE VIDA Y MUERTE by Mercedes Rein, Mario Morgan, with Estela Medina

LA DAMA DUENDE by Pedro Calderon de la Barca, with Virginia Rambal, Mirtha Cartaya, Braulio Villar, Roberto Antonio, Teresa Yenque, Julio Hara, Nino Roger, Mateo Gomez, Patricia Jimenez Rojo

Gerry Goodstein Photos

**Virginia Rambal, Robert Antonio, Julio Hara
in "La Dama Duende"**

Left Center: "Los Fantastikos"

STAGE ONE THEATRE LAB

Boston, Massachusetts
July 20–December 20, 1976

Artistic Director, Kaleel Sakakeeny; Technical Director, Robin Doty

COMPANY

Michael Fulginiti, Wendie Flagg, Kevin Kuhlke, Maggie Browning, Debra Margolies, Sheryl Munn, Sheila Greene, John Wright

PRODUCTIONS

"Masques," *World Premiere* of "The Munch Piece"

Robin Doty Photos

Stage One Theatre Lab Company

STAGE WEST

West Springfield, Massachusetts
November 13, 1976–May 1, 1977

Managing Director, Stephen E. Jays; Artistic Director, Rae Allen; Press, Jeff Wilson, Ellen Kennedy; Assistant to Miss Allen, Dan Eaton; Stage Managers, Steven Woolf, Nancy Finn, Rick Mannheim; Technical Director, Michael Degitz; Costumes, Sigrid Insull, Carr Garnett, Susan Tucker; Sets, Jerry Rojo, Edward Cesaitis; Guest Artists, Grover Dale, Davey Marlin-Jones, Jamie Gallagher, Ron Wallace, Barbara Harris, Larry King, Fredda Slavin, Susan Tucker

PRODUCTIONS AND CASTS

SLEUTH with Peter Walker, Christopher Romilly

YOU CAN'T TAKE IT WITH YOU with Elizabeth Parrish, Nancy Sellin, Yolande Bryant, Brad Sullivan, A.J. Moein, Steven Worth, Bari K. Willerford, Wyman Pendleton, Chris Waering, Rick Manheim, Chris Romilly, Renos Mandis, Bev Lubin, Gwyllum Evans, Dorothy Marie, Ed Beckman, Roman Alis, Scott Clement, Leigh Plakias

THE TOOTH OF CRIME with Clyde Burton, Sharon Ernster, Renos Mandis, Ray Aranha, Chris Romilly, Wyman Pendleton, Mark Metcalf, Jeremy Lawrence

WHEN WE DEAD AWAKEN with Ronald Bishop, Nancy Sellin, Gwyllum Evans, Timothy Near, Dorrie Kavanaugh, Brad Sullivan, Michael Lesker, Maryl Splane Wragg, Scott Clement, Allen Frenyea, Kevin Callahan, Amelia Hays

THE HOT L BALTIMORE with Clyde Burton, Kathy Tolen, Elizabeth Parrish, Dorothy Marie, Carol Morley, Wyman Pendleton, Nancy Sellin, Jeremy Lawrence, Gwyllum Evans, Timothy Near, Neil Musante, Chris Romilly, Mary Lou Wragg, Arland Russell, Scott Clement

JACQUES BREL IS ALIVE AND WELL AND LIVING IN PARIS with Rae Allen, Nina Menge, Jim Canavan, William Michael, Avram Schackman

TAKE A FABLE with Nancy Sellin, Bev Lubin, Chris Romilly, Steven Worth, Rick Manheim

GOLLIWHOPPERS! with Derek Meader, Ann Cohen, Linda Russell, Bari K. Willerford, Linda Thomas Wright, Kevin Bacon

Alan Epstein Photos

Nancy Sellin, Elizabeth Parrish, Yolande Bryant in "You Can't Take It with You" Above: Mark Metcalf, Clyde Burton in "The Tooth of Crime"

STUDIO ARENA THEATRE

Buffalo, N. Y.
October 8, 1976–June 11, 1977
Twelfth Season

Executive Producer, Neal DuBrock; Associate Producer, Gintare Sileika; Management Director, Charles W. Raison; Press, Blossom Cohan; Executive Assistant, Michael Healy; Company Manager, Jane Abbott; Stage Managers, Bernard Jay Adler, Ryan Kelly; Technical Directors, Ed Collins, Steven J. Normandale; Props, Ralph Fetterly, Carl John; Wardrobe, Diane R. Schaller, Mary-Camille Schwindler; Sound, Richard Menke; Sets, William Ritman, James Tilton, Jack Arnone, Karl Eigsti, Scott Johnson, Ben Edwards; Costumes, Jane Greenwood, Clifford Capone, Karl Eigsti, David James, Theoni V. Aldredge; Lighting, Marc B. Weiss, David Zierk, Patrika Brown, Peter Gill, Robert Crawley, Ben Edwards; Directors, Terry Schreiber, Tony Tanner, Woodie King, Jr., Larry Carpenter, Warren Enters, Edwin Sherin

PRODUCTIONS AND CASTS

THE ECCENTRICITIES OF A NIGHTINGALE by Tennessee Williams. See Broadway Calendar

DEATH OF A SALESMAN by Arthur Miller, with Pat Hingle, Joan Lorring, Ralph Farnworth, Kathleen Gaffney, Suzanne Gilbert, Richard Greene, Max William Jacobs, Pat McNamara, Philip Piro, Marcus Smythe, Robert Tennenhouse, Joan Calkin, Sharon Smith

VANITIES by Jack Heifner, with Ann McCurry, Nancy New, Cecelia Riddett

SIZWE BANZI IS DEAD by Athol Fugard, John Kani, Winston Ntshona, with D'Urville Martin, Joe Seneca

EMLYN WILLIAMS AS CHARLES DICKENS, and DYLAN THOMAS GROWING UP, solo performances by Emlyn Williams

ELIZABETH THE QUEEN by Maxwell Anderson, with Kim Hunter, George Chakiris, Marshall Borden, Kermit Brown, Eric Conger, Harriet Hall, Edward Holmes, David Sabin, Howard Shalwitz, Albert Verdesca, Richard Vernon, Norman Weiler, Douglas Crane, Geoffrey Giuliano, William Wright

A VERY PRIVATE LIFE by Neal Du Brock (*World Premiere*), with Celeste Holm, Betty Buckley, Thomas Callaway, Franklyn Seales

Phototech Studio Photos

**Thomas Callaway, Celeste Holm
in "A Very Private Life"**

**Pat Hingle in "Death of a Salesman"
Top Left: George Chakiris, Kim Hunter in
"Elizabeth the Queen"**

SYRACUSE STAGE

Syracuse, N. Y.
October 16, 1976–April 9, 1977

Producing Director, Arthur Storch; Managing Director, James Clark; Assistant Manager, Diane Malecki; Press, Susan Kindlund; Stage Directors, Arthur Storch, Marshall Oglesby, Bill Ludel, Robert Mandel, John Going; Sets, John Doepp, Sandro La Ferla, Stuart Wurtzel, Marjorie Kellogg, Elmon Webb, Virginia Dancy; Costumes, Lowell Detweiler, Patricia McGourty, Nanzi Adzima, Jennifer von Mayrhauser, James Berton Harris; Lighting, Judy Rasmuson, James Stephens, Lee Watson, Edward Effron, Arden Fingerhut; Stage Managers, David Cunningham, Marjorie Horne, Peter Dowling, Dave Clow, David Semonin; Production Manager, Mark Luking

PRODUCTIONS AND CASTS

A QUALITY OF MERCY by Roma Greth (*World Premiere*), with Janet Ward, Brad Sullivan, Kathleen Tolan, William Carden, Prudence Wright Holmes, Sheila Coonan

WHAT THE BUTLER SAW by Joe Orton, with Robert Moberly, Nicholas Hormann, Elaine Bromka, Madeleine le Roux, John Guerrasio, Douglas Fisher

TWELFTH NIGHT by William Shakespeare, with Richard Pilcher, Joseph Regalbuto, Scott C. Searfoss, Paul Tellstrom, Deborah Mayo, Keith Taylor, Haskell Gordon, Bobo Lewis, Tony Aylward, Stephanie Braxton, Alan Kass, Erik Fredericksen, Alan Rosenberg, William Spitz, John Ahlin, J. G. Kennelly, Lori Burgess

THE SEA GULL by Anton Chekhov, with Rita Gam, Pirie MacDonald, Rudy Bond, Natalie Priest, Thomas Ruisinger, Suzanne Toren, Mark Winkworth, Jack R. Marks, Tony Aylward, Trish Hawkins, William Spitz, Paul Tellstrom, Millie Sovik

SLEUTH by Anthony Shaffer, with Nicholas Woodeson, Sam Gray

A STREETCAR NAMED DESIRE by Tennessee Williams, with Virginia Kiser, David Canary, Dorothy Fielding, Conrad McLaren, Jay Devlin, Marjorie Lovett, Gerard E. Moses, Eleanor E. Russell, Paul Tellstrom, Ruth Fenster, Geraldine O. Clark, Keith Taylor, Ron George, Donna Stuccio, Dave Anderson

Robert Lorenz Photos

Prudence Wright Holmes, Kathleen Tolan in "A Quality of Mercy" Top Left: David Canary, Virginia Kiser in "A Streetcar Named Desire" Below: Sam Gray, Nicholas Woodeson in "Sleuth"

Natalie Priest, Rita Gam
in "The Sea Gull"

221

STAIRCASE THEATRE

Santa Cruz, California
June 6, 1976–May 28, 1977

Executive Producer, Karen Weinschenker; Artistic Director, Paul Ventura; Associate Producer, Greydon Morley; Administrative Director, W. Terry Poland; General Manager, Susan Edelman; Directors, Paul Ventura, Rena Down, David Ostwald, Robert Gatto, Donna Lachman, Rick Prindle, Alexander Kinney, Richard Poe; Sets and Lighting, Lee Bauer, Evan Parker, Lloyd Elliott Scott, Dana McDermott, Kevin Constant, Susan Edelman, Brian O'Donnell, Jon Webster, Nancy Godfrey; Costumes, Carol McPeek, Susan Ruttan, Wendi Pope, Lloyd Elliott Scott, Moira Mallison; Sound, Ron Holman, W. G. Wills, Kevin Constant; Stage Managers, Larry Arsenault, George Myers, Susan Edelman, Bruce Jordan, Wendi Pope, Lyllah Penacchio; Technical Directors, Kevin Constant, Lee Bauer, Phil Hofstetter

COMPANY

Scott Anderson, Douglas Barry, Lee Bauer, Dennis Berkefeldt, Wendy Bowers, Tom Busk, Shane Davis, Susan Edelman, Bruce Fairbairn, Patty Free, Robert Gatto, Ellen Himelfarb, Bruce Jordan, Mel Kinder, Susan Morgenstern, Greydon Morley, Teck Murdock, Lori Muttersbach, Richard Poe, Vicki Oswald, W. Terry Poland, Wendi Pope, Robyn Roberts, Susan Ruttan, Rochelle Singer, Richard Stone, Jay Vaughn, Jerry Walls, Irving Washkov, Karen Weinschenker, Coleman Wright

PRODUCTIONS

"Man of La Mancha," "Born Yesterday," "Lysistrata," "Sweet Bird of Youth," "Gypsy," "The Real Inspector Hound," "Who's Afraid of Virginia Woolf?," "The Tooth of Crime," "Kennedy's Children," "Butterflies Are Free"

Kent Eaton Photos

**Richard Poe, Billie Harris
in "Sweet Bird of Youth"
Top: Lee Bauer, James King, Douglas
Barry in "Kennedy's Children"**

THEATRE BY THE SEA

Portsmouth, New Hampshire
September 30, 1976–May 29, 1977

Producing Director, Jon Kimbell; Directors, Russell Treys, Fred Goldrich, Leon Odenz, Harrison Fisher; Designers, Bob Phillips, T. Winberry; Stage Manager, Michael Spellman; Costume Mistress, Anne Sylvester; Business Manager, Kathleen Kimbell; Press, Sandi Bianco; Administrative Assistant, Marie Harris; Staff Assistants, Gwen Lacey, Connie Barron

COMPANY

Jill Atonson, Holly Barron, Gary Brubach, Robin Hoff, Sara Louise, Frederic Major, Jeff McCarthy, David Penhale, Alan Tongret, Stephanie Voss, Nancy Walton, Scott Weintraub, Doris Yeager GUEST ARTISTS: Helen Auerbach, Eleanor Barbour, le Clanc du Rand, Barbara Lea, Katharine Manning, Tad Motyka, Anthony McKay, Jo Ann Yeoman

PRODUCTIONS

"Company" by Stephen Sondheim and George Furth, "Anna Christie" by Eugene O'Neill, "The Mousetrap" by Agatha Christie, "Vanities" by Jack Heifner, "Afternoons in Vegas" by Jack Gilhooley (*U. S. Premiere*), "Under Milk Wood" by Dylan Thomas, "Man with a Load of Mischief" by John Clifton and Ben Tarver

Phil McGuire Photos

**Holly Barron, Sara Louise, Robin Hoff
in "Afternoons in Vegas"**

222

**Left Center: le Clanche du Rand, Anthony McKay
in "Anna Christie"**

TRINITY SQUARE REPERTORY COMPANY

Providence, Rhode Island
September 24, 1976–May 21, 1977

Director, Adrian Hall; Administrator, G. David Black; General Manager, E. Timothy Langan; Press, Marion Simon, John Pantalone, Patricia Schwadron; Musical Director, Richard Cumming; Sets, Eugene Lee, Robert D. Soule; Lights, John Custer, Eugene Lee; Costumes, James Berton Harris, Betsey Potter, Franne Lee; Technical Director, David Ward; Props, Sandra Nathanson, Tom Waldon; Stage Managers, William Radka, Maureen Gibson, Jay Adler; Directors, Adrian Hall, Robert Mandel, George Martin, Don Price

COMPANY

Richard P. Bennett, Robert Black, Steven Brown, Vincent Ceglie, Timothy Crowe, William Damkoehler, Timothy Donahue, John Garrick, Peter Gerety, Bradford Gottlin, Tom Griffin, Ed Hall, Richard Jenkins, David C. Jones, Melanie Jones, Richard Kavanaugh, David Kennett, Richard Kneeland, Howard London, Mina Manente, George N. Martin, Derek Meader, Barbara Meek, Nancy Nichols, Barbara Orson, Julie Pember, Ricardo Pitts-Wiley, Bonnie Sacks, Margo Skinner, Norman Smith, Cynthia Strickland, Bonnie Strickman, Daniel Von Bargen, Diane Warren, Rose Weaver

PRODUCTIONS

"Of Mice and Men," "The Boys from Syracuse," "King Lear," "Seven Keys to Baldpate," "A Flea in Her Ear," "Knock Knock," "Rich and Famous," "Bad Habits"

William L. Smith Photos

Right: Richard Kneeland in "King Lear"
Top: Timothy Donahue, Barbara Orson, Peter Gerety in "Boys from Syracuse"

Barbara Meek, Richard Jenkins, Timothy Crowe in "Rich and Famous"

Howard London, Margo Skinner, Richard Kavanaugh, George Martin in "Knock Knock"

VIRGINIA MUSEUM THEATRE REPERTORY COMPANY

Richmond, Virginia
October 1, 1976–March 26, 1977

Artistic Director, Keith Fowler; General Manager, Loraine Slade; Assistant Director, James Kirkland; Production Manager, Terry A. Bennett; Musical Director, William Stancil; Stage Directors, Roderick Cook, Keith Fowler, James Kirkland; Sets, Terry A. Bennett, Richard Bryant, Robert Franklin, Richard Carleton Hankins, Sandro LaFerla; Costumes, Terry A. Bennett, Frederick N. Brown, Paige Southard; Lighting, James D. Bloch, Michael Orris Watson; Stage Managers, Rachael Lindhart, Doug Flinchum; Press, Michael P. Hickey

COMPANY

David Addis, Steven Andresen, Janet Bell, Sarah Brooke, Leigh Burch, Dalton Cathey, Townes C. Coates, J. Chris Crow, Laura Cruger, Beth Dixon, Sally Drayer, Maury Erickson, Dillon Evans, April Foreman, Roger Foreman, Keith Fowler, Reid Freeman, Kimberly Gaisford, Sonny Goff, Matt Gresge, Margaret Gwenver, Mark Hattan, Tracy Heffernan, Ellen Herrnstadt, Richard G. Holmes, W. M. Hunt, Mary Jones, George E. M. Kelly, James Kirkland, Kathleen Klein, Susan Larson, Marjorie Lerstrom, Philip LeStrange, Ken Letner, Pamela Lewis, Rachael Lindhart, Michael Martin, Joseph Martinez, Sam Maupin, Carmella Maurizi, Kurt Negaard, Laurie Null, Brad O'Hare, Barbara Parker, Jack Parrish, Wyman Pendleton, William Pitts, Craig Purinton, Jessica Regelson, Walter Rhodes, Susan Roderer, Brooks Rogers, Ed Sala, Peter Sheeha, Marie Goodman Shelton, Nancy Shocket, Cindy Shifflett, Stephen D. Spera, William Stancil, Edward Stevlingson, Jeremiah Sullivan, Jack Swanson, Judith Tillman, David J. Williams, John W. Winn III

PRODUCTIONS

"The Country Wife" by William Wycherley, "The Mousetrap" by Agatha Christie, "Oh! Coward!" devised by Roderick Cook with words and music by Noel Coward, "A Christmas Carol" adapted by Keith Fowler from Charles Dickens' novel, "The Caretaker" by Harold Pinter," "Hamlet" by William Shakespeare, "Childe Byron" by Romulus Linney (*World Premiere*)

Ron Jennings, Dennis McWaters, Katherina Wetzel Photos

Dillon Evans, Keith Fowler in "The Caretaker"
Top: Jeremiah Sullivan in "Childe Byron"

WHOLE THEATRE COMPANY

Montclair, New Jersey
October 8, 1976–May 28, 1977

Managing Director, Karen Ann Shafer; Business Manager, Sylvia Traeger; Press, Lucy Stille; Production Manager, Thom Shovestull; Directors, Apollo Dukakis, Larry Spiegel, Ernie Schenk, E. H. Cornell, Bernard Hiatt; Musical Director, Rod Derefinko; Sets, Ernie Schenk, Susan Hilferty, Raymond C. Recht, Paul Dorphley; Costumes, Ruth Brand, Susan Hilferty, Julie Schwollow, Veronica Deisler; Lighting, Marshall Spiller; Stage Managers, Charles Traeger, Peter Alyea, Harold Apter

COMPANY

Maggie Abeckerly, Jessica Allen, Remi Barclay, Jason Bosseau, Tom Brennan, Lynn Clifton, Judith Delgado, Paul Dorphley, Apollo Dukakis, Olympia Dukakis, Gerald Fierst, Marjorie Fierst, Glenna Jones, W. T. Martin, Arnold Mittelman, Stefan Peters, Ernie Schenk, Louis Zorich

PRODUCTIONS

"The Rose Tattoo," "Three Men on a Horse," "The Maids," "The Lover," "The School for Wives," "Berlin to Broadway with Kurt Weill"

Keith Scott Morton Photos

**Stefan Peters, Olympia Dukakis
in "The Rose Tattoo"**

224

YALE REPERTORY THEATRE

New Haven, Connecticut
October 1, 1976–May 15, 1977

Director, Robert Brustein; Associate Director, Alvin Epstein; Managing Director, Robert J. Orchard; Business Manager, Abigail Fearon; Press, Jan Geidt; Production Supervisor, John Robert Hood; Technical Directors, Bronislaw Sammler, George Lindsay, Jonathan Seth Miller, Stage Managers, Frank S. Torok, James F. Ingalls; Costumer, Courtney Boyd Davis; Props, Hunter Nesbitt Spence; Assistant Managing Directors, Jacqueline L. Grant, Edward Strong; Sets, Tony Straiges, Michael Yeargan, Christopher Phelps Clarens, David Lloyd Gropman, Krystyna Zachwatowicz; Costumes, Jeanne Button, Jess Goldstein, Kathleen M. Armstrong, Dunya Ramicova, Krystyna Zachwatowicz; Lighting, William B. Warfel, Paul Gallo, James H. Gage, Tom Skelton, Lewis Folden; Movement, Carmen de Lavallade; Conductors, Kirk Nurock, Paul Schierhorn

COMPANY

Blanche Baker, Bever-Leigh Banfield, Richard Bey, Guy Boyd, Norma Brustein, Robert Brustein, William Carden, Elzbieta Chezevsha, Alma Cuervo, Clifford David, Carmen de Lavallade, Robert Drivas, John Doolittle, Alvin Epstein, Ron Faber, Joyce Fideor, Jeremy Geidt, Laurence Gerwitz, Joseph Grifasi, Ben Halley, Jr., William Hickey, Thomas Hill, Anne Louise Hoffman, Ron Leibman, Charles Levin, Brian McEleney, Kate McGregor-Stewart, Lynn Oliver, Barry Press, Stephen Rowe, Baker Salsbury, Paul Schierhorn, Eugene Troobnick, Mary Van Dyke, Margaret Whitton, Carol Williard, James Zitlow

PRODUCTIONS

"Julius Caesar" by William Shakespeare, "Suicide in B-Flat" by Sam Shepard with music by Lawrence Wolf (*World Premiere*), "Ivanov" by Anton Chekhov, "The Vietnamization of New Jersey (A American Tragedy) by Christopher Durang (*World Premiere*), "The Durango Flash" by William Hauptman (*World Premiere*), "Mister Puntila and His Chauffeur Matti" by Bertolt Brecht translated by Gerhard Nellnaus, "White Marriage" by Tadeusz Roseqicz translated by Adam Czerniawski (*American Premiere*)

Eugene Cook Photos

Right: Elzbieta Chezevska, Margaret Whitton, Alvin Epstein in "Ivanov" Top: Blanche Baker, Carol Williard in "White Marriage"

Ron Leibman, Eugene Troobnick, Robert Drivas in "Julius Caesar"

William Hickey, Clifford David in "Suicide in B-Flat"

PULITZER PRIZE PRODUCTIONS

1918–Why Marry?, **1919**– No award, **1920**–Beyond the Horizon, **1921**–Miss Lulu Bett, **1922**–Anna Christie, **1923**–Icebound, **1924**–Hell-Bent fer Heaven, **1925**–They Knew What They Wanted, **1926**–Craig's Wife, **1927**–In Abraham's Bosom, **1928**–Strange Interlude, **1929**–Street Scene, **1930**–The Green Pastures, **1931**–Alison's House, **1932**–Of Thee I Sing, **1933**–Both Your Houses, **1934**–Men in White, **1935**–The Old Maid, **1936**–Idiot's Delight, **1937**–You Can't Take It with You, **1938**–Our Town, **1939**–Abe Lincoln in Illinois, **1940**–The Time of Your Life, **1941**–There Shall Be No Night, **1942**–No award, **1943**–The Skin of Our Teeth, **1944**–No award, **1945**–Harvey, **1946**–State of the Union, **1947**–No award, **1948**–A Streetcar Named Desire, **1949**–Death of a Salesman, **1950**–South Pacific, **1951**–No award, **1952**–The Shrike, **1953**–Picnic, **1954**–The Teahouse of the August Moon, **1955**–Cat on a Hot Tin Roof, **1956**–The Diary of Anne Frank, **1957**–Long Day's Journey into Night, **1958**–Look Homeward, Angel, **1959**–J. B., **1960**–Fiorello!, **1961**–All the Way Home, **1962**–How to Succeed in Business without Really Trying, **1963**–No award, **1964**–No award, **1965**–The Subject Was Roses, **1966**–No award, **1967**–A Delicate Balance, **1968**–No award, **1969**–The Great White Hope, **1970**–No Place to Be Somebody, **1971**–The Effect of Gamma Rays on Man-in-the-Moon Marigolds, **1972**–No award, **1973**–That Championship Season, **1974**–No award, **1975**–Seascape, **1976**–A Chorus Line, **1977**–The Shadow Box

NEW YORK DRAMA CRITICS CIRCLE AWARDS

1936–Winterset, **1937**–High Tor, **1938**–Of Mice and Men, Shadow and Substance, **1939**–The White Steed, **1940**–The Time of Your Life, **1941**–Watch on the Rhine, The Corn is Green, **1942**–Blithe Spirit, **1943**–The Patriots, **1944**–Jacobowsky and the Colonel, **1945**–The Glass Menagerie, **1946**–Carousel, **1947**–All My Sons, No Exit, Brigadoon, **1948**–A Streetcar Named Desire, The Winslow Boy, **1949**–Death of a Salesman, The Madwoman of Chaillot, South Pacific, **1950**–The Member of the Wedding, The Cocktail Party, The Consul, **1951**–Darkness at Noon, The Lady's Not for Burning, Guys and Dolls, **1952**–I Am a Camera, Venus Observed, Pal Joey, **1953**–Picnic, The Love of Four Colonels, Wonderful Town, **1954**–Teahouse of the August Moon, Ondine, The Golden Apple, **1955**–Cat on a Hot Tin Roof, Witness for the Prosecution, The Saint of Bleecker Street, **1956**–The Diary of Anne Frank, Tiger at the Gates, My Fair Lady, **1957**–Long Day's Journey into Night, The Waltz of the Toreadors, The Most Happy Fella, **1958**–Look Homeward Angel, Look Back in Anger, The Music Man, **1959**–A Raisin in the Sun, The Visit, La Plume de Ma Tante, **1960**–Toys in the Attic, Five Finger Exercise, Fiorello!, **1961**–All the Way Home, A Taste of Honey, Carnival, **1962**–Night of the Iguana, A Man for All Seasons, How to Succeed in Business without Really Trying, **1963**–Who's Afraid of Virginia Woolf?, **1964**–Luther, Hello, Dolly!, **1965**–The Subject Was Roses, Fiddler on the Roof, **1966**–The Persecution and Assassination of Marat as Performed by the Inmates of the Asylum of Charenton under the Direction of the Marquis de Sade, Man of La Mancha, **1967**–The Homecoming, Cabaret, **1968**–Rosencrantz and Guildenstern Are Dead, Your Own Thing, **1969**–The Great White Hope, 1776, **1970**–The Effect of Gamma Rays on Man-in-the-Moon Marigolds, Borstal Boy, Company, **1971**–Home, Follies, The House of Blue Leaves, **1972**–That Championship Season, Two Gentlemen of Verona, **1973**–The Hot l Baltimore, The Changing Room, A Little Night Music, **1974**–The Contractor, Short Eyes, Candide, **1975**–Equus, The Taking of Miss Janie, A Chorus Line, **1976**–Travesties, Streamers, Pacific Overtures, **1977**–Otherwise Engaged, American Buffalo, Annie

AMERICAN THEATRE WING
ANTOINETTE PERRY (TONY) AWARD PRODUCTIONS

1948–Mister Roberts, **1949**–Death of a Salesman, Kiss Me, Kate, **1950**–The Cocktail Party, South Pacific, **1951**–The Rose Tattoo, Guys and Dolls, **1952**–The Fourposter, The King and I, **1953**–The Crucible, Wonderful Town, **1954**–The Teahouse of the August Moon, Kismet, **1955**–The Desperate Hours, The Pajama Game, **1956**–The Diary of Anne Frank, Damn Yankees, **1957**–Long Day's Journey into Night, My Fair Lady, **1958**–Sunrise at Campobello, The Music Man, **1959**–J. B., Redhead, **1960**–The Miracle Worker, Fiorello! tied with Sound of Music, **1961**–Becket, Bye Bye Birdie, **1962**–A Man for All Seasons, How to Succeed in Business without Really Trying, **1963**–Who's Afraid of Virginia Woolf?, A Funny Thing Happened on the Way to the Forum, **1964**–Luther, Hello, Dolly!, **1965**–The Subject Was Roses, Fiddler on the Roof, **1966**–The Persecution and Assassination of Marat as Performed by the Inmates of the Asylum of Charenton under the Direction of the Marquis de Sade, Man of La Mancha, **1967**–The Homecoming, Cabaret, **1968**–Rosencrantz and Guildenstern Are Dead, Hallelujah, Baby!, **1969**–The Great White Hope, 1776, **1970**–Borstal Boy, Applause, **1971**–Sleuth, Company, **1972**–Sticks and Bones, Two Gentlemen of Verona, **1973**–That Championship Season, A Little Night Music, **1974**–The River Niger, Raisin, **1975**–Equus, The Wiz, **1976**–Travesties, A Chorus Line, **1977**–The Shadow Box, Annie

1977 THEATRE WORLD AWARD WINNERS

TRAZANA BEVERLEY
of "For Colored Girls. . . ."

MICHAEL CRISTOFER
of "The Cherry Orchard"

JOE FIELDS
of "The Basic Training of Pavlo Hummel"

JOANNA GLEASON
of "I Love My Wife"

CECILIA HART
of "Dirty Linen"

JOHN HEARD
of "G. R. Point"

KEN PAGE
of "Guys and Dolls"

GLORIA HODES
of "The Club"

ANDREA McARDLE
of "Annie"

JONATHAN PRYCE
of "Comedians"

CHICK VENNERA
of "Jockeys"

JULIETTE KOKA
of "Piaf . . . A Remembrance"

1977 THEATRE WORLD AWARDS PARTY, Thursday, May 26, 1977: Top: Earle Hyman, Dorothy Loudon, Fritz Weaver, Carol Channing, John Willis, Michael Cristofer, Christopher Plummer, Estelle Parsons, Ralph Carter; Page Johnson; Estelle Parsons, Ralph Carter, Tovah Feldshuh, James Naughton, Patricia Elliott **Below:** Trazana Beverley Carol Channing, Beatrice Winde (for Joe Field); Patricia Elliott; John Heard, Rosemary Harris; **Second row from bottom:** Rosemary Harris, Jennifer Ehle, Eva Le Gallienne, Andrea McArdle; Christopher Plummer; Michael Cristofer, Estelle Parsons **Bottom row:** Alexander Cohen (for Jonathan Pryce), Tovah Feldshuh; Julie McKenzie, Reid Shelton, Millicent Martin; Andrea McArdle

Top: Frank Spiering (for Chick Vennera), Gloria Hodes, Anthony Perkins and wife Berry Berenson, Juliette Koka Below: John Heard, Russ Thacker, Bill Como, Gretchen Wyler, Ken Page, Linda Miller Second row from bottom: Joanna Gleason, James Naughton; Marti Rolph; Cecilia Hart; Carol Channing, Eva Le Gallienne, Dorothy Loudon Bottom: Carol Channing, Ralph Carter; Richard Barr, Eva Le Gallienne; Earle Hyman, David Powers, Fritz Weaver

Photos by Alberto Cabrera, Ron Reagan, Evan Romero, Van Williams

| **Warren
Beatty** | **Jane
Alexander** | **Al
Pacino** | **Faye
Dunaway** | **Cliff
Robertson** |

PREVIOUS THEATRE WORLD AWARD WINNERS

1944–45: Betty Comden, Richard Davis, Richard Hart, Judy Holliday, Charles Lang, Bambi Linn, John Lund, Donald Murphy, Nancy Noland, Margaret Phillips, John Raitt

1945–46: Barbara Bel Geddes, Marlon Brando, Bill Callahan, Wendell Corey, Paul Douglas, Mary James, Burt Lancaster, Patricia Marshall, Beatrice Pearson

1946–47: Keith Andes, Marion Bell, Peter Cookson, Ann Crowley, Ellen Hanley, John Jordan, George Keane, Dorothea MacFarland, James Mitchell, Patricia Neal, David Wayne

1947–48: Valerie Bettis, Edward Bryce, Whitfield Connor, Mark Dawson, June Lockhart, Estelle Loring, Peggy Maley, Ralph Meeker, Meg Mundy, Douglass Watson, James Whitmore, Patrice Wymore

1948–49: Tod Andrews, Doe Avedon, Jean Carson, Carol Channing, Richard Derr, Julie Harris, Mary McCarty, Allyn Ann McLerie, Cameron Mitchell, Gene Nelson, Byron Palmer, Bob Scheerer

1949–50: Nancy Andrews, Phil Arthur, Barbara Brady, Lydia Clarke, Priscilla Gillette, Don Hanmer, Marcia Henderson, Charlton Heston, Rick Jason, Grace Kelly, Charles Nolte, Roger Price

1950–51: Barbara Ashley, Isabel Bigley, Martin Brooks, Richard Burton, James Daly, Cloris Leachman, Russell Nype, Jack Palance, William Smothers, Maureen Stapleton, Marcia Van Dyke, Eli Wallach

1951–52: Tony Bavaar, Patricia Benoit, Peter Conlow, Virginia de Luce, Ronny Graham, Audrey Hepburn, Diana Herbert, Conrad Janis, Dick Kallman, Charles Proctor, Eric Sinclair, Kim Stanley, Marian Winters, Helen Wood

1952–53: Edie Adams, Rosemary Harris, Eileen Heckart, Peter Kelley, John Kerr, Richard Kiley, Gloria Marlowe, Penelope Munday, Paul Newman, Sheree North, Geraldine Page, John Stewart, Ray Stricklyn, Gwen Verdon

1953–54: Orson Bean, Harry Belafonte, James Dean, Joan Diener, Ben Gazzara, Carol Haney, Jonathan Lucas, Kay Medford, Scott Merrill, Elizabeth Montgomery, Leo Penn, Eva Marie Saint

1954–55: Julie Andrews, Jacqueline Brookes, Shirl Conway, Barbara Cook, David Daniels, Mary Fickett, Page Johnson, Loretta Leversee, Jack Lord, Dennis Patrick, Anthony Perkins, Christopher Plummer

1955–56: Diane Cilento, Dick Davalos, Anthony Franciosa, Andy Griffith, Laurence Harvey, David Hedison, Earle Hyman, Susan Johnson, John Michael King, Jayne Mansfield, Sarah Marshall, Gaby Rodgers, Susan Strasberg, Fritz Weaver

1956–57: Peggy Cass, Sydney Chaplin, Sylvia Daneel, Bradford Dillman, Peter Donat, George Grizzard, Carol Lynley, Peter Palmer, Jason Robards, Cliff Robertson, Pippa Scott, Inga Swenson

1957–58: Anne Bancroft, Warren Berlinger, Colleen Dewhurst, Richard Easton, Tim Everett, Eddie Hodges, Joan Hovis, Carol Lawrence, Jacqueline McKeever, Wynne Miller, Robert Morse, George C. Scott

1958–59: Lou Antonio, Ina Balin, Richard Cross, Tammy Grimes, Larry Hagman, Dolores Hart, Roger Mollien, France Nuyen, Susan Oliver, Ben Piazza, Paul Roebling, William Shatner, Pat Suzuki, Rip Torn

1959–60: Warren Beatty, Eileen Brennan, Carol Burnett, Patty Duke, Jane Fonda, Anita Gillette, Elisa Loti, Donald Madden, George Maharis, John McMartin, Lauri Peters, Dick Van Dyke

1960–61: Joyce Bulifant, Dennis Cooney, Sandy Dennis, Nancy Dussault, Robert Goulet, Joan Hackett, June Harding, Ron Husmann, James MacArthur, Bruce Yarnell

1961–62: Elizabeth Ashley, Keith Baxter, Peter Fonda, Don Galloway, Sean Garrison, Barbara Harris, James Earl Jones, Janet Margolin, Karen Morrow, Robert Redford, John Stride, Brenda Vaccaro

1962–63: Alan Arkin, Stuart Damon, Melinda Dillon, Robert Drivas, Bob Gentry, Dorothy Loudon, Brandon Maggart, Julienne Marie, Liza Minnelli, Estelle Parsons, Diana Sands, Swen Swenson

1963–64: Alan Alda, Gloria Bleezarde, Imelda De Martin, Claude Giraud, Ketty Lester, Barbara Loden, Lawrence Pressman, Gilbert Price, Philip Proctor, John Tracy, Jennifer West

1964–65: Carolyn Coates, Joyce Jillson, Linda Lavin, Luba Lisa, Michael O'Sullivan, Joanna Pettet, Beah Richards, Jaime Sanchez, Victor Spinetti, Nicolas Surovy, Robert Walker, Clarence Williams III

1965–66: Zoe Caldwell, David Carradine, John Cullum, John Davidson, Faye Dunaway, Gloria Foster, Robert Hooks, Jerry Lanning, Richard Mulligan, April Shawhan, Sandra Smith, Lesley Ann Warren

1966–67: Bonnie Bedelia, Richard Benjamin, Dustin Hoffman, Terry Kiser, Reva Rose, Robert Salvio, Sheila Smith, Connie Stevens, Pamela Tiffin, Leslie Uggams, Jon Voight, Christopher Walken

1967–68: David Birney, Pamela Burrell, Jordan Christopher, Jack Crowder (Thalmus Rasulala), Sandy Duncan, Julie Gregg, Stephen Joyce, Bernadette Peters, Alice Playten, Michael Rupert, Brenda Smiley, Russ Thacker

1968–69: Jane Alexander, David Cryer, Blythe Danner, Ed Evanko, Ken Howard, Lauren Jones, Ron Leibman, Marian Mercer, Jill O'Hara, Ron O'Neal, Al Pacino, Marlene Warfield

1969–70: Susan Browning, Donny Burks, Catherine Burns, Len Cariou, Bonnie Franklin, David Holliday, Katharine Houghton, Melba Moore, David Rounds, Lewis J. Stadlen, Kristoffer Tabori, Fredricka Weber

1970–71: Clifton Davis, Michael Douglas, Julie Garfield, Martha Henry, James Naughton, Tricia O'Neil, Kipp Osborne, Roger Rathburn, Ayn Ruymen, Jennifer Salt, Joan Van Ark, Walter Willison

1971–72: Jonelle Allen, Maureen Anderman, William Atherton, Richard Backus, Adrienne Barbeau, Cara Duff-MacCormick, Robert Foxworth, Elaine Joyce, Jess Richards, Ben Vereen, Beatrice Winde, James Woods

1972–73: D'Jamin Bartlett, Patricia Elliott, James Farentino, Brian Farrell, Victor Garber, Kelly Garrett, Mari Gorman, Laurence Guittard, Trish Hawkins, Monte Markham, John Rubinstein, Jennifer Warren, Alexander H. Cohen (Special Award)

1973–74: Mark Baker, Maureen Brennan, Ralph Carter, Thom Christopher, John Driver, Conchata Ferrell, Ernestine Jackson, Michael Moriarty, Joe Morton, Ann Reinking, Janie Sell, Mary Woronov, Sammy Cahn (Special Award)

1974–75: Peter Burnell, Zan Charisse, Lola Falana, Peter Firth, Dorian Harewood, Joel Higgins, Marcia McClain, Linda Miller, Marti Rolph, John Sheridan, Scott Stevensen, Donna Theodore, Equity Library Theatre (Special Award)

1975–76: Danny Aiello, Christine Andreas, Dixie Carter, Tovah Feldshuh, Chip Garnett, Richard Kelton, Vivian Reed, Charles Repole, Virginia Seidel, Daniel Seltzer, John V. Shea, Meryl Streep, A Chorus Line (Special Award)

Ernest Abuba

Brandy Alexander

Steven Alex-Cole

Jane Altman

Daniel Arden

BIOGRAPHIES OF THIS SEASON'S CAST

ABRAHAM, F. MURRAY. Born Oct. 24, 1939 in Pittsburgh, Pa. Attended UTex. OB bow 1967 in "The Fantasticks," followed by "An Opening in the Trees," "Fourteenth Dictator," "Young Abe Lincoln," "Tonight in Living Color," "Adaptation," "Survival of St. Joan," "The Dog Ran Away," "Fables," "Richard III," "Little Murders," "Scuba Duba," "Where Has Tommy Flowers Gone?," "Miracle Play," "Blessing," "Sexual Perversity in Chicago," Bdwy in "The Man in the Glass Booth" (1968), "6 Rms Riv Vu.," "Bad Habits," "The Ritz," "Legend."

ABUBA, ERNEST. Born Aug. 25, 1947 in Honolulu, HI. Attended Southwestern Col. Bdwy debut 1976 in "Pacific Overtures."

ACKERMAN, LONI. Born Apr. 10, 1949 in NYC. Attended New School. Bdwy debut 1968 in "George M!," followed by "Dames at Sea" (OB), "No, No, Nanette," "So Long 174th Street," "Magic Show," "Starting Here Starting Now" (OB).

ACKROYD, DAVID. Born May 30, 1940 in Orange, N.J. Graduate Bucknell, Yale. Bdwy debut 1971 in "Unlikely Heroes" followed by "Full Circle," "Hamlet" (LC). "Isadora Duncan Sleeps with the Russian Navy" (OB).

ADAMS, MASON. Born Feb. 26, 1919 in NYC. Graduate UWisc. Has appeared in "Get Away, Old Man," "Public Relations," "Career Angel," "Violet," "Shadow of My Enemy," "Tall Story," "Inquest," "Trial of the Catonsville 9," "Sign in Sidney Brustein's Window," "Meegan's Game" (OB), "Shortchanged Review," (LC), "Checking Out," "The Soft Touch" (OB).

AGRESS, TED. Born Apr. 20, 1945 in Brooklyn, NY. Attended Adelphi U. Bdwy debut 1965 in "Hello, Dolly!" followed by "Dear World," "Look Me Up" (OB), "Shenandoah."

AGRIN, GLEN. Born Feb. 9, 1952 in NYC. Graduate Hofstra U. Debut OB 1976 in "Fiorella!"

AIELLO, DANNY. Born June 20, 1935 in NYC. Debut 1975 in "Lamppost Reunion" for which he received a Theatre World Award, followed by "Wheelbarrow Closers," "Gemini."

ALANN, LLOYD. Born Aug. 15, 1952 in The Bronx, NY. Attended Lehman Col. Bdwy debut 1975 in "Grease."

ALBERT, DONNIE RAY. Born Jan. 10, 1950 in New Orleans LA. Graduate LSU, SMU. Bdwy debut 1976 in "Porgy and Bess."

ALDREDGE, TOM. Born Feb. 28, 1928 in Dayton, O. Attended Dayton U., Goodman Theatre. Bdwy bow 1959 in "The Nervous Set," followed by "UTBU," "Slapstick Tragedy," "Everything in the Garden," "Indians," "Engagement Baby," "How the Other Half Loves," "Sticks and Bones," "Where's Charley?," "Leaf People," "Rex," "Vieux Carre," OB in "The Tempest," "Between Two Thieves," "Henry V," "The Premise," "Love's Labour's Lost," "Troilus and Cressida," "Butter and Egg Man," "Ergo," "Boys in the Band," "Twelfth Night," "Colette," "Hamlet," "The Orphan," "King Lear," "Iceman Cometh."

ALEXANDER, BRANDY. Born Aug. 17, 1943 in Portland, ME. Attended Boston Conservatory. After many club engagements, made debut OB in "Triple Play" (1968), Bdwy 1976 in "Let My People Come."

ALEXANDER, C. K. Born May 4, 1920 in Cairo, Egypt. Graduate American U. Bdwy debut 1946 in "Hidden Horizon," followed by "The Happy Time," "Flight into Egypt," "Mr. Pickwick," "Can-Can," "Fanny," "The Matchmaker," "La Plume de Ma Tante," "Rhinoceros," "Carnival," "Tovarich," "Poor Bitos," "Ari," OB in "The Dragon," "Corruption in the Palace of Justice," "Justice Box," "Threepenny Opera," "The Cherry Orchard" (LC).

ALEXANDER, TERRY. Born Mar. 23, 1947 in Detroit, MI. Wayne State U. graduate. Bdwy debut 1971 in "No Place to be Somebody" OB in "Rashomon," "Glass Menagerie," "Breakout," "Naomi Court," "Streamers."

ALEXANDRINE, DRU. Born Apr. 23, 1950 in Cheshire, Eng. Studied at Royal Ballet School. Bdwy debut 1973 in "Pajama Game," followed by "My Fair Lady" (1976)

ALEX-COLE, STEVEN. Born Jan. 6, 1949 in Baltimore, MD. Graduate Union Col., UStockholm. Debut 1975 OB in "Let My People Come," followed by Bdwy in "Treemonisha" (1975), "Porgy and Bess."

ALLEN, NORMAN. Born Dec. 24, 1939 in London. Bdwy bow 1963 in "Chips with Everything," followed by "Half a Sixpence," "Rockefeller and the Red Indians," "Get Thee to Canterbury" (OB), "Borstal Boy," "Vivat! Vivat Reginal," "Jockey Club Stakes," "Comedians."

ALLEN, SCOTT. Born Aug. 29, 1948 in Morristown, NJ. Attended Union Col., Upsala Col., AMDA. Bdwy debut 1975 in "A Chorus Line."

ALMQUIST, GREGG. Born Dec. 1, 1948 in Minneapolis, MN. Graduate UMinn. Debut OB 1974 in "Richard III," followed by "A Night at the Black Pig."

ALTMAN, JANE. Born Sept. 7 in Philadelphia, Pa. Temple U. graduate. Debut OB in "Importance of Being Ernest," followed by "Taming of the Shrew," "Candida," "A Doll's House," "Magda," "The Three Musketeers," "And So to Bed," "Saints."

ANDALMAN, JEAN. Born May 5, 1951 in Chicago, IL. Graduate Sarah Lawrence Col. Debut 1972 OB in "The Bar That Never Closes," followed by "Thoughts," Bdwy 1976 in "Oh! Calcutta!"

ANDERMAN, MAUREEN. Born Oct. 26, 1946 in Detroit, MI. Graduate U. Mich. Bdwy debut 1970 in ASF's "Othello," followed by "Moonchildren" for which she received a Theatre World Award, "An Evening with Richard Nixon and. . . .," "The Last of Mrs. Lincoln," "Seascape," "Hamlet" (LC), "Who's Afraid of Virginia Woolf?"

ANDERSON, JANE. Born July 28, 1954 in Los Altos, CA. Attended Emerson Col., Ohio U. Debut 1976 OB in "Sexual Perversity in Chicago."

ANDRE, JILL. Born Feb. 16, 1935 in NYC. Attended CCNY, Columbia U. Debut OB 1952 in "Madwoman of Chaillot," followed by "Dark of the Moon," "Last Analysis," "Horseman Pass By," "From Here Inside My Head," "Kennedy's Children," "Stop the Parade," "Monkey, Monkey," "Battle of Angels," "Four Friends," "Augusta," Bdwy in "Sunrise at Campobello," "Great White Hope," "An Evening with Richard Nixon. . . .," "The Trip Back Down."

ANDREAS, CHRISTINE. Born Oct. 1, 1951 in Camden, NJ. Bdwy debut 1975 in "Angel Street," followed by "My Fair Lady," for which she received a Theatre World Award.

ANDREWS, GEORGE LEE. Born Oct. 13, 1942 in Milwaukee, WI. Debut OB 1970 in "Jacques Brel Is Alive. . . .," followed by "Starting Here Starting Now," Bdwy 1973 in "A Little Night Music."

ANGELA, JUNE. Born Aug. 18, 1959 in NYC. Bdwy debut 1970 in "Lovely Ladies, Kind Gentlemen," followed by "The King and I" (1977).

ARDEN, DANIEL. Born Oct. 30, 1954 in Los Angeles, CA. Graduate NC School of Arts. Bdwy debut 1977 in "Equus"

ARGO, ALLISON. Born Dec. 23, 1953 in Richmond, VA. Debut OB 1974 in "Neighbors," followed by Bdwy in "Lady from the Sea" (1976), "Night of the Iguana."

ARI, BOB. Born July 1, 1949 in NYC. Graduate Carnegie-Mellon U. Debut OB 1976 in "Boys from Syracuse" (ELT).

ASHLEY, ELIZABETH. Born Aug. 30, 1939 in Ocala, FL. Attended Neighborhood Playhouse. Bdwy debut 1959 in "The Highest Tree," followed by "Take Her, She's Mine" for which she received a Theatre World Award, "Barefoot in the Park," "Ring Round the Bathtub," "Cat on a Hot Tin Roof," "The Skin of Our Teeth," "Legend," "Caesar and Cleopatra."

ASHLEY, MARY ELLEN. Born June 11, 1938 in Long Island, City, NY. Queens College graduate. Bdwy debut 1943 in "The Innocent Voyage," followed by "Bobino," "By Appointment Only," "Annie Get Your Gun," "Yentl," OB in "Carousel," "Yentl the Yeshiva Boy," "Polly," "Panama Hattie" (ELT), "Soft Touch."

ASSANTE, ARMAND. Born Oct. 4, 1949 in NYC. Attended AADA. Debut OB 1971 in "Lake of the Woods," followed by "Yankees 3, Detroit 0," "Rubbers," "Boccacio," Bdwy in "Comedians," "Romeo and Juliet."

ATTLES, JOSEPH. Born Apr. 7, 1903 in Charleston, SC. Attended Harlem Musical Conservatory. Bdwy bow in "Blackbirds of 1928," followed by "John Henry," "Porgy and Bess," "Kwamina," "Tambourines to Glory," "The Last of Mrs. Lincoln," "Bubbling Brown Sugar," OB in "Jerico-Jim Crow," "Cabin in the Sky," "Prodigal Son," "Day of Absence," "Cry of Players," "King Lear," "Duplex."

| **Jack Axelrod** | **Verona Barnes** | **Peter Bartlett** | **Betsy Beard** | **Jon Benson** |

AUBERJONOIS, RENE. Born June 1, 1940 in NYC. Graduate Carnegie Inst. With LCRep in "A Cry of Players," "King Lear," and "Twelfth Night," Bdwy in "Fire," "Coco," "Tricks," "The Good Doctor," BAM Co. in "The New York Idea" and "Three Sisters."

AUSTIN, ANTHONY. Born June 6, 1966 in NYC. Debut OB 1974 in "Merry Wives of Windsor," followed by "Billy Irish," Bdwy 1977 in "Exiles."

AUSTIN, BETH. Born May 23, 1952 in Philadelphia, PA. Graduate Point Park Col., Pittsburgh Playhouse. Debut OB 1977 in "Wonderful Town" (ELT), Bdwy 1977 in "Sly Fox."

AVALOS, LUIS. Born Sept. 2, 1946 in Havana, Cuba. Debut OB in "Never Jam Today," followed by "Rules for Running of Trains," LC's "Camino Real," "Beggar on Horseback," "Good Woman of Setzuan," and "Kool Aid," "The Architect and the Emperor," "As You Like It," "El Grande de Coca Cola," "Zoo Story," "Payment as Pledged," "Armenians," "Marco Polo."

AXELROD, JACK. Born Jan. 25, 1930 in Los Angeles, CA. Graduate UCal. Debut OB 1969 in "Macbeth," followed by "Gandhi," Bdwy 1976 in "Herzl."

AYR, MICHAEL. Born Sept. 8, 1953 in Great Falls, MT. Graduate SMU. Debut 1976 OB in "Mrs. Murray's Farm," followed by "The Farm."

AZITO, ANTONIO. Born July 18, 1948 in NYC. Attended Juilliard. Debut OB 1971 in "Red, White and Black," followed by "Players Project," "Secrets of the Citizens' Correction Committee," "Threepenny Opera." Bdwy 1977 in "Happy End."

BACIGALUPI, ROBERT. Born Oct. 21, 1949 in San Francisco, CA. Juilliard graduate. Debut 1975 in "The Robber Bridegroom," followed by "Edward II," "The Time of Your Life."

BAFF, REGINA. Born Mar. 31, 1949 in The Bronx, NY. Attended Western Reserve, Hunter Col. Debut 1969 OB in "The Brownstone Urge," followed by "Patrick Henry Lake Liquors," "The Cherry Orchard," "Domino Courts," Bdwy in "Story Theatre," "Metamorphosis," "Veronica's Room."

BAIRD, MARY E. Born June 26, 1947 in Berkeley, CA. Attended Chabot Col. Debut OB 1974 in "At Sea with Benchley, Kalmar & Ruby," followed by "Rubbers," "Peg O' My Heart."

BAKER, LENNY. Born Jan. 17, 1945 in Boston, MA. Debut OB 1969 in "Frank Gagliano's City Scene," followed by "The Year Boston Won the Pennant," "The Time of Your Life," "Summertree," "Early Morning," "Survival of Joan," "Gallery," "Barbary Shore," "Merry Wives of Windsor," "Pericles," "Secret Service," "Boy Meets Girl," "Henry V," "Measure for Measure," Bdwy in "Freedom of the City" (1974), "I Love My Wife."

BALSAM, MARTIN. Born Nov. 4, 1919 in NYC. Attended Actors Studio. Debut 1935 in "Pot Boiler" (OB), followed by "Ghost for Sale," "The Closing Door," "Sundown Beach," "Macbeth," "The Rose Tattoo," "Camino Real," "Middle of the Night," "The Porcelain Year," "You Know I Can't Hear You When the Water's Running," "Cold Storage" (OB).

BARNES, VERONA. Born June 2, 1940 in Wilson, NC. Graduate Winston-Salem State Col. Bdwy debut 1968 in "The Great White Hope," OB in "Sleep," "The Cherry Orchard," "House Party," "All God's Chillun," "Divine Comedy."

BARRETT, LAURINDA. Born in NYC in 1931. Attended Wellesley Col., RADA. OB in "The Misanthrope," "Palm Tree in a Rose Garden," "All Is Bright," Bdwy in "Too Late the Phalarope," "The Girls in 509," "The Milk Train Doesn't Stop Here Anymore," "UTBU," "I Never Sang for My Father," "Equus."

BARRETT, LESLIE. Born Oct. 30, 1919 in NYC. Bdwy debut 1936 in "But for the Grace of God," followed by "Enemy of the People," "Dead End," "Sunup to Sundown," "There's Always a Breeze," "Primrose Path," "Stroke of 8," "Horse Fever," "Good Neighbor," "All in Favor," "Counsellor-at-Law," "Deadfall," "Rhinoceros," "The Investigation," OB in "Hamp," "The Contractor," "Play Me, Zoltan," "Savages."

BARRIE, BARBARA. Born May 23, 1931 in Chicago, IL. Graduate UTex. Bdwy debut 1955 in "The Wooden Dish," followed by "Happily Never After," "Company," "Selling of the President," "Prisoner of Second Avenue," "California Suite," OB in "The Crucible," "Beaux Stratagem," "Taming of the Shrew," "Twelfth Night," "All's Well That Ends Well," "Horseman, Pass By," "Killdeer."

BARROWS, DIANA. Born Jan. 23, 1966 in NYC. Bdwy debut 1975 in "Cat on a Hot Tin Roof," followed by "Panama Hattie" (ELT), "Annie."

BARTLETT, D'JAMIN. Born May 21 in NYC. Attended AADA. Bdwy debut 1973 in "A Little Night Music" for which she received a Theatre World Award, OB in "The Glorious Age," "Boccacio." "2 by 5," "Lulu."

BARTLETT, PETER. Born Aug. 28, 1942 in Chicago, IL. Attended Loyola U., LAMDA. Bdwy debut 1969 in "A Patrot for Me," followed by "Gloria and Esperanza," OB in "Boom Boom Room," "I Remember the House Where I Was Born," "The Crazy Locomotive."

BARTON, DONALD. Born May 2, 1928 in Eastland, TX. Attended UTex. Credits include "Design for a Stained Glass Window," "Paint Your Wagon," "Wonderful Town," "Goldilocks," "Much Ado about Nothing," "The Royal Family."

BARTZ, JAMES ALLAN. Born Apr. 23, 1948 in Racine, WI. Graduate UWisc. Bdwy debut 1976 in "Wheelbarrow Closers."

BATES, KATHY. Born June 28, 1948 in Memphis, TN. Graduate Southern Methodist U. Debut OB 1976 in "Vanities."

BATTEN, TOM. Born in Oklahoma City, OK. Graduate USC. Bdwy debut 1961 in "How to Succeed in Business . . . ," followed by "Mame," "Gantry," "Mack and Mabel," "She Loves Me."

BATTISTA, LLOYD. Born May 14, 1937 in Cleveland, OH. Graduate Carnegie Tech. Bdwy debut 1966 in "Those That Play the Clowns," followed by "The Homecoming," OB in "The Flame and the Rose," "Murder in the Cathedral," "The Miser," "Gorky," "Sexual Perversity in Chicago."

BAXLEY, BARBARA. Born Jan. 1, 1925 in Porterville, CA. Attended Pacific Col., Neighborhood Playhouse. Bdwy debut 1948 in "Private Lives," followed by "Out West of Eighth," "Peter Pan," "I Am a Camera," "Bus Stop," "Camino Real," "Frogs of Spring," "Oh, Men! Oh, Women!," "Flowering Peach," "Period of Adjustment," "She Loves Me," "Three Sisters," "Plaza Suite," "Me Jack, You Jill," "Best Friend," OB in "Brecht on Brecht," "Measure for Measure," "To Be Young, Gifted and Black," "Oh, Pioneers."

BEACHNER, LOUIS. Born June 9, 1923 in Jersey City, NJ. Bdwy bow 1942 in "Junior Miss," followed by "No Time for Sergeants," "Georgy," "The Changing Room," "National Health," "Where's Charley?," OB in "Time to Burn," "The Hostage," "Savages."

BEAN, REATHEL. Born Aug. 24, 1942 in Missouri. Graduate Drake U. OB in "America Hurrah," "San Francisco's Burning," "The Love Cure," "Henry IV," "In Circles," "Peace," "Journey of Snow White," "Wanted," "The Faggot," "Lovers," "Not Back with the Elephants."

BEARD, BETSY. Born Nov. 9, 1949 in Tulsa, OK. Graduate Tulsa U. Bdwy debut 1975 in "Shenandoah," followed by "Equus," OB in "Polly," "Antigone."

BEDFORD, BRIAN. Born Feb. 16, 1935 in Morley, Eng. Attended RADA. Bwdy bow 1960 in "Five Finger Exercise," followed by "Lord Pengo," "The Private Ear," "The Knack" (OB). "The Astrakhan Coat," "The Unknown Soldier and His Wife," "Seven Descents of Myrtle," "Jumpers," with APA in "Misanthrope," "Cocktail Party," and "Hamlet," "Private Lives," "School for Wives."

BEDFORD, PATRICK. Born May 30, 1932 in Dublin IR. Appeared with Dublin Gate Theatre before Bdwy bow 1966 in "Philadelphia Here I Come," followed by "The Mundy Scheme," "Small Craft Warnings" (OB), "Equus."

BELACK, DORIS. Born Feb. 26 in NYC. Attended AADA. Debut OB 1956 in "World of Sholom Aleichem," followed by "P.S. 193," Bdwy in "Middle of the Night," "The Owl and the Pussycat," "The Heroine," "You Know I Can't Hear You When the Water's Running," "90 Day Mistress," "Last of the Red Hot Lovers," "Bad Habits," "The Trip Back Down."

BELL, GLYNIS. Born July 30, 1947 in London. Attended Oakland U., AADA. Debut 1975 OB in "The Devils," followed by "The Time of Your Life," "The Robber Bridegroom," "Three Sisters."

BELL, JOAN. Born Feb. 1, 1935 in Bombay, Ind. Studied at Sylvia Bryant Stage Sch. Bdwy debut 1963 in "Something More," followed by "Applause," "Chicago."

BELLOMO, JOE. Born Apr. 12, 1938 in NYC. Attended Manhattan Sch. of Music. Bdwy bow 1960 in "New Girl in Town," followed by CC's "South Pacific" and "Guys and Dolls," OB in "Cindy," "Fantasticks."

BENNETT, MEG. Born Oct. 4, 1948 in Los Angeles, CA. Graduate Northwestern U. Debut OB 1971 in "Godspell," on Bdwy 1972 in "Grease."

BENSON, JON PETER. Born Oct. 9 In Mentor, OH. Graduate Principia Col., LAMDA. Debut OB 1976 in "The Prince of Homburg."

| Joanne Beretta | David Berk | Kathleen Betsko | Bill Biskup | Leila Blake |

BERETTA, JOANNE. Born Nov. 14 in San Francisco, CA. Attended San Francisco State Col. Debut 1976 OB in "The Club."

BEREZIN, TANYA. Born Mar. 25, 1941 in Philadelphia, Pa. Attended Boston U. Debut OB 1967 in "The Sandcastle," followed by "Three Sisters," "Great Nebula in Orion," "him," "Amazing Activity of Charlie Contrare," "Battle of Angels," "Mound Builders," "Serenading Louie," "My Life."

BERGER, SUSAN. Born Sept. 20, 1943 in Buffalo, NY. Graduate UGa., UHawaii. Debut OB 1972 in "Masquerade," followed by Bdwy 1976 in "The Robber Bridegroom."

BERK, DAVID. Born July 20, 1932 in NYC. Graduate Manhattan Sch. of Music. Debut OB 1958 in "Eloise," followed by "Carnival" (CC). "So Long 174th Street," "Wonderful Town" (ELT).

BERRY, ERIC. Born Jan. 9, 1913 in London. Graduate RADA. NY debut 1954 in "The Boy Friend," followed by "Family Reunion," "The Power and the Glory," "Beaux Stratagem," "Broken Jug," "Pictures in the Hallway," "Peer Gynt," "Great God Brown," "Henry IV," "The White House," "White Devil," "Charley's Aunt," "The Homecoming" (OB), "Capt. Brassbound's Conversion," "Pippin."

BETHENCOURT, FRANCIS. Born Sept. 5, 1924 in London. Attended Mayfield Col. Bdwy debut 1948 in "Anne of the Thousand Days," followed by "Happy Times," "Dial 'M' for Murder," "Visit to a Small Planet," "Ross," "Right Honourable Gentleman," "Borstal Boy," "Dirty Linen," OB in "Hamp," "Pygmalion."

BETSKO, KATHLEEN. Born May 6, 1939 in Conventry, Eng. Graduate UNH. Bdwy debut 1976 in "Equus," OB in "Ring Round the Moon," "A Slight Ache."

BEVERLEY, TRAZANA. Born Aug. 9, 1945 in Baltimore, MD. Graduate NYU. Debut 1969 OB in "Rules for Running Trains," followed by "Les Femmes Noires," "Geronamo," Bdwy in "My Sister, My Sister," "For Colored Girls Who Have Considered Suicide When the Rainbow Is Enuf" for which she received a Theatre World Award.

BINDIGER, EMILY. Born May 10, 1955 in Brooklyn, NY. Graduate HS Performing Arts. Debut 1973 OB in "Sisters of Mercy," Bdwy 1977 in "Shenandoah."

BIRNEY, REED. Born Sept. 11, 1954 in Alexandria, Va. Attended Boston U. Bdwy debut 1977 in "Gemini."

BISHOP, KELLY (formerly Carole) Born Feb. 28, 1944 in Colorado Springs, CO. Bdwy debut 1967 in "Golden Rainbow," followed by "Promises, Promises," "On The Town," "Rachel Lily Rosenbloom," "A Chorus Line."

BISKUP, BILL. Born Dec. 11, in Springfield, MA. Graduate Ithaca Col. Debut OB 1971 in "F. Jasmine Addams," followed by "Fiorello!" (ELT), Bdwy 1974 in "In Praise of Love."

BITTNER, JACK. Born in Omaha, NE. Graduate UNeb. Has appeared OB in "Nathan the Wise," "Land of Fame," "Beggar's Holiday," "Rip Van Winkle," "Dear Oscar," "What Every Woman Knows," "By Bernstein," "The Philanderer."

BLAIR, PAMELA. Born Dec. 5, 1949 in Arlington, VT. Attended Ntl. Acad. of Ballet. Made Bdwy debut in 1972 in "Promises, Promises," followed by "Sugar," "Seesaw," "Of Mice and Men," "Wild and Wonderful," "A Chorus Line," OB in "Ballad of Boris K."

BLAISDELL, BRAD. Born Mar. 15, 1949 in Baltimore, MD. NY debut OB 1975 in ELT's "Tenderloin," followed by 1976 in "Going Up."

BLAKE, LEILA. Born in Southsea, Eng. Attended LAMDA, Aida Foster Sch. Bdwy debut 1977 in "Dirty Linen."

BLANTON, JEREMY. Born Dec. 31, 1939 in Memphis, TN. Attended Memphis State U. Debut OB 1975 in "Oklahoma!" (JB), Bdwy 1976 in "My Fair Lady."

BLAXILL, PETER. Born Sept. 27, 1931 in Cambridge, MA. Graduate Bard Col. Debut OB 1967 in "Scuba Duba," followed by "The Fantasticks," "The Passion of Antigona Perez," Bdwy in "Marat/de Sade," "The Littlest Circus," "The Innocents."

BLOOM, VERNA. Born Aug. 7 in Lynn, MA. Graduate Boston U. Bdwy debut 1967 in "Marat/Sade," followed by OB "Kool Aid," "The Cherry Orchard."

BLUE, JAYANT. Born Jan. 9, 1946 in Bangalore, India. Graduate Indian Inst. of Science, AADA. Bdwy debut 1976 in "Comedians."

BLUM, MARK. Born May 14, 1950 in Newark, NJ. Graduate UPa., UMinn. Debut 1976 OB in "The Cherry Orchard."

BOBBIE, WALTER. Born Nov. 18, 1945 in Scranton, Pa. Graduate UScranton, Catholic U. Bdwy bow 1971 in "Frank Merriwell," followed by "Grass Harp," "Grease," "Drat!" (OB), "Tricks," "Going Up."

BODIN, DUANE. Born Dec. 31, 1932 in Duluth MN. Bdwy debut 1961 in "Bye Bye Birdie," followed by "La Plume de Ma Tante," "Here's Love," "Fiddler on the roof," "1776," "Fiddler on the Roof" (1976).

BOND, RALEIGH. Born July 20, 1935 in Chicago, IL. Graduate Northwestern U. Debut 1961 OB in "Donogoo," followed by "Abe Lincoln in Illinois," "Evenings with Chekhov," "Red Roses for Me," "Taming of the Shrew," "Shortchanged Review," "Beaux Stratagem," Bdwy 1977 in "Sly Fox."

BOND, RUDY. Born Oct. 1, 1915 in Philadelphia, PA. Attended UPa. Bdwy in "Streetcar Named Desire," "Bird Cage," "Two Blind Mice," "Romeo and Juliet," "Glad Tidings," "Golden Boy," "Fiorello!," "Illya Darling," "Night Watch," OB in "O'Daniel," LCRep's "After the Fall," and "Incident at Vichy," "Big Man," "Match-Play," "Papp," "12 Angry Men," "The Birds," "Joan of Lorraine," "Bread," "Armenians," "Dream of a Blacklisted Actor," "From the Memoirs of Pontius Pilate."

BOOCKVOR, STEVE. Born Nov. 18, 1942 in NYC. Attended Queens Col., Juilliard. Bdwy debut 1966 in "Anya," followed by "A Time for Singing," "Cabaret," "Mardi Gras," "Jimmy," "Billy," "The Rothchilds," "Follies," "Over Here," "The Lieutenant," "Musical Jubilee," "Annie."

BOOTH, ERIC. Born Oct. 18, 1950 in NYC. Graduate Emerson Col., Stanford U. Bdwy debut 1977 in "Caesar and Cleopatra."

BORDO, ED. Born Mar. 3, 1931 in Cleveland, OH. Graduate Allegheny Col., LAMDA. Bdwy bow 1964 in "The Last Analysis," followed by "Inquest," "Zalmen or the Madness of God," "Annie," OB in "The Dragon," "Waiting for Godot," "Saved."

BORRELLI, JIM. Born Apr. 10, 1948 in Lawrence, MA. Graduate Boston Col. NY Debut OB 1971 in "Subject to Fits," followed by "Grease."

BOSCO, PHILIP. Born Sept. 26, 1930 in Jersey City, NJ. Graduate Catholic U. Credits: "Auntie Mame," "Rape of the Belt," "Ticket of Leave Man" (OB), "Donnybrook," "Man for All Seasons," "Mrs. Warren's Profession," with LCRep in "The Alchemist," "East Wind," "Galileo," "St. Joan," "Tiger at the Gate," "Cyrano," "King Lear," "A Great Career," "In the Matter of J. Robert Oppenheimer," "The Miser," "The Time of Your Life," "Camino Real," "Operation Sidewinder," "Amphitryon," "Enemy of the People," "Playboy of the Western World," "Good Woman of Setzuan," "Antigone," "Mary Stuart," "Narrow Road to the Deep North," "The Crucible," "Twelfth Night," "Enemies," "Plough and the Stars," "Merchant of Venice," and "A Streetcar Nemed Desire," "Henry V," "Threepenny Opera," "Streamers."

BOSTWICK, BARRY. Born Feb. 24, 1945 in San Mateo, CA. Graduate Cal-Western, NYU. Bdwy debut with APA in "War and Peace," followed by "Pantagleize," "Misanthrope," "Cock-a-Doodle Dandy," "Hamlet," "Grease," "The Robber Bridegroom," "She Loves Me," OB in "Salvation," "Colette," "Soon," "Screens," "They Knew What They Wanted."

BOVA, JOSEPH. Born May 25, in Cleveland, OH. Graduate Northwestern U. Debut OB 1959 in "On the Town," followed by "Once upon a Mattress," "House of Blue Leaves," "Comedy," "The Beauty Part," "NYSF's "Taming of the Shrew," "Richard III," "Comedy of Errors," "Invitation to a Beheading," "Merry Wives of Windsor," "Henry V," "Streamers," Bdwy in "Rape of the Belt," "Irma La Douce," "Hot Spot," "The Chinese," "American Millionaire."

BRADLEY, HENRY. Born Nov. 23, 1931 in Albany, NY. Attended AmTh-Wing, Black Theatre Workshop. Debut OB 1977 in "On-the Lock-In."

BRAHA, HERBERT. (formerly Herb Simon) Born Sept. 18, 1946 in Hyannis, MA. Attended Carnegie Tech. Debut 1971 OB in "Godspell," followed by "The Shortchanged Review," "Soft Touch."

BRAND, GIBBY. Born May 20, 1946 in NYC. Graduate Ithaca Col. Debut OB 1977 in "The Castaways."

BREMSETH, LLOYD. Born July 27, 1948 in Minneapolis, MN. Attended UMinn. Debut OB 1968 in "Kiss Rock," followed by "Klara," "Sweet Shoppe Myriam," "Kiss Now," "Godspell."

BRENNAN, MAUREEN. Born Oct. 11, 1952 in Washington, DC. Attended UCincinnati. Bdwy debut 1974 in "Candide" for which she received a Theatre World Award, followed by "Going Up," "Knickerbocker Holiday."

BREWER-MOORE, CATHY. Born Jan. 9, 1948 in Brunswick, GA. Attended New School, AADA. Bdwy debut 1973 in "Seesaw," followed by "Wonderful Town" (ELT).

BRILL, FRAN. Born Sept. 30, 1946 in Pa. Attended Boston U. Bdwy debut 1969 in "Red, White and Maddox," OB in "What Every Woman Knows," "Scribes."

BRISEBOIS, DANIELLE. Born June 28, 1969 in Brooklyn, NY. Bdwy debut 1977 in "Annie."

BRISTOL, ALYSON. Born Sept. 26, 1952 in Garden City, NY. Graduate UCincinnati. Bdwy debut 1976 in "My Fair Lady," followed by "Knickerbocker Holiday."

BROCKSMITH, ROY. Born Sept. 15, 1945 in Quincy, IL. Debut OB 1971 in "Whip Lady," followed by "The Workout," "Beggar's Opera," "Polly," "Threepenny Opera," Bdwy 1975 in "The Leaf People."

BROOK, PAMELA. Born Jan. 21, 1947 in London, Ont., Can. Graduate UToronto, UMinn. Debut OB 1976 in "The Philanderer."

BROOKE, JACOB. Born May 29, 1942 in London, Eng. Attended Loughborough Col. Bdwy debut 1977 in "Dirty Linen/New-Found-Land."

BROOKS, GERALDINE. Born Oct. 29, 1925 in NYC. Attended Neighborhood Playhouse, AADA, Actors Studio. Bdwy debut 1944 in "Follow the Girls," followed by "Winter's Tale," "Time of the Cuckoo," "Brighttower," "Fiddler on the Roof" (JB), "Jules Feiffer's Hold Me" (OB).

BROTHERSON, ERIC. Born May 10, 1911 in Chicago, IL. Attended UWisc. Bdwy debut 1937 in "Between the Devil," followed by "Set to Music," "Lady in the Dark," "My Dear Public," "Gentlemen Prefer Blondes," "Room Service," "The Hot Corner," "Musical Jubilee," "My Fair Lady," "Knickerbocker Holiday."

BROWN, CANDY A. Born Aug. 19 in San Rafael, CA. Attended MacAlester Col. Bdwy debut 1969 in "Hello, Dolly," followed by "Purlie," "Pippin," "Chicago."

BROWN, GRAHAM. Born Oct. 24, 1924 in NYC. Graduate Howard U. OB in "Widower's Houses," "The Emperor's Clothes," "Time of Storm," "Major Barbara," "Land Beyond the River," "The Blacks," "Firebugs," "God Is a (Guess What?)," "An Evening of One Acts," "Man Better Man," "Behold! Cometh the Vanderkellans," "Ride a Black Horse," "Great MacDaddy," "Eden," on Bdwy in "Weekend," "Man in the Glass Booth," "The River Niger," "Pericles," "Black Picture Show" (LC), "Kings."

BROWN, GWENDOLYN. (formerly Gwen Saska) Born Sept. 9, 1939 in Mishawaka, IN. Northwestern and Columbia graduate. Debut 1969 OB in "Geese," followed by "Macbeth," "In the Boom Boom Room," "Secret Service," "Boy Meets Girl," Bdwy 1977 in "The Trip Back Down."

BROWN, KERMIT. Born Feb. 3, 1937 in Asheville, NC. Graduate Duke U. With APA in "War and Peace," "Judith," "Man and Superman," "The Show-Off," "Pantagleize," "The Cherry Orchard," OB in "The Millionairess," "Things," "Lulu," "Heartbreak House" (ELT).

BRUCE, SHELLEY. Born May 5, 1965 in Passaic, NJ. Debut OB 1973 in "The Children's Mass," Bdwy 1977 in "Annie."

BRUMMEL, DAVID. Born Nov. 1, 1942 in Brooklyn. Bdwy debut 1973 in "The Pajama Game," followed by "Music Is," OB in "Cole Porter," "Fantasticks."

BRUNEAU, RALPH. Born Sept. 22, 1952 in Phoenix, AZ. Graduate UNotre Dame. Debut 1974 OB in "The Fantasticks," followed by "Saints."

BRYANT, DAVID. Born May 26, 1936 in Nashville, TN. Attended TN State U. Bdwy debut 1972 in "Don't Play us Cheap," followed by "Bubbling Brown Sugar."

BRYGGMAN, LARRY. Born Dec. 21, 1938 in Concord, CA. Attended CCSF, AmThWing. Debut 1962 OB in "A Pair of Pairs," followed by "Live like Pigs," "Stop, You're Killing Me," "Mod Donna," "Waiting for Godot," "Ballymurphy," "Marco Polo Sings a Solo," "Brownsville Raid," Bdwy in "Ulysses in Nighttown," "Checking Out," "Basic Training of Pavlo Hummel."

BRYNNER, YUL. Born June 15, 1915 in Sakhalin Island, Japan. Bdwy debut 1946 in "Lute Song," followed by "The King and I," (also 1977 revival), "Home Sweet Homer."

BUCKLEY, BETTY. Born July 3, 1947 in Big Spring, TX. Graduate TCU. Bdwy debut 1969 in "1776," followed by "Pippin," OB in "Ballad of Johnny Pot," "What's a Nice Country Like You Doing in a State Like This?," "Circle of Sound."

BULFAIR, BLAISE. Born Feb. 17, 1959 in NYC. Debut 1975 in "A Midsummer Night's Dream," followed by "Joe Egg," Bdwy 1977 in "The Trip Back Down."

BULOS, YUSEF. Born Sept. 14, 1940 in Jerusalem. Attended Beirut Am.U., AADA. Debut OB 1965 with American Savoyards in repertory, followed by "Saints," Bdwy in "Indians," "Capt. Brassbound's Conversion."

BURGE, JAMES. Born Dec. 3, 1943 in Miami, FL. Graduate U Okla., Wayne State U. Bdwy bow 1970 in "Grin and Bare It," followed by "The Royal Family."

BURGOS, ROBERT. Born Sept. 30, 1942 in NYC. Attended AADA. Debut OB 1960 in "Dead End," followed by "Hamlet," " 'Tis Pity She's a Whore," "Banquet for the Moon," "Fair of Opinion," "Jack Gelber's New Play."

BURK, TERENCE. Born Aug. 11, 1947 in Lebanon, IL. Graduate S.IL.U. OB in "Religion," "The Future," "Sacred and Profane Love," Bdwy debut 1976 in "Equus."

BURNELL, PETER. Born Apr. 29, 1950 in Johnstown, NY. OB in "Henry IV," "Antony and Cleopatra," "The Tempest," "Macbeth," "Olathe Response," "Ubu Roi/Ubu Bound," "Dancing for the Kaiser," "The Prince of Homburg," Bdwy debut 1974 in "In Praise of Love" for which he received a Theatre World Award.

BURSTYN, ELLEN. Born Dec. 7, 1932 in Detroit, MI. Attended Actors Studio. Bdwy debut 1957 (as Ellen McRae) in "Fair Game," followed by "Same Time, Next Year," BAM Co.'s "Three Sisters."

BUTURLA, STAN. Born Aug. 17, 1948 in Brooklyn, NY. Graduate Hofstra U. Debut 1977 OB in "Twelfth Night" (ELT).

BYERS, CATHERINE. Born Oct. 7 in Sioux City, IA. Graduate UIowa, LAMDA, Bdwy debut 1971 in "The Philanthropist," followed by "Don't Call Back," "Equus," OB in "Petrified Forest," "All My Sons."

BYRDE, EDYE. Born Jan. 19, 1929 in NYC. Bdwy debut 1975 in "The Wiz."

CALLAN, CHRISTOPHER. Born July 14, 1944 in Fresno, CA. Graduate San Francisco State Col. Debut 1968 in CC's "Brigadoon," followed by Bdwy in "I'm Solomon," "1776," "Desert Song," "Over Here," "Rodgers and Hart," "Fiddler on the Roof" (1977).

CAMPO, ROGER. Born June 18, 1963 in NYC. Attended HB Studio. Bdwy debut 1977 in "Caesar and Cleopatra."

CANNING, JAMES J. Born July 2, 1946 in Chicago, IL. Graduate DePaul U. Debut 1972 in "Grease."

CAPERS, VIRGINIA. Born Sept. 22, 1925 in Sumter, SC. Attended Juilliard. Bdwy debut 1973 in "Raisin."

CAREW, PETER. Born Nov. 8, 1922 in Old Forge, PA. Graduate NYU. Debut OB 1948 in "Coffee House," followed by "Street Scene," "Ah, Wilderness," "Antigone," "Waiting for Lefty," "12 Angry Men," "Falling from Heaven," "Go Show me a Dragon," "A Stage Affair," "King of the Whole Damn World," "Purple Canary," "Kiss Mama," "A View from the Bridge," "He Who Gets Slapped," "Istanbul," "Great White Hope" (Bdwy 1969), "Thunder Rock," "Monsters."

CARIOU, LEN. Born Sept. 30, 1939 in Winnipeg, Can. Bdwy debut 1968 in "House of Atreus," followed by "Henry V" and "Applause" for which he received a Theatre World Award, "Night Watch," "A Little Night Music," OB in "A Sorrow beyond Dreams."

CARLIN, CHET. Born Feb. 23, 1940 in Malverne, NY. Graduate Ithaca Col., Catholic U. Bdwy bow 1972 in "An Evening with Richard Nixon and . . . ," OB in "Under Gaslight," "Lou Gehrig Did not Die of Cancer," "Graffiti!," "Crystal and Fox," "Golden Honeymoon," "Arms and the Man," "Arsenic and Old Lace" (ELT).

CARLING, P. L. Born Mar. 31. Graduate Stanford U., UCLA. Debut 1955 OB in "The Chairs," followed by "In Good King Charles' Golden Days," "Magistrate," "Picture of Dorian Gray," "The Vise," "Lady from the Sea," "Booth Is Back in Town," "Ring Round the Moon," "Philadelphia, Here I Come," "Sorrows of Frederick," Bdwy in "The Devils" (1965), "Scratch," "Shenandoah."

CARLSEN, ALLAN. Born Feb. 7 in Chicago, IL. Attended UPa. Bdwy debut 1974 in "The Freedom of the City," OB in "The Morning after Optimism," "Iphigenia in Aulis," "Peg O' My Heart."

CARLSON, DEBORAH. Born Dec. 21, 1952 in Bridgeport, CT. Graduate UConn. Debut OB 1977 in "Movie Buff."

CARNEY, GRACE. Born Sept. 15, 1911 in Harford, CT. Attended Columbia U, CCNY. Debut OB 1959 in "A Family Portrait," followed by "Billygoat Eddie," "Whitsuntide," Bdwy in "Donnybrook," "Eccentricites of a Nightingale," "Vieux Carre."

CARROLL, DAVID-JAMES. Born July 30, 1950 in Rockville Centre, NY. Graduate Dartmouth Col. Debut 1975 in "A Matter of Time," followed by "Joseph and the Amazing Technicolor Dreamcoat," Bdwy "Rodgers and Hart" (1975), "Where's Charley?"

CARRUTHERS, JAMES. Born May 26, 1931 in Morristown, NJ. Attended Lafayette Col., HB Studio. Debut 1959 OB in "Our Town," followed by "Under the Sycamore Tree," "Misalliance," "The Hostage," "Telemachus Clay," "Shadow of a Gunman," "Masks," "Lulu," Bdwy 1976 in "Poor Murderer."

CARTER, DIXIE. Born May 25, 1939 in McLemoresville, TN. Graduate Memphis State U. Debut 1963 OB in "The Winter's Tale," followed by LC's "Carousel," "Merry Widow," "The King and I," "Sextet," "Jesse and the Bandit Queen" for which she received a Theatre World Award, Bdwy 1976 in "Pal Joey."

CARVER, MARY. Born May 3, 1924 in Los Angeles, CA. Graduate USC. Debut 1950 OB in "Bury the Dead," followed by "Rhinoceros," Bdwy in "Out West of 8th," "Low and Behold," "The Shadow Box."

CASSIDY, TIM. Born Mar. 22, 1952 in Alliance, OH. Attended UCincinnati. Bdwy debut 1974 in "Good News," followed by "A Chorus Line."

CAUSEY, CLAY. Born Dec. 26, 1948 in Atlanta, GA. Graduate UGa. Bdwy debut 1977 in "Knickerbocker Holiday."

CELLARIO, MARIA. Born June 19, 1948 in Buenos Aires, Arg. Graduate Ithaca Col. Bdwy debut 1975 in "The Royal Family."

 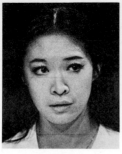   

| Peter Burnell | Tisa Chang | Walter Charles | Nora Cole | Jerome Collamore |

CHALFANT, KATHLEEN. Born Jan. 14, 1945 in San Francisco, CA. Graduate Stanford U. Bdwy debut 1975 in "Dance With Me," followed by "Jules Feiffer's Hold Me" (OB).

CHAMBERLAIN, RICHARD. Born Mar. 31, 1935 in Beverly Hills, CA. Attended Pomona Col. Bdwy debut 1976 in "Night of the Iguana."

CHANG, TISA. Born Apr. 5 in Chungking, CH. Attended CCNY. Bdwy debut 1970 in "Lovely Ladies, Kind Gentlemen," followed by "Brother" (OB), "Basic Training of Pavlo Hummel."

CHANNING, CAROL. Born Jan. 31, 1921 in Seattle, Wash. Attended Bennington Col. Bdwy debut 1941 in "No for an Answer," followed by "Let's Face It," "Proof Through the Night," "Lend an Ear" for which she received a Theatre World Award, "Gentlemen Prefer Blondes," "Wonderful Town," "The Vamp," "Show Girl," "Hello Dolly!," "Four on a Garden," "Lorelei."

CHAPMAN, ROGER. Born Jan. 1, 1947 in Cheverly, MD. Graduate Rollins Col. Debut 1976 OB in "Who Killed Richard Cory?," followed by "My Life."

CHAPMAN, WILLIAM. Born Apr. 30, 1923 in Los Angeles, CA. Attended USCal. On Bdwy in "Candide," "Maria Golovin," "Greenwillow," "South Pacific" (CC 1961), "Shenandoah."

CHARLES, PAUL. Born July 29, 1947 in NYC. Attended Quintano Sch. Has appeared in "Best Foot Forward" (OB), "Kelly," "Royal Hunt of the Sun," "A Joyful Noise," "La Strada," "A Chorus Line."

CHARLES, WALTER. Born Apr. 4, 1945 in East Stroudsburg, PA. Graduate Boston U. Bdwy debut 1973 in "Grease," followed by "1600 Pennsylvania Avenue," "Knickerbocker Holiday."

CHARNEY, DIDI. Born Aug. 1, 1951 in NYC. Graduate Carleton Col. Debut OB 1976 in "Heartbreak House," followed by "Twelfth Night" (ELT), "My Life."

CHARTOFF, MELANIE. Born Dec. 15, 1948 in New Haven, CT. Graduate Adelphi U. Debut OB 1971 in "The Proposition," followed by "Do I Hear a Waltz?," "Via Galactica" (Bdwy 1972), "Love Song."

CHINN, LORI. Born July 7 in Seattle, WA. Bdwy debut 1970 in "Lovely Ladies, Kind Gentlemen," OB in "Coffins for Butterflies," "Hough in Blazes," "Peer Gynt," "King and I," "Children," "Secret Life of Walter Mitty," "Bayou Legend," "The Primary English Class," "G. R. Point."

CHODER, JILL. Born Dec. 14, 1948 in Pittsburg, PA. Attended NYU. Bdwy debut 1962 in "Bye Bye Birdie," followed by "Stop the World. . . .," "The Roar of the Greasepaint," OB in "Best Foot Forward," "Your Own Thing," "Boccaccio."

CHRIS, MARILYN. Born May 19 in NYC. Attended CCNY. Appeared in "The Office," "Birthday Party," "7 Descents of Myrtle," "Lenny," OB in "Nobody Hears a Broken Drum," "Fame," "Judas Applause," "Junebug Graduates Tonight," "Man Is Man," "In the Jungle of Cities," "Good Soldier Schweik," "The Tempest," "Ride a Black Horse," "Screens," "Kaddish," "Lady from the Sea," "Bread," "Leaving Home," "Curtains."

CHRISMAN, CAROLYN. Born in NYC. Has appeared OB in "Games," "Fantastic Gardens," "Home Again," "Something for Kitty Genovese," "Greenwillow," "Dinner at the Ambassador's," "The Boy Friend," "Man's Estate," "Play Me, Zoltan."

CHRISTIAN, ROBERT. Born Dec. 27, 1939 in Los Angeles. Attended UCLA. OB in "The Happening," "Hornblend," "Fortune and Men's Eyes," "Boys in Band," "Behold! Cometh the Vanderkellans," "Mary Stuart," "Narrow Road to the Deep North," "Twelfth Night," "The Past Is the Past," "Going through Changes," "Black Sunlight," "Terraces," "Blood Knot," "Boesman and Lena," Bdwy in "We Bombed in New Haven," "Does a Tiger Wear a Necktie?," "An Evening with Richard Nixon," "All God's Chillun."

CHRISTOPHER, THOM. Born Oct. 5, 1940 in Jackson Heights, NY. Attended Ithaca Col., Neighborhood Playhouse. Debut 1972 in "One Flew over the Cuckoo's Nest," Bdwy bow 1973 in "Emperor Henry IV," followed by "Noel Coward in Two Keys" for which he received a Theatre World Award, "Caesar and Cleopatra."

CILENTO, WAYNE. Born Aug. 25, 1949, in The Bronx, NY. Graduate State U. Brockport. Bdwy in "Irene," "Rachel Lily Rosenbloom," "Seesaw," "A Chorus Line."

CISSEL, CHUCK. Born Oct. 3, 1948, in Tulsa, OK. Graduate UOkla. Bdwy debut 1971 in "Purlie," followed by "Lost in the Stars," "Via Galactica," "Don't Bother Me, I Can't Cope," "A Chorus Line."

CLAIRE, LUDI. Born Apr. 15 in Indiana. Attended Ecole Intn'l. Appeared in "The Small Hours," "Gramercy Ghost," "Tower Beyond Tragedy," "Venus Observed," "Someone Waiting," "Legend of Lovers," "Silk Stockings," "First Gentleman," "Country Wife," "Duel of Angels," "Hamlet," "Prisoner of Second Avenue."

CLANTON, RALPH. Born Sept. 11, 1914 in Fresno, CA. Attended Pasadena Playhouse. On Bdwy in "Victory Belles," "Macbeth," "Richard III," "Othello," "Lute Song," "Cyrano," "Antony and Cleopatra," "Design for a Stained Glass Window," "Taming of the Shrew," "Burning Glass," "Vivat! Vivat Reginal," "The Last of Mrs. Lincoln," OB in "Ceremony of Innocence," "Endecott and the Red Cross," "The Philanderer," BAM Co.'s "New York Idea," and "Three Sisters."

CLARK, CHERYL. Born Dec. 7, 1950 in Boston, MA. Attended Ind.U., NYU. Bdwy debut 1972 in "Pippin," followed by "Chicago," "A Chorus Line."

CLARKSON, JOHN. Born Jan. 19, 1932 in London. Graduate Oxford U. NY debut OB 1971 in "Murderous Angels," followed by "An Evening with Ma Bell," "Staircase," Bdwy in "No Sex Please, We're British" (1973), "My Fair Lady."

CLEMENTE, RENE. Born July 2, 1950 in El Paso, TX. Graduate West Tex. State U. Bdwy debut 1977 in "A Chorus Line."

CLOSE, GLENN. Born May 19, 1947 in Greenwich, CT. Graduate William & Mary Col. Bdwy debut 1974 with Phoenix Co. in "Love for Love," "Member of the Wedding," and "Rules of the Game," followed by "Rex," OB in "The Crazy Locomotive."

COCO, JAMES. Born Mar. 21, 1930 in NYC. Debut OB 1956 in "Salome," followed by "Moon in the Yellow River," "Squat Betty/The Sponge Room," "That 5 A.M. Jazz," "Lovey," "The Basement," "Fragments," "Witness," "Next," "Monsters" (The Transfiguration of Benno Blimpie), Bdwy in "Hotel Paradiso," "Everybody Loves Opal," "Passage to India," "Arturo Ui," "The Devils," "The Man of La Mancha," "The Astrakhan Coat," "Here's Where I Belong," "Last of the Red Hot Lovers."

COE, JOHN. Born Oct. 19, 1925 in Hartford CT. Graduate Boston U. On Bdwy in "Passion of Josef D," "Man in the Glass Booth," "La Strada," "Happy End," OB in "Marrying Maiden," "Thistle in My Bed," "John," "Wicked Cooks," "June Bug Graduates Tonight," "Drums in the Night," "America Hurrah," "Father Uxbridge Wants to Marry," "Nobody Hears a Broken Drum," "Dylan," "Screens," "The Kid."

COEN, DANA. Born Oct. 16, 1946 in Leominster, MA. Graduate Boston U. Debut 1971 OB in "Touch," followed by Light Opera of Manhattan, "As You Like It," "In the Boom Boom Room," "Boys from Syracuse."

COGGIN, BARBARA. Born Feb. 27 in Chattanooga, TN. Attended Peabody Col. Bdwy debut 1970 in "Lovely Ladies, Kind Gentlemen," followed by "Poor Murderer," OB in "The Drunkard," "One for the Money, etc.," "Judy: A Garland of Songs," "Rag Doll," "Museum."

COHEN, MARGERY. Born June 24, 1947 in Chicago, IL. Attended UWisc, UChicago. Bdwy debut 1968 in "Fiddler on the Roof," followed by "Jacques Brel Is Alive. . . .," OB in "Berlin to Broadway," "By Bernstein," "Starting Here Starting Now."

COHEN, MARK. Born Apr. 2, 1949 in Boston, MA. Graduate Yale U, London's Guildhall Sch. Debut 1977 OB in "The Days of the Turbins," Bdwy 1977 in "Romeo and Juliet."

COLE, KAY. Born Jan. 13, 1948 in Miami, Fl. Bdwy debut 1961 in "Bye Bye Birdie," followed by "Stop the World I Want to Get Off," "Roar of the Greasepaint . . . ," "Hair," "Jesus Christ Superstar," "Words and Music," "Chorus Line," OB in "The Cradle Will Rock," "Two if by Sea," "Rainbow," "White Nights," "Sgt. Pepper's Lonely Hearts Club Band."

COLE, NORA. Born Sept. 10, 1953 in Louisville, KY. Attended Beloit Col, Goodman Sch. of Drama. Debut 1977 OB in "Movie Buff."

COLES, ZAIDA. Born Sept. 10, 1933 in Lynchburg, VA. Credits OB: "The Father," "Pins and Needles," "Life and Times of J. Walter Smintheus," "The Cherry Orchard," "Bayou Legend," "Divine Comedy," on Bdwy in "Weekend," "Zelda."

COLLAMORE, JEROME. Born Sept. 25, 1891 in Boston, MA. Debut 1918 with Washington Square Players in "Salome," subsequently in, among others, "Christopher Bean," "Hamlet," "Romeo and Juliet," "Kind Lady," "Androcles and the Lion," "George Washington Slept Here," "The Would-Be Gentleman," "Cheri," "Abraham Cochran," "That Hat," BAM Co.'s "New York Idea."

| Suzanne Collins | Robert Colson | Murphy Cross | Darryl Croxton | Deborah Crowe |

COLLINS, STEPHEN. Born Oct. 1, 1947 in Des Moines, IO. Graduate Amherst Col. Bdwy debut 1972 in "Moonchildren," followed by "No Sex Please, We're British," "The Ritz," OB in "Twelfth Night," "More Than You Deserve," "Macbeth" (LC), "Last Days of British Honduras," BAM Co.'s "New York Idea" and "Three Sisters."

COLLINS, SUZANNE. Born in San Francisco, CA. Graduate USan Francisco. Debut 1975 OB in "Trelawny of the Wells," followed by "The Cherry Orchard."

COLSON, ROBERT. Born May 7 in Jefferson, OH. Graduate Western Reserve U. Debut 1963 OB in "The Importance of Being Earnest," followed by "Awakening of Spring," Bdwy 1977 in "Vieux Carre."

COLYER, AUSTIN. Born Oct. 29, 1935 in Brooklyn, NY. Attended SMU. Has appeared in "Darwin's Theories," "Let it Ride," "Maggie Flynn," CC revivals of "Brigadoon," "Music Man," and "How to Succeed in Business . . . ," "Show Me Where the Good Times Are" (OB), "Jimmy," "Desert Song," "Pal Joey" (1976).

COMBS, DAVID. Born June 10, 1949 in Reno, NV. Graduate UNev., Wayne State U. Bdwy debut 1975 in "Equus."

COMDEN, BETTY. Born May 3, 1919 in Brooklyn, NY. Graduate NYU. Appeared with nightclub act "The Revuers" before Bdwy debut in 1944 in "On the Town" for which she received a Theatre World Award, followed by "A Party with Betty Comden and Adolph Green" (OB) which was revived in 1977 on Bdwy.

CONAWAY, JEFF. Born Oct. 5, 1950 in NYC. Attended NYU. Bdwy debut 1960 in "All the Way Home," followed by "Grease."

CONNELL, GORDON. Born Mar. 19, 1923 in Berkeley, CA. Graduate UCal., NYU. Bdwy bow 1961 in "Subways Are for Sleeping," followed by "Hello, Dolly!," "Lysistrata," OB in "Beggar's Opera."

CONNELLY, R. BRUCE. Born Aug. 22, 1949 in Meriden, CT. Graduate S. Conn. State Col. Debut 1975 OB in "Godspell."

CONNOLLY, GEORGE DAVID. Born Oct. 26, 1944 in Boston, MA. Bdwy debut 1968 in "The Happy Time," followed by "Borstal Boy," "The Last of Mrs. Lincoln," "She Loves Me," OB in "Up Eden," BAM Co.'s "New York Idea."

CONRIED, HANS. Born in 1917 in Baltimore, MD. Attended Columbia U. Bdwy debut 1953 in "Can-Can," followed by "Tall Story," "70 Girls 70," "Irene," "Something Old Something New."

CONROY, JARLATH. Born Sept. 30, 1944 in Galway, IR. Attended RADA. Bdwy debut 1976 in "Comedians."

COOK, JAMES. Born Mar. 7, 1937 in NYC. Attended AADA. OB in "The Fantasticks," "Goa," "Cyrano," "A Cry of Players," "King Lear," "Playboy of the Western World," "Good Woman of Setzuan," "Enemy of the People," "In the Matter of J. Robert Oppenheimer," "The Architect and the Emperor," "Arsenic and Old Lace," Bdwy in "Great White Hope," "Wrong Way Light Bulb."

COOLEY, DENNIS. Born May 11, 1948 in Huntington Park, Ca. Attended Northwestern U. Bdwy debut 1970 in "Hair," followed by "Jesus Christ Superstar," "Creation of the World and Other Business," "Where's Charley?," "Shenandoah."

COOTE, ROBERT. Born Feb. 4, 1909 in London. Bdwy debut 1953 in "The Love of Four Colonels," followed by "Dear Charles," "My Fair Lady" (1956, 1976), "Jockey Club Stakes."

COPELAND, JOAN. Born June 1, 1922 in NYC. Attended Bklyn Col., AADA. Debut 1945. OB in "Romeo and Juliet," followed by "Othello," "Conversation Piece," "Delightful Season," "End of Summer," Bdwy in "Sundown Beach," "Detective Story," "Not for Children," "Handful of Fire," "Something More," "The Price," "Two by Two," "Pal Joey," "Checking Out."

COPELAND, MAURICE. Born June 13, 1911 in Rector, AR. Graduate Pasadena Playhouse. Bdwy debut 1974 in "The Freedom of the City," followed by "Henry V" (OB).

CORMAN, PAUL A. Born Apr. 22, 1946 in Dallas, TX. Graduate Antioch Col., NYU. Debut 1976 in "Maggie Flynn," followed by "Fiddler on the Roof."

COSTEN, RUSSELL. Born May 15, 1945 in Boston, MA. Graduate St. John's U. Bdwy debut 1970 in "J. B.," OB in "Caligula," "Danton's Death," "Othello," "Birthday Party," "Three Musketeers," "Mary Tudor," "Arsenic and Old Lace."

COSTER, NICOLAS. Born Dec. 3, 1934 in London. Attended Neighborhood Playhouse. Bdwy bow 1960 in "Becket," followed by "90 Day Mistress," "But Seriously," "Twigs," "Otherwise Engaged," OB in "Epitaph for George Dillon," "Shadow and Substance," "Thracian Horses," "O, Say Can You See," "Happy Birthday, Wanda June," "Naomi Court.," "Old Glory."

COSTIGAN, KEN. Born Apr. 1, 1934 in NYC. Graduate Fordham U., Yale U. Debut 1960 OB in "Borak," followed by "King of the Dark Chamber," "The Hostage," "Next Time I'll Sing to You," "Curley McDimple," "The Runner Stumbles," "Peg o' My Heart," Bdwy 1962 in "Gideon."

COULLET, RHONDA. Born Sept. 23, 1945 in Magnolia, AR. Attended UArk., UDenver. Debut 1973 OB in "National Lampoon Lemmings," Bdwy 1976 in "The Robber Bridegroom."

COUNCIL, RICHARD. Born Oct. 1, 1947 in Tampa, Fl. Graduate UFla. Debut OB 1973 in "Merchant of Venice," followed by "Ghost Dance," "Look We've Come Through," "Arms and the Man," "Isadora Duncan Sleeps with the Russian Navy," Bdwy 1975 in "The Royal Family."

COURTENAY, TOM. Born Feb. 25, 1937 in Hull, Eng. Graduate RADA. Made Bdwy debut 1977 in "Otherwise Engaged."

COWAN, EDIE. Born Apr. 14 in NYC. Graduate Butler U. Bdwy debut 1964 in "Funny Girl," followed by "Sherry," "Annie."

CRAIG, DONALD. Born Aug. 14, 1941 in Abilene, TX. Graduate Hardin-Simmons Col., UTex. Debut 1975 OB in "Do I Hear a Waltz?" (ELT), Bdwy 1977 in "Annie."

CRAIG, JOEL. Born Apr. 26 in NYC. Attended Brandeis U. Bdwy debut 1961 in "Subways Are for Sleeping," followed by "Nowhere to Go but Up," "Hello, Dolly!," "Follies," "Out of This World" (OB), "Cyrano," "Very Good Eddie."

CRAIG, NOEL. Born Jan. 4 in St. Louis, MO. Attended Northwestern U., Goodman Theatre, London Guildhall. Bdwy debut 1967 in "Rosencrantz and Guildenstern Are Dead," followed by "A Patriot for Me," "Conduct Unbecoming," "Vivat! Vivat Regina!," "Going Up," OB in "Pygmalion," "Promenade," "Family House," "Inn at Lydda."

CRAWLEY, TOM. Born Aug. 4, 1940 in Central Falls, RI. Graduate UNeb., NYU. Debut 1970 OB in "The Persians," followed by "The Measure Taken," "Ghosts," "The Snob," "Heartbreak House."

CRESWELL, SAYLOR. Born Nov. 18, 1939 in Pottstown, PA. Graduate Brown U. Debut OB 1968 in "Carving a Statue," followed by "Room Service," "Savages," Bdwy 1976 in "Herzl."

CRISTOFER, MICHAEL. Born Jan. 22, 1945 in Trenton, NJ. Attended Catholic U. Made debut 1977 OB in "The Cherry Orchard" for which he received a Theatre World Award.

CROFOOT, LEONARD JOHN. Born Sept. 20, 1948 in Utica, NY. Bdwy debut 1968 in "The Happy Time," followed by "Come Summer," "Gigi," OB in "Circus," "Joseph and the Amazing Technicolor Dreamcoat."

CRONIN, JANE. Born Apr. 4, 1936 in Boston, MA. Attended Boston U. Bdwy debut 1965 in "Postmark Zero," OB in "Bald Soprano," "One Flew over the Cuckoo's Nest," "Hot 1 Baltimore," "The Gathering."

CROSS, MURPHY. Born June 22, 1950 in Baltimore, MD. Graduate NC School of Arts. Debut 1972 OB in "Look Me Up," Bdwy 1976 in "Bubbling Brown Sugar."

CROSSLEY, KAREN. Born May 20 in Cleveland, OH. Attended Case Western Reserve. Bdwy debut 1975 in "Very Good Eddie."

CROWE, DEBORAH L. Born Aug. 6, 1952 in Atlanta, GA. Attended Newberry Col., Ga. State. Debut 1974 OB in "Take Me Along," Bdwy 1976 in "Going Up."

CROXTON, DARRYL. Born Apr. 5, 1946 in Baltimore, MD. Attended AADA. Appeared OB in "Volpone," "Murder in the Cathedral," "The Taking of Miss Janie," "Volpone," "Old Glory," "Divine Comedy," "Jack Gelber's New Play," Bdwy debut 1969 in "Indians," followed by "Sly Fox."

CULLUM, JOHN. Born Mar. 2, 1930 in Knoxville, TN. Graduate U. Tenn. Bdwy bow 1960 in "Camelot," followed by "Infidel Caesar," "The Rehearsal," "Hamlet," "On a Clear Day You Can See Forever" for which he received a Theatre World Award, "Man of LaMancha," "1776," "Vivat! Vivat Regina!," "Shenandoah," "Kings," "The Trip Back Down," OB in "Three Hand Reel," "The Elizabethans," "Carousel," "In the Voodoo Parlor of Marie Leveau," "The King and I" (JB).

CUMMINGS, KAY. Born in NYC. Graduate Elmira Col. Debut 1976 OB in "2 by 5."

Mike Dantuono

Rebecca Darke

Lloyd Davis, Jr.

Connie Day

Kevin Lane
Dearinger

CURRY, CHRISTOPHER. Born Oct. 22, 1948, in Grand Rapids, MI. Graduate UMich. Debut 1974 OB in "When You Comin' Back, Red Ryder?" followed by "The Cherry Orchard," "Spelling Bee," "Ballymurphy," "Isadora Duncan Sleeps with the Russian Navy."

CURTIS, KEENE. Born Feb. 15, 1925 in Salt Lake City, UT. Graduate UUtah. Bdwy bow 1949 in "Shop at Sly Corner," with APA in "School for Scandal," "The Tavern," "Anatole," "Scapin," "Right You Are," "Importance of Being Earnest," "Twelfth Night," "King Lear," "Seagull," "Lower Depths," "Man and Superman," "Judith," "War and Peace," "You Can't Take It with You," "Pantagleize," "Cherry Orchard," "Misanthrope," "Cocktail Party," "Cock-a-Doodle Dandy" and "Hamlet," "A Patriot for Me," "The Rothschilds," "Night Watch," "Via Galactica," OB in "Colette," "Ride across Lake Constance."

CWIKOWSKI, BILL. Born Aug. 4, 1945 in Newark, NJ. Graduate Monmouth and Smith Cols. Debut 1972 OB in "Charlie the Chicken," followed by "Summer Brave," "Desperate Hours," "Mandragola," "Two by John Ford Noonan," "Soft Touch."

DAMON, CATHRYN. Born Sept. 11 in Seattle, WA. Bdwy debut 1954 in "By the Beautiful Sea," followed by "The Vamp," "Shinbone Alley," "A Family Affair," "Foxy," "Flora, The Red Menace," "UTBU," "Come Summer," "Criss-Crossing," "A Place for Polly," "Last of the Red Hot Lovers," OB in "Boys from Syracuse," "Secret Life of Walter Mitty," "Show Me Where The Good Times Are," "Effect of Gamma Rays on Man-in-the-Moon Marigolds," "Siamese Connections," "Prodigal," "Down by the River . . . ," "Sweet Bird of Youth," "The Cherry Orchard."

DANA, LEORA. Born Apr. 1, 1923 in NYC. Attended Barnard Col., RADA. Bdwy debut 1947 in "Madwoman of Chaillot," followed by "Happy Time," "Point of No Return," "Sabrina Fair," "Best Man," "Beekman Place," "The Last of Mrs. Lincoln," "The Women," "Mourning Pictures," OB in "In the Summer House," "Wilder's Triple Bill," "Collision Course," "Bird of Dawning Singeth All Night Long," "Increased Difficulty of Concentration," "Place without Mornings," "Rebel Women."

DANGLER, ANITA. Born Sept. 26 in NYC. Attended NYU. Bdwy debut 1956 in "Affair of Honor," followed by "The Hostage," APA's "Right You Are," "You Can't Take It with You" and "War and Peace," "Hamlet" (CP), "Cyrano," "Comedy of Errors" (CP), OB in "Trelawny of the Wells," "Isadora Duncan Sleeps with the Russian Navy."

DANIELE, GRACIELA. Born Dec. 8, 1939 in Buenos Aires. Bdwy debut 1964 in "What Makes Sammy Run?" followed by "Here's Where I Belong," "Promises, Promises," "Follies," "Chicago."

DANNER, BLYTHE. Born in Philadelphia, PA. Graduate Bard Col. Debut OB 1966 in "The Infantry," followed by "Collision Course," "Summertree," "Up Eden," "Someone's Comin' Hungry," LCRep's "Cyrano" and "The Miser" for which she received a Theatre World Award, "Twelfth Night," Bdwy 1969 in "Butterflies Are Free," BAM Co.'s "New York Idea."

DANSON, TED. Born Dec. 29, 1947 in San Diego, CA. Graduate Carnegie Tech. Debut 1972 OB in "The Real Inspector Hound," followed by "Comedy of Errors," Bdwy in "Status Quo Vadis," "Comedians."

DANTUONO, MIKE. Born July 30, 1942 in Providence, RI. Debut 1974 OB in "How to Get Rid of It," followed by "Maggie Flynn," Bdwy 1977 in "Caesar and Cleopatra."

DARKE, REBECCA. Born Dec. 6, 1935 in Brooklyn, NY. Credits: OB in "The Midnight Caller," "Who'll Save the Plowboy," "Undercover Man," "A Party for Divorce," "A Piece of Blue Sky," Bdwy 1977 in "The Basic Training of Pavlo Hummel."

DARNAY, TONI. Born Aug. 11 in Chicago, IL. Attended Northwestern U. Debut 1942 OB in "Name Your Poison," followed by "When the Bough Breaks," "Nocturne in Daylight," "The Gold Watch," "Possibilities," Bdwy 1944 in "Sadie Thompson," followed by "Affair of Honor," "Life with Father" (CC), "The Women," "Molly," "The Heiress," "Vieux Carre."

DAVID, CLIFFORD. Born June 30, 1932 in Toledo, OH. Attended Toledo U., Actors Studio. Bdwy bow 1960 in "Caligula," followed by "Wildcat," "Aspern Papers," "On a Clear Day You Can See Forever," "A Joyful Noise," "1776," OB in "Boys from Syracuse," "Camino Real," "Museum."

DAVIDSON, JACK. Born July 17, 1936 in Worcester, MA. Graduate Boston U. Debut 1968 OB in "Moon for the Misbegotten," followed by "Battle of Angels," "Midsummer Night's Dream," "Hot l Baltimore," "A Tribute to Lili Lamont," Bdwy in "Capt. Brassbound's Conversion" (1972), "Anna Christie."

DAVIDSON, LORRAINE. Born Oct. 11, 1945 in Boston, MA. Attended HB Studio. Debut OB 1974 in "Let My People Come" (also Bdwy 1976).

DAVIS, LLOYD, JR. Born May 25, 1954 in Baltimore, MD. Graduate Middlebury Col. Debut 1977 OB in "Hagar's Children."

DAY, CONNIE. Born Dec. 26, 1940 in NYC. Debut 1971 OB in "Look Me Up," followed by "Molly" (Bdwy 1973), "Show Boat" (JB).

DeANGELIS, ROSEMARY. Born Apr. 26, 1933 in Brooklyn, NY. Graduate Fashion Inst. Debut 1959 OB in "Time of Vengeance," followed by "Between Two Thieves," "To Be Young, Gifted and Black," "In the Summerhouse," "Monsters" (The Transfiguration of Benno Blimpie).

DEARINGER, KEVIN LANE. Born Nov. 23, 1951 in Versailles, KY. Graduate UKy. Bdwy debut 1976 in "My Fair Lady."

DEERING, OLIVE. Born in the Bronx, NY. Attended Actors Studio. Bdwy debut 1932 in "Girls in Uniform," followed by "Growing Pains," "Searching for the Sun," "Daughters of Atreus," "Richard II," "Medicine Show," "They Walk Alone," "Nathan the Wise," "Skydrift," "Front Page," "Dark Legend," "Devil's Advocate," "Marathon '33," "Vieux Carre," OB in "Ceremony of Innocence," "Two by Tennessee," "Winter Chicken."

DeFABEES, RICHARD. Born Apr. 4, 1947 in Englewood, NJ. Georgetown U. graduate. Debut 1973 OB in "Creeps," followed by "Monsters" (Sideshow), Bdwy 1975 in "The Skin of Our Teeth."

DeFILIPPS, RICK. Born Apr. 16, 1950 in Binghamton, NY. Attended AMDA. Debut 1976 OB in "Panama Hattie" (ELT), followed by "Wonderful Town."

DeFRANK, ROBERT. Born Nov. 29, 1945. Graduate Towson State, Essex Community Col. Debut 1977 OB in "The Crazy Locomotive."

DEGIDON, TOM. Born Sept. 17, 1928 in Trenton, NJ. Graduate NYU. Debut 1959 OB in "Enemy of the People," followed by "Machinal," "Happy Is Larry," "One Day More," "Dirty Hands," "Little Murders," "Empty Handed Piper," Bdwy in "You Know I Can't Hear You When the Water's Running," "Wheelbarrow Closers."

DeKOVEN, ROGER. Born Oct. 22, 1907 in Chicago, IL. Attended UChicago, Northwestern, Columbia. Bdwy bow 1926 in "Juarez and Maximilian," followed by "Mystery Man," "Once in a Lifetime," "Counsellor-at-Law," "Murder in the Cathedral," "Eternal Road," "Brooklyn U.S.A.," "The Assassin," "Joan of Lorraine," "Abie's Irish Rose," "The Lark," "Hidden River," "Compulsion," "Miracle Worker," "Fighting Cock," "Herzl," OB in "Deadly Game," "Steal the Old Man's Bundle," "St. Joan," "Tiger at the Gates," "Walking to Waldheim," "Cyrano de Bergerac," "An Enemy of the People," "Ice Age," "Prince of Homburg."

DELL, MARLENE. Born Dec. 23, 1932 in Union City, NJ. Attended Sarah Lawrence Col. Debut 1959 OB in "On the Town," followed by "The Club," Bdwy in "Conquering Hero" (1961), "Roar of the Grease Paint."

DELOY, GEORGE. Born Nov. 23, 1953 in Uruguay. Attended UUtah. Debut 1975 OB in "El Grande de Coca-Cola," Bdwy 1976 in "The Robber Bridegroom."

DEMAS, CAROLE. Born May 16, 1940 in Bklyn. Attended UVt., NYU. OB in "Morning Sun," "The Fantasticks," "How to Steal an Election," "Rondelay," Bdwy debut 1965 in "Race of Hairy Men," followed by "Grease."

DEMPSEY, JEROME. Born Mar. 1, 1929 in St. Paul, MN. Toledo U graduate. Bdwy bow 1959 in "West Side Story," followed by "The Deputy," "Spofford," "Room Service," "Love Suicide at Schofield Barracks," OB in "Cry of Players," "Year Boston Won the Pennant," "The Crucible," "Justice Box," "Trelawny of the Wells," "The Old Glory," "Six Characters in Search of an Author," "Threepenny Opera."

DeMUNN, JEFFREY P. Born Apr. 25, 1947 in Buffalo, NY. Graduate Union Col. Debut 1975 OB in "Augusta," Bdwy 1976 in "Comedians."

DENGEL, JAKE. Born June 19, 1933 in Oshkosh, WI. Graduate Northwestern U. Debut OB in "The Fantasticks," followed by "Red Eye of Love," "Fortuna," "Abe Lincoln in Illinois," "Dr. Faustus," "An Evening with Garcia Lorca," "Shrinking Bride," APA's "Cock-a-Doodle Dandy" and "Hamlet," "Where Do We Go from Here?," "Woyzeck," "Endgame," "Measure for Measure," Bdwy in "Royal Hunt of the Sun," "The Changing Room."

DENNIS, RONALD. Born Oct. 2, 1944 in Dayton, OH, Debut OB 1966 in "Show Boat," followed by "Of Thee I Sing," "Moon Walk," "Please Don't Cry," Bdwy 1975 in "A Chorus Line."

| **Shelly Desai** | **Nancy Donohue** | **John Dorrin** | **Candice Earley** | **Peter Dvorsky** |

DENNIS, SANDY. Born Apr. 27, 1937 in Hastings, NE. Bdwy debut 1957 in "The Dark at the Top of the Stairs," followed by "Burning Bright" (OB), "Face of a Hero," "Complaisant Lover," "A Thousand Clowns" for which she received a Theatre World Award, "Any Wednesday," "Daphne in Cottage D," "How the Other Half Loves," "Let Me Hear You Smile," "Absurd Person Singular," "Same Time Next Year."

DENNISTON, LESLIE. Born May 19, 1950 in San Francisco, CA. Attended HB Studio. Bdwy debut 1976 in "Shenandoah."

DESAI, SHELLY. Born Dec. 3, 1935 in Bombay, India. Graduate Okla.State U. Debut 1968 OB in "The Indian Wants the Bronx," followed by "Babu," "Wonderful Year," "Jungle of Cities," "Gandhi," "Savages."

DeSALVO, ANNE. Born Apr. 3 in Philadelphia, PA. OB in "Iphigenia in Aulis," "Lovers and Other Strangers," "The First Warning," "Warringham Roof," Bdwy 1977 in "Gemini."

DeSHIELDS, ANDRE. Born Jan. 12, 1946 in Baltimore, MD. Graduate U Wisc. Bdwy debut 1973 in "Warp," followed by "Rachel Lily Rosenbloom," "The Wiz," OB in "2008½."

DEVLIN, JAY. Born May 8, 1929 in Ft. Dodge, IA. OB in "The Mad Show," "Little Murders," "Unfair to Goliath," "Boys in the Band," "Ballymurphy."

DEWHURST, COLLEEN. Born June 3, 1926 in Montreal, Can. Attended Downer Col., AADA. Bdwy debut 1952 in "Desire under the Elms," followed by "Tamburlaine the Great," "Country Wife," "Caligula," "All the Way Home," "Great Day in the Morning," "Ballad of the Sad Cafe," "More Stately Mansions," "All Over," "Mourning Becomes Electra," "Moon for the Misbegotten," "Who's Afraid of Virginia Woolf?," OB in "Taming of the Shrew," "The Eagle Has Two Heads," "Camille," "Macbeth," "Children of Darkness" for which she received a Theatre World Award, "Antony and Cleopatra" (CP), "Hello and Goodbye," "Good Woman of Setzuan" (LC), "Hamlet" (NYSF).

DICKSON, CURTIS. Born Mar. 25, 1947 in Roanoke, VA. Graduate UKan., Northwestern U. Bdwy debut 1976 in "Porgy and Bess."

DINELLI, MICHAEL. Born Jan. 22, 1953 in Los Angeles, CA. Debut OB 1976 in "In the Boom Boom Room," Bdwy 1977 in "The Basic Training of Pavlo Hummel."

DISHY, BOB. Born in Brooklyn, NY. Graduate Syracuse U. Bdwy debut 1955 in "Damn Yankees," followed by "Can-Can" (CC'62), "Flora the Red Menace," "Something Different," "The Goodbye People," "A Way of Life," "The Creation of the World and Other Business," "American Millionaire," "Sly Fox," OB in "Chic," "When the Owl Screams," "Wrecking Ball," "By Jupiter," "Unknown Soldier and His Wife."

DIXON, ED. Born Sept. 2, 1948 in Oklahoma. Attended OklaU. Bdwy in "Student Prince," "No, No, Nanette," "Knickerbocker Holiday," OB in "By Bernstein," "Wonderful Town."

DONLEY, ROBERT. Born in Cumberland Township, PA. Attended Waynesburg Col., Atlantic U. Debut 1947 on Bdwy in "Crime and Punishment," followed by "Andersonville Trial," "Something about a Soldier," "Unsinkable Molly Brown," "The Visit," "Twigs," "Anna Christie."

DONOHUE, NANCY. Born Nov. 2, 1938 in Orange, NJ. Graduate Conn. Col. Bdwy debut 1964 in "Never Too Late," followed by OB "Canadian Gothic," "Prometheus Bound," "Little Eyolf," "The Runner Stumbles," "The Gathering."

DOOLEY, PAUL. Born Feb. 22, 1928 in Parkersburg, WVa. Graduate WVa. U. Bdwy debut in "The Odd Couple," OB in "Threepenny Opera," "Toinette," "Fallout," "Dr. Willy Nilly," "Second City," "Adaptation," "White House Murder Case," "Jules Feiffer's Hold Me!"

DORN, JAN. Born Mar. 12, 1954 in Jackson, TN. Graduate UCLA. Debut OB 1977 in "Hagar's Children."

DORRIN, JOHN. Born July 17, 1920 in Omaha, NE. Attended Los Angeles City Col. Bdwy debut 1944 in "Song of Norway," followed by "Silk Stockings," "Most Happy Fella," "Best Man," "My Fair Lady," "What Makes Sammy Run?," "Fade Out, Fade In," "Carousel," "Annie Get Your Gun," "Finian's Rainbow," "St. Joan," "I'm Solomon," "Oklahoma" (JB), "New Girl in Town" (ELT), "Gigi," "Show Boat" (JB), "Knickerbocker Holiday."

DOUGLASS, PI. Born in Sharon, CT. Attended Boston Conserv. Bdwy debut 1969 in "Fig Leaves Are Falling," followed by "Hello, Dolly!," "Georgy," "Purlie," "Ari," "Jesus Christ Superstar," "Selling of the President," "The Wiz," OB in "Of Thee I Sing."

DOYLE, LEE H. Born Apr. 20, 1928 in Cleveland, OH. Attended Tokyo U. Debut 1965 OB in "By Jupiter," followed by "Threepenny Opera," "Here Come The Clowns," "Woyzek," Bdwy 1976 "Going Up."

DREMAK, W. P. Born Aug. 2 in Akron, OH. Graduate Carnegie Tech. Debut 1967 OB in "Jonah," followed by Bdwy "Jesus Christ Superstar" (1972), "Eccentricities of a Nightingale."

DRIVAS, ROBERT. Born Nov. 20, 1943 in Chicago. Bdwy debut 1958 in "The Firstborn," followed by "One More River," "The Wall," "Lorenzo," "Irregular Verb to Love," "And Things That Go Bump in the Night," "The Ritz," OB in "Mrs. Dally Has a Lover" for which he received a Theatre World Award, "Sweet Eros," "Where Has Tommy Flowers Gone," "Breeze from the Gulf," "Monsters" (Sideshow).

DRUMMOND, ALICE. Born May 21, 1929 in Pawtucket, RI. Attended Pembroke Col. OB in "Royal Gambit," "Go Show Me a Dragon," "Sweet of You to Say So," "Gallows Humor," "American Dream," "Giants' Dance," "Carpenters," "Charles Abbott & Son," "God Says There Is No Peter Ott," "Enter a Free Man," "Memory of Two Mondays," "Secret Service," "Boy Meets Girl," "Savages," Bdwy debut 1963 in "Ballad of the Sad Cafe," followed by "Malcolm," "The Chinese," "Thieves," "Summer Brave."

DUELL, WILLIAM. Born Aug. 30, in Corinth, NY. Attended Ill. Wesleyan, Yale. OB in "Portrait of the Artist . . . ," "Barroom Monks," "Midsummer Night's Dream," "Henry IV," "Taming of the Shrew," "The Memorandum," "Threepenny Opera," Bdwy in "A Cook for Mr. General," "Ballad of the Sad Cafe," "Ilya, Darling," "1776," "Kings."

DUFF-MacCORMICK, CARA. Born Dec. 12 in Woodstock, Can. Attended AADA. Debut 1969 OB in "Love Your Crooked Neighbor," followed by "The Wager," "Macbeth" (LC), "A Musical Merchant Of Venice," "Ladyhouse Blues," "The Philanderer," Bdwy 1972 in "Moonchildren" for which she received a Theatre World Award, followed by "Out Cry."

DUKES, DAVID. Born June 6, 1945 in San Francisco, CA. Attended Mann College. Bdwy debut 1971 in "School for Wives," followed by "Don Juan," "The Play's the Thing," "The Visit," "Chemin de Fer," "Holiday," "Rules of the Game," "Love for Love," "Travesties," OB in "Rebel Women."

DUNNOCK, MILDRED. Born Jan 25 in Baltimore, MD. Graduate Goucher Col., Columbia U. Bdwy debut 1932 in "Life Begins," followed by "The Corn Is Green," "Richard III," "Only the Heart," "Foolish Notion," "Lute Song," "Another Part of the Forest," "The Hallams," "Death of a Salesman," "Pride's Crossing," "The Wild Duck," "In the Summer House," "Cat on a Hot Tin Roof," "Child of Fortune," "The Milk Train Doesn't Stop Here Anymore," "Traveller without Luggage," "Days in the Trees," OB in "The Trojan Women," "Phedre," "Willie Doesn't Live Here Anymore," "Colette," "A Place without Doors."

DVORSKY, PETER. Born Aug. 27, 1948 in Komarno, Czech. Antioch Col. graduate. Debut OB 1972 in "School for Scandal," followed by "Lower Depths," Bdwy in "Three Sisters" (1973), "Beggar's Opera," "Measure for Measure," "Edward II," "The Time of Your Life," "The Robber Bridegroom."

DYBAS, JAMES. Born Feb. 7, 1944 in Chicago, IL. Bdwy debut 1965 in "Do I Hear a Waltz?," followed by "George M!," "Via Galactica," "Pacific Overtures."

EARLEY, CANDICE. Born Aug. 18, 1950 in Ft. Hood, TX. Attended Trinity U. Bdwy debut 1971 in "Hair," followed by "Jesus Christ Superstar," "Grease," "Civilization and Its Discontents" (OB).

EASTERBROOK, LESLIE. Born July 29, 1949 in Los Angeles, CA. Stephens Col. graduate. Bdwy debut 1976 in "California Suite."

EBERT, JOYCE. Born June 26, 1933 in Homestead, PA. Graduate Carnegie Tech. Debut 1956 OB in "Liliom," followed by "Sign of Winter," "Asmodee," "King Lear," "Hamlet," "Under Milkwood," "Trojan Women," "White Devil," "Tartuffe," Bdwy in "Solitaire/Double Solitaire" (1971), "The Shadow Box."

eda-YOUNG, BARBARA. Born Jan. 30, 1945 in Detroit, MI. Bdwy debut 1968 in "Lovers and Other Strangers," OB in "The Hawk," LCRep's "The Time of Your Life," "Camino Real," "Operation Sidewinder," "Kool Aid" and "A Streetcar Named Desire," "The Gathering."

Susan Edwards   **Bill Elverman**   **Claris Erickson**   **Terry Eno**   **Barbara Erwin**

EDE, GEORGE. Born Dec. 22, 1931 in San Francisco, CA. Bdwy debut 1969 in "A Flea in Her Ear," followed by "Three Sisters," "The Changing Room," "The Visit," "Chemin de Fer," "Holiday," "Love for Love," "Rules of the Game," "Member of the Wedding," "Lady from the Sea," "The Philanderer" (OB).

EDENFIELD, DENNIS. Born July 23, 1948 in New Orleans, LA. Attended Le Petite Theatre. Debut OB 1970 in "The Evil That Men Do," Bdwy 1973 in "Irene."

EDMEAD, WENDY. Born July 6, 1956 in NYC. Graduate NYCU. Bdwy debut 1974 in "The Wiz."

EDWARDS, BRANDT. Born Mar. 22, 1947 in Holly Springs, MS. Graduate UMiss. NY debut off and on Bdwy in "A Chorus Line."

EDWARDS, SUSAN. Born Aug. 24, 1950 in Levittown, NY. Graduate Hofstra U. Bdwy debut 1976 in "Bubbling Brown Sugar," followed by OB in "Jazz Babies," "The Boys from Syracuse" (ELT).

EGAN, JENNY. Born in NYC. Graduate Grinnell Col., NYU, Neighborhood Playhouse. Bdwy debut 1953 in "The Crucible," followed by "Ballad of the Sad Cafe," "The Cuban Thing," OB in "Illusion," "Mary Stuart," "The Chairs," "The Bald Soprano," "Jack," "Under Milk Wood," "American Dream."

ELDER, JUDYANN. Born Aug. 18 in Cleveland, OH. Graduate Emerson Col. Debut 1967 OB in "Song of the Lusitanian Bogey," followed by "Daddy Goodness," "Kongi's Harvest," "God Is a (Guess What?)," "Ceremonies in Dark Old Men," "Five on the Black Hand Side," Bdwy 1976 in "I Have a Dream."

ELIZONDO, HECTOR. Born Dec. 12, 1936 in NYC. Attended CCNY. Bdwy debut 1968 in "The Great White Hope," followed by "Prisoner of Second Avenue," "Sly Fox," OB in "Drums in the Night," "Steambath," "Dance of Death" (LC).

ELLIOTT, DENHOLM. Born May 31, 1922 in London. Attended Malvern Col., RADA. Bdwy debut 1951 in "Ring 'Round the Moon," followed by "The Green Bay Tree," "Monique," "Write Me a Murder," "The Seagull," NRT's "Imaginary Invalid," "Touch of the Poet" and "Tonight at 8:30," BAM Co's "New York Idea" and "Three Sisters."

ELLIOTT, PATRICIA. Born July 21, 1942 in Gunnison, CO. Graduate U. Colo., London Academy. Debut with LCRep 1968 in "King Lear," and "A Cry of Players," followed by OB in "Henry V," "The Persians," "A Doll's House," "Hedda Gabler," "In Case of Accident," "Water Hen," "Polly," "But Not for Me," "By Bernstein," "Prince of Homburg," Bdwy bow 1973 in "A Little Night Music" for which she received a Theatre World Award, "The Shadow Box."

ELLIS, ANTONIA. Born Apr. 30, 1944 in Newport, Isle of Wight. Bdwy debut 1975 in "Pippin."

ELMORE, STEVE. Born July 12, 1936 in Niangua, MO. Debut 1961 OB in "Madame Aphrodite," followed by "Golden Apple," "Enclave," Bdwy in "Camelot," "Jenny," "Fade In Fade Out," "Kelly," "Company," "Nash at 9," "Chicago."

ELVERMAN, BILL. Born Nov. 14, 1951 in Kenosha, WI. Graduate UWisc. Debut 1977 OB in "Museum."

ENEY, WOODY. Born June 8, 1937 in Canberra, Aust. Attended RADA. Debut OB 1974 in "The Desperate Hours," followed by "Click," "G. R. Point."

ENGSTROM, JON. Born in Fresno, CA. Bdwy debut 1971 in "No, No, Nanette," followed by "The Pajama Game," "Very Good Eddie."

ENO, TERRY. Born June 5, 1946 in Miami, FL. Attended Miami U., HB Studio. Bdwy debut in "Irene," followed by "Good News," OB in "Buy Bonds Buster," "Joseph and the Amazing Technicolor Dreamcoat."

ENSERRO, MICHAEL. Born Oct. 5, 1918 in Soldier, PA. Attended Allegheny Col., Pasadena Playhouse. Bdwy in "Me and Molly," "Passion of Josef D," "Song of the Grasshopper," "Mike Downstairs," "Camino Real," "Saturday Sunday Monday," OB in "Penny Change," "Fantasticks," "The Miracle," "The Kitchen," "Rome, Rome," "The Jar."

ENSSLEN, DICK. Born Dec. 19, 1926 in Reading PA. Attended Musical Theatre Academy. Bdwy debut 1964 in "Anyone Can Whistle," followed by "Bajour," "Education of Hyman Kaplan," "Canterbury Tales," "Desert Song," "Annie."

ENTEN, BONI. Born Feb. 20, 1947 in Baltimore, MD. Attended TCU. Bdwy debut 1965 in "Roar of the Grease Paint," followed by "Rocky Horror Show," "Pal Joey," OB in "You're a Good Man, Charlie Brown," "Oh! Calcutta!," "Salvation," "The Real Inspector Hound."

EPSTEIN, PIERRE. Born July 27, 1930 in Toulouse, France. Graduate UParis, Columbia. Bdwy bow 1962 in "A Shot in the Dark," followed by "Enter Laughing," "Bajour," "Black Comedy," "Thieves," "Fun City," OB in "Incident at Vichy," "Threepenny Opera," "Too Much Johnson," "Second City," "People vs. Ranchman," "Promenade," "Cakes with Wine," "Little Black Sheep," "Comedy of Errors," "A Memory of Two Mondays," "They Knew What They Wanted," "Museum."

ERIC, DAVID. Born Feb. 28, 1949 in Boston, MA. Graduate Neighborhood Playhouse. Debut OB 1971 in "Ballad of Johnny Pot," followed by "Love Me, Love My Children," Bdwy in "Yentl" (1975), "Shenandoah."

ERICKSON, CLARIS. Born Dec. 13, 1940 in Aurora, IL. Graduate Northwestern U., UEdinburgh. Debut 1962 OB in "Little Eyolf," followed by "A Tribute to Lili Lamont."

ERWIN, BARBARA. Born June 30, 1937 in Boston, MA. Debut 1973 OB in "The Secret Life of Walter Mitty," followed by "Broadway," Bdwy 1977 in "Annie."

ESTERMAN, LAURA. Born Apr. 12, in NYC. Attended Radcliffe, LAMDA. Debut 1969 OB in "The Time of Your Life" (LCR), followed by "Pig Pen," "The Carpenters," "Ghosts," "Waltz of the Toreadors," "Macbeth" (LC), "The Seagull," "Rubbers," "Yanks 3, Detroit 0," "Golden Boy," Bdwy 1974 "God's Favorite."

EVANKO, ED. Born in Winnipeg, Can. Studied at Bristol Old Vic. Bdwy debut 1969 in "Canterbury Tales" in which he received a Theatre World Award, followed by "Rex," "Knickerbocker Holiday," OB in "Love Me, Love My Children," "Leaves of Grass."

EVERHART, REX. Born June 13, 1920 in Watseka, IL. Graduate UMo., NYU. Bdwy bow 1955 in "No Time for Sergeants," followed by "Tall Story," "Moonbirds," "Tenderloin," "Matter of Position," "Rainy Day in Newark," "Skyscraper," "How Now Dow Jones," "1776," "The Iceman Cometh," "Chicago."

FAGA, GARY. Born Nov. 23, 1953 in Brooklyn, NY. Attended Bklyn Col. Debut OB 1975 in "Hustlers," followed by "Dance with Me," Bdwy 1976 in "Equus."

FAIRBANK, SPRING. Born Mar. 15, 1941 in Chicago, IL. Attended New Eng. Conserv. Debut 1968 in "My Fair Lady" (CC), followed by "Oh, Lady, Lady" (ELT), Bdwy 1975 in "Very Good Eddie."

FANN, ALBERT. Born Feb. 21, 1933 in Cleveland, OH. Attended Cleveland Inst. of Music. Debut 1970 OB in "King Heroin," Bdwy 1975 in "The Wiz."

FARALDO, DANIEL. Born Nov. 4, 1949 in Buenos Aires, AR. Graduate Argentin Consv. of Dramatic Arts. Debut 1977 OB in "Jockeys."

FARENTINO, JAMES. Born Feb. 24, 1938 in Brooklyn, NY. Attended AADA. Bdwy debut 1961 in "Night of the Iguana," followed by "Death of a Salesman," OB in "Days and Nights of Beebee Fenstermaker," "In the Summer House," LC's "Streetcar Named Desire," for which he received a Theatre World Award.

FARR, KIMBERLY. Born Oct. 16, 1948 in Chicago. UCLA graduate. Bdwy debut 1972 in "Mother Earth," followed by "The Lady from the Sea," "Going Up," OB in "More than You Deserve," "The S.S. Benchley," "At Sea with Benchley."

FASO, LAURIE. Born Apr. 11, 1946 in Buffalo, NY. Graduate Denison U., Carnegie Tech. Debut OB 1974 in "Godspell," followed by "The Glorious Age," "Comedy of Errors" (CP), Bdwy 1976 in "Godspell."

FAYE, JOEY. Born July 12, 1910 in NYC. Bdwy bow 1938 in "Sing Out the News," followed by "Room Service," "Meet the People," "Man Who Came to Dinner," "Milky Way," "Boy Meets Girl," "Streets of Paris," "Allah Be Praised," "The Duchess Misbehaves," "Tidbits of 1948," "High Button Shoes," "Top Banana," "Tender Trap," "Man of LaMancha," "70 Girls 70," OB in "Lyle," "Naomi Court."

FEARL, CLIFFORD. Born in NYC. Graduate Columbia U. Bdwy debut 1950 in "Flahooley," followed by "Three Wishes for Jamie," "Two's Company," "Kismet," "Happy Hunting," "Oh, Captain," "Redhead," "Let It Ride," "110 in the Shade," "Ben Franklin in Paris," "Mame," "La Plume de Ma Tante," "Dear World," "Jimmy," "My Fair Lady."

FELDER, CLARENCE. Born Sept. 2, 1938 in St. Matthews, SC. Debut OB 1964 in "The Room," followed by "Are You Now or Have You Ever Been," "Claw," "Henry V," Bdwy in "Red, White and Maddox" (1969), "Love for Love," "Rules of the Game," "Golden Boy," "A Memory of Two Mondays," "They Knew What They Wanted."

241

FELDSHUH, TOVAH. Born Dec. 27 in NYC. Graduate Sarah Lawrence Col. Bdwy debut 1973 in "Cyrano," followed by "Dreyfus in Rehearsal," "Rodgers and Hart," "Yentl" for which she received a Theatre World Award, OB in "Yentl the Yeshiva Boy," "Straws in the Wind," BAM Co.'s "Three Sisters."

FERRELL, ANDY. Born Sept. 9, 1950 in Wilson, NC. Graduate NC State U. Debut 1976 OB in "The Boys from Syracuse."

FIELDS, JOE. Born Jan. 23, 1935 In Uniontown, AL. Attended Karmu Theatre Sch. Debut 1969 OB in "Ceremonies in Dark Old Men," followed by "Of Mice and Men," "As You Like It," Bdwy in "Ain't Supposed to Die a Natural Death" (1971), "The Basic Training of Pavlo Hummel" for which he received a Theatre World Award.

FIERRON, ERNIE. Born Feb. 10, 1933 in San Antonio, TX. Attended Actors Studio. Debut 1960 OB in "White Cargo," followed by "No Exit," "A Strange Kind of Romance," "The Cage," "Savages."

FISKE, ELLEN. Born May 1 in Paterson, NJ. Graduate Wilmington Col., Ohio U. Debut 1974 OB in "Arms and the Man," Bdwy 1976 in "The Royal Family."

FITCH, ROBERT. Born Apr. 29, 1934 in Santa Cruz, CA. Attended U Santa Clara. Bdwy debut 1961 in "Tenderloin," followed by "Do Re Mi," "My Fair Lady" (CC), "Girl Who Came to Supper," "Flora the Red Menace," "Baker Street," "Sherry," "Mack and Mabel," "Henry, Sweet Henry," "Mame," "Promises, Promises," "Coco," "Lorelei," "Annie," OB in "Lend an Ear," "Half-Past Wednesday," "Anything Goes," "Crystal Heart," "Broadway Dandies," "One Cent Plain."

FITZGERALD, FERN. Born Jan. 7, 1947 in Valley Stream, NY. Bdwy debut 1976 in "Chicago," followed by "A Chorus Line."

FITZGERALD, GERALDINE. Born Nov. 24, 1914 in Dublin, Ire. Bdwy debut 1938 in "Heartbreak House," followed by "Sons and Soldiers," "Doctor's Dilemma," "King Lear," "Hide and Seek," "Ah, Wilderness," "The Shadow Box," OB in "Cave Dwellers," "Pigeons," "Long Day's Journey into Night," "Everyman and Roach."

FITZPATRICK, JIM. Born Nov. 26, 1950 in Omaha, NE. Attended UNeb. Debut 1977 OB in "Arsenic and Old Lace."

FITZPATRICK, LYNN. Born in Philadelphia, PA. Graduate Ohio Dominican Col. Bdwy debut 1972 in "Ambassador," followed by "You Never Know" (OB), "My Fair Lady."

FLANAGAN, NEIL. Born May 3, 1934 in Springfield, Il. Debut 1966 OB in "Fortune and Men's Eyes," followed by "Haunted Host," "Madness of Lady Bright," "Dirtiest Show in Town," "The Play's the Thing," "As You Like It," "Hedda Gabler," "Design for Living," "him," "Partnership," "Down by the River....," "Lisping Judas," "Elephant in the House," "Exiles," Bdwy in "Sheep on the Runway," "Secret Affairs of Mildred Wild," "Knock Knock."

FLANAGAN, PAULINE. Born June 29, 1925 in Sligo, IRe. Debut 1958 OB in "Ulysses in Nighttown," followed by "Pictures in the Hallway," LCRep's "Antigone," "The Crucible," and "The Plough and the Stars," Bdwy in "God and Kate Murphy," "The Living Room," "The Innocents."

FLANAGAN, WALTER. Born Oct. 4, 1928 in Ponta, TX. Graduate Houston U. On Bdwy in "Once for the Asking," "A Texas Trilogy," OB in "Bedtime Story," "Coffee and Windows," "Opening of a Window," "The Moon Is Blue," "Laughwind," "The Dodo Bird."

FLANINGAM, LOUISA. Born May 5, 1945 in Chester, SC. Graduate UMd. Debut 1971 OB in "The Shrinking Bride," Bdwy 1976 in "The Magic Show."

FLEISCHMAN, MARK. Born Nov. 25, 1935 in Detroit, MI. Attended UMich. Bdwy debut 1955 in "Tonight in Samarkand," followed by "A Distant Bell," "The Royal Family," OB in "What Every Woman Knows," "Lute Song," "The Beautiful People," "Big Fish, Little Fish."

FOGARTY, JACK. Born Oct. 23, 1923 in Liverpool, Eng. Attended Fordham and Columbia U. Debut 1952 OB in "No Exit," followed by "Hogan's Goat," "Sweeney Todd," "The Fantasticks."

FOOTE, GENE. Born Oct. 30, 1936 in Johnson City, TN. Attended ETSU. Bdwy debut 1961 in "Unsinkable Molly Brown," followed by "Bajour," "Sweet Charity," "Golden Rainbow," "Applause," "Pippin," "Chicago," "Celebration" (OB).

FORBES, BRENDA. Born Jan. 14, 1909 in London. Bdwy debut 1931 in "Barretts of Wimpole Street," followed by "Candida," "Lucrece," "Flowers of the Forest," "Pride and Prejudice," "Storm over Patsy," "Heartbreak House," "One for the Money," "Two for the Show," "Three to Make Ready," "Yesterday's Magic," "Morning Star," "Suds in Your Eyes," "Quadrille," "The Reluctant Debutante," "Loves of Cass McGuire," "Darling of the Day," "The Constant Wife," "My Fair Lady."

FORBES, DONNA LIGGITT. Born Sept. 9, 1947 in Wilson, NC. Graduate E. Car. U. Debut 1972 on Bdwy in "Hurry Harry," OB in "Smile, Smile, Smile," "Wonderful Town."

FORD, RUTH. Born July 7, 1915 in Hazelhurst, MS. Bdwy debut 1938 in "Shoemaker's Holiday," followed by "Danton's Death," "Swingin' the Dream," "No Exit," "This Time Tomorrow," "Clutterbuck," "House of Bernarda Alba," "Island of Goats," "Requiem for a Nun," "The Milk Train Doesn't Stop Here Anymore," "Grass Harp," OB in "Glass Slipper," "Miss Julie," "Madame de Sade," "A Breeze from the Gulf."

FORELLA, MICHAEL. Born May 11, 1947 in The Bronx, NY. Graduate Carnegie-Mellon U. Bdwy debut 1970 in "Room Service," followed by "Boccaccio," "Romeo and Juliet," OB in "Godspell."

FORLOW, TED. Born Apr. 29, 1931 in Independence, MO. Attended Baker U. Bdwy debut 1957 in "New Girl in Town," followed by "Juno," "Destry Rides Again," "Subways Are for Sleeping," "Can-Can," "Wonderful Town" (CC), "A Funny Thing Happened on the Way to the Forum," "Milk and Honey," "Carnival" (CC), "Man of LaMancha," "A Night at the Black Pig" (OB).

FORSLUND, CONNIE. Born June 19, 1950 in San Diego, CA. Graduate NYU. Debut 1970 OB in "The Divorce of Judy and Jane," followed by "The Cretan Bull," "The Kiss-Off," Bdwy in "The Women" (1973), "Habeas Corpus," "Unexpected Guests."

FORSYTHE, HENDERSON. Born Sept. 11, 1917 in Macon, MO. Attended UIowa. OB in "The Iceman Cometh," "The Collection," "The Room," "A Slight Ache," "Happiness Cage," "Waiting for Godot," "In Case of Accident," "Not I" (LC), "An Evening with the Poet-Senator," "Museum," Bdwy in "The Cellar and the Well," "Miss Lonelyhearts," "Who's Afraid of Virginia Woolf?," "Malcolm," "Right Honourable Gentleman," "Delicate Balance," "Birthday Party," "Harvey," "Engagement Baby," "Freedom of the City," "Texas Trilogy."

FORTUS, DANIEL. Born Jan. 6, 1953 in Brooklyn, NY. Bdwy debut 1963 in "Oliver," followed by "Minnie's Boys," "Molly," OB in "Friends and Enemies," "A Day in the Life of Just about Everyone," "2 by 5."

FOSTER, FRANCES. Born June 11 in Yonkers, NY. Bdwy debut 1955 in "The Wisteria Trees," followed by "Nobody Loves an Albatross," "Raisin in the Sun," "The River Niger," "First Breeze of Summer," OB in "Take a Giant Step," "Edge of the City," "Tammy and the Doctor," "The Crucible," "Happy Ending," "Day of Absence," "An Evening of One Acts," "Man Better Man," "Brotherhood," "Akokawe," "Rosalee Pritchett," "Sty of the Blind Pig," "Ballet Behind the Bridge," "Good Woman of Setzuan" (LC), "Behold! Cometh the Vanderkellans," "Orrin," "Boesman and Lena."

FOSTER, NORAH. Born Feb. 25, 1954 in Wilmington, NC. Graduate Neighborhood Playhouse. Bdwy debut 1976 in "Wheelbarrow Closers."

FOWKES, CONARD. Born Jan. 4, 1933 in Washington, DC. Yale graduate. Bdwy bow 1958 in "Howie," followed by "The Wall," "Minor Miracle," "All the Girls Came out to Play," OB in "Look Back in Anger," "That Thing at the Cherry Lane," "America Hurrah," "The Reckoning," "Istanbul," "Sleep," "Domino Courts."

FRANK, JIM. Born June 1 in Houston, TX. Attended Lon Morris Col. Debut 1972 OB in "No Strings," followed by "Dance on a Country Grave."

FREED, SAM. Born Aug. 29, 1948 in York, PA. Graduate Pa. State U. Debut OB 1972 in "The Proposition," followed by "What's a Nice Country Like You...," "Dance on a Country Grave," Bdwy 1974 in "Candide."

FRENCH, ARTHUR. Born in NYC. Attended Brooklyn Col. Debut 1962 OB in "Raisin' Hell in the Sun," followed by "Ballad of Bimshire," "Day of Absence," "Happy Ending," "Jonah," "Black Girl," "Ceremonies in Dark Old Men," "An Evening of One Acts," "Man Better Man," "Brotherhood," "Perry's Mission," "Rosalee Pritchett," "Moonlight Arms," "Dark Tower," "Brownsville Raid," Bdwy in "Ain't Supposed to Die a Natural Death," "The Iceman Cometh," "All God's Chillun Got Wings."

FRENCH, VALERIE. Born in London. Bdwy debut 1965 in "Inadmissible Evidence," followed by "Help Stamp Out Marriage," "Mother Lover," "Children, Children," OB in "Tea Party," "Trelawny of the Wells," "Studs Edsel," "Henry V," "John Gabriel Borkman."

FREY, LEONARD. Born Sept. 4, 1938 in Brooklyn. Attended Cooper Union, Neighborhood Playhouse. Debut OB in "Little Mary Sunshine," "Funny House of a Negro," "Coach with Six Insides," "Boys in the Band," "Time of Your Life," "Beggar on Horseback," "People Are Living There," "Twelfth Night," "Troilus and Cressida," on Bdwy in "Fiddler on the Roof," "The National Health," "Knock Knock."

FRIESEN, RICK. Born Nov. 29, 1943 in Minneapolis, MN. Graduate UKan. Debut 1972 OB in "Mystery Play," Bdwy 1976 in "Fiddler on the Roof."

FUJII, TIMM. Born May 26, 1952 in Detroit, MI. Attended CalStateU. Bdwy debut 1976 in "Pacific Overtures."

FULLER, JANICE. Born June 4 in Oakland, CA. Attended RADA. Debut OB 1975 in "Ice Age," followed by "A Night at the Black Pig."

GABLE, JUNE. Born June 5, 1945 in NY. Graduate Carnegie Tech. OB in "MacBird," "Jacques Brel Is Alive and Well and Living In Paris," "A Day in the Life of Just about Everyone," "Mod Donna," "Wanted," "Lady Audley's Secret," "Comedy of Errors," Bdwy 1974 in "Candide."

GALIANO, JOSEPH. Born Mar. 26, 1944 in Beaumont, TX. Graduate SMU. Debut 1976 OB in "The Fantasticks."

GALLAGHER, MICHAEL. Born Mar. 27, 1947 in Austin, TX. Graduate TCU. Debut 1976 on Bdwy in "Going Up," followed by OB in "Wonderful Town" (ELT).

GALLOWAY, JANE. Born Feb. 27, 1950 in St. Louis, MO. Attended Webster Col. Debut 1976 OB in "Vanities," followed by "Domino Courts," "Comanche Cafe."

GAMMON, WILLIAM. Born Sept. 22, 1943 in Bristol, TN. Graduate Fla. State U. Bdwy debut 1969 in "Red, White and Maddox," followed by "Porgy and Bess," OB in "Friends," "The Smile in the Third Row."

Ellen Fiske   **Mark Fleischman**   **Terry Gene**   **Chip Garnett**   **Jeanne Grant**

GARDENIA, VINCENT. Born Jan. 7, 1923 in Naples, Italy. Debut 1955 OB in "In April Once," followed by "Man with the Golden Arm," "Volpone," "Brothers Karamazov," "Power of Darkness," "Machinal," "Gallows Humor," "Theatre of the Absurd," "The Lunatic View," "Little Murders," "Passing Through from Exotic Places," "The Carpenters," Bdwy in "The Visit" (1958), "Rashomon," "The Cold Wind and the Warm," "Only in America," "The Wall," "Daughter of Silence," "Seidman & Son," "Dr. Fish," "Prisoner of Second Avenue," "God's Favorite," "California Suite."

GARNETT, CHIP. Born May 8, 1953 in New Kensington, PA. Attended Indiana U. Debut 1973 OB in "Inner City," followed by Bdwy "Candide" (1974), "Bubbling Brown Sugar" for which he received a Theatre World Award.

GARNETT, GALE. Born July 23, 1946 in Auckland, NZ. Debut 1959 OB in "Jack," followed by "Sisters of Mercy," "Greatest Fairy Story Ever Told," "Cracks," "Ladyhouse Blues," Bdwy in "World of Suzie Wong," "Ulysses in Nighttown."

GARRATY, TRI. Born Apr. 6, 1955 in Washington, DC. Attended Georgetown U. Debut 1977 OB in "Hagar's Children."

GARRETT, BOB. Born Mar. 2, 1947 in NYC. Graduate Adelphi U. Debut OB 1971 in "Godspell," Bdwy in "Grease."

GARY, HAROLD. Born May 7, 1910 in NYC. Bdwy bow 1928 in "Diamond Lil," followed by "Crazy with the Heat," "A Flag Is Born," "Guys and Dolls," "Oklahoma!," "Arsenic and Old Lace," "Billion Dollar Baby," "Fiesta," "The World We Make," "Born Yesterday," "Will Success Spoil Rock Hunter?," "Let It Ride," "Counting House," "Arturo Ui," "A Thousand Clowns," "Enter Laughing," "Illya, Darling," "The Price," "Roosebloom (OB)," "The Sunshine Boys," "Pal Joey."

GATES, LARRY. Born Sept. 24, 1915 in St. Paul, MN. Attended U Minn. Bdwy bow 1939 in "Speak of the Devil," followed by "Twelfth Night," "Bell, Book and Candle," "Taming of the Shrew," "Love of Four Colonels," "Teahouse of the August Moon," "Sing Me No Lullaby," "Carefree Tree," "Poor Murderer," OB in "A Case of Libel," "Carving a Statue," "Hamlet."

GAVON, IGORS. Born Nov. 14, 1937 in Latvia. Bdwy bow 1961 in "Carnival," followed by "Hello, Dolly," "Marat/deSade," "Billy," "Sugar," "Mack and Mabel," "Musical Jubilee," OB in "Your Own Thing," "Promenade," "Exchange," "Nevertheless They Laugh," "Polly," "The Boss."

GAZZARA, BEN. Born Aug. 28, 1930 in NYC. Attended CCNY. Bdwy debut 1953 in "End as a Man" for which he received a Theatre World Award, followed by "Cat on a Hot Tin Roof," "Hatful of Rain," "Night Circus", "Strange Interlude," "Traveller without Luggage," "Hughie," "Duet," "Who's Afraid of Virginia Woolf?"

GEFFNER, DEBORAH. Born Aug. 26, 1952 in Pittsburgh, PA. Attended Juilliard, HB Studio. Debut 1975 OB in "Tenderloin," Bdwy in "Pal Joey," "A Chorus Line."

GENE, TERRY. Born Jan. 30, 1954 in NYC. Bdwy debut 1975 in "Hello, Dolly!," OB in "Wonderful Town" (ELT)

GENTLES, AVRIL. Born Apr. 2, 1929 in Upper Montclair, NJ. Graduate UNC. Bdwy debut 1955 in "The Great Sebastians," followed by "Nude with Violin," "Present Laughter," "My Mother, My Father and Me," "Jimmy Shine," "Grin and Bare It," "Lysistrata," "Texas Trilogy," OB in "Dinny and the Witches," "The Wives," "Now Is the Time," "Man with a Load of Mischief."

GIBSON, KAREN. (formerly Karen Zenker) Born Jan. 9 in Columbus, OH. Attended Ohio State U. Debut 1975 OB in ELT's "Three Musketeers," followed by Bdwy 1976 in "My Fair Lady."

GIELGUD, JOHN. Born Apr. 14, 1904 in London. Attended RADA. Bdwy debut 1928 in "The Patriot," followed by "Hamlet," "Importance of Being Earnest," "Love for Love," "Crime and Punishment," "The Lady's Not for Burning," "Medea," "Ages of Man," "School for Scandal," "Homage to Shakespeare," "Tiny Alice," "Home," "No Man's Land."

GILCHRIST, REBECCA. Born June 10, 1948 in Parkersburg, WV. Graduate WVa. U. Debut OB 1972 in "The Proposition," Bdwy debut 1974 in "Grease."

GILFORD, JACK. Born July 25 in NYC. Bdwy debut 1940 in "Meet the People," followed by "They Should Have Stood in Bed," "Count Me In," "The Live Wire," "Alive and Kicking," "Once over Lightly," "Diary of Anne Frank," "Romanoff and Juliet," "The Tenth Man," "A Funny Thing Happened on the Way to the Forum," "Cabaret," "3 Men on a Horse," "No, No, Nanette," "The Sunshine Boys," "Sly Fox."

GILL, TERI. Born July 16, 1954 in Long Island City, NY. Graduate USIU. Bdwy debut 1976 in "Going Up."

GILLETTE, ANITA. Born Aug. 16, 1938 in Baltimore, MD. Debut 1960 OB in "Russell Patterson's Sketchbook" for which she received a Theatre World Award, followed by Bdwy's "Carnival," "All American," "Mr. President," "Guys and Dolls" (CC), "Don't Drink the Water," "Cabaret," "Jimmy," "Rich and Famous" (OB).

GIRVIN, T. GALEN. Born Apr. 7, 1948 in Coatesville, PA. Graduate Westminster Col. Debut 1974 OB in "Pop!," followed by "Boys from Syracuse" (ELT).

GLASS, GIBSON. Born Feb. 16, 1950 in Stamford, CT. Attended UDubuque, Goodman Theatre. Debut 1974 OB in "The Tempest," followed by "Pullman Car Hiawatha," "Gammer Gurton's Needle," "Love's Labours Lost," "Peg o' My Heart."

GLEASON, JOANNA. Born June 2, 1950 in Toronto, Can. Graduate UCLA. Bdwy debut 1977 in "I Love My Wife" for which she received a Theatre World Award.

GLENN, BETTE. Born Dec. 13, 1946 in Atlantic City, NJ. Graduate Montepelier Col. Debut 1971 OB in "Ruddigore," followed by "Maggie Flynn," Bdwy in "Irene," "She Loves Me."

GOLDSMITH, MERWIN. Born Aug. 7, 1937 in Detroit, MI. Graduate UCLA. Studied at Old Vic. Bdwy debut 1970 in "Minnie's Boys," followed by "The Visit," "Chemin de Fer," "Rex," "Dirty Linen," OB in "Hamlet as a Happening," "Chickencoop Chinaman," "Wanted," "Comedy," "Rubbers," "Yankees 3, Detroit O," "Trelawny of the Wells."

GORDON, CARL. Born Jan. 20, 1932 in Richmond, VA. Bdwy bow 1966 in "Great White Hope," followed by "Ain't Supposed to Die a Natural Death," OB in "Day of Absence," "Happy Ending," "Strong Breed," "Trials of Brother Jero," "Kongi's Harvest," "Welcome to Black River," "Shark," "Orrin and Sugar Mouth," "A Love Play," "The Great MacDaddy."

GOULD, ELEANOR CODY. Born in Bradford, PA. Attended Elkins Col., AADA ... where she became a teacher for many years. Returned to acting and appeared OB in "Ice Age."

GRAFF, ILENE. Born Feb. 28 in NYC. Graduate Ithaca Col. Bdwy debut 1968 in "Promises, Promises," followed by "Grease," "I Love My Wife."

GRAHAM, DONNA. Born Sept. 28, 1964 in Philadelphia, PA. Bdwy debut 1977 in "Annie."

GRAMMIS, ADAM. Born Dec. 8, 1947 in Allentown, PA. Graduate Kutztown State Col. Bdwy debut 1971 in "Wild and Wonderful," followed by "Shirley MacLaine Show," "A Chorus Line," OB in "Dance Continuum," "Joseph and the Amazing Technicolor Dreamcoat."

GRANT, JEANNE. Born Dec. 18, 1925 in Chicago, IL. Graduate UChicago. Bdwy debut 1947 in "Brigadoon," followed by "The King and I," "Damn Yankees," "A Tree Grows in Brooklyn," "The Consul," "Saint of Bleecker Street," "3 Wishes for Jamie," "Goldilocks," "Gay Life," "Fiddler on the Roof" ('76).

GRAVES, ERNEST. Born May 5, 1919 in Chicago, IL. Attended Goodman Theatre. Bdwy bow 1941 in "Macbeth," followed by "The Russian People," "Cyrano de Bergerac," "Eastward in Eden," "Venus Is," "Ceremony of Innocence" (OB), "Poor Murderer."

GREEN, ADOLPH. Born Dec. 2 in NYC. Appeared in nightclubs with "The Revuers" before Bdwy debut 1944 in "On the Town," followed by "A Party with Betty Comden and Adolph Green" (OB) and revived on Bdwy in 1977.

GREENE, ELLEN. Born Feb. 22 in NYC. Attended Ryder Col. Debut 1973 in "Rachel Lily Rosenbloom," followed by "In the Boom Boom Room," "Threepenny Opera."

GREENE, RICHARD. Born Jan. 8, 1946 in Miami, FL. Graduate Fla. Atlantic U. Debut 1971 with LCRep in "Macbeth," followed by "Play Strindberg," "Mary Stuart," "Narrow Road to the Deep North," "Twelfth Night," and "The Crucible," Bdwy 1977 in "Romeo and Juliet."

GREGORIO, ROSE. Born in Chicago, IL. Graduate Northwestern U, Yale. Debut 1962 OB in "The Days and Nights of Beebee Fenstermaker," followed by "Kiss Mama," "The Balcony," "Bivouac at Lucca," "Journey to the Day," Bdwy in "The Owl and the Pussycat," "Daphne in Cottage D," "Jimmy Shine," "The Cuban Thing," "The Shadow Box."

243

Kristin Griffith   **Bob Gunton**   **Sandra Halperin**   **Dorian Harewood**   **Helen Harrelson**

GREY, JOEL. Born Apr. 11, 1932 in Cleveland, OH. Attended Cleveland Playhouse. Bdwy debut 1951 in "Borscht Capades," followed by "Come Blow Your Horn," "Stop the World—I Want to Get Off," "Half a Sixpence," "Cabaret," "George M!," "Goodtime Charley," OB in "The Littlest Revue," "Harry, Noon and Night," "Marco Polo Sings a Solo."

GRIFFIN, SEAN G. Born Oct. 14, 1942 in Limerick, Ire. Graduate Notre Dame, U Kan. Bdwy debut 1974 in "The National Health," followed by "Poor Murderer."

GRIFFITH, KRISTIN. Born Sept. 7, 1953 in Odessa, TX. Juilliard graduate. Bdwy debut 1976 in "A Texas Trilogy."

GRIMES, TAMMY. Born Jan. 30, 1934 in Lynn, MA. Attended Stephens Col., Neighborhood Playhouse. Debut 1956 OB in "The Littlest Revue," followed by "Clerambard," Bdwy in "Look after Lulu" (1959) for which she received a Theatre World Award, "The Unsinkable Molly Brown," "Rattle of a Simple Man," "High Spirits," "The Only Game in Town," "Private Lives," "Musical Jubilee," "California Suite."

GRIZZARD, GEORGE. Born Apr. 1, 1928 in Roanoke Rapids, VA. Graduate UNC. Bdwy bow 1954 in "All Summer Long," followed by "The Desperate Hours," "Happiest Millionaire" for which he received a Theatre World Award, "Disenchanted," "Big Fish, Little Fish," with APA 1961–62, "Who's Afraid of Virginia Woolf?," "Glass Menagerie," "You Know I Can't Hear You ...," "Noel Coward's Sweet Potato," "Gingham Dog," "Inquest," "Country Girl," "Creation of the World and Other Business," "Crown Matrimonial," "The Royal Family," "California Suite."

GROLLMAN, ELAINE. Born Oct. 22, 1928 in The Bronx, NY. Debut 1974 OB in "Yentl the Yeshiva Boy," followed by "Kaddish," "The Water Hen," "Millions of Miles," "Come Back, Little Sheba," Bdwy 1975 in "Yentl."

GUILLAUME, ROBERT. Born Nov. 30, 1937 in St. Louis, MO. Bdwy debut 1961 in "Kwamina," followed by "Finian's Rainbow," "Tambourines to Glory," "Golden Boy," "Purlie," "Guys and Dolls," OB in "Charlie Was Here and Now He's Gone," "Life and Times of J. Walter Smintheus," "Jacques Brel Is Alive ...," "Music! Music!," "Miracle Play," "Apple Pie."

GUITTARD, LAURENCE. Born July 16, 1939 in San Francisco, CA. Graduate Stanford U. Bdwy debut 1965 in "Baker Street," followed by "Anya," "Man of La Mancha," "A Little Night Music" for which he received a Theatre World Award, "Rodgers and Hart," "She Loves Me."

GULACK, MAX. Born May 19, 1928 in NYC. Graduate CCNY, Columbia U. Debut OB 1952 in "Bonds of Interest," followed by "Warrior's Husband," "Worm in the Horseradish," "Marcus in the High Grass," "Country Scandal," "Song for the First of May," "Threepenny Opera."

GUNN, MOSES. Born Oct. 2, 1929 in St. Louis, MO. Graduate UTN. AIU, UKan. OB in "Measure for Measure," "Bohikee Creek," "Day of Absence," "Happy Ending," "Baal," "Hard Travelin'," "Lonesome Train," "In White America," "The Blacks," "Titus Andronicus," "Song of the Lusitanian Bogey," "Summer of the 17th Doll," "Kongi's Harvest," "Daddy Goodness," "Cities in Bezique," "Perfect Party," "To Be Young, Gifted and Black," "Sty of the Blind Pig," "Twelfth Night," Bdwy in "A Hand Is on the Gate," "Othello," "First Breeze of Summer," "The Poison Tree," "I Have a Dream."

GUNTON, BOB. Born Nov. 15, 1945 in Santa Monica, CA. Attended UCal. Debut 1971 OB in "Who Am I?," followed by "The Kid," "Desperate Hours," OB and Bdwy 1977 in "Happy End."

GWILLIM, JACK. Born Dec. 15, 1915 in Canterbury, Eng. Attended Central School. Bdwy debut 1956 in "Macbeth," followed by "Romeo and Juliet," "Richard II," "Troilus and Cressida," "Laurette," "Ari," "Lost in the Stars," "The Iceman Cometh," "The Constant Wife," "Romeo and Juliet" ('77), OB in "The Farm."

GWYNNE, FRED. Born July 10, 1926 in NYC. Harvard Graduate. Bdwy debut 1952 in "Mrs. McThing," followed by "Love's Labour's Lost," "Frogs of Spring," "Irma La Douce," "Here's Love," "The Lincoln Mask," "More Than You Deserve" (OB), "Cat on a Hot Tin Roof," "A Texas Trilogy."

HADARY, JONATHAN. Born Oct. 11, 1948 in Chicago, IL. Attended Tufts U. Debut 1974 OB in "White Nights," followed by "El Grande de Coca-Cola," "Songs from Pins and Needles," "Gemini" (also Bdwy 1977).

HAFNER, JULIE J. Born June 4, 1952 in Dover, OH. Graduate Kent State U. Debut 1976 OB in "The Club."

HAIGH, KENNETH. Born Mar. 25, 1930 in Yorkshire, Eng. Attended Central School. Bdwy debut 1957 in "Look Back in Anger," followed by "Caligula," "Endecott and the Red Cross" (OB), "California Suite."

HALE, ELIZABETH. Born Jan. 15, 1947 in Brooklyn, NY. Graduate Emerson Col. Bdwy debut 1976 in "Fiddler on the Roof."

HALL, GRAYSON. Born in Philadelphia, PA. Attended Temple U., Cornell U. Debut 1953 OB in "Man and Superman," followed by "La Ronde," "Six Characters in Search of an Author," "The Balcony," "The Buskers," "The Love Nest," "Shout from the Rooftops," "The Last Analysis," "Friends and Relations," "The Screens," "Secrets of the Citizens Correction Committee," "The Sea," "What Every Woman Knows," "Jack Gelber's New Play," "Happy End," Bdwy in "Subways Are for Sleeping," "Those That Play the Clowns," "The Leaf People," "Happy End."

HALLIDAY, GORDON. Born Apr. 2, 1952 in Providence, RI. Attended RI Col., AADA. Bdwy debut 1975 in "Shenandoah."

HALPERIN, SANDRA. Born Feb. 16, 1951 in Los Angeles, CA. Juilliard graduate. Bdwy debut 1975 in "The Three Sisters," followed by "The Time of Your Life," "The Robber Bridegroom."

HAMILTON, MARGARET. Born Dec. 9, 1902 in Cleveland, OH. Attended Cleveland Playhouse. Bdwy debut 1932 in "Another Language," followed by "Dark Tower," "Farmer Takes a Wife," "Outrageous Fortune," "The Men We Marry," "Fancy Meeting You Again," "Annie Get Your Gun" (CC), "Goldilocks," "UTBU," LC's "Show Boat" and "Oklahoma!," "Come Summer," "Our Town," BAM Co.'s "New York Idea" and "Three Sisters."

HAMILTON, ROGER. Born in San Diego, CA., May 2, 1928. Attended San Diego Col., RADA. OB in "Merchant of Venice," "Hamlet," "Live Like Pigs," "Hotel Passionato," "Sjt. Musgrave's Dance," Bdwy in "Someone Waiting," "Separate Tables," "Little Moon of Alban," "Luther," "The Deputy," "Rosencrantz and Guildenstern Are Dead," "The Rothschilds," "Pippin."

HAMMIL, JOHN. Born May 9, 1948 in NYC. Attended UCLA. Bdwy debut 1972 in "Purlie," followed by "Oh! Calcutta!," OB in "El Grande de Coca-Cola."

HAMPTON, DONALD. Born Feb. 28, 1947 in McKinney, TX. Graduate Schiller Col., U Tex. Debut 1977 OB in "Piaf . . . A Remembrance."

HANLEY, KATIE. Born Jan. 17, 1949 in Evanston, IL. Attended Carnegie-Mellon U. Debut 1971 OB in "Godspell," followed by "Grease."

HARADA, ERNEST. Born Oct. 20, 1946 in Honolulu, HI. Attended Syracuse U., LAMDA. Bdwy debut 1976 in "Pacific Overtures."

HARDIN, B. J. Born Jan. 1, 1954 in Hattiesburg, MS. Attended U Ark. Bdwy debut 1976 in "The Robber Bridegroom."

HAREWOOD, DORIAN. Born Aug. 6, in Dayton, OH. Attended U Cincinnati. Bdwy debut 1972 in "Two Gentlemen of Verona," followed by "Over Here," "Don't Call Back" for which he received a Theatre World Award, "Streamers."

HARGER, GARY. Born Aug. 19, 1951 in New Haven, CT. Ithaca Col. graduate. Bdwy debut 1975 in "Shenandoah."

HARNEY, BEN. Born Aug. 29, 1952 in Brooklyn, NY. Bdwy debut 1971 in "Purlie," followed by "Pajama Game," "Treemonisha," "Pippin," OB in "Don't Bother Me, I Can't Cope."

HARPER, J. W. Born Oct. 8, 1948 in Bell, CA. Attended Marin Col., Juilliard. Bdwy debut 1975 in "The Robber Bridegroom," followed by "Edward II," "The Time of Your Life," "Three Sisters."

HARRELSON, HELEN. Born in Missouri; graduate Goodman Theatre Sch. Bdwy debut 1950 in "The Cellar and the Well," followed by "Death of a Salesman," "Days in the Trees," "Romeo and Juliet," OB in "Our Town," "His and Hers," "House of Atreus."

HARRINGTON, DELPHI. Born Aug. 26 in Chicago, IL. Graduate Northwestern U. Debut 1960 OB in "Country Scandal," followed by "Moon for the Misbegotten," "Baker's Dozen," "The Zykovs," Bdwy in "Thieves," "Everything in the Garden," "Romeo and Juliet."

HARRIS, BAXTER. Born Nov. 18, 1940 in Columbus, KS. Attended U Kan. Debut 1967 OB in "America Hurrah," followed by "The Reckoning," "Wicked Women Revue," "More Than You Deserve," "Pericles," "him," "Battle of Angels," "Down by the River. . . .," Bdwy 1976 in "A Texas Trilogy."

HARRIS, CHARLENE. Born Mar. 16, 1925 in Chicago, IL. Bdwy debut 1950 in "Bless You All," OB in "Divine Comedy."

Nick Harrison

Trish Hawkins

Winston DeWitt Hemsley

Jo Henderson

Judd Hirsch

HARRIS, CYNTHIA. Born in NYC. Graduate Smith Col. Bdwy debut 1963 in "Natural Affection, followed by "Any Wednesday," "Best Laid Plans," "Company," OB in "The Premise," "3 by Wilder," "America Hurrah," "White House Murder Case," "Mystery Play," "Bad Habits," "Merry Wives of Windsor," "Beauty Part," "Jules Feiffer's Hold Me!"

HARRIS, JULIE. Born Dec. 2, 1925 in Grosse Point, MI. Attended Yale. Bdwy debut 1945 in "It's a Gift," followed by "Henry V," "Oedipus," "The Playboy of the Western World," "Alice in Wonderland," "Macbeth," "Sundown Beach" for which she received a Theatre World Award, "The Young and The Fair," "Magnolia Alley," "Montserrat," "The Member of the Wedding," "I Am a Camera," "Mlle Colombe," "The Lark," "Country Wife," "Warm Peninsula," "Little Moon of Alban," "A Shot in the Dark," "Marathon '33," "Ready When You Are, C. B.," "Hamlet" (CP), "Skyscraper," "40 Carats," "And Miss Reardon Drinks A Little," "Voices," "The Last of Mrs. Lincoln," "The Au Pair Man" (LC), "In Praise of Love," "Belle of Amherst."

HARRIS, ROSEMARY. Born Sept. 19, 1930 in Ashby, Eng. Attended RADA. Bdwy debut 1952 in "Climate of Eden" for which she received a Theatre World Award, followed by "Troilus and Cressida," "Interlock," "The Disenchanted," "The Tumbler," in APA's "The Tavern," "School for Scandal," "Seagull," "Importance of Being Earnest," "War and Peace," "Man and Superman," "Judith" and "You Can't Take It with You," "Lion in Winter," "Old Times," LC's "Merchant of Venice" and "Streetcar Named Desire," "Royal Family," BAM Co.'s "New York Idea" and "Three Sisters."

HARRIS, TOM. Born Feb. 17, 1949 in Kingston, PA. Graduate King's Col. Debut 1971 OB in "The Basic Training of Pavlo Hummel," followed by "Fishing," Bdwy bow 1972 in "Grease."

HARRISON, KEN. Born Oct. 26, 1947 in Santa Barbara, CA. Studied at American Conservatory Theatre. Bdwy debut 1977 in "Anna Christie."

HARRISON, NICK. Born May 28, 1938 in Cincinnati, OH. Attended Ohio State. Debut 1971 OB in "The Cage," followed by "Speakeasy," "Line," "Come Back, Little Sheba."

HARRISON, REX. Born Mar. 5, 1908 in Huyten, Eng. Attended Liverpool Col. Bdwy debut 1936 in "Sweet Aloes," followed by "Anne of a Thousand Days," "Bell, Book and Candle," "Venus Observed," "Love of Four Colonels," "My Fair Lady," "Fighting Cock," "Emperor Henry IV," "In Praise of Love," "Caesar and Cleopatra."

HART, CECILIA. Born June 6 in Cheyenne, WY. Graduate Emerson Col. Debut 1974 OB in "Macbeth," followed by "Emperor of Late Night Radio," Bdwy in "The Heiress" (1976), "Dirty Linen" for which she received a Theatre World Award.

HAWKINS, TRISH. Born Oct. 30, 1945 in Hartford, CT. Attended Radcliffe, Neighborhood Playhouse. Debut OB 1970 in "Oh! Calcutta!" followed by "Iphigenia," "The Hot l Baltimore" for which she received a Theatre World Award, "him", "Come Back, Little Sheba," "Battle of Angels," "Mound Builders," "The Farm."

HAYNES, TIGER. Born Dec. 13, 1907 in St. Croix, VI. Bdwy bow 1956 in "New Faces," followed by "Finian's Rainbow," "Fade Out—Fade In," "The Pajama Game," "The Wiz."

HEARD, JOHN. Born Mar. 7, 1946 in Washington, DC. Graduate Clark U. Debut 1974 OB in "The Wager," followed by "Macbeth," "Hamlet," "Fishing," "G. R. Point" for which he received a Theatre World Award, "Creditors," Bdwy in "Warp" (1973)

HEATH, GORDON. Born Sept. 20, 1918 in NYC. Attended CCNY. Bdwy debut 1945 in "Deep Are the Roots," OB in "Oedipus," "Endgame."

HEATH, SIGRID. Born Jan. 29, 1947 in St. Lucia, BWI. Attended UNC. Debut 1976 OB in "Lovesong."

HECHT, PAUL. Born Aug. 16, 1941 in London. Attended McGill U. OB in "Sjt. Musgrave's Dance," "MacBird," Bdwy in "Rosencrantz and Guildenstern Are Dead," "1776," "The Rothschilds," "Ride Across Lake Constance" (LC), "Great God Brown," "Don Juan," "Emperor Henry IV," "Herzl," "Caesar and Cleopatra."

HECKART, EILEEN. Born Mar. 29, 1919 in Columbus, OH. Graduate Ohio State U. Debut OB in "Tinker's Dam," followed by Bdwy in "Our Town," "They Knew What They Wanted," "The Traitor," "Hilda Crane," "In Any Language," "Picnic" for which she received a Theatre World Award, "Bad Seed," "View from the Bridge," "Dark at the Top of the Stairs," "Invitation to a March," "Pal Joey," "Everybody Loves Opal," "And Things That Go Bump in the Night," "Barefoot in the Park," "You Know I Can't Hear You When the Water's Running," "Mother Lover," "Butterflies Are Free," "Veronica's Room," "Ladies at the Alamo."

HEFFERNAN, JOHN. Born May 30, 1934 in NYC. Attended CCNY, Columbia, Boston U. OB in "The Judge," "Julius Caesar," "Great God Brown," "Lysistrata," "Peer Gynt," "Henry IV," "Taming of the Shrew," "She Stoops to Conquer," "The Plough and the Stars," "Octoroon," "Hamlet," "Androcles and the Lion," "A Man's a Man," "Winter's Tale," "Arms and the Man," "St. Joan" (LCR), "Peer Gynt" (CP), "Memorandum," "Invitation to a Beheading," "Shadow of a Gunman," "The Sea," Bdwy in "Luther," "Tiny Alice," "Postmark Zero," "Woman Is My Idea," "Morning, Noon and Night," "Purlie," "Bad Habits," "Lady from the Sea," "Knock Knock," "Sly Fox."

HEIST, KARL. Born June 14, 1950 in West Reading, PA. Graduate McMurry Col. Debut 1976 OB in "Fiorello," followed by "Silk Stockings."

HEMSLEY, WINSTON DeWITT. Born May 21, 1947 in Brooklyn, NY. Bdwy debut 1965 in "Golden Boy," followed by "A Joyful Noise," "Hallelujah, Baby," "Hello, Dolly!," "Rockabye Hamlet," "A Chorus Line," OB in "Buy Bonds Buster."

HENDERSON, JO. Born in Buffalo, NY. Attended Western Mich. U. OB in "Camille," "Little Foxes," "An Evening with Merlin Finch," "20th Century Tar," "A Scent of Flowers," "Revival," "Dandelion Wine," "Ladyhouse Blues," "My Life."

HENNING, DOUG. Born May 3, 1947 in Winnipeg, Can. Graduate McMaster U. Bdwy debut 1974 in "The Magic Show."

HEPBURN, KATHARINE. Born Nov. 9, 1909 in Hartford, CT. Graduate Bryn Mawr. Bdwy debut 1928 in "Night Hostess," followed by "These Days," "A Month in the Country," "Art and Mrs. Bottle," "Warrior's Husband," "The Lake," "Philadelphia Story," "Without Love," "As You Like It," "The Millionairess," "Coco," "A Matter of Gravity."

HEWETT, CHRISTOPHER. Born Apr. 5 in England; attended Beaumont Col. Bdwy debut 1956 in "My Fair Lady," followed by "First Impressions," "Unsinkable Molly Brown," "Kean," "The Affair," "Hadrian VII," "Music Is," OB in "Tobias and the Angel," "Trelawny of the Wells."

HEYMAN, BARTON. Born Jan. 24, 1937 in Washington, DC. Attended UCLA. Bdwy debut 1969 in "Indians," followed by "Trial of the Catonsville 9," OB in "Midsummer Night's Dream," "Sleep," "Phantasmagoria Historia," "Enclave," "Henry V."

HIGGINS, DENNIS. Born Aug. 25, 1942 in Washington, DC. Attended Geo. Wash. U., AADA. Debut 1969 OB in "Tom Jones," followed by "Greenwillow" (ELT), "Isadora Duncan Sleeps with the Russian Navy."

HIGGINS, JOEL. Born Sept. 28, 1943 in Bloomington, IL. Graduate Mich. State U. Bdwy debut 1975 in "Shenandoah" for which he received a Theatre World Award, followed by "Music Is."

HIGGINS, MICHAEL. Born Jan. 20, 1926 in Bklyn. Attended Theatre Wing. Bdwy bow 1946 in "Antigone," followed by "Our Lan'," "Romeo and Juliet," "The Crucible," "The Lark," "Equus," OB in "White Devil," "Carefree Tree," "Easter," "The Queen and the Rebels," "Sally, George and Martha," "L'Ete," "Uncle Vanya," "The Iceman Cometh."

HINES, PATRICK. Born Mar. 17, 1930 in Burkesville, TX. Graduate Tex. U. Debut OB in "Duchess of Malfi," followed by "Lysistrata," "Peer Gynt," "Henry IV," "Richard III," Bdwy in "Great God Brown," "Passage to India," "The Devils," "Cyrano," "The Iceman Cometh," "A Texas Trilogy," "Caesar and Cleopatra."

HIRSCH, JUDD. Born Mar. 15, 1935 in NYC. Attended AADA. Bdwy debut 1966 in "Barefoot in the Park," followed OB by "On the Necessity of Being Polygamous," "Scuba Duba," "Mystery Play," "Hot l Baltimore," "Prodigal," "Knock Knock."

245

Ann Hodapp **David Hodo** **Ruby Holbrook,** **Matthew Inge** **Karen Jablons**

HODAPP, ANN. Born May 6, 1946 in Louisville, Ky. Attended Hunter Col., NYU. Debut 1968 OB in "You're a Good Man, Charlie Brown," followed by "A Round with Ring," "House of Leather," "Shoestring Revue," "God Bless Coney," "What's A Nice Country Like You . . . ," "Oh, Lady! Lady!," "House-wives Cantata," "A Day in the Port Authority," "A Little Wine with Lunch," "Fiorello."

HODES, GLORIA. Born Aug. 20 in Norwich, CT. Operatic training before Bdwy debut 1969 in "Gantry," followed by OB's "The Club" for which she received a Theatre World Award.

HODO, DAVID. Born July 7, 1950 in Palo Alto, CA. Graduate Cal. State U. Bdwy debut 1975 in "Doctor Jazz," followed by "Pal Joey."

HOFFMANN, JACK. Born Mar. 6, 1950 in Indianapolis, IN. Graduate Denison U. Debut 1974 OB in "Anna K.," followed by "Dear Oscar," " Waiting for Godot," "Boys from Syracuse" (ELT).

HOGAN, JONATHAN. Born June 13, 1951 in Chicago, IL. Graduate Goodman Theatre. Debut OB 1972 in "The Hot l Baltimore," followed by "Mound Builders," "Harry Outside," Bdwy 1976 in "Comedians."

HOLBROOK, HAL. Born Feb. 17, 1925 in Cleveland, OH. Graduate Denison U. Bdwy bow 1961 in "Do You Know the Milky Way?," followed by "Glass Menagerie," "Mark Twain Tonight" (1959, '66, '77), "The Apple Tree," "I Never Sang for My Father," "Man of LaMancha," "Does a Tiger Wear a Necktie?," OB in "Henry IV," "Richard II," "Abe Lincoln in Illinois," "Marco Millions," "Incident at Vichy," "Tartuffe," "After the Fall," "Lake of the Woods."

HOLBROOK, RUBY. Born Aug. 28, 1930 in St. John's, Newfoundland. Attended Denison U. Debut 1963 OB in "Abe Lincoln in Illinois," followed by "Hamlet," "James Joyce's Dubliners," "Measure for Measure," "The Farm."

HOLLANDER, JACK. Born Jan. 29, 1918 in Chicago, IL. Graduate Goodman Theatre. Bdwy debut 1959 in "Miracle Worker," followed by "All the Way Home," "Gideon," "Impossible Years," "Man in the Glass Booth," "Inquest," "Birthday Party," "Zalmen, or the Madness of God," OB in "Girl of the Golden West," "Dybbuk," "Journey to the Day," "Titus Andronicus," "Comedy of Errors," "Ergo," "Phantasmagoria Historia . . . ," "Troilus and Cressida," "Jack Gelber's New Play," "From the Memoirs of Pontius Pilate."

HOLLIDAY, DAVID. Born Aug. 4, 1937 in Illinois. Attended Carthage Col. Bdwy debut 1968 in "Man of La Mancha," followed by "Coco" for which he received a Theatre World Award, "Nevertheless, They Laugh" (OB), "Music Is."

HOLLIDAY, KENE. Born June 25, 1949 in NYC. Graduate UMd. Debut 1976 OB in "Streamers."

HOLMES, PRUDENCE WRIGHT. Born in Boston, MA. Attended Carnegie Tech. Debut 1971 OB in "Godspell," followed by "Polly," "The Crazy Locomotive," Bdwy 1977 in "Happy End."

HORMANN, NICHOLAS. Born Dec. 22, 1944 in Honolulu, HI. Graduate Oberlin, Yale. Bdwy debut 1973 in "The Visit," followed by "Chemin de Fer," "Holiday," "Love for Love," "Rules of the Game," "Member of the Wedding," OB in "Ice Age," "Marco Polo."

HORNE, CHERYL. Born Nov. 15 in Stamford, CT. Graduate SMU. Debut 1975 OB in "The Fantasticks."

HORTON, RUSSELL. Born Nov. 11, 1941 in Los Angeles, CA. Graduate UCLA. Debut 1966 OB in "Displaced Person," followed by "How's the World Treating You?," LC's "Galileo" and "Antigone," "What Did We Do Wrong?," "The Last Resort," "Scribes."

HOSBEIN, JAMES. Born Sept. 24, 1946 in Benton Harbor, MI. Graduate UMich. Debut 1972 OB in "Dear Oscar," followed by "Darrel and Carol and Kenny and Jenny," Bdwy 1977 in "Annie."

HOTY, TONY. Born Sept. 29, 1949 in Lakewood, OH. Attended Ithaca Col., WVaU. Debut 1974 OB in "Godspell" (also Bdwy 1976), followed by "Joseph and the Amazing Technicolor Dreamcoat."

HOWARD, JOE. Born Nov. 24, 1948 in Yonkers, NY. Graduate Hamilton Col. Bdwy debut 1976 in "So Long, 174th Street," followed by "Shenandoah."

HOWARD, KEN. Born Mar. 28, 1944 in El Centro, CA. Yale graduate, Bdwy debut 1968 in "Promises, Promises," followed by "1776" for which he received a Theatre World Award, "Child's Play," "Seesaw," "Little Black Sheep" (LC), "The Norman Conquests," "1600 Pennsylvania Avenue."

HOWARD, STEPHEN. Born Feb. 11, 1947 in Kansas City, MO. Attended UKan., HB Studio. Debut 1977 OB in "Wonderful Town" (ELT).

HOWARD, TULANE B. II. Born Oct. 4, 1953 in Washington, DC. Graduate Tarkio Col. Debut 1975 OB in "Wonderful Woman," Bdwy 1976 in "Let My People Come."

HUDGINS, WAYNE. Born June 19, 1950 in Amarillo, TX. Graduate UWash. Bdwy debut 1976 in "Shenandoah."

HUDSON, TRAVIS. Born Feb. 2 in Amarillo, TX. Graduate U Tex. Bdwy debut in "New Faces of 1962," followed by "Pousse Cafe," "Very Good Eddie," OB in "Triad," "Tattooed Countess," "Young Abe Lincoln," "Get Thee to Canterbury," "Golden Apple."

HUGHES, BARNARD. Born July 16, 1915 in Bedford Hills, N. Y. Attended Manhattan Col. OB in "Rosmersholm," "A Doll's House," "Hogan's Goat," "Line," "Older People," "Hamlet" "Merry Wives of Windsor," "Pericles," BAM Co.'s "Three Sisters," Bdwy in "The Ivy Green," "Dinosaur Wharf," "Teahouse of the August Moon" (CC), "A Majority of One," "Advise and Consent," "The Advocate," "Hamlet," "I Was Dancing," "Generation," "How Now, Dow Jones?," "Wrong Way Light Bulb," "Sheep On The Runway," "Abelard and Heloise," "Much Ado About Nothing," "Uncle Vanya," "The Good Doctor," "All Over Town."

HURT, WILLIAM. Born Mar. 20, 1950 in Washington, DC. Graduate Tufts U., Juilliard. Debut 1976 OB in "Henry V," followed by "My Life."

HYMAN, EARLE. Born Oct. 11, 1926 in Rocky Mount, NC. Attended New School, Theatre Wing. Bdwy debut 1943 in "Run, Little Chillun," followed by "Anna Lucasta," "Climate of Eden," "Merchant of Venice," "Othello," "Julius Caesar," "The Tempest," "No Time for Sergeants," "Mr. Johnson" for which he received a Theatre World Award, "St Joan," "Hamlet," "Waiting for Godot," "Duchess of Malfi," "Les Blancs," OB in "The White Rose and the Red," "Worlds of Shakespeare," "Jonah," "Life and Times of J. Walter Smintheus," "Orrin," "Cherry Orchard," "House Party," "Carnival Dreams."

HYMAN, LARRY. Born Oct. 21, 1955 in Los Angeles, CA. Bdwy debut 1976 in "Rockabye Hamlet," followed by "Going Up."

ING, ALVIN. Born May 26, 1938 in Honolulu, HI. Graduate Columbia U. Bdwy debut 1959 in "World of Suzie Wong," followed by "Two Gentlemen of Verona," "Pacific Overtures," OB in "Tenth of an Inch," "Cranes and Peonies," "Coffins for Butterflies," "Six."

INGE, MATTHEW. Born May 29, 1950 in Fitchburg, MA. Attended Boston U., Harvard. Bdwy debut 1976 in "Fiddler on the Roof."

INNERARITY, MEMRIE. Born Feb. 11, 1945 in Columbus, MS. Attended USMiss. Debut 1976 OB in "The Club."

IVES, ANNE. Born in Providence, RI. Attended Sargent's Sch., AmThWing. Bdwy debut 1906 in "The Chorus Lady," followed by "Point of No Return," "Masquerade," "Uncle Vanya," "Unexpected Guests," OB in "The Crucible," "Effect of Gamma Rays . . . ," "Good Woman of Setzuan," "The Contractor," "Ice Age."

JABLONS, KAREN. Born July 19, 1951 in Trenton, NJ. Juilliard graduate. Debut 1969 OB in "The Student Prince," followed by "Sound of Music," "Funny Girl," "Boys from Syracuse," Bdwy in "Ari," "Two Gentlemen of Verona," "Lorelei," "Where's Charley?," "A Chorus Line."

JACKSON, ANNE. Born Sept. 3, 1926 in Allegheny, PA. Attended Neighborhood Playhouse. Bdwy debut 1945 in "Signature," followed by "Yellow Jack," "John Gabriel Borkman," "The Last Dance," "Summer and Smoke," "Magnolia Alley," "Love Me Long," "Lady from the Sea," "Never Say Never," "Oh, Men! Oh, Women!," "Rhinoceros," "Luv," "The Exercise," "Inquest," "Promenade All!," "Waltz of the Toreadors," OB in "The Tiger," "The Typists," "Marco Polo Sings a Solo."

JACKSON, ERNESTINE. Born Sept. 18 in Corpus Christi, TX. Graduate Del Mar Col., Juilliard. Debut 1966 in LC's "Show Boat," followed by "Finian's Rainbow" (CC), "Hello, Dolly!," "Applause," "Jesus Christ Superstar," "Tricks," "Raisin" for which she received a Theatre World Award, "Guys and Dolls."

JAMES, CLIFTON. Born May 29, 1921 in Spokane, WA. Attended Ore. U., Actors Studio. Has appeared in "The Time of Your Life" (CC), "The Cave Dwellers," "Great Day in the Morning," "Andorra," "And Things That Go Bump in the Night," "The Coop" (OB), "Trial of Lee Harvey Oswald," "The Shadow Box."

JAMES, JESSICA. Born Oct. 31, 1933 in Los Angeles, CA. Attended USC. Bdwy debut 1970 in "Company," followed by "Gemini," OB in "Nourish the Beast," "Hothouse," "Loss of Innocence," "Rebirth Celebration of the Human Race," "Silver Bee," "Gemini."

Don Jay

Nicki Kaplan

Page Johnson

Kate Kellery

Jeff Keller

JAMES, WILLIAM. Born Apr. 29, 1938 in Jersey City, NJ. Graduate NJ State Teachers Col. Bdwy bow 1962 in "Camelot," followed by "Maggie Flynn," "Coco," "My Fair Lady," (CC & 1976), "Where's Charley?" (CC), "She Loves Me," OB in "Anything Goes," "Smith."

JANIS, CONRAD. Born Feb. 11, 1928 in NYC. Bdwy debut 1942 in "Junior Miss," followed by "Dark of the Moon," "The Next Half Hour," "Brass Ring" for which he received a Theatre World Award, "Time Out for Ginger," "Terrible Swift Sword," "Visit to a Small Planet," "Make a Million," "Sunday in New York," "Marathon '33," "Front Page," "No Hard Feelings," "Same Time Next Year."

JANSEN, JIM. Born July 27, 1945 in Salt Lake City, UT. Graduate U Utah. NYU, Debut OB in "Moonchildren," followed by "Marco Polo Sings a Solo," Bdwy 1974 in "All Over Town."

JARKOWSKY, ANDREW. Born in NYC. Graduate CCNY. Debut OB 1974 in "Festival of Short Plays," followed by "Cakes with Wine," "The Boss," Bdwy 1977 in "The Trip Back Down."

JAROSLOW, RUTH. Born May 22 in Brooklyn, NY. Attended HB Studio. Debut 1964 OB in "That 5 A.M. Jazz," followed by "Jonah," Bdwy in "Mame," "Fiddler on the Roof," (original and 1977), "The Ritz."

JASPER, ZINA. Born Jan. 29, 1939 in the Bronx, NY. Attended CCNY. Bdwy debut 1967 in "Something Different," followed by "Paris Is Out," OB in "Saturday's Children," "Moondreamers," "A Dream out of Time," "Quail Southwest."

JAY, DON. Born in Calif. Bdwy debut 1965 in "The Zulu and the Zayda," followed by "Hello, Dolly!," "Two Gentlemen of Verona," "Raisin," OB in "On the Lock-In."

JEANNETTE, GERTRUDE. Born Nov. 28, 1918 in Little Rock, AR. Attended New School. Has appeared in "Lost in the Stars," "The Long Dream," "Amen Corner," "Nobody Loves an Albatross," "The Skin of Our Teeth," "Vieux Carre," OB in "This Way Forward," "Deep Are the Roots," "417," "Moon on a Rainbow Shawl," "To Be Young, Gifted and Black."

JEROME, TIMOTHY. Born Dec. 29, 1943 in Los Angeles, CA. Graduate Ithaca Col. Bdwy debut 1969 in "Man of La Mancha," followed by "The Rothschilds," "Creation of the World and Other Business," OB in "Beggar's Opera," "Pretzels," "Civilization and Its Discontents."

JOHANSON, ROBERT. Born Apr. 17, 1951 in Wilmington, DE. Graduate Ithaca Col. Bdwy debut 1977 in "Shenandoah."

JOHNSON, PAGE. Born Aug. 25, 1930 in Welch, WV. Graduate Ithaca Col. Bdwy bow 1951 in "Romeo and Juliet," followed by "Electra," "Oedipus," "Camino Real," "In April Once" for which he received a Theatre World Award, "Red Roses for Me," "The Lovers," "Equus," OB in "The Enchanted," "Guitar," "4 in 1," "Journey of the Fifth Horse," "School for Scandal," "The Tavern" and "The Seagull," APA's "Odd Couple," "Boys In The Band," "Medea."

JOHNSTON, JUSTINE. Born June 13 in Evanston, IL. Debut 1959 OB in "Little Mary Sunshine," followed by "The Time of Your Life" (CC), "The Dubliners," Bdwy in "Pajama Game," "Milk and Honey," "Follies," "Irene," "Molly," BAM Co.'s "New York Idea."

JONES, CHARLOTTE. Born Jan. 1, in Chicago. Attended Loyola, DePaul U. OB in "False Confessions," "Sign of Jonah," "Girl on the Via Flaminia," "Red Roses for Me," "Night is Black Bottles," "Camino Real," "Plays for Bleecker St.," "Pigeons," "Great Scot!," "Sjt. Musgrave's Dance," "Papers," "Johnny Johnson," "Beggar's Opera," "200 Years of American Furniture," Bdwy in "Camino Real," "Buttrio Square," "Mame," "How Now Dow Jones," "Skin of Our Teeth," "Matter of Gravity."

JONES, JAMES EARL. Born Jan. 17, 1931 in Arkabutla, MI. Graduate Mich U. OB in "The Pretender," "The Blacks," "Clandestine on the Morning Line," "The Apple," "A Midsummer Night's Dream," "Moon on a Rainbow Shawl" for which he received a Theatre World Award. "PS 193," "Last Minstrel," "Love Nest," "Bloodknot," "Othello," "Baal," "Danton's Death" (LC), "Boesman and Lena," "Hamlet" (NYSF) "Cherry Orchard," Bdwy in "The Egghead," "Sunrise at Campobello," "The Cool World," "A Hand Is on the Gate," "Great White Hope," "Les Blancs," "King Lear," "The Iceman Cometh," "Of Mice and Men."

JONES, JEFFREY. Born Sept. 28, 1947 in Buffalo, NY. Graduate Lawrence U., LAMDA. Debut OB 1973 in "Lotta," followed by "The Tempest," "Trelawny of the Wells," "Secret Service," "Boy Meets Girl," "Scribes."

JONES, JEN. Born Mar. 23, 1927 in Salt Lake City, UT. Attended UUtah. Debut 1960 OB in "Drums under the Window," followed by "Long Voyage Home," "Diff'rent," "Creditors," "Look at Any Man," "I Knock at the Door," "Pictures in the Hallway," "The Grab Bag," "Bo Bo," Bdwy in "Dr. Cook's Garden," "But Seriously," "Eccentricities of a Nightingale."

JORDAN, ALAN. Born Mar. 21, 1943 in Toronto, Can. Graduate Neighborhood Playhouse. Debut 1974 OB in "The Proposition," followed by "Battle of Angels," "Exiles."

JOSLYN, BETSY. Born Apr. 19, 1954 in Staten Island, NY. Graduate Wagner Col. Debut 1976 OB in "The Fantasticks."

JOYCE, STEPHEN. Born Mar. 7, 1933 in NYC. Attended Fordham U. Bdwy bow 1966 in "Those That Play the Clowns," followed by "The Exercise," "The Runner Stumbles," OB in "Three Hand Reel," "Galileo," "St. Joan," "Stephen D" for which he received a Theatre World Award, "Fireworks," "School for Wives," "Savages," "Scribes."

JULIA, RAUL. Born Mar. 9, 1940 in San Juan, PR. Graduate UPR. OB in "Macbeth," "Titus Andronicus" (CP), "Theatre in the Streets," "Life Is a Dream," "Blood Wedding," "Ox Cart," "No Exit," "Memorandum," "Frank Gagliano's City Scene," "Your Own Thing," "Persians," "Castro Complex," "Pinkville," "Hamlet," "King Lear," "As You Like It," "Emperor of Late Night Radio," "Threepenny Opera," "The Cherry Orchard," Bdwy bow 1968 in "The Cuban Thing," followed by "Indians," "Two Gentlemen of Verona," "Via Galactica," "Where's Charley?"

JUNG, CALVIN. Born Feb. 17, 1945 in NYC. Graduate Hillsdale Col. Debut 1972 OB in "Chickencoop Chinaman," followed by "Dawn Song," "Year of the Dragon," "A Memory of Two Mondays," "They Knew What They Wanted," Bdwy 1976 in "Sly Fox."

KAGAN, DIANE. Born in Maplewood, NJ. Graduate Fla. State U. Debut OB 1963 in "Asylum," followed by "Days and Nights of Beebee Fenstermaker," "Death of the Well-Loved Boy," "Madam de Sade," "Blue Boys," "Alive and Well in Argentina," "Little Black Sheep," "The Family," Bdwy in "Chinese Prime Minister," "Never Too Late," "Any Wednesday," "Venus Is," "Tiger at the Gates" (LC), "Vieux Carre."

KAHN, MADELINE. Born Sept. 29, 1942 in Boston, MA. Graduate Hofstra U. Bdwy debut 1968 in "New Faces of 1968," followed by "Two by Two," "She Loves Me," OB in "Promenade," "Boom Boom Room," "Marco Polo Sings a Solo."

KAPLAN, NICKI. Born May 23, 1938 in NYC. Graduate Syracuse U. Debut 1975 OB in "Another Language."

KAREMAN, FRED. Born June 24, 1934 in Asbury Park, NJ. Attended Rutgers U., Neighborhood Playhouse. Debut 1955 OB in "Salvage," followed by "Taming of the Shrew," "Days and Nights of Beebee Fenstermaker," Bdwy in "The Skin of Our Teeth," "The Time of Your Life" (CC), "Re-Education of Horse Johnson," "A Cook for Mr. General."

KARR, PATTI. Born July 10 in St. Paul, MN. Attended TCU. Bdwy debut 1953 in "Maggie," followed by "Carnival in Flanders," "Pipe Dream," "Bells Are Ringing," "New Girl in Town," "Body Beautiful," "Bye Bye Birdie," "New Faces of 1962," "Come on Strong," "Look to the Lilies," "Different Times," "Lysistrata," "Seesaw," "Irene," "Pippin," OB in "A Month of Sundays," "Up Eden."

KATCHER, HOPE. Born June 22, 1951 in Brooklyn, NY. Graduate Boston U. Bdwy debut 1976 in "Fiddler on the Roof."

KAVA, CAROLINE. Born in Chicago, IL. Attended Neighborhood Playhouse. Debut 1975 OB in "Gorky," followed by "Threepenny Opera."

KEITH, LAWRENCE. Born Mar. 4, 1931 in Brooklyn, NY. Graduate Brooklyn Col., Indiana U. Bdwy debut 1960 in "My Fair Lady," followed by "High Spirits," "I Had a Ball," "Best Laid Plans," "Mother Lover," OB in "The Homecoming," "Conflict of Interest," "Brownsville Raid."

KELL, MICHAEL. Born Jan. 18, 1944 in Jersey City, NJ. Attended HB Studio. Debut 1972 OB in "One Flew over the Cuckoo's Nest," followed by "Boom Boom Room," "Golden Boy," "Streamers."

KELLER, JEFF. Born Sept. 8, 1947 in Brooklyn. Graduate Monmouth Col. Bdwy debut 1974 in "Candide," followed by "Fiddler on the Roof."

KELLERY, KATE. Born Aug. 23, 1950 in Washington, DC. Graduate Temple, Catholic U. Bdwy debut 1975 in "The Skin of Our Teeth."

KELLIN, MIKE. Born Apr. 26, 1922 in Hartford, CT. Attended Trinity Col., Yale. Bdwy bow 1949 in "At War with the Army," followed by "Bird Cage," "Stalag 17," "The Emperor's Clothes," "The Time of Your Life," "Pipe Dream," "Who Was That Lady?," "God and Kate Murphy," "Ankles Aweigh," "Rhinoceros," "Odd Couple," "Mother Courage," OB in "Taming of the Shrew," "Diary of a Scoundrel," "Purple Dust," "Tevya and His Daughters," "Winkelberg," "Winterset," "Joan of Lorraine," "Bread," "American Buffalo," "Duck Variations."

KELLSTROM, GAIL. Born June 24, 1944 in Newark, NJ. Graduate Rutgers U., Penn State. Debut 1970 OB in "Second Cummings," followed by "Yerma," "In White America," "Dance on a Country Grave."

KELLY, K. C. Born Nov. 12, 1952 in Baraboo, WI. Attended UWisc. Debut 1976 OB in "The Chicken Ranch," followed by Bdwy 1977 in "Romeo and Juliet."

KELTON, RICHARD. Born Apr. 29, 1943 in Lincoln, NB. Graduate UKan. Bdwy debut 1976 in "Who's Afraid of Virginia Woolf?" for which he received a Theatre World Award.

KENNEDY, MIMI. Born Sept 25, 1948 in Rochester, NY. Graduate Smith College. Bdwy debut 1975 in "Grease."

KERMOYAN, MICHAEL. Born Nov. 29, 1925 in Fresno, CA. Attended Stanford U., USC. Bdwy bow 1954 in "The Girl in Pink Tights," followed by "Whoop-Up," "Happy Town," "Camelot," "Happiest Girl in the World," "Fly Blackbird," "Ross," "Tovarich," "Anya," "The Guide," "Desert Song," "The King and I," OB in "Carousel," "Sandhog," "Angels of Anadarko."

KERNAN, DAVID. Born June 23, 1939 in London, Eng. Bdwy debut 1977 in "Side by Side by Sondheim."

KERR, PHILIP. Born Apr. 9, 1940 in NYC. Attended Harvard, LAMDA. Bdwy debut 1969 in "Tiny Alice," followed by "A Flea in Her Ear," "Three Sisters," "Jockey Club Stakes," OB in "Hamlet," "The Rehearsal."

KERT, LARRY. Born Dec. 5, 1934 in Los Angeles, CA. Attended LACC. Bdwy bow 1953 in "John Murray Anderson's Almanac," followed by "Ziegfeld Follies," "Mr. Wonderful," "Walk Tall," "Look, Ma, I'm Dancin'," "Tickets Please," "West Side Story," "A Family Affair," "Breakfast at Tiffany's," "Cabaret," "La Strada," "Company," "Two Gentlemen of Verona," "Music! Music!," "Musical Jubilee," "Side by Side by Sondheim."

KEZER, GLENN. Born Apr. 2, 1923 in Okemah, OK. Graduate UOkla. Bdwy in "My Fair Lady," "Camelot," "Fade Out—Fade In," "Half a Sixpence," "Little Murders," "Trial of Lee Harvey Oswald," "The Other Man," OB in "Walk in Darkness," "Brigadoon" (CC), "Oh, Say Can You See L.A.," "Firebugs," "The David Show," "Promenade," "Threepenny Opera."

KILEY, RICHARD. Born Mar. 31, 1922 in Chicago, IL. Attended Loyola U. Bdwy debut 1953 in "Misalliance" for which he received a Theatre World Award, followed by "Kismet," "Sing Me No Lullaby," "Time Limit!" "Redhead," "Advise and Consent," "No Strings," "Here's Love," "I Had a Ball," "Man of La Mancha" (also LC), "Her First Roman," "The Incomparable Max," "Voices," "Absurd Person Singular," "The Heiress," "Knickerbocker Holiday."

KILLMER, NANCY. Born Dec. 16, 1936 in Homewood, IL. Graduate Northwestern U. Bdwy debut 1969 in "Coco," followed by "Goodtime Charley," "So Long, 174th Street," OB in "Exiles."

KILTY, JEROME. Born June 24, 1922 in Pala Indian Reservation, CA. Attended Guildhall Sch., London. Bdwy debut 1950 in "The Relapse," followed by "Love's Labour's Lost" (CC), "Misalliance," "A Pin to See the Peepshow," "Frogs of Spring," "Quadrille," "Othello," "Henry IV," OB in "Dear Liar."

KIMMINS, KENNETH. Born Sept. 4, 1941 in Brooklyn, NY. Graduate Catholic U. Debut 1966 OB in "The Fantasticks," followed by "Adaptation," "All My Sons," Bdwy in "Fig Leaves Are Falling," "Gingerbread Lady," "Company," "Status Quo Vadis," "Magic Show."

KING, JOHN MICHAEL. Born May 13, 1926 in NYC. Attended AADA. Bdwy debut 1951 in "Courtin' Time," followed by "Music in the Air," "Of Thee I Sing," "Buttrio Square," "Me and Juliet," "Ankles Aweigh," "Hit the Trail," "Fanny," "My Fair Lady" for which he received a Theatre World Award, "Anya," "On a Clear Day You Can See Forever," "The King and I," (1977), OB in "Have I Got One for You," "Sound of Music" (JB).

KIRSCH, CAROLYN. Born May 24, 1942 in Shreveport, LA. Bdwy debut 1963 in "How to Succeed . . .," followed by "Folies Bergere," "La Grosse Valise," "Skyscraper," "Breakfast at Tiffany's," "Sweet Charity," "Hallelujah, Baby!," "Dear World," "Promises, Promises," "Coco," "Ulysses in Nighttown," "A Chorus Line," OB in "Silk Stockings."

KISER, TERRY. Born Aug. 1, 1939 in Omaha, NE. Graduate U. Kan. Debut OB 1966 in "Night of the Dunce," followed by "Fortune and Men's Eyes" for which he received a Theatre World Award, "Horseman, Pass By," "Frank Gagliano's City Scene," "The Ofay Watcher," "Castro Complex," "In Case of Accident," "The Children," "More Than You Deserve," Bdwy in "Paris is Out," "Shelter," "God's Favorite."

KLINE, KEVIN. Born Oct. 24, 1947 in St. Louis, MO. Graduate Ind. U., Juilliard. Debut 1970 OB in "Wars of Roses," followed by "School for Scandal," "Lower Depths," "The Hostage," "Women Beware Women," "Robber Bridegroom," "Edward II," "The Time of Your Life," "Beware the Jubjub Bird," "Dance on a Country Grave." Bdwy in "Three Sisters," "Measure for Measure," "Beggar's Opera," "Scapin."

KLUNIS, TOM. Bdwy debut 1961 in "Gideon," followed by "The Devils," "Henry V," "Romeo and Juliet," OB in "The Immoralist," "Hamlet," "Arms and the Man," "Potting Shed," "Measure for Measure," "Romeo and Juliet," "The Balcony," "Our Town," "Man Who Never Died," "God Is My Ram," "Rise, Marlowe," "Iphigenia in Aulis," "Still Life."

KNIGHT, SHIRLEY. Born July 5 in Goessel, KS. Attended Phillips U., Wichita U. Bdwy debut 1964 in "The Three Sisters," followed by "We Have Always Lived in a Castle," "The Watering Place," "Kennedy's Children," OB in "Journey to the Day," "Rooms," "Happy End."

KNUDSON, KURT. Born Sept. 7, 1936 in Fargo, ND. Attended NDState U., Hamline U, UMiami. Debut 1976 OB in "The Cherry Orchard."

KOKA, JULIETTE. Born Apr. 4, 1930 in Finland. Attended Helsinki Sch. of Dramatic Arts. Debut 1977 OB in "Piaf . . . A Remembrance" for which she received a Theatre World Award.

KOLBA, MICHAEL. Born Oct. 1, 1947 in Moorhead, MN. Graduate Moorhead U., UHawaii. Debut 1976 OB in "The Cherry Orchard," followed by "Measure for Measure."

KOPYC, FRANK. Born Aug. 6, 1948 in Troy, NY. Graduate Yankton Col. Debut 1973 OB in "Pop," followed by "Fiorello!" (ELT).

KOREY, ALEXANDRA. Born May 14 in Brooklyn, NY. Graduate Columbia U. Debut 1976 OB in "Fiorello!" (ELT).

KORZEN, ANNE. Born Nov. 8, 1938 in NYC. Graduate Bard Col. Debut 1976 OB in "Fiorello!" (ELT).

KOTTKE, DAVID. Born Nov. 8, 1952 in Detroit, MI. Attended Butler U., NYSU Fredonia. Debut 1976 OB in "Don't Step on My Olive Branch."

KOVENS, EDWARD. Born June 26, 1934 in NYC. Attended NY Inst. of Arts. Bdwy debut 1964 in "The Three Sisters," OB in "Modern Statuary," "Never Ending Rain," "Waiting for Godot," "Dirty Hands," "Country Girl," "Deer Park," "Fortune and Men's Eyes," "42 Seconds from Broadway," "From the Memoirs of Pontius Pilate."

KRAMER, JOEL. Born July 1, 1943 in The Bronx, NY. Graduate Queens Col., UMich. Debut 1963 OB in "St. Joan of the Stockyards," followed by "Playboy of the Western World," "Measure for Measure," "Man Who Corrupted Hadleyburg," "Call Me Madam," "Castaways."

KRAUS, PHILIP. Born May 10, 1949 in Springville, NY. Carnegie Tech graduate. Bdwy debut 1973 in "Shelter," followed by "Equus."

KUHLMAN, RON. Born Mar. 6, 1948 in Cleveland, OH. Graduate Ohio U. Debut 1972 OB in "A Maid's Tragedy," followed by "A Chorus Line" (Bdwy 1975).

KURNITZ, JULIE. Born Sept. 8, 1942 in Mt. Vernon, NY. Attended UWisc., NYU. Debut 1968 OB in "In Circles," followed by "Peace," "Joan," "The Faggot," "Not Back with the Elephants," Bdwy bow 1970 in "Minnie's Boys."

KURTZ, SWOOSIE. Born Sept. 6, 1944 in Omaha, NE. Attended USCal., LAMDA. Debut 1968 OB in "The Firebugs," followed by "The Effect of Gamma Rays. . . .," "Enter a Free Man," "Children," "Museum," Bdwy 1975 in "Ah, Wilderness."

LADD, DIANE. Born Nov. 29, 1932 in Meridian, MS. Attended Actors Studio. Appeared OB in "Orpheus Descending," "One Night Stands of a Noisy Passenger," Bdwy 1976 in "A Texas Trilogy" (Lu Ann Laverty Oberlander).

LADD, MARGARET. Born Nov. 8, 1942 in Providence, RI. Graduate Bard Col. OB in "The Knack," "Free, Free, Free," "The Experiment," "Museum," Bdwy in "The Great Indoors," "Sheep on the Runway."

LAGERFELT, CAROLYN. Born Sept. 23 in Paris. Graduate AADA. Bdwy debut 1971 in "The Philanthropist," followed by "4 on a Garden," "Jockey Club Stakes," "The Constant Wife," "Look Back in Anger" (OB), "Otherwise Engaged."

LAM, DIANE. Born Mar. 6, 1945 in Honolulu, HI. Graduate UHi., SMU. Bdwy debut 1976 in "Pacific Overtures."

LAMONT, ROBIN. Born June 2, 1950 in Boston, MA. Attended Carnegie-Mellon U. Debut 1971 OB in "Godspell," followed by "Thoughts," Bdwy 1976 in "Godspell."

LaMOTTA, JOHN. Born Jan. 8, 1939 In Brooklyn, NY. Bdwy bow 1967 in "Illya, Darling," followed by "I'm Solomon," "Zorba," "She Loves Me," OB in " Dead Survivors," "God Bless Coney."

LAMPERT, ZOHRA. Born May 13, 1936 in NYC. Attended Chicago U. Bdwy debut 1956 in "Major Barbara," followed by "Maybe Tuesday," "Look, We've Come Through," "First Love," "Mother Courage," "Nathan Weinstein, Mystic, Conn.," "Lovers and Other Strangers," "The Sign in Sidney Brustein's Window," "Unexpected Guests," OB In "Venus Observed," "Diary of a Scoundrel," LCRep's "After the Fall" and "Marco Millions."

LANCASTER, LUCIE. Born Oct. 15, 1907 in Chicago, IL. Bdwy debut 1947 in "Heads or Tails," followed by "Mr. Pickwick," "The Girl Who Came to Supper," "Bajour," "How Now, Dow Jones," "Little Boxes" (OB), "70 Girls 70," "Pippin."

LANCHESTER, ROBERT. Born Aug. 2, 1941 In Boston, MA. Graduate MIT, UCBerkeley. Bdwy debut 1969 in "A Flea in Her Ear," followed by "Three Sisters," "OB in "Greenwillow," "King Lear," "A Perfect Mollusc."

LANDERS, MATT. Born Oct. 21, 1952 in Mohawk Valley, NY. Attended Boston Cons. Debut OB 1974 in "Godspell," followed by Bdwy 1975 in "Grease."

LANDON, SOFIA. Born Jan. 24, 1949 in Montreal, Can. Attended Northwestern U. Debut 1971 OB in "The Red, White and Black," followed by "Gypsy," "Missouri Legend," "Heartbreak House," "Peg o' My Heart."

LANE, BETTY. Born in Detroit, MI. Graduate Juilliard. Bdwy debut 1976 in "Porgy and Bess."

LANE, GENETTE. Born Oct. 13, 1940 in Brooklyn, MD. Attended Peabody Cons., AmThWing. OB in "Peter Rabbit," "The Adventures of High Jump," "The Drunkard," "Ruddigore," Bdwy 1977 in "Knickerbocker Holiday."

| Richard Kelton | Margaret Ladd | Bruce Lea | Louise Larabee | Bob Levine |

LANE, NANCY. Born June 16, 1951 in Passaic, NJ. Attended Va. Commonwealth U., AADA. Debut 1975 OB and Bdwy in "A Chorus Line."

LANGE, HOPE. Born Nov. 28, 1933 in Redding Ridge, CT. Attended Reed Col. Bdwy debut 1943 in "The Patriots," followed by "The Hot Corner," "Same Time, Next Year."

LANGELLA, FRANK. Born Jan. 1, 1940 in Bayonne, NJ. Graduate Syracuse U. Debut 1963 OB in "The Immoralist," followed by "The Old Glory," "Good Day," "White Devil," "Yerma," "Iphigenia in Aulis," "A Cry of Players," "Prince of Homburg," Bdwy in "Seascape."

LANSING, JOHN. Born Oct. 16, 1949 in Baldwin, NY. Attended Hofstra Col. Bdwy debut 1972 in "The Sign in Sidney Brustein's Window," followed by "Grease."

LARABEE, LOUISE. Born Apr. 9 in Bremerton, WA. Has appeared in "Angel Island," "The Land Is Bright," "Guest in the House," "Junior Miss," "Sleep No More," "The Number," "A Date with April," "Picnic," "Right Honourable Gentleman," "Carousel" (CC), OB in "The Last Resort."

LARSON, LISBY. Born Oct. 23, 1951 in Washington, DC. Graduate Ukan. Debut 1976 OB in "The Boys from Syracuse."

LATHRAM, ELIZABETH. Born Apr. 23, 1947 in Washington, DC. Graduate UOre. Debut 1971 OB in "Godspell," followed by "Moonchildren," Bdwy 1976 in "Godspell."

LAUDICINA, DINO. Born Dec. 22, 1939 in Brooklyn, NY. Bdwy bow 1960 in "Christine," followed by "Rosencrantz and Guildenstern Are Dead," "Indians," "Scratch," "The Innocents," OB in "King of the Dark Chamber," "Dollar."

LAUGHLIN, SHARON. Graduate UWash. Bdwy debut 1964 in "One by One," followed by "The Heiress," OB in "Henry IV," "Huui, Huui," "Mod Donna," "Subject to Fits," "The Minister's Black Veil," "Esther," "Rag Doll," "Four Friends," "Heartbreak House."

LAURENSON, AMELIA. Born Oct. 12, 1939 in Columbus, OH. Graduate Denison U. Bdwy debut 1977 in "Night of the Iguana."

LAVIZZO, VALCOUR. Born Sept. 7, 1953 in Atlanta, Ga. Attended AADA, HB Studio. Debut 1971 OB in "The Screens," followed by "Kaddish," "Rain," "Savages."

LAWRENCE, ANTHONY. Born Mar. 19, 1952 in Bessemer, AL. Graduate UTenn. Debut 1976 OB in "The Boys from Syracuse."

LEA, BRUCE. Born Mar. 9, 1949 in New Orleans, La. Graduate TCU. Bdwy debut 1971 in "On the Town," followed by "Irene," "Debbie," OB in "DuBarry Was a Lady."

LEAGUE, JANET. Born Oct. 13 in Chicago, IL. Attended Goodman Theatre. Debut 1969 OB in "To Be Young, Gifted and Black," followed by "Tiger at the Gates," "The Screens," "Mrs. Snow," "Pease Don't Cry and Say No," Bdwy in "First Breeze of Summer," (1975) "For Colored Girls Who Have Considered . . ."

LEDERER, SUZANNE. Born Sept. 29, 1948 in Great Neck, NY. Graduate Hofstra U. Bdwy debut 1974 in "The National Health," followed by "Days in the Trees."

LEEDS, MICHAEL. Born Nov. 14, 1951 in NYC. Graduate Ithaca Col. Bdwy debut 1976 in "Pal Joey."

LeGALLIENNE, EVA. Born Jan. 11, 1899 in London, Eng. Bdwy debut 1915 in "Mrs. Boltay's Daughters," followed by "Bunny," "Melody of Youth," "Mr. Lazarus," "Saturday to Monday," "Lord and Lady Algy," "Off Chance," "Lusmore," "Elsie Janis and Her Gang," "Not So Long Ago," "Lilliom," "Sandro Botticelli," "The Rivals," "The Swan," "Assumption of Hannele," "LaVierge Folle," "Call of Life," "Master Builder," "John Gabriel Borkman," "Saturday Night," "Three Sisters," "Mistress of the Inn," "Twelfth Night," "Cradle Song," "Inheritors," "Good Hope," "First Stone," "Improvisations in June," "Hedda Gabler," "Would-Be Gentleman," "Cherry Orchard," "Peter Pan," "Sunny Morning," "Seagull," "Living Corpse," "Romeo and Juliet," "Siegfried," "Alison's House," "Camille," "Dear Jane," "Alice in Wonderland," "L'Aiglon," "Rosmersholm," "Women Have Their Way," "Prelude to Exile," "Madame Capet," "Frank Fay's Music Hall," "Uncle Harry," "Therese," "Henry VIII," "What Every Woman Knows," "Ghosts," "The Corn Is Green" (CC), "Starcross Story," "Southwest Corner," "Mary Stuart," "Exit the King," "The Royal Family."

LEIBMAN, RON. Born Oct. 11, 1937 in NYC. Attended Ohio Wesleyan, Actors Studio. Bdwy debut 1963 in "Dear Me, the Sky Is Falling," followed by "Bicycle Ride to Nevada," "The Deputy," "We Bombed in New Haven," for which he received a Theatre World Award, "Cop-Out," OB in "The Academy," "John Brown's Body," "Scapin," "Legend of Lovers," "Dead End," "Poker Session," "The Premise," "Transfers," "Room Service," "Love Two," "Rich and Famous."

LeMASSENA, WILLIAM. Born May 23, 1916 in Glen Ridge, NJ. Attended NYU. Bdwy bow 1940 in "Taming of the Shrew," followed by "There Shall Be No Night," "The Pirate," "Hamlet," "Call Me Mister," "Inside U.S.A.," "I Know, My Love," "Dream Girl," "Nina," "Ondine," "Fallen Angels," "Redhead," "Conquering Hero," "Beauty Part," "Come Summer," "Grin and Bare It," "All over Town," "A Texas Trilogy," OB in "The Coop," "Brigadoon," "Life with Father," "F. Jasmine Addams."

LEMMON, SHIRLEY. Born May 15, 1948 in Salt Lake City, UT. Graduate Utah State U. Bdwy debut 1971 in "Company," followed by "Smith," "Words and Music," OB in "2 by 5."

LeNOIRE, ROSETTA. Born Aug. 8, 1911 in NYC. Attended Theatre Wing. Bdwy debut 1936 in "Macbeth," followed by "Bassa Moona," "Hot Mikado," "Marching with Johnny," "Janie," "Decision," "Three's a Family," "Destry Rides Again," "Finian's Rainbow," "South Pacific," "Sophie," "Tambourines to Glory," "Blues for Mr. Charlie," "Great Indoors," "Lost in the Stars," "The Royal Family," OB in "Bible Salesman," "Double Entry," "Clandestine on the Morning Line," "Cabin in the Sky," "Lady Day," LC in "Show Boat," "A Cry of Players," and "Streetcar Named Desire."

LEO, TOM. Born Nov. 28, 1936 in Teaneck, NJ. Graduate UToronto. Debut 1974 OB in "More Than You Deserve," followed by "Beethoven/Karl," "A Little Wine with Lunch."

LEON, JOSEPH. Born June 8, 1923 in NYC. Attended NYU, UCLA. Bdwy debut 1950 in "Bell, Book and Candle," followed by "Seven Year Itch," "Pipe Dream," "Fair Game," "Gazebo," "Julia, Jake and Uncle Joe," "Beauty Part," "Merry Widow," "Henry, Sweet Henry," "Jimmy Shine," "All over Town," "California Suite," OB in "Come Share My House," "Dark Corners," "Interrogation of Havana," "Are You Now or Have You Ever Been."

LESTER, BARBARA. Born Dec 27, 1928 in London, Eng. Graduate Columbia U. Bdwy debut 1956 in "Protective Custody," followed by "Legend of Lizzie," "Luther," "Inadmissible Evidence," "Johnny No-Trump," "Grin and Bare It," "Butley," OB in "Electra," "Queen after Death," "Summer of the 17th Doll," "Richard II," "Much Ado about Nothing," "One Way Pendulum," "Abelard and Heloise," "There's One in Every Marriage."

LeVAGGI, JAMES. Born in San Francisco, CA. Graduate USF. Debut 1967 OB in "Damn Yankees," followed by "The Telephone," "Can-Can," "Full Moon," "Silk Stockings."

LEVENE, SAM. Born Aug. 28, 1905 in NYC. Graduate AADA. Bdwy debut 1927 in "Wall Street," followed by "3 Men on a Horse," "Dinner at 8," "Room Service," "Margin for Error," "Sound of Hunting," "Light up the Sky," "Guys and Dolls," "Hot Corner," "Fair Game," "Make a Million," "Heartbreak House," "Good Soup," "Devil's Advocate," "Let It Ride," "Seidman & Son," "Cafe Crown," "Last Analysis," "Nathan Weinstein, Mystic, Conn.," "The Impossible Years," "Paris Is Out," "A Dream out of Time" (OB), "The Sunshine Boys," "Dreyfus in Rehearsal," "The Royal Family."

LEVINE, ROBERT. Born Sept. 4, 1931 in Brooklyn, NY. Graduate Syracuse U. Debut 1960 OB in "Opening of a Window," followed by "Enemy of the People," "The Miser," "King Lear," "A Cry of Players," "Suggs," "Good Woman of Setzuan," "The Time of Your Life," "Bananas," "In the Matter of J. Robert Oppenheimer," "The Last Resort."

LEVITT, JUDY. Born Sept. 17, 1945 in Detroit, MI. Graduate UKan. Debut 1977 OB in "Twelfth Night."

LIDE, MILLER. Born Aug. 10, 1935 in Columbia, SC. Graduate USC, Am ThWing. Debut 1961 OB in "Three Modern Japanese Plays," followed by "Trial at Rouen," "Street Scene," "Joan of Arc at the Stake," Bdwy in "Ivanov" (1966), "Halfway up the Tree," "Who's Who in Hell," "We Interrupt This Program," "The Royal Family."

LINAHAN, DONALD. Born Feb. 22, 1936 in Uniontown, PA. Graduate William and Mary Col. Bdwy debut 1975 in "All God's Chillun Got Wings," followed by "Cracks" (OB), "Days in the Trees."

LINDIG, JILLIAN. Born Mar. 19, 1944 in Johnson City, TX. Debut 1969 OB in "Brownstone Urge," followed by "AC/DC," Bdwy in "Equus."

Abraham Lind-Oquendo   **Ruth Livingston**   **Peter Lownds**   **Rosamond Lynn**   **Edmund Lyndeck**

LIND-OQUENDO, ABRAHAM. Born in NYC. Graduate Manhattan Sch. of Music. Bdwy debut 1976 in "Porgy and Bess."

LIPSCOMB, DENNIS. Born Mar. 1, 1942 in Brooklyn, NY. Graduate Clarkson Col., UIowa, LAMDA. Debut 1975 OB in "The Rivals," followed by "The Boss," "The Crazy Locomotive," Bdwy 1977 in "Romeo and Juliet."

LIPSON, PAUL. Born Dec. 23, 1913 in Brooklyn. Attended Ohio State, Theatre Wing. Bdwy bow 1942 in "Lily of the Valley," followed by "Heads or Tails," "Detective Story," "Remains to Be Seen," "Carnival in Flanders," "I've Got Sixpence," "The Vamp," "Bells Are Ringing," "Fiorello" (CC), "Sound of Music," "Fiddler on the Roof," (original and 1976) OB in "Deep Six the Briefcase," "The Inn at Lydda," "Golden Boy."

LIPTON, MICHAEL. Born Apr. 27, 1925 in NYC. Attended Queens Col. Appeared in "Caesar and Cleopatra," "The Moon Is Blue," "Sing Me No Lullaby," "Wake Up, Darling," "Tenth Man," "Separate Tables," "Inquest," OB in "Lover," "Trigon," "Long Christmas Dinner," "Hamp," "Boys in the Band," "Justice Box," "Cold Storage."

LITHGROW, JOHN. Born in Rochester, NY. Graduate Harvard U. Bdwy debut 1973 in "The Changing Room," followed by "My Fat Friend," "Comedians," "Anna Christie," OB in "Hamlet," "Trelawny of the Wells," "A Memory of Two Mondays," "Secret Service," "Boy Meets Girl."

LITTLE, CLEAVON. Born June 1, 1939 in Chickasha, OK. Attended San Diego State U., AADA. Debut 1967 in "MacBird," followed by "Hamlet," "Someone's Coming Hungry," "Ofay Watcher," "Scuba Duba," "Narrow Road to the Deep North," "Great MacDaddy," "Joseph and the Amazing Technicolor Dreamcoat," Bdwy in "Jimmy Shine," "Purlie," "All over Town," "The Poison Tree."

LIVERT, RICHARD. Born July 31, 1944 in Brooklyn, NY. Attended S.Ill.U. Debut 1973 OB in "A Recent Killing," followed by "Tubstrip," "From the Memoirs of Pontius Pilate."

LIVINGSTON, RUTH. Born March 25 in New Haven, CT. Graduate UMich., AmThWing. Debut OB in "The Rimers of Eldritch," followed by "Play Me, Zoltan," Bdwy 1977 in "Romeo and Juliet."

LLOYD, CHRISTOPHER. Born Oct. 22, 1938 in Stamford, CT. Attended Neighborhood Playhouse. Bdwy debut 1969 in "Red, White and Maddox," followed by "Happy End," OB in "Kaspar," "Total Eclipse," "Macbeth," "The Seagull," "In the Boom Boom Room," "Happy End."

LOMBARD, MICHAEL. Born Aug. 8, 1934 in Brooklyn, NY. Graduate Bklyn Col., Boston U. OB in "King Lear," "Merchant of Venice," "Cages," "Pinter Plays," "LaTurista," "Elizabeth the Queen," "Room Service," "Mert and Phil," Bdwy in "Poor Bitos," "The Devils," "Gingerbread Lady," "Bad Habits," "Otherwise Engaged."

LONDON, ROY. Born May 3, 1943 in NYC. Graduate Antioch Col. Bdwy debut 1967 in "Little Murders," followed by "The Birthday Party," "Gingham Dog," OB in "Three by de Ghelderode," "Once in a Lifetime," "Viet Rock," "America Hurrah," "Monopoly," "New York! New York!," "End of Summer," "Ballymurphy."

LONG, AVON. Born June 18, 1910 in Baltimore, MD. Attended New Eng. Cons. Bdwy debut 1942 in "Porgy and Bess," followed by "Memphis Bound," "Carib Song," "Beggar's Holiday," "Don't Play Us Cheap," "Bubbling Brown Sugar," OB in "Ballad of Jazz Street."

LOUDON, DOROTHY. Born Sept. 17, 1933 in Boston, MA. Attended Emerson Col., Syracuse U. Debut 1961 OB in "World of Jules Feiffer," Bdwy 1963 in "Nowhere to Go but Up" for which she received a Theatre World Award, followed by "Noel Coward's Sweet Potato," "Fig Leaves Are Falling," "Three Men on a Horse," "The Women," "Annie."

LOVE, EDWARD. Born June 29, 1952 in Toledo, OH. Graduate Ohio U, NYU. Debut 1972 OB in "Ti-Jean and His Brothers," Bdwy 1975 in "Raisin," followed by "A Chorus Line."

LOWELL, JOAN. Born Nov. 22, 1938 in NYC. Debut 1977 OB in "Come Back, Little Sheba" (ELT).

LOWNDS, PETER. Born Aug. 5, 1944 in NYC. Yale graduate. Debut 1976 OB in "Benito Cereno," followed by "The Hostage," "Isadora Duncan Sleeps with the Russian Navy."

LUCKINBILL, LAURENCE. Born Nov. 21, 1938 in Ft. Smith, AR. Graduate UArk., Catholic U. Bdwy debut in "A Man for All Seasons," followed by "Beekman Place," "Poor Murderer," "The Shadow Box," OB in "Oedipus Rex," "There Is a Play Tonight," "Fantasticks," "Tartuffe," "Boys in the Band," "Horseman, Pass By," "Memory Bank," "What the Butler Saw," "A Meeting by the River," "Alpha Beta."

LUNA, BARBARA. Born Mar. 2 in NYC. Bdwy debut 1951 in "The King and I," followed by "West Side Story" (LC), "A Chorus Line."

LuPONE, PATTI. Born Apr. 21, 1949 in Northport, NY. Juilliard graduate. Debut 1972 OB in "School for Scandal," followed by "Women Beware Women," "Next Time I'll Sing to You," "Beggar's Opera," "Scapin," "Robber Bridegroom," "Edward II," "The Time of Your Life."

LuPONE, ROBERT. Born July 29, 1946 in Brooklyn, NY. Juilliard graduate. Bdwy debut 1970 in "Minnie's Boys," followed by "Jesus Christ Superstar," "The Rothschilds," "The Magic Show," "A Chorus Line," OB in "Charlie Was Here and Now He's Gone."

LUSTIK, MARLENA. Born Aug. 22, 1944 in Milwaukee, WI. Attended Marquette U. Bdwy debut 1966 in Pousse Cafe," followed by "Days in the Trees," OB in "Effect of Gamma Rays on. . . ."

LUZ, FRANK C. Born Dec. 22, in Cambridge, MA. Attended NMex. State U. Debut 1974 OB in "The Rivals," followed by "Fiorello!"

LYMAN, DEBRA. Born July 17, 1940 in Philadelphia, PA. Graduate Phila. Col. Debut 1967 OB in "By Jupiter," Bdwy in "Sugar" (1972), "My Fair Lady," "Chicago."

LYNCH, RICHARD. Born Feb. 12, 1940 in Brooklyn, NY. Attended Actors Studio. Bdwy debut 1965 in "The Devils," followed by "Lady from the Sea," "Basic Training of Pavlo Hummel," OB in "Live Like Pigs," "One Night Stands of a Noisy Passenger," "Things That Almost Happen," "12 Angry Men," "The Orphan," "Action."

LYNDECK, EDMUND. Born Oct. 4,1925 in Baton Rouge, LA. Graduate Montclair State Col., Fordham U. Bdwy debut 1969 in "1776," followed by "The King and I" (JB), OB in "Mandragola," "A Safe Place," "Amoureuse." "Piaf . . . A Remembrance."

LYNN, ROSAMOND. Born Dec. 31, in Palo Alto CA. Bdwy debut 1973 in "Much Ado about Nothing," followed by "A Matter of Time" (OB), "Pal Joey."

MacGRATH, LEUEEN. Born July 3, 1914 in London, Eng. Attended RADA. Bdwy debut 1948 in "Edward, My Son," followed by "The Enchanted," "High Ground," "Fancy Meeting You Again," "Love of 4 Colonels," "Tiger at the Gates," "Potting Shed," OB in "The Seagull," "A Tribute to Lili Lamont."

MADDEN, DONALD. Born Nov. 5, 1933 in NYC. Attended CCNY. Bdwy debut 1958 in "Look Back in Anger," followed by "First Impressions," "Step on a Crack," "One by One," "White Lies," "Black Comedy," OB in "Julius Caesar" for which he received a Theatre World Award, "Lysistrata," "Pictures in a Hallway," "Henry IV," "She Stoops to Conquer," "Octoroon," "Hamlet," "Ceremony of Innocence," "Henry VI," "Richard III," "A Doll's House," "Hedda Gabler," "The Philanderer," "Scribes."

MADDEN, SHARON. Born July 8, 1947 in St. Louis, MO. Debut 1975 OB in "Battle of Angels," followed by "The Hot 1 Baltimore," "Who Killed Richard Cory?," "Mrs. Murray's Farm," "The Passing of Corky Brewster."

MAGGART, BRANDON. Born Dec. 12, 1933 in Carthage, TN. Graduate U. Tenn. OB in "Sing Muse!," "Like Other People," "Put It In Writing" for which he received a Theatre World Award, "Wedding Band," "But Not for Me," Bdwy in "Kelly," "New Faces of 1968," "Applause," "Lorelei," "We Interrupt This Program."

MAGUIRE, GEORGE. Born Dec. 4, 1946 in Wilmington, DE, Graduate UPa. Debut 1975 OB in "Polly," followed by "Follies," "Antigone."

MAHER, JOSEPH. Born Dec. 29, 1933 in Westport, Ire. Bdwy bow 1964 in "The Chinese Prime Minister," followed by "The Prime of Miss Jean Brodie," "Henry V," "There's One in Every Marriage," "Who's Who in Hell," "Days in the Trees," OB in "The Hostage," "Live Like Pigs," "Importance of Being Earnest," "Eh?," "Local Stigmatic," "Mary Stuart," "The Contractor," "Savages."

MAJORS, DALIENNE. Born Feb. 26, 1950 in San Antonio, TX. Juilliard graduate. Debut 1977 OB in "Jules Feiffer's Hold Me!"

| Maureen Maloney | Ezra Jack Maret | Jan Maris | Gene Masoner | Beverly May |

MALIS, CLAIRE. Born Feb. 17, 1944 in Gary, IN. Graduate UInd., AADA. Debut 1969 OB in "The Man with the Flower in His Mouth," followed by "Berkeley Square," "My Life."

MALONEY, MAUREEN. Born Jan. 3, 1948 in NYC. Debut 1969 OB in "Rondelay," followed by "Let Yourself Go," "I'll Die if I Can't Live Forever," "Castaways," Bdwy in "Goodtime Charley" (1975).

MANN, PJ. Born Apr. 9, 1953 in Pasadena, CA. Bdwy debut 1976 in "Home Sweet Homer."

MARCH, ELLEN. Born Aug. 18, 1948 in Brooklyn. Graduate AMDA. Debut OB 1967 in "Pins and Needles," Bdwy 1973 in "Grease."

MARCHAND, NANCY. Born June 19, 1928 in Buffalo, NY. Graduate Carnegie Tech. Debut 1951 in "Taming of the Shrew" (CC), followed by "Merchant of Venice," "Much Ado about Nohing," "Three Bags Full," "After the Rain," LC's "The Alchemist," "Yerma," "Cyrano de Bergerac," "Mary Stuart," "Enemies" and "The Plough and the Stars," "40 Carats," "And Miss Reardon Drinks a Little," "Veronica's Room," OB in "The Balcony," "Children."

MARCUM, KEVIN. Born Nov. 7, 1955 in Danville, IL. Attended UIll. Bdwy debut 1976 in "My Fair Lady."

MARET, EZRA JACK. Born June 27, 1948 in Maywood, CA. Debut 1977 OB in "On-the-Lock-In."

MARGULIES, DAVID. Born Feb. 19, 1937 in NYC. Graduate CCNY. Debut 1958 OB in "Golden Six," followed by "Six Characters in Search of an Author," "Tragical Historie of Dr. Faustus," "Tango," "Little Murders," "Seven Days of Mourning," "Last Analysis," "An Evening with the Poet Senator," "Kid Champion," Bdwy in "The Iceman Cometh," (1973) "Zalmen, or the Madness of God," "Comedians."

MARIS, JAN. Born Sept. 18, 1947 in Waco, TX. Graduate Baylor U., AADA. Debut 1977 OB in "Silk Stockings" (ELT).

MARLOWE, LYNN. Born Oct. 13, 1952 in Springfield, Il. Graduate UIll. Debut 1975 OB in "Do I Hear a Waltz?," followed by "The Boys from Syracuse."

MARRIOTT, JOHN. Born Sept. 30, 1900 in Boley, OK. Attended Wilberforce U. Bdwy debut 1934 in "Too Many Boats," followed by "Sweet River," "Chalked Out," "Little Foxes," "Janie," "No Way Out," "The Iceman Cometh," "How I Wonder," "Respectful Prostitute," "The Ponder Heart," "Season of Choice" (OB), "More Stately Mansions," "Weekend," "Texas Trilogy."

MARSHALL, LARRY. Born Apr. 3, 1944 in Spartanburg, SC. Attended Fordham, Xavier, New Eng. Consv. Bdwy debut in "Hair," followed by "Two Gentlemen from Verona," "Midsummer Night's Dream" (LC), "Rockabye Hamlet," "Porgy and Bess."

MARTIN, JOYCE. Born Mar. 8, 1949 in St. Paul, MN. Attended UMinn. Bdwy debut 1976 in "Fiddler on the Roof."

MARTIN, MILLICENT. Born June 8, 1934 in Romford, Eng. Attended Italia Conti Sch. Bdwy debut 1954 in "The Boy Friend," followed by "Side by Side by Sondheim."

MARTIN, NAN. Born in Decatur, IL. Attended UCLA, Actors Studio. Bdwy debut 1950 in "A Story for a Sunday Evening," "The Constant Wife," "J. B.," "Great God Brown," "Under the Yum-Yum Tree," "Summer Brave," "Eccentricities of a Nightingale," OB in "Saturday Night Kid," "Sweet Confession," "Lysistrata," "Much Ado about Nothing," "Phaedra," "Merchant of Venice," "Taming of the Shrew," "Hamlet."

MARTIN, VIRGINIA. Born Dec. 2, 1932 in Chattanooga, TN. Attended Theatre Wing. Appeared in "South Pacific," "Pajama Game," "Ankles Aweigh," "New Faces of 1956," "How to Succeed in Business . . .," "Little Me," OB in "Buy Bonds Buster," "Joseph and the Amazing Technicolor Dreamcoat."

MASONER, GENE. Born Jan. 22, in Kansas City, KS. Attended UKan., HB Studio. Debut OB 1969 in "Your Own Thing," followed by "White Devil," "Cherry," "3 Drag Queens from Datona," Bdwy 1975 in "Shenandoah."

MASSMAN, PAIGE. Born Oct. 13, 1946. Graduate Webster Col., Purdue U. Debut 1976 OB In "The Boys from Syracuse."

MASTERS, BEN. Born May 6, 1947 in Corvallis, OR. Graduate UOre. Debut 1970 OB in "Boys in the Band," followed by "What the Butler Saw," "The Cherry Orchard," Bdwy in "Capt. Brassbound's Conversion."

MASTERS, DAVID. Born Feb. 26, 1924 in St. Paul, MN. Graduate Wm. & Mary, NYU. Debut 1953 OB in "Madwoman of Chaillot," followed by "What Every Woman Knows" (CC), "The Anatomist," "The Big Knife," "Measure for Measure," Bdwy in "Fiddler on the Roof" (1967 & '76).

MATESKY, JARED. Born May 30, 1947 in Washington, DC. Graduate UMd., Catholic U. Debut 1977 OB in "Twelfth Night." (ELT)

MATHEWS, WALTER. Born Oct. 10. 1926 in NYC. Graduate NYU, Ohio U. Bdwy debut 1951 in "St. Joan," followed by "The Long Dream," "King Lear," "Mr. Roberts," "Equus."

MATHEWSON, JOSEPH. Born Sept. 22, 1938 in Ashland, KY. Yale graduate. Debut 1969 OB in "Tom Jones," followed by "The Sorrows of Frederick," "The Runner Stumbles."

MATHIS, SHERRY. Born Feb. 2, 1949 in Memphis, TN. Attended Memphis State U. Bdwy debut 1973 in "A Little Night Music," followed by "Music Is."

MATSUSAKA, TOM. Born Aug. 8 in Wahiawa, HI. Graduate Mich. State U. Bdwy bow 1968 in "Mame," followed by "Pacific Overtures," OB in "Jungle of Cities," "Ride the Winds," "Santa Anita '42."

MAURICE, MICHAEL. Born Feb. 17, 1952 in Detroit, MI. Attended MStateU., Actors Studio. Debut 1975 OB in "The Three Musketeers," followed by "Twelfth Night."

MAXWELL, ROBERTA. Born in Canada. Debut 1958 OB in "Two Gentlemen of Verona," followed by "A Whistle in the Dark," "Slag," "The Plough and the Stars," "Merchant of Venice," "Ashes," Bdwy in "The Prime of Miss Jean Brodie" (1968), "Henry V," "House of Atreus," "The Resistible Rise of Arturo Ui," "Othello," "Hay Fever," "There's One in Every Marriage," "Equus."

MAY, BEVERLY. Born Aug. 11, 1927 in East Wellington, BC, Can. Graduate Yale U. Debut 1976 OB in "Female Transport," Bdwy 1977 in "Equus."

MAYER, CHARLES. Born Apr. 4, 1904 in Germany. Attended State Th. Sch. Debut OB 1944 in "Korbin," followed by "Beavercoat," "Marriage Proposal," "Jacknife," "Boubouroche," "Golden Boy," "The Lawyer," "Flight into Egypt," "Ice Age," Bdwy in "A Bell for Adano," "Red Mill," "Now I Lay Me Down to Sleep," "Springtime Folly," "Thieves," "Fiddler on the Roof" (1976).

McARDLE, ANDREA. Born Nov. 5, 1963 in Philadelphia, PA. Bdwy debut 1977 in "Annie" for which she received a Theatre World Award.

McCALL, JANET. Born June 26, 1935 in Washington, DC. Graduate Penn. State. Debut 1960 OB in "The Golden Apple," followed by "Life Is a Dream," "Tattooed Countess," "The Bacchantes," "Jacques Brel Is Alive . . .," "How to Get Rid of It," "Cockeyed Tiger," Bdwy in "Camelot," "1776," "2 by 2," "Jacques Brel . . .," "She Loves Me."

McCALLUM, DAVID. Born Sept. 19, 1933 in Scotland. Attended Chapman Col. Bdwy debut 1968 in "The Flip Side," followed by "California Suite."

McCARTHY, KEVIN. Born Feb. 15, 1914 in Seattle, WA. Attended UMinn. Bdwy debut 1938 in "Abe Lincoln in Illinois," followed by "Flight to the West," "Winged Victory," "Truckline Cafe," "Joan of Lorraine," "Death of a Salesman," "Anna Christie," "Deep Blue Sea," "Red Roses for Me," "Day the Money Stopped," "Two for the Seesaw," "Advise and Consent," "Something about a Soldier," "Three Sisters," "A Warm Body," "Cactus Flower," "Happy Birthday, Wanda June," "Poor Murderer," OB in "The Children," "Rapists," "Harry Outside."

McCARTY, MARY. Born in 1923 in Kansas. Bdwy debut 1948 in "Sleepy Hollow" for which she received a Theatre World Award, followed by "Small Wonder," "Miss Liberty," "Bless You All," "A Rainy Day in Newark," "Follies," "Chicago," "Anna Christie."

McCLANAHAN, RUE. Born Feb. 21 in Healdton, OK. Bdwy debut 1965 in "Best Laid Plans," followed by "Jimmy Shine," "Father's Day," "Sticks and Bones," "California Suite," OB in "Secret Life of Walter Mitty," "Big Man," "MacBird," "Tonight in Living Color," "Who's Happy Now?," "Dark of the Moon," "God Says There Is No Peter Ott," "Dylan," "Crystal and Fox."

McCONNELL, TY. Born Jan. 13, 1940 in Coldwater, MI. Graduate UMich. Debut OB 1962 in "The Fantasticks," followed by "Promenade," "Contrast," "Fashion," "The Dubliners," "Lovesong," Bdwy in "Lion in Winter," "Dear World."

McCOWEN, ALEC. Born May 26, 1925 in Tunbridge Wells, Eng. Attended RADA. Bdwy debut 1951 in "Antony and Cleopatra," followed by "Caesar and Cleopatra," "King Lear," "Comedy of Errors," "After the Rain," "Hadrian VII," "The Philanthropist," "The Misanthrope," "Equus."

McDERMOTT, KEITH. Born in Houston, TX. Attended LAMDA. Bdwy debut 1976 in "Equus."

McGILL, EVERETT. Born Oct. 21, 1945 in Miami Beach, FL. Graduate UMo., RADA. Debut OB 1971 in "Brothers," followed by "The Father," "Enemies," Bdwy in "Equus" (1974), "A Texas Trilogy."

McGREEVEY, ANNIE. Born in Brooklyn, NY. Graduate AADA. Bdwy debut 1971 in "Company," followed by "The Magic Show," OB in "Booth Is Back in Town."

McGUIRE, DOROTHY. Born June 14, 1918 in Omaha, NE. Attended Pine Manor Col. Bdwy debut 1938 in "Our Town," followed by "Swingin' the Dream," "Kind Lady," "Claudia," "Legend of Lovers," "Winesburg, Ohio," "Night of the Iguana."

McKECHNIE, DONNA. Born in Nov. 1944 in Detroit, MI. Bdwy debut 1961 in "How to Succeed . . ." followed by "Promises, Promises," "Company," "On the Town," "Music! Music!" (CC), "A Chorus Line."

McKINLEY, BARBARA. Born Aug. 12, 1949 in Detroit, MI. Graduate UGa. Bdwy debut 1976 in "Going Up."

McMILLAN, KENNETH. Barn July 2, 1934 in Brooklyn. Bdwy debut 1970 in "Borstal Boy" followed by "American Buffalo," OB in "Red Eye of Love," "King of the Whole Damn World," "Little Mary Sunshine," "Babes in the Wood," "Moonchildren," "Merry Wives of Windsor," "Where Do We Go from Here?", "Kid Champion," "Streamers."

McMILLIAN, LARRY. Born Jan. 15, 1949 in Birmingham, AL. Graduate UAla. Bdwy debut 1975 in "Very Good Eddie."

McMURRAY, SAM. Born Apr. 15, 1952 in NYC. Graduate Washington U. Debut OB 1975 in "The Taking of Miss Janie," followed by "Merry Wives of Windsor," "Clarence," "Ballymurphy."

McWILLIAMS, CAROLINE. Born Apr. 4, in Seattle, WA. Attended Carnegie Tech. Pasadena Playhouse. Bdwy debut 1971 in "The Rothschilds," followed by "Cat on a Hot Tin Roof," OB in "An Ordinary Man," "Boccacio," "Measure for Measure."

MEARS, DeANN. Born in Ft. Fairfield, ME. Attended Westbrook Col. Debut 1961 OB in "Decameron," followed by "Ernest in Love," "Sound of Silence," "House of Blue Leaves," "Desire under the Elms," "Arthur," "Dear Liar," Bdwy in "Too True to Be Good," "Tiny Alice," "Abelard and Heloise."

MERCADO, HECTOR. Born in NYC in 1949. Graduate H. S. Performing Arts. Attended Harkness Ballet Sch., HB Studio. Bdwy debut 1960 in "West Side Story," followed by "Man of LaMancha," "Mass," "Dr. Jazz," "1600 Pennsylvania Ave.," "Your Arms Too Short to Box with God."

MERIN, EDA REISS. Born July 31 in NYC. Attended Hunter Col. Bdwy debut 1939 in "My Heart's in the Highlands," followed by "Trio," "Lovers," "Sophie," "A Flag Is Born," "A Far Country," OB in "Private Life of the Master Race," "Tower Beyond Tragedy," "Square in the Eye," "Huui, Huui," "Inner Journey," "Good Woman of Setzuan," "A Doll's House," "Hedda Gabler," "Uncle Vanya."

MERSON, SUSAN. Born Apr. 25, 1950 in Detroit, MI. Graduate Boston U. Bdwy debut 1974 in "Saturday Sunday Monday," followed by OB "Vanities."

METCALF, MARK. Born Mar. 11 in Findlay, OH. Attended UMich. Debut OB 1973 in "Creeps," followed by "The Tempest," (LC), "Beach Children," "Hamlet," "Patrick Henry Lake Liquors," "Streamers."

METZO, WILLIAM. Born June 21, 1937 in Wilkes-Barre, PA. Graduate King's Col. Debut 1963 OB in "The Bald Soprano," followed by "Papers," "A Moon for the Misbegotten," "Arsenic and Old Lace," Bdwy 1973 in "Cyrano."

MEYERS, MAIDA. Born May 2, 1954 in Philadelphia, PA. Graduate Temple U. Bdwy debut 1977 in "Knickerbocker Holiday."

MICHAELS, JOSHUA. Born Apr. 6, 1950 in Detroit, MI. Attended Cal. State U. Debut 1976 OB in "Follies," followed by "The Boys from Syracuse."

MILES, ROSS. Born in Poughkeepsie, NY. Bdwy debut 1962 in "Little Me," followed by "Baker Street," "Pickwick," "Darling of the Day," "Mame," "Jumpers," "Goodtime Charley," "Chicago."

MILES, SYLVIA. Born Sept. 9, 1934 in NYC. Attended Pratt Inst., Actors Studio. Debut 1954 OB in "A Stone for Danny Fisher," followed by "The Iceman Cometh," "The Balcony," "Chekhov Sketch Book," "Matty, Moron and Madonna," "The Kitchen," "Rosebloom," "Nellie Toole & Co.," "American Night Cry," Bdwy in "The Riot Act," "Night of the Iguana."

MILGRIM, LYNN. Born Mar. 17, 1944 in Philadelphia, PA. Graduate Swarthmore Col., Harvard U. Debut 1969 OB in "Frank Gagliano's City Scene," followed by "Crimes of Passion," "Macbeth," "Charley's Aunt," "The Real Inspector Hound," Bdwy 1977 in "Otherwise Engaged."

MILLER, MARTHA. Born Aug. 30, 1929 in New Bedford, MA. Graduate Carnegie-Mellon U. Debut OB 1956 in "House of Connolly," followed by "A Place without Morning," "Julius Caesar," "Major Barbara," "In the Summer House," "Merry Wives of Windsor," "Rimers of Eldritch," "Heartbreak House."

MILLER, MICHAEL. Born Sept. 1, 1931 in Los Angeles, CA. Attended Bard Col. Debut 1961 OB in "Under Milk Wood," followed by "The Lesson," "A Memory of 2 Mondays," "Little Murders," "Tom Paine," "Morning, Noon and Night," "Enemy of the People," "Whitsuntide," "Say When," "Case against Roberta Guardino," "Dandelion Wine," "Museum," Bdwy in "Ivanov," "Black Comedy," "Trial of Lee Harvey Oswald."

MILLIGAN, JACOB. Born Mar. 25, 1949 in Kansas City, MO. Graduate UKC. Bdwy debut 1976 in "Equus."

MILLS, STEPHANIE. Born in 1959 in Brooklyn, NY. Bdwy debut 1975 in "The Wiz."

MINER, JAN. Born Oct. 15, 1917 in Boston, MA. Debut 1958 OB in "Obligato," followed by "Decameron," "Dumbbell People," "Autograph Hound," Bdwy in "Viva Madison Avenue," "Lady of the Camelias," "Freaking Out of Stephanie Blake," "Othello," "Milk Train Doesn't Stop Here Anymore," "Butterflies Are Free," "The Women," "Pajama Game," "Saturday Sunday Monday," "The Heiress," "Romeo and Juliet."

MIXON, ALAN. Born Mar. 15, 1933 in Miami, FL. Attended UMiami. Bdwy bow 1962 in "Something about a Soldier," followed by "Sign in Sidney Brustein's Window," "The Devils," "The Unknown Soldier and His Wife," "Love Suicide at Schofield Barracks," "Equus," OB in "Suddenly Last Summer," "Desire under the Elms," "Trojan Women," "Alchemist," "Child Buyer," "Mr. and Mrs. Lyman," "A Whitman Portrait," "Iphigenia in Aulis," "Small Craft Warnings," "Mourning Becomes Electra," "The Runner Stumbles," "Old Glory," "The Gathering."

MIYAMOTO, ANNE. Born in Honolulu, HI. Graduate UHaw., NYU. Debut 1962 OB in "Yanks Are Coming," Bdwy 1977 in "Basic Training of Pavlo Hummel."

MOBERLY, ROBERT. Born Apr. 15, 1939 in Excelsior Springs, MO. Graduate UKan. Debut 1967 OB in "Arms and the Man," followed by "The Millionairess," "A Gun Play," "Shadow of a Gunman," Bdwy "A Place for Polly," "A Matter of Gravity."

MONFERDINI, CAROLE. Born in Eagle Lake, TX. Graduate North Tex. State U. Debut 1973 OB in "The Foursome," followed by "The Club."

MOONEY, WILLIAM. Born in Bernie, MO. Attended UCol. Bdwy debut 1961 in "A Man for All Seasons," followed by "A Place for Polly," OB in "Half Horse, Half Alligator," "Strike Heaven on the Face," "Conflict of Interest," "Overnight," "Brownsville Raid."

MOORE, JONATHAN. Born Mar. 24, 1923 in New Orleans, LA. Attended Piscator's Sch. Debut OB 1961 in "After the Angels," followed by "Berkeley Square," "Checking Out," Bdwy in "Dylan," "1776."

MORELL, DEBBIE. Born June 26, 1954 in NYC. Attended Manhattanville Col., Actors Studio. Debut 1976 OB in "Fiorello!"

MORENO, RITA. Born Dec, 11, 1931 in Humacao, PR. Bdwy debut 1945 in "Skydrift," followed by "West Side Story," "Sign in Sidney Brustein's Window," "Last of the Red Hot Lovers," "The National Health," "The Ritz," "She Loves Me."

MORENZIE, LEON. Born in Trinidad, WI. Graduate Sir George William U. Debut 1972 OB in "Ti-Jean and His Brothers," followed by "The Cherry Orchard," "Cockeyed Tiger," Bdwy in "The Leaf People."

MORFOGEN, GEORGE. Born Mar. 30, 1933 in NYC. Graduate Brown U., Yale. Debut 1957 OB in "Trial of D. Karamazov," followed by "Christmas Oratorio," "Othello," "Good Soldier Schweik," "Cave Dwellers," "Once in a Lifetime," "Total Eclipse," "Ice Age," "Prince of Homburg," Bdwy in "The Fun Couple."

MORIARTY, MICHAEL. Born Apr. 5, 1941 in Detroit, MI. Graduate Dartmouth, LAMDA. Debut OB 1963 in "Antony and Cleopatra," followed by "Peanut Butter and Jelly," "Long Day's Journey into Night," "Henry V," Bdwy in "Trial of the Catonsville 9," "Find Your Way Home" for which he received a Theater World Award, "Richard III" (LC).

MORSE, RICHARD. Born May 31 in Brookline, MA. Attended Principia Col., Neighborhood Playhouse. Debut 1955 OB in "Teach Me How to Cry," followed by "Thor with Angels," "Makropoulis Secret," "All Kinds of Giants," "Aria Da Capo," "Mime Theatre," Bdwy in "Mother Courage," "Fiddler on the Roof."

MORTON, JOE. Born Oct. 18, 1947 in NYC. Attended Hofstra U. Debut OB 1968 in "Month of Sundays," followed by "Salvation," "Charlie Was Here and Now He's Gone," "G. R. Point," Bdwy in "Hair," "Two Gentlemen of Verona," "Tricks," "Raisin" for which he received a Theatre World Award.

MOSTEL, JOSHUA. Born Dec. 21, 1946 in NYC. Graduate Brandeis U. Debut 1971 OB in "The Proposition," followed by "More Than You Deserve," Bdwy in "Unlikely Heroes," "American Millionaire," "A Texas Trilogy."

MOSTEL, ZERO. Born Feb. 28, 1915 in Brooklyn, NY. Graduate CCNY, NYU. Bdwy debut 1942 in "Keep 'Em Laughing," followed by "Concert Varieties," "Beggar's Holiday," "Flight into Egypt," "Good as Gold," "Rhinoceros," "A Funny Thing Happened on the Way to the Forum," "Ulysses in Nighttown" (also OB), "Fiddler on the Roof" (1964 & 1976).

MOUSKOURI, NANA. Born Oct. 13 in Athens, Greece. Attended Athens Cons. of Music. Bdwy debut 1977 in concert.

MULLIKIN, BILL. Born Apr. 1, 1927 in Baltimore, MD. Graduate Loyola U. Bdwy debut in "New Faces of 1952," followed by "The Boy Friend" (OB), "Hello Dolly!"

MULREAN, LINDA. Born Nov. 17, 1950 in Boston, MA. Graduate Manhattanville Col. Debut 1973 OB in "The Karl Marx Play," followed by "Fashion," "Antigone."

MURPHY, PETER. Born Sept. 13, 1925 in Glenarm, Ireland. Attended ULondon, RADA. Debut 1956 OB in "The Comedian," followed by "Macbeth," "Ghosts," "The Fantasticks," "When We Dead Awaken," "Dancing for the Kaiser," "Heartbreak House."

MURPHY, ROSEMARY. Born Jan. 13, 1927 in Munich, Ger. Attended Neighborhood Playhouse, Actors Studio. Bdwy debut 1950 in "Tower beyond Tragedy," followed by "Look Homeward, Angel," "Period of Adjustment," "Any Wednesday," "Delicate Balance," "Weekend," "Death of Bessie Smith," "Butterflies Are Free," "Ladies at the Alamo."

MURRAY, BRIAN. Born Oct. 9, 1939 in Johannesburg, SA. Debut 1964 OB in "The Knack," followed by "King Lear," "Ashes," Bdwy in " All in Good Time," "Rosencrantz and Guildenstern Are Dead," "Sleuth."

Josh Mostel   **Jan Neuberger**   **Don Nute**   **Mary Ann Niles**   **Gabriel Oshen**

MURRAY, DON. Born July 31, 1929 in Hollywood, CA. Attended AADA. Debut 1948 in "The Insect Comedy" (CC), followed by "The Rose Tattoo," "The Skin of Our Teeth" (1955), "The Hot Corner," "The Norman Conquests," "Same Time Next Year."

MURRAY, MARY. Born Nov. 13, 1953 in Ridgewood, NJ. Attended Ramapo Col., Juilliard. Bdwy debut 1976 in "The Robber Bridegroom."

MURRAY, PEG. Born in Denver, CO. Attended Western Reserve U. OB in "Children of Darkness," followed by "A Midsummer Night's Dream," "Oh, Dad, Poor Dad . . .," "Small Craft Warnings," "Enclave," Bdwy in "The Great Sebastians" (1956), "Gypsy," "Blood, Sweat and Stanley Poole," "She Loves Me," "Anyone Can Whistle," "The Subject Was Roses," "Something More," "Cabaret," "Fiddler on the Roof," "Royal Family."

NAUGHTON, JAMES. Born Dec. 6, 1945 in Middletown, CT. Graduate Brown, Yale U. Debut 1971 OB in "Long Day's Journey into Night" for which he received a Theatre World Award, followed by "I Love My Wife" (Bdwy 1977).

NEGRO, MARY-JOAN. Born Nov. 9, 1948 in Brooklyn, NY. Debut 1972 OB in "The Hostage," followed by "Lower Depths," "Women Beware Women," "Ladyhouse Blues," Bdwy in "Three Sisters," "Measure for Measure," "Beggar's Opera."

NEILSON, RICHARD. Born Nov. 30, 1924 in London, Eng. Debut 1959 OB in "Heloise," followed by "O Say Can You See," "Tea Party," Bdwy in "Pickwick (1964)," "Wise Child," "My Fair Lady," "Equus."

NETTLETON, DENISE. Born June 9, 1948 in Branford, Can. Bdwy debut 1974 in "Grease."

NEUBERGER, JAN. Born. Jan 21, 1953 in Amityville, NY. Attended NYU. Bdwy debut 1974 in "Gypsy," OB in "Silk Stockings" (ELT)

NEVILLE-ANDREWS, JOHN. Born Aug. 23, 1948 in Woking Surrey, Eng. Attended Westminster Tech. Col. Debut 1973 OB in "El Grande de Coca-Cola," followed by "Bullshot Crummond."

NEWELL, JAMES S. Born Nov. 20, 1940 in Chicago, IL. Graduate Xavier U., St. Louis U., Wayne State U. Debut 1976 OB in "The Fantasticks."

NEWMAN, STEPHEN D. Born Jan. 20, 1943 in Seattle, WA. Stanford graduate. Debut 1971 OB in Judith Anderson's "Hamlet," followed by "School for Wives," "Beggar's Opera," "Pygmalion," "In the Voodoo Parlour of Marie Leveau," "Richard III," "Santa Anita '42," "Polly," Bdwy in "An Evening with Richard Nixon and . . .," "Emperor Henry IV," "Habeas Corpus," "Rex," "Dirty Linen."

NEWMAN, WILLIAM. Born June 15, 1934 in Chicago, IL. Graduate UWash., Columbia U. Debut 1972 OB in "The Beggar's Opera," followed by "Are You Now or Have You Ever Been," "Conflict of Interest," "Mr. Runaway," "Uncle Vanya," Bdwy in "Over Here," "Rocky Horror Show."

NICKERSON, SHANE. Born Jan. 29, 1964 in Miami, FL. Bdwy debut 1972 in "Pippin."

NICOL, LESSLIE. Born May 27 in Dundee, Scot. NY debut OB in "Man with a Load of Mischief," Bdwy 1973 in "Grease."

NILES, MARY ANN. Born May 2, 1933 in NYC. Attended Miss Finchley's Ballet Acad. Bdwy debut in "Girl from Nantucket," followed by "Dance Me a Song," "Call Me Mister," "Make Mine Manhattan," "La Plume de Ma Tante," "Carnival," "Flora the Red Menace," "Sweet Charity," "George M!," "No, No, Nanette," "Irene," OB in "The Boys from Syracuse," CC's "Wonderful Town" and "Carnival."

NIMOY, LEONARD. Born Mar. 26, 1931 in Boston, MA. Attended Boston Col., Pasadena Playhouse. Bdwy debut 1973 in "Full Circle," followed by "Equus."

NOLTE, BILL. Born June 4, 1953 in Toledo, OH. Graduate Cincinnati Conservatory of Music. Debut 1977 OB in "Wonderful Town."

NORTH, ALAN. Born Dec. 23, 1927 in NYC. Attended Columbia U. Bdwy bow 1955 in "Plain and Fancy," followed by "South Pacific"(CC), "Summer of the 17th Doll," "Requiem for a Nun," "Never Live Over a Pretzel Factory," "Dylan," "Spofford," OB in "Scribes."

NUTE, DON Born Mar. 13, in Connellsville, Pa. Attended Denver U. Debut OB 1965 in "The Trojan Women," followed by "Boys in the Band," "Mad Theatre for Madmen," "The Eleventh Dynasty," "About Time," "The Urban Crisis," "Christmas Rappings," "The Life of a Man," "A Look at the Fifties."

OAKLAND, SIMON. Born Aug. 28, 1920 in Brooklyn, NY. Attended Columbia U. Bdwy debut 1948 in "Skipper Next to God," followed by "Light Up the Sky," "Caesar and Cleopatra," "Harvey," "The Shrike," "Sands of Negev," "The Great Sebastians," "Angela," "Twigs," "The Shadow Box."

O'BRIEN, SYLVIA. Born May 4, 1924 in Dublin, Ire. Debut OB 1961 in "O Marry Me," followed by "Red Roses for Me," "Every Other Evil," "3 by O'Casey," "Essence of Woman," "Dear Oscar," Bdwy in "Passion of Josef D," "Right Honourable Gentleman," "Loves of Cass McGuire," "Hadrian VII," "Conduct Unbecoming," "My Fair Lady."

O'DELL, K. LYPE. Born Feb. 2, 1939 in Claremore, OK. Graduate Los Angeles State Col. Debut 1972 OB in "Sunset," followed by "Our Father," "Ice Age," "Prince of Homburg."

OH, SOON-TECK. Born June 29, 1943 in Korea. Attended UCLA, Neighborhood Playhouse. Bdwy debut 1976 in "Pacific Overtures."

OKARSKI, DAVE. Born June 21, 1950 in NYC. Graduate Beloit Col. Debut 1977 OB in "Come Back, Little Sheba." (ELT)

O'KEEFE, PAUL C. Born Apr. 27, 1951 in Boston, MA. Graduate Columbia U. Bdwy debut 1958 in "The Music Man," followed by "Sail Away, "Oliver," "A Texas Trilogy."

ORBACH, JERRY. Born Oct. 20, 1935 in NYC. Attended Northwestern U. Bdwy debut 1961 in "Carnival," followed by "Guys and Dolls," "Carousel," "Annie Get Your Gun," "The Natural Look," "Promises, Promises," "6 Rms Riv Vu," "Chicago," OB in "Threepenny Opera," "The Fantasticks," "The Cradle Will Rock," "Scuba Duba."

ORFALY, ALEXANDER. Born Oct. 10, 1935 in Brooklyn, NY. Appeared in "South Pacific" (LC), "How Now, Dow Jones," "Ari," "Sugar," "Cyrano," "Fiddler on the Roof"(1976), OB in "The End of All Things Natural," "Mahogonny," "Johnny Johnson," "Ride the Winds," "Polly."

O'SHEA, MILO. Born June 2, 1926 in Dublin, Ire. Bdwy debut 1968 in "Staircase," followed by "Dear World," "Mrs. Warren's Profession"(LC), "Comedians."

OSHEN, GABRIEL. Born Oct. 8, 1950 in NYC. Bdwy debut 1974 in "Equus."

OTTENHEIMER, ALBERT M. Born Sept. 6, 1904 in Tacoma, WA. Graduate UWash. Bdwy debut 1946 in "Affair of Honor," followed by "West Side Story," "Deputy," "Yentl," OB in "Monday's Heroes," "Tiger," "Mother Riba," "A Christmas Carol," "Juno and the Paycock," "Italian Straw Hat," "The Iceman Cometh," "Call It Virtue," "The Immoralist," "The Cat and the Canary," "Exhaustion of Our Son's Love," "Deadly Game," "Brother Gorski," "The Kid," "Holy Ghosts," "Yentl the Yeshiva Boy."

OWENS, EDWIN. Born May 8, 1942 in Chicago, IL. Graduate Carnegie Tech, LAMDA. Bdwy debut 1970 in "Conduct Unbecoming," followed by "The Changing Room," "That Championship Season," "Caesar and Cleopatra," OB in "The Basic Training of Pavlo Hummel"(1971).

OWENS, ELIZABETH. Born Feb. 26, 1938 in NYC. Attended New School, Neighborhood Playhouse. Debut 1955 OB in "Dr. Faustus Lights the Lights," followed by "Chit Chat on a Rat," "The Miser," "The Father," "Importance of Being Earnest," "Candida," "Trumpets and Drums," "Oedipus," "Macbeth," "Uncle Vanya," "Misalliance," "Master Builder," "American Gothics," "The Play's the Thing," "The Rivals," "Death Story," "The Rehearsal," "Dance on a Country Grave," Bdwy in "The Lovers," "Not Now Darling," "The Play's the Thing."

PACINO, AL. Born Apr. 25, 1940 in NYC. Attended Actors Studio. Bdwy bow 1969 in "Does a Tiger Wear a Necktie?" for which he received a Theatre World Award, followed by "The Basic Training of Pavlo Hummel," OB in "Why Is A A Crooked Letter?," "Peace Creeps," "The Indian Wants the Bronx," "Local Stigmatic," "Camino Real" (LC).

PAGE, GERALDINE. Born Nov. 22, 1924 in Kirksville, MO. Attended Goodman Theatre. OB in "7 Mirrors," "Summer and Smoke" for which she received a Theatre World Award, "Macbeth," "Look Away," "The Stronger," Bdwy debut 1953 in "Midsummer," followed by "The Immoralist," "The Rainmaker," "Innkeepers," "Separate Tables," "Sweet Bird of Youth," "Strange Interlude," "Three Sisters," "P.S. I Love You," "The Great Indoors," "White Lies," "Black Comedy," "The Little Foxes," "Angela," "Absurd Person Singular."

PAGE, KEN. Born Jan. 20, 1954 in St. Louis, MO. Attended Fontbonne Col. Bdwy debut 1976 in "Guys and Dolls" for which he received a Theatre World Award, followed by "The Wiz."

PAGENT, ROBERT. Born Dec. 12, 1917 in Pittsburgh, PA. Attended Ind.U. On Bdwy in "Oklahoma!," "One Touch of Venus," "Carousel," JB in "Show Boat."

253

| Stuart Pankin | Joan Pape | Glover Parham | Verna Pierce | Hardy Phippen |

PALMER, BETSY. Born Nov. 1, 1929 in East Chicago, IN. Graduate DePaul U., Actors Studio. Bdwy debut 1955 in "The Grand Prize," followed by "Affair of Honor," "Roar Like a Dove," "South Pacific" (CC), "Cactus Flower," "Eccentricities of a Nightingale."

PALMER, LELAND. Born June 16, 1945 in Port Washington, NY. Bdwy debut 1966 in "Joyful Noise," followed by "Applause," "Pippin," OB in "Your Own Thing."

PALMIERI, JOSEPH. Born Aug. 1, 1939 in Bklyn. Attended Catholic U. With NYSF 1965–6, "Cyrano de Bergerac" (LCR), OB in "Butter and Egg Man," "Boys in the Band," "Beggar's Opera," "The Family," "The Crazy Locomotive," Bdwy in "Lysistrata," "Candide."

PANKIN, STUART. Born Apr. 8, 1946 in Philadelphia, PA. Graduate Dickinson Col., Columbia U. Debut OB 1968 in "Wars of the Roses," followed by "Richard III," "Timon of Athens," "Cymbeline," "Mary Stuart," "Narrow Road to the Deep North," "Twelfth Night," "The Crucible," "Wings," "A Glorious Age," "Joseph and The Amazing Technicolor Dreamcoat," BAM's "3 Sisters."

PAPE, JOAN. Born Jan. 23, 1944 in Detroit, MI. Graduate Purdue U., Yale. Debut 1972 OB in "Suggs," followed by "Bloomers," "Museum," Bdwy in "The Secret Affairs of Mildred Wild," "Cat on a Hot Tin Roof."

PARHAM, GLOVER. Born Jan. 14, 1945 in Birmingham, AL. Graduate Oberlin Consv. Bdwy debut 1975 in "Treemonisha," followed by "Porgy and Bess."

PARKER, ELLEN. Born Sept. 30, 1949 in Paris, Fr. Graduate Bard Col. Debut 1971 OB in "James Joyce Liquid Memorial Theatre," Bdwy 1977 in "Equus."

PARKER, PAULA. Born Aug. 14, 1950 in Chicago, IL. Graduate S. Ill. U. Debut 1971 OB in "The Debate," followed by "Maggie Flynn."

PARSONS, ESTELLE. Born Nov. 20, 1927 in Lynn, MA. Attended Boston U., Actors Studio. OB in "Threepenny Opera," "Automobile Graveyard," "Mrs. Dally Has a Lover" for which she received a Theatre World Award, "In the Summer House." "Monopoly," "Peer Gynt," "Mahagonny," "Silent Partner," "Barbary Shore," "Oh Glorious Tintinnabulation," with LCR in "East Wind," "Galileo," "People Are Living There," and "Mert and Phil," Bdwy in "Happy Hunting," "Whoop-Up!," "Beg, Borrow or Steal," "Ready When You Are, C. B.," "Malcolm," "Seven Descents of Myrtle," "A Way of Life," "And Miss Reardon Drinks a Little," "Norman Conquests," "Ladies at the Alamo."

PASEKOFF, MARILYN. Born Nov. 7, 1949 in Pittsburgh, PA. Graduate Boston U. Debut 1975 OB in "Godspell," followed by "Words."

PASSELTINER, BERNIE. Born Nov. 21, 1931 in NYC. Graduate Catholic U. OB in "Square in the Eye," "Sourball," "As Virtuously Given," "Now Is the Time for All Good Men," "Rain," "Kaddish," "Against the Sun," "End of Summer," "Yentl, the Yeshiva Boy," "Heartbreak House," Bdwy in "The Office," "The Jar," "Yentl."

PASTENE, ROBERT. Born Jan. 29, 1918 in Brockton, MA. Attended MIT, Wash. U. Has appeared in "The First Crocus," "Hamlet," "Crime and Punishment," "Taming of the Shrew," "St. Joan," "Children's Hour," "In the Counting House," "House of Atreus," "Arturo Ui," OB in "Journey to the Day," "John Gabriel Borkman."

PATELLA, DENNIS. Born July 24, 1945 in Youngstown, OH. Graduate Wayne State U. Debut 1974 OB in "The Cherry Orchard," followed by "Original Cast," "Three Sisters," "LaRonde," Bdwy in "Romeo and Juliet."

PATIK VICKIE. Born June 14, 1950 in Los Angeles, CA. Graduate Los Angeles State U. Bdwy debut 1976 in "My Fair Lady."

PATTERSON, DICK. Born in Clear Lake, IA. Graduate UCLA. Bdwy debut in "Vintage 1960," followed by "The Billy Barnes People," "Bye Bye Birdie," "Fade-Out, Fade-In," "Something Old, Something New."

PAULSON, WILLIAM. Born Mar. 17, 1954 in NYC. Attended Hunter Col., Neighborhood Playhouse. Bdwy debut 1976 in "Night of the Iguana."

PAYTON-WRIGHT, PAMELA. Born Nov. 1, 1941 in Pittsburgh, PA. Graduate Birmingham Southern Col., RADA. Bdwy debut 1967 with APA in "The Show-Off," followed by "Exit the King," "The Cherry Orchard," "Jimmy Shine," "Mourning Becomes Electra," "Glass Menagerie," "Romeo and Juliet," OB in "Effect of Marigolds . . .," "The Crucible."

PEARL, IRWIN. Born Oct. 14, 1945 in Brooklyn, NY. Graduate Hofstra U. Bdwy bow 1970 in "Minnie's Boys," followed by "Fiddler on the Roof" (1976), OB in "Big Hotel," "Ergo," "Invitation to a Beheading," "Babes in Arms" (ELT).

PELIKAN, LISA. Born July 12 in Paris, France. Attended Juilliard. Debut 1975 OB in "Spring's Awakening," followed by "Elephant in the House," Bdwy in "Romeo and Juliet" (1977).

PENDLETON, AUSTIN. Born Mar. 27, 1940 in Warren, OH. Attended Yale U. Appeared with LC Rep. Co. 1962–63, and in "Oh, Dad, Poor Dad . . .," "Fiddler on the Roof," "Hail Scrawdyke," "The Little Foxes," "An American Millionaire," "The Runner Stumbles," OB in "The Last Sweet Days of Isaac," BAM Co.'s "Three Sisters."

PENN, EDWARD. Born In Washington, DC. Studied at HB studio. Debut 1965 OB in "The Queen and the Rebels," followed by "My Wife and I," "Invitation to a March," "Of Thee I Sing," "Fantasticks," "Greenwillow," "One for the Money," "Dear Oscar," "Speed Gets the Poppys," "Man with a Load of Mischief." Bdwy bow 1975 in "Shenandoah."

PERCASSI, DON. Born Jan. 11 in Amsterdam, NY. Bdwy debut 1964 in "High Spirits," followed by "Walking Happy," "Coco," "Sugar," "Molly," "Mack and Mabel," "A Chorus Line."

PERETZ, SUSAN. Born in NYC. Graduate U. Buffalo. Debut 1972 OB in "American Gothics," followed by "42 Seconds from Broadway," "Comedy of Errors," Bdwy 1975 in "Ladies at the Alamo."

PERKINS, ANTHONY. Born Apr. 4, 1932 in NYC. Attended Rollins Col., Columbia U. Bdwy debut 1954 in "Tea and Sympathy" for which he received a Theatre World Award, followed by "Look Homeward, Angel," "Greenwillow," "Harold," "Star Spangled Girl," "Steambath" (OB), "Equus."

PERKINS, DON. Born Oct. 23, 1928 in Boston, MA. Graduate Emerson Col. OB in "Drums under the Window," "Henry VI," "Richard III," "The Dubliners," "The Rehearsal," Bdwy 1970 in "Borstal Boy."

PERLEY, WILLIAM. Born Nov. 24, 1942 in NYC. Graduate U. Fla. Debut 1975 OB in "Tenderloin," Bdwy 1977 in "Vieux Carre."

PESATURO, GEORGE. Born July 29, 1949 in Winthrop, MA. Graduate Manhattan Col. Bdwy debut 1976 in "A Chorus Line."

PETERS, MARK. Born Nov. 20, 1952 in Council Bluffs, IA. Yale graduate. Debut 1977 OB in "The Crazy Locomotive."

PETERSON, KURT. Born Feb. 12, 1948 in Stevens Point, WI. Attended AMDA. Bdwy debut 1969 in "Dear World," followed by "Follies," "Knickerbocker Holiday," OB in "An Ordinary Miracle," "West Side Story" (LC), "Dames at Sea," "By Bernstein."

PETERSON, RICHARD. Born Apr. 25, 1945 in Palo Alto, CA. Graduate Boston U. Debut 1972 OB in "Antony and Cleopatra," followed by "Titanic," "Twelfth Night" (ELT)

PETRICOFF, ELAINE. Born in Cincinnati, OH. Graduate Syracuse U. Bdwy debut 1971 in "The Me Nobody Knows," OB in "Hark!," "Ride the Winds," "Cole Porter," Bdwy debut 1973 in "Grease."

PHELPS, ELEANOR. Born in Baltimore, MD. Vassar graduate. Bdwy debut 1928 in "Merchant of Venice," followed by "Richard II," "Criminal Code," "Trick for Trick," "Seen But Not Heard," "Flight to the West," "Queen Bee," "We the People," "Six Characters in Search of an Author," "Mr. Big," "Naughty-Naught," "The Disenchanted," "Picnic," "My Fair Lady" (1956 & 76), "40 Carats," "Crown Matrimonial," "Royal Family," OB in "Garden District," "Color of Darkness."

PHIPPEN, HARDY, JR. Born July 9, 1946 in Chicago, IL. Harvard graduate. Debut 1976 OB in "Fiorello!" (ELT)

PIAZZA, FRANK. Born Aug. 31, 1945 in Bridgeport, CT. Graduate Quinnipiac Col. Bdwy debut 1977 in "Unexpected Guests."

PICARDO, ROBERT. Born Oct. 27, 1953 in Philadelphia, PA. Graduate Yale U. Debut 1975 OB in "Sexual Perversity in Chicago," followed by "Visions of Kerouac," "The Primary English Class," "Gemini" (also Bdwy '77)

PICON, MOLLY. Born Feb. 28, 1898 in NYC. Star of Yiddish Theatre, on Bdwy in "Morning Star," "For Heaven's Sake, Mother," "Milk and Honey," "How to Be a Jewish Mother," "Front Page," "Paris Is Out," "Something Old, Something New."

PIERCE, VERNA. Born in NJ. Attended U. Kan. AADA. Bdwy debut 1974 in "A Little Night Music," followed by "Pippin," "Fiorello!" (ELT/OB).

Shelli Place   **Barry Preston**   **Lizabeth Pritchett**   **Patrick Quinn**   **Teri Ralston**

PIERRE, CHRISTOPHE. Born Dec. 25, 1949 in New Orleans, LA. Attended Theological Seminary. Bdwy debut 1973 in "Don't Bother Me, I Can't Cope," followed by "The Wiz," "Guys and Dolls."

PITCHFORD, DEAN. Born July 29, 1951 in Honolulu, HI. Graduate Yale U. Debut 1971 OB in "Godspell," Bdwy 1973 in "Pippin," "Saints" (OB).

PLACE, SHELLI. Born Jan. 9, 1951 in Oak Park, IL. Graduate SMU. Debut 1977 OB in "Come Back, Little Sheba" (ELT).

PLASKOW, MERRILL W. 2nd. Born July 2, 1946 in Philadelphia, PA. Graduate Southampton Col., Penn. State U. Bdwy debut 1976 in "Fiddler on the Roof."

PLIMPTON, SHELLEY. Born in 1947 in Roseburg, OR. Debut 1967 OB in "Hair," followed by "Nightclub Cantata."

PLUMLEY, DON. Born Feb. 11, 1934 in Los Angeles, CA. Pepperdine Col. graduate. Debut 1961 OB in "The Cage," followed by "A Midsummer Night's Dream," "Richard II," "Cymbeline," "Much Ado about Nothing," "Saving Grace," "A Whistle in the Dark," "Operation Sidewinder," "Enemy of the People," "Back Bog Beast Bait," "The Kid," Bdwy 1974 in "Equus."

PLYMALE, TRIP. Born Nov. 15 in Raleigh, NC. Attended NC Sch. of Arts. Bdwy debut 1976 in "The Robber Bridegroom."

POLE, FRANCES. Born June 12, 1907 in St. Paul, MN. Debut 1958 OB in " 'Tis Pity She's a Whore," followed by "Mornings at 7," "Ice Age," "Arsenic and Old Lace."

POMERANTZ, JEFFREY DAVID. Born July 2, 1945 in NYC. Attended Northwestern U., RADA. Bdwy debut (as Jeffrey David-Owen) 1971 in "The Leaf People," followed by "The Ritz," "Equus," OB in "John Gabriel Borkman."

PONAZECKI, JOE. Born Jan. 7, 1934 in Rochester, NY. Attended Rochester U., Columbia. Bdwy bow 1959 in "Much Ado about Nothing," followed by "Send Me No Flowers," "Call on Kuprin," "Take Her, She's Mine," "Fiddler on the Roof," "Xmas in Las Vegas," "3 Bags Full," "Love in E-Flat," "90 Day Mistress," "Harvey," "Trial of the Catonsville 9," "Country Girl," "Freedom of the City," "Summer Brave," "Music Is," OB in "The Dragon," "Muzeeka," "Witness," "All Is Bright," "The Dog Ran Away," "Dream of a Blacklisted Actor."

POTTER, CAROL. Born May 21, 1948 in NYC. Graduate Radcliffe Col. Debut 1974 OB in "The Last Days of British Honduras," followed by "Gemini" (1977 OB & Bdwy).

PRADO, FRANCISCO. Born Nov. 3, 1941 in San Juan, PR. Graduate UPR. Debut 1977 OB in "G. R. Point."

PREBLE, ED. Born Nov. 9, 1919 in Chicago, IL. Bdwy bow 1957 in "Inherit the Wind," followed by "Family Way," "Kings," OB in "Press Cuttings," "Failures," "Krapp's Last Tape," "Marcus in the High Grass," "A Figleaf in Her Bonnet," "Calling in Crazy," "The Family."

PREMICE, JOSEPHINE. Born July 21, 1926 in Brooklyn, NY. Graduate Columbia, Cornell U. Bdwy debut 1945 in "Blue Holiday," followed by "Caribbean Carnival," "Mr. Johnson," "Jamaica," "A Hand Is on the Gate," "Bubbling Brown Sugar," OB in "House of Flowers," "Cherry Orchard," "American Night Cry."

PRESTON, BARRY. Born May 31, 1945 in Brooklyn, NY. Attended Utah State Col. Bdwy debut 1964 in "Something More," followed by "A Joyful Noise," "Bubbling Brown Sugar."

PRESTON, ROBERT. Born June 8, 1918 in Newton Highlands, MA. Attended Pasadena Playhouse. Bdwy debut 1951 in "20th Century," followed by "The Male Animal," "Men of Distinction," "His and Hers," "The Magic and the Loss," "Tender Trap," "Janus," "Hidden River," "Music Man," "Too True to Be Good," "Nobody Loves an Albatross," "Ben Franklin in Paris," "The Lion in Winter," "I Do! I Do!," "Mack and Mabel," "Sly Fox."

PRESTON, WILLIAM. Born Aug. 26, 1921 in Columbia, PA. Graduate Penn. State U. Debut OB 1972 in "We Bombed in New Haven," followed by "Hedda Gabler," "Whisper into My Good Ear," "A Nestless Bird," "Friends of Mine," "Iphigenia in Aulis," "Midsummer," "The Fantasticks."

PRIMROSE, ALEK. Born Aug. 20, 1934 in San Joaquin, CA. Attended Col. of the Pacific. OB in "Good King Charles' Golden Days," "Golem," "Leave It to Jane," "The Balcony," "Rules of the Game," "A Man's a Man," "In White America," "The Kitchen," "Trials of Oz," "Incident at Vichy," "Tartuffe," BAM's "New York Idea." Bdwy in "A Cook for Mr. General," "House of Atreus," "Arturo Ui," "Room Service," "Ring Round the Bathtub," "The Lincoln Mask."

PRITCHETT, LIZABETH. Born Mar. 12, 1920 in Dallas, TX. Attended SMU. Bdwy debut 1959 in "Happy Town," followed by "Sound of Music," "Maria Golovin," "The Yearling," "A Funny Thing Happened on the Way to the Forum," OB in "Cindy," "The Real Inspector Hound," "The Karl Marx Play," "Show Boat" (JB).

PROFANATO, GENE. Born Dec. 9, 1964 in NYC. Bdwy debut 1970 in "Lovely Ladies, Kind Gentlemen," followed by "The King and I" (1977).

PRYCE, JONATHAN. Born June 1, 1947 in Wales, UK. Attended RADA. Bdwy debut 1976 in "Comedians" for which he received a Theatre World Award.

PURSLEY, DAVID. Born July 13, 1938 in Lewisburg, PA. Graduate Harvard, Baylor U. Debut 1969 OB in "Peace," followed by "The Faggott," "Wings," "Three Musketeers," "Happy End" (1977 Bdwy).

QUARRY, RICHARD. Born Aug. 9, 1944 in Akron, OH. Graduate U. Akron, NYU. Bdwy bow 1970 in "Georgy," followed by "Oh! Calcutta!," "Grease."

QUINN, PATRICK. Born Feb. 12, 1950 in Philadelphia, PA. Graduate Temple U. Bdwy debut 1976 in "Fiddler on the Roof."

RABB, ELLIS. Born June 20, 1930 in Memphis, TN. Attended Carnegie Tech., Yale. Debut OB 1956 in "Midsummer Night's Dream," followed by "Misanthrope," "Mary Stuart," "The Tavern," "Twelfth Night," "The Importance of Being Earnest," "King Lear," "Man and Superman," Bdwy in "Look after Lulu," "Jolly's Progress," "Right You Are . . .," "Scapin," "Impromtu at Versailles," "Lower Depths," "School for Scandal," "Pantagleize," "Cock-a-Doodle Dandy," "Hamlet," "The Royal Family." Founder and director of APA.

RAGNO, JOSEPH. Born Mar. 11, 1936 in Brooklyn, NY. Attended Allegheny Col. Debut 1960 OB in "Worm in the Horseradish," followed by "Elizabeth the Queen," "A Country Scandal," "The Shrike," "Cymbeline," "Love Me, Love My Children," "Interrogation of Havana," "The Birds," "Armenians," "From the Memoirs of Pontius Pilate," Bdwy in "Indians" (1969), "The Iceman Cometh."

RALSTON, TERI. Born Feb. 16, 1943 in Holyoke, CO. Graduate San Francisco State Col. Debut 1969 OB in "Jacques Brel Is Alive. . . .," Bdwy in "Company" (1970), followed by "A Little Night Music."

RAMSAY, REMAK. Born Feb. 2, 1937 in Baltimore, MD. Graduate Princeton U. Debut 1964 OB in "Hang Down Your Head and Die," followed by "The Real Inspector Hound," Bdwy in "Half a Sixpence," "Sheep on the Runway," "Lovely Ladies, Kind Gentlemen," "On the Town," "Jumpers," "Private Lives," "Dirty Linen."

RAMSEY, JOHN. Born Jan. 23, 1940 in Scranton, PA. Graduate Brown U., Yale. Debut 1964 OB in "Sunset," followed by Bdwy in "House of Atreus," "Find Your Way Home," "Sly Fox."

RANDALL, CHARLES. Born Mar. 15, 1923 in Chicago, IL. Attended Columbia U. Bdwy bow 1953 in "Anastasia," followed by "Enter Laughing," "Trial of Lee Harvey Oswald," OB in "The Adding Machine," "The Cherry Orchard," "Brothers Karamazov," "Susan Slept Here," "Two for Fun," "Timon of Athens," "Endgame."

RANDELL, RON. Born Oct. 8, 1920 in Sydney, Aust. Attended St. Mary's Col. Bdwy debut 1949 in "The Browning Version," followed by "A Harlequinade," "Candida," "World of Suzie Wong," "Sherlock Holmes," "Mrs. Warren's Profession" (LC), "Measure for Measure" (CP).

RAWLINS, LESTER. Born Sept. 24, 1924 in Farrell, PA. Attended Carnegie Tech. Bdwy in "Othello," "King Lear," "The Lovers," "A Man for All Seasons," "Herzl," "Romeo and Juliet," OB in "Endgame," "Quare Fellow," "Camino Real," "Hedda Gabler," "Old Glory," "Child Buyer," "Winterset," "In the Bar of a Tokyo Hotel," "The Reckoning," "Nightride."

RAYSON, BENJAMIN. Born in NYC. Bdwy debut 1953 in "Can-Can," followed by "Silk Stockings," "Bells Are Ringing," "A Little Night Music," "Happy End."

REA, KITTY. Born Jan. 13, 1952 in Bethesda, MD. Graduate San Francisco State U. Debut OB 1974 and Bdwy 1976 in "Godspell."

REAMS, LEE ROY. Born Aug. 23, 1942 in Covington, KY. Graduate U. Cinn. Cons. Bdwy debut 1966 in "Sweet Charity," followed by "Oklahoma!" (LC). "Applause," "Lorelei," "Show Boat" (JB).

REDGRAVE, LYNN. Born in London Mar. 8, 1943. Attended Central Schl. of Speech. Bdwy debut 1967 in "Black Comedy," followed by "My Fat Friend," "Mrs. Warren's Profession" (LC), "Knock Knock."

REED, VIVIAN. Born June 6, 1947 in Pittsburgh, PA. Attended Pittsburgh Musical Inst., Juilliard. Bdwy debut 1971 in "That's Entertainment," followed by "Don't Bother Me, I Can't Cope," "Bubbling Brown Sugar" for which she received a Theatre World Award.

REESE, ROXANNE. Born June 6, 1952 in Washington, DC. Graduate Howard U. Debut 1974 OB in "Freedom Train," followed by "Feeling Good," "No Place to Be Somebody," Bdwy 1976 in "For Colored Girls Who Have Considered . . ."

REEVE, CHRISTOPHER. Born Sept. 25, 1952 in NYC. Graduate Cornell U., Juilliard. Debut 1975 OB in "Berkeley Square," followed by "My Life," Bdwy 1976 in "A Matter of Gravity."

REID, ELLIOTT. Born Jan. 16, 1920 in NYC. Attended Actors Studio. Bdwy debut 1937 in "Julius Caesar," followed by "Shoemaker's Holiday," "My Sister Eileen," "Macbeth," "Two Blind Mice," "Live Wire," "Two on the Aisle," "From A to Z."

REILEY, ORRIN. Born Aug. 12, 1946 in Santa Monica, CA. Graduate UCLA. Bdwy debut 1969 in "Dear World," followed by "Man of LaMancha," "Applause," "On the Town," "Seesaw," "Knickerbocker Holiday."

REILLY, JOHN WILLIAM. Born Apr. 3, 1949 in NYC. Graduate SUNY. Bdwy debut 1977 in "Vieux Carre."

REIMUELLER, ROSS. Born Nov. 16, 1937 in Dayton, OH. Graduate Oberlin Col., New Eng. Consv. Bdwy debut 1976 in "Porgy and Bess."

REINKING, ANN. Born Nov. 10, 1949 in Seattle, WA. Attended Joffrey Sch., HB Studio. Bdwy debut 1969 in "Cabaret," followed by "Coco," "Pippin," "Over Here" for which she received a Theatre World Award, "Goodtime Charley," "A Chorus Line," "Chicago."

REMME, JOHN. Born Nov. 21, 1935 in Fargo, ND. Attended U. Minn. Debut 1972 OB in "One for the Money," Bdwy 1975 in "The Ritz," followed by "The Royal Family."

REPOLE, CHARLES. Born May 24 in Brooklyn, NY. Graduate Hofstra U. Bdwy debut 1975 in "Very Good Eddie" for which he received a Theatre World Award.

REXROAD, DAVID. Born Jan. 11, 1950 in Parkersburg, WV. Graduate WVa. U. Debut OB 1973 in "The Fantasticks."

REYNOLDS, DEBBIE. Born Apr. 1, 1932 in El Paso, TX. Bdwy debut 1973 in "Irene," followed by "The Debbie Reynolds Show."

RICE, SARAH. Born Mar. 5, 1955 in Okinawa. Attended Ariz State U. Debut 1974 OB in "The Fantasticks."

RICHARDS, CAIN. Born June 15, 1929 in Lancaster, PA. Attended Penn State U., AADA. OB in "Moor Born," "Life and Times of J. Walter Sminthius," "Let Them Down Gently," Bdwy 1977 in "Caesar and Cleopatra."

RICHARDS, JESS. Born Jan. 23, 1943 in Seattle, WA. Attended U. Wash. Bdwy debut 1966 in "Walking Happy," followed by "South Pacific" (LC). "Blood Red Roses," "Two by Two," "On the Town" for which he received a Theatre World Award, "Mack and Mabel," OB in "One for the Money," "Lovesong."

RICHARDS, JIM. Born May 11, 1953 in NYC. Graduate U. Miami. Debut 1977 OB in "Movie Buff."

RICHARDSON, IAN. Born Apr. 7, 1934 in Edinburgh, Scot. Attended Royal Scottish Acad. Debut 1964 at LC with Royal Shakespeare Co. in "King Lear," "Comedy of Errors," BAM 1975–6 in "Richard II," "Summerfolk," "Love's Labours Lost," "He That Plays the King," Bdwy in "Marat/Sade" (1965), "My Fair Lady" (1976).

RICHARDSON, RALPH. Born Dec. 19, 1902 in Cheltenham, Eng. Bdwy debut 1935 in "Romeo and Juliet," followed by "Henry IV, Parts I & II," "Uncle Vanya," "Oedipus," "The Critic," "Waltz of the Toreadors," "School for Scandal," "Home," "No Man's Land."

RICKETTS, JIM. Born May 11, 1948 in NYC. Attended Ill. Wesleyan U., AMDA. Debut 1977 OB in "Peg o' My Heart."

RIDGE, JOHN. Born May 13, 1924 in Brooklyn, NY. Attended LIU, NYU, Pratt Inst. Debut OB 1969 in "The Triumph of Robert Emmet," Bdwy 1972 in "Mourning Becomes Electra," followed by "Threepenny Opera" (LC).

RIEGERT, PETER. Born Apr. 11, 1947 in NYC. Graduate U. Buffalo. Debut 1975 OB in "Dance with Me," followed by "Sexual Perversity in Chicago."

RIFICI, JOE. Born Nov. 25, 1952 in NYC. Graduate Wagner Col. Bdwy debut 1975 in "Grease."

RIGBY, TERENCE. Born Jan. 2, 1937 in Birmingham, Eng. Graduate RADA. Bdwy debut 1967 in "The Homecoming," followed by "No Man's Land."

RINALDI, JOY. Born in Yonkers, NY. Graduate Stephens Col., AADA. Debut OB 1969 in "Satisfaction Guaranteed," Bdwy 1973 in "Grease."

RISEMAN, NAOMI. Born Oct. 6, 1930 in Boston, MA. Graduate NYU, Columbia U. Debut 1959 OB in "Boo Hoo East Lynn," followed by "Merry Wives of Windsor," "The Lady's Not for Burning," "Romeo and Juliet," "Earnest in Love," "Will the Mail Train Run Tonight?," "Once in a Lifetime," "Promenade," "Heartbreak House," Bdwy in "Status Quo Vadis" (1973), "How to Be a Jewish Mother," "Fiddler on the Roof."

RIVERA, CHITA. Born Jan. 23, 1933 in Washington, DC. Attended Am. Sch. of Ballet. Bdwy debut 1950 in "Guys and Dolls," followed by "Call Me Madam," "Can-Can," "Shoestring Revue" (OB), "Seventh Heaven," "Mr. Wonderful," "West Side Story," "Bye Bye Birdie," "Bajour," "Chicago."

ROBBINS, REX. Born in Pierre, SD. Bdwy debut 1964 in "One Flew Over the Cuckoo's Nest," followed by "Scratch," "The Changing Room," "Gypsy," "Comedians," OB in "Servant of Two Masters," "The Alchemist," "Arms and the Man," "Boys in the Band." "A Memory of Two Mondays," "They Knew What They Wanted," "Secret Service," "Boy Meets Girl," BAM Co.'s "Three Sisters."

ROBERTS, BILL. Born May 25, 1948 in Sealy, TX. Graduate Sam Houston State U. Debut OB 1976 in "Maggie Flynn," followed by "Twelfth Night."

ROBERTS, RALPH. Born Aug. 17 in Salisbury, NC. Attended UNC. Debut 1948 in CC's "Angel Street," followed by "4 Chekhov Comedies," "S. S. Glencairn," "Madwoman of Chaillot," "Witness for the Prosecution," "The Lark," "Bells Are Ringing," "The Milk Train Doesn't Stop Here Anymore," "Love Suicide at Schofield Barracks," "Siamese Connections" (OB), "A Texas Trilogy."

ROBERTSON, JANE. Born May 17, 1948 in Bartlesville, OK. Attended U. Okla. Debut 1970 OB in "Shoestring Revue," followed by "DuBarry Was a Lady," "Buy Bonds Buster," Bdwy in "A Matter of Time," "Rachel Lily Rosenbloom."

ROBERTSON, WILLIAM. Born Oct. 9, 1908 in Portsmouth, VA. Graduate Pomona Col. Bdwy debut 1936 in "Tapestry in Grey," followed by "Cup of Trembling," "Liliom," "Our Town," "Caesar and Cleopatra," OB in "Uncle Harry," "Shining Hour," "Aspern Papers," "Madame Is Served," "Tragedian in spite of Himself," "Kibosh," "Sun-Up," "The Last Pad," "Hamlet," "Girls Most Likely to Succeed," "The Petrified Forest," "The Minister's Black Veil," "Santa Anita," "Babylon," "Midsummer Night's Dream," "A Touch of the Poet," "The Zykovs," "Rimers of Eldritch."

ROBINSON, HAL. Born in Bedford, IN. Graduate Ind. U. Debut 1971 OB in "Memphis Store-Bought Teeth," followed by "From Berlin to Broadway," "The Fantasticks."

ROCCO, MARY. Born Sept. 12, 1933 in Brooklyn, NY. Graduate Queens Col., CCNY. Debut 1976 OB in "Fiorello!"

RODGERS, SHEV. Born Apr. 9, 1928 in Holister, CA. Attended SF State Col. Bdwy bow 1959 in "Redhead," followed by "Music Man," "Man of La Mancha" (also LC), "Home Sweet Homer," "Legend," OB in "Get Thee to Canterbury," "War Games," "Moonchildren," "Marco Polo Sings a Solo."

ROE, PATRICIA. Born Sept. 18, 1932 in NYC. Attended, Columbia U., Actors Studio. Bdwy debut 1951 in "Romeo and Juliet," followed by "Cat on a Hot Tin Roof," "Compulsion," "By the Beautiful Sea," "Night Circus," "A Distant Bell," "Look after Lulu," "Night of the Iguana," "A Texas Trilogy," OB in "The Collection," "After the Fall," "But for Whom Charlie," "The Homecoming," "Bananas," "Transfers."

ROERICK, WILLIAM. Born Dec. 17, 1912 in NYC. Bdwy bow 1935 in "Romeo and Juliet," followed by "St. Joan," "Hamlet," "Our Town," "Importance of Being Earnest," "The Land is Bright," "Autumn Hill," "This Is the Army," "Magnificent Yankee," "Tonight at 8:30," "The Heiress," "Medea," "Macbeth," "Burning Glass," "Right Honourable Gentleman," "Marat/deSade," "Homecoming," "We Bombed in New Haven," "Elizabeth the Queen" (CC), "Waltz of the Toreadors," "Night of the Iguana," OB in "Madam, Will You Walk," "Cherry Orchard," "Come Slowly, Eden," "A Passage to E. M. Forster," "Trials of Oz."

ROGERS, GINA. Born Sept. 25, 1949 in Brooklyn, NY. Graduate U. Bridgeport. Debut 1976 OB in "Sexual Perversity in Chicago."

ROLFING, TOM. Born Sept. 6, 1949 in Cedar Rapids, IA. Carnegie Tech Graduate. Debut 1973 OB in "Godspell," Bdwy in "Godspell," "Equus."

ROLPH, MARTI. Born March 8 in Los Angeles, CA. Occidental Col. graduate. Bdwy debut 1971 in "Follies," followed by "Good News" for which she received a Theatre World Award. OB in "Saints."

ROSE, GEORGE. Born Feb. 19, 1920 in Bicester, Eng. Bdwy debut with Old Vic 1946 in "Henry IV," followed by "Much Ado about Nothing," "A Man for All Seasons," "Hamlet," "Royal Hunt of the Sun," "Walking Happy," "Loot," "My Fair Lady" (CC '68). "Canterbury Tales," "Coco," "Wise Child," "Sleuth," "My Fat Friend." "My Fair Lady." "She Loves Me."

ROSE, JOHN. Born Aug. 24, 1939 in Ottawa, KS. Attended City Col. San Francisco, USC. Bdwy debut 1976 in "The Night of the Iguana."

ROSEN, ROBERT. Born Apr. 24, 1954 in NYC. Attended Indiana U., HB Studio. Bdwy debut 1975 in "Shenandoah."

ROSENBLUM, MARSHALL. Born May 14, 1946 in NYC. Graduate Mich. State U., U. Cincinati. Debut 1976 OB in "Heartbreak House."

ROSS, HOWARD. Born Aug. 21, 1934 in NYC. Attended Juilliard, NYU. Bdwy debut 1965 in "Oliver," followed by "1600 Pennsylvania Avenue," OB in "Jacques Brel Is Alive . . .," "Beggar's Opera," "Philemon," "Isadora Duncan Sleeps with the Russian Navy."

ROSS, JOHN B. Born Mar. 7, 1953 in Topeka, KS. Attended U. Tex. Bdwy debut 1976 in "Porgy and Bess."

ROSS, JUSTIN. Born Dec. 15, 1954 in Brooklyn, NY. Debut 1974 OB in "More Than You Deserve," Bdwy 1975 in "Pippin," followed by "A Chorus Line."

ROUNDS, DAVID. Born Oct. 9, 1930 in Bronxville, NY. Attended Denison U. Bdwy debut 1965 in "Foxy" followed by "Child's Play" for which he received a Theatre World Award, "The Rothschilds," "The Last of Mrs. Lincoln," "Chicago," "Romeo and Juliet," OB in "You Never Can Tell," "Money," "The Real Inspector Hound," "Epic of Buster Friend," "Enter a Free Man."

Lee Roy Reams

Joy Rinaldi

Charles Repole

Jana Schneider

Richard Seer

ROUSSEAU, CAROLLE. Born Jan. 21 in La Bouverie, Belg. Debut 1976 OB in "Henry V."

ROWE, HANSFORD. Born May 12, 1924 in Richmond, VA. Graduate U. Richmond. Bdwy debut 1968 in "We Bombed in New Haven," followed by "Porgy and Bess," OB in "Curley McDimple," "The Fantasticks," "Last Analysis," "God Says There Is No Peter Ott," "Mourning Becomes Electra," "Bus Stop," "Secret Service," "Boy Meets Girl."

RUANE, JANINE. Born Dec. 17, 1963 in Philadelphia, PA. Bdwy debut 1977 in "Annie."

RUBENSTEIN, BARBARA. Born in Chicago, IL. Graduate Northwestern U. Debut OB 1969 in "Your Own Thing," followed by "Wings," Bdwy in "Much Ado about Nothing" (1972), "Bubbling Brown Sugar."

RUDD, PAUL. Born May 15, 1940 in Boston, MA. OB in "Henry IV," followed by "King Lear," "A Cry of Players," "Midsummer Night's Dream," "An Evening with Merlin Finch," "In the Matter of J. Robert Oppenheimer," "Elagabalus," "Streamers" (LC), "Henry V" (CP), Bdwy in "The Changing Room," "The National Health," "The Glass Menagerie," "Ah, Wilderness!," "Romeo and Juliet."

RULE, CHARLES. Born Aug. 4, 1928 in Springfield, MO. Bdwy bow 1951 in "Courtin' Time," followed by "Happy Hunting," "Oh, Captain!," "Conquering Hero," "Donnybrook," "Bye, Bye Birdie," "Fiddler on the Roof," "Henry, Sweet Henry," "Maggie Flynn," "1776," "Cry for Us All," "Gypsy," "Goodtime Charley."

RUPERT, MICHAEL. Born Oct. 23, 1951 in Denver, CO. Attended Pasadena Playhouse. Bdwy debut 1968 in "The Happy Time" for which he received a Theatre World Award, followed by "Pippin."

RUSKIN, JEANNE. Born Nov. 6 in Saginaw, MI. Graduate NYU. Bdwy debut 1975 in "Equus."

RUSSAK, GERARD. Born Sept. 11, 1927 in Paterson, NJ. Attended NY Col of Music. Bdwy bow 1967 in "Marat/deSade," followed by "Zorba," "Knickerbocker Holiday," OB in "The Fantasticks."

RUSSELL, DAVID. Born Aug. 9, 1949 in Allenwood, PA. Ithaca Col. graduate. Bdwy debut 1975 in "Shenandoah."

RUSSOM, LEON. Born Dec. 6, 1941 in Little Rock, AR. Attended Southwestern U. Debut 1968 OB in "Futz," followed by "Cyrano," "Boys in the Band," "Oh! Calcutta!," "Trial of the Catonsville 9," "Henry VI," "Richard III," "Shadow of a Gunman," BAM Co.'s "New York Idea," "Three Sisters."

RUVOLO, DANNY. Born May 22, 1956 in East Rockaway, NY. Attended HB Studio. Bdwy debut 1974 in "Ulysses in Nighttown," followed by "A Chorus Line."

RYAN, CHARLENE. Born in NYC. Bdwy debut 1964 in "Never Live over a Pretzel Factory," followed by "Sweet Charity," "Fig Leaves Are Falling," "Coco," "A Funny Thing Happened on the Way to the Forum," "Chicago."

SABIN, DAVID. Born Apr. 24, 1937 in Washington, DC. Graduate Catholic U. Debut 1965 OB in "The Fantasticks," followed by "Now Is the Time for All good Men," "Threepenny Opera" (LC), Bdwy in "The Yearling," "Slapstick Tragedy," "Jimmy Shine," "Gantry," "Ambassador," "Celebration." "Music Is."

SACKS, DAVIA. Born July 10 in Flushing, NY. Attended Dade Jr. Col. Debut 1973 OB in "Swiss Family Robinson," followed by "Zorba," Bdwy 1976 in "Fiddler on the Roof."

SADUSK, MAUREEN. Born Sept. 8, 1948 in Brooklyn, NY. Attended AADA. Debut 1969 OB in "We'd Rather Switch," followed by "O Glorious Tintinnabulation," "New Girl in Town," "Fiddler on the Roof" (1976).

ST. JAMES, DAVID. Born Sept. 4, 1947 in Honolulu, HI. Graduate UGa. Debut 1977 OB in "Silk Stockings" (ELT)

SAKREN, JARED. Born June 18, 1950 in Danbury, CT. Attended Juilliard. Debut 1972 OB in "School for Scandal," followed by "Lower Depths," "The Hostage," "Next Time I'll Sing to You," "Women Beware Women," "Beware the Jubjub Bird."

SALATA, GREGORY. Born July 21, 1949 in NYC. Graduate Queens Col. Bdwy debut 1975 in "Dance with Me," followed by "Equus.", OB in "Piaf . . . A Remembrance."

SAPPINGTON, FAY. Born May 22, 1906 in Galveston, TX. Attended UTx., Pasadena Playhouse. Bdwy debut 1950 in "Southern Exposure," followed by "The Cellar and the Well," "Glad Tidings," "J. B.," "The Yearling," "Golden Rainbow," "Pippin," OB in "Campbells of Boston," "In Case of Accident."

SARANDON, CHRIS. Born July 24, 1942 in Beckley, WVa. Graduate UWVa., Catholic U. Bdwy debut 1970 in "The Rothschilds," followed by "Two Gentlemen of Verona," OB in "Marco Polo Sings a Solo."

SARNO, JANET. Born Nov. 18, 1933 in Bridgeport, CT. Graduate SCTC, Yale U. Bdwy debut 1963 in "Dylan," followed by "Equus," OB in "6 Characters in Search of an Author," "Who's Happy Now," "Closing Green," "Fisher," "Survival of St. Joan," "The Orphan."

SCALZO, JOSEPH. Born Feb. 13, 1949 in Danbury, CT. Graduate Hartwick Col. Debut 1974 OB in "The Window," Bdwy 1977 in "Caesar and Cleopatra."

SCARDINO, DON. Born in Feb. 1949 in NYC. Attended CCNY. On Bdwy in "Loves of Cass McGuire," "Johnny No-Trump," "My Daughter, Your Son," "Godspell" OB in "Shout from the Rooftops," "Rimers of Eldritch," "The Unknown Solider and His Wife," "Godspell," "Moonchildren," "Kid Champion," "Comedy of Errors," "Secret Service," "Boy Meets Girl.", "Scribes."

SCHACT, SAM. Born Apr. 19, 1936 in The Bronx, NY. Graduate CCNY. OB in "Fortune and Men's Eyes," "Cannibals," "I Met a Man," "The Increased Difficulty of Concentration" (LCR), "One Night Stands of a Noisy Passenger." "Owners," "Jack Gelber's New Play," Bdwy in "The Magic Show."

SCHAEFER, CRAIG. Born Aug. 24, 1953 in San Gabriel, CA. Attended UCLA. Debut 1975 OB in "Tenderloin.", followed by "Joseph and the Amazing Technicolor Dreamcoat."

SCHELL, MARIA. Born Jan. 15, 1926 in Vienna. Bdwy debut 1976 in "Poor Murderer."

SCHLEE, ROBERT. Born June 13, 1938 in Williamsport, PA. Lycoming Col. graduate. Debut 1972 OB in "Dr. Selavy's Magic Theatre," followed by "Hotel for Criminals," "Threepenny Opera."

SCHNEIDER, JANA. Born Oct. 24, 1951 in McFarland, WI. Graduate UWisc. Debut 1976 OB in "Women Behind Bars," Bdwy 1976 in "The Robber Bridegroom."

SCHWAB, SOPHIE. Born Feb. 23, 1954 in Miami, FL. Graduate Northwestern U. Debut 1976 OB in "Fiorello!"

SCHWEID, CAROLE. Born Oct. 5, 1946 in Newark, NJ. Graduate Boston U., Juilliard. Bdwy debut 1970 in "Minnie's Boys," followed by "A Chorus Line," OB in "Love Me, Love My Children," "How To Succeed in Business . . .","Silk Stockings" (ELT).

SCIPIO, ANTHONY. Born Apr. 19, 1941 in Philadelphia, PA. Graduate St. Joseph's Col. Debut 1977 OB in "Arsenic and Old Lace" (ELT).

SCOTT, GEORGE C. Born Oct. 18, 1927 in Wise, Va. OB in "Richard II" for which he received a Theatre World Award, followed by "As You Like It," "Children of Darkness," "Desire under the Elms," Bdwy in "Comes a Day," "Andersonville Trial," "The Wall," "General Seeger,' "Little Foxes," "Plaza Suite," "Uncle Vanya," "Death of a Salesman.", "Sly Fox."

SCOTT, STEPHEN. Born Feb. 8, 1928 in London, Eng. Attended Central Speech Sch. Bdwy debut 1967 in "There's a Girl in My Soup," followed by "Borstal Boy," "Vivat! Vivat Regina!," "Dirty Linen," OB in "Rosmersholm."

SCOTTI, DON. Born Apr. 20, 1947 in Brooklyn, NY. Attended CCNY, AMDA. Debut 1971 OB in "Emerald Slippers," Bdwy 1976 in "Let My People Come."

SEER, RICHARD. Born Oct. 13, 1949 in Anchorage, AK. Graduate Cal. State U. Debut 1972 OB in "Hey Day," followed by "Joseph and the Amazing Technicolor Dreamcoat."

SEFF, RICHARD. Born Sept. 23, 1927 in NYC. Attended NYU. Bdwy debut 1951 in "Darkness at Noon," followed by "Herzl," OB in "Big Fish, Little Fish."

SEIDEL, VIRGINIA. Born July 26 in Harvey, IL. Attended Roosevelt U. Bdwy debut 1975 in "Very Good Eddie" for which she received a Theatre World Award.

SELDES, MARIAN. Born Aug. 23, 1928 in NYC. Attended Neighborhood Playhouse. Bdwy debut 1947 in "Medea," followed by "Crime and Punishment," "That Lady," "Tower Beyond Tragedy," "Ondine," "On High Ground," "Come of Age," "Chalk Garden," "The Milk Train Doesn't Stop Here Anymore," "The Wall," "A Gift of Time," "A Delicate Balance," "Before You Go," "Father's Day," "Equus," OB in "Different," "Ginger Man," "Mercy Street," "Candle in the Wind," "Isadora Duncan Sleeps with the Russian Navy."

SELDIN, ROCHELLE. Born Aug. 22, 1954. Attended Monmouth Col., AADA. Debut 1976 OB in "Fiorello!"

SELL, JANIE. Born Oct. 1, 1941 in Detroit, MI. Attended U. Detroit. Debut OB 1966 in "Mixed Doubles," followed by "Dark Horses," "Dames at Sea," "By Bernstein," Bdwy in "George M!," "Irene," "Over Here" for which she received a Theatre World Award, "Pal Joey," "Happy End."

SERBAGI, ROGER. Born July 26, 1937 in Waltham, MA. Attended AmTh-Wing. Bdwy debut 1969 in "Henry V," OB in "A Certain Young Man," "Awake and Sing," "The Partnership," "Monsters."

SERRA, RAYMOND. Born Aug. 13, 1937 in NYC. Attended Rutgers U., Wagner Col. Debut 1975 OB in "The Shark," Bdwy 1976 in "Wheelbarrow Closers."

SERRECCHIA, MICHAEL. Born Mar. 26, 1951 in Brooklyn, NY. Attended Brockport State U. Teachers Col. Bdwy debut 1972 in "The Selling of the President," followed by "Heathen!," "Seesaw," "A Chorus Line," OB in "Lady Audley's Secret."

SETRAKIAN, ED. Born Oct. 1, 1928 in Jenkintown,WVa. Graduate Concord Col., NYU. Debut 1966 OB in "Drums in the Night," followed by "Othello," "Coriolanus," "Macbeth," "Hamlet," "Baal," "Old Glory," "Futz," Bdwy 1976 in "Days in the Trees."

SHAKAR, MARTIN. Born Jan. 1, 1940 in Detroit, MI. Attended Wayne State U. Bdwy bow 1969 in "Our Town," in "Lorenzaccio," "Macbeth," "The Infantry," "Americana Pastoral," "No Place to be Somebody," "World of Mrs. Solomon," "And Whose Little Boy are You?," "Investigation of Havana," "Night Watch," "Owners," "Actors," "Richard III," "Transfiguration of Benno Blimpie," "Jack Gelber's New Play."

SHAWN, DICK. Born Dec. 1 in Buffalo, NY. Attended U. Miami. Bdwy debut 1948 in "For Heaven's Sake, Mother," followed by "A Funny Thing Happened on the Way . . .," "The Egg," "Peterpat," "Fade Out-Fade In," "I'm Solomon," "Musical Jubilee," OB in "Rebirth Celebration of the Human Race." "The Greatest Entertainer in the Whole Wide World."

SHEA, JOHN V. Born Apr. 14 in North Conway, NH. Graduate Bates Col., Yale. Debut OB 1974 in "Yentl, the Yeshiva Boy," followed by "Gorky," "Battering Ram," Bdwy in "Yentl" (1975) for which he received a Theatre World Award., "Romeo and Juliet."

SHEARER, DENNY. Born July 30, 1941 in Canton, OH. Attended HB Studio. Debut 1968 OB in "Up Eden," Bdwy in "Music Is" (1976), "Bubbling Brown Sugar."

SHELLEY, CAROLE. Born Aug. 16, 1939 in London, Eng. Bdwy debut 1965 in "The Odd Couple," followed by "The Astrakhan Coat," "Loot," "Noel Coward's Sweet Potato," "Little Murders" (OB), "Hay Fever," "Absurd Person Singular," "The Norman Conquests."

SHELTON, REID. Born Oct. 7, 1924 in Salem, OR. Graduate U. Mich. Bdwy bow 1952 in "Wish You Were Here," followed by "Wonderful Town," "By the Beautiful Sea," "Saint of Bleecker Street," "My Fair Lady," "Oh! What a Lovely War!," "Carousel" (CC), "Canterbury Tales," "Rothschilds," "1600 Pennsylvania Avenue," "Annie," OB in "Phedre," "Butterfly Dream," "Man with a Load of Mischief," "Beggars Opera," "The Contractor," "Cast Aways."

SHELTON, SLOANE. Born Mar. 17, 1934 in Asheville, NC. Attended Berea Col., RADA. Bdwy debut 1967 in "Imaginary Invalid," followed by "Touch of the Poet," "Tonight at 8:30," "I Never Sang for My Father," "Sticks and Bones," "The Runner Stumbles," OB in "Androcles and the Lion," "The Maids," "Basic Training of Pavlo Hummel."

SHERMAN, BRUCE. Born June 20, 1953 in Philadelphia, PA. Graduate UFla., Neighborhood Playhouse. Debut 1976 OB in "The Boys from Syracuse" (ELT).

SHERMAN, GERALDINE. Born in London, Eng. Attended Burlington Sch. Bdwy debut 1972 in "Butley," OB in "Claw."

SHERWOOD, WAYNE. Born in Olivia, MN. Graduate UOre. Bdwy bow 1955 in "Catch a Star," followed by "Wonderful Town" (CC), OB in "Jacques Brel is Alive . . .," "Johnny Johnson," "Castaways."

SHIMERMAN, ARMIN. Born Nov. 5, 1949 in Lakewood, NJ. Graduate UCLA. Debut 1976 OB in "Threepenny Opera" (LC), followed by "Silk Stockings" (ELT).

SHIMODA, YUKI. Born Aug. 10, 1921 in Sacramento, CA. Graduate Sacramenta Jr. Col. Bdwy debut 1952 in "Teahouse of the August Moon," followed by "Auntie Mame," "Pacific Overtures."

SHIMONO, SAB. Born in Sacramento, Cal. Graduate UCal. Bdwy bow 1965 in "South Pacific," (CC), followed by "Mame," "Lovely Ladies, Kind Gentlemen," "Pacific Overtures," OB in "Santa Anita," "Ride the Winds."

SHOWALTER, MAX. Born June 2, 1917 in Caldwell, KS. Attended Pasadena Playhouse. Bdwy bow 1938 in "Knights of Song," followed by "Very Warm for May," "My Sister Eileen," "Show Boat," "John Loves Mary," "Make Mine Manhattan," "Hello, Dolly!," "Grass Harp," "Show Boat" (JB).

SIDNEY, SYLVIA. Born Aug. 8, 1910 in NYC. Attended Theatre Guild Sch. Bdwy debut 1926 in "Prunella," followed by "The Squall," "Crime," "Mirrors," "The Breaks," "Gods of the Lightning," "Nice Women," "Crossroads," "Many a Slip," "Bad Girl," "To Quito and Back," "Gentle People," "We Will Never Die," "Fourposter," "Very Special Baby," "Enter Laughing," "Barefoot in the Park," "Riverside Drive" (OB), "Me Jack, You Jill," "Vieux Carre."

SIEGEL, HARVEY. Born Feb. 28, 1945 in NYC. Attended Stella Adler Studio. Debut 1971 OB in "Out of the Death Cart," followed by "The Team," "June Moon," Bdwy 1976 in "Wheelbarrow Closers."

SILLIMAN, MAUREEN. Born Dec. 3 in NYC. Attended Hofstra U. Bdwy debut 1975 in "Shenandoah."

SILLS, PAWNEE. Born in Castalia, NC. Attended Bklyn Col. Debut OB 1962 in "Raisin Hell in the Sun," followed by "Mr. Johnson," "Black Happening," "One Last Look," "NY and Who to Blame it On," "Cities in Bezique," "I'd Go to Heaven if I was Good," "Oakville, U.S.A.," "Hocus-Pocus," "And So to Bed." Bdwy 1977 in "Caesar and Cleopatra."

SILVER, SHELDON. Born Nov. 30 in Philadelphia, PA. Graduate Temple U., Ill. State U. Debut 1976 OB in "Fiorello!"

SIMON, MARK. Born Sept. 11, 1948 in NYC. Attended NYU. Debut OB 1974 in "Naked Lunch," followed by "Henry V," "Measure for Measure," "Hagar's Children."

SIMPSON, THOMAS. Born Nov. 15, 1953 in Chicago, IL. Graduate Grinnell Col. Debut 1977 OB in "Hagar's Children."

SIMS, MARLEY. Born Feb. 23, 1948 in NYC. Graduate Hofstra U. Debut OB 1971 in "The Me Nobody Knows," followed by "Godspell." (OB and Bdwy).

SIROLA, JOSEPH. Born Oct. 7, 1929 in Carteret, NJ. Graduate Columbia U. Debut 1959 OB in "Song for a Certain Midnight," followed by "Phaedra," Bdwy in "The Unsinkable Molly Brown," "Golden Rainbow," "Pal Joey."

SKINNER, RANDY. Born Mar. 5, 1952 in Colubus, OH. Graduate Ohio State U. Debut 1976 OB in "The Boys from Syracuse."

SKIPITARIS, LOUKAS. Born Dec. 7 in Thessaloniki, Greece. Bdwy debut 1967 in "Illya, Darling," followed by "Zorba," "Wonderful Town" (ELT).

SLACK, BEN. Born July 23, 1937 in Baltimore, MD. Graduate Catholic U. Debut 1971 OB in "Oedipus at Colonus," followed by "Interrogation of Havana," "Rain," "Thunder Rock," "Trelawny of the Wells," "Heartbreak House," Bdwy 1976 in "Legend."

SMITH, BARREY. Born in Presque Isle, ME. Graduate Wheaton Col., Princeton. Bdwy debut 1973 in "Grease."

SMITH, CAMERON. Born Aug. 13 in Dayton, OH. Graduate Ohio U. Debut 1975 OB in "Three Musketeers," followed by "Twelfth Night."

SMITH, GARNETT. Born Sept. 22, 1937 in Richmond, VA. Bdwy debut 1967 in "Rosencrantz and Guildenstern Are Dead," followed by "Canterbury Tales," OB in "Cambridge Circus," "Dear Oscar," "Pavlov, Palov," "Greatest Fairy Story Ever Told," "Crazy Locomotive."

SMITH, TIMOTHY. Born May 4, 1955 in Gaylord, MI. Attended HB Studio. Bdwy debut 1976 in "My Fair Lady," followed by "A Chorus Line."

SNYDER, ARLEN DEAN. Born Mar. 3, 1933 in Rice, KS. Graduate UTulsa, UIowa. Bdwy bow 1965 in "The Family Way," followed by "The Trip Back Down," OB "Benito Cereno," "Hogan's Goat," "Miss Pete," "Open 24 Hours," "Candyapple," "June Moon," "Big Broadcast," "Thunder Rock," "Streamers."

SNYDER, DREW. Born Sept. 25, 1946 in Buffalo, NY. Graduate Carnegie Tech. Bdwy debut 1968 with APA in "Pantagleize," followed by "Cocktail Party," "Cock-a-doodle Dandy," and "Hamlet," NYSF's "Henry VI," "Richard III," and "Sticks and Bones," "The Cretan Bull," "Quail Southwest."

SNYDER, MICHAEL. Born Oct. 8, 1953 in Tampa, FL. Graduate SUNY. Bdwy debut 1977 in "Equus."

SNYDER, NANCY E. Born Dec. 2, 1949 in Kankakee, IL. Graduate Webster Col., Neighborhood Playhouse. Bdwy debut 1976 in "Knock, Knock," OB in "The Farm," "My Life."

SOCKWELL, SALLY. Born June 14 in Little Rock, AR. Debut 1976 OB in "Vanities."

SOLEN, PAUL. Born Mar. 27, 1941 in Cincinnati, O. Bdwy debut 1964 in "Hello, Dolly!," followed by "Breakfast at Tiffany's," "Dear World," "Pippin," "Chicago."

SOMMER, JOSEF. Born June 26, 1934 in Greifswald, Ger. Graduate Carnegie Tech. Bdwy bow 1970 in "Othello," followed by "Children, Children," "Trial of the Catonsville 9," "Full Circle," "Who's Who in Hell," "The Shadow Box," OB in "Enemies," "Merchant of Venice," "The Dog Ran Away."

SONDERGAARD, GALE. Born in Litchfield, MN. Graduate UMinn. Bdwy debut 1923 in "What's Your Wife Doing?" followed by "Faust," "Major Barbara," "Strange Interlude," "Karl and Anna," "Red Dust," "Alison's House," "American Dream," "Dr. Monica," "Invitation to a Murder," "Cue for Passion," OB in "Woman," "Kicking The Castle Down," "John Gabriel Borkman."

SOREL, THEODORE. Born Nov. 14, 1936 in San Francisco, CA. Graduate Col. of Pacific. OB in "Arms and the Man," "Moon Mysteries," Bdwy 1977 in "Sly Fox."

SPELMAN, LEON. Born July 29, 1945 in Kingsport, TN. Attended CCNY, AADA. Bdwy debut 1972 in "Via Galactica," followed by "Fiddler on the Roof" (1976).

SPIEGEL, BARBARA. Born Mar. 12 in NYC. Debut 1969 in LCRep in "Camino Real," "Operation Sidewinder" and "Beggar on Horseback," followed by "Feast for Flies," "Museum."

SQUIBB, JUNE. Born Nov. 6 in Vandalia, IL. Attended Cleveland Play House, HB Studio. Debut 1956 OB in "Sable Brush," followed by "Boy Friend," "Lend an Ear," "Another Language," "Castaways," Bdwy in "Gypsy" (1960), "The Happy Time."

STALEY, JAMES. Born May 20, 1948 in Oklahoma City, OK. Graduate Okla.U. Bdwy debut 1972 in "Promenade All!," followed by "Of Mice and Men," "A Texas Trilogy," OB in "Siamese Connections," "Felix."

| John V. Shea | Sloane Shelton | Mark Simon | Susan Streater | George Taylor |

STAPLETON, MAUREEN. Born June 21, 1925 in Troy, NY. Attended HB Studio. Bdwy debut 1946 in "Playboy of the Western World," followed by "Antony and Cleopatra," "Detective Story," "Bird Cage," "Rose Tattoo" for which she received a Theatre World Award, "The Emperor's Clothes," "The Crucible," "Richard III," "The Seagull," "27 Wagons Full of Cotton," "Orpheus Descending," "The Cold Wind and the Warm," "Toys in the Attic," "Glass Menagerie," (1965 & 1975), "Plaza Suite," "Norman, Is That You?," "Gingerbread Lady," "Country Girl," "Secret Affairs of Mildred Wild."

STENBORG, HELEN. Born Jan. 24, 1925 in Minneapolis, MN. Attended Hunter Col. OB in "A Doll's House," "A Month in the Country," "Say Nothing," "Rosmersholm," "Rimers of Eldrich," "Trial of the Catonsville 9," "Hot l Baltimore," "Pericles," "A Doll's House," "Elephant in the House," "A Tribute to Lili Lamont," "Museum," Bdwy in "Sheep on the Runway."

STEPHENS, GARN. Born in Tulsa, OK. Graduate Calif. Western U., Pasadena Playhouse. Bdwy debut 1972 in "Grease."

STERNHAGEN, FRANCES. Born Jan. 13, 1932 in Washington, DC. Vassar Graduate. OB in "Admirable Bashful," "Thieves' Carnival," "Country Wife," "Ulysses in Nighttown," "Saintliness of Margery Kemp," "The Room," "A Slight Ache," "Displaced Person," "Playboy of the Western World" (LC), Bdwy in "Great Day in the Morning," "Right Honourable Gentleman," with APA in "Cocktail Party," and "Cock-a-doodle Dandy," "The Sign in Sidney Brustein's Window," "Enemies" (LC), "The Good Doctor," "Equus."

STEVENSEN, SCOTT. Born May 4, 1951 in Salt Lake City, UT. Attended USCal. Bdwy debut 1974 in "Good News," for which he received a Theatre World Award, followed OB in "2 by 5."

STEVENSON, MARGOT. Born Feb. 8, 1918 in NYC. Brearley School graduate. Bdwy debut 1932 in "Firebird," followed by "Evensong," "A Party," "Barretts of Wimpole Street," "Symphony," "Truly Vallant," "Call It a Day," "Stage Door," "You Can't Take It With You," "Golden Wings," "Little Women" (CC), "Rugged Path," "Leading Lady," "The Young and Beautiful," "The Apple Cart," "Triple Play," "Lord Pengo," "Hostile Witness," "The Royal Family," OB in "Autumn Ladies and Their Lovers' Lovers," "Quail Southwest."

STEWART, VINCENT. Born Oct. 18, 1962 in Brooklyn, NY. Bdwy debut 1977 in "The Shadow Box."

STILLER, JERRY. Born June 8, 1931 in NYC. Graduate Syracuse U., HB Studio, Debut 1953 OB in "Coriolanus," followed by "The Power and the Glory," "Golden Apple," "Measure for Measure," "Taming of the Shrew," "Carefree Tree," "Diary of a Scoundrel," "Romeo and Juliet," "As You Like It," "Two Gentlemen of Verona," Bdwy in "The Ritz," "Unexpected Guests."

STREATER, SUSAN. Born Oct. 19, 1952 in Dallas, TX. Attended SMU. Debut 1977 OB in "Wonderful Town" (ELT).

STREEP, MERYL. Born Sept. 22 in Summit, NJ. Graduate Vassar, Yale. Debut 1975 OB in "Trelawny of the Wells," followed by "27 Wagons Full of Cotton" for which she received a Theatre World Award, "A Memory of Two Mondays," "Secret Service," "Henry V," "Measure for Measure" (CP), "The Cherry Orchard," (LC), Bdwy in "Happy End" (1977).

STRICKLER, DAN. Born Feb. 4, 1949 in Los Angeles, CA. Graduate Cal.-State U., Temple U. Debut 1977 OB in "Jules Feiffer's Hold Me!"

STRUDWICK, SHEPPERD. Born Sept. 22, 1907 in Hillsboro, NC. Graduate UNC. Bdwy bow 1929 in "Yellow Jacket," followed by "Both Your Houses," "Let Freedom Ring," "End of Summer," "As You Like It," "Christopher Blake," "Affairs of State," "Ladies of the Corridor," "Doctor's Dilemma," "The Seagull," "Night Circus," "Desert Incident," "Only in America," "J. B.," "Who's Afraid of Virginia Woolf?," "The Devils," "The Price," "Galileo," "Measure for Measure," "Timon of Athens," "Desert Song," "Eccentricities of a Nightingale."

STUART, IAN. Born May 25, 1940 in London, Eng. Attended St. Ignatius Col. Debut 1972 OB in "Misalliance," Bdwy 1977 in "Caesar and Cleopatra."

STUART, WENDY. Born June 9, 1950 in Summit, NJ. Attended Juilliard. Debut 1977 OB in "Silk Stockings" (ELT).

SULLIVAN, BRAD. Born Nov. 18, 1931 in Chicago, IL. Graduate UMaine., AmThWing. Debut 1961 OB in "Red Roses for Me," followed by "South Pacific" (LC), "Hot-house," Bdwy 1977 in "Basic Training of Pavlo Hummel."

SULLIVAN, JEREMIAH. Born Sept. 22, 1937 in NYC. Harvard graduate. Bdwy debut 1957 in "Compulsion," followed by "The Astrakhan Coat," "Philadelphia, Here I Come!," "Lion in Winter," "Hamlet," OB in "Ardele," "A Scent of Flowers," "House of Blue Leaves," "Gogol."

SUNDSTEN, LANI. Born Feb. 27, 1949 in NYC. Attended Am. Col. in Paris. Bdwy debut 1970 in "The Rothschilds," followed by "Tricks," "California Suite," OB in "Carousel," "Boom Boom Room."

SUTORIUS, JAMES. Born Dec. 14, 1944 in Euclid, OH. Graduate Ill. Wesleyan, AMDA. Bdwy debut 1970 in "The Cherry Orchard," followed by "The Changing Room," OB in "Servant of Two Masters," "Hamlet," "Sexual Perversity in Chicago."

SWANSEN, LARRY. Born Nov. 10, 1930 in Roosevelt, OK. Graduate OKU. Bdwy debut 1966 in "Those That Play the Clowns," followed by "Great White Hope," "The King and I," OB in "Dr. Faustus Lights the Lights," "Thistle in My Bed," "A Darker Flower," "Vincent," "MacBird," "Unknown Soldier and His Wife," "Sound of Music," "Conditioning of Charlie One," "Ice Age," "Prince of Homburg."

SWEET, DOLPH, Born July 18, 1920 in NYC. Graduate Columbia U. Bdwy debut 1960 in "Rhinoceros," followed by "Romulus," "The Advocate," "Sign in Sidney Brustein's Window," "Great Indoors," "Natural Look," "Billy," "Penny Wars," OB in "The Dragon," "Too Much Johnson," "Sjt. Musgrave's Dance," "Ceremony of Innocence," "Death of J.K.," "Bread," "Streamers."

SWIFT, ALLEN. Born Jan. 16, 1924 in NYC. Debut 1961 OB in "Portrait of the Artist," followed by "Month of Sundays," Bdwy in "Student Gypsy" (1963), "Checking Out."

SWITKES, WILLY. Born Nov. 12, 1929 in New Haven, CT. Graduate Catholic U. Debut 1960 OB in "A Country Scandal," followed by "The Firebugs," "Conerico Was Here to Stay," Bdwy 1976 in "Sly Fox."

SYERS, MARK. Born Oct. 25, 1952 in Trenton, NJ. Graduate Emerson Col. Bdwy debut in "Pacific Overtures."

TABOR, SUSAN. Born May 28, 1939 in Detroit, MI. Skidmore, NYU graduate. Debut 1962 OB in "Electra," followed by "What Every Woman Knows," Bdwy in "Inadmissible Evidence" (1965), "California Suite."

TABORI, KRISTOFFER. Born Aug. 4, 1952 in Calif. Bdwy debut 1969 in "The Penny Wars," followed by "Henry V," "Habeas Corpus," OB in "Emile and the Detectives," "Guns of Carrar," "A Cry of Players," "Dream of a Blacklisted Actor," "How Much, How Much?" for which he received a Theatre World Award, "The Wager," "Scribes."

TAMBOR, JEFFREY. Born July 8, 1944 in San Francisco, CA. Attended SF State Col., Wayne State U. Debut 1976 OB in "Measure for Measure," Bdwy 1976 in "Sly Fox."

TANNER, MELINDA, Born Oct. 5, 1946 in Los Angeles, CA. Attended LACC. Debut 1975 in "The Sea," followed by "Godspell," Bdwy 1976 in "The Robber Bridegroom."

TARTEL MICHAEL. Born Mar. 21, 1936 in Newark, NJ. Attended Manhattan Col. Debut OB 1969 in "The Fantasticks," Bdwy 1969 in "Billy" followed by "Going Up."

TAYLOR, CLARICE, Born Sept. 20, in Buckingham County, VA. Attended New Theater School. Debut 1943 OB in "Striver's Row," followed by "Major Barbara," "Family Portrait," "Trouble in Mind," "The Egg and I," "A Medal for Willie," "Nat Turner," "Simple Speaks His Mind," "Gold Through the Trees," "The Owl Answers," "Song of the Lusitanian Bogey," "Summer of the 17th Doll," "Kongi's Harvest," "Daddy Goodness," "God Is a (Guess What?)," "An Evening of One Acts," "5 on the Black Hand Side," "A Man Better Man," "Day of Absence," "Brotherhood," "Akokawe," "Rosalee Pritchett," "Sty of the Blind Pig," "Duplex" (LC), "Wedding Band," Bdwy 1975 in "The Wiz."

TAYLOR, GEORGE. Born Sept. 18, 1930 in London, Eng. Attended AADA. Debut 1972 OB in "Hamlet," followed by "Enemies" (LC), "The Contractor," "Scribes," Bdwy in "Emperor Henry IV," "The National Health."

TAYLOR, HOLLAND. Born Jan 14, 1943 in Philadelphia, PA. Graduate Bennington Col. Bdwy debut 1965 in "The Devil," followed by "Butley," "We Interrupt This Program," "Something Old, Something New," OB in "Poker Session," "The David Show," "Tonight in Living Color," "Colette," "Fashion," "Nightlight," "Children."

THACKER, RUSS. Born June 23, 1946 in Washington, DC. Attended Montgomery Col. Debut 1967 in "Life with Father" (CC), followed OB by "Your Own Thing" for which he received a Theatre World Award, "Dear Oscar," "Once I Saw A Boy Laughing," Bdwy in "Grass Harp," "Heathen," "Music! Music!" (CC), "Home Sweet Homer," "Me Jack You Jill."

THEODORE, DONNA. Born July 25, 1945 in Oakland, CA. Debut 1974 OB in "Oh, Lady, Lady," followed by "Dance on a Country Grave." Bdwy 1975 in "Shenandoah" for which she received a Theatre World Award.

THOMAS, MADELON. Born Jan. 26, 1946 in Salt Lake City, UT. Attended UUtah, AADA. Debut 1977 OB in "John Gabriel Borkman."

THOMAS, WILLIAM, JR. Born in Columbus, O. Graduate Ohio State U Debut OB 1972 in "Touch," followed by "Natural," "Godspell," Bdwy 1976 in "Your Arms Too Short to Box with God."

THOME, DAVID. Born July 24, 1951 in Salt Lake City, UT. Bdwy debut 1971 in "No, No, Nanette," followed by "Different Times," "Good News," "Rodgers and Hart," "A Chorus Line."

THOMPSON, TAZEWELL. Born May 27, 1950 in NYC. Attended Actors Co. Sch. Debut 1968 OB in "Goa," followed by Bdwy in "The National Health" (1974), "Checking Out."

THORNE, RAYMOND. Born Nov. 27, 1934 in Lackawanna, NY. Graduate UConn. Debut 1966 OB in "Man with a Load of Mischief," followed by "Rose," "Dames at Sea," "Love Course," "Blue Boys," Bdwy 1977 in "Annie."

TILLINGER, JOHN. Born June 28, 1938 in Tabriz, Iran. Attended URome. Bdwy debut 1966 in "How's the World Treating You?," followed by "Halfway up the Tree," "The Changing Room," OB in "Tea Party," "Pequod," "A Scent of Flowers," "Crimes of Passion," "Claw," "Ashes."

TIMMONS, DEBRA. Born Mar. 14, 1951 in South Carolina. Attended HB Studio. Debut 1971 OB in "Spring's Awakening," Bdwy 1976 in "Fiddler on the Roof."

TOBIN, MATTHEW. Born Aug. 10, 1933 in Indianapolis, IN. Graduate Carnegie Tech. Debut 1959 OB in "Hasty Heart," followed by "Boys from Syracuse," "The Mad Show," "Boys in the Band," "Empire Builders," "Lyle," "Survival of St. Joan," "Any Resemblance to Persons Living or Dead," "Festival of Short Plays," "Kaboom," "Room Service," "Drums at Yale," Bdwy in "Redhead" (1959), "Love Suicide at Schofield Barracks," "Sherlock Holmes," "Something Old, Something New."

TOLAYDO, MICHAEL. Born July 23, 1946 in Nairobi, Kenya. Attended Houston Baptist Col., AADA. Bdwy debut 1970 in "The Cherry Orchard," followed by "Robber Bridegroom," "Edward II," "The Time of Your Life," "Three Sisters," "Dirty Linen," OB in "Hamlet."

TOMLIN, LILY. Born Sept. 1, 1936 in Highland Park, MI. Attended Wayne State U. Appeared at Upstairs at the Downstairs in revues, Bdwy in "Arf," "The Great Airplane Snatch," and on Bdwy (1977) in her solo show "Appearing Nitely."

TOMMON, MARIE. Born Apr. 13, 1945 in England. Attended AADA. Bdwy debut 1975 in "Private Lives," followed by "Twelfth Night" (OB).

TONER, THOMAS. Born May 25, 1928 in Homestead, PA. Graduate UCLA. Bdwy debut 1973 in "Tricks," followed by "The Good Doctor," "All Over Town," "A Texas Trilogy," OB in "Pericles," "Merry Wives of Windsor," "Midsummer Night's Dream," "Richard III."

TORN, RIP. Born Feb. 6, 1931 in Temple, TX. Graduate UTx. Bdwy bow 1956 in "Cat on a Hot Tin Roof," followed by "Sweet Bird of Youth," "Daughter of Silence," "Strange Interlude," "Blues for Mr. Charlie," "Country Girl" (CC), "Glass Menagerie," OB in "Chapparal" (1958) for which he received a Theatre World Award, "The Cuban Thing," "The Kitchen," "Deer Park," "Dream of a Blacklisted Actor," "Dance of Death," "Macbeth," "Barbary Shore," "Creditors."

TORRES, ANDY. Born Aug. 10, 1945 in Ponce, PR. Attended AMDA. Bdwy debut 1969 in "Indians," followed by "Purlie," "Don't Bother Me, I Can't Cope," "The Wiz," "Guys and Dolls," OB in "Billy Noname."

TOVATT, ELLEN. Born in NYC. Attended Antioch Col., LAMDA. Debut 1962 OB in "Taming of the Shrew," followed by Bdwy in "The Great God Brown," "The Visit," "Chemin de Fer," "Holiday," "Love for Love," "Rules of the Game," "Herzl."

TOWERS, CONSTANCE. Born May 20, 1933 in Whitefish, MT. Attended Juilliard, AADA. Bdwy debut 1965 in "Anya," followed by "Show Boat" (LC), "Carousel" (CC), "Sound of Music" (CC'67, JB '70 & '71), "Engagement Baby," "The King and I" (CC'68, JB '72, Bdwy '77).

TROY, LOUISE. Born Nov. 9, in NYC. Attended AADA. Debut 1955 OB in "The Infernal Machine," followed by "Merchant of Venice," "Conversation Piece," "Salad Days," "O, Oysters!," "A Doll's House," "Last Analysis," "Judy and Jane," Bdwy in "Pipe Dream" (1955), "A Shot in the Dark," "Tovarich," "High Spirits," "Walking Happy," "Equus."

TUCCI, MARIA. Born June 19, 1941 in Florence, Italy. Attended Actors Studio. Bdwy debut 1963 in "The Milk Train Doesn't Stop Here Anymore," followed by "Rose Tattoo" (CC), "Little Foxes," "Cuban Thing," "Great White Hope," "School for Wives," OB in "Corruption in the Palace of Justice," "Five Evenings," "Trojan Women," "White Devil," "Horseman Pass By," "Yerma," "Shepherd of Avenue B," "The Gathering."

TUCCI, MICHAEL. Born Apr. 15, 1946 in NYC. Graduate C. W. Post Col. Debut 1974 OB in "Godspell," followed by "Jules Feiffer's Hold Me!," Bdwy 1975 in "Grease."

TUNE, TOMMY. Born Feb. 28, 1939 in Wichita Falls, TX. Graduate UTex. Bdwy debut 1965 in "Baker Street," followed by "A Joyful Noise," "How Now Dow Jones," "Seesaw," OB in "Ichabod."

TYRRELL, JOHN, Born Nov. 24, 1948 in Perth Amboy, NJ. Graduate Marquette U., Neighborhood Playhouse. Bdwy debut 1974 in "Equus."

ULLMANN, LIV. Born Dec. 16, 1938 in Touro, Japan. Debut 1975 in "A Doll's House" (LC), Bdwy 1977 in "Anna Christie."

URMSTON, KENNETH. Born Aug. 6, 1929 in Cincinnati, OH. Attended Xavier U. Bdwy debut 1950 in "Make A Wish," followed by "Top Banana," "Guys and Dolls," "John Murray Anderson's Almanac," "Can-Can," "Silk Stockings," "Oh Captain!," "Bells Are Ringing," "Redhead," "Madison Avenue," "Tenderloin," "We Take the Town," "Lovely Ladies, Kind Gentlemen," "Follies," "Pippin."

VALE, MICHAEL. Born June 28, 1922 in Brooklyn, NY. Attended New Sch. Bdwy debut 1961 in "The Egg," followed by "Cafe Crown," "Last Analysis," "Impossible Years," "Saturday, Sunday, Monday," "Unexpected Guests," "California Suite," OB in "Autograph Hound," "Moths," "Now There's the Three of Us," "Tall and Rex," "Kaddish," "42 Seconds from Broadway," "Sunset."

VALENTINE, JAMES. Born Feb. 18, 1933 in Rockford, IL. Attended ULondon, Central Sch. of Drama. Bdwy debut 1958 in "Cloud 7," followed by "Epitaph for George Dillon," "Duel of Angels," "Ross," "Caesar and Cleopatra."

VAN BENSCHOTEN, STEPHEN. Born Aug. 27, 1943 in Washington, DC. Graduate LaSalle Col., Yale. Debut 1967 OB in "King John," Bdwy in "Unlikely Heroes," "Grease."

VAN DEVERE, TRISH. Born Mar. 9, 1947 in Englewood Cliffs, NJ. Graduate Ohio Wesleyan U. Debut 1967 OB in "Kicking Down the Castle," Bdwy 1975 in "All God's Chillun Got Wings," followed by "Sly Fox."

VAN NORDEN, PETER. Born Dec. 16, 1950 in NYC. Graduate Colgate U., Neighborhood Playhouse. Debut 1975 OB in "Hamlet," followed by "Henry V," "Measure for Measure," "A Country Scandal," "Hound of the Baskervilles," "Tartuffe," "Antigone," "Bingo," "The Balcony," Bdwy 1977 in "Romeo and Juliet."

VAN VACTER, BEN. Born Dec. 20, 1951 in Elk City, OK. Graduate UOkla. Bdwy debut 1976 in "Night of the Iguana."

VARRONE, GENE. Born Oct. 30, 1929 in Brooklyn, NY. Graduate LIU. Bdwy in "Damn Yankees," "Take Me Along," "Ziegfeld Follies," "Goldilocks," "Wildcat," "Tovarich," "Subways Are for Sleeping," "Bravo Giovanni," "Drat! The Cat!" "Fade Out—Fade In," "Don't Drink the Water," "Dear World," "Coco," "A Little Night Music," "So Long, 174th Street," "Knickerbocker Holiday," OB in "Promenade."

VENNEMA, JOHN C. Born Aug. 24, 1948 in Houston, TX. Graduate Princeton U., LAMDA. Bdwy debut 1976 in "The Royal Family."

VENNERA, CHICK. Born Mar. 27, 1952 in Herkimer, NY. Attended Pasadena Playhouse. Debut 1977 OB in "Jockeys" for which he received a Theatre World Award.

VERDON, GWEN. Born Jan. 13, 1926 in Culver City, CA. Bdwy debut 1950 in "Alive and Kicking," followed by "Can-Can" for which she received a Theatre World Award, "Damn Yankees," "New Girl in Town," "Redhead," "Sweet Charity," "Children, Children," "Chicago."

VERNON, RICHARD. Born Jan. 19, 1946 in Washington, DC. Graduate Catholic U. Bdwy debut 1976 in "Poor Murderer."

VIDNOVIC, MARTIN. Born Jan. 4, 1948 in Falls Church, VA. Attended Cincinnati Consv. of Music. Debut 1972 OB in "The Fantasticks," followed by Bdwy in "Home Sweet Homer" (1976), "The King and I."

VILLAIRE, HOLLY. Born Apr. 11, 1944 in Yonkers, NY. Graduate UDetroit, UMich. Debut 1971 OB in "Arms and the Man," followed by "Purity," "Eyes of Chalk," "Anna-Luse," "Village Wooing," "The Fall and Redemption of Man," BAM Co.'s "New York Idea" and "Three Sisters," Bdwy in "Scapino" (1974), "Habeas Corpus."

VINOVICH, STEVE. Born Jan. 22, 1945 in Peoria, IL. Graduate UIll., UCLA, Juilliard. Debut 1974 OB in "The Robber Bridegroom," followed by "King John," "Father Uxbridge Wants to Marry," Bdwy in "Robber Bridegroom" (1976), "The Magic Show."

VITA, MICHAEL. Born in 1941 in NYC. Studied at HB Studio. Bdwy debut 1967 in "Sweet Charity," followed by "Golden Rainbow," "Promises, Promises," "Chicago," OB in "Sensations," "That's Entertainment."

VON SCHERLER, SASHA. Born Dec. 12. in NYC. Bdwy debut 1959 in "Look after Lulu," followed by "Rape of the Belt," "The Good Soup," "Great God Brown," "First Love," "Alfie," "Harold," "Bad Habits," OB in "Admirable Bashville," "The Comedian," "Conversation Piece," "Good King Charles' Golden Days," "Under Milk Wood," "Plays for Bleecker Street," "Ludlow Fair," "Twelfth Night," "Sondra," "Cyrano de Bergerac," "Crimes of Passion," "Henry VI," "Trelawny of the Wells," "Screens," "Soon Jack November," "Pericles," "Kid Champion," "Henry V," "Comanche Cafe," "Museum."

VOSKOVEC, GEORGE. Born June 19, 1905 in Sazava, Czech. Graduate Dijon U. Bdwy debut 1945 in "The Tempest," followed by "Love of 4 Colonels," "His and Hers," "The Seagull," "Festival," "Uncle Vanya," "A Call on Kuprin," "Tenth Man," "Big Fish, Little Fish," "Do You Know the Milky Way?," "Hamlet," "Cabaret," "Penny Wars," "All Over," OB in "The Alchemist," "East Wind," "Galileo," "Oh Say Can You See L. A.?," "Room Service," "Brecht on Brecht," "All Is Bright," "The Cherry Orchard," "Agamemnon."

| Russ Thacker | Sasha von Scherler | Steve Vinovich | Alyce E. Webb | Arn Weiner |

WAGER, MICHAEL. Born Apr. 29, 1925 in NYC. Harvard graduate. Bdwy bow 1949 in "Streetcar Named Desire," followed by "Small Hours," "Bernardine," "Merchant of Venice," "Misalliance," "The Remarkable Mr. Pennypacker," "Othello," "Henry IV," "St. Joan," "Firstborn," "The Cradle Will Rock," "Three Sisters," "The Cuban Thing," OB in "Noontide," "Brecht on Brecht," "Sunset," "Penny Friend," "Trelawny of the Wells," "Taming of the Shrew," "Inn at Lydda," "Richard III."

WAITE, JOHN THOMAS. Born Apr. 19, 1948 in Syracuse, NY. Attended Syracuse U. Debut 1976 OB in "The Fantasticks."

WALDROP, MARK. Born July 30, 1954 in Washington, DC. Graduate Cincinnati Consv. of Music. Debut 1977 OB in "Movie Buff."

WALKEN, CHRISTOPHER. Born Mar. 31, 1943 in Astoria, NY. Attended Hofstra U. Bdwy debut 1958 in "J. B.," followed by "High Spirits," "Baker Street," "The Lion in Winter," "Measure for Measure," (CP), "Rose Tattoo" (CC'66) for which he received a Theatre World Award, "Unknown Soldier and His Wife," "Rosencrantz and Guildenstern Are Dead," "Scenes from American Life," (LC), "Cymbeline" (NYSF), LC's "Enemies," "The Plough and the Stars," "Merchant of Venice," "The Tempest," "Troilus and Cressida," and "Macbeth," "Sweet Bird of Youth," OB in "Best Foot Forward," "Iphigenia in Aulis," "Lemon Sky," "Kid Champion."

WALKER, CHET. Born June 1, 1954 in Stuttgart, AR. Bdwy debut 1972 in "On the Town," followed by "Ambassador," "Pajama Game," "Lorelei," "Pippin."

WALKER, KATHRYN. Born in Jan. in Philadelphia, PA. Graduate Wells Col., Harvard, LAMDA. Debut 1971 OB in "Slag," followed by "Alpha Beta," "Kid Champion," "Rebel Women," Bdwy in "The Good Doctor" (1973) "Mourning Pictures."

WALLACE, EMETT "BABE". Born June 24, 1909 in Brooklyn, NY. Bdwy debut 1946 in "Lysistrata," followed by "Guys and Dolls" (1976), OB in "Justice," "The Bald Soprano," "House Party," "Reminiscing with Sissle and Blake."

WALLACE, LEE. Born July 15, 1930 in NYC. Attended NYU. Debut OB 1966 in "Journey of the Fifth Horse," followed by "Saturday Night," "An Evening with Garcia Lorca," "Macbeth," "Booth Is Back In Town," "Awake and Sing," "Shepherd of Avenue B," "Basic Training of Pavlo Hummel," "Curtains," Bdwy in "Secret Affairs of Mildred Wild," "Molly," "Zalmen, or the Madness of God."

WALLACE, TIMOTHY. Born July 24, 1947 in Racine, WI. Graduate UWisc. Penn State U. Debut 1976 OB in "The Rimers of Eldritch" (ELT)., followed by "Dance on a Country Grave."

WALSH, FRANCIS. Born in Buffalo, NY. Debut 1976 OB in "A Tribute to Lili Lamont."

WALSH, THOMAS J. Born Mar. 15, 1950 in Auburn, NY. Attended Boston Consv. Bdwy debut 1973 in "Seesaw," followed by "Rachel Lily Rosenbloom," "Music! Music!," "A Chorus Line."

WARD, DOUGLAS TURNER. Born May 5, 1930 in Burnside, LA. Attended UMich. Bdwy bow 1959 in "A Raisin in the Sun," followed by "One Flew over the Cuckoo's Nest," "Last Breeze of Summer," OB in "The Iceman Cometh," "The Blacks," "Pullman Car Hiawatha," "Bloodknot," "Happy Ending," "Day of Absence," "Kongi's Harvest," "Ceremonies in Dark Old Men," "The Harangues," "The Reckoning," "Frederick Douglass through His Own Words," "River Niger," "The Brownsville Raid."

WARDEN, JAMES, JR. Born May 2, 1958 in Brooklyn, NY. Debut 1976 OB in "Eden."

WARFIELD, DONALD. Born Aug. 25 in Rhinelander, WI. Graduate Brown U., Yale. Debut 1968 OB in "People VS. Ranchman," followed by "War Games," "Saved," "Love Your Crooked Neighbor," "Mystery Play," "The Children's Mass," "G. R. Point," Bdwy in "Watercolor" (1970)

WASHINGTON, VERNON. Born Aug. 10, 1927 in Hartford CT. Attended Wholter School of Drama. OB in "Cabin in the Sky," "The Strong Breed," "Trials of Brother Jero," "Scuba Duba," "Hocus-Pocus," Bdwy 1976 in "Bubbling Brown Sugar."

WATERSTON, SAM. Born Nov. 15, 1940 in Cambridge, MA. Graduate Yale. Bdwy bow 1963 in "Oh, Dad, Poor Dad . . .," followed by "First One Asleep Whistle," "Halfway up the Tree," "Indians," "Hay Fever," "Much Ado About Nothing," OB in "As You Like it," "Thistle in My Bed," "The Knack," "Fitz," "Biscuit," "La Turista," "Posterity For Sale," "Ergo," "Muzeeka," "Red Cross," "Henry IV," "Spitting Image," "I Met a Man," "Brass Butterfly," "Trial of the Catonsville 9," "Cymbeline," "Hamlet," "A Meeting by the River," "The Tempest," "A Doll's House," "Measure for Measure."

WATSON, DOUGLASS. Born Feb. 24, 1921 in Jackson, GA. Graduate UNC. Bdwy bow 1947 in "The Iceman Cometh," followed by "Antony and Cleopatra," for which he received a Theatre World Award, "Leading Lady," "Richard III," "Happiest Years," "That Lady," "Wisteria Trees," "Romeo and Juliet," "Desire under the Elms," "Sunday Breakfast," "Cyrano de Bergerac," "Confidential Clerk," "Portrait of a Lady," "Miser," "Young and Beautiful," "Little Glass Clock," "Country Wife," "Man for All Seasons," "Chinese Prime Minister," "Marat/deSade," "Prime of Miss Jean Brodie," "Pirates of Penzance," NYSF's "Much Ado about Nothing," "King Lear," and "As You Like It," "Over Here," OB in "The Hunger," "Dancing for the Kaiser," "Money," "My Life."

WEAVER, FRITZ. Born Jan. 19, 1926 in Pittsburgh, PA. Graduate UChicago. Bdwy debut 1955 in "Chalk Garden," for which he received a Theatre World Award, followed by "Protective Custody," "Miss Lonelyhearts," "All American," "Lorenzo," "The White House," "Baker Street," "Child's Play," "Absurd Person Singular," OB in "The Way of the World," "White Devil," "Doctor's Dilemma," "Family Reunion," "The Power and the Glory," "Great God Brown," "Peer Gynt," "Henry IV," "My Fair Lady" (CC), "Lincoln."

WEBB, ALYCE, E. Born June 1, 1934 in NYC. Graduate NYU. Bdwy debut 1946 in "Street Scene," followed by "Lost in the Stars," "Finian's Rainbow," "Porgy and Bess," "Show Boat," "Guys and Dolls," "Kiss Me, Kate," "Wonderful Town," "Hello, Dolly!," "Purlie," OB in "Simply Heavenly," "Ballad of Bimshire," "Trumpets of the Lord," "Streetcar Named Desire" (LC), "Show Boat" (JB).

WEBB, ROBB. Born Jan. 29, 1939 in Whitesburg, KY. Attended Ohio State U. Debut 1976 OB in "Who Killed Richard Cory?" Bdwy 1976 in "Sly Fox."

WEDGEWORTH, ANN. Born Jan. 21 in Abilene, TX. Attended UTex. Bdwy debut 1958 in "Make A Million," followed by "Blues for Mr. Charlie," "Last Analysis," "Thieves," OB in "Chaparral," "The Crucible," "Days and Nights of Beebee Fenstermaker," "Ludlow Fair," "Line."

WEIL, ROBERT E. Born Nov. 18, 1914 in NYC. Attended NYU. Bdwy bow in "New Faces of 1942," followed by "Burlesque," "Becket," "Once upon a Mattress," "Blood, Sweat and Stanley Poole," "Night Life," "Arturo Ui," "Beggar on Horseback" (LC), "Lenny," "Happy End," OB in "Love Your Crooked Neighbor," "Felix."

WEINER, ARN. Born July 19, 1931 in Brooklyn, NY. Attended Pratt, LACC. Bdwy debut 1966 in "Those That Play the Clowns," followed by "Yentl." OB in "Come Walk with Me," "Saving Grace," "Come Out, Carlo," "Evenings with Chekhov," "Sunset."

WELCH, CHARLES C. Born Feb. 2, 1921 in New Britain, CT. Attended Randall Sch., AmThWing, Bdwy debut 1958 in "Cloud 7," followed by "Donny Brook," "Golden Boy," "Little Murders," "Holly Go Lightly," "Darling of the Day," "Dear World," "Follies," "Status Quo Vadis," "Shenandoah," OB in "Half-Past Wednesday," "Oh, Lady! Lady!"

WELDON, CHARLES. Born June 1, 1940 in Wetumka, OK. Bdwy debut 1969 in "Big Time Buck White," followed by "River Niger," OB in "Ride a Black Horse," "Long Time Coming and a Long Time Gone," "Jamimma," "In the Deepest Part of Sleep," "Brownsville Raid," "Great MacDaddy."

WELLER, PETER. Born June 24, 1947 in Stevens Point, WI. Graduate AADA. Bdwy bow 1972 in "Sticks and Bones," followed by "Full Circle," "Summer Brave," OB in "Children," "Merchant of Venice," "Macbeth," "Rebel Women," "Streamers."

WELLS, CYNTHIA. Born Mar. 6, 1942 in Jackson, MN. Graduate Macalester Col., UMinn. Bdwy debut 1975 in "Very Good Eddie."

WENTZ, EARL. Born Mar. 22, 1938 in Charlotte, NC. Attended Charlotte, Wingate, and Queens Cols. Debut 1976 OB in "Missouri Legend."

Penney White   Richard Woods   Janet Wong   Jerry Yoder   Penny Worth

WESTON, MARK. Born Feb. 13, 1931 in The Bronx, NY. Attended UWisc. Debut 1955 in "Billy Budd," followed by "The Trial of Mary Surratt," "Come Back, Little Sheba," Bdwy in "Time Limit!" (1956).

WHITE, PENNEY. Born Oct. 28 in Pensacola, FL. Graduate Northwestern U. Bdwy debut 1971 in "Metamorphoses," OB in "Second City," "Some Other Time" (LC), "Inside My Head," "Telemachus Clay," "Bag of Flies," "Museum."

WHITE, TERRI. Born Jan. 24, 1953 in Palo Alto, CA. Attended USIU. Debut OB 1976 in "The Club."

WHITEHEAD, PAXTON. Born in Kent, Eng. Attended Webber-Douglas Drama Sch. Bdwy debut 1962 in "The Affair," followed by "Beyond the Fringe," "Candida," "Habeas Corpus," OB in "Gallows Humour," "One Way Pendulum," "A Doll's House," "Rondelay."

WHITESIDE, CHARLES. Born Sept. 7, 1951 in Detroit, MI. Attended NC Sch. of Arts, HB Studio. Debut 1975 OB in "Celebration," followed by "Silk Stockings," Bdwy 1976 in "Let My People Come."

WHITNEY, IRIS. Born Feb. 20 in Pasadena, CA. Attended UCLA. Bdwy debut 1937 in "Plumes in the Dust," followed by "Abe Lincoln in Illinois," "Juno and the Paycock," "The Flying Gerardoes," "The Strings, My Lord, Are False," "Dark of the Moon," "The Remarkable Mr. Pennypacker," "A Touch of the Poet," "Build with One Hand," "The Awakening of Spring" (OB), "Three Bags Full," "Vieux Carre."

WIDDOES, KATHLEEN. Born Mar. 21, 1939 in Wilmington, DE. Attended Paris' Theatre des Nations. Bdwy debut 1958 in "The Firstborn," followed by "World of Suzy Wong," "Much Ado about Nothing," OB in "Three Sisters," "The Maids," "You Can't Take It with You," "To Clothe the Naked," "World War 2 1/2," "Beggar's Opera," "As You Like It," "Midsummer Night's Dream," "Castaways."

WIDLOCK, JOHN. Born Mar. 16, 1944 in Springfield, MO. Graduate Queens Col., Hunter Col. Debut 1977 OB in "Jockeys."

WILCOX, RALPH. Born Jan. 30, 1951 in Milwaukee, WI. Attended UWisc. Debut 1971 OB in "Dirtiest Show In Town," followed by "Broadway," "Miracle Play," Bdwy in "Ain't Supposed to Die a Natural Death," "The Wiz"

WILLARD, DEL. Born May 8, 1935 in Rutland, VT. Debut OB 1963 in "The Brig," followed by "A Recent Killing," "Come Back, Little Sheba."

WILLIAMS, BILLY DEE. Born Apr. 6, 1938 in NYC. Attended Ntl. Acad. of Fine Arts. Bdwy debut 1945 in "Fireband of Florence," followed by "Cool World," "A Taste of Honey," "Hallelujah, Baby!," "I Have a Dream," OB in "Blue Boy in Black," "Firebugs," "Ceremonies in Dark Old Men," "Slow Dance on the Killing Ground."

WILLIAMS, EMLYN. Born Nov. 26, 1905 in Mostyn, Wales. Bdwy debut 1927 in "And So To Bed," followed by "Criminal at Large," "Night Must Fall," "Montserrat," "Bleak House," "A Boy Growing Up," "Daughter of Silence," "Man For All Seasons," "The Deputy," "Readings from Charles Dickens," OB in "Dylan Thomas Growing Up," "Emyln Williams as Charles Dickens."

WILLIAMS, SAMMY. Born Nov. 13, 1948 in Trenton, NJ. Bdwy debut 1969 in "The Happy Time," followed by "Applause," "Seesaw," "A Chorus Line."

WILLISON, WALTER. Born June 24, 1947 in Monterey Park, CA. Bdwy debut 1970 in "Norman, Is that You?," followed by "Two by Two" for which he received a Theatre World Award, "Wild and Wonderful," "Pippin."

WILLOUGHBY, RONALD. Born June 3, 1937 in Goss, MS. Graduate Milsaps Col., Northwestern U. Debut 1963 OB in "Walk in Darkness," followed by "Little Eyolf," "Antony and Cleopatra," "Balm in Gilead," "Dracula: Sabbat," "The Faggot," "The King of the U.S.," "Twelfth Night."

WILSON, ELIZABETH. Born Apr. 4, 1925 in Grand Rapids, MI. Attended Neighborhood Playhouse, Bdwy debut 1953 in "Picnic," followed by "Desk Set," "Tunnel of Love," "Big Fish, Little Fish," "Sheep on the Runway," "Sticks and Bones," "Secret Affairs of Mildred Wild," OB in "Plaza 9," "Eh?," "Little Murders," "Good Woman of Setzuan," "Uncle Vanya," "Threepenny Opera."

WILSON, KEVIN. Born May 26, 1950 in Indianapolis, IN. Graduate UMd., HB Studio. Debut 1977 in "Shenandoah."

WILSON, MARY LOUISE. Born Nov. 12, 1936 in New Haven, CT. Graduate Northwestern. OB in "Our Town," "Upstairs at the Downstairs," "Threepenny Opera," "A Great Career," "Whispers on the Wind," "Beggar's Opera," Bdwy in "Hot Spot," "Flora, the Red Menace," "Criss-Crossing," "Promises, Promises," "The Women," "Gypsy," "The Royal Family."

WINDE, BEATRICE. Born Jan. 6 in Chicago, Ill. Debut 1966 OB in "In White America," followed by "June Bug Graduates Tonight," "Strike Heaven on the Face." "Divine Comedy," Bdwy 1971 in "Ain't Supposed to Die a Natural Death" for which she received a Theatre World Award.

WINDSLOW, ROBERT. Born Oct. 11, 1950 in Vancouver, BC, Can. Graduate AMDA. Debut 1977 OB in "The New York Idea" and "The Three Sisters" (BAM Co.)

WINSTON, LEE. Born Mar. 14, 1941 in Great Bend, KS. Graduate UKan. Debut 1966 OB in "The Drunkard," followed by "Show Boat" (LC), "Little Mahaganny," "Good Soldier Schweik," Bdwy 1976 in "1600 Pennsylvania Avenue."

WINTERS, NEWTON. Born in Henderson, NV. Bdwy debut 1976 in "Bubbling Brown Sugar."

WINTERS, WARRINGTON. Born July 28, 1909 in Bigstone Country, MN Graduate UMinn. Debut OB 1975 in ELT's "Another Language," followed by "A Night at the Black Pig."

WOLF, CATHERINE. Born in Philadelphia, PA. Attended Neighborhood Playhouse. Bdwy debut 1976 in "The Innocents."

WONG, JANET. Born Aug. 30, 1951 in Berkeley, CA. Attended UCal. Bdwy debut 1977 in "A Chorus Line."

WOODS, RICHARD. Born May 9, 1921 in Buffalo, NY. Graduate Ithaca Col. Bdwy in "Beg, Borrow or Steal," "Capt. Brassbound's Conversion," "Sail Away," "Coco," "Last of Mrs. Lincoln," "Gigi," "Sherlock Holmes," "Murder among Friends," "The Royal Family," OB in "The Crucible," "Summer and Smoke," "American Gothic," "Four-in-One," "My Heart's in the Highlands," "Eastward in Eden," "The Long Gallery," "The Year Boston Won the Pennant," "In the Matter of J. Robert Oppenheimer" (LC), with APA in "You Can't Take It with You," "War and Peace," "School for Scandal," "Right You Are," "The Wild Duck," "Pantagleize," "Exit the King," "The Cherry Orchard," "Cock-a-doodle Dandy," and "Hamlet."

WORTH, IRENE. Born June 23, 1916 in Nebraska. Graduate UCLA. Bdwy debut 1943 in "The Two Mrs. Carrolls," followed by "The Cocktail Party," "Mary Stuart," "Toys in the Attic," "King Lear," "Tiny Alice," "Sweet Bird of Youth," "The Cherry Orchard" (LC).

WORTH, PENNY. Born Mar. 2, 1950 in London, Eng. Attended Sorbonne, Paris. Bdwy debut 1970 in "Coco," followed by "Irene," "Annie."

WRIGHT, EDDIE, JR. Born Aug. 14, 1951 in Jersey City, NJ. Attended Rutgers U. Bdwy debut 1972 in "Wild and Wonderful," followed by "Thoughts" (OB), "Guys and Dolls" (1976).

WRIGHT, WILLIAM. Born Jan. 21, 1943 in Los Angeles, CA. Graduate UUtah, Bristol Old Vic. Debut 1973 OB in "Merchant of Venice" (LC), Bdwy 1976 in "Equus."

WYLER, GRETCHEN. Born Feb. 16, 1932 in Oklahoma City, OK. Bdwy debut 1950 in "Where's Charley?," followed by "Guys and Dolls," "Silk Stockings," "Damn Yankees," "Rumple," "Bye Bye Birdie," "Sly Fox."

WYMAN, NICHOLAS. Born May 18, 1950 in Portland, ME. Graduate Harvard. Bdwy debut 1975 in "Very Good Eddie."

YODER, JERRY. Born in Columbus, OH. Graduate Ohio State U. Bdwy debut 1973 in "Seesaw," followed by "Goodtime Charley," "Chicago," OB in "The Boys from Syracuse."

ZAKS, JERRY. Born Sept. 7, 1946 in Germany, Graduate Dartmouth, Smith Col. Bdwy debut 1973 in "Grease," OB in "Death Story," "Dream of a Blacklisted Actor," "Kid Champion," "Golden Boy," "Marco Polo."

ZANG, EDWARD. Born Aug. 19, 1934 in NYC. Graduate Boston U. OB in "Good Soldier Schweik," "St. Joan," "Boys in the Band," "The Reliquary of Mr. And Mrs. Potterfield," "Last Analysis," "As You Like it," "More than You Deserve," "Polly," "Threepenny Opera," BAM Co.'s "New York Idea."

ZIMMERMAN, MARK. Born Apr. 19, 1952 in Harrisburg, PA. Graduate UPa. Debut 1976 OB in "Fiorello!," followed by "Silk Stockings."

ZORICH, LOUIS. Born Feb. 12, 1924 in Chicago, IL. Attended Roosevelt U. OB in "Six Characters in Search of an Author," "Crimes and Crimes," "Henry V," "Thracian Horses," "All Women Are One," "Good Soldier Schweik," "Shadow of Heroes," "To Clothe the Naked," "Sunset," "A Memory of Two Mondays," "They Knew What They Wanted," "The Gathering," Bdwy in "Becket," "Moby Dick," "The Odd Couple," "Hadrian VII," "Moonchildren," "Fun City," "Goodtime Charley," "Herzl."

OBITUARIES

WARNER ANDERSON, 65, New-York-born stage, film and tv actor, died Aug. 26, 1976 in Santa Monica, CA. Before going to Hollywood he appeared on Bdwy in such productions as "Medea," "Within Four Walls," "The Criminals," "War and Peace," "Maytime," "Happiness," "Broken Journey," "Mr. & Mrs. North," "Remains to Be Seen." He appeared in over 50 films, but was probably best known for the tv series "The Line-up." His widow and a son, Michael, survive.

LEOPOLD BADIA, 74, Spanish-born actor, died July 2, 1976 in NYC. After his Bdwy debut in 1927 in "Speakeasy," he appeared in many plays, including "Machinal," "Siege," "One Third of a Nation," "The Cradle Will Rock," "The Big Story," "A Bell for Adano," "Cyrano de Bergerac," "Richard III," "Sixth Finger in a Five Finger Glove." He left no immediate survivors.

EDITH BARRETT, 64, Massachusetts-born stage and film actress, died of a heart attack Feb. 22, 1977 in Albuquerque, NM. After her debut with Walter Hampden in 1923 in "Cyrano de Bergerac," she appeared in "Trelawny of the Wells," "Merchant of Venice," "Immortal Thief," "Hamlet," "Caponsacchi," "Phantom Lover," "Becky Sharp," "Michael and Mary," "Mrs. Moonlight" (her greatest success), "Troilus and Cressida," "Perfect Marriage," "Strange Orchestra," "Moor Born," "Allure," "Piper Paid," "Symphony," "Parnell," "Wise Tomorrow," "Shoemaker's Holiday," and "Wuthering Heights." She was divorced from actor Vincent Price. A son survives.

GEORGE BAXTER, 72, stage, film and tv actor, died Sept. 10, 1976 in NYC. His stage credits include "Sweet Nell of Old Drury," "Windows," "Milgrim's Progress," "Caesar and Cleopatra," "Glass Slipper," "Night Duel," "No Foolin'," "We Americans," "Rio Rita," "Perfect Marriage," "Behind the Red Lights," "3 Waltzes," "Madame Capet," "George Washington Slept Here," "Mr. Big," "Early to Bed," "For Keeps," "Rebecca," "Devils Galore," "A Flag Is Born," "Louisiana Lady." No reported survivors.

SAMUEL (TONY) BICKLEY, 67, stage, radio and tv actor, died June 19, 1976 in Norwalk, CT. His Bdwy credits include "Days of Our Youth," "Without Love," "Made in Heaven," "Man and Superman," "Grey-Eyed People," "The Best Man." He appeared in many radio and tv shows. Surviving are his widow and two daughters.

KERMIT BLOOMGARDEN, 71, Brooklyn-born producer of many distinguished plays, died from a brain tumor on Sept. 20, 1976 in his NYC home. His productions include "Heavenly Express," "Deep Are the Roots," "Woman Bites Dog," "Command Decision," "Montserrat," "The Man," "Legend of Sarah," "Autumn Garden," "The Children's Hour," "The Crucible," "Wedding Breakfast," "View from the Bridge," "A Memory of Two Mondays," "The Lark," Pulitzer-Prize winning "Death of a Salesman," "Diary of Anne Frank," and "Look Homeward, Angel," "Most Happy Fella," "Night of the Auk," "Music Man," "The Gang's All Here," "Toys in the Attic," "The Wall," "The Gay Life," "Moon on a Rainbow Shawl," "Nowhere to Go but Up," "My Mother, My Father and Me," "Anyone Can Whistle," "The Playroom," "Illya Darling," "Hello and Goodbye," "The Hot l Baltimore," and "Equus." He is survived by two sons, John who worked with him, and David.

JIM BOLES, 63, stage, film, radio and tv actor died May 26, 1977 from a heart seizure in Sherman Oaks, CA. He had appeared in more than a thousand radio and tv shows, and on Bdwy in "Goodbye Again," "The Victors," "All That Fall." He had played in over 30 films. Surviving are a son Eric, and two daughters, Sue and Barbara.

JOAN BOWLUS, 86, oldest of the Ziegfeld Follies girls, died July 2, 1976 in Venice, CA. She was born in England and began her career as a dancer, and joined the "Follies" in 1916. No reported survivors.

SAXE BRADBURY, 33, stage and film actress, was killed Nov. 13, 1976 in a private plane crash in Arizona. She had appeared in the revival of "Gypsy," and in "Saturday, Sunday, Monday." No reported survivors.

ROMNEY BRENT, 74, Mexican-born (nee Romulo Larrade) stage, and film actor, director, playwright, and teacher, died Sept. 24, 1976 in Mexico City. After his debut in 1922 he had appeared in such Bdwy productions as "Lucky One," "The Tidings Brought to Mary," "Peer Gynt," "Flame of Love," "Garrick Gaities," "Androcles and the Lion," "The Chief Thing," "The Squall," "Loud Speaker," "Katy Did," "Merchant of Venice," "Phantom Lover," "Be Your Age," "The Little Show," "Inspector General," "Getting Married," "Streets of New York," "Pillars of Society," "Warrior's Husband," "Words and Music," "Simpleton of the Unexpected Isles," "Three Men on a Horse," "Love for Love," "Bird in Hand," "The Deep Mrs. Sykes," "Winter's Tale," "Joan of Lorraine," "Parisienne," "Tovarich," "The International Set." He wrote "The Mad Hopes," "Tomorrow's a Holiday!," and with Cole Porter "Nymph Errant." He directed "Night Before Christmas," "The Lady Comes Across," "Winter's Tale," and "Teahouse of the August Moon." A daughter survives.

MARTIN BURTON, 71, stage and film actor, died Aug. 4, 1976 after a lengthy illness in Santa Monica, CA. Before going to Hollywood in 1931 he appeared in "Crime," "Night Hawk," "Playing the Game," "Cafe de Danse," "Love Duel," "Death Takes a Holiday," "Merchant of Venice," "It Pays to Sin." He Co-Produced "Broken Journey," "Feathers in a Gale," "The Joyous Season," and "The Magnificent Yankee." He retired in 1954. No known survivors.

GODFREY CAMBRIDGE, 43, NY-born stage and film actor, nightclub comedian, and recording artist, died of a heart attack on a movie set in Burbank, CA., Nov. 29, 1976. After his stage debut in 1956 in "Take a Giant Step," he appeared in "Nature's Way," "Androcles and the Lion," "Shakespeare in Harlem," "The Blacks," "Purlie Victorious," "The Living Premise." His widow and two daughters survive.

Kermit Bloomgarden

Romney Brent (1941)

Godfrey Cambridge (1967)

263

Jack Cassidy (1975)

Ethel Barrymore Colt

Marjorie Gateson (1948)

JACK CASSIDY, 49, NY-born actor-singer-dancer of stage, film and tv, was burned to death Dec. 12, 1976 in his Los Angeles, CA. apartment. After his Bdwy debut (1943) in "Something for the Boys," he performed in "Sadie Thompson," "Around the World," "Inside U.S.A.," "Small Wonder," "Music in My Heart," "Alive and Kicking," "Wish You Were Here," "Witness for the Prosecution," "Importance of Being Earnest," "Sandhog," "Shangri-La," "Beggar's Opera," "She Loves Me" for which he received a "Tony," "Fade Out—Fade In," "It's a Bird..It's a Plane..It's Superman!," "Maggie Flynn," "The Mundy Scheme," and "Murder among Friends." He received an "Emmy" for his tv performance in "The Andersonville Trial." He was married and divorced from actresses Evelyn Ward and Shirley Jones. Three sons survive, including rock singer David Cassidy.

ETHEL BARRYMORE COLT, 65, actress and singer, and daughter of the late Ethel Barrymore, died May 22, 1977 of cancer at her home in NYC. She made her professional debut in 1930 in support of her mother in "Scarlet Sister Mary," subsequently appearing in "Scandals," "George White's Scandals," "Under Glass," "Laura Garnett," "L'Aiglon," "London Assurance," "Orchids Preferred," "Whiteoaks," "Come of Age," "Curtains Up!," "Take It from the Top," "A Madrigal of Shakespeare," and "Follies." She had also appeared with the NYC Opera. She was the widow of petroleum executive Romeo Miglietta. A son, actor John Miglietta, survives.

LILLIAN KEMBLE COOPER, 85, English-born leading Bdwy singer and actress in the 1920's and '30's, died May 4, 1977 in Los Angeles, CA. She was from a well-known British theatrical family and came to the U.S. in 1918. Her NY appearances include "Night Boat," "New Morality," "National Anthem," "The Mountebank," "The New Poor," "Our Betters," "Twelfth Night," "For Services Rendered," "Roman Servant," "Tonight at 8:30," and "I Know My Love." Twice divorced; a brother survives, actor Anthony Kemble Cooper.

FLORENCE DUNLAP, 94, actress, died May 3, 1977 in NYC. Among the many plays in which she appeared are "Dead End," "The Children's Hour," "Personal Appearance," "Tobacco Road," "One Touch of Venus," "Fanny," "Happy Hunting." She was a widow with no survivors reported.

MYLES EASON, 61, Australian-born actor, died of a heart attack while vacationing on Grand Cayman Island. After his Bdwy debut in 1958 in "The Visit," he appeared in "Much Ado about Nothing," "Julia, Jake and Uncle Joe," "My Fair Lady"(CC), "A Midsummer Night's Dream." He had recently been in the tv series "The Guiding Light." His widow survives.

DAME EDITH EVANS, 88, one of England's most celebrated actresses, died Oct. 14, 1976 after a brief illness in her Cranbrook, Kent, Eng., home. She had been active on stage and in films until her death. After her Bdwy debut in 1931 in "The Lady with a Lamp," she returned to appear in "Romeo and Juliet," "Evensong," "Bull-Dog Drummond," "Daphne Laureola," "Homage to Shakespeare." She was the widow of engineer George Booth.

TIM EVERETT, 38, stage and tv actor-dancer-choreographer and teacher, died in his sleep March 4, 1977 in NYC apparently from heart failure. Montana-born, he made his Bdwy debut 1954 in "On Your Toes," followed by "Damn Yankees," "Livin' the Life," "The Dark at the Top of the Stairs" for which he received a Theatre World Award, "The Cold Wind and the Warm," "Marathon '33." He is survived by his parents and two sisters, actresses Sherrye and Tanya Everett.

NORMAN FOSTER, 72, Indiana-born stage and film actor, and film director, died July 7, 1976 of cancer in Santa Monica, CA. Before going to Hollywood he appeared on Bdwy in "Just Life," "Sure Fire!," "The Barker," "The Racket," "Night Hostess," "Tin Pan Alley," "Carnival," and "June Moon." Surviving are his widow, former actress Sally Blane, a son and a daughter.

JAMES W. GARDINER, 57, producer and former actor, died Nov. 6, 1976 of a heart attack in Las Vegas, NV. Among the productions he co-produced are "Are You With It?," "Plain and Fancy," "Ziegfeld Follies." As an actor, he had appeared in "Early to Bed," among others. No reported survivors.

MARJORIE GATESON, 86, Brooklyn-born stage, film and tv actress, died in NYC Apr. 17, 1977 of pneumonia. After her Bdwy debut in 1912 in "The Dove of Peace," her credits include "American Maid," "Mlle. Modiste," "Little Cafe," "Around the Map," "Her Soldier Boy," "Fancy Free," "Little Simplicity," "Shubert Gaieties," "Little Miss Charity," "Rose Girl," "Love Letter," "Lady Butterfly," "Strange Bedfellows," "Man in Evening Clothes," "Blond Sinner," "Oh! Ernest!," "Hidden," "The Great Necker," "Midsummer Night's Dream," "As Good as New," "Street Scene," "Sweethearts," "Show Boat"(CC). She appeared in over 100 films, and several tv serials. For many years was on the governing board of Actors Equity. No reported survivors.

BEN GRAUER, 68, actor and radio announcer, newsman, commentator, interviewer, moderator and host, died from a heart ailment May 31, 1977 in NYC. Before becoming "NBC's All-Around Man," he appeared on Bdwy in "Penrod," "The Blue Bird," and "Processional." He retired in 1973. He leaves his widow, interior designer Melanie Kahane, and a stepdaughter.

EDITH GRESHAM, 79, stage, radio and tv actress, died Dec. 31, 1976 in Riverdale, NY. She made her Bdwy debut in 1919 in "39 East," and subsequently appeared in "Whispering Friends," "Girls in Uniform," "Frederika," "Run Sheep Run," "The Women," "Sing Out the News," "Three's a Family," "Oklahoma!," "Debut," "The Visit," "Conquering Hero," "The Country Wife," "The Unsinkable Molly Brown." A sister survives.

MARGARET (MAGGIE) HAYES, 63, stage film and tv actress, died Jan. 26, 1977 in Miami, FL. In addition to acting, she had been a fashion model, fashion editor, department store executive, and most recently a jewelry designer and boutique owner. Her Bdwy credits include "I Must Love Someone," "Bright Rebel," "Many Happy Returns," "Little Women," "The Family," "One Shoe Off," "Happily Ever After," "Pink Jungle," "Step on a Crack," "Fair Game for Lovers." Three children survive.

HENRY HULL, 87, stage and film character actor, died Mar. 8, 1977 at the home of his daughter in Cornwall, Eng. After his NY debut in 1911 in "Green Stockings," he appeared in "Believe Me," "Xantippe," "The Man Who Came Back," "39 East," "When We Are Young," "The Trial of Joan of Arc," "Everyday," "The Cat and the Canary," "Roger Bloomer," "In Love with Love," "The Other Rose," "The Youngest," "Lulu Belle," "Ivory Door," "The Gray Fox," "Young Alexander," "Congratulations" which he wrote, "Ladies Leave," "Veneer," "Michael and Mary," "Grand Hotel," "The Roof," "The Bride the Sun Shines On," "Moon in the Yellow River," "Foreign Affairs," "Springtime for Henry," "Tobacco Road," "Plumes in the Dust," "Masque of Kings," "Foolish Notion," "Mister Roberts," "Happy Town." He was in 46 movies. His daughter survives.

JOSEPH HYMAN, 80, Colorado-born producer, died Feb. 25, 1977 in NYC. Either alone, or with Moss and Bernard Hart, he produced, "There's Always a Breeze," "Dear Ruth," "The Secret Room," "Mr. Peebles and Mr. Hooker," "Make Mine Manhattan," "Light Up the Sky," "The Climate of Eden," "Anniversary Waltz," "Christopher Blake," "Winged Victory," and "Fair Game." Surviving are his widow and a daughter.

MILT KAMEN, 55, NY-born actor, nightclub comedian and satirist, died Feb. 24, 1977 of a heart attack at his Beverly Hills, CA., home. In NY he had appeared in "Safari!," "Across the Boards on Tomorrow Morning," "A Thurber Carnival," "The Typists," "The Tiger," "The Passion of Josef D." He is survived by his widow and his father.

LEO KERZ, 64, Berlin-born producer and designer for costumes, sets and lighting, died of cancer Nov. 4, 1976 in NYC. He was associated with over 40 productions, including "Flamingo Road," "Christopher Blake," "Antony and Cleopatra," "Clerambard," and "Rhinoceros." His third wife, and two sons survive.

GERALD R. (JERRY) LAWS, 64, Connecticut-born actor, singer and stage manager, died Sept. 7, 1976 in NYC of a heart attack. He had appeared in "Blackbirds of 1939," "Porgy and Bess," "St. Louis Woman," "Finian's Rainbow," "Along Came a Spider," "The Great White Hope." He was most recently the stage manager for "The Wiz." Surviving are his widow, a son, and a daughter.

JUDITH LOWRY, 86, NJ-born stage, film and tv actress, died of a heart attack Nov. 29, 1976, while walking with her son in NYC. After her Bdwy debut in 1915 in "Romeo and Juliet," she appeared in many productions, including "Crime in the Whistler Room," "Goat Song," "Easter," "Beyond the Horizon," "Nightstick," "The Light of Asia," "Fall," "J.B.," and "The Effect of Gamma Rays on Man-in-the-Moon Marigolds." She was probably best known for her appearances as Mother Dexter on the tv series "Phyllis." Surviving are nine children.

LEO LUCKER, 64, Chicago-born actor and teacher, died Feb. 1, 1977 in NYC. Among his NY credits are "Twilight Walk," "School for Scandal," "Little Clay Cart," "Absalom," "Carousel," "Annie Get Your Gun," "Auntie Mame," "Season of Choice," "Susannah and the Elders," "Damask Drum," "Hans' Crime," "The French Way," "The Wives," and "Night of the Iguana." Since 1967 he had worked for the Health and Hospital Corp. No reported survivors.

HERBERT MACHIZ, 57, NYC-born actor, director and teacher, died Aug. 27, 1976 of a heart attack in his home in Brewster, NY. Among his NY productions are "The Immortal Husband," "A Streetcar Named Desire"(CC with Tallulah Bankhead), "Absalom," "Eugenia," "Garden District," "The Milk Train Doesn't Stop Here Anymore," "Wives," "Elizabeth the Queen," "In the Bar of a Tokyo Hotel," "Street Scene," and "Gertrude Stein's First Reader." He was on the faculty of AADA. A brother and sister survive.

SUE MacMANAMY, 84, retired actress, died June 10, 1976 following a stroke in her home in Bel Air, CA. Among her Bdwy credits are "True to Form," "Nature's Nobleman," "Thumbs Down," "High Stakes," "The Four Flusher," "Human Nature," "Ink," "Angels Don't Kiss." She was the widow of actor Otto Kruger, and retired after their marriage that lasted 55 years. Surviving is a daughter, actress Ottilie Kruger.

RITA MARKS, 68, retired dancer-actress, died Nov. 11, 1976 in Hollywood, FL. After her debut at 17 in "No, No, Nanette," she subsequently appeared in "Yes, Yes, Yvette," "Good News," "Grand Street Follies," "New Moon," "Blossom Time," "Show Boat"(1932), "Music in the Air." She is survived by her husband, Prof. Edward Girden, and a daughter.

JOHN MARRIOTT, 83, Oklahoma-born stage, film and tv actor, died Apr. 5, 1977 in NYC. His credits include "Too Many Boats," "Sweet River," "Chalked Out," "The Little Foxes," "Janie," "No Way Out," "The Iceman Cometh," "How I Wonder," "The Respectful Prostitute," "The Small Hours," "Green Pastures," "Dinosaur Wharf," "The Ponder Heart," "Orpheus Descending," "Interlock," "Of Mice and Men," "Season of Choice," "Miracle Worker," "Bicycle Ride to Nevada," "Death of a Well-Loved Boy," "More Stately Mansions," "Weekend," "Three Men on a Horse," "A Texas Trilogy." Surviving are his widow, a son, and a daughter.

WALTER McGINN, 40, stage, film and tv actor, died Mar. 31, 1977 in a Los Angeles, CA., hospital from injuries in an auto accident. His NY appearances include "The Subject Was Roses," "Willie Doesn't Live Here Anymore," "Here's Where I Belong," "Spitting Image," "Anthony and Cleopatra," "Twelfth Night," "As You Like It," "A Winter's Tale," "That Championship Season," "The Iceman Cometh"(1973). Survivors include his widow, actress Robyn Goodman, and his father.

JACK McGOWAN, 81, former singer-actor, playwright, and screen writer, died May 28, 1977 in NYC. As an actor, he appeared in "Mary," "Rose of Stamboul," "George White's Scandals," "The Rise of Rosie O'Reilly," "Little Nelly Kelly." He wrote "Tenth Avenue," "Excess Baggage," "Hold Everything," "Parade," "Flying High," "Heigh-Ho Everybody," "Vanities," "Say When." He went to Hollywood in the 1930's and became a screenwriter. He had been in retirement for 15 years. No reported survivors.

FRANK MILAN, 71, Tennessee-born stage and film actor, died of a heart attack Apr. 8, 1977 in NYC. After his 1930 debut in "Penal Law 2010," his credits include "Petrified Forest," "The Great Necker," "Goodbye My Fancy," "Two Blind Mice," "The Desk Set," "Who Was That Lady I Saw You With?," "Once More, with Feeling," "The Highest Tree," and "Brigadoon." Two sisters survive.

Henry Hull (1965)

Jerry Laws

Herbert Machiz (1968)

Rosalind Russell (1965)

Onslow Stevens (1956)

Linda Watkins (1931)

RICHARD MYERS, 76, Philadelphia-born composer and former producer, died March 12, 1977 in Perigueux, France. He composed the music for songs in such shows as "Greenwich Village Follies," "Murder at the Vanities," "Garrick Gaieties," "Earl Carroll Vanities," "Ziegfeld Follies." He produced, usually in partnership, "Give Us This Day," "I Want a Policeman!," "Lorelei," "Importance of Being Earnest," "Margin for Error," "My Dear Children," "Cue for Passion," "Plan M," "Sons and Soldiers," "The Moon Is Blue," "Dear Charles," "Hotel Paradiso," "Requiem for a Nun." His widow and a son survive.

MARY NASH, 92, retired Bdwy star and film actress, died Dec. 3, 1976 in her home in Brentwood, CA. After her NY debut in 1905 in "Alice-Sit-by-the-Fire," her credits include "The City," "The Woman," "The Lure," "The Man Who Came Back," "Big Chance," "Thy Name Is Woman," "Capt. Applejack," "The Mysterious Way," "The Lady," "Hassan," "A Lady's Virtue," "Two Orphans," "Fate's Messenger," "Command to Love," "A Strong Man's House," "Diana," "A Woman Denied," "The Devil Passes," "Uncle Tom's Cabin." She began her Hollywood career in 1936 and appeared in 18 films. She was divorced from actor Jose Ruben. No reported survivors.

SEAMUS O'BRIEN, 44, London-born actor, died May 14, 1977 after being fatally stabbed in his NYC apartment during a robbery. He had appeared OB in "The Eagle with Two Heads," "Salome," and for 5 years had played the Old Actor in "The Fantasticks." His Bdwy debut was in 1972 in "Vivat! Vivat Regina!" Surviving is a daughter.

RUSSELL PATTERSON, 82, Omaha-born designer, illustrator and cartoonist who created the "flapper" of the 1920's, died Mar. 17, 1977 of heart failure in Atlantic City, NJ. The "Patterson Girl" was the style-setter for the 1920's, and his comic strip "Mamie" became the trend-setter for the 1930's. He was a costume and scenic designer, as well as a producer and director for Bdwy. His credits include "The Gang's All Here," "Ballyhoo of 1932," "Hold Your Horses," "Ziegfeld Follies," "Fools Rush In," "Russell Patterson's Sketch Book," "Scandals," and "George White's Scandals." Surviving are his widow, musician and song-writer Ruth Cleary, and a daughter.

VIRGINIA PAYNE, 66, stage and radio actress died Feb. 10, 1977 in Cincinnati, OH. For 27 years she was the voice of Ma Perkins on the CBS radio serial. In NY she appeared on stage in "Right You Are if You Think You Are," "The Mousetrap," "An Evening with Katherine Mansfield," "Fade Out—Fade in." She was active in the organization of AFRA that later merged and became AFTRA. A sister survives.

MAUREEN PRYOR, 52, English-born actress, died May 5, 1977 of a heart ailment in London. Her Bdwy debut in 1965 in "Boeing, Boeing," was followed by appearances in "After the Rain," and "Little Boxes"(OB). No reported survivors.

WILLIAM REDFIELD, 49, NY-born stage, screen and tv actor, died in NYC Aug. 17, 1976 of a respiratory ailment complicated by leukemia. After his Bdwy debut in "Swing Your Lady" (1936), his credits include "Excursion," "Virginia," "Stop-Over," "Our Town," "Junior Miss," "Snafu," "Barefoot Boy with Cheek," "Bruno and Sidney," "Montserrat," "Miss Liberty," "Out of This World," "Misalliance," "Double in Hearts," "The Making of Moo," "U.S.A.," "Midgie Purvis," "A Man for All Seasons," "Hamlet," "A Minor Adjustment," "Love Suicide at Schofield Barracks," "Dude." He was a founding member of Actors Studio. Surviving are his second wife, a son and a daughter.

ROBERT RONAN, 41, NY-born actor and director, died Apr. 6, 1977 of injuries received when fire destroyed his home in Franklin Park, NY. He appeared OB in "The Tragical Historie of Dr. Faustus," "Colombe," "Troilus and Cressida," "All's Well That Ends Well," "Richard III," "Shoemaker's Holiday," "The Memorandum," "Henry IV Part II," "Invitation to a Beheading," "Twelfth Night," and "Trelawny of the Wells" which he also directed, "Love's Labour's Lost," "Timon of Athens." No reported survivors.

ARLENE ROTHLEIN, 37, NY-born actress, dancer and choreographer, died in Brooklyn Nov. 20, 1976 of meningitis. She had appeared in several OB productions, and in 1968 received an "Obie" for her performance in "The Little Match Girl." Surviving are her husband, George McGrath, and a daughter.

ROSALIND RUSSELL, 64, Connecticut-born stage and film star, died Nov. 28, 1976 in her Beverly Hills, CA., home of cancer complicated by rheumatoid arthritis. After her Bdwy debut in "The Garrick Gaieties"(1930), she appeared in "Company's Coming," "Talent," "Bell, Book and Candle"(on tour), "The Second Man," "Wonderful Town" and "Auntie Mame." In 1933 she went to Hollywood and became one of its brightest stars. She is survived by her husband of 35 years, producer Frederick Brisson, and a son.

DON SHELTON, 64, actor, died June 19, 1976 in Los Angeles, CA. His credits include "Birthright," "After Such Pleasures," "Shatter'd Lamp," "Ah, Wilderness!," "Plumes in the Dust," "Two on an Island," "Eight O'Clock Tuesday," "The Story of Mary Surratt." His wife, actress Mary Bear, died in 1972. No reported survivors.

ONSLOW STEVENS, 70, Los Angeles-born stage and film actor, was found dead Jan. 5, 1977 in a Van Nuys, CA., nursing home. The cause of death was under investigation, although listed as pneumonia. After his Bdwy debut in "Stage Door"(1936), he appeared in "The Two Mrs. Carrolls," "Eastward in Eden," "The Millionairess," "Dame Nature," "Michael Drops In," "The Ghost of Elsinore," and "A Clearing in the Woods." He is survived by his third wife.

MURVYN VYE, 63, Massachusetts-born stage, screen and tv actor, died Aug. 17, 1976 while on vacation in Pompano Beach, FL. He had appeared in burlesque, nightclubs, in 48 films, and almost 200 tv shows, not including the series "The Untouchables." His Bdwy credits include "Hamlet," "As You Like It," "Oklahoma!," "Carousel" in which he created the role of Jigger, "The Live Wire," "The Number," "Arturo Ui," "South Pacific," "One Touch of Venus," "The Caucasian Chalk Circle." No reported survivors.

LINDA WATKINS, 68, Boston-born stage and film actress, died Oct. 31, 1976 in Santa Monica, CA. After her Bdwy debut in 1926 in "The Devil in the Cheese," she appeared in 22 productions, including "The Ivory Door," "The Wild Duck," "Hedda Gabler," "Lady from the Sea," "June Moon," "Sweet Stranger," "In the Meantime," "Midnight," "Love and Babies," "Give Us This Day," "They Shall Not Die," "Say When," "County Chairman," "Penny Wise," "I Am My Youth," and "Janie." After going to Hollywood, she had roles in 11 movies. She was the widow of lawyer Gabriel Hess.

INDEX

269

275

277

283

284